How to Build a Digital Library

The Morgan Kaufmann Series in Multimedia Information and Systems

Series Editor, Edward A. Fox, Virginia Polytechnic University

How to Build a Digital Library
Ian H. Witten and David Bainbridge

Digital Watermarking
Ingemar J. Cox, Matthew L. Miller, and Jeffrey A. Bloom

Readings in Multimedia Computing and Networking
Edited by Kevin Jeffay and HongJiang Zhang

Introduction to Data Compression, Second Edition
Khalid Sayood

Multimedia Servers: Applications, Environments, and Design
Dinkar Sitaram and Asit Dan

Managing Gigabytes: Compressing and Indexing Documents and Images,
Second Edition
Ian H. Witten, Alistair Moffat, and Timothy C. Bell

Digital Compression for Multimedia: Principles and Standards
Jerry D. Gibson, Toby Berger, Tom Lookabaugh, Dave Lindbergh, and
Richard L. Baker

Practical Digital Libraries: Books, Bytes, and Bucks
Michael Lesk

Readings in Information Retrieval
Edited by Karen Sparck Jones and Peter Willett

How to Build a
Digital Library

Ian H. Witten

Computer Science Department
University of Waikato

David Bainbridge

Computer Science Department
University of Waikato

MORGAN KAUFMANN PUBLISHERS

AN IMPRINT OF ELSEVIER SCIENCE

AMSTERDAM   BOSTON   LONDON   NEW YORK
OXFORD   PARIS   SAN DIEGO   SAN FRANCISCO
SINGAPORE   SYDNEY   TOKYO

Publishing Director	Diane D. Cerra
Assistant Publishing Services Manager	Edward Wade
Senior Developmental Editor	Marilyn Uffner Alan
Editorial Assistant	Mona Buehler
Project Management	Yonie Overton
Cover Design	Frances Baca Design
Text Design	Mark Ong, Side by Side Studios
Composition	Susan Riley, Side by Side Studios
Copyeditor	Carol Leyba
Proofreader	Ken DellaPenta
Indexer	Steve Rath
Printer	The Maple-Vail Book Manufacturing Group

Designations used by companies to distinguish their products are often claimed as trademarks or registered trademarks. In all instances in which Morgan Kaufmann Publishers is aware of a claim, the product names appear in initial capital or all capital letters. Readers, however, should contact the appropriate companies for more complete information regarding trademarks and registration.

Morgan Kaufmann Publishers
An imprint of Elsevier Science
340 Pine Street, Sixth Floor
San Francisco, CA 94104-3205
www.mkp.com

07 06 05 04 03   5 4 3 2 1

Library of Congress Control Number: 2002107327
ISBN: 1-55860-790-0

This book is printed on acid-free paper.

Contents

Figures

Tables

Foreword

by Edward A. Fox

Computer science addresses important questions, offering relevant solutions. Some of these are recursive or self-referential. Accordingly, I am pleased to testify that a suitable answer to the question carried in this book's title is the book itself! Witten and Bainbridge have indeed provided a roadmap for those eager to build digital libraries.

Late in 2001, with a draft version of this book in hand, I planned the introductory unit for my spring class Multimedia, Hypertext, and Information Access (CS4624), an elective computer science course for seniors. Departmental personnel installed the Greenstone software on the 30 machines in our Windows lab. Students in both sections of this class had an early glimpse of course themes as they explored local and remote versions of Greenstone, applied to a variety of collections. They also built their own small digital libraries—all within the first few weeks of the course.

When the CS4624 students selected term projects, one team of three asked if they could work with Roger Ehrich, another computer science professor, to build a digital library: the Germans from Russia Heritage Society (GRHS) Image Library. After exploring alternatives, they settled on Greenstone. I gave them my draft copy of this book and encouraged them throughout the spring of 2002 as they worked with the software and with the two GRHS content collections: photographs and document images. They learned about documents and metadata, about macros and images, about installation and setting up servers, about user accounts and administration, about prototyping and documentation. They learned how to tailor the interface, to load and index the collection, and to satisfy the requirements of their client. Greenstone was found useful for yet another community!

Ian Witten has given numerous tutorials and presentations about digital libraries, helping thousands understand key concepts, as well as how the Greenstone software can be of use. Talking with many of those attending these sessions, I have found his impact to be positive and beneficial. This book should extend the reach of his in-person contact to a wider audience, helping fill the widely felt need to understand "digital libraries" and to be able to deploy a "digital library in a box." Together with David Bainbridge, Witten has prepared this book, greatly extending his tutorial overviews and drawing upon a long series of articles from the New Zealand Digital Library Project—some of the very best papers in the digital library field.

This book builds upon the authors' prior work in a broad range of related areas. It expands upon R&D activities in the compression, information retrieval, and multimedia fields, some connected with the MG system (and the popular book *Managing Gigabytes*, also in this book series). It brings in a human touch, explaining how digital libraries have aided diverse communities, from Uganda to New Zealand, from New Mexico to New York, from those working in physics to those enjoying popular music. Indeed, this work satisfies the "5S" checklist that I often use to highlight the key aspects of digital libraries, involving societies, scenarios, spaces, structures, and streams.

Working with UNESCO and through the open source community, the New Zealand team has turned Greenstone into a tool that has been widely deployed by *Societies* around the globe, as explained at both the beginning and end of the book. Greenstone's power and flexibility have allowed it to serve a variety of needs and support a range of user tasks, according to diverse *Scenarios*. Searching and browsing, involving both phrases and metadata and through both user requests and varied protocols, can support both scholars and those focused on oral cultures.

With regard to *Spaces,* Greenstone supports both peoples and resources scattered around the globe, with content originating across broad ranges of time. Supporting virtual libraries and distributed applications, digital libraries can be based in varied locations. Spaces also are covered through the 2D user interfaces involved in presentation, as well as internal representations of content representation and organization.

Structures are highlighted in the chapters on documents as well as markup and metadata. Rarely can one find a clear explanation of character encoding schemes such as Unicode, or page description languages such as PostScript and PDF, in addition to old standbys such as Word and LaTeX, and multimedia schemes like GIF, PNG, JPEG, TIFF, and MPEG. Seldom can one find a clearer discussion of XML, CSS, and XSL, in addition to MARC and Dublin Core. From key elements (acronyms, phrases, generic entities, and references) to collections, from lists to classification structure, from metadata to catalogs, the organizational aspects of digital libraries are clearly explicated.

Digital libraries build upon underlying *Streams* of content: from characters to words to texts, from pixels to images, and from tiny fragments to long audio and video streams. This book covers how to handle all of these, through flexible plugins and classifiers, using macros and databases, and through processes and protocols. Currently popular approaches are discussed, including the Open Archives Initiative, as well as important themes like digital preservation.

Yes, this book satisfies the "5S" checklist. Yes, this book can be used in courses at both undergraduate and graduate levels. Yes, this book can support practical projects and important applications. Yes, this book is a valuable reference, drawing upon years of research and practice. I hope, like me, you will read this book many times, enjoying its engaging style, learning both principles and concepts, and seeing how digital libraries can help you in your present and future endeavors.

Preface

On the top floor of the Tate Modern Art Gallery in London is a meeting room with a magnificent view over the River Thames and down into the open circle of Shakespeare's Globe Theatre reconstructed nearby. Here, at a gathering of senior administrators who fund digital library projects internationally, one of the authors stood up to introduce himself and ended by announcing that he was writing a book entitled *How to Build a Digital Library*. On sitting down, his neighbor nudged him and asked with a grin, "A work of fiction, eh?" A few weeks earlier and half a world away, the same author was giving a presentation about a digital library software system at an international digital library conference in Virginia, when a colleague in the audience noticed someone in the next row who, instead of paying attention to the talk, downloaded that very software over a wireless link, installed it on his laptop, checked the documentation, and built a digital library collection of his e-mail files—all within the presentation's 20-minute time slot.

These little cameos illustrate the extremes. Digital libraries?—colossal investments, which like today's national libraries will grow over decades and centuries, daunting in complexity. Conversely: digital libraries?—off-the-shelf technology; just add documents and stir. Of course, we are talking about very different things: a personal library of ephemeral notes hardly compares with a national treasure-house of information. But don't sneer at the "library" of e-mail: this collection gives its user valued searching and browsing facilities, and with half a week's rather than half an hour's work one could create a document management system that stores documents for a large multinational corporation.

Digital libraries are organized collections of information. Our experience of the World Wide Web—vibrant yet haphazard, uncontrolled and uncontrollable—daily reinforces the impotence of information without organization. Likewise, experience of using online public access library catalogs from the desktop—impeccably but stiffly organized, and distressingly remote from the actual documents themselves—reinforces the frustrations engendered by organizations without fingertip-accessible information. Can we not have it both ways? Enter digital libraries.

Whereas physical libraries have been around for 25 centuries, digital libraries span a dozen years. Yet in today's information society, with its Siamese twin, the knowledge economy, digital libraries will surely figure among the most important and influential institutions of this new century. The information revolution not only supplies the technological horsepower that drives digital libraries, but fuels an unprecedented demand for storing, organizing, and accessing information. If information is the currency of the knowledge economy, digital libraries will be the banks where it is invested.

We do not believe that digital libraries are supplanting existing bricks-and-mortar libraries—not in the near- and medium-term future that this book is about. And we certainly don't think you should be burning your books in favor of flat-panel displays! Digital libraries are new tools for achieving human goals by changing the way that information is used in the world. We are talking about new ways of dealing with knowledge, not about replacing existing institutions.

What is a digital library? What does it look like? Where does the information come from? How do you put it together? Where to start? The aim of this book is to answer these questions in a plain and straightforward manner, with a strong practical "how to" flavor.

We define digital libraries as

> focused collections of digital objects, including text, video, and audio, along with methods for access and retrieval, and for selection, organization, and maintenance.

To keep things concrete, we show examples of digital library collections in an eclectic range of areas, with an emphasis on cultural, historical, and humanitarian applications, as well as technical ones. These collections are formed from different kinds of material, organized in different ways, presented in different languages. We think they will help you see how digital libraries can be applied to real problems. Then we show you how to build your own.

The Greenstone software

A comprehensive software resource has been created to illustrate the ideas in the book and form a possible basis for your own digital library. Called the Greenstone Digital Library Software, it is freely available as source code on the World Wide Web (at *www.greenstone.org*) and comes precompiled for many popular platforms. It is a complete industrial-strength implementation of essentially all the techniques covered in this book. A fully operational, flexible, extensible system for constructing easy-to-use digital libraries, Greenstone is already widely deployed internationally and is being used (for example) by United Nations agencies and related organizations to deliver humanitarian information in developing countries. The ability to build new digital library collections, particularly in developing countries, is being promoted in a joint project in which UNESCO is supporting and distributing the Greenstone digital library software.

Although some parts of the book are tightly integrated with the Greenstone software—for it is hard to talk specifically and meaningfully about practical topics of building digital libraries without reference to a particular implementation—we have worked to minimize this dependence and make the book of interest to people using other software infrastructure for their digital collections. Most of what we say has broad application and is not tied to any particular implementation. The parts that are specific to Greenstone are confined to two chapters (Chapters 6 and 7), with a brief introduction in Chapter 1 (Section 1.4), and the Appendix. Even these parts are generally useful, for those not planning to build upon Greenstone will be able to use this material as a baseline, or make use of Greenstone's capabilities as a yardstick to help evaluate other designs.

How the book is organized

The gulf between the general and the particular has presented interesting challenges in organizing this book. As the title says, our aim is to show you how to build a digital library, and we really do want you to build your own collections (it doesn't have to take long, as the above-mentioned conference attendee discovered). But to work within a proper context you need to learn something about libraries and information organization in general. And if your practical work is to proceed beyond a simple proof-of-concept prototype, you will need to come to grips with countless nitty-gritty details.

We have tried to present what you need to know in a logical sequence, introducing new ideas where they belong and developing them fully at that point. However, we also want the chapters to function as independent entities that can be read in different ways. We are well aware that books like this are seldom read through from cover to cover! The result is, inevitably, that some topics are scattered throughout the book.

We cover three rather different themes: the intellectual challenges of libraries and digital libraries, the practical standards involved in representing documents digitally, and how to use Greenstone to build your own collections. Many academic readers will want a textbook, some a general text on digital libraries, others a book with a strong practical component that can support student projects.

For a general introduction to digital libraries, read Chapters 1 and 2 to learn about libraries and library organization, then Chapter 3 to find out about what digital libraries look like from a user's point of view, and then skip straight to Chapter 9 to see what the future holds.

To learn about the standards used to represent documents digitally, skim Chapter 1; read Chapters 4, 5, and 8 to learn about the standards; and then look at Chapter 3 to see how they can be used to support interfaces for searching and browsing. If you are interested in converting documents to digital form, read Section 2.4 as well.

To learn how to build a digital library as quickly as possible, skim Chapter 1 (but check Section 1.4) and then turn straight to Chapter 6. You will need to consult the Appendix when installing the Greenstone software. If you run into things you need to know about library organization, different kinds of interfaces, document formats, or metadata formats, you can return to the intervening material.

For a textbook on digital libraries without any commitment to specific software, use all of the book in sequence but omit Chapters 6 and 7. For a text with a strong practical component, read all chapters in order—and then turn your students loose on the software!

We hate acronyms and shun them wherever possible—but in this area you just can't escape them. A glossary of terms is included near the end of the book to help you through the swamp.

What the book covers

We open with four scenarios intended to dispel any ideas that digital libraries are no more than a routine development of traditional libraries with bytes instead of books. Then we discuss the concept of a *digital library* and set it in the historical context of library evolution over the ages. One thread that runs through the book is internationalization and the role of digital libraries in developing countries—for we believe that here digital libraries represent a "killer app" for computer technology. After summarizing the principal features of the Greenstone software, the first chapter closes with a discussion of issues involved in copyright and "harvesting" material from the Web.

Recognizing that many readers are itching to get on with actually *building* their digital library, Chapter 2 opens with an invitation to skip ahead to the start of Chapter 6 for an account of how to use the Greenstone software to create a plain but utilitarian collection that contains material of your own choice. This is very easy to do and should only take half an hour if you restrict yourself to a demonstration prototype with a small volume of material. (You will have to spend a few minutes downloading and installing the software first; turn to the Appendix to get started.) We want you to slake your natural curiosity about what is involved in building digital collections, so that you can comfortably focus on learning more about the foundations. We then proceed to discuss where the material in your library might come from (including the process of optical character recognition or OCR) and describe traditional methods of library organization.

As the definition of *digital library* given earlier implies, digital libraries involve two communities: end users who are interested in access and retrieval, and librarians who select, organize, and maintain information collections. Chapter 3 takes the user's point of view. Of course, digital libraries would be a complete failure if you had to study a book in order to learn how to use them— they are supposed to be easy to use!—and this book is really directed at the library builder, not the library user. Nevertheless it is useful to survey what different digital libraries look like. Examples are taken from domains ranging from human development to culture, with audiences ranging from children to library professionals, material ranging from text to music, and languages ranging from Māori to Chinese. We show many examples of browsing structures, from simple lists to hierarchies, date displays, and dynamically generated phrase hierarchies.

Next we turn to documents, the digital library's raw material. Chapter 4 begins with character representation, in particular Unicode, which is a way of representing all the characters used in all the world's languages. Plain text formats introduce some issues that you need to know about. Here we take the opportunity to describe full-text indexing, the basic technology for searching text, and also digress to introduce the question of segmenting words in languages like Chinese. We then describe popular formats for document representation: PostScript; PDF (Portable Document Format); RTF (Rich Text Format); the native format used by Microsoft Word, a popular word processor; and LaTeX, commonly used for mathematical and scientific documents. We also introduce the principal international standards used for representing images, audio, and video.

Besides documents, there is another kind of raw material for digital libraries: metadata. Often characterized as "data about data," metadata figures prominently in this book because it forms the basis for organizing both digital and traditional libraries. The related term *markup*, which in today's consumer society we usually associate with price increases, has another meaning: it refers to the process of annotating documents with typesetting information. In recent times this has been extended to annotating documents with structural information—including metadata—rather than (or as well as) formatting commands. Chapter 5 covers markup and metadata and also explains how metadata is expressed in traditional library catalogs. We introduce the idea of extracting metadata from the raw text of the documents themselves and give examples of what can be extracted.

Up to this point the book has been quite general and applies to any digital library. Chapters 6 and 7 are specific to the Greenstone software. There are two parts to a digital library system: the offline part, preparing a document collection for presentation, and the online part, presenting the collection to the user through an appropriate interface. Chapter 6 describes the first part: how to build Greenstone collections. This involves configuring the digital library and creating the full-text indexes and metadata databases that are needed to make it work. Given the desired style of presentation and the input that is available, you come up with a formal description of the facilities that are required and let the software do the rest.

To make the digital library as flexible and tailorable as possible, Greenstone uses an object-oriented software architecture. It defines general methods for presentation and display that can be subclassed and adapted to particular collections. To retain full flexibility (e.g., for translating the interface into different languages) a macro language is used to generate the Web pages. A communications protocol is also used so that novel user interface modules can interact with the digital library engine underneath to implement radically different presentation styles. These are described in Chapter 7.

In Chapter 8 we reach out and look at other standards and protocols, which are necessary to allow digital libraries to interoperate with one another and with related technologies. For example, electronic books—e-books—are becoming popular, or at least widely promoted, and digital libraries may need to be able to export material in such forms.

Finally we close with visions of the future of digital libraries and mention some important related topics that we have not been able to develop fully. We hope that this book will help you learn the strengths and pitfalls of digital libraries, gain an understanding of the principles behind the practical organization of information, and come to grips with the tradeoffs that arise when implementing digital libraries. The rest is up to you. Our aim will have been achieved if you actually *build a digital library*!

Acknowledgments

The best part of writing a book is reflecting on all the help you have had from your friends. This book is the outcome of a long-term research and development effort at the University of Waikato—the New Zealand Digital Library Project. Without the Greenstone software the book would not exist, and we begin by thanking Rodger McNab, who charted our course by making the major design decisions that underlie Greenstone. Rodger left our group some time ago, but the influence of his foresight remains—a legacy that this book exploits. Next comes Stefan Boddie, the man who has kept Greenstone going over the years, who steers the ship and navigates the shoals with a calm and steady hand on the tiller. Craig Nevill-Manning had the original inspiration for the expedition: he showed us what could be done, and left us to it.

Every crew member, past and present, has helped with this book, and we thank them all. Most will have to remain anonymous, but we must mention a few striking contributions (in no particular order). Te Taka Keegan and Mark Apperley undertook the Māori Newspaper project described in Chapter 3. Through Te Taka's efforts we receive inspiration every day from the magnificent Māori *toki* that resides in our laboratory and can be seen in Figure 1.10, a gift from the Māori people of New Zealand that symbolizes our practical approach to building digital libraries. Lloyd Smith (along with Rodger and Craig) created the music collections that are illustrated here. Steve Jones builds many novel user interfaces, especially ones involving phrase browsing, and some of our key examples are his. Sally Jo Cunningham is the resident expert on library organization and related matters. Stuart Yeates designed and built the acronym extraction module and helped in countless other ways, while Dana McKay worked on such things as extracting date metadata, as well as drafting the Greenstone manuals that eventually turned into Chapters 6 and 7. YingYing Wen was our chief source of information on the Chinese language and culture, while Malika Mahoui took care of the Arabic side. Matt Jones from time to time provided us with sage and well-founded advice.

Many others in the digital library lab at Waikato have made substantial—nay, heroic—technical contributions to Greenstone. Gordon Paynter, researcher and senior software architect, built the phrase browsing interface, helped design the Greenstone communication protocol, and improved many aspects of metadata handling. Hong Chen, Kathy McGowan, John McPherson, Trent Mankelow, and Todd Reed have all worked to improve the software. Geoff Holmes and Bill Rogers helped us over some very nasty low-level Windows problems. Eibe Frank worked on key-phrase extraction, while Bernhard Pfahringer helped us conceptualize the Collector interface. Annette Falconer worked on a Women's History collection that opened up new avenues of research. There are many others: we thank them all.

Tucked away as we are in a remote (but very pretty) corner of the Southern Hemisphere, visitors to our department play a crucial role: they act as sounding boards and help us develop our thinking in diverse ways. Some deserve special mention. George Buchanan came from London for two long and productive spells. He helped develop the communications protocol and built the CD-ROM writing module, and continues to work with our team. Elke Duncker, also from London, advised us on cultural and ethical issues. Dave Nichols from Lancaster worked on the Java side of Greenstone and, with Kirsten Thomson, helped evaluate the Collector interface. The influence of Carl Gutwin from Saskatoon is particularly visible in the phrase browsing and key-phrase extraction areas. Gary Marsden from Cape Town also made significant contributions. Dan Camarzan, Manuel Ursu, and their team of collaborators in Brasov, Romania, have worked hard to improve Greenstone and put it into the field. Alistair Moffat from Melbourne, Australia, along with many of his associates, was responsible for MG, the full-text searching component, and he and Tim Bell of Christchurch, New Zealand, have been instrumental in helping us develop the ideas expressed in this book.

Special thanks are due to Michel Loots of Human Info in Antwerp, who has encouraged, cajoled, and occasionally bullied us into making our software available in a form designed to be most useful to people in developing countries, based on his great wealth of experience. We are particularly grateful to him for opening up this new world to us; it has given us immense personal satisfaction and the knowledge that our technological efforts are materially helping people in need. We acknowledge the support of John Rose of UNESCO in Paris, Maria Trujillo of Colombia, and Chico Fernandez-Perez of the FAO in Rome. Rob Akscyn in Pittsburgh has been a continual source of inspiration, and his wonderful metaphors occasionally enliven this book. Until he was so sadly and unexpectedly snatched away from us, we derived great benefit from the boundless enthusiasm of Ferrers Clark at CISTI, the Canadian national science and technology library. We have learned much from conversations with Dieter Fellner of Braunschweig, particularly with respect to generalized documents, and from Richard Wright at the BBC in London. Last but by no means least, Harold Thimbleby in London has been a constant source of material help and moral support.

We would like to acknowledge all who have translated the Greenstone interface into different languages—at the time of writing we have interfaces in Arabic, Chinese, Dutch, French, German, Hebrew, Indonesian, Italian, Māori, Portuguese, Russian, and Spanish. We are very grateful to Jojan Varghese and his team from Vergis Electronic Publishing, Mumbai, India, for taking the time to explain the intricacies of Hindi and related scripts. We also thank everyone who has contributed to the GNU-licensed packages included in the Greenstone distribution.

The Department of Computer Science at the University of Waikato has supported us generously in all sorts of ways, and we owe a particular debt of gratitude to Mark Apperley for his enlightened leadership, warm encouragement, and financial help. In the early days we were funded by the New Zealand Lotteries Board and the New Zealand Foundation for Research, Science and Technology, which got the project off the ground. We have also received support from the Ministry of Education, while the Royal Society of New Zealand Marsden Fund supports closely related work on text mining and computer music. The Alexander Turnbull Library has given us access to source material for the Māori Niupepa project, along with highly valued encouragement.

Diane Cerra and Marilyn Alan of Morgan Kaufmann have worked hard to shape this book, and Yonie Overton, our project manager, has made the process go very smoothly for us. Angela Powers has provided excellent support at the Waikato end. Ed Fox, the series editor, contributed enthusiasm, ideas, and a very careful reading of the manuscript. We gratefully acknowledge the efforts of the anonymous reviewers, one of whom in particular made a great number of pertinent and constructive comments that helped us improve this book significantly.

Much of this book was written in people's homes while the authors were traveling around the world, including an extraordinary variety of delightful little villages—Killinchy in Ireland, Great Bookham and Welwyn North in England, Pampelonne in France, Mascherode in Germany, Canmore in Canada—as well as cities such as London, Paris, Calgary, New Orleans, and San Francisco. You all know who you are—thanks! Numerous institutions helped with facilities, including Middlesex University in London, Braunschweig Technical University in Germany, the University of Calgary in Canada, and the Payson Center for International Development and Technology Transfer in New Orleans. The generous hospitality of Google during a two-month stay is gratefully acknowledged: this proved to be a very stimulating environment in which to think about large-scale digital libraries and complete the book.

All our traveling has helped spin the threads of internationalization and human development that are woven into the pages that follow. Our families—Annette, Pam, Anna, and Nikki—have supported us in countless ways, sometimes journeying with us, sometimes keeping the fire burning at home in New Zealand. They have had to live with this book, and we are deeply grateful for their sustained support, encouragement, and love.

About the Web site

You can view the book's full color figures at Morgan Kaufmann's *How to Build a Digital Library* Web site at *www.mkp.com/DL*. There you will also find two online appendices: a greatly expanded version of the printed appendix, *Installing and Operating Greenstone*, and another appendix entitled *Greenstone Source Code* for those who want to delve more deeply into the system. There is also a novel full-text index to the book that allows you to locate the pages in which words and word combinations appear.

1 Orientation

The world of digital libraries

Example One: Supporting human development

Kataayi is a grassroots cooperative organization based in the village of Kakunyu in rural Uganda. In recent years its enterprising members have built ferro-cement rainwater catchment tanks, utilized renewable energy technologies such as solar, wind, and biogas, and established a local industry making clay roofing tiles—among many other projects. But amid such human resourcefulness, information resources are scarce. The nearest public phone, fax, library, newspapers, and periodicals are found in the district town, Masaka, 20 km distant over rough roads. Masaka boasts no e-mail or Internet access. The difficulty of getting there effectively discourages local inhabitants from taking advantage of the information and communication technologies that we take for granted in developed countries.

The Kataayi community believe that an information and communication center will have a major development impact in their area. They laid the groundwork by acquiring a computer and solar power generation equipment. They established an e-mail connection via cellular phone and set up a computer training program. They constructed a brick building to house the center (Figure 1.1). And they gathered several books. But they need more information resources—lots more. They are looking for books covering topics such as practical technology,

Figure 1.1 Kataayi's information and communication center.

fair-trade marketing, agriculture, environmental conservation, spirituality, and social justice issues.

Then they discovered digital libraries. The Humanity Development Library is a compendium of some 1,200 authoritative books and periodicals on just such topics, produced by many disparate organizations—UN agencies and other international organizations. In print these books would weigh 340 kg, cost $20,000, and occupy a small library bookstack. Instead the collection takes the form of a digital library and is distributed on a single CD-ROM throughout the developing world at essentially no cost. Related digital library collections cover topics such as disaster relief, agriculture, the environment, medicine and health, food and nutrition; more are coming. These digital libraries will increase Kataayi's information resources immeasurably, at a miniscule fraction of the cost of paper books.

Example Two: Pushing on the frontiers of science

Leave this local community and enter a very different one that operates internationally and on a far larger scale. For the last decade physicists have been using automated archives to disseminate the results of their research. The first archive, in high-energy physics, began in the early 1990s. It targeted a tiny group of fewer than 200 physicists working on a particular set of research problems, who wanted to communicate their progress. Within months the clientele had grown fivefold. Numerous other physics databases sprang into existence. Within a few years these archives served tens of thousands of researchers; by the year 2000 they had grown to 150,000 papers and processed 150,000 requests per day.

The physics archival digital libraries are entirely automated. To submit a research paper, contributors fill out title, author, and abstract on an electronic form and transmit the full text of the paper. Upon receipt, which is instantaneous, the paper immediately and automatically becomes part of the archive, permanently accessible to others. The contributions are not reviewed or moderated in any way, except for a quick scan to ensure that they are relevant to the discipline. The chaff is simply ignored by the community. The upshot is that research results are communicated on a dramatically accelerated timescale, and the expense and waste of hard-copy distribution is eliminated.

For some areas of physics, online archives have already become the dominant means of communicating research progress. Many people believe that the scheme has effectively replaced commercial publication as a way of conveying both topical and archival research information. Why don't researchers in every discipline follow suit? Soon, perhaps, they will. Proponents of these online archives forecast the imminent demise of commercially published research journals and believe that communicating research results using "chemicals adsorbed onto sliced processed dead trees" will rapidly become a quaint anachronism. On the other hand, many disagree: they argue that peer review is still highly valued in most scientific disciplines, and that even in the small, specialized communities where they are used, online archives augment rather than replace peer-reviewed journals.

Example Three: Preserving a traditional culture

The physics archive is centered at the Los Alamos National Laboratory in New Mexico. Only 36 miles away as the crow flies, but light-years distant in other respects, is the Zia Pueblo, home of one of a score of Native American tribes in New Mexico (Figure 1.2). By 1900 the population had fallen to less than 100,

Figure 1.2 The Zia Pueblo village.

and the tribe was expected to die out during the 20th century. With the return of some land, and medicine and education provided by U.S. government programs, fortunes have improved and the people now number 600. But a major problem is facing the Zia Pueblo today: the loss of its language and traditional culture. Young people are not learning the Zia Pueblo traditions, nor Keresan, its language. This is a common complaint in traditional societies, overexposed as we all are to the deafening voice of popular commercial culture blaring everywhere from television, radio, and advertising billboards.

To preserve the Zia language and traditions, a digital library has been proposed. It will include an oral history compilation, with interviews of tribal elders conducted in their native language. It will include an anthology of traditional songs, with audio recordings, musical scores transcribed from them, and lyrics translated by a native speaker. It will include video recordings of tribal members performing Pueblo dances and ceremonies, along with a synopsis describing each ceremony and a transcription and translation of the recorded audio. The goal is to produce a multimedia artifact, the purpose of which is not so much to archive the material as to make it publicly available and to involve members of the tribe in collecting and disseminating it.

Example Four: Exploring popular music

Turn from this small, esoteric group in New Mexico to the wide-ranging, disorganized, eclectic panoply of music that is played in the Western world today. In all human societies music is an expression of popular culture. Different generations identify strongly with different musical styles and artists. People's taste in music reflects their personality and sense of identity: teenagers, in particular, regard their musical preferences as being strongly bound up with who they are. Music is a medium that is both popular and international. Pop music culture transcends social boundaries, be they national borders or socioeconomic groupings. Yet music also exhibits strong cultural diversity: folk music is specific to a particular country or region, and different styles characterize local ethnic groupings.

Imagine a digital music library that reflects popular taste, a library that people from all walks of life will want to use. From an immense music collection you can retrieve tunes in many ways: by humming a theme, by recalling words from the title or lyrics, by giving the composer's name—or you can specify any combination of these. Flexible browsing facilities allow you to meander through the collection, listening to tunes rendered by a synthesizer, or indeed to live recordings. Almost any song you can think of is there, often in dozens of different versions.

Experimental versions of such libraries already exist. A huge volume of musical material is already on the Web in the form of MIDI files, the musical representation used by synthesizers. It is easy to locate and download hundreds of thousands of files covering a wide range of styles, from classical symphonies to current pop songs, from jazz classics to ethnic folk songs. In a very real sense these reflect popular taste, comprising whatever people have decided to spend their time entering. You will find a score of versions of the Beatles' *Yellow Submarine* and Bach's *Air on a G-string*. All these tunes can be indexed by automatically identifying melodic themes and extracting text containing the title, artist, composer, and lyrics. Contentious copyright issues can be avoided by leaving all source material on its home site: what the library provides is not a repository but a catalog and means of access. And the Web is a prolific source of other musical resources, from record stores to guitar tablatures for popular tunes. Having found a tune, you can listen to samples of recordings by different artists, obtain a CD, watch a rock video, or buy sheet music.

The scope of digital libraries

These four examples, at different stages of development and deployment, hint at the immense range of digital libraries. From the perspective of ordinary people, libraries often seem scholarly and esoteric. But they are not necessarily so. Practical topics are of interest to practical people like Kataayi's members. Academic libraries have as their purpose research and education: high-energy physicists already base their research activity on electronic document collections. Digital libraries offer unique ways of recording, preserving, and propagating culture in multimedia form. Collections that reflect popular taste in music (or film, or TV) will become a mass-market consumer product, with delivery to teenagers on miniature, mobile, Web-capable, pocket devices.

An application that makes a sustained market for a promising but underutilized technology is often called a "killer app." The term was coined in the mid-1980s for the Lotus spreadsheet, then the major driving force behind the business market for IBM PCs. (VisiCalc had previously played a similar role in the success of the Apple II.) The World Wide Web is often described as the Internet's killer app. The killer app for digital libraries may well be music collections; in turn, we will see in Section 1.3 that as far as the developing world is concerned, digital libraries themselves may be killer apps for computer technology.

1.1 Libraries and digital libraries

Is a digital library an institution or a piece of technology? The term *digital library*, like the word *library*, means different things to different people. Many people think of libraries as bricks and mortar, a quiet place where books are kept. To professional librarians, they are institutions that arrange for the preservation of literature, their collection, organization, and access. And not just for books: there are

Figure 1.3 The New York Public Library.

libraries of art, film, sound recordings, botanical specimens, and cultural objects. To researchers, libraries are networks that provide ready access to the world's recorded knowledge, wherever it is held. Today's university students of science and technology, sadly, increasingly think of libraries as the World Wide Web—or rather, they misguidedly regard the Web as the ultimate library.

But a digital library is not really a "digitized library." We hope that you, dear reader, are reading *How to Build a Digital Library* because you are thinking of building a digital library. But we do not imagine that you are the director of the New York Public Library, contemplating replacing that magnificent edifice by a computer (Figure 1.3). Nor do we want you to think, even for a moment, of burning your books at home and sitting by the fireside on winter evenings absorbed in a flat-panel computer display. (Some say that had books been invented after computers were, they would have been hailed as a great advance.) Rather, we hope that you are inspired by a vision—perhaps something like the scenarios above—of achieving new human goals by changing the way that information is used in the world. Digital libraries are about new ways of dealing with knowledge: preserving, collecting, organizing, propagating, and accessing it—not about deconstructing existing institutions and putting them in an electronic box.

In this book, a digital library is conceived as an organized collection of information,

> a focused collection of digital objects, including text, video, and audio, along with methods for access and retrieval, and for selection, organization, and maintenance of the collection.

This broad interpretation of "digital objects"—not just text—is reflected in the scenarios above. Beyond audio and video we also want to include such things as 3D objects, simulations, dynamic visualizations, and virtual-reality worlds. The second and third parts of the definition deliberately accord equal weight to user (access and retrieval) and librarian (selection, organization, and maintenance). The librarian functions are often overlooked by digital library proponents, who generally have a background in technology and approach their work from this perspective rather than from the viewpoint of library or information science.

But selection, organization, and maintenance are central to the notion of a library. If *data* is characterized as recorded facts, then *information* is the set of patterns, or expectations, that underlie the data. You could go on to define *knowledge* as the accumulation of your set of expectations, and *wisdom* as the value attached to knowledge. All information is not created equal, and it is wisdom that librarians put into the library by making decisions about what to include in a collection—difficult decisions!—and following up with appropriate ways of organizing and maintaining the information. Indeed it is exactly these features that will distinguish digital libraries from the anarchic mess that we call the World Wide Web.

Digital libraries do tend to blur what has traditionally been a sharp distinction between user and librarian. The collections in the scenarios above were not, in the main, created by professional librarians. Nevertheless it is important to keep in mind the distinction between the two roles. Digital library software supports users as they search and browse the collection; equally it supports librarians as they strive to provide appropriate organizational structures and maintain them effectively.

Digital libraries are libraries without walls. But they do need boundaries. The very notion of a collection implies a boundary: the fact that some things are in the collection means that others must lie outside it. And collections need a kind of presence, a conceptual integrity, that gives them cohesion and identity: that is where the wisdom comes in. Every collection should have a well-articulated *purpose*, which states the objectives it is intended to achieve, and a set of *principles*, which are the directives that will guide decisions on what should be included and—equally important—what should be excluded. These decisions are difficult ones; we return to them in Section 2.1.

Digital collections often present an appearance that is opaque: a screen—typically a Web page—with no indication of what, or how much, lies beyond. Is it a carefully selected treasure or a morass of worthless ephemera? Are there half a dozen documents or many millions? At least physical libraries occupy physical space, present a physical appearance, and exhibit tangible physical organization. When standing on the threshold of a large bricks-and-mortar library, you gain a sense of presence and permanence that reflects the care taken in building and maintaining the collection inside. No one could confuse it with a dung heap! Yet in the virtual world the difference is not so palpable.

We draw a clear distinction between a digital library and the World Wide Web: the Web lacks the essential features of selection and organization. We also want to distinguish a digital library from a Web site—even one that offers a focused collection of well-organized material. Existing digital libraries invariably manifest themselves in this way. But a Web site that provides a wealth of digital objects, along with appropriate methods of access and retrieval, should not necessarily be considered a "library." Libraries are storehouses to which new material can easily be added. Most well-organized Web sites are created manually through hand-crafted hypertext linkage structures. But just as adding new acquisitions to a physical library does not involve delving into the books and rewriting parts of them, so it should be possible for new material to become a first-class member of a digital library without any need for manual updating of the structures used for access and retrieval.

What connects a new acquisition into the structure of a physical library is partly where it is placed on the shelves, but more important is the information about it that is included in the library catalog. We call this information *metadata*—data about data—and it will figure prominently in the digital libraries described in this book.

1.2   The changing face of libraries

Libraries are society's repositories for knowledge: temples, if you like, of culture and wisdom. Born in an era where agriculture was humankind's greatest preoccupation, libraries experienced a resurgence with the invention of printing in the Renaissance, and really began to flourish when the industrial revolution prompted a series of inventions that mechanized the printing process—the steam press, for example.

Libraries have been around for more than 25 centuries, although only one individual library has survived more than about 5 centuries, and most are far younger. The exception is a collection of more than 2,000 engraved stone slabs or "steles," situated in Xi'an, an ancient walled city in central China with a long and distinguished history. The collection was established in the Song dynasty (ca. 1100 A.D.) and has been gradually expanded with new work since that time. Each stele stands 2 or 3 meters high and is engraved with a poem, story, or historical record (Figure 1.4). For example, Confucius's works are here, as is much classic poetry, and an account of how a Christian sect spread eastward to China along the Silk Road. Chinese writing is an art form, and this library gathers together the works of many outstanding calligraphers over a period of two millennia. It also contains the heaviest books in the world!

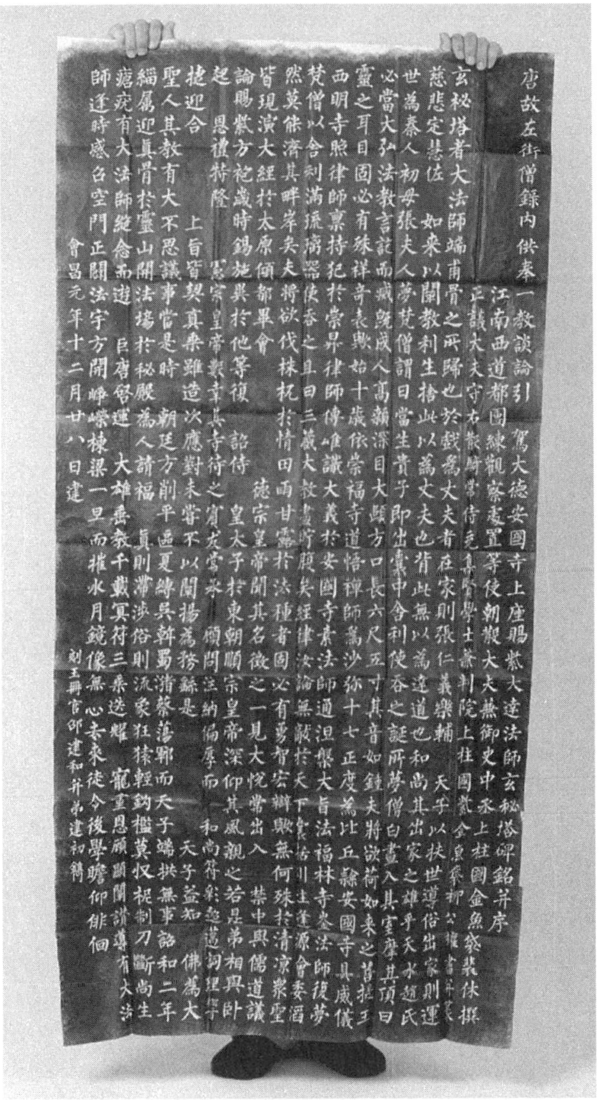

Figure 1.4 Rubbing from a stele in Xi'an.

We think of the library as the epitome of a stable, solid, unchanging institution, and indeed the silent looming presence of 2,000 enormous stone slabs—often called the "forest of steles"—certainly projects a sense of permanence. But this is an exception. Over the years libraries have evolved beyond recognition. Originally intended for storage and preservation, libraries have refocused to place users at the center, with increased emphasis on information exchange.

Ancient libraries were only useful to the small minority of people who could read and were accessible within stringent limitations imposed by social conditions.

Medieval monastic and university libraries held chained copies of books in public reading areas. Other copies were available for loan, although substantial security was demanded for each volume borrowed.

The public library movement took hold in the 19th century. Still, the libraries of the day had bookstacks that were closed to the public: patrons perused the catalog and chose their books, which were then handed out over the counter. In continental Europe, most libraries still operate this way. However, progressive 20th century librarians came to realize the advantage of allowing readers to browse among the shelves and make their own selections, and the idea of open-access libraries became widely adopted in English-speaking countries, marking the fulfillment of the principle of free access to the contents of libraries by all—the symbolic snapping of the links of the chained book.

Today we stand on the threshold of the digital library. The information revolution not only supplies the technological horsepower that drives digital libraries, but fuels an unprecedented demand for storing, organizing, and accessing information—a demand which is, for better or worse, economically driven rather than curiosity driven as in days gone by. If information is the currency of the knowledge economy, digital libraries will be the banks where it is invested. Indeed Goethe once said that visiting a library was like entering the presence of great wealth which was silently paying untold dividends.

In the beginning

The fabled library of Alexandria is widely recognized as the world's first great library—although long before it, Assyrian king Assurbanipal (668–626 B.C.) established a comprehensive, well-organized collection of tens of thousands of clay tablets, and long before that, Chinese written records began, having a history extending at least as far back as the 18th century B.C. Created around 300 B.C., the Alexandrian Library grew at a phenomenal rate and, according to legend, contained some 200,000 volumes within 10 years.

The work of the acquisitions department was rather more dramatic than in the libraries of today. During a famine, for example, the king refused to sell grain to the Athenians unless he received in pledge the original manuscripts of some leading authors. The manuscripts were diligently copied and the copies returned to the owners, while the originals went into the library. By far the largest single acquisition occurred when Mark Antony stole the rival library of Pergamum and gave it lock, stock, and barrel—200,000 volumes—to Cleopatra as a love token; she passed it over to Alexandria for safekeeping.

By the time Julius Caesar set fire to the ships in the harbor of Alexandria in 47 B.C. and the fire spread to the shore, the library had grown to 700,000 volumes. More than 2,000 years would pass before any other library would attain this size, notwithstanding technological innovations such as the printing press. Tragically the Alexandrian library was destroyed. Much remained after Caesar's fire, but this was willfully laid waste (according to the Moslems) by Christians in 391 A.D. or (according to the Christians) by Moslems in 641 A.D. In the Arab conquest, Amru, the captain of Caliph Omar's army, would apparently have been willing to spare the library, but the fanatical Omar is said to have disposed of the problem of information explosion with the immortal words, "If these writings of the Greeks agree with the Koran, they are useless and need not be preserved; if they disagree, they are pernicious and ought to be destroyed."

The information explosion

Moving ahead a thousand years, let us peek at what was happening in a library at a major university near the center of European civilization a century or two after Gutenberg's introduction of the movable-type printing press around 1450.[1] Trinity College, Dublin, one of the oldest universities in Western Europe, was founded in 1592 by Queen Elizabeth I. In 1600 the library contained a meager collection of 30 printed books and 10 handwritten manuscripts. This grew rapidly, by several thousand, when two of the Fellows mounted a shopping expedition to England, and by a further 10,000 when the library received the personal collection of Archbishop Ussher, a renowned Irish man of letters, on his death in 1661.

At the time, however, even this collection was dwarfed by Duke August's of Wolfenbüttel, Germany, whose collection had reached 135,000 imprints by his death in 1666 and was the largest contemporary library in Europe, acclaimed as the eighth wonder of the world. These imprints were purchased in quires (i.e., unbound) and shipped to the duke in barrels, who had them bound in 31,000 volumes with pale parchment bindings that you can still see today. Incidentally this collection inspired Casanova, after spending seven days visiting the library in 1764, to declare that "I have sometimes thought that the life of those in heaven may be somewhat similar to [this visit]." Coming from the world's most renowned lover, this is high praise indeed!

Returning to Ireland, another great event in the development of Trinity College occurred in 1801, when an act was passed by the British Parliament decreeing that a copy of every book printed in the British Isles was to be donated to the Trinity College Library. This privilege extends to this day and is shared by five other libraries—the British National Library, the University Libraries of Oxford and Cambridge, and the National Libraries of Scotland and Wales. This "legal

---

1. The printing press was invented in China much earlier, around five centuries before Gutenberg.

deposit" law had a much earlier precedent in France, where King François I decreed in 1537 that a copy of every book published was to be placed in the Bibliothèque du Roi (long since incorporated into the French National Library). Likewise the Library of Congress receives copies of all books published in the U.S. But we digress.

There were no journals in Ussher's collection. The first scholarly journals appeared just after his death: the *Journal des Sçavans* began in January 1665 in France, and the *Philosophical Transactions* of the Royal Society began in March 1665 in England. These two have grown, hydralike, into hundreds of thousands of scientific journals today—although, as we have seen, some are being threatened with replacement by electronic archives.

In the 18th century the technology of printing really took hold. For example, more than 30,000 titles were published in France during a 60-year period in the mid-1700s. The printing press that Gutenberg had developed in order to make the Bible more widely available became the vehicle for disseminating the European Enlightenment—an emancipation of human thinking from the weight of authority of the church—some 300 years later.

In the U.S., President John Adams created a reference library for Congress when the seat of government was moved to the new capital city of Washington in 1800. He began by providing $5,000 "for the purchase of such books as may be necessary for the use of Congress—and for putting up a suitable apartment for containing them therein." The first books were ordered from England and shipped across the Atlantic in 11 hair trunks and a map case. The library was housed in the new Capitol until August 1814, when—in a miniature replay of Julius Caesar's exploits in Alexandria—British troops invaded Washington and burned the building. The small congressional library of some 3,000 volumes was lost in the fire. Another fire destroyed two-thirds of the collection in 1851. Unlike Alexandria, however, the Library of Congress has regrown—indeed its rotunda is a copy of the one in Wolfenbüttel two centuries earlier. In fact today it contains approximately 22 million volumes.

The information explosion began to hit home in Ireland in the middle of the 19th century. Work started in 1835 on the production of a printed catalog for the Trinity College Library (Figure 1.5), but by 1851 only the first volume, covering letters *A* and *B*, had been completed. The catalog was finally finished in 1887, but only by restricting the books that appeared in it to those published up to the end of 1872. Other libraries, however, were wrestling with much larger volumes of information. By the turn of the century, the Trinity College Library had around a quarter of a million books, while the Library of Congress had nearly three times that number. Both were dwarfed by the British Museum (now part of the British National Library), which at the time had nearly 2 million books, and the French National Library in Paris with over 2.5 million.

— Resolutie van de staten generael der Vereenighde Nederlanden, dienende tot antwoort op de memorie by de ambassadeurs van sijne majesteyt van Vranckrijck.
's Graven-hage, 1678. 4°.   Fag. H. 2. 80. N°. 20.
        Fag. H. 2. 85. N°. 17. Fag. H. 3. 42. N°. 4.

— Tractaet van vrede gemaeckt tot Nimwegen op den 10 Augusty, 1678, tusschen de ambassadeurs van [LOUIS XIV.] ende de ambassadeurs vande staten generael der Vereenighde Nederlanden.
                Fag. H. 2. 85. N°. 21.

— Nederlantsche absolutie op de Fransche belydenis.
Amsterdam, 1684. 4°.   Fag. H. 2. 50. N°. 22.

— Redenen dienende om aan te wijsen dat haar ho. mog. [niet] konnen verhindert werden een vredige afkomst te maken op de conditien by memorien van den grave d' Avaux van de 5 en 7 Juny, 1684, aangeboden.
[*s. l.*] 1684. 4°.   Fag. H. 2. 86. N°. 3.
        Fag. H. 2. 96. N°. 8. Fag. H. 3. 44. N°. 52.

— Redenen om aan te wijsen dat de bewuste werving van 16000 man niet kan gesustineert werden te zullen hebben konnen strekken tot het bevorderen van een accommodement tusschen Vrankrijk en Spaigne.
[*s. l.*] 1684. 4°.   Fag. H. 2. 86. N°. 4.
                Fag. H. 2. 96. N°. 2.

— D' oude mode van den nieuwen staat van oorlogh.
[*s. l.* 1684]. 4°.   Fag. H. 2. 86. N°. 12.
                Fag. H. 2. 96. N°. 3.

— Aenmerkingen over de althans swevende verschillen onder de leden van den staat van ons vaderlant.
[*s. l.*] 1684. 4°.   Fag. H. 2. 92. N°. 1.
        Fag. H. 2. 98. N°. 16. Fag. H. 3. 1. N°. 18.

— Missive van de staten generael der Vereenighde Nederlanden, . . . 14 Maert, 1684.
's Graven-hage, 1684. 4°.   Fag. H. 2. 92. N°. 10.

— Missive van de staaten generael der Vereenigde Nederlanden, . . . 11 July, 1684.
[*sin. tit.* 1684]. 4°.   Fag. H. 2. 96. N°. 13.
                Fag. H. 3. 44. N°. 69.

— Resolutie vande staten generael der Vereenighde Nederlanden, . . . 2 Maart, 1684.
's Gravenhage, 1684. 4°.   Fag. H. 2. 92. N°. 11.
                Fag. H. 3. 44. N°. 9.

— Extract uyt de resolutien van de staten generael, . . . 31 Maert, 1684.
[*s. l.*] 1684. 4°.   Fag. H. 2. 92. N°. 13.
        Fag. H. 2. 96. N°. 25. Fag. H. 3. 44. N°. 11.
                . Fag. H. 3. 44. N°. 15.

— Antwoort van de staten generael der Vereenighde Nederlanden op de propositie van wegen sijne churf. doorl. van Ceulen, Maert 23, 1684, gedaen.
's Gravenhage, 1684. 4°.   Fag. H. 2. 92. N°. 12.

Figure 1.5 A page of the original Trinity College Library catalog.

The Alexandrian principle

In an early statement of library policy, an Alexandrian librarian was reported as being "anxious to collect, if he could, all the books in the inhabited world, and, if he heard of, or saw, any book worthy of study, he would buy it"—and two millennia later this was formulated as a self-evident principle of librarianship: *It is a librarian's duty to increase the stock of his library.* When asked how large a library should be, librarians answered, "Bigger. And with provision for further expansion."

Only recently has the Alexandrian principle begun to be questioned. In 1974, following a 10-year building boom then unprecedented in library history, the *Encyclopedia Britannica* noted that "even the largest national libraries are . . . doubling in size every 16 to 20 years" and gently warned that "such an increase can hardly be supported indefinitely." And the struggle continues. In the past decade the national libraries of the U.K., France, Germany, and Denmark all opened new buildings. The ones in London and Paris are monumental in scale: their country's largest public buildings of the century. Standing on the bank of the Seine River, the Bibliothèque Nationale de France consists of four huge towers that appear like open books, surrounding a sunken garden plaza (Figure 1.6). The reading rooms occupy two levels around the garden, with bookshelves encircling them on the outer side.

Sustained exponential growth cannot continue. A collection of essays published in 1976 entitled *Farewell to Alexandria: Solutions to Space, Growth, and Performance Problems of Libraries* dwells on the problems that arise when growth must end. Sheer limitation of space has forced librarians to rethink their principles. Now they talk about "aggressive weeding" and "culling," "no-growth libraries," the "optimum size for collections," and some even ask, "Could smaller be better?" In a striking example of aggressive weeding, the library world was rocked in 1996 by allegations that the San Francisco Public Library had surreptitiously dumped 200,000 books, or 20 percent of its collection, into landfills, because its new building, though lavishly praised by architecture critics, was too small for all the books.

The notion of focused collections is replacing the Alexandrian model that the ideal library is vast and eternally growing. The notion of service to library users is replacing the idea of a library as a storehouse of all the world's knowledge. These movements will surely be reinforced by the experience of the World Wide Web, which amply illustrates the anarchy and chaos that inevitably result from sustained exponential growth. The events of the last quarter century have even shaken librarians' confidence in the continued existence of the traditional library. Defensive tracts with titles like *Future Libraries: Dreams, Madness and Reality* deride "technolust" and the empty promises of the technophiles.

Figure 1.6 The Bibliothèque Nationale de France.
Dominique Perrault, architect; © Alain Goustard,
photographer.

Early technodreams

Let us, for a moment at least, give an ear to the technophiles. Over 60 years ago,
science fiction writer H. G. Wells was promoting the concept of a "world brain"
based on a permanent world encyclopedia which "would be the mental background of every intelligent [person] in the world. It would be alive and growing
and changing continually under revision, extension and replacement from the
original thinkers in the world everywhere," and he added sardonically that "even
journalists would deign to use it."

Eight years later, Vannevar Bush, the highest-ranking scientific advisor in the
U.S. war effort, urged us to "consider a future device for individual use, which is
a sort of mechanized private file and library . . . a device in which an individual

Figure 1.7 Artist's conception of the Memex, Bush's automated library. Courtesy of Mary and Alfred Crimi Estate.

stores all his books, records, and communications, and which is mechanized so that it may be consulted with exceeding speed and flexibility" (Figure 1.7).

Fifteen years later, J. C. R. Licklider, head of the U.S. Department of Defense's Information Processing Techniques Office, envisioned that human brains and computing machines would be tightly coupled together and supported by a "network of 'thinking centers' that will incorporate the functions of present-day libraries together with anticipated advances in information storage and retrieval."

Toward the end of the 20th century we became accustomed to hearing similar pronouncements from the U.S. Presidential Office, rising above the road noise of the information superhighway.

The library catalog

Wells, Bush, Licklider, and other visionary thinkers were advocating something very close to what we might now call a *virtual library*. To paraphrase the dictionary definition, something is *virtual* if it exists in essence or effect though not in actual fact, form, or name. A virtual library is a library for all practical purposes, but a library without walls—or books.

In truth a virtual representation of books has been at the core of libraries right from the beginning: the catalog. Even before Alexandria, libraries were arranged by subject and had catalogs that gave the title of each work, the number of lines, the contents, and the opening words. In 240 B.C. an index was produced to provide access to the books in the Alexandrian library that was a classified subject catalog, a bibliography, and a biographical dictionary all in one.

A library catalog is a complete model that represents, in a predictable manner, the universe of books in the library. Catalogs provide a summary of, if not a surrogate for, library contents. Today we call this "metadata." And it is highly valuable in its own right. As a late 19th century librarian wrote, "Librarians classify and catalog the records of ascertained knowledge, the literature of the whole past. In this busy generation, the librarian makes time for his fellow mortals by saving it. And this function of organizing, of indexing, of time-saving and thought-saving, is associated peculiarly with the librarian of the 19th century."

Other essential aids to information-seeking in libraries are published bibliographies and indexes. Like catalogs, these are virtual representations—metadata—and they provide the traditional means of gaining access to journal articles, government documents, microfiche and microfilm, and special collections.

A possible interpretation of "digital library"—which is quite different from the concept developed in this book—is a system designed to automate traditional library functions by helping librarians to manage physical books. Computer-searchable catalogs are standard in libraries today. And there are many other functions that are automated: acquisitions, loans, recalls, interlibrary services, and library planning. However, this kind of library automation system is not closely related to the digital libraries we encountered in the opening scenarios.

The changing nature of books

The technophile visionaries whose dreams we shared above were not talking about a virtual library in the sense of an automated catalog. They wanted the full text of all documents in the library to be automated, not just a metadata surrogate. They took it for granted that books are adequately represented by the information they contain: the physical object is of no consequence.

The information in library catalogs and bibliographies can be divided into two kinds: the first having reference to the contents of books; the second treating their external character and the history of particular copies. Intellectually only the abstract content of a book—the information contained therein—seems important. But the strong visceral element of books cannot be neglected and is often cited as a reason why book collections will never become "virtual."

Bibliophiles love books as much for the statements they make as objects as for the statements they contain as text. Indeed early books were works of art. The steles in Xi'an are a monumental example, studied as much for their calligraphic beauty as for the philosophy, poetry, and history they record, a priceless, permanent record

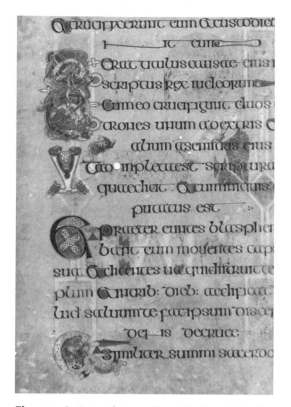

Figure 1.8 Part of a page from the *Book of Kells*.

of earlier civilizations. The *Book of Kells* in Ireland, produced by Irish monks at the scriptorium of Iona about 1,200 years ago, is one of the masterpieces of Western art. Figure 1.8 shows part of a page and illustrates the extraordinary array of pictures, interlaced shapes, and ornamental details. Indeed Giraldus Cambrensis, a 13th century scholar, fancifully wrote that "you might believe it was the work of an angel rather than a human being."

Beautiful books have always been highly prized for their splendid illustrations, for colored impressions, for heavily decorated illuminated letters, for being printed on uncommon paper, or uncommon materials, for their unusual bindings, and for their rarity and historic significance. In India one can see ancient books—some 2,000 years old—written on palm leaves, bound with string threaded through holes in the leaves. Figure 1.9 shows an example, which includes a picture of a deity (Sri Ranganatha) reclining with his consort on a serpent (Adishesha). In the castle library of Königsburg are 20 books bound in silver, richly adorned with large and beautifully engraved gold plates. Whimsical bindings abound: a London bookseller had Fox's *History of King James II* bound

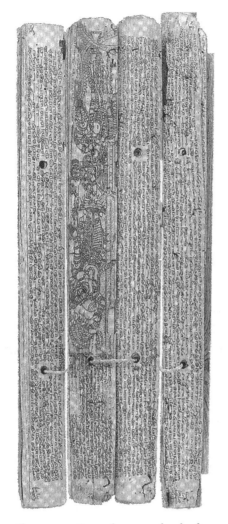

Figure 1.9 Pages from a palm-leaf manuscript
in Thanjavur, India. Thanjavur Maharaja
Serfoji's Sarasvat Mahal Library, Thanjavur,
Tamil Nadu (1995).

in fox skin. History even provides many instances of books bound in human
skin. It is hard to resist just one macabre example: a book in the Boston
Athenaeum collection.

James Allen, alias George Walton, was a burglar, bank robber, horse thief and highwayman when, in 1833, he attacked John Fenno Jr. on the Massachusetts Turnpike with
intent to rob. Fenno resisted his attacker and was shot, but saved by a suspender buckle.
Allen fled, was caught and sent to prison where he wrote a boastful autobiographical

account of his life of crime called *The Highwayman*. Admiring Fenno's bravery, he asked that Fenno be given a copy of his book bound in the author's skin.

On July 17, 1837 upon Allen's death, Massachusetts General Hospital "accepted his body for anatomical and pathological studies" and removed enough skin to provide the covering of his book. Bookbinder Peter Low treated the skin to look like gray deerskin and edged it with gold tooling. It is embossed with the Latin inscription "Hic Liber Waltonis Cute Compactus Est" (This book by Walton is bound in his own skin).

Those who feel nauseous may find this the best argument of all for digital libraries!

Catalogs and bibliographies comprise metadata: virtual information about books. In the kind of virtual library sketched in the early technodreams above, the very concept of the book as an individual physical entity seems to be at risk. However, technology has advanced to the point where it need not be: surrogates can substitute for physical works. A picture of the cover may be displayed as a "tangible"—or at least memorable—emblem of the physical book itself. Users can browse the collection using graphical techniques of virtual reality. Maybe they will even be able to caress the virtual cover, smell the virtual pages. But it is unlikely, perhaps inappropriate, that readers will love simulated books the way that bibliophiles love real ones, and eventually surrogates may become anachronistic and fade away. For what really matters in libraries is information, even knowledge. Ask Kataayi.

1.3   Digital libraries in developing countries

It sometimes happens that technological advances in developing countries leapfrog those in developed ones. This occurs because established infrastructure, a strong and necessarily conservative force, is absent. Alternative sources such as solar energy are widely used in place of traditional power generation and distribution, while many developing countries have experienced far higher levels of mobile phone growth than developed ones. Digital libraries provide another example, compensating for the failure of traditional distribution mechanisms to address local requirements and deliver information where it is needed.

Many current technology trends are not benefiting developing countries—indeed, some bring serious negative consequences. Just as industrialization and globalization have increased the gulf between haves and have-nots, so information and communications technology is creating a chasm between "knows" and "know-nots." By and large, developing countries are not participating in the information revolution, although knowledge is critical for development. The knowledge gap between rich and poor is widening.

In the developing world digital libraries provide perhaps the first really compelling raison d'être for computing technology. Priorities in these countries include health, food, hygiene, sanitation, and safe drinking water. Though computers are not a priority, simple, reliable access to targeted information meeting these basic needs certainly is. Digital libraries give system developers a golden opportunity to help reverse the negative impact of information technology on developing countries.

Disseminating humanitarian information

Traditional publishing and distribution mechanisms have tragically failed the developing world. Take medicine, a field of great importance in this context. Whereas a U.S. medical library subscribes to about 5,000 journals, the Nairobi University Medical School Library, long regarded as a flagship center in East Africa, received just 20 journals in 1998 (compared with 300 a decade before). In Brazzaville, Congo, the university has only 40 medical books and a dozen journals, all from before 1993, and the library in a large district hospital consists of a single bookshelf filled mostly with novels.

Digital libraries, by decoupling production and distribution costs from intellectual property charges, offer a desperately needed lifeline. A wealth of essential humanitarian material is produced by various international organizations, such as the United Nations, as well as national units such as the U.S. Peace Corps. Being produced by internationally oriented, nonprofit organizations, funded by all people on the planet, this information is—at least in principle—in the public domain: it could be made freely available in the form of networked digital libraries. While those 5,000 medical journals cannot be distributed for free because copyright on the articles is held by commercial publishers, this problem does not arise in many areas of physics, as we have seen. The world is changing, and the rate of change will accelerate.

Disaster relief

Natural disasters such as earthquakes or hurricanes, and man-made ones such as terrorist attacks or nuclear accidents, demand immediate and informed response. Disaster relief situations are complex and are addressed by a broad range of players in a variety of organizations acting in parallel. They present an overwhelming need for information: information that is tailored for the problem at hand, organized so that it can be accessed effectively, and distributed even in the absence of an effective network infrastructure. The response to a crisis is characterized by the generation of large amounts of unstructured multimedia data that must be acquired, processed, organized, and disseminated sufficiently rapidly to be of use to crisis responders.

Digital library technology allows organized collections of information, graced with comprehensive searching and browsing capabilities, to be created rapidly. Intelligence specific to the nature of a disaster, the geographical region, and the logistic resources available for the relief effort can all be gathered into a built-to-order digital library collection that combines targeted knowledge with general medical and sanitary information.

Preserving indigenous culture

Libraries and their close relatives, museums, have always been involved in preserving culture. These institutions collect literature and artifacts and use them to disseminate knowledge and understanding of different times and cultures. Digital libraries, however, open up the possibility of flexible and coherent multimedia collections that are both fully searchable and browsable in multiple dimensions—and permit more active participation by indigenous people in preserving and disseminating their own culture. The scenario described above with the Zia Pueblo provides a good example. The principal participants here are by definition the indigenous people themselves: the technological world assumes the role of catalyst, midwife, and consumer; for once indigenous culture has been recorded, it will find a fascinated, sympathetic, and perhaps influential audience elsewhere.

Information about indigenous culture takes many guises: oral history in the form of narration and interviews; artifacts in the form of images and descriptions; songs in the form of audio recordings, music transcriptions, and lyrics; dances and ceremonies in the form of video, audio, written synopses, and interpretations. Multimedia digital libraries allow such information to be integrated, recorded, browsed, and searched, all within a uniform user interface.

Because language is the vehicle of thought, communication, and cultural identity, a crucial feature of digital libraries for culture preservation is the ability to work in local languages. This strengthens individual cultures, promotes diversity, and reduces the dominance of English in the global information infrastructure.

Locally produced information

In digital library applications for culture preservation, the relevant information is, of necessity, readily available locally. But there are countless other scenarios that involve creating and distributing locally produced information collections. At first glance one might think that there is such a wealth of content on the Internet that surely there must be something of benefit to everyone. However, this ignores not only the problem of language—most information is available only in English or other major languages—but also the fact that there are many local community content issues that contribute toward effective information use.

Teachers prepare educational material that addresses specific community problems, and they adapt published material to employ local examples. Indigenous people have invaluable medicinal knowledge based on local plants or long-acquired knowledge of the cultivation and protection of local species. Such knowledge is vital: more than half of the world's most frequently prescribed drugs are derived from plants or synthetic copies of plant chemicals—and this trend is growing.

Local groups assemble information collections that describe and reflect neighborhood conditions, providing new material for sociocultural studies, fostering cultural exchange while retaining diversity, and increasing international understanding. Web sites for community and social development might include information on health problems endemic to a particular African community, or information on commodity prices of a particular good traded in Brazilian markets, or examples of curricular projects suitable for use in Indian schools.

The development of content that addresses the specific needs of a particular community stimulates the demand for information technology among that community. Getting learners to produce their own content is one of the best ways to exploit information technology in learning situations. Not only does it improve the learning experience, it also creates material that benefits the community. Teachers and students can work together to create their own content that has value for the community, and for the nation too.

Effective human development blossoms from empowerment rather than gifting. As the Chinese proverb says, "Give a man a fish and he will eat for a day; teach him to fish and he will eat for the rest of his days." Disseminating information originating in the developed world is a useful activity for developing countries, as Kataayi members will testify. But a more effective strategy for sustained long-term human development is to disseminate the capability of creating information collections, rather than the collections themselves. This will allow developing countries to participate actively in our information society, rather than observing it from outside. It will stimulate the creation of new industry. And it will help ensure that intellectual property remains where it belongs, in the hands of those who produce it.

The technological infrastructure

Computers are not so hard to come by in developing countries as one might think. Their extraordinarily rapid rate of obsolescence, coupled with the developed world's voracious appetite for the latest and greatest, makes low-end machines essentially free: instead of clogging landfill sites many (though certainly not enough) find their way to developing countries. A 1998 World Bank survey of developing countries found 3 to 30 PCs per 1,000 people, depending on the poverty level. With growth predicted at 20 percent per year, we estimate that at the turn of the millennium there were fifty million PCs in developing countries, serving a population of four billion.

A more serious obstacle is that network access varies widely around the globe. Whereas in 1998 more than a quarter of the U.S. population was surfing the Internet, the figure for Latin America and the Caribbean was 0.8 percent, for Sub-Saharan Africa 0.1 percent, and for South Asia 0.04 percent. Schools and hospitals in developing countries are poorly connected. Even in relatively well-off South Africa, many hospitals and 75 percent of schools have no telephone line. Universities are better equipped, but even there up to 1,000 people can depend on just one terminal. The Internet is failing the developing world. While global satellite communication networks may eventually bring relief, this takes time and money.

Because of the difficulty of network access, the structure and organization of digital libraries should be separated from their distribution media. Physical distribution of information on recordable devices can provide an attractive alternative to networks. Compact disk read-only memory, CD-ROM, is a practical format for areas with little Internet access. Their 650 Mb capacity can hold a useful volume of information, such as the 1,200 fully illustrated and fully indexed books in the Humanity Development Library. Most of the space in a collection such as this is consumed by pictures: several times as many books could be included if they were not so lavishly illustrated. CDs are giving way to digital versatile disk, DVD, which can hold from 5 to 20 Gb of data. A year's supply of those 5,000 medical journals mentioned above could fit, fully indexed, on a single DVD. And save lives.

1.4   The Greenstone software

This is a practical book about *how to build* a digital library. While the concepts developed in the book are quite general, we keep it tightly focused and practically oriented by using a particular digital library system throughout the book: the Greenstone Digital Library software from the New Zealand Digital Library Project at the University of Waikato. Illustrations in the book are nearly all taken from collections built with this software, or with associated software tools: this serves to keep our feet firmly on the ground. For example, three of the four opening scenarios use Greenstone: the Humanity Development Library is built with it (along with many other humanitarian collections), the Zia Pueblo collec-

Figure 1.10 Māori *toki* or ceremonial adze, emblem of
the Greenstone project.

tion is a planned project that will use it (along with other heritage-preservation
projects), and the popular music library is a research project that centers around
it (along with many other music library activities). The fourth, the physics
archives, could use Greenstone quite easily—as similar collections readily testify.

The Greenstone software provides a convenient way of organizing information and making it available over the Internet. A *collection* of information comprises several (typically several thousand, or several million) documents. A *document*, in turn, is any information-bearing message in electronically recorded
form. Documents are the fundamental unit from which information collections
are built, although they may have their own substructure and associated files.
Documents generally comprise text, although they may be images, sound files,
or video. A collection may contain many different types of documents. Each collection provides a uniform interface through which all documents in it can be
accessed—although the way that documents are displayed will depend on their

medium and format. A *library* generally includes many different collections, each organized differently—although there is a strong family resemblance in how collections are presented.

Making information available using this system is far more than just "putting it on the Web." The collection becomes maintainable, searchable, and browsable. Prior to presentation, each collection undergoes a building process that, once established, is completely automatic. This process creates all the structures that are used at runtime for accessing the collection. Searching is based on various indexes involving full text and metadata. Browsing is based on various metadata and on phrase structures, and other information, abstracted from the full text of the documents. Support structures for both are created during the building operation. When new material appears, it can be fully incorporated into the collection by rebuilding.

To address the exceptionally broad requirements of digital libraries, the Greenstone system is public and extensible. It is issued under the GNU General Public License, and, in the spirit of open-source software, users are invited to contribute modifications and enhancements. Only through an international cooperative effort will digital library software become sufficiently comprehensive to meet the world's needs. Currently the Greenstone software has been used by several United Nations agencies, including the Food and Agriculture Organization in Rome, UNESCO in Paris, the United Nations University in Tokyo, and the Centre for Human Settlements (Habitat) in Nairobi. It is used at sites throughout the world, and interfaces and collections exist in languages ranging from Portuguese to Chinese, from Māori to Arabic. Collections range from newspaper articles to technical documents, from educational journals to oral history, from visual art to folk songs. Further details, and many examples, can be obtained over the Internet from *www.nzdl.org*.

Throughout the book we will learn about the needs of digital libraries and how the Greenstone software helps to meet them. To give an idea of the breadth of these requirements, here is a list of features of the software.

Accessible via Web browser

Collections are accessed through a standard Web browser (e.g., Netscape or Internet Explorer). The browser is used for both local and remote access.

Runs on Windows and Unix

Collections can be served on either Windows (3.1/3.11, 95/98/ME/, NT/2000, and XP) or Unix (for example, Linux or SunOS); any of these can operate as a Web server.

Permits full-text and fielded search

The user can search the full text of the documents or choose among indexes built from different parts of the documents. Some collections have an index of full documents, an index of sections, an index of titles, and an index of authors, each of which can be searched for particular words or phrases. Results can be ranked by relevance or sorted by a metadata element.

Offers flexible browsing facilities	The user can browse lists of authors, lists of titles, lists of dates, classification structures, and so on. Different collections offer different browsing opportunities, and even within a collection a broad variety of browsing facilities are available. Browsing and searching interfaces are constructed during the building process, according to collection configuration information.
Creates access structures automatically	All collections are easy to maintain. Searching and browsing structures are built directly from the documents themselves. No links are inserted by hand. This means that if new documents in the same format become available, they can be merged into the collection automatically. However, existing links in the original documents, leading both within and outside the collection, are preserved.
Makes use of available metadata	Metadata may be associated with each document, or with individual sections within documents, and forms the raw material for browsing indexes. It must be provided explicitly or derivable automatically from the source documents. Standard schemes for expressing metadata are used, with provision for extensions as necessary.
Capabilities can be extended by plug-ins	"Plug-ins" can be written to accommodate new document types. Plug-ins currently exist for plain text files, HTML documents, Microsoft Word, RTF, PDF, PostScript, Powerpoint, and Excel files, e-mail, some proprietary formats, and for generic tasks such as recursively traversing directory structures containing such documents. A collection may have source documents in different forms. To build browsing indexes from metadata, an analogous scheme of "classifiers" is used: classifiers create browsing indexes of various kinds, based on metadata.
Can handle documents in any language	Unicode is used throughout the software, allowing any language to be processed in a consistent manner. To date, collections have been built containing French, Spanish, Māori, Russian, Chinese, Arabic, and English. On-the-fly conversion is used to convert from Unicode to an alphabet supported by the user's Web browser.
Can display user interface in multiple languages	The interface can be presented in multiple languages. Currently the system is available in Arabic, Chinese, Dutch, French, German, Hebrew, Indonesian, Italian, Māori, Portuguese, Russian, Spanish, and English. New languages can be added easily.
Can handle collections of text, pictures, audio, and video	Greenstone collections can contain text, pictures, audio, and even video clips. Most nontextual material is either linked to the textual documents or accompanied by textual descriptions (such as figure captions) to allow full-text searching and browsing. However, the architecture permits implementation of plug-ins and classifiers for nontextual data.
Allows hierarchical browsing	Hierarchical phrase and key-phrase indexes of text or any metadata can be created using standard classifiers.
Designed for multi-gigabyte collections	Collections can contain millions of documents, making the Greenstone system suitable for collections up to several gigabytes.

Uses compression techniques	Compression is used to reduce the size of the indexes and text. Small indexes have the added advantage of faster retrieval.
Permits authentication of users	A built-in access control mechanism allows collections, and even individual documents, to be restricted to authorized users using a password protection scheme.
Offers user logging	All queries made to every Greenstone collection can be recorded in user logs.
Provides an administrative function	An "administrative" function enables specified users to authorize other users to build collections, have access to protected collections, examine the composition of all collections, turn logging on and off, and so on.
Updates and adds new collections dynamically	Collections can be updated and new ones brought online at any time, without bringing the system down; the process responsible for the user interface will notice (through periodic polling) when new collections appear and will add them to the list presented to the user. End users can easily build new collections in the same style as existing ones from material on the Web or in local files—or both.
Publishes collections on CD-ROM	Greenstone collections can be published, in precisely the same form, on a self-installing CD-ROM. The interaction is identical to accessing the collection on the Web (Netscape is provided on each disk)— except that response times are faster and more predictable.
Supports distributed collections	A flexible process structure allows different collections to be served by different computers, yet be presented to the user in the same way, on the same Web page, as part of the same digital library. The Z39.50 protocol is fully supported, both for accessing external servers and for presenting Greenstone collections to external clients.
Everything you see, you can get	The Greenstone Digital Library is open-source software, available from the New Zealand Digital Library (*www.nzdl.org*) under the terms of the GNU General Public License. The software includes everything described above: Web serving, CD-ROM creation, collection building, multilingual capability, and plug-ins and classifiers for a variety of different source document types. It includes an autoinstall feature to allow easy installation on both Windows and Unix. In the spirit of open-source software, users are encouraged to contribute modifications and enhancements.

1.5 The pen is mighty: Wield it wisely

Collecting information and making it widely available to others has far-ranging social implications, and those who build digital libraries must act responsibly by making themselves aware of the legal and ethical issues that surround their particular application. Copyright is the place to begin.

Copyright

Digital libraries can easily be made far more accessible than physical ones. And the fact that they are widely accessible brings its own problems: access to the information in digital libraries is generally less controlled than it is in physical collections. Putting information into a digital library has the potential to make it immediately available to a virtually unlimited audience.

This is great news. For the user, information around the world becomes available wherever you are. For the author, a greater potential audience can be reached than ever before. And for publishers, new markets open up that transcend geographical limitations. But there is a flip side. Authors and publishers ask how many copies of a work will be sold if networked digital libraries enable worldwide access to an electronic copy of it. Their nightmare is that the answer is *one*. How many books will be published online if the entire market can be extinguished by the sale of one electronic copy to a public library?

How will publishers react to this situation? The threat for users is that publishers will adopt technical and legal means to implement restrictive policies governing access to the information they sell—for example, by restricting access to the purchaser (no lending to friends) or imposing expiry dates (no permanent collections). The net result could easily damage the flow of information far beyond the current status quo.

Possessing a copy of a document certainly does not constitute ownership in terms of copyright law. Though there may be many copies, each document has only one copyright owner. This applies not just to physical copies of books, but to computer files too, whether they have been digitized from a physical work or created electronically in the first place—"born digital." When you buy a copy of a document, you can resell it, but you certainly do not buy the right to redistribute it. That right rests with the copyright owner.

Who owns a particular work? The initial copyright owner is the creator, unless the work is made for hire. Works made for hire are ones created by employees within the scope of their employment, or under a specific contract that explicitly designates the work as being made for hire, in which case it is the employer or contracting organization that owns the copyright. The owner can transfer or "assign" copyright to another party through a specific contract, made in writing and signed by the owner.

Copyright protection begins and ends at different times, depending on when the work was created. In the U.S., older works are protected for 95 years after the date of first publication. Through the 1998 Copyright Extension Act, newer ones are protected from the "moment of their fixation in a tangible medium of expression" until 70 years after the author's death. Works for hire are protected for 95 years after publication or 120 years after creation, whichever comes first.

Copyright law is complex, arcane, and varies from one country to another. Most countries are signatories to the Berne Convention, which governs international copyright law. Most countries allow material to be copied for research purposes by individuals, a concept known as *fair use*. However, making copies for distribution, or resale, is prohibited. Copyright law applies regardless of whether the document bears the international copyright symbol ©. Unlike patents, it is not necessary to register documents for copyright—it applies automatically.

The legal situation with regard to computer files, and particularly documents published on the World Wide Web, is murky. Lawyers have questioned whether it is legal even to view a document on the Web, since one's browser inevitably makes a local copy, which has not explicitly been authorized. Of course, it is widely accepted that you can view Web documents—after all, that's what they're there for. If we allow that you can view them, next comes the question of whether you can save them for personal use. Or link to them. Or distribute them to others. Note that documents are copied and saved behind the scenes all over the place: to economize on network traffic and accelerate delivery, Web cache mechanisms save copies of documents locally and deliver them to other users.

The way that computers in general, and the Web in particular, work has led people to question whether the notion of a "copy" is perhaps no longer the appropriate foundation for copyright law in the digital age. Legitimate copies of digital information are made so routinely that restrictions on the act of copying no longer serve to regulate and control use on behalf of copyright owners. Computers make many internal copies when they are used to access information: the fact that a copy has been made says little about the legitimacy of the behavior. In the digital world, copying is so bound up with the way computers work that controlling it provides unexpectedly broad powers, far beyond those intended by copyright law.

Many digital library projects involve digitizing documents. First you must consider: Is the work to be digitized in the public domain, or does it attempt to faithfully reproduce a work in the public domain? If the answer to either question is yes, you may digitize the work without securing anyone's permission. Of course, the result of your own digitizing efforts will not be protected by copyright either, unless you produce something more than a faithful reproduction of the original. If material has been donated to your institution for digitizing, and the donor was the copyright owner, you can certainly go ahead provided the donor gave your institution the right to digitize—perhaps in a written form using words such as "the right to use the work for any institutional purpose, in any medium." Even without a written agreement, it may reasonably be assumed that the donor implicitly granted the right to take advantage of new media, provided the work continues to be used for the purpose for which it was donated. You do need to ensure, of course, that the donor is the original copyright owner and has not transferred copyright. You cannot, for example, assume permission to digitize letters written by others.

If you want to digitize documents and the above considerations do not apply, you should consider whether you can go ahead under the concept of fair use. This is a difficult judgment to make. You need to reflect on how things look from the copyright owner's point of view and address those concerns. Institutional policies about who can access the material, backed up by practices that restrict access appropriately, can help. Finally, if you conclude that fair use does not apply, then you will have to obtain permission to digitize the work or acquire access to it by licensing it.

If you are building a digital library, you must pay serious attention to the question of copyright. Digital library projects must be undertaken with a full understanding of ownership rights and with full recognition that permissions are essential to convert materials that are not in the public domain. Because of the potential for legal liability, any prudent library builder will consider seeking professional advice. A full account of the legal situation is far beyond the scope of this book, but the "Notes and sources" section at the end of the chapter (Section 1.6) does contain some pointers to sources of further practical information about the copyright question. These sources include information on how fair use can be interpreted and discuss the issues involved when negotiating copyright permission or licensing.

Looking at the situation from an ethical rather than a legal point of view helps to shed light on the fundamental issues. It is unethical to steal: deriving profit by distributing a book on which someone else has rightful claim to copyright is wrong. It is unethical to deprive someone of the fruit of their labor: giving away electronic copies of a book on which someone else has rightful claim to copyright is wrong. It is unethical to pass someone else's work off as your own: making a digital library collection without due acknowledgment is wrong. It is unethical to willfully misrepresent someone else's point of view: modifying documents before including them in the collection is wrong even though authorship is acknowledged.

Collecting from the Web

All of these points have an immediate and practical impact on digital libraries. Digital libraries are organized collections of information. The Web is full of unorganized information. Downloading parts of it in order to organize information into focused collections and make the material more useful to others is a prime application area for digital libraries.

Search engines, one of the most widely used services on the Internet, provide a good example. They use software "robots" to continually download huge portions of the Web and create indexes to them. Although they may retain documents on their own computers, users are presented with a summary and directed to the original source documents rather than to local copies. Search engines are commercial operations. Their services are not sold directly to users, however, but revenue is derived from advertising—in effect, a tax on the user's attention. Although they are widely accepted as a good thing, their legal status is unclear.

Web sites can safeguard against indiscriminate downloading. A generally accepted *robot exclusion protocol* allows individual Web sites to prevent portions of their sites from being downloaded and indexed. Although compliance with this protocol is entirely voluntary, widely used search engines certainly do so. But the onus of responsibility has been shifted. Previously, to use someone else's information legitimately, one had to request explicit permission from the information provider. Now search engines automatically assume permission unless the provider has set up an exclusion mechanism. This is a key development with wide ramifications. And some Web sites threaten dire consequences for computers that violate the robot exclusion protocol—for example, denial-of-service attacks on the violating computer. This is law enforcement on the wild Web frontier.

Different, but equally fascinating, copyright issues are raised by projects that are archiving the entire World Wide Web. The reason for doing this is to offer services such as supplying documents that are no longer available and providing a "copy of record" for publicly available documents, in effect supplying the raw material for historical studies. Creating this archive raises many interesting issues involving privacy and copyright, issues that are not easily resolved.

What if a college student created a Web page that had pictures of her then-current boyfriend? What if she later wanted to "tear them up," so to speak, yet they lived on in the archive? Should she have the right to remove them? In contrast, should a public figure—a U.S. senator, for instance—be able to erase data posted from his or her college years? Does collecting information made available to the public violate the "fair use" provisions of copyright law?

Most digital libraries aim to provide more comprehensive searching and browsing services than do search engines. Like archives, they most likely want to store documents locally, to ensure their continued availability. Documents are more likely to be seen as part of the library, rather than as products of their originating Web site. Digital libraries are more likely to modify documents as an aid to the user, least invasively by highlighting search terms or adding metadata, more invasively by re-presenting them in a standard format, most invasively by producing computer-generated summaries of documents, or extracting keywords and key phrases automatically.

Those responsible for such libraries need to consider carefully the ethical issues above. It is important to respect robot exclusion protocols. It is important to provide mechanisms whereby authors can withdraw their works from the library. It is helpful if explicit permission can be sought to include material. If information is automatically derived from, or added to, the source documents, it is necessary to be sensitive to possible issues of misrepresentation.

The world is changing. Digital libraries are pushing at the frontiers of what is possible by way of organizing anthologies of material. And they are pushing at the frontiers of society's norms for dealing with the distribution of intellectual property. Those who run large-scale Internet information services tell interesting "war stories" of people's differing expectations of what it is reasonable for their services to do.

For example, search engine operators frequently receive calls from computer users who have noticed that some of their documents are indexed when they think they shouldn't be. Sometimes users feel their documents couldn't possibly have been captured legitimately because there are no links to them. Most search engines have a facility for locating any documents that link to a specified one and can easily find the offending link. On other occasions people put confidential documents into a directory that is open to the Web, perhaps just momentarily while they change the directory permissions, only to have them grabbed by a search engine and made available for all the world to find.

Search technology makes information readily available that may previously have been public in principle, but impossible to find in practice. When a major search engine took over the archives of USEnet, a huge corpus of Internet discussion groups on a wide range of topics, it received many pleas from contributors to retract indiscreet postings from the past because, being easily available for anyone to find, they were now causing their authors considerable embarrassment.

A system that downloads research papers from the Web, extracts citations from them, and compiles them into a citation index receives many complaints about incorrect references, complaints that should be directed to the authors of the citing papers rather than to the extraction service. Indeed it had to be pointed out to one irate user that a particular, incorrect reference to one of his papers that he had noticed on the system had actually been extracted from another paper on the complainant's own Web site.

As a final example, several years ago a researcher was describing to an audience at a major U.S. university an early, noncommercial digital library collection of research reports. The reports had been downloaded from the Internet (using the FTP file transfer protocol, for which there is no established exclusion protocol). One member of the audience indignantly denounced this as theft of information; others volubly defended the system as providing a useful service to researchers using publicly available material. The detractor demanded that all reports from that university be immediately withdrawn from the collection; the others requested that they be retained because they helped publicize their research.

Illegal and harmful material

Some material is illegal and harmful and clearly inappropriate for public presentation. Examples are distasteful. A 1999 UNESCO Expert Meeting on Paedophilia on the Internet noted,

> Violence and pornography have invaded the Internet. Photos and videos of children and young teenagers engaged in sexual acts and various forms of paedophilia are readily available. Reports of children being kidnapped, beaten, raped and murdered abound. . . . The Internet has in many cases replaced the media of paedophiliac magazines, films and videos. It is a practical, cheap, convenient and untraceable means for conducting business as well as for trafficking in paedophilia and child pornography. The Internet has also become the principal medium for dialogue about paedophilia and its perpetuation.

UNESCO has taken the lead on breaking the silence on this topic and is engaged in a number of initiatives to provide safety nets for children online.

Whether information is considered harmful or not often depends on the cultural, religious, and social context in which it is circulated. Standards vary enormously both within and among nations. However, the international nature of the Internet means that it is no longer possible to police the transfer of information. The difficulty of sustaining local legal and cultural standards is a huge challenge that faces society today. It revolves around the dilemma of balancing freedom of expression against citizens' rights to be protected from illegal or harmful material.

A well-publicized example of different views on access to information arose in early 2000 around information concerning online sales of Nazi memorabilia on U.S. Web sites accessed using the Yahoo Internet portal. A Paris judge ruled that the sites are barred under French law and ordered them to be blocked. However, the sites are governed by less restrictive U.S. laws, and a U.S. judge ruled that the First Amendment protects content generated in the U.S. by American companies from being regulated by authorities in countries that have more restrictive laws on freedom of expression. Suit and countersuit followed, and the matter is still not settled as this book goes to press two years later.

Online gambling, where laws are restrictive (or at best muddy) in countries such as the U.S., China, and Italy, provides another example. Some international gambling sites claim to comply with local laws by checking the geographical origin of the user (a difficult and unreliable procedure which is easily circumvented) and refusing to offer their services in countries where gambling is illegal.

Cultural sensitivity

Most digital libraries are international. More often than not they are produced by people from European and North American backgrounds, yet the majority of people in the world live in countries that have very different cultures. Some digital libraries are specifically aimed at people in different parts of the world: collections for developing countries, for example, or collections aimed at preserving and promoting indigenous cultures. It is clearly essential for digital library developers to consider how their creations will affect other people.

We pointed out earlier that language is the vehicle of thought, communication, and cultural identity, and so digital library users should be able to work in whatever language suits them. But the need for cultural sensitivity goes deeper than this. Particular labels can have strong, and unexpected, connotations: certain car models have failed to sell in certain countries because the manufacturer's name had a serious negative association. So too for icons: dogs, for example, are offensive in Arabic cultures, and users will transfer negative associations if they are adopted as user interface icons. Different cultures have different color preferences, and particular colors have different associations.

In Polynesian cultures the concept of *tapu*, usually translated as "sacred," has rich and complex connotations that are difficult for those from Western cultures to appreciate. Many objects have different degrees of *tapu*, and it is rude and offensive to refer to them inappropriately, in the same way that many Westerners find blasphemy rude and offensive. One particular example that can affect digital library design is that representations of people—including pictures—are *tapu*, and it is generally inappropriate for them to be on public display.

1.6 Notes and sources

To avoid breaking up the flow of the main text, all references and explanatory notes are collected in a section at the end of each chapter. This first "Notes and sources" section describes information sources, papers, books, and other resources relevant to the material covered in Chapter 1.

We learned about the Kataayi Cooperative from Emmanuel Kateregga-Ndawulu, the chairman. If you would like to learn more about this fascinating initiative, a Web search for *Kataayi* will turn up some interesting information (and, at least at the time of writing, no false hits!). Jon Miller kindly provided the photographs in Figure 1.1 (and Figure 9.3 in Chapter 9). The Humanity Development Library is produced by Michel Loots of the Humanity Libraries Project in Antwerp, Belgium, using the Greenstone software, and widely distributed in the developing world. The development of the physics archives is described by Paul Ginsparg, its originator, in a paper called "Winners and losers in the global research village" (Ginsparg, 1996); he is responsible for the memorable "sliced dead trees" metaphor. (Note incidentally that *adsorbed* is a physics term, not a misprint; it means the assimilation of dissolved matter by the surface of a solid.) Lloyd Smith at New Mexico Highlands University conceived of the

Zia Pueblo project and came up with the vision described here; the Zia Pueblo kindly supplied the photograph in Figure 1.2. The digital music library is ongoing work in the Department of Computer Science at Waikato, initiated by Rodger McNab and Lloyd Smith and currently led by one of the authors (Bainbridge et al., 1999; Bainbridge, 2000).

The definition of *killer app* is from the online Jargon File (version 4.2.2, at *http://info.astrian.net/jargon/Preface.html*), a comprehensive compendium of hacker slang. Our definition of *digital library* in Section 1.1 is from Akscyn and Witten (1998); it is abstracted from 10 definitions of the term *digital library* culled from the literature by Ed Fox (on the Web at *http://ei.cs.vt.edu/fox/dlib/def.html*). It was the computer pioneer Maurice Wilkes who said that books would be hailed as a great advance if they were invented today. The "data . . . information . . . knowledge . . . wisdom" sequence and characterization is due to Harold Thimbleby at University College, London.

A good source for the development of libraries is Thompson (1997), who formulates some principles of librarianship, including the one quoted, that it is a librarian's duty to increase the stock of his library. Thompson is the source of some of the material with which Section 1.2 begins, including the metaphor about snapping the links of the chained book—in fact, he formulates open access as another principle: *libraries are for all*. The imaginative architectural developments that have occurred in physical libraries at the close of the 20th century are documented, and beautifully illustrated, by Wu (1999). Gore (1976b) recounts the fascinating history of the Alexandrian Library; he edited the book entitled *Farewell to Alexandria* (Gore, 1976a). The information on Trinity College, Dublin, was kindly supplied by David Abrahamson; that on the Library of Congress was retrieved from the Internet. Much of the other historical information is from an excellent and thought-provoking paper by Gaines that is well worth reading (Gaines, 1993). Thomas Mann (1993), a reference librarian at the Library of Congress, has produced a wonderful source of information on libraries and librarianship, full of practical assistance on how to use conventional library resources to find things.

H. G. Wells's "world brain" idea was published in 1938 and not long ago was still being pursued (Wells, 1938; Goodman, 1987). Vannevar Bush's vision was described in the year the United Nations was founded (Bush, 1947)—although certainly no connection between virtual libraries and the plight of developing countries was made in those days. Licklider's vision dates from 1960 (Licklider, 1960), while the U.S. Presidential Office weighed in early in 1993 (Clinton and Gore, 1993).

The 19th-century librarian who "makes time for his fellow mortals" is Bowker (1883), quoted by Crawford and Gorman (1995), while the quotation about Allen's human-skin book is from Kruse (1994). The modern term "metadata" is an impressive-sounding moniker, but the catchphrase "data about data" is glib but not very enlightening. In some sense, *all* data is about data: where does one stop and the other begin? We return to this discussion at the beginning of Chapter 5. Meanwhile we continue to use the term freely, always in the context of digital library collections in which it is clear that the metadata is information about a particular resource.

More information on the promise of digital libraries in developing countries can be found in Witten et al. (2001). The figures on the Nairobi and Brazzaville universities are from the United Nations *Human Development Report* (United Nations, 1999), as is some of the information on Internet penetration in developing countries. Arunachalam (1998) tells how the Internet is "failing the developing world." Statistics on the numbers of computers available in developing countries can be found in the World Bank's (2000) *World Development Indicators.* Information on mobile phone penetration can be found in an International Telecommunication Union report (1999). There is much information on the "digital divide," the widening knowledge gap between rich and poor: read the United Nations' 1997 statement on *Universal Access to Basic Communication and Information Services*, the International Telecommunication Union's 1998 World telecommunication development report, or the World Bank's 1998/99 *World Development Report.* Some of the examples of the potential uses of locally produced information in Section 1.3 come from an excellent article that Mark Warschauer is writing, entitled "What is the digital divide?"—it's available on his Web site at *www.gse.uci.edu/markw*.

The Greenstone software is produced by the New Zealand Digital Library Project and is described by Witten et al. (1999b, 2000). Information about the GNU General Public License can be obtained from *www.gnu.org/copyleft/gpl.html*. The *toki* (adze) shown in Figure 1.10 was a gift from the Māori people in recognition of the Digital Library's contributions to indigenous language preservation; it resides in the project laboratory at the University of Waikato. In Māori culture there are several kinds of *toki*, with different purposes. This one is a ceremonial adze, *toki pou tangata*, a symbol of chieftainship. The *rau* (blade) is sharp, hard, and made of *pounamu* or greenstone—hence the Greenstone software, at the cutting edge of digital library technology. There are three figures carved into the *toki*. The forward-looking one looks out to where the *rau* is pointing to ensure that the *toki* is appropriately targeted. The backward-looking one at the top is a sentinel that guards where the *rau* can't see. There is a third head at the bottom of the handle which makes sure that the chief's decisions—to which the *toki* lends authority—are properly grounded in reality. The name of this *taonga*, or art treasure, is *Toki Pou Hinengaro*, which translates roughly as "the adze that shapes the excellence of thought." *Haramai te toki, haumi e, hui e, tāiki e.*

Samuelson and Davis (2000) provide an excellent and thought-provoking overview of copyright and related issues in the information age, which is a synopsis of a larger report published by the National Academy of Sciences Press

(Committee on Intellectual Property Rights, 2000). Section 1.5 draws heavily on this material. An earlier paper by Samuelson (1998) discusses specific digital library issues raised by copyright and intellectual property law, from a U.S. perspective. The Association for Computing Machinery has published a collection of papers that give a wide-ranging discussion of the effect of emerging technologies on intellectual property issues (White, 1999).

There's plenty of information on copyright on the Web. For example, *http://scholar.lib.vt.edu/copyright* is a useful Web site developed by staff at Virginia Tech to share what they learned about policies and common practices that relate to copyright. It includes interpretations of U.S. copyright law, links to the text of the law, sample letters to request permission to use someone else's work, links to publishers' e-mail addresses, advice for authors about negotiating to retain some rights, as well as current library policies. Georgia Harper at the University of Texas at Austin has created an excellent *Crash Course in Copyright* (*www.utsystem.edu/ogc/intellectualproperty/cprtindx.htm*) that is delightfully presented and well worth reading. The information about the duration of copyright protection is from Lolly Gasaway, director of the Law Library and professor of law at the University of North Carolina, through his Web site at *www.unc.edu/~unclng/public-d.htm*.

The Internet archiving project is described in a *Scientific American* article by Brewster Kahle (1997); this is the source for the hypothetical college student scenario. The war stories will remain unattributed. Information on the UNESCO initiative to attack paedophilia on the Internet can be found at *www.unesco.org/webworld/child_screen/conf_index.html*. Elke Duncker is a marvelous source of information on cultural sensitivity and user interfaces: some of her experiences with user interface issues in different cultures are described in Duncker (2000).

Standard library automation systems are described by Cooper (1996). The first book on digital libraries is *Practical Digital Libraries* by Lesk (1997), a pioneering work that gives a fascinating early account of this emerging field. In contrast, Crawford and Gorman (1995) fear that virtual libraries are virtual nonsense that threatens to devastate the cultural mission of libraries. Chen (1998) describes the past, present, and future of digital libraries from his perspective as Program Director of the NSF/DARPA/NASA Digital Libraries Initiative in the U.S. from 1993–1995. Sanders (1999) offers an edited collection of papers that give a librarian's perspective on many aspects of digital libraries and their use. Although Borgman's (2000) title focuses on the global information infrastructure, most of her material is relevant to the kind of digital libraries discussed here. Arms (2000) gives an authoritative, comprehensive, and balanced account of digital libraries from many different perspectives. He includes a historical perspective, a survey of the state of the art, and an account of current research.

2 Preliminaries

Sorting out the ingredients

Building a library is a major undertaking that needs to be carefully planned. Before beginning, you should reflect on the fact that distributing any kind of information collection carries certain responsibilities. There are legal issues of copyright: being able to access documents doesn't necessarily mean you can give them to others. There are social issues: collections should respect the customs of the community out of which the documents arise. And there are ethical issues: some things simply should not be made available to others. The pen is mightier than the sword!—be sensitive to the power of information and use it wisely.

One of the first questions to ask when building a digital library is what technology will be used. You are probably reading this book because you are a practical person and are itching to get on with actually *building* your library. If you plan to use the Greenstone software introduced in Section 1.4, on which the implementation-dependent aspects of this book (Chapters 6 and 7) are based, now is a good time to turn to the first section of Chapter 6 and construct an initial collection to give you a preview of how things will work. The technical part of building a digital library is easy if you know what you want and it matches what can be done with the tools you have available. Section 6.2 leads you through the process of building a collection with Greenstone. First, to download and install the software, you need to consult the Appendix.

Having laid your mind at rest regarding the technology, begin by fixing some broad parameters of your digital library. The other chapters in this book assume that the raw material for your library is provided in machine-readable form. Of course, one overriding question is where it is going to come from. There are three broadly different answers to this question, leading to three rather different kinds of digital library. We discuss these in Section 2.1.

As well as the raw material, you also need metadata—summary information about the documents in your collection. Librarians are expert in creating metadata and using it to facilitate access to large information collections. If you are building a sizable digital library, the team will include people with training in library science—and you will need to know something about their job. Section 2.2 introduces the principles and practices of bibliographic organization in conventional libraries.

You must also consider what kinds of access your digital library will support, and we review some of the possibilities, and the pitfalls, in Section 2.3.

Probably the single most important issue in contemplating a digital library project is whether you plan to digitize the material for the collection from ordinary books and papers. Because this inevitably involves manually handling physical material, and probably also involves manual correction of computer-based text recognition, it generally represents the vast bulk of the work involved in building a digital library. Section 2.4 describes the process of digitizing textual documents, by far the most common form of library material. Most library builders end up outsourcing the operation to a specialist; this section alerts you to the issues you will need to consider when planning this part of the project.

2.1 Sources of material

There are fundamental questions about the nature of the library you are building: what its purpose is, what the principles are for including documents, and when one document differs from another. While we cannot help you in making these decisions, it is essential that you ask—and answer—these questions.

Next we consider three scenarios for where your digital library material originates:

- You have an existing library that you wish to convert to digital form.
- You have access to a collection of material that you want to offer as a digital library.
- You want to provide an organized portal into a focused subset of material that already appears on the Web.

These scenarios are neither exclusive nor exhaustive, and in practice you often encounter a mixture. But they are useful in helping to focus on the questions that should be asked before embarking on a digital library construction project.

Ideology

Begin by formulating a clear conception of what it is that you intend to achieve with your proposed digital library collection—this might be called the "ideology" of your enterprise. The ideology can be formulated in terms of the collection's *purpose*, the objectives it is intended to achieve, and its *principles*, the directives that will guide decisions on what should be included and—equally important— what should be excluded. These decisions are difficult ones. Section 1.1 introduced "wisdom" as the value attached to knowledge and argued that librarians exercise wisdom when they make decisions about what to include in a collection.

Whenever you build a digital library collection, you should formulate its purpose and state it clearly as an introduction to the collection. You should make it plain to users what principles have been adopted to govern what is included. You should also include a description of how the collection is organized.

We assume that you have established the purpose of the digital library collection and its scope in terms of what works it will include. You will also have to decide what to do about different manifestations of a single work. In the traditional library world, there is an important, but rather slippery, distinction between a *work* and a *document*. A work is the disembodied content of a message and might be thought of as pure information. In traditional libraries a document is a particular physical object (say a book) that embodies or manifests the work. We will elaborate on this distinction in Section 2.2 below.

In the case of digital libraries, a document is a particular electronic encoding of a work. The work/document distinction surfaces when we have to deal with different versions of a document. Digital representations of a work are far easier than printed ones to both copy and change. You will have to decide not only which documents to include and which to exclude, but also when two documents are the same and when they are different. Collections often contain many exact duplicates of documents; should duplicate copies be retained? And when a new version of a document appears, should it supersede the old one, or should both be kept? The answers will depend on the purpose of your collection. Archival or historical records must not be allowed to change, but errors in collections of practical or educational information must be correctable.

Here's a further complication that affects the identity of documents. Digital libraries are not ephemeral, but have a continued existence over time. For example, they often keep records of the interaction history of individual users to facilitate future interaction. When identifiers are allocated to documents, decisions must be made about whether duplicates are significant and when new versions of documents supersede old ones. For instance, one way of assigning identifiers is to compute a number from the word sequence that makes up the document. This is attractive because exact copies receive the same identifier and are therefore mapped into the same object. However, sometimes you might want to make an updated version of a document supersede the original by giving it exactly the same identifier even though its content is slightly different, and you cannot do this if identifiers are computed from the content.

Converting an existing library

Converting a conventional library into digital form, often the image that springs to mind when people first mention digital libraries, is the most ambitious and expensive kind of digital library project. It involves digitizing the contents of an existing paper-based collection, which is usually a huge and daunting undertaking.

Before embarking on such a task, you need to consider carefully whether there is really a need. Digital libraries have three principal advantages over conventional ones: they are easier to access remotely, they offer more powerful searching and browsing facilities, and they serve as a foundation for new value-added services. You should look at the customer base for the existing library and assess how advantageous it will be for customers to access the new digital library instead. You should look at the value of the collections in the library and consider whether the customer base will expand if the information can be made available electronically. You should look at what new services the digital library could support, such as automatic notification of new documents that match clients' interest profiles, and assess the demand for them. You need to evaluate the cost/benefit of the proposed digital library.

There are many further questions to ask. Will the new digital library coexist with the existing physical one, or supplant it? Maintaining two separate libraries will be a continual drain on resources. At what rate is the collection growing, or changing? In many situations digitization of material is not just a one-time capital cost, but an ongoing operational expenditure. Should you outsource the whole digital library operation? There exist organizations that can arrange fully searchable Web access to, for example, newspapers of your choice. Such organizations provide a full range of services, including conversion of existing documents and ongoing digitization of new material. Services like these are growing dramatically.

Can user needs be satisfied, or partially satisfied, in alternative ways? For example, it might be possible to buy access to part of your holdings through external organizations that amortize their costs by supplying services to a whole range of other customers. Converting an existing library is such a large and expensive proposition that all alternatives should be carefully explored before making a commitment.

Once you have decided to go ahead, a key question will be how to prioritize material for conversion. Library materials can be divided into three classes: special collection and unique materials, such as rare books and manuscripts; high-use items that are currently in demand for teaching and research; and low-use items including less frequently used research materials. One set of criteria for digital conversion includes the intellectual content or scholarly value of the material, the desire to enhance access to it, and available funding opportunities. Another concerns the educational value, whether for classroom support, background reading, or distance education. A third may be the need to reduce handling of fragile originals, especially if they are heavily used. Other reasons are institutional: promoting special strengths such as unique collections of primary source material—the jewels in the crown of a research library—or resource-sharing partnerships with other libraries. Cost and space savings may also play a role. Of course copyright will have a crucial influence and is the first thing to consider (see Section 1.5).

Six principles have been identified that drive the development of library collections.

- *Priority of utility:* Usefulness is the ultimate reason behind all collection decisions. Predicting utility is, however, notoriously difficult.
- *Local imperative:* Local collections are built to support local needs, and expenditure of local resources must have a demonstrable local benefit.
- *Preference for novelty:* Although historical collections are essential for research, only limited resources can be devoted to the collection and maintenance of older material.
- *Implication of intertextuality:* To add an item to a collection is to create a relationship between it and other items. Building a collection always creates new textual relationships.
- *Scarcity of resources:* All collection development decisions have to balance scarce resources: funding, staff time, shelf space, and user time and attention.
- *Commitment to the transition:* More and more information will become available in digital form. Libraries are responsible for promoting this transition and assisting users to adjust to it.

These principles apply equally well to the selection of material for digitization.

Building a new collection

We argued in Chapter 1 that digital libraries are about new ways of dealing with knowledge—of achieving new human goals by changing the way that information is used in the world—rather than about deconstructing existing institutions. Many digital library projects build new collections of new material, rather than digitizing existing libraries.

If this is what you plan to do, you should ask—and answer!—the question, "Why you?" Are other organizations better placed to undertake this task? For a start, do you own the material?—or, more to the point, do you own the copyright? If not, you need to quickly ascertain whether you will be able to acquire permission for your project from the copyright holders before going any further. Copyright holders are naturally cautious about permitting their material to be made available electronically because of the potential for uncontrolled access (whether intended or not). The natural organization to create a digital collection is the copyright holder; if that is not you, you need to have strong arguments as to why your organization is the appropriate one for the job.

The scale of your library-building project will be largely determined by whether the material is already available electronically, or whether material in conventional paper form needs to be digitized. If everything is already electronic, things are immeasurably easier. Even if operations such as collecting and organizing files, and converting formats, are necessary, they will be far cheaper than digitizing the material because once the appropriate procedures have been determined, the computer can be used to apply them rapidly and on a large scale.

The next question to consider is where the metadata will come from. Obtaining the necessary metadata and converting it to electronic form is likely to be a major task. Indeed, in situations where the raw documents are already available electronically, manual input of metadata will usually dominate the cost of the digital library project. When digitizing an existing library the metadata is already available, but when making new collections it imposes a substantial burden.

Virtual libraries

Another kind of digital library provides a portal to information that is available electronically elsewhere. This is sometimes referred to as a *virtual library* to emphasize that the library does not itself hold content. Librarians have used this term for a decade or more to denote a library that provides access to distributed information in electronic format through pointers provided locally. As we noted in Chapter 1, the Web lacks the essential digital library features of selection and organization. But it does contain a vast wealth of useful information. People who sift through this information and build organized subcollections of the Web do a useful job, and an important subclass of digital libraries comprises those that provide access to information that is already available on the Web.

Information portals usually concentrate on a specific topic or focus on a particular audience. Commercial Web search engines are unable to produce consistently relevant results, given their generalized approach, the immense amount of territory they cover, and the great number of audiences they serve. The problem is likely to be exacerbated by the increasing use of the Web for commerce. Search engine companies strive to support themselves by enhancing the level of service they provide for commercial activity, with the aim of becoming attractive vehicles for advertising.

Virtual libraries present new challenges. Clearly the source information is already available electronically, in a form that can be readily displayed with a

Web browser. Some metadata will also be present—notably title and possibly author. The value that is added by imposing a digital library organization on a subset of the Web is twofold: selection of content and the provision of further metadata whereby it can be organized.

First, consider content selection. You need to define a purpose or theme for your library, and then discover and select material on the Web that relates to this theme. You can do this by manually seeking and filtering information, using whatever tools are available—search engines and the like. You can also attempt it automatically, with programs that crawl the Web, following links and seeking out new information that is relevant to the defined theme. Such systems typically start with a small and focused selection of relevant documents and traverse the Web seeking new documents to augment the collection. In a domain-specific search the Web is not explored indiscriminately, but in a directed fashion that seeks relevant documents efficiently. This raises interesting questions of how to direct and control the search. Focused Web crawling is an important topic that is likely to develop into a major technique for information discovery. In practice, to build a high-quality collection it will probably always be necessary to manually filter the results of automatic Web crawling.

Second, consider the provision of further metadata. Like content selection, this can also be done either manually or automatically. Categorizing and classifying Web pages helps to connect researchers and students with important scholarly and educational resources. Of course techniques for automatically assigning metadata are extremely valuable for any digital library, and in Chapter 5 we will encounter various metadata operations, ranging from phrase extraction to acronym identification. In libraries of material gathered from the Web, these techniques assume a special importance since they constitute the bulk of the raison d'être for a digital library portal.

A good example of a virtual library is INFOMINE, a cooperative project of the University of California and California State University (among others). Run by librarians, it covers most major academic disciplines through access to important databases, e-journals, e-texts, and other digital collections. It contains descriptions and links to a wealth of scholarly and educational Internet resources, each of which has been selected and described by a professional academic librarian who is a specialist in the subject and in resource description generally. Librarians see this as an important expenditure of effort for their users, a natural evolution of their traditional task of collecting and organizing information in print.

It takes an hour or two to prepare a traditional library catalog entry for a new book or journal. At the other extreme, Web search engines provide no metadata and no access mechanism other than searching the text for particular words and phrases, but automatically recrawl and reindex the entire Web every few weeks. Virtual libraries occupy an intermediate position. INFOMINE asks human catalogers to complete each record in 25 minutes on average. In addition a variety of semiautomated techniques are used to determine when information has been moved or altered significantly, and to automatically update links, or flag the site for manual reindexing, accordingly.

In general the higher the scholarly or educational value of a resource, the greater the amount of expert time that can be invested in its description. A scenario for semiautomated resource discovery and description might involve three levels of material:

1. Automatically generated, with URL, author-supplied metadata, significant keywords and phrases extracted from the full text, and generalized subjects assigned automatically
2. Manually reviewed by a human expert who edits and enriches the automatically derived metadata, checking it for accuracy and adding annotations and subject headings
3. Intensively described by a human expert who provides extensive metadata from scratch

Information could move from the first to the second level if it is judged to be sufficiently central to the collection's focus on the basis of automatic classification information, and from the second to the third level on the basis of sufficiently high usage.

2.2 Bibliographic organization

We have discussed where the documents in the digital library might originate. Now let's talk about how the metadata is produced: the summary information that provides the hooks on which all library collections are organized.

Organizing information on a large scale is far more difficult than it seems at first sight. In his 1674 Preface to the Catalogue for the Bodleian Library in Oxford, Thomas Hyde lamented the lack of understanding shown by those who had never been charged with building a catalog:

> "What can be more easy (those lacking understanding say), having looked at the title-pages than to write down the titles?" But these inexperienced people, who think making an index of their own few private books a pleasant task of a week or two, have no conception of the difficulties that arise or realize how carefully each book must be examined when the library numbers myriads of volumes. In the colossal labor, which exhausts both body and soul, of making into an alphabetical catalogue a multitude of books gathered from every corner of the earth there are many intricate and difficult problems that torture the mind.

In this section we will look at traditional principles of bibliographic organization, and at current practice. Librarians have a wealth of experience in classifying and organizing documents in a way that makes relevant information easy to find. Although some features are less relevant to digital libraries—such as the physical constraint of arranging the library's contents on a linear shelving system—there is nevertheless a great deal to be learned from their experience, and would-be digital librarians would be foolish to ignore it. Most library users locate information by finding one relevant book on the shelves and then looking around for others in the same area. In fact conventional libraries provide far more powerful retrieval structures.

Objectives of a bibliographic system

It was not until the late 19th century, long after Thomas Hyde bemoaned the difficulty of building a catalog, that the objectives of a bibliographic system were first explicitly formulated. There were three: *finding*, *collocation*, and *choice*.

The first objective, *finding*, was to enable a person to find a book of which either the author, title, or subject is known. In modern terms this involves finding information in a database, confirming its identity, and perhaps ascertaining its whereabouts and availability. The user is assumed to be seeking a known document and has in hand author, title, or subject information. The modern library catalog is designed expressly to support these features.

The second objective, *collocation*, was to show what the library has by a given author, on a given subject, or in a given kind of literature. To "collocate" means to place together or in proper order. This objective is concerned with locating information that is nearby in one of several information spaces. The organization of the library catalog and the spatial arrangement of the books on the shelves help satisfy the objective.

The third objective, *choice*, was to assist in the choice of a book either bibliographically, in terms of its edition, or topically, in terms of its character. The assumption is that the reader is faced with a number of different documents—perhaps several different editions of a work—and must choose among them.

In the last few decades these three objectives have been refined and restated several times. Recently they have been expanded into the following five.

1. To *locate* entities in a file or database as the result of a search using attributes or relationships of the entities:
   a. To find a single entity, that is, a document
   b. To locate sets of entities representing
      - all documents belonging to the same work
      - all documents belonging to the same edition
      - all documents by a given author
      - all documents on a given subject
      - all documents defined by "other" criteria

2. To *identify* an entity, that is, to confirm that the entity described in a record corresponds to the entity sought, or to distinguish among several entities with similar characteristics

3. To *select* an entity that is appropriate to the user's needs with respect to content, physical format, and the like

4. To *acquire* or obtain access to the entity described, through purchase, loan, and so on, or by online access to a remote computer

5. To *navigate* a bibliographic database: to find works related to a given one by generalization, association, and aggregation; to find attributes related by equivalence, association, and hierarchy

The Latin word *entity* lacks the Anglo-Saxon directness of *book* and *work*. It serves to broaden the scope of the objectives beyond books and documents to include audio, video, and both physical and digital objects. It also serves to broaden the search criteria from the particular metadata of author, title, and subject. The existence of a catalog of metadata is acknowledged explicitly as the basis of searching, along with the use of attributes and relationships. A new *acquisition* objective has been added, along with a *navigation* objective that greatly generalizes the traditional notion of collocation expressed by objective 1b.

Bibliographic entities

The principal entities in a bibliography are *documents*, *works*, *editions*, *authors*, and *subjects*. Sets of these, such as document collections, the authors of a particular document, and the subjects covered by a document, are also bibliographic entities. Other entities are more directly related to the production process: for example, an *imprint* is the set of printings of a document that preserve the image of a previous printing. We also deal below with *titles* and *subject classifications*, which strictly speaking are attributes of works rather than entities in their own right.

Documents

Documents are the basic inhabitants of the physical bibliographic universe. We characterized them in Section 2.1 as particular physical objects that embody or manifest the intellectual content of a work. Although traditional documents are physical objects, they are not necessarily physically independent of other objects: an article in a journal or a chapter in an edited collection is really a document in its own right.

In the case of digital libraries, a document is a particular electronic encoding of a work. Since one document can form an integral part of another, documents have a fundamental hierarchical structure that can be more faithfully reflected in a digital library than in a physical one. On the other hand, digital documents have a kind of impermanence and fluidity that makes them hard to deal with.

They can be instantly (and unthinkingly) duplicated, they frequently have uncertain boundaries, and they can change dynamically. This creates difficulties that we have already met in Section 2.1: helpful digital libraries need to present users with an image of stability and continuity, as though electronic documents were identifiable, discrete objects like physical ones.

Works

Works are the basic inhabitants of the intellectual bibliographic universe. They can be conceptualized as the disembodied content of documents. In practice an important operational question for traditional librarians is this: when are two documents sufficiently alike that they can be considered to represent the same work? For books, operations such as revision, updating, expansion, and translation into different languages are generally held to preserve the identity of a work. Translation to another medium may or may not. An audiotape of a book would likely be considered the same work; a video production would generally not.

The distinction between a work and a document may appear to be an abstract one, far removed from the world of real libraries. However, it has important practical consequences. A particular work may appear in several different editions. Some editions of children's books may be lavishly illustrated, others plain. New editions of scientific books may contain important revisions or substantial additional material. Editions may appear in different languages. They may be condensed versions ("Reader's Digest" editions) or expanded with scholarly annotations and footnotes. Assuming that different manifestations all have the same, or approximately the same, intellectual content, they may be considered to represent the same work. However, whether the differences are significant or not really depends on the reader's orientation and purpose.

A work's identity is even more seriously compromised when it is reinterpreted in a different medium. Different movie versions of a story usually represent radically different interpretations and are generally considered to be different works. The case of poetry or story readings is less clear-cut. If, as Marshall McLuhan claimed, the medium really is the message, then interpretations in different media certainly do imply different works.

Editions

Editions are the book world's traditional technique for dealing with two difficult problems: different presentation requirements, and managing change of content. The various editions of a work share essentially the same information but differ with respect to both printing details and updated content. A large-font edition for the visually impaired or a pocket edition for the traveler address different presentation requirements. Revised editions correct and update the content.

Electronic documents generally indicate successive modifications to the same work using terms such as *version*, *release*, and *revision* rather than *edition*. These terms are not standardized, and different people use them in different ways. No matter what term you use, the underlying problem is that new editions of an electronic document may be produced extraordinarily rapidly, unencumbered by traditional processes of physical book production. We cannot even estimate how many versions we have generated of the present book while writing it, if a new version had been declared every time a file was saved. Yet these changes over time could easily have been captured by a dynamic digital library that always presented the current incarnation of the work but allowed you to examiner earlier versions too.

Authors

Of all bibliographic entities, authors seem the most straightforward, and authorship has been the primary attribute used to identify works since medieval times. All Western libraries provide an author catalog that places books by the same author together. However, authorship is not always straightforward. Some works appear to emanate from organizations or institutions; are they then "authors"? Modern scientific and medical papers often have numerous authors because of the complex and collaborative nature of the work and institutional conventions about who should and should not be included. Many works are anthologies: is the editor to be regarded as an "author"? If not, what about anthologies that include extensive commentaries by the editors; when is this deemed worthy of authorship? And what about ghostwriters?

For a concrete example of some of the difficulties, turn to the "References" section at the end of the book and locate the entry under "Library of Congress (1998)." Who is the author of this book? A particular person or group of people? The Library of Congress? The Library of Congress Cataloging Policy and Support Office?

In the digital world, documents may or may not represent themselves as being written by particular authors. If they do, authorship is commonly taken at face value. Of course many documents may end up authorless by this criterion. However, even if many works are anonymous, when authorship is clearly identifiable, users of a digital library will expect to be able to locate documents by author.

Taking authorship at face value has significant drawbacks—not so much because people misrepresent authorship, but because differences often arise in how names are written. For one thing, authors sometimes use pseudonyms. But a far greater problem is simply inconsistency in spelling and formatting. Traditional librarians go to great pains to normalize names into a standard form.

Table 2.1, admittedly an extreme example, illustrates just how difficult the problem can become. It shows different ways in which the name of *Muammar Qaddafi* (the Libyan leader) is represented on documents that have been received

Table 2.1 Spelling variants of the name Muammar Qaddafi.		
Qaddafi, Muammar	Muammar al-Qadhafi	Qathafi, Muammar
Gadhafi, Mo ammar	Mu ammar al-Qadhdhafi	Gheddafi, Muammar
Kaddafi, Muammar	Qadafi, Mu ammar	Muammar Gaddafy
Qadhafi, Muammar	El Kazzafi, Moamer	Muammar Ghadafi
El Kadhafi, Moammar	Gaddafi, Moamar	Muammar Ghaddafi
Kadhafi, Moammar	Al Qathafi, Mu ammar	Muammar Al-Kaddafi
Moammar Kadhafi	Al Qathafi, Muammar	Muammar Qathafi
Gadafi, Muammar	Qadhdhafi, Mu ammar	Muammar Gheddafi
Mu ammar al-Qadafi	Kaddafi, Muammar	Khadafy, Moammar
Moamer El Kazzafi	Muammar al-Khaddafi	Qudhafi, Moammar
Moamar al-Gaddafi	Mu amar al-Kad'afi	Qathafi, Mu'Ammar el
Mu ammar Al Qathafi	Kad'afi, Mu amar al-	El Qathafi,Mu'Ammar
Muammar Al Qathafi	Gaddafy, Muammar	Kadaffi, Momar
Mo ammar el-Gadhafi	Gadafi, Muammar	Ed Gaddafi, Moamar
Muammar Kaddafi	Gaddafi, Muammar	Moamar el Gaddafi
Moamar El Kadhafi	Kaddafi, Muamar	

by the Library of Congress. The Library catalog chooses one of these forms, ostensibly the form in which the author is most commonly known—*Qaddafi, Muammar* in this case—and then groups all variants under this one spelling—with appropriate cross-references in the catalog from all of the variant spellings. In this case, ascribing authorship by taking documents at face value would end up with 47 different authors!

The creation of standardized names for authors is called *authority control*, and the files that librarians use to record this information are called *authority files*. This is one instance of a general idea: using a *controlled vocabulary* or set of *preferred terms* to describe entities. Terms that are not preferred are *deprecated* (a technical term that does not necessarily imply disapproval) and are often listed explicitly with a reference to the associated preferred term—as in Table 2.1. Controlled vocabularies are to be contrasted with the gloriously uncontrolled usage found in free text, where there are no restrictions at all on how authors may choose to express what they want to say.

Titles

Titles are really attributes of works rather than entities in their own right. Obviously they are important elements of any bibliographic system. In digital collections, titles, like authors, are often taken at face value from the documents

Table 2.2 Title pages of different editions of Hamlet.	
Amleto, Principe di Danimarca	*Montale Traduce Amleto*
Der erste Deutsche Buhnen-Hamlet	*Shakespeare's Hamlet*
The First Edition of the Tragedy of Hamlet	*Shakspeare's Hamlet*
Hamlet, A Tragedy in Five Acts	*The Text of Shakespeare's Hamlet*
Hamlet, Prince of Denmark	*The Tragedy of Hamlet*
Hamletas, Danijos Princas	*The Tragicall Historie of Hamlet*
Hamleto, Regido de Danujo	*La Tragique Histoire d'Hamlet*
The Modern Reader's Hamlet	

themselves. However, in the world of books they can show considerable variation, and librarians use vocabulary control for titles as well as for authors. For example, Table 2.2 shows the titles that are represented on the title pages of 15 different editions of *Hamlet*.

Subjects

Subjects rival authors as the predominant gateway to library contents. Although physical library catalog systems boasted card-based subject catalogs, which were sometimes a useful retrieval tool, computer-based catalogs have breathed new life into subject searching and are now widely used in libraries. However, subjects are far harder to assign objectively than authorship, and involve a degree of, well, subjectivity. Interestingly, the dictionary defines *subjective* as both

> Pertaining to the real nature of something; essential

and

> Proceeding from or taking place within an individual's mind such as to be unaffected by the external world.

Perhaps the evident conflict between these two meanings says something about the difficulty of defining subjects objectively!

As with authorship, digital documents sometimes explicitly represent what they are about by including some kind of subject descriptors. Otherwise there are two basic approaches to automatically ascribing subject descriptors or "key phrases" to documents. One is key-phrase *extraction*, where phrases that appear in the document are analyzed in terms of their lexical or grammatical structure, and with respect to phrases that appear in a corpus of documents in the same domain. Phrases, particularly noun phrases, that appear frequently in this document but rarely in others in the same domain are good candidates for subject descriptors. The second is key-phrase *assignment*, where documents are automatically classified with respect to a large corpus of documents for which subject descriptors have already been determined (usually manually), and documents inherit descriptors that have been ascribed to similar documents. We return to this topic in Chapter 5 (Section 5.6).

It is far easier to assign subject descriptors to scientific documents than to literary ones, particularly works of poetry. Many literary compositions and artistic works—including audio, pictorial, and video compositions—have subjects that cannot readily be named. Instead they are distinguished as having a definite style, form, or content, using artistic categories such as *genre*.

The Library of Congress Subject Headings (LCSH) are a comprehensive and widely used controlled vocabulary for assigning subject descriptors. They currently occupy five large printed volumes, amounting to about 6,000 pages each, commonly referred to by librarians as "the big red books." The aim is to provide a standardized vocabulary for all categories of knowledge, descending to quite a specific level, so that books—books on any subject, in any language—can be described in a way that allows all books on a given subject to be easily retrieved.

The red books contain a total of around two million entries, written in three columns on each page. Perhaps 60 percent of them are full entries like the one for *Agricultural Machinery* in the first row of Table 2.3. This entry indicates that *Agricultural Machinery* is a preferred term, and should be used instead of the three terms *Agriculture—Equipment and supplies*, *Crops—Machinery*, and *Farm machinery*. *UF* stands for "use for." Each of these three deprecated terms has its own one-line entry that indicates (with a *USE* link) that *Agricultural Machinery* should be used instead; these deprecated terms account for the remaining 40 percent of entries in the red books. The *UF/USE* links, which are inverses, capture the relationship of *equivalence* between terms. One of each group of equivalent terms is singled out as the preferred one, not because it is intrinsically special but purely as a matter of convention.

Another relationship captured by the subject headings is the *hierarchical* relationship of broader and narrower topics. These are expressed by *BT* (broader topic) and *NT* (narrower topic), respectively, which again are inverses. The *Agricultural Machinery* example of Table 2.3 stands between the broader topic *Machinery* and narrower topics such as *Agricultural implements* and *Agricultural instruments*—there are many more not shown in the table. Each of these narrower topics will have links back to the broader topic *Agricultural Machinery*; and *Agricultural Machinery* will appear in the (long) list of specializations under the term *Machinery*.

The abbreviation *RT* stands for "related topics" and gives an *associative* relationship between a group of topics that are associated but neither equivalent nor hierarchically related. The fact that *Farm equipment* is listed as a related topic under *Agricultural Machinery* indicates that the converse is also true: *Agricultural machinery* will be listed as a related topic under *Farm Equipment*.

Table 2.3 Library of Congress Subject Heading entries.

Agricultural Machinery		Machinery		
UF	Agriculture—Equipment and supplies	UF	...	
	Crops—Machinery	BT	...	
	Farm machinery	RT	...	
		SA	...	
BT	Machinery	NT	...	
RT	Farm equipment			Agricultural machinery
	Farm mechanization			...
	Machine-tractor stations			
SA	subdivision Machinery under names of crops, e.g., Corn—Machinery	**Agricultural Implements**		
		UF	...	
NT	Agricultural implements	BT		Agricultural machinery
	Agricultural instruments	...		
	...			
		Farm Equipment		
Agriculture—Equipment and supplies		UF	...	
USE	Agricultural Machinery	BT	...	
		RT		Agricultural machinery
Crops—Machinery				...
USE	Agricultural Machinery			
		...		
Farm machinery				
USE	Agricultural Machinery			

Finally, the *SA* or "see also" entry indicates a whole group of subject headings, often specified by example—like the *e.g., Corn—Machinery* under *Agricultural Machinery* in Table 2.3. The dash in this example indicates that there is a subheading *Machinery* under the main entry for *Corn*. However, there is no back reference from this entry to *Agricultural machinery*.

Subject classifications

Books on library shelves are usually arranged by subject. Each work is assigned a single code or *classification*, and books representing the work are physically placed in lexicographic code order. Note that the classification code is not the same as the subject headings discussed above: any particular item has several subject headings but only one classification code. The purpose of a library classification scheme is to place works into topic categories, so that volumes treating the same or similar topics fall close to one another. Subject classification systems that are in wide use in the English-speaking world are the Library of Congress Classification (originating from the U.S.), the Dewey Decimal Classification (from England), and the Colon Classification System (used in India).

Physically browsing library shelves is a popular way of finding related material. Of course readers who browse books in this way have access to the full content of the book, which is quite different from browsing catalog entries that give only a small amount of summary metadata. Indeed most readers—even scholars—remain blithely unaware that there is any way of finding related books other than browsing library shelves, despite the existence of the elaborate and carefully controlled subject heading scheme described above. Physical placement on library shelves, being a one-dimensional linear arrangement, is clearly a far less expressive way of linking content than the rich hierarchy that subject headings provide.

Placing like books together adds an element of serendipity to searching. You catch sight of an interesting book whose title seems unrelated, and a quick glance inside—the table of contents, chapter headings, illustrations, graphs, examples, tables, bibliography—gives you a whole new perspective on the subject. Catalog records—even ones that include abstracts or summaries of the contents—are nowhere near as informative as full text, and no mere catalog can substitute for the experience of browsing full texts of related works. This helps to explain why most readers perform a simple author or title search for a specific book, or one with a suitable title, and then follow up by browsing through nearby books—ignoring the whole machinery of controlled vocabularies and subject classifications that librarians have taken such pains to provide.

Whereas physical libraries are constrained to a single linear arrangement of books, digital libraries, of course, are not restricted to such an organization. The entire contents of a digital collection can (in principle) be rearranged at the click of a mouse, and rearranged again, and again, and again, in different ways depending on how you are thinking. The whole reason for the subject classification vanishes: there is no single linear arrangement of works. The only circumstance in which you might need subject classifications is when you reach outside the library to systems whose users are not so fortunate as to have access to full texts.

2.3 Modes of access

The purpose of libraries is to give people access to information, and digital libraries have the potential to increase access tremendously. Now you do not have to go to the library, it comes to you—in your office and home, in your hotel while traveling, even at the café, on the beach, and in the plane.

Most digital libraries are on the Web (although many restrict access to in-house use). This provides convenient and universal access—at least in the developed world, and for people who possess the necessary technology. You can work in the library whenever you want, wherever you are, and so can others.

If a physical library decides to offer a digital library service to the general public, terminals will need to be installed for people to use. Service is no longer confined to a central library building; terminals can be deployed in publicly accessible locations that are closer to individual user groups. Each workstation may need additional equipment for library use, such as printed reference material and a color printer for users, along, perhaps, with general application software and other devices such as scanners. Reliance on external networks may be reduced by configuring clusters of workstations with local servers that contain a copy of the entire digital library—this is often called *mirroring*.

As we learned in Chapter 1, Web access may be infeasible or inappropriate in situations such as developing countries and disaster relief operations. In this case digital libraries may be delivered on read-only mass-storage consumer devices such as CD-ROM or DVD. Even when this is not necessary for logistic reasons, users may like to own a physical, permanent, immutable copy of the library contents. Sometimes this is valuable psychologically. A large private collection of hardly read books makes many people feel that they somehow possess the knowledge therein. Also, on the Web you are always at the mercy of someone else. Finally, one way of controlling access is to distribute the library on tangible physical devices instead of putting it on universal networks.

You can have the best of both worlds. Digital library collections can coexist both on the Web and on read-only mass storage devices, and be accessible in exactly the same way from either medium.

From a user interface point of view, Web browsers implement a lowest common denominator that falls well below the state of the art in interface technology. Apart from a few local operations—scrolling, menu selection, button highlighting—the only possible response to a user action is to display a new page, and response time is unpredictable and often far from immediate. The many small differences among browsers, and different versions of browsers, exacerbate the lowest common denominator effect and suck up inordinate quantities of development effort. Of course the use of scriptable browsers (e.g., JavaScript) and local applets (e.g., in Java) helps to some extent. However, fully reactive user interfaces call for tighter coupling between the user's workstation or "client" and the central digital library server.

Again you can have the best of both worlds. A digital library system can provide a basic end-user service over the Web, as well as a more intimate connection with the digital library server using an established protocol (such as the "common object request broker architecture" or CORBA protocol). Then more sophisticated user interfaces can be implemented that use the protocol to access the basic library services of searching, browsing, and delivery of documents and metadata. Experimental or special-purpose interfaces can share the same central library system with ordinary users who work on standard Web browsers. Such interfaces might provide services as varied as virtual reality interfaces for physically navigating through a digital library, or query visualization using Venn diagrams, or content visualization via dynamic three-dimensional cluster diagrams. If necessary, network delays can be mitigated by temporary caching or by permanently mirroring the digital library contents locally.

Some digital library applications—notably video libraries and reactive interfaces involving sophisticated visualizations—need higher bandwidth than can be provided by general-purpose network technology. These call for special treatment and are beyond the scope of this book.

Even though the library is delivered by the Web, access may have to be restricted to authorized users. Software firewalls that restrict access to particular named sites are one solution; password protection is another. Since the basic Web infrastructure provides universal access, password protection must be implemented within the digital library system itself. Access can be restricted to the library as a whole, or to certain collections within it, or to certain documents, or even to certain pages or paragraphs. For example, any user may be allowed to present text searches and view the results in the form of extracts or summaries of the target documents, but users may have to authenticate themselves when it comes to viewing the full text of a document—or of particular "classified" documents. The basic technology of reliable password protection is well-developed and easy to provide.

Digital watermarking is another control mechanism: it guards against unauthorized distribution of information taken from the library. While data can be encrypted to prevent unauthorized access during transmission, it is difficult to devise reliable technical means that prevent a user authorized to read a document from copying and distributing it—particularly remote users who are capable of installing their own software on library workstations. Instead documents in the form of pictures and document images can be "watermarked" by embedding a secret, imperceptible, ineradicable code into their structure. This may not prevent copying, but it does ensure that the owner of the copied material can be identified. To help track down the source of the leak, different watermarks can be used that identify the workstation to which the material was served.

Another form of access is communicating with other digital library systems. Conventional library systems use an international standard communication protocol (Z39.50; see Chapter 8) to give individual users and other libraries remote access to their catalog records. Digital libraries may offer their users integrated access to the world's library catalogs by integrating "client" software into the user interface. Furthermore, by embedding a "server" for the standard protocol, they can offer their own content to external libraries and their users.

Finally, a digital library system may be implemented as a distributed system. Replicated servers on different computers—perhaps widely dispersed—offer their own collections, or their own parts of a single collection. The servers communicate among themselves and present a single unified view to users. Some collections may be replicated in different places, perhaps to reduce network traffic by permitting local responses to local users, or perhaps to accelerate access by dispatching different queries to different processors. Other collections may be geographically distributed, the results from different servers being integrated before presentation to the user, who perceives a single seamless collection. Such an architecture permits "virtual" digital libraries that do not actually hold their own library material but merely act as a broker to information served elsewhere.

2.4 Digitizing documents

One of the first things to consider when starting to build a digital library is whether you need to digitize existing documents. Digitization is the process of taking traditional library materials, typically in the form of books and papers, and converting them to electronic form where they can be stored and manipulated by a computer. Digitizing a large collection is an extremely time-consuming and expensive process, and should not be undertaken lightly.

There are two stages in digitization, illustrated in Figure 2.1. The first produces a digitized image of each page using a process known as *scanning*. The second produces a digital representation of the textual content of the pages using a process called *optical character recognition* (OCR). In many digital library systems it is the result of the first stage that is presented to library readers: what they see are page images, electronically delivered. The second stage is necessary if a full-text index is to be built automatically for the collection that allows you to locate any combination of words, or if any automatic metadata extraction technique is contemplated, such as identifying the titles of documents by finding them in the text.

Sometimes the second stage may be unnecessary, but this is rare because a prime advantage of digital libraries is automatic searching of the full textual content of the documents. If, as is usually the case, the second stage is undertaken, this raises the possibility of using the OCR result as an alternative way of displaying the page contents. This will be more attractive if the OCR system is not only able to interpret the text in the page image, but can retain the page layout as well. Whether or not it is a good idea to display its output depends on how well the page content and format is captured by the OCR process. We will see examples in the next chapter of collections that illustrate these different possibilities.

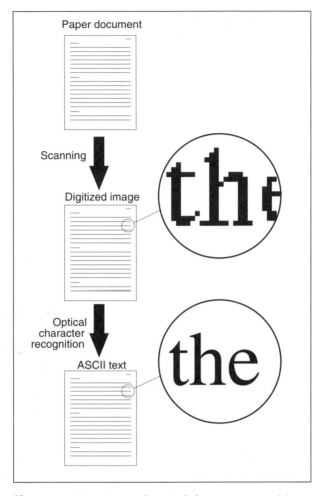

Figure 2.1 Scanning and optical character recognition.

Scanning

The result of the first stage is a digitized image of each page. These images resemble digital photographs, although it may be that each picture element or *pixel* is either black or white—whereas photos have pixels that come in color, or at least in different shades of gray. Text is well represented in black and white, but if the images include nontextual material such as pictures, or contain artifacts like coffee stains or creases, grayscale or color images will resemble the original pages more closely.

When digitizing documents by scanning page images, you will need to decide whether to use black-and-white, grayscale, or color, and you will also need to determine the resolution of the digitized images—that is, the number of pixels

Table 2.4 An assortment of devices and their resolutions.

Device	Resolution (dpi)	Depth (bits)
Laptop computer screen (14-inch diagonal, 1024×768 resolution)	92×92	8, 16, 24, or 32
Fax machine	200×100 or 200×200	1
Scanner	300×300 or 600×600	1, 8, or 24
Laser printer	600×600	1
Phototypesetter	4800×4800	1

per linear unit. For example, ordinary faxes have a resolution of around 200 dpi (dots per inch) in the horizontal direction and 100 dpi vertically, and each pixel is either black or white. Faxes vary a great deal because of deficiencies in the low-cost scanning mechanisms that are typically used. Another familiar example of black-and-white image resolution is the ubiquitous laser printer, which generally prints 600 dots per inch in both directions. Table 2.4 shows the resolution of several common imaging devices.

The number of bits used to represent each pixel also helps to determine image quality. Most printing devices are black and white: one bit is allocated to each pixel. When putting ink on paper, this representation is natural—a pixel is either inked or not. However, display technology is more flexible, and many computer screens allow several bits per pixel. Monochrome displays often show 16 or 256 levels of gray, while color displays range up to 24 bits per pixel, encoded as 8 bits for each of the colors red, green, and blue, or even 32 bits per pixel, encoded in a way that separates the chromatic, or color, information from the achromatic, or brightness, information. Grayscale and color scanners can be used to capture images having more than 1 bit per pixel.

More bits per pixel can compensate for a lack of linear resolution and vice versa. Research on human perception has shown that if a dot is small enough, its brightness and size are interchangeable—that is, a small bright dot cannot be distinguished from a larger, dimmer one. The critical size below which this phenomenon takes effect depends on the contrast between dots and their background. It corresponds roughly to a 640×480 pixel display at normal viewing levels and distances.

When digitizing documents for a digital library, think about what you want the user to be able to see. How closely does what you get from the digital library need to resemble the original document pages? Are you concerned about preserving artifacts? What about the pictures in the text? Will users see one page on the screen at a time? Will they be allowed to magnify the images?

You will need to obtain scanned versions of several sample pages, choosing the test pages to cover the various kinds and quality of images in the collection, digitized to a range of different qualities—different resolutions, different numbers of gray levels, color and monochrome. You should perform trials with end users of the digital library to determine what quality is necessary for actual use.

It is always tempting to say that quality should be as high as it possibly can be! But there is a cost: the downside of accurate representation is increased storage space on the computer and—probably more importantly—increased time for page access by users, particularly remote users. Doubling the linear resolution quadruples the number of pixels, and although this increase is ameliorated somewhat by compression techniques, users still pay a toll in access time. Your trials should take place on typical computer configurations using typical communications facilities, so that you can assess the effect of download time as well as image quality. You might also consider generating thumbnail images, or images at several different resolutions, or using a "progressive refinement" form of image transmission (see Chapter 4), so that users who need high-quality pictures can be sure that they've got the right one before embarking on a lengthy download.

Optical character recognition

The second stage of digitizing library material is to transform the scanned image into a digitized representation of the page *content*—in other words, a character-by-character representation rather than a pixel-by-pixel one. This is known as "optical character recognition" or OCR. Although the OCR process itself can be entirely automatic, subsequent manual cleanup is invariably necessary and is usually the most expensive and time-consuming process involved in creating a digital library from printed material. You might characterize the OCR operation as taking "dumb" page images that are nothing more than images, and producing "intelligent" electronic text that can be searched and processed in many different ways.

As a rule of thumb, you need an image resolution of 300 dpi to support OCR of regular fonts of size 10-point or greater, and an image resolution of 400 to 600 dpi for smaller font sizes (9-point or less). Note that some scanners take up to four times longer for 600 dpi scanning than for 300 dpi. Many OCR programs can tune the brightness of grayscale images appropriately for the text being recognized, so grayscale scanning tends to yield better results than black-and-white scanning. However, if you scan offline, black-and-white images generate much smaller files than grayscale ones.

Not surprisingly the quality of the output of an OCR program depends critically on the kind of input that is presented. With clear, well-printed English, on clean pages, in ordinary fonts, digitized to an adequate resolution, laid out on the page in the normal way, with no tables, images, or other nontextual material, the result of a leading OCR engine is likely to be 99.9 percent accurate or above—say 1 to 4 errors per 2,000 characters, which is a little under a page of this book. Accuracy continues to increase, albeit slowly, as technology improves. Replicating the exact format of the original image is more difficult, although for simple pages an excellent approximation will be achieved.

Unfortunately life rarely presents us with favorable conditions. Problems occur with proper names, with foreign names and words, and with special terminology—like Latin names for biological species. They also occur with strange fonts, and particularly foreign alphabets with accents or diacritical marks, or non-Roman characters. With all kinds of mathematics. With small type or smudgy print. With overdark characters that have smeared or bled together, or overlight ones whose characters have broken up. With tightly packed or loosely set text where, to justify the margins, character and word spacing diverge widely from the norm. With hand annotation that interferes with the print. With water-staining, or extraneous marks such as coffee stains or squashed insects. With multiple columns, particularly when set close together. With any kind of pictures or images—particularly ones that contain some text. With tables, footnotes, and other floating material. With unusual page layouts. When the text in the images is skewed, or the lines of text are bowed from trying to place book pages flat on the scanner platen, or when the book binding has interfered with the scanned text. These problems may sound arcane, but even modest OCR projects often encounter many of them.

The highest and most expensive level of accuracy attainable from commercial service bureaus is typically 99.995 percent, or 1 error in 20,000 characters of text (approximately seven pages of this book). Such levels are often most easily achievable by keyboarding. Regardless of whether the material is rekeyed or processed by OCR with manual correction, each page is processed twice, by different operators, and the results are compared automatically. Any discrepancies are resolved manually.

As a rule of thumb, OCR becomes less efficient than manual keying when the error rate drops below 95 percent. Moreover, once the initial OCR pass is complete, costs tend to double with each additional percentage increase in accuracy that is required. However, the distribution of errors over pages in a large image conversion project is generally far from uniform: often 80 percent of the errors come from 20 percent of the page images. It may be worth considering having the worst of the pages manually keyed and performing OCR on the remainder.

Interactive OCR

Because of the difficulties mentioned above, OCR is best performed as an interactive process. Human intervention is useful both before the actual recognition, when cleaning up the image, and afterward, when cleaning up the text produced. The actual recognition part can be time-consuming—times of one or two minutes per page are not unusual—and it is useful to be able to perform interactive preprocessing for a batch of page images, have them recognized offline, and return to the batch for interactive cleanup. Careful attention to such practical details can make a great deal of difference in a large-scale OCR project.

Interactive OCR involves six steps: image acquisition, cleanup, page analysis, recognition, checking, and saving.

Acquisition

In the initial scanning step, images are acquired either by inputting them from a document scanner or by reading a file that contains predigitized images. In the former case the document is placed on the scanner platen and the program produces a digitized image. Most digitization software can communicate with a wide variety of image acquisition devices: this is done using a standard interface specification called *TWAIN*. Your OCR program may be able to scan many page images in one batch and let you work interactively on the other steps afterward; this will be particularly useful if you have an automatic document feeder.

Cleanup

The cleanup stage applies certain image-processing operations to the whole image, or to parts of it. For example, a despeckle filter cleans up isolated pixels or "pepper and salt" noise. It may be necessary to rotate the image by 90 or 180 degrees, or to automatically calculate a skew angle and deskew the image by rotating it back by that angle. Images may be converted from white-on-black to the standard black-on-white representation, and double-page spreads may be converted to single image pages. These operations may be invoked manually or automatically. If you don't want to recognize certain parts of the image, or if it contains large artifacts—such as photocopied parts of the document's binding—you may need to remove them manually by selecting the unwanted area and clearing it.

Page analysis

The page analysis stage examines the layout of the page and determines which parts of it to process, and in what order. Again this can take place either manually or automatically. The result is to segment the page into blocks of different types. Typical types include text blocks, which will be interpreted as ordinary running text, table blocks, which will be further processed to analyze the layout before reading each table cell, and picture blocks, which will be ignored in the character recognition stage. During page analysis multicolumn text layouts are detected and sorted into correct reading order.

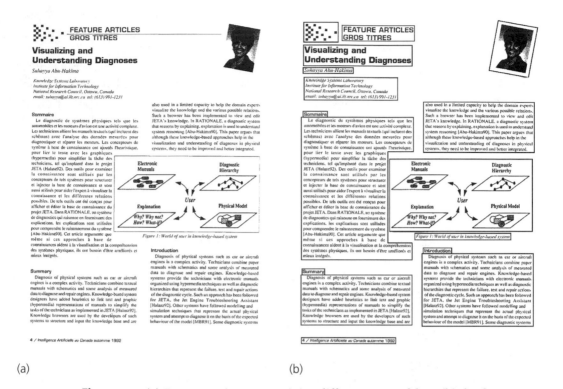

(a)   (b)

Figure 2.2 (a) Document image containing different types of data; (b) the document image segmented into different regions. Copyright © 1992 *Canadian Artificial Intelligence Magazine.*

Figure 2.2a shows an example of a scanned document with regions that contain different types of data: text, two graphics, and a photographic image. In Figure 2.2b, bounding boxes have been drawn (manually in this case) around these regions. This particular layout is interesting because it contains a region—the large text block halfway down the left-hand column—that is clearly nonrectangular, and another region—the halftone photograph—that is tilted. Because layouts such as this present significant challenges to automatic page analysis algorithms, many interactive OCR systems show users the result of automatic page analysis and offer the option of manually overriding it.

It is also useful to be able to set up manually a template layout pattern that applies to a whole batch of pages. For example, you may be able to define header and footer regions, and specify that each page contains a double column of text—perhaps even giving the bounding boxes of the columns. Perhaps the whole page analysis process should be circumvented by specifying in advance that all pages contain single-column running text, without headers, footers, pictures, or tables.

Finally, although word spacing is usually ignored, in some cases spaces may be significant—as when dealing with formatted computer programs.

Tables are particularly difficult to handle. For each one, the user may be able to specify interactively such things as whether the table has one line per entry or contains multiline cells, and whether the number of columns is the same throughout or some rows contain merged cells. As a last resort it may be necessary for the user to specify every row and column manually.

Recognition

The recognition stage reads the characters on the page. This is the actual "OCR" part. One parameter that may need to be specified is the font type, whether regular typeset text, fixed-width typewriter print, or dot matrix characters. Another is the alphabet or character set, which is determined by the language in question. Most OCR packages only deal with the Roman alphabet; some accept Cyrillic, Greek, and Czech too. Recognizing Arabic text, the various Indian scripts, or ideographic languages like Chinese and Korean is a task that calls for specialist software.

Even within the Roman alphabet there are some character-set variations. While English speakers are accustomed to the 26-letter alphabet, many languages do not employ all the letters— Māori, for example, uses only 15. Documents in German include an additional character, ß or *scharfes s*, which is unique because unlike all other German letters it exists only in lowercase. (A recent change in the official definition of the German language has replaced some, but not all, occurrences of ß by *ss*.) European languages use accents: the German umlaut (*ü*); the French acute (*é*), grave (*à*), circumflex (*ô*), and cedilla (*ç*); the Spanish tilde (*ñ*). Documents may, of course, be multilingual.

For certain document types it may help to create a new "language" to restrict the characters that can be recognized. For example, a particular set of documents may be all in uppercase, or consist of nothing but numbers and associated punctuation.

In some OCR systems, the recognition engine can be trained to attune it to the peculiarities of the documents being read. Training may be helpful if the text includes decorative fonts, or special characters such as mathematical symbols. It may also be useful when recognizing large batches of text (100 pages or more) in which the print quality is low.

For example, the letters in some particular character sequences may have bled or smudged together on the page so that they cannot be separated by the OCR system's segmentation mechanism. In typographical parlance they form a *ligature:* a combination of two or three characters set as a single glyph—such as *fi, fl* and *ffl* in the font in which this book is printed. Although OCR systems recognize standard ligatures as a matter of course, printing occasionally contains unusual ligatures, as when particular sequences of two or three characters are systematically joined together. In these cases it may be helpful to train the system to recognize each combination as a single unit.

Training is accomplished by making the system process a page or two of text in a special training mode. When an unrecognized character is encountered, the user has an opportunity to enter it as a new pattern. It may first be necessary to adjust the bounding box to include the whole pattern and exclude extraneous fragments of other characters. Recognition accuracy will improve if several examples of each new pattern are supplied. When naming a new pattern, its font properties (italic, bold, small capitals, subscript, superscript) may need to be specified along with the actual characters that comprise the pattern.

There is a limit to the amount of extra accuracy that can be achieved with training. OCR still does not perform well with more stylized type styles, such as Gothic, that are significantly different from modern ones—and training may not help much.

Obviously, better OCR results can be obtained if a language dictionary is incorporated into the recognition process. It is far easier to distinguish letters such as *o*, *0*, *O*, and *Q* if they are interpreted in the context of the words in which they occur. Most OCR systems include predefined language dictionaries and are able to use domain-specific dictionaries containing such things as technical terms, common names, abbreviations, product codes, and the like. Particular words may be constrained to particular styles of capitalization. Regular words may appear with or without an initial capital letter and may also be written in all capitals. Proper names must begin with a capital letter (and may be written in all capitals too). Some acronyms are always capitalized, while others may be capitalized in fixed but arbitrary ways.

Just as the particular language determines the basic alphabet, many letter combinations are impossible in a given language. Such information can greatly constrain the recognition process, and some OCR systems allow it to be provided by the user.

Checking

The next stage of OCR is manual checking of the output. The recognized page is displayed on the screen, with problems highlighted in color. One color may be reserved for unrecognized and uncertainly recognized characters, another for words that do not appear in the dictionary. Different display options allow some of this information to be suppressed. The original image itself will be displayed for the user's convenience, perhaps with an auxiliary magnification window that zooms in on the region in question. An interactive dialog, similar to that provided by word processors in spell-check mode, focuses on each error and allows the user to ignore this instance, ignore all instances, correct the word, or add it to the dictionary as a new word. Other options allow you to ignore words with digits and other nonalphabetic characters, ignore capitalization mismatches, normalize spacing around punctuation marks, and so on.

You may also want to edit the format of the recognized document, including font type, font size, character properties such as italics and bold, margins, indentation, table operations, and so on. Ideally, general word-processor options will be offered within the same package, to save having to alternate between the OCR program and a standard word processor.

Saving

The final stage is to save the OCR result, usually to a file (alternatives include copying it to the clipboard or sending it by e-mail). Supported formats might include plain text, HTML, RTF, Microsoft Word, and PDF. There are many possible options. You may want to remove all formatting information before saving, or include the "uncertain character" highlighting in the saved document, or include pictures in the document. Other options control such things as page size, font inclusion, and picture resolution. In addition, it may be necessary to save the original page image as well as the OCR text. In PDF format (described in Chapter 4), you can save the text and pictures only, or save the text under (or over) the page image, where the entire image is saved as a picture and the recognized text is superimposed upon it, or hidden underneath it. This hybrid format has the advantage of faithfully replicating the look of the original document—which can have useful legal implications. It also reduces the requirement for super-accurate OCR. Alternatively you might want to save the output in a way that is basically textual, but with the image form substituted for the text of uncertainly recognized words.

Page handling

Let us return to the process of scanning the page images in the first place and consider some practical issues. Physically handling the pages is easiest if you can "disbind" the books by cutting off their bindings; obviously this destroys the source material and is only possible when spare copies exist. At the other extreme, source material can be unique and fragile, and specialist handling is essential to prevent its destruction. For example, most books produced between 1850 and 1950 were printed on paper made from acid-process wood pulp, and their life span is measured in decades—far shorter than earlier or later books. Toward the end of their lifetime they decay and begin to fall apart. (We return to this in Chapter 9.)

Sometimes the source material has already been collected on microfiche or microfilm, and the expense associated with manual paper handling can be avoided by digitizing these forms directly. Although microfilm cameras are capable of recording at very high resolution, quality is inevitably compromised because an additional generation of reproduction is interposed; furthermore, the original microfilming may not have been done carefully enough to permit digitized images of sufficiently high quality for OCR. Even if the source material is not already in this form, microfilming may be the most effective and least damaging means of preparing content for digitization. It capitalizes on substantial institutional and vendor expertise, and as a side benefit the microfilm masters provide a stable long-term preservation format.

Generally the two most expensive parts of the whole process are handling the source material on paper, and the manual interactive processes of OCR. A balance must be struck. Perhaps it is worth using a slightly inferior microfilm to reduce paper handling at the expense of more labor-intensive OCR; perhaps not.

Microfiche is more difficult to work with than microfilm, since it is harder to reposition automatically from one page to the next. Moreover, it is often produced from an initial microfilm, in which case one generation of reproduction can be eliminated by digitizing directly from the film.

Image digitization may involve other manual processes apart from paper handling. Best results may be obtained by manually adjusting settings like contrast and lighting individually for each page or group of pages. The images may be skewed, that is, slightly rotated from their correct orientation on the scanning platen, and a deskewing operation may have to be applied. This can be done either manually or automatically. It may be necessary to split double-page spreads into single-page images; again this may be manual or automatic. In some cases pictures and illustrations will need to be copied from the digitized images and pasted into other files.

Planning an image digitization project

Any significant image digitization project will normally be outsourced. As a rough ballpark estimate, you can expect to pay $1 to $2 per page for scanning and OCR if the material is in a form that can easily be handled (e.g., books whose bindings can be removed), the text is clear and problem-free, there are few images and tables that need to be handled manually, and you have a significant volume of material. If difficulties arise, costs increase to many dollars per page. Companies that perform image digitization often contract the labor-intensive parts of the process to specialists in other countries.

Using a third-party service bureau eliminates the need for you to become a state-of-the-art expert in image digitization and OCR. However, it will be necessary for you to set standards for the project and ensure that they are adhered to.

Most of the factors that affect image digitization can only be evaluated by practical tests. You should arrange for samples of the material to be scanned and

OCR'd by competing commercial organizations and compare the results. For practical reasons (because it is expensive or infeasible to ship valuable source materials around), the scanning and OCR stages may be contracted out separately. Once scanned, images can be transmitted electronically to potential OCR vendors for evaluation. You should probably obtain several different scanned samples—at different resolutions, different numbers of gray levels, from different sources such as microfilm and paper—to give OCR vendors a range of different conditions. You should select sample images that span the range of challenges that your material presents.

Once sample pages have been scanned and OCR'd, you might consider building a small digital library prototype that will allow others to assess the look and feel of the planned collection. This is often a good way to drum up support by getting others excited about the project.

Quality control of the scanned images is obviously an important concern in any image digitization project. The obvious way is to load the images into your system as soon as they arrive from the vendor and check them for acceptable clarity and skew. Images that are rejected are then returned to the vendor for rescanning. However, this strategy is time-consuming and may not provide sufficiently timely feedback to allow the vendor to correct systematic problems. It may be more effective to decouple yourself from the vendor by batching the work. Quality can then be controlled on a batch-by-batch basis, where you review a statistically determined sample of the images and accept or reject whole batches.

Inside an OCR shop

Being labor-intensive, OCR work is often outsourced from the Western world to developing countries such as India, the Philippines, and Romania. In 1999 one of the authors visited an OCR shop in a small two-room unit on the ground floor of a high-rise building in a country town in Romania. It contained about a dozen terminals, and every day from 7:00 AM through 10:30 PM they were occupied by operators who were clearly working with intense concentration. There are two shifts a day, with about a dozen people in each shift and two supervisors—25 employees in all.

Most of the workers are university students and are delighted to have this kind of employment—it compares well with the alternatives available in their town. Pay is by results, not by the hour—and this is quite evident as soon as you walk into the shop and see how hard people work! In effect, they regard their shift at the terminal as an opportunity to earn money, and they make the most of it.

This firm uses two different commercial OCR programs. One is better for processing good copy, has a nicer user interface, and makes it easy to create and modify custom dictionaries. The other is preferred for tables and forms; it has a larger character set with many unusual alphabets (e.g., Cyrillic). The firm does not necessarily use the latest version of these programs; sometimes earlier versions have special advantages that are absent in subsequent ones.

The principal output formats are Microsoft Word and HTML. Again, the latest release of Word is not necessarily the one that is used—obsolete versions have advantages for certain operations. A standalone program is used for converting Word documents to HTML because it greatly outperforms Word's built-in facility. These people are expert at decompiling software and patching it. For example, they were able to fix some errors in the conversion program that affected how nonstandard character sets are handled. Most HTML is written by hand, although they do use an HTML editor for some of the work.

A large part of the work involves writing scripts or macros to perform tasks semiautomatically. Extensive use is made of Word Basic to write macros. Although Photoshop is used extensively for image work, they also employ a scriptable image processor for repetitive operations. MYSQL, an open-source SQL implementation, is used for forms databases. Java is used for animation and for implementing Web-based questionnaires.

These people have a wealth of detailed knowledge about the operation of different versions of the software packages they use, and they keep their finger on the pulse as new releases emerge. But perhaps their chief asset is their set of in-house procedures for dividing up work, monitoring its progress, and checking the quality of the result. An accuracy of around 99.99 percent is claimed for characters, or 99.95 percent for words—an error rate of 1 word in 2,000. This is achieved by processing every document twice, with different operators, and comparing the result. In 1999 throughput was around 50,000 pages/month, although capability is flexible and can be expanded rapidly on demand. Basic charges for ordinary work are around $1 per page (give or take a factor of two), but vary greatly depending on the difficulty of the job.

An example project

In the New Zealand Digital Library we undertook a project to put a collection of historical New Zealand Māori newspapers on the Web, in fully indexed and searchable form. There were about 20,000 original images, most of them double-page spreads. Figure 2.3 shows an example image, an enlarged version of the beginning, and some of the text captured using OCR. This particular image is a difficult one to work with because some areas are smudged by water-staining. Fortunately not all the images were so poor. As you can see by attempting to decipher it yourself, high accuracy requires a good knowledge of the language in which the document is written.

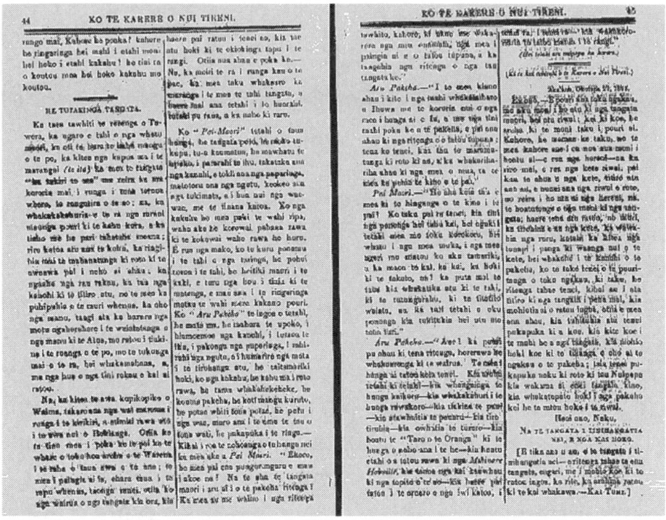

(a)

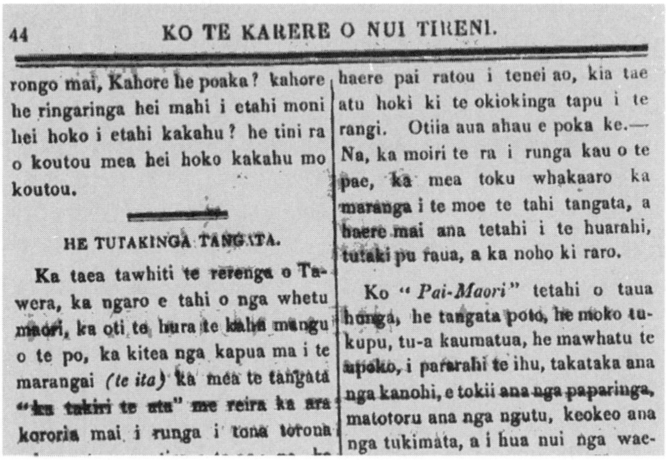

44 KO TE KARERE O NUI TIRENI.

rongo mai, Kahore he poaka? kahore he ringaringa hei mahi i etahi moni hei hoko i etahi kakahu? he tini ra o koutou mea hei hoko kakahu mo koutou.

HE TUTAKINGA TANGATA.

Ka taea tawhiti te rerenga o Tawera, ka ngaro e tahi o nga whetu maori, ka oti te hura te kaha mangu o te po, ka kitea nga kapua ma i te marangai *(te ita)* ka mea te tangata "ka takiri te ata" me reira ka ara kororia mai i runga i tona torona

haere pai ratou i tenei ao, kia tae atu hoki ki te okiokinga tapu i te rangi. Otiia aua ahau e poka ke.—Na, ka moiri te ra i runga kau o te pae, ka mea toku whakaaro ka maranga i te moe te tahi tangata, a haere mai ana tetahi i te huarahi, tutaki pu taua, a ka noho ki raro.

Ko "*Pai-Maori*" tetahi o taua hunga, he tangata poto, he moko tukupu, tu-a kaumatua, he mawhatu te upoko, i pararahi te ihu, takataka ana nga kanohi, e tokii ana nga paparinga, matotoru ana nga ngutu, keokeo ana nga tukimata, a i hua nui nga wae-

(b)

44 KO TE KARERE O NUI TIRENI.
Rongo mai, Kahore he poaka? kahore
he ringaringa hei mahi i etahi moni
hei hoko i etahi kakahu? he tini ra
o koutou mea hei hoko kakahu mo
koutou.

HE TUTAKINGA TANGATA
Ka taea tawhiti te rerenga o Tawera, ka ngaro e tahi o nga whetu
maori, ka oti te hura te kaha mangu
o te po, ka kitea nga kapua ma te
marangai *(te ita)* ka mea te tangata
"ka takiri te ata" me reira ka ara
kororia mai i runga i tona torona
whero, te rangatira o te ao; na, ka

…
haere pai ratou i tenei ao, kia tae
atu hoki ki te okiokinga tapu i te
rangi. Otiia aua ahau e poka ke.—
Na, ka moni te ra i runga kau o te
pae, ka mea toku whakaaro ka
maranga i te moe te tahi tangata, a
haere mai ana tetahi i te huarahi,
tutaki pu taua, a ka noho ki raro.
Ko "*Pai-Maori*" tetahi o taua
hunga, he tangata poto, he moko tukupu, tu a kaumatua, he mawhatu te
upoko, i pararahi te ihu, takataka ana
nga kanohi, e tokii ana nga paparinga,
matotoru ana nga ngutu, keokeo ana
nga tukimata, a hua nui nga wae-

(c)

Figure 2.3 (a) Double-page spread of a Māori newspaper; (b) enlarged version; (c) OCR text.

The first task was to scan the images into digital form. Gathering together paper copies of the newspapers would have been a massive undertaking, for the collection comprises 40 different newspaper titles which are held in a number of libraries and collections scattered throughout the country. Fortunately New Zealand's national archive library had previously produced a microfiche containing all the newspapers for the purposes of historical research. The library provided us with access not just to the microfiche result, but also to the original 35-mm film master from which it had been produced. This simultaneously reduced the cost of scanning and eliminated one generation of reproduction. The photographic images were of excellent quality because they had been produced specifically to provide microfiche access to the newspapers.

Having settled on the image source, the quality of scanning depends on scanning resolution and the number of gray levels or colors. These factors also determine how much storage is required for the information. After conducting some tests, we determined that a resolution corresponding to approximately 300 dpi on the original printed newspaper was adequate for the OCR process. Higher resolutions yielded no noticeable improvement in recognition accuracy. We also found that OCR results from a good black-and-white image were as accurate as those from a grayscale one. Adapting the threshold to each image, or each batch of images, produced a black-and-white image of sufficient quality for the OCR work. However, grayscale images were often more satisfactory and pleasing for the human reader.

Following these tests, the entire collection was scanned to our specifications by a commercial organization. Because we supplied the images on 35-mm film, the scanning could be automated and proceeded reasonably quickly. We asked for both black-and-white and grayscale images to be generated at the same time to save costs, although it was still not clear whether we would be using both forms. The black-and-white images for the entire collection were returned on eight CD-ROMs; the grayscale images occupied approximately 90 CD-ROMs.

Once the images had been scanned, the OCR process began. Our first attempts used Omnipage, a widely used proprietary OCR package. But we encountered a problem: this software is language-based and insists on utilizing one of its known languages to assist the recognition process. Because our source material was in the Māori language, additional errors were introduced when the text was automatically "corrected" to more closely resemble English. Although other language versions of the software were available, Māori was not among them. And it proved impossible to disable the language-dependent correction mechanism.[2] The result was that recognition accuracies of not much more than 95 percent

---

2. In previous versions of Omnipage one can subvert the language-dependent correction by simply deleting the dictionary file, and we know of one commercial OCR organization that uses an obsolete version for precisely this reason.

were achieved at the character level. This meant a high incidence of word errors in a single newspaper page, and manual correction of the Māori text proved extremely time-consuming.

A number of alternative software packages and services were considered. For example, a U.S. firm offered an effective software package for around $10,000 and demonstrated its use on some of our sample pages with impressive results. The same firm offers a bureau service and was prepared to undertake the basic OCR form for only $0.16 per page (plus a $500 setup fee). Unfortunately this did not include verification, which we had identified as being the most critical and time-consuming part of the process—partly because of the Māori language material.

Eventually we did locate a reasonably inexpensive software package that had high accuracy and allowed us to establish our own language dictionary. We determined to undertake the OCR process in house. This proved to be an excellent decision, and we would certainly go this route again. However, it is heavily conditioned on the unusual language in which the collection is written, and the local availability of fluent Māori speakers.

A parallel task to OCR was to segment the double-page spreads into single pages for the purposes of display, in some cases correcting for skew and page-border artifacts. We produced our own software for segmentation and skew detection and used a semiautomated procedure in which the system displayed segmented and deskewed pages for approval by a human operator.

2.5   Notes and sources

A useful source of information on criteria for selecting material for digitization is de Stefano (2000), who is specifically concerned with digital conversion. The problem of selecting for preservation raises similar issues, described by Atkinson (1986) in the predigital era. The six principles for the development of library collections are Atkinson's.

McCallum et al. (2000) describe methods for using machine learning techniques to automate the construction of Internet portals, that is, virtual libraries. Their techniques, which are still under development, help to automate the creation and maintenance of domain-specific virtual libraries. As an example, a virtual library of computer science research papers is available on the Web at *www.cora.justresearch.com*.

The term *virtual library* was characterized in 1993 as "remote access to the contents and services of libraries and other information resources, combining an on-site collection of current and heavily used materials in both print and electronic form, with an electronic network which provides access to, and delivery from, external worldwide library and commercial information and knowledge sources" (Gapen, 1993, p. 1). The pioneering INFOMINE project is described by Mason et al. (2000), an inspiring paper from which much of our information about virtual libraries was taken. Begun in January 1994, INFOMINE now provides organized and annotated links to over 20,000 scholarly and educational Internet resources, all selected and described by professional librarians. This project shows how librarians and librarian-designed finding tools can play a welcome role in making the Web a more useful environment for researchers and students.

The person who first formulated the objectives of a bibliographic system was Charles Ammi Cutter, an outstanding late Victorian library systematizer (Cutter, 1876). He was a great champion of users who astonished dyed-in-the-wool librarians with radical opinions such as "the convenience of the user must be put before the ease of the cataloger." According to Svenonius (2000), he practiced what he preached, rejecting the traditional European classified catalog, designed for scholars, in favor of a new alphabetic subject approach more suitable for the person in the street.

Section 2.2 on bibliographic organization has been strongly influenced by two classic works: *The Intellectual Foundations of Information Organization* by Svenonius (2000), and *Library Research Models* by Mann (1993). It is difficult, perhaps, to make books on library science racy, but these come as close as one is ever likely to find. The five objectives of a bibliographic system are from Svenonius. Mann's book has already been cited in Chapter 1 as a wonderful source of information on libraries and librarianship.

Development of the Library of Congress Subject Headings began in 1898, and the first edition came out in 1909. A recent edition of the big red books was published in 1998 (Library of Congress, 1998).

A good source of further information to help stimulate thought on the basic structure and parameters of your digital library is *The Digital Library Toolkit* from Sun Microsystems (2000). This provides a series of questions that people undertaking a digital library construction project should consider. It also raises issues that affect the planning and implementation of a digital library, summarizes a host of technological resources (with Web pointers), and briefly reviews existing digital library systems.

Steganography takes one piece of information and hides it in another. Digital watermarking is a kind of steganography where what is hidden is a trademark or identification code. Brassil et al. (1994) wrote an early article on watermarking textual images; Katzenbeisser and Petitcolas (1999) have collected a number of papers on all aspects of digital watermarking; and Cox, Miller, and Bloom (2001) have written a comprehensive reference book on the subject.

High-performance OCR products are invariably proprietary: we know of no public-domain systems that attain a level of performance comparable to commonly used proprietary ones. However, at least two promising projects are underway. One is GOCR (for "Gnu OCR"), which aims to produce an advanced open-source OCR system; its current status is available at *http://jocr.sourceforge.net*. Another is Clara OCR, which is intended for large-scale digitization projects and runs under X Windows; it is available at *www.claraocr.org/*.

The interactive OCR facilities described in Section 2.4 are well exemplified by the Russian OCR program FineReader (ABBYY Software, 2000), an excellent example of a commercial OCR system. Lists of OCR vendors are easily found on the Web, as are survey articles that report the results of performance comparisons for different systems. The newsgroup for OCR questions and answers is comp.ai.doc-analysis.ocr. Price-Wilkin (2000) gives a nontechnical review of the process of creating and accessing digital image collections, including a sidebar on OCR by Kenn Dahl, the founder of a leading commercial OCR company. The OCR shop we visited in Romania is *Simple Words* (*www.sw.ro*), a well-organized and very successful private company that specializes in high-volume work for international and nongovernment organizations.

The Māori language has fifteen sounds: the five vowels *a*, *e*, *i*, *o*, and *u*, and ten consonant sounds written *h*, *k*, *m*, *n*, *p*, *r*, *t*, *w*, *ng*, and *wh*. Thus the language is written using fifteen different letters. The first eight consonant sounds are pronounced as they are in English; the last two are digraphs pronounced as the *ng* in *singer* and the *wh* in *whale*, or as *f*. Each vowel has a short and long form, the latter being indicated by a macron as in the word *Māori*.

The ß or *scharfes s* character in German has been the source of great controversy in recent years. In 1998 a change in the official definition of German replaced some, but not all, occurrences of ß by *ss*. However, spelling reform has proven unpopular in German-speaking countries. Indeed in August 2000 Germany's leading daily newspaper, the *Frankfurter Allgemeine Zeitung*, returned to traditional German spelling. Acting on its own and virtually alone among Germany's major newspapers, *FAZ* suddenly announced that it was throwing out the new spelling and returning to the previous rules. Today there are ever-increasing calls for a "reform of the reform."

TWAIN is an image-capture application programming interface, originally released in 1992 for the Microsoft Windows and Apple Macintosh operating systems, which is typically used as an interface between image processing software and a scanner or digital camera. The TWAIN Working Group, an organization that represents the imaging industry, can be found at *www.twain.org*. According to *The Free On-Line Dictionary of Computing* (at *www.foldoc.org*), the name comes from the phrase "and never the twain shall meet" in Kipling's *The Ballad of East and West*. It reflects the difficulty, at the time, of connecting scanners and personal computers. On being uppercased to TWAIN to make it more distinctive, people incorrectly began to assume that it was an acronym. There is no official interpretation, but the phrase "Technology Without An Interesting Name" continues to haunt the standard.

The design and construction of the "Niupepa" (the Māori word for "newspapers") collection of historical New Zealand newspapers sketched at the end of Section 2.4 is given by Keegan et al. (2001). A more accessible synopsis by Apperley et al. (2001) is available, while Apperley et al. (in press) give a comprehensive description. The project was undertaken in conjunction with the Alexander Turnbull Library, a branch of the New Zealand National Library, whose staff gathered the material together and created the microfiche that was the source for the digital library collection. This work is being promoted as a valuable social and educational resource and is partially funded by the New Zealand Ministry of Education.

3 Presentation

User interfaces

How do you build a digital library? Where do you start? How do you *explain* how to build a digital library? "Begin at the beginning," the King of Hearts said gravely, "and go on till you come to the end: then stop" (Figure 3.1). But we will ignore his advice and begin our story at the end: what you might expect the final library system to look like. Then in the next two chapters we jump to the beginning and look at the forms in which the library material might be provided. Chapters 6 and 7 fill in the middle by explaining how it's all done. Despite the Red King's words, this is quite logical. It corresponds to looking first at the goal, what you hope to achieve; then at the starting point, what you have to work with; and finally in between, how you get from where you are now to where you want to be.

Our *digital library* definition from Chapter 1 begins

a focused collection of digital objects, including text, video, and audio . . .

and a good place to start is with the objects themselves. We will mostly be concerned with textual objects—we call them *documents*—and how they appear on the user's screen. The next section illustrates how different documents can appear within a digital library system. There are many possibilities, and we include just a smattering: structured text documents, unstructured text documents, page images, page images along with the accompanying text, speech

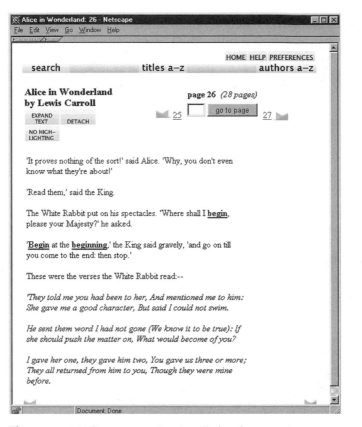

Figure 3.1 Finding a quotation in *Alice's Adventures in Wonderland*.

audio, photographic pictures, and videos. A digital library might include "non-standard" information such as music, which has many different representations—synthesized audio, music notation, page images, recorded MIDI performances, recorded audio performances. We also take the opportunity, when surveying examples of documents, to illustrate the wide range of uses to which digital libraries are being put.

In addition to documents, digital libraries include metadata of the kind used conventionally for bibliographic organization as discussed in Section 2.2, although metadata potentially involves a wider range of information and formats. We next examine some examples of metadata display, which will help convey the idea of what kind of metadata might accompany a digital library collection.

The definition goes on to say

... along with methods for access and retrieval ...

The second part of this chapter illustrates different methods for access and retrieval. Conventionally these are divided into *searching* and *browsing*, although in truth the distinction is not a sharp one. We first examine interfaces that allow you to locate words and phrases in the full text of the document collection. Searching is also useful for metadata—such as finding words in title and author fields—and we look at digital library interfaces that allow these searches, and combinations of them, to be expressed. It is often useful to be able to recall and modify past searches: *search history* interfaces allow you to review what you have done and reuse parts of it. Next we examine browsing interfaces for metadata, such as titles, authors, dates, and subject hierarchies, and show how these relate to the structure that is implicit within the metadata itself.

But searching and browsing are not really different activities: they are different parts of a spectrum. In practice people want to be able to interact with information collections in different ways, some involving searching for particular words, some involving convenient browsing—perhaps browsing the results of searching. We examine two schemes that effectively combine searching and browsing. Both are based on phrases extracted automatically from the documents in a digital library: one on an enormous—almost exhaustive—set of phrases that appear in the text; the other on carefully selected sets of key phrases for each document.

The final part of the definition is

. . . and for selection, organization, and maintenance of the collection.

We will not address this activity explicitly in this chapter, except insofar as browsing structures reflect the organization of the collection. In truth this entire book is about organizing and maintaining digital libraries—or rather, about organizing them in such a way that they are easy to maintain.

Figure 3.1, like most of the illustrations here, shows a screen shot from a Web browser. However, the browser does not show a static Web page: the digital library software has constructed this page dynamically at the time it was called up for display. The navigation bar at the top, the book title at the top left, the buttons underneath, and the page selector at the top right are all composed together with the text at display time, every time the page is accessed. The information is actually stored in compressed form in a textual database system. If you look on the computer that is the Web server for this digital library, you will not find this page stored there. Likewise in the next examples, in Figure 3.2, these pages are also put together, along with all images and links, at the time requested—not before. And in Figures 3.3a and b, the cover picture at the top left and the table of contents at the top right are stored internally in such a way that they can be accessed, and searched, and browsed, independently of the text.

(a)   (b)

Figure 3.2 Different-looking digital libraries: (a) Kids' Digital Library (Middlesex University, London, England); (b) School Journal Digital Library (Learning Media Limited, Wellington, New Zealand).

This is why in Chapter 1 we distinguished a digital library from a Web site—even one that offers a focused collection of well-organized material. The fact that documents are treated as structured objects internally enhances the prospects for providing comprehensive searching and browsing facilities.

The general look and feel of a digital library system can easily be altered by changing the way the screen is laid out and the icons used on it. Figure 3.2a shows the front page of the Kids' Digital Library, which uses a hand-printed font, chunky, hand-drawn icons, and bright pastel shades to promote a feeling of friendliness and informality—contrasting strongly with the austere, businesslike image conveyed by Figure 3.1. Figure 3.2b shows a page of a collection taken from a School Journal (we will return to this collection and give more information about it shortly): again, colorful pictures are available and are used wherever possible in place of textual descriptions, and the logo at the top is designed to help communicate the intended feeling. Exactly the same underlying technology can be used to support many different styles of digital library. Because all Web pages are generated dynamically from an internal representation, it is easy to change the entire look and feel of all pages associated with a collection—immediately, at runtime, without regenerating or even touching the content of the collection. None of the underlying information need be altered, just the output processing routines.

3.1 Presenting documents

If you want to build a digital library, the first questions that need to be answered are: What form are the documents in? What structure do they have? How do you want them to look?

Hierarchically structured documents

Figure 3.3 shows a book in the Humanity Development Library entitled *Village Level Brickmaking*. A picture of the front cover is displayed as a graphic on the left of Figure 3.3a, and the table of contents appears to its right. Below this is the start of the main text, which begins with title, author, and publisher. The books in this collection are generously illustrated: many pictures are included in the text. On the screen these images appear in-line, just as they did in the paper books from which the collection was derived. Figures 3.3c and d show some of the images, obtained by scrolling down from Figure 3.3b.

All books in this collection have front-cover images, and the appropriate image always appears at the top of any page where a book, or part of a book, is displayed. This ever-present picture gives a feeling of physical presence, a constant reminder of the context in which you are reading. The user interface look and feel may be a poor substitute for the real look and feel of a physical book—the heft, the texture of the cover, the crinkling sound of pages turning, the smell of the binding, highlighting and marginal notes on the pages, dog-eared leaves, coffee stains, the pressed wildflower that your lover always used as a bookmark—but it's a lot better than nothing.

The books in the Humanity Development Library are structured into sections and subsections. The small folder icons in Figure 3.3a indicate chapters—there are chapters on *Standardization*, *Clay Preparation*, *Moulding*, and so on. The small text-page icons beside the *Preface*, *Extraction*, and *Acknowledgements* headings indicate leaves of the hierarchy: sections that contain text but no further subsection structure.

Clicking on *Moulding* in Figure 3.3a produces the page in Figure 3.3b, which shows the chapter's structure in the form of a table of contents of its sections. Here the user has opened the book to the *Sand moulding* section by clicking on its text-page icon; that section heading is shown in bold and its text appears below. By clicking on other headings the reader can learn about such topics as *Slop moulding*, *How to mould bricks*, and *Drying*.

You can read the beginning of the *Sand moulding* section in Figure 3.3b: the scroll bar to the right of the screen indicates that there is more text underneath. Figures 3.3c and d show the effect of scrolling further down the same page.

Sometimes you want to see the full table of contents, with all chapters and their sections and subsections included. Sometimes you want to see the text of

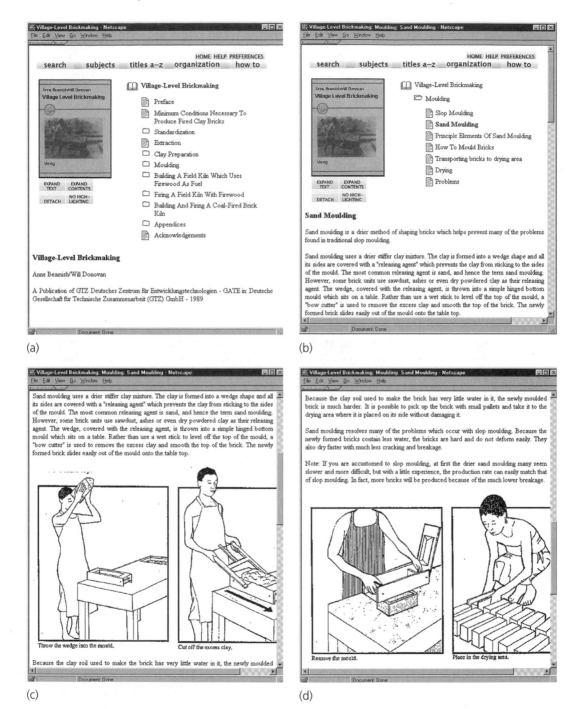

Figure 3.3 *Village-Level Brickmaking:* (a) the book; (b) the chapter on *Moulding;* (c, d) some of the pages. Beamish, A., and Donovan, W. *Village-Level Brickmaking.* Copyright © 1989 GTZ Deutsches Zentrum für Entwicklungstechnologien-GATE in Deutsche Gusellschaft für Technische Zusammenarbeit (GTZ) GmbH.

the whole book—apart from getting a complete view, a common reason for doing this is in order to print it out. In Figure 3.3 the button labeled "Expand contents" expands the table of contents into its full hierarchical structure. Likewise the Expand Text button expands the text of the section being displayed. If we pressed Expand Text in Figure 3.3a we would get the text of the entire book, including all chapters and subsections; if we pressed it in Figure 3.3b we would get the complete text of the *Moulding* chapter, including all subsections. Finally, the Detach button duplicates this window on the screen, so that you can leave the text in it while you go and look at another part of the library in the other window—invaluable when comparing multiple documents.

The Humanity Development Library is a large compendium of practical material that covers diverse areas of human development, from agricultural practice to foreign policy, from water and sanitation to society and culture, from education to manufacturing, from disaster mitigation to microenterprises. It contains 1,230 publications—books, reports, and magazines—totaling 160,000 pages, which as noted in Chapter 1 would weigh 340 kg in print form and occupy a small library bookstack.

This material was carefully selected and put together by a dedicated collection editor, who acquired the books, arranged for permission to include each one, organized a massive OCR operation to convert them into electronic form, set and monitored quality control standards for the conversion, decided what form the digital library should take and what searching and browsing options should be provided, entered the metadata necessary to build these structures, and checked the integrity of the information and the look and feel of the final product. The care and attention put into the collection is reflected by its high quality. Nevertheless it is not perfect: there are small OCR errors, and some of the 30,000 in-text figures (of which examples can be seen in Figures 3.3c and d) are inappropriately sized. The amount of effort required to edit a high-quality collection of a thousand or more books is staggering—just ask a publisher what goes into the production of a single conventional book like this one.

Plain, unstructured text documents

Figure 3.4, and Figure 3.1 earlier, show screen shots from a far plainer collection, a set of documents that have been treated as unstructured text. There is no hierarchical structure here—at least none that is known to the digital library system. Neither are there front-cover images. In place of Figure 3.3's cover picture and table of contents at the top of each page, Figure 3.4 shows a more prosaic display: the title of the book and a page selector that lets you turn from one page to another. Browsing is less convenient because there is less structure to work with. Even the "pages" do not correspond to physical pages, but are arbitrary breaks

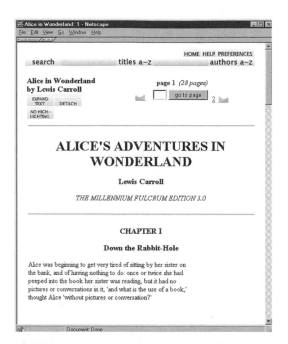

Figure 3.4 *Alice's Adventures in Wonderland.*

made by the computer every few hundred lines—that's why *Alice's Adventures in Wonderland* appears to have only 28 pages! The only reason for having pagination at all is to prevent your Web browser from downloading the entire book every time you look at it.

In fact, this book *does* have chapters—in Figure 3.4 you can see the beginning of Chapter 1, *Down the rabbit-hole.* However, this structure is not known to the digital library system: the book is treated as a long scroll of plain text. At some extra cost in effort when setting up the collection, it would have been possible to identify the beginning of each chapter, and its title, and incorporate this information into the library system to permit more convenient chapter-by-chapter browsing—as has been done in the Humanity Development Library. The cost depends on how similar the books in the collection are to one another and how regular the structure is. For any given structure, or any given book, it is easy to do; but in real life any large collection (of, say, thousands of books) will exhibit considerable variation in format. As we mentioned before, the task of proof-reading thousands of books is not to be undertaken lightly!

Another feature of this collection is that the books are stored as raw ASCII text, with the end of each line hard-coded in the document, rather than (say) HTML. That is why the lines of text in Figure 3.4 are quite short: they always remain exactly the same length and do not expand to fill the browser window. Compared with the Humanity Development Library, this is a low-quality, unattractive collection.

Removing the end-of-line codes would be easy for the text visible in Figure 3.4, but a simple removal algorithm would destroy the line breaks in tables of contents and displayed bullet points. It is surprisingly difficult to do such things reliably on large quantities of real text—reliably enough to avoid the chore of manual proofreading.

Figure 3.1 shows another feature: the words *begin* and *beginning* are highlighted in boldface. This is because the page was reached by a text search of the entire library contents (described in Section 3.3), to find the quotation with which this chapter begins. This digital library system highlights search terms in (almost) every collection: there is a button at the top that turns highlighting off if it becomes annoying. In contrast, standard Web search engines do not highlight search terms in target documents—partly because they do not store the target documents but instead direct the user to the document held at its original source location.

Alice's Adventures in Wonderland is a book in the Gutenberg collection. The goal of Project Gutenberg is to encourage the creation and distribution of electronic text. Although conceived in 1971 with the exceedingly ambitious aim of a trillion electronic literature files by the year 2001, work did not begin in earnest until 1991, and the aim was scaled back to 10,000 electronic texts within ten years. The first achievement was an electronic version of the U.S. Declaration of Independence, followed by the Bill of Rights and the Constitution. Then came the Bible and Shakespeare—unfortunately, however, the latter was never released because of copyright restrictions. The growth rate of the collection was planned to double each year, with one book per month added in 1991, two in 1992, four in 1993, and so on; at this rate the final goal should have been reached in 2001. At the time of writing the project was a little behind schedule, with nearly 4,500 books entered by the end of 2001 and a rate of increase of perhaps 100 per month.

Project Gutenberg is a grassroots phenomenon. Text is input by volunteers, each of whom can enter a book a year or even just one book in a lifetime. The project does not direct the volunteers' choice of material; instead people are encouraged to choose books they like and enter them in the manner in which they feel most comfortable. Central to the project's philosophy is to represent books as plain text, with no formatting and no metadata other than title and author. Professional librarians look askance at amateur efforts like this, and indeed quality control is a serious problem. However, for a vision that dates back more than two decades before the advent of the World Wide Web, Gutenberg is remarkably farsighted and gives an interesting perspective on the potential role of volunteer labor in placing society's literary treasures in the public domain.

In keeping with the Project Gutenberg spirit, little effort has been made to "pretty up" this digital library collection. It represents the opposite end of the spectrum to the Humanity Development Library. It took a few hours for a person to download the Project Gutenberg files and create the collection and a few

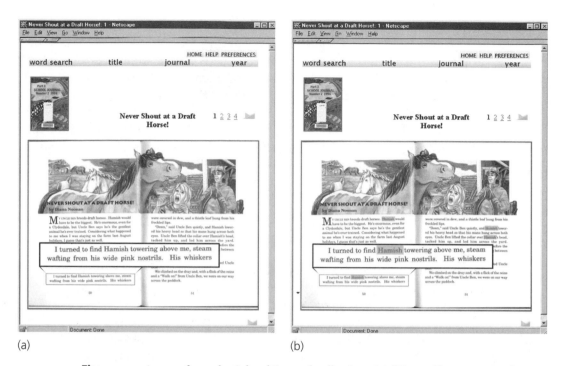

(a)   (b)

Figure 3.5 *A* story from the School Journal collection: (a) "Never Shout at a Draft Horse!"; (b) with search term highlighted (mock-up). "Never Shout at a Draft Horse" by Diana Noonan. New Zealand School Journal, 1994, Part 3, No. 2.

hours of computer time to build it. Despite the tiny amount of effort spent constructing it, it is fully searchable—which makes it indispensable for finding obscure quotations—and includes author and title lists. If you want to know the first sentence of *Moby Dick*, or whether Hermann Melville wrote other popular works, or whether "Ishmael" appears as a central character in any other books, or the relative frequencies of the words *he* and *her*, *his* and *hers* in a large collection of popular English literature, this is where to come.

Page images

The page of the children's story "Never Shout at a Draft Horse!" shown in Figure 3.5 is represented not as text but as a facsimile of the original printed version. This example is taken from a collection of literature written for children, the New Zealand School Journal. The collection's designer decided to show digitized images of the books' pages rather than text extracted from them. From a technical point of view there is a big difference: a textual representation generally occupies only about one-twentieth as much storage space as a page image, greatly reducing the space required to store the collection and the time needed to download each page. However, the picture of the horse would have to be represented as an image, just as the pictures are in Figures 3.3c and d, sacrificing some of the storage space gained.

One good reason for showing page images rather than extracted text in this collection is because the optical character recognition (OCR) process that identifies and recognizes the text content of page images is inevitably error-prone. When schoolchildren are the target audience, special care must be taken not to expose them to erroneous text. Of course errors can be detected and corrected manually, as in the Humanity Development Library, but at a substantial cost, well beyond the resources that could be mustered for this particular project.

Text is indeed extracted from the New Zealand School Journal pages using OCR, and that text is used for searching. But the reader never sees it. The consequence of OCR errors is that some searches may not return all the pages they should. If a word on a particular page was misrecognized, then a search for that word will not return that page. It is also possible that a word on the page is misinterpreted as a different word, in which case a search for *that* word will incorrectly return the page, in addition to other pages on which the word really does appear. However, neither of these errors was seen as a big problem—certainly not so serious as showing children corrupted text.

Figure 3.5 shows the journal cover at the top left and a page selector at the right that lets you browse around the story more conveniently than the numeric selector in Figure 3.2. These stories are short: "Never Shout at a Draft Horse" (Figure 3.5) has only four pages.

A disadvantage of showing page images is that it is hard to find search terms on the page. In Figure 3.1 the terms *begin* and *beginning* are in boldface. While it is easy to highlight words in a page of text, it is more difficult to highlight them in a page *image*. It is not impossible—Figure 3.5b shows the same page with the word *Hamish* highlighted as though it had been marked with a yellow marker pen. It looks impressive, and indeed it is not difficult to process the page image in this way to simulate yellow highlighting. However, it is necessary to find out exactly where the word occurs in the page in order to know what areas to highlight. It is difficult to infer from the page image the information required to do this, although some OCR systems generate information on word positions.

The *School Journal* is a magazine for New Zealand schoolchildren, delivered free to schools throughout the nation by the Ministry of Education. Its purpose is to provide quality writing that is relevant to the needs and interests of New Zealand children, and the real aim is to foster a love of reading. The material it contains is widely used throughout the school curriculum. Not only is it used for teaching reading, but also for social studies, science, and many other subjects.

The magazine originated over 90 years ago, and the cover of the very first issue is the top left image in Figure 3.2b. Like most children's literature of the time, the content of early issues was based around conveying attitudes and values of society at large. During the 1930s the journal began to encourage children's intellectual curiosity by relating the material to the student's environment. This collection of a small sample of School Journals gives a fascinating historical perspective on the development of attitudes toward children's education—and indeed the development of society in general—throughout the 20th century.

Page images and extracted text

While readers of the School Journal digital library collection see page images only, in other situations it is useful to provide a facility for viewing the extracted text as well. Figure 3.6 shows an example from a collection of historical New Zealand Māori newspapers, in both image and text form. As you can see, the tabular information at the top of the page just beneath the masthead and issue details, which represents sums of money (although it is difficult to make out), is missing from the text version. Because it is the text version that supports searching, this information is not visible to searches. On the other hand, the word *Rotorua*, which was the search term for this page, is highlighted in the text but not in the page image.

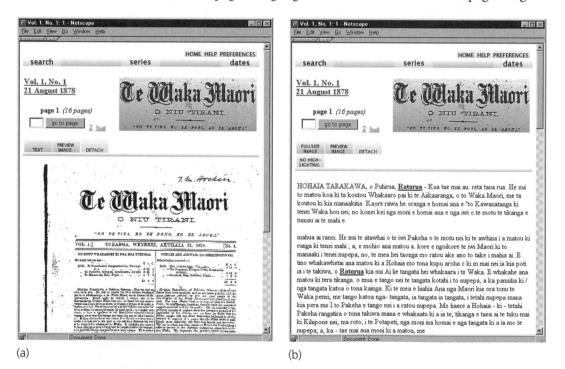

(a)   (b)

Figure 3.6 A historic Māori newspaper: (a) page image; (b) extracted text.

Both forms are provided in this collection because the advantage of being able to locate search terms in these rather long pages was deemed to outweigh any damage that might be wrought by showing readers incorrect versions of the text. The reader can choose whether to view text or image and can move quickly from one to the other. A magnified version of each page image is also available, should it be required—this facility is provided in most image collections.

The Māori newspapers record fascinating historical information that is useful from many points of view. They were published from 1842 to 1933, a formative period in the development of New Zealand, which, being so far from Europe, was colonized quite late. Far-reaching political developments took place during these years, and the collection is a significant resource for historians. It is also an interesting corpus for linguists, for changes in the Māori language were still taking place and can be tracked through the newspapers.

The collection contains 40 different newspaper titles that were published during the period. They are mostly written in Māori, though some are in English and a few have parallel translations. There are a total of 12,000 images, varying from A4 to double-page tabloid spreads—these images contain a total of around 20,000 newspaper pages. The images had previously been collected on microfiche. They are in a variety of conditions: some are crisp, others are yellowish, and still others are badly water-stained.

Construction and distribution of the microfiche was an enormous effort and was undertaken to make this national treasure available to scholars. However, the material was entirely unindexed. Although a research project has begun that is producing summaries of the articles, these will take many years to complete. The digital library collection completely transforms access to the material. First, the documents are available over the Web, which makes them readily accessible to a far wider audience. Second, they can be fully searched, which makes almost any kind of research immeasurably easier. Third, the collection does not require any research skills to use, so that ordinary people can discover things that they would never otherwise know about their heritage, ancestry, or home town.

Audio and photographic images

Some years ago the public library in the small New Zealand town where we live began a project to collect local history. Concerned that knowledge of what it was like to grow up here in the 1930s, 1940s, and 1950s would soon be permanently lost, they decided to interview older people about their early lives. Armed with tape recorders, local volunteers conducted semistructured interviews with residents of the region and accumulated many cassette tapes of recorded reminiscences, accompanied by miscellaneous photographs from the interviewees' family albums. From these tapes, the interviewer developed a brief typewritten summary of each interview, dividing it into sections representing themes or events covered in the interview. And then the collection sat in a cardboard box behind the library's circulation desk, largely unused.

Recently all the tapes and photos were digitized and made into a digital library collection, along with the summaries. Figure 3.7 shows it in use. The small control panel in the center is being used to replay a particular recording, using a standard software audio-player that sports regular tape-recorder functions—pause, fast forward, and so on. You don't have to wait until the whole audio file is downloaded: the software starts playing the beginning of the file while the rest is being transmitted. Behind the control panel is the interview summary. In the background on the right can be seen a photograph—in this

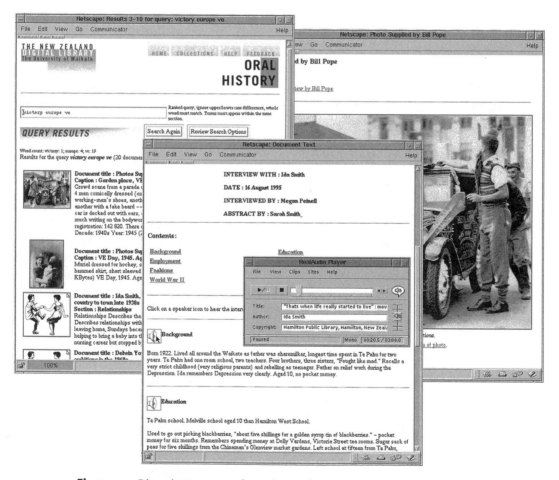

Figure 3.7 Listening to a tape from the Oral History collection. Hamilton Public Library, Hamilton, New Zealand.

case of the celebrations in our town on VE Day near the end of the Second World War—and on the left is the query page that was used to locate this information.

The interview page is divided into sections with a summary for each. Clicking on one of the speaker icons plays back the selected portion of the audio interview; interviews also can be played back in full using buttons at the top of the page (not visible in Figure 3.7). When the tapes were digitized, timings were generated for the beginning and end of each section. Flipping through a tape in this way, scanning a brief textual synopsis and clicking on interesting parts to hear them, is a far more engaging and productive activity than trying to scan an audiotape with a finger on the fast-forward button.

It is the contents of the interview pages that are used for text searching. Although they do not contain a full transcript of the interview, most keywords that you might want to search on are included. In addition, brief descriptions of each photograph were entered, and these are also included in the text search. These value-adding activities were done by amateurs, not professionals. Standard techniques such as deciding in advance on the vocabulary with which objects are described—a so-called controlled vocabulary—were not used. Nevertheless it seems to be easy for people to find material of interest.

Imagine the difference in access between a box of cassette tapes at the library's circulation desk and the fully indexed, Web-accessible digital library collection depicted in Figure 3.7. Text searching makes it easy to find out what it was like at the end of the war, or to study the development of a particular neighborhood, or to see if certain people are mentioned—and you can actually hear senior citizens reminisce about these things. Casual inquiries and browsing immediately become simple and pleasurable—in striking contrast to searching through a paper file, then a box of tapes, and finally trying to find the right place on the tape using a cassette tape player. In fact, although this collection can be accessed from anywhere on the Web, the audio files are only available to users on terminals in the local public library because when the interviews were made the subjects were not asked for consent to distribute their voices worldwide. There is a message here for those engaged in local history projects—think big!

Video

Including videos as documents in digital libraries is just as easy as including audio or photographic images. Web browsers, suitably equipped with plug-ins, are capable of playing video in a variety of formats. Of course a great deal of storage space will be required for a large collection of videos. And the feasibility of downloading video material over the Internet depends on numerous technical factors, such as the bandwidth of the connection.

Just as the oral history audiotapes are accessed through textual summaries of the interviews and descriptions of the photographs, so with videos it is possible to supply appropriate descriptive text so that they can be located. Summaries and reviews are readily available and provide a good start.

Music

As Chapter 1 mentioned, digital collections of music have the potential to capture popular imagination in ways that more scholarly libraries will never do. Figure 3.8 shows the process of trying to find the tune *Auld Lang Syne*. The player in the front window is controlling playback of audio generated by a music synthesizer program from an internal representation of the music. Also visible is the musical notation for the tune, which is generated from the same internal representation, this time by a music-typesetting program that produces an image suitable for display in a Web browser. In this collection the same internal representation supports musical searching: we return to this in Chapter 9.

Figure 3.8 Finding *Auld Lang Syne* in a digital music library.

The music representation for this collection was produced by an optical music recognition (OMR) program—similar to an OCR program but working in the domain of printed music—from a scanned page of a music book that includes the tune. Not shown in Figure 3.8, but just a click away for the user, is an image of the actual book page that contains the song. Also available are the lyrics. In other music collections it is easy to locate and listen to prerecorded renditions of the tune that people have keyed into their computer and stored in the widely used MIDI (musical instrument digital interface) format, which is a standard adopted by the electronic music industry for recording and controlling electronic instruments. It is even possible to click through to music sites that contain actual recordings and play those too.

The twin keys to creating a rich digital library music collection that is interesting and entertaining to search and browse are (1) being able to convert between the different forms that music takes, and (2) making resourceful use of the Web to locate relevant information. There are several possible representations of music:

- printed notation
- human-produced MIDI file
- audio replayed from a human MIDI file
- audio synthesized from an internal representation
- audio file representing a human performance
- internal representation, suitable for searching

An internal representation can be generated without difficulty from a human-produced MIDI file, though not from a human audio performance (at least not without excessive difficulty). And it is certainly not possible for a computer to synthesize a human performance! All other conversions are possible, with varying quality of results. For example, using optical music recognition to convert from printed notation to an internal representation is by no means a perfect process; printed music generated from a MIDI file is nowhere near as legible as professionally typeset music.

Foreign languages

We have already seen an example of a foreign-language collection: the Māori newspapers in Figure 3.6. Māori uses the standard Roman character set, although it does include one diacritical mark, a bar that occurs over vowels to lengthen them. In Chapter 5 (Section 5.1) we show how to represent such characters in Web documents.

Figure 3.9 shows interfaces in French and Portuguese. The French illustration is from a UNESCO collection called Sahel Point Doc that contains information

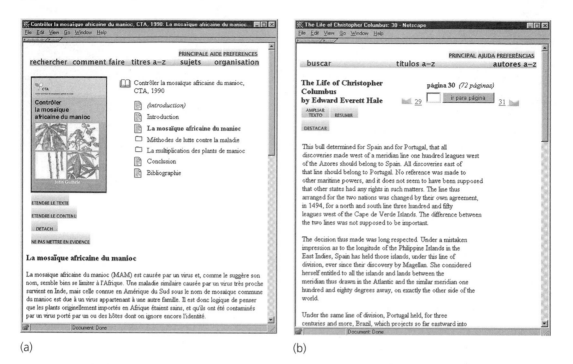

(a)   (b)

Figure 3.9 Foreign-language collections: (a) French (*Contrôler la mosaïque africaine du manioc* by J. Guthrie, CTA, 1990); (b) Portuguese interface to an English collection (*The Life of Christopher Columbus* by Edward Everett Hale, Electric Umbrella Publishing).

about the Sahel region of sub-Saharan Africa. Everything in this collection is in French: all target documents, the entire user interface, and the help text. Figure 3.9b shows a Portuguese interface to an English-language collection—the same Gutenberg collection that we examined earlier. Again, the entire user interface (and help text) has been translated into Portuguese, but in this case the target documents are in English. In fact the user interface language is a user-selectable option on a Preferences page: you can instantaneously switch to languages such as German, Dutch, Spanish, and Māori too.

Figure 3.10 shows documents from two different Chinese collections. The first comes from a collection of rubbings of Tang poetry—not unlike those stone steles described in Chapter 1, the world's oldest surviving library. These documents are images, not machine-readable text. Like the School Journal collection, there are machine-readable versions of each document—although in this case they were entered manually rather than by OCR—but the user never sees them: they are used only for searching. Because of the difficulty of locating particular words in the images, search terms are not highlighted in this collection.

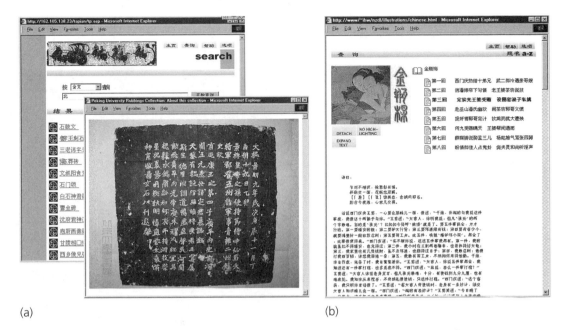

(a)   (b)

Figure 3.10 Documents from two Chinese collections: (a) rubbings of Tang poetry; (b) classic literature.

The second Chinese example is from a small collection of classic literature. Here books are represented in the same way as they are in the Humanity Development Library, with chapters shown by folders. The work illustrated is here *The Plum in the Golden Vase,* an anonymous early 17th-century satirical novel that recounts the domestic life of a corrupt merchant with six wives and concubines who slowly destroys himself with conspicuous consumption, political imbroglios, and sexual escapades. One of the three most famous Ming Dynasty novels, it reflects the debaucheries of society at the time—and is still banned in China. In this collection, being textual, search terms are highlighted by putting them in bold. Boldface characters (and indeed italics) are used in Chinese just as they are in Western languages.

It's easy to display documents in exotic languages within Web browsers. In the early days you had to download a special plug-in for the character set being used, but today's browsers incorporate support for many languages. Figure 3.11 shows pages from an Arabic collection of information on famous mosques, displayed using an ordinary browser. If your browser does not support a particular character set, you may need to download an appropriate plug-in.

As Figures 3.10a and 3.11b imply, the text of both the Chinese and Arabic collections (as well as all other languages) is fully searchable. Again, the browser does the hard part, facilitating character entry and ensuring that Arabic text is

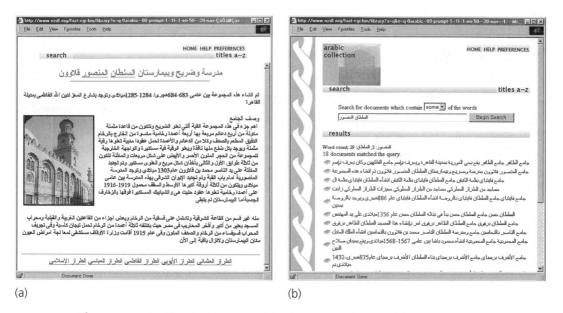

Figure 3.11 An Arabic collection: (a) a document; (b) searching.

composed from right to left, not from left to right as in other languages. To enter ideographic languages like Chinese, which go beyond the normal keyboard, you need special software. All documents in this digital library system are represented internally in Unicode, and the system converts between this and the representation supported by the browser (which can differ from one browser to another). We discuss how to handle different character sets in Chapter 4 (Section 4.1), while Chapter 5 (Section 5.1) mentions how to embed them in Web documents.

3.2 Presenting metadata

As we saw in Chapter 2, traditional libraries manage their holdings using catalogs that contain information about every object they own. Metadata, characterized in Chapter 1 as "data about data," is a recent term for such information. Metadata is information in a structured format, whose purpose is to provide a description of other data objects to facilitate access to them. Whereas the data objects themselves—the books, say—generally contain information that is not structured, or (as in the Gutenberg collection in Figure 3.4) whose structure is not apparent to the system, the essential feature of metadata is that its elements *are* structured. Moreover, metadata elements are standardized so that the same type of information can be used in different systems and for different purposes.

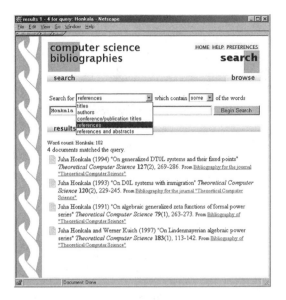

Figure 3.12 Bibliography display.

In the computer's representation of a book it may not be obvious what is the title, the author, the publisher, the source of the original copy, and so on. However, if this information is represented in metadata, it is done so in a standard way using standard elements, so that the computer can identify these fields and operate on them.

Figure 3.12 shows metadata presented as a conventional bibliographic listing. These items have been located in a large collection of computer science references: the hyperlinks at the end of each reference link to the source bibliographies. Many of the bibliographic entries have abstracts, which are viewed by clicking the page icon to the left of each entry. In this case all the icons are grayed out, indicating that no abstracts are available. The metadata here includes title, author, date, the title of the publication in which the article appears, volume number, issue number, and page numbers. These are standard bibliographic metadata items. Also included are the URL of the source bibliography and the abstract—although you may argue whether this is structured enough to really constitute metadata.

Metadata has many different aspects, corresponding to different kinds of information that might be available about an item, that are not included in the abbreviated reference format of Figure 3.12. Historical features describe provenance, form, and preservation history. Functional ones describe usage, condition, and audience. Technical ones provide information that promotes interoperability between different systems. Relational metadata covers links and citations. And, most important of all, intellectual metadata describes the content or subject.

Metadata provides assistance with search and retrieval; gives information about usage in terms of authorization, copyright, or licensing; addresses quality issues such as authentication and rating; and promotes system interoperability.

Figure 3.13a shows a metadata record retrieved over the Internet from the Library of Congress information service and displayed within a simple interface that shows all the fields in the record (only half of which are visible). The more common fields are named, while obscure ones are labeled with identification numbers (e.g., field 35). You can see that there is some redundancy: the principal author appears in both the *Personal Name* field and a subfield of the title; the other authors also appear further down the record in separate *Author Note–Name* fields. This metadata was retrieved using an information interchange standard called Z39.50 that is widely used throughout the library world (described in Section 8.5) and is represented in a record format called MARC, for "machine-readable cataloging," that is also used by libraries internationally (described in Section 5.4).

Library metadata is standardized—although, as is often the case with standards, there are many different ones to choose from. (Indeed MARC itself comes in more than 20 variants, produced for different countries.) Metadata is important in contexts other than bibliographic records, but these areas often lack any

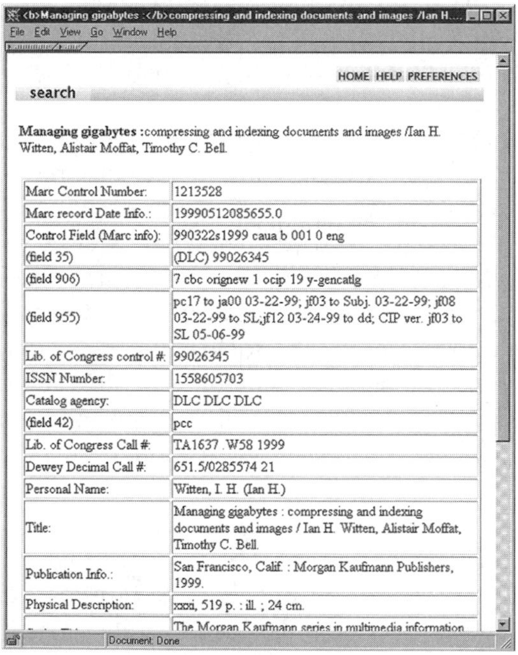

(a)  (b)

Figure 3.13 Metadata examples: (a) bibliography record retrieved from the Library of Congress; (b) description of a BBC television program.

accepted standard. Figure 3.13b shows a record from a BBC catalog of radio and television programs and gives information pertinent to this context—program title, item title, date, medium, format, several internal identifiers, a description, and a comments field. This database also includes many other fields.

Metadata descriptions often grow willy-nilly, in which case the relatively unstructured technique of text searching becomes a more appropriate way of locating records than the conventional way of searching a structured database with predefined fields. Because of increased interest in communicating information about radio and television programs internationally, people in the field are working on developing a new metadata standard for this purpose. Developing international standards requires a lot of hard work, negotiation, and compromise; it takes years.

3.3   Searching

Electronic document delivery is the primary raison d'être for most digital libraries. But searching comes a close second—in particular, searching the full text of the documents' contents. Whereas conventional automated library catalog searches are restricted to metadata, digital libraries have access to the entire contents of the objects they contain. This is a great advantage.

Figure 3.14a shows a request for the search that was used to find this chapter's opening quotation: it seeks paragraphs in English that contain both the words *begin* and *beginning*. Figure 3.14b shows the computer's response: a list of documents that contain paragraphs matching the query. These pages provide a deliberately plain, stripped-down, unadorned search mechanism with only rudimentary functionality. In digital libraries—particularly ones targeted at nonacademic users—simple facilities should be available to satisfy the basic things that most people want most of the time. Options may be provided for more advanced interactions, but not at the expense of simplicity for the casual user. As Alan Kay, a leading early proponent of the visually based paradigm of human-computer interaction, said, "Simple things should be simple, complex things should be possible."

The screens shown in Figure 3.14 allow readers to choose the unit that is searched, the language, and the type of search. The units that can be chosen vary from collection to collection. They typically include such items as *paragraphs, sections, documents*; also *section titles, document titles*, and *authors*. The first group of items involves the full text. The second group is quite different in that it involves metadata elements—but it is unnecessary to point this out explicitly to the user, at least for casual users.

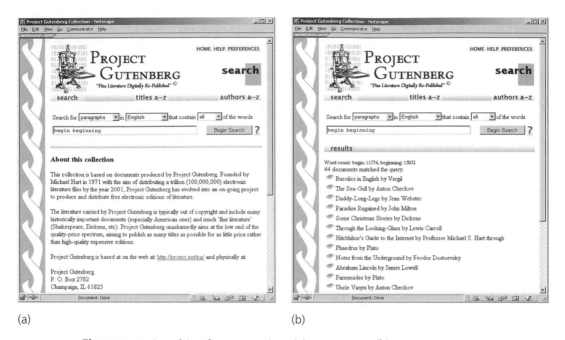

Figure 3.14 Searching for a quotation: (a) query page; (b) query response.

What is returned, as shown in Figure 3.14b, is a list of the titles of the documents. Even though the search may be for *paragraphs*, not just the relevant paragraph is returned, but also the enclosing document in its entirety. In this digital library system, the units that the user finally sees on the screen as the result of searching or browsing operations are defined to be the "documents." If you wanted the system to present paragraphs as individual units, you would need to define paragraphs to be the "documents"—and arrange for paragraphs to include internal links, perhaps to preceding and succeeding ones. This is not hard to do.

In multilingual collections it is useful to restrict searches to a specified language in order to avoid false hits on words in other languages. The type of search, in this interface, can be either *all of the words* (as chosen in Figure 3.14) or *some of the words* (not shown). Technically these are interpreted as a Boolean AND query and a ranked query respectively.

Types of query

In the field of information retrieval, an important distinction is made between *Boolean* and *ranked* queries. Both comprise a list of *terms*—words to be sought in the text. In a Boolean query, terms are combined using the connectives AND, OR, and NOT, and the *answers*, or *responses*, to the query are those units of text that satisfy the stipulated condition. In a ranked query, the list of terms is treated as a small document in its own right, and units of text that are "similar" to it are sought, ranked in order of the degree of match. It may be more logical to view ranking as a separate operation that can be applied to any kind of query; from this perspective what we are calling a *ranked query* is usually interpreted as an OR query, which seeks documents containing *any* of the specified words, followed by a ranking operation. In both Boolean and ranked retrieval, what is searched may be units of text such as *paragraphs* or metadata elements such as *authors*, whichever the reader chooses. The unit returned is not necessarily the same as the unit searched—in the above examples the entire enclosing document is returned regardless of what search unit is specified.

AND is the most common Boolean query type, and this is how *all of the words* is interpreted in Figure 3.14. A query such as

digital AND *library*

might be used to retrieve books on the same subject as this one. Both terms (or lexical variants that are considered equivalent, as described below) must occur somewhere in every answer. They need not be adjacent, nor need they appear in any particular order. Documents containing phrases such as *library management in the digital age* will be returned as answers. Also returned would be a document containing the text *a software library for digital signal processing*—perhaps not quite what is sought, but nonetheless a correct answer to this Boolean query. And a document in which the word *library* appeared in the first paragraph and *digital* in the last would be considered equally correct.

Retrieval systems inevitably return some answers that are not relevant, and users must filter these out manually. There is a difficult choice between casting a broad query to be sure of retrieving all relevant material, albeit diluted with many irrelevant answers, and a narrow one, where most retrieved documents are of interest but others slip through the net because the query is too restrictive. A broad search that identifies virtually all the relevant documents is said to have *high recall*, while one in which virtually all retrieved documents are relevant has *high precision*.

An enduring theme in information retrieval is the tension between these two virtues. When searching you must decide whether you prefer high precision or high recall and formulate your query appropriately. In typical Web searches, for example, precision is generally more sought after than recall. There is so much out there that you probably don't want to find *every* relevant document—you likely couldn't handle them all anyway—and you certainly don't want to have to pay the price of checking through a lot of irrelevant documents. However, if you are counsel for the defense looking for precedents for a legal case, you probably care a great deal about recall—you want to be sure that you have checked *every* relevant precedent, because the last thing you want is for the prosecutor to spring a nasty surprise in court.

Another problem is that small variations of a query can lead to quite different results. Although you might think the query *electronic* AND *document* AND *collection* is similar to *digital* AND *library*, it is likely to produce a very different answer. To catch all desired documents, professional librarians become adept at adding extra terms, learning to pose queries such as

(*digital* OR *virtual* OR *electronic*) AND (*library* OR (*document* AND *collection*))

where the parentheses indicate operation order.

Until around 1990 Boolean retrieval systems were the primary means of access to online information in commercial and scientific applications. However, Internet search engines have taught us that they are not the only way a database can be queried.

Rather than seeking exact Boolean answers, people—particularly nonprofessional and casual users—often prefer simply to list words that are of interest and have the retrieval mechanism supply whatever documents seem most relevant. For example, to locate books on digital libraries, a list of terms such as

digital, virtual, electronic, library, document, collection, large-scale, information, retrieval

is, to a nonprofessional at least, probably a clearer encapsulation of the topic than the Boolean query cited earlier.

Identifying documents relevant to a list of terms is not just a matter of converting the terms to a Boolean query. It would be fruitless to connect these particular terms with AND operators, since vanishingly few documents are likely to match. (We cannot say that no documents will match. This page certainly does.) It would be equally pointless to use OR connectives since far too many documents will match and few are likely to be useful answers.

The solution is to use a *ranked query*, which applies some kind of artificial measure that gauges the similarity of each document to the query. Based on this numeric indicator, a fixed number of the closest matching documents are returned as answers. If the measure is good, and only a few documents are returned, they will contain predominantly relevant answers—high precision. If many documents are returned, most of the relevant documents will be included—high recall. In practice, low precision invariably accompanies high recall since many irrelevant documents will almost certainly come to light before the last of the relevant ones appears in the ranking. Conversely, when the precision is high, recall will probably be low, since precision will be high only near the beginning of the ranked list of documents, at which point only a few of the total set of relevant ones will have been encountered.

Great effort has been invested over the years in a quest for similarity measures and other ranking strategies that succeed in keeping both recall and precision reasonably high. Simple techniques just count the number of query terms that appear somewhere in the document: this is often called *coordinate matching*. A document that contains five of the query terms will be ranked higher than one containing only three, and documents that match just one query term will be ranked lower still. An obvious drawback is that long documents are favored over short ones since by virtue of size alone they are more likely to contain a broader selection of the query terms. Furthermore common terms appearing in the query tend to discriminate unfairly against documents that do not happen to contain them, even ones that match on highly specific ones. For example, a query containing *the digital library* might rank a document containing *the digital age* alongside or even ahead of one containing *a digital library*. Words such as *the* in the query should probably not be given the same importance as *library*.

Many ranking techniques assign a numeric weight to each term based on its frequency in the document collection. Common terms receive low weight. These techniques also compensate for the length of the document, so that long ones are not automatically favored.

It is difficult to describe ranking mechanisms in a few words. It is difficult even to describe the *idea* of ranking to end users in a way that is both succinct and comprehensible. That is why the digital library system illustrated ducks the issue, in the simple form of interface illustrated in Figure 3.14, by mentioning only that answers should match "some of the words." Hopefully the reader will not be too confused by the responses he or she receives.

Professional information retrieval specialists like librarians want to understand exactly how their query will be interpreted and are prepared to issue complex queries provided that the semantics are clear. For most tasks they prefer precisely targeted Boolean queries. These are especially appropriate if it is metadata that is being searched, and particularly if professional catalogers have entered it, for the terms that are used are relatively unambiguous and predictable. Casual users, on the other hand, may not want to grapple with the complex matter of how queries are interpreted; they prefer to trust the system to do a good job and are prepared to scroll further down the ranked list if they want to expend more effort on their search. They like ranked queries. These are especially appropriate if full text is being searched, for term usage is relatively unpredictable.

A compromise between Boolean and ranked queries emerged in early Internet search engines. By default they treated queries as ranked, but allowed users more precise control by indicating certain words that must appear in the text of every answer (usually by a preceding + sign) and others that must not appear (preceded by –). Of course there are many other possibilities, and as the Web grew and the quest for precision began to dominate recall, some search engines began to return only documents that contained all of the search terms, corresponding to a ranked Boolean AND. An obvious generalization of these ideas is to undertake a full Boolean search and rank the results. And many other schemes have been proposed. Some use nonstandard logic, such as fuzzy logic, instead of the standard Boolean operators; this provides an alternative rationale for ranking the results.

It is difficult to design querying methods that scale up satisfactorily to hundreds of millions of documents—particularly given the additional constraint that it must be possible to implement the scheme so that queries are answered almost immediately. The usual one- or two-word query soon becomes completely inadequate except for very special queries. Long Boolean expressions are hard to enter, manage, and refine, tipping the balance toward automatic methods of ranking to assist users in their quest for satisfactory means of information retrieval.

Case-folding and stemming

Two operations that are often needed when querying are *case-folding* and *stemming*. Figure 3.15 shows a Preferences page that allows users to choose between different types of query interface and different query options. In the lower part, case-folding and stemming options are selected. An attempt has been made in the interface to describe these operations in three or four words whose meaning

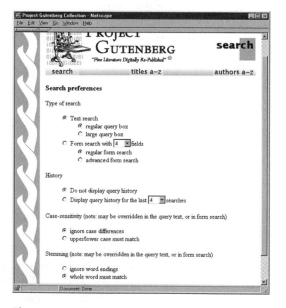

Figure 3.15 Choosing search preferences.

will hopefully be grasped immediately by casual users; here we discuss them in more detail.

In our earlier example queries, uppercase versions of words—such as *Digital* and *DIGITAL, Library* and *LIBRARY*—should probably be considered equivalent to the query terms *digital* and *library*, respectively. This is easily accomplished by case-folding—in other words, replacing all uppercase characters in the query with their lowercase equivalents. There will be situations where users wish to disable this feature and perform an exact-match search, perhaps looking for documents containing *Digital* AND *Equipment* AND *Corporation* (the now-defunct computer manufacturer), to avoid being flooded with answers about *corporation policy on capital equipment for digital libraries*. Users need to be able to specify either option in their query.

The second process, *stemming*, relaxes the match between query terms and words in the documents so that, for example, the term *libraries* is accepted as equivalent to *library*. Stemming involves reducing a word by stripping off one or more suffixes, converting it to a neutral *stem* that is devoid of tense, number, and—in some languages—case and gender information.

The process of altering words by adding suffixes (and, in some languages, affixes) is governed by many linguistic rules. Converting the *y* in *library* to the *ies* in *libraries* is one simple example; another is the final-consonant doubling when the word *stem* is augmented to *stemming*. The process of reducing a word to its root form, which is called *morphological reduction*, is correspondingly complex and typically requires a language dictionary that includes information about which rules apply to which words.

However, for the purposes of information retrieval, simpler solutions suffice. All that is necessary is for different variants of a word to be reduced to an unambiguous common form—the stem. The stem does not have to be the same as the morphological root form. So long as all variants of a word are reduced to the same stem, and no other words reduce to that stem, the desired effect will be obtained. There is a further simplification: only certain kinds of suffixes need be considered. Linguists use the word *inflectional* to describe suffixes that mark a word for grammatical categories. In contrast, *derivational* suffixes modify the major category of a word—for example, when *-less* is appended to words such as *hope* or *cloud*, it converts a noun to an adjective. Derivational suffixes should not be stripped because they alter the meaning—radically, in this example.

Like case-folding, stemming is not necessarily appropriate for all queries, particularly those involving names and other known items.

Stemming is language-dependent: an algorithm for English will not work well on French words and vice versa. If no stemmer is available for the language under consideration, it is probably best not to stem. Indeed the very concept of stemming differs widely from one language to another. Many languages use prefixes as well as suffixes to indicate derivational forms; others involve complex compound words that should be split into constituent parts before taking part in a query. Case-folding, too, is not relevant to certain languages, such as Chinese and Arabic.

Stemming and case-folding complicate the task of highlighting search terms in the retrieved documents. You cannot simply find the stem and highlight all words that contain it, for this would often highlight the wrong word. For example, a particular system might stem both *library* and *libraries* to *librar* so that they match, but avoid stemming *librarian* because this is a derivational suffix that changes the meaning of the word. (In practice, many stemmers are not so sophisticated.) However, the form *librarian* does contain the letters *librar* and so will be highlighted if this is based on a simple textual match—incorrectly, for this system. And this method may fail to highlight a correct term—a different stemming algorithm might stem *libraries* to the root form *library*, and then fail to match when the text is highlighted.

Correct results would be obtained by stemming each word in the retrieved document using the same stemming algorithm and seeing if the result matched the stemmed query word, but this is likely to be prohibitively time-consuming. An alternative is for the information retrieval system to record the stemmed form of each word and expand the query by adding each stemmed form of these terms prior to the highlighting operation.

Phrase searching

Users often want to specify that the search is for contiguous groups of words, or *phrases*. Indeed, most of our examples—*digital library*, *Digital Equipment Corporation*—would be better posed as phrase searches. Phrases are generally indicated in a query by putting the phrase in quotation marks.

Although from a user's point of view phrase searching is a simple and natural extension of the idea of searching, it is more complex from an implementation perspective. Users think phrase searching is as easy and natural as, say, Boolean searching, because they visualize the computer looking through all the documents, just as they would, but faster—a lot faster! Given that you can find the individual words in all those documents, surely it doesn't make much difference if you have to check that they come together as a phrase.

Actually it does. When computers search, they don't scan through the text as we would: that would take too long. Computers are not all that fast at working through masses of text. For one thing the documents will be stored on disk, and access to the disk is by no means instantaneous. Instead computers first create an index that records, for each word, the documents that contain that word. Every word in the query is looked up in the index, to get a list of document numbers. Then the query is answered by manipulating these lists—in the case of a Boolean AND query, by checking which documents are in all the lists. (The process is described in a little more detail in Section 4.2.)

Phrase searching changes everything. No longer can queries be answered simply by manipulating the lists of document numbers. There are two quite different ways of proceeding. The first is to look inside the documents themselves: checking through all documents that contain the query terms to see if they occur together as a phrase. We refer to this as a *postretrieval scan*. The second is to record word numbers as well as document numbers in the index—the position of each occurrence of the word in the document as well as the documents it occurs in. We refer to this as a *word-level index*. Then when each word in the query is looked up in the index, the computer can tell from the resulting list of word positions if the words occur together in a phrase by checking whether they are numbered consecutively.

The mechanism that is used to respond to phrase queries greatly affects the resources required by an information retrieval system. With a postretrieval scan, only a document-level index is needed. But it can take a great deal of time to respond to a phrase query because—depending on how common the terms are—many documents might have to be scanned. Phrases containing unusual words can be processed quickly, for few documents include them and therefore few need be scanned for the occurrence of the phrase. But phrases containing common words, such as *digital library*, will require substantial computer time, and response will be slow.

With a word-level index, the exact position of each occurrence of each word is recorded, instead of just the documents in which it occurs. This makes the index significantly larger. Not only are word numbers larger than document numbers, and hence require more storage space, but any given word probably appears several times in any given document and each occurrence must be recorded.

Which mechanism is employed also affects how phrases can be used in queries. For example, people often want to specify proximity: the query terms must appear within so many words of each other, but not necessarily contiguously in a phrase. If word numbers are stored, responding to a proximity query is just a matter of checking that the positions do not differ by more than the specified amount. If phrase scanning is employed, proximity searching is far more difficult.

Users sometimes seek a phrase that includes punctuation and even white space. A word-level index treats the documents as sequences of words, and punctuation and spacing are generally ignored. Distinguishing between differently punctuated versions of phrases requires a postretrieval scan even if a word-level index is available—unless the index also includes word separators.

Phrases complicate ranked searching. Ranking uses the frequency of a query term throughout the corpus as a measure of how influential that word should be in determining the ranking of each document—common words like *the* are less influential than rare ones like *aspidistra*. However, if a phrase is used in the query, it should really be the frequency of the phrase, not the frequency of the individual words in it, that determines its influence. For example, the English words *civil*, *rights*, and *movement* are used in many contexts, but the phrase *civil rights movement* has a rather specific meaning. The importance of this phrase relative to other words in a query should be judged according to the frequency of the phrase, not of the constituent words.

As we have seen, the simple idea of including phrases in queries complicates things technically. In practice, building digital library systems involves pragmatic decisions. A word-level index will be included if it is feasible, if phrase searching is likely to be common, and if the space occupied by the system is not a significant constraint. In simple systems a postretrieval scan will be used, particularly if phrase searching will be rare or if phrases might contain punctuation. In either case ranking will be based on individual word frequencies, not phrase frequencies, for practical reasons.

One of the problems in digital libraries is ensuring that users grasp what is happening. As we have seen, it is difficult to fully understand what is happening in phrase searching! An alternative is the kind of phrase browsing technique described in Section 3.5: this provides a natural interface whose workings are easy to grasp.

Different query interfaces

Different query interfaces are suitable for different tasks, and users can choose different search preferences, as shown in Figure 3.15, to suit what they are doing.

For example, the search pages we have seen (e.g., Figure 3.14) have miniscule query boxes, encouraging users to type just one or two terms. In reality many queries contain only a few words. Indeed studies have shown that the most common number of terms in actual queries to actual Web search systems is—zero! Most often people just hit the search button, or the Return key, without typing anything in, presumably either by accident or without understanding what is going on. The second most common type of query has just one term. Note that for single-term queries, the difference between Boolean and ranked retrieval is moot. There *is* a difference—most Boolean systems will return the retrieved documents in a particular, predetermined, order—say, date order—whereas ranked systems will return them in order of how often they contain the query term (normalized by document length). But the user probably doesn't focus on this difference and is just as likely to enter the query term in either mode—or far more likely, in practice, to use whatever default the system provides. The third

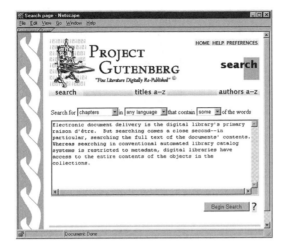

Figure 3.16 Large-query search interface.

most common query has two terms; after that, frequency falls off rapidly with query length.

Most search systems implicitly encourage short queries by not providing enough space on the screen for users to specify long ones! But modern search engines are capable of dealing with large queries: indeed they can often be processed more efficiently than small ones because they are more likely to contain rare words, which greatly restricts the scope of the search. Figure 3.16 shows a large query box into which users can paste paragraph-sized chunks of text—and it is scrollable to facilitate even larger queries.

A useful feature for all kinds of search is to allow users to examine and reuse their search history. "Those who ignore history," to adapt George Santayana's famous dictum, "will be forced to retype it." New queries are routinely constructed by modifying old ones—adding new terms if the query is too broad, to increase precision at the expense of recall, or removing terms if it is too restrictive, to increase recall. Figure 3.17 shows an interface that presents the last four queries issued by the user. If one of the buttons to the left is clicked, the corresponding query is reentered into the search box, where it can be further modified. For example, clicking on the button to the left of the field containing *begin beginning* will place those words in the search box. The interface, and the number of history items displayed, is selected by making appropriate choices on the Preferences page in Figure 3.15.

A slightly awkward situation arises when the user changes search options, or even collections, between queries. It could be misleading to display query history in a way that ignores this. And it is possible that the user is experimenting with these options to ascertain their effect on a query—to see if the number of results changes if stemming is enabled, for example, or determine whether one

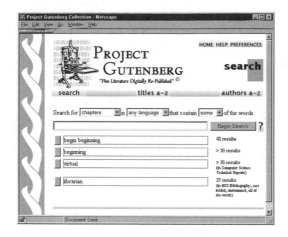

Figure 3.17 Query with history.

collection or the other contains more potential answers. This is why details are given alongside the history item when such changes occur, as can be seen in Figure 3.17. In most situations these details never appear, because users rarely alter their query options. The details, when they do appear, clarify the context within which the query history should be interpreted.

The query facilities shown so far let users search the full document text, or certain metadata fields which were chosen when the collection was created. Often, particularly for academic study, searches on different fields need to be combined. You might be seeking a book by a certain author with a particular word in the title or with a particular phrase in the main text. Library catalog systems provide a search form that consists of several individual fields into which specifications can be entered.

Figure 3.18a shows a form for a fielded search. The user types each field specification into one of the entry boxes, uses the menu selector to the right of the box to select which field it applies to, and decides whether to seek documents that satisfy *some* or *all* of these conditions. If you need more than four entry boxes, the Preferences page (Figure 3.15) gives further options.

Using the form in Figure 3.18b, more complex fielded searches can be undertaken. Again, up to four specifications are placed in the entry boxes, and the fields to which they apply are selected. Case-folding and stemming can be determined for each field individually, rather than being set globally using the Preferences page as before. The selection boxes that precede the fields allow Boolean operators: they give the three options *and*, *or*, and *and not*. In fact, completely general Boolean queries cannot be specified using this form because the user cannot control the order of operation—there is no place to insert parentheses. The specifications are executed in sequential order: each one applies to all the fields beneath it.

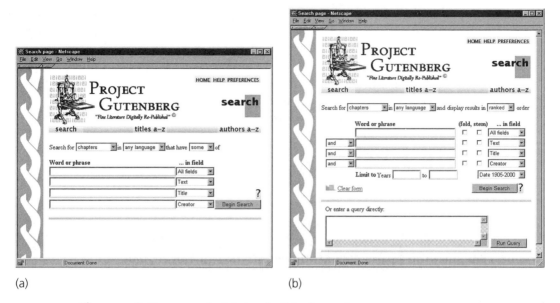

(a)   (b)

Figure 3.18 Form search: (a) simple; (b) advanced.

The line near the top, just beneath the navigation bar, allows users to decide whether the results should be sorted into *ranked* or *natural* order (the latter is the order in which documents appear in the collection, usually date order). Below the field specification boxes there is an opportunity to limit the search to certain date ranges. In some collections more than one date may be associated with each document, corresponding to different kinds of metadata. For example, in a historical collection there is a big difference between the period that a document covers and the date it was written. If the metadata involves multiple date fields, a particular one is chosen using the selection box to the right of the year specifications—and here the beginning and end year is shown as well, to clarify what it is sensible to type in as a "limit" specification.

This interface is intended for expert users. However, experts often find it frustrating to have to specify what they want by filling out a form: they prefer to type textual queries rather than having to click from one field to another. Behind the form-based interface is an underlying textual specification of queries, and users may prefer to enter their queries directly in this query language.

The box at the bottom of Figure 3.18b allows queries to be entered textually. Whenever a form-based query is executed, its textual equivalent appears in this box, above the query results. The query specification language used is CCL, standing for "common command language." This was a popular language for expressing queries in the library world, especially before the widespread availability of graphical interfaces—which are universally preferred by nonexpert users. CCL is described in Section 8.4.

This system makes it particularly easy to learn the language syntax because queries entered on the form are automatically converted to CCL and displayed underneath when the query is executed. Users who are unsure about the precedence order in which their field specifications are interpreted can look at the CCL equivalent (which is fully bracketed) to find out—and alter the interpretation order by inserting brackets into the textual query and reexecuting it. This provides a relatively easy path for frequent users of the form interface to evolve into power users of CCL.

It is difficult to provide a useful history facility with a forms-based interface because the representation of previous queries is cumbersome—several copies of a form consume a lot of screen space and are only rarely informative. However, the textual query language provides a natural way of utilizing history within the advanced search interface. Previous queries can be expressed in CCL and displayed in boxes just like those of Figure 3.17. They can be recalled into the query specification box, and reexecuted, or modified, there.

3.4   Browsing

Browsing is often described as the other side of the coin from searching, but really there is an entire spectrum between the two. Our dictionary describes browsing as "inspecting in a leisurely and casual way," whereas searching is "making a thorough examination in order to find something." Other dictionaries are more loquacious. According to Webster's, browsing is

to look over casually (as a book), skim;

to skim through a book reading at random passages that catch the eye;

to look over books (as in a store or library), especially in order to decide what one wants to buy, borrow, or read;

to casually inspect goods offered for sale, usually without prior or serious intention of buying;

to make an examination without real knowledge or purpose.

The word *browse* originally referred to animals nibbling on grass or shoots, and its use in relation to reading, which is now far more widespread, appeared much later. Early in the 20th century, the library community adopted the notion of browsing as "a patron's random examination of library materials as arranged for use" when extolling the virtues of open book stacks over closed ones—the symbolic snapping of the links of the chained book mentioned in Section 1.3.

In contemporary information retrieval terms, searching is purposeful, whereas browsing tends to be casual. Terms such as *random*, *informal*, *unsystematic*, and *without design* are used to capture the unplanned nature of browsing and the lack of a specific plan of action for reaching a goal—if indeed one exists.

Searching implies that you know what you're looking for, whereas in browsing the most you can say is that you'll know it when you see it—and the activity is often far less directed than that, perhaps even no more than casually passing time. But the distinction is not clear—pedants are quick to point out that if when searching you *really* know what you're looking for, then there's no need to find it! The truth is that we do not have a good vocabulary to describe and discuss various forms or degrees of browsing.

The metadata provided with the documents in a collection offer handles for different kinds of browsing activities. Information collections that are entirely devoid of metadata can be searched—that is one of the real strengths of full-text searching—but they cannot be browsed in any meaningful way unless some additional browsing structures are present. The structure that is implicit in metadata is the key to providing browsing facilities that are based on it. And now it's time for some examples.

Browsing alphabetical lists

The simplest and most rudimentary of structures is the ordered list. In Figure 3.19a a plain alphabetical list of document titles is presented for browsing. The list is quite short: if it were not, it might take a long time to download over a network connection, and the user would have to scroll through it using the browser's scroll bar—which is an inconvenient way to find things in extremely long lists.

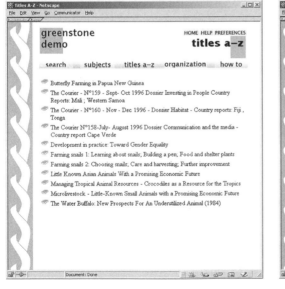

(a)   (b)

Figure 3.19 Browsing an alphabetical list of titles: (a) plain list; (b) with A–Z tags.

Notice incidentally that the ordering is not strictly alphabetical: the article *The* (and also *A*) is ignored at the beginning of titles. This is common practice when presenting sorted lists of textual items. For special kinds of text the ordering may be different yet again: for example, names are conventionally ordered alphabetically by surname even though they may be preceded by first names and initials.

Figure 3.19b shows part of a much larger list, with tags at the top to select alphabetic ranges. The user clicks on a tag, and the list of titles beginning with that letter appears underneath. The letter ranges are automatically chosen so that each one covers a reasonable number of documents. That is, letters in the three ranges *J–L*, *Q–R* and *U–Y* have been merged, because the number of documents that fall under each of these letters is rather small. In fact Figure 3.19a was generated by exactly the same scheme—but in this case there were so few documents that no alphabetic ranges were generated at all.

With very many documents, this interface becomes cumbersome. It is inconvenient to use tabs with multiletter labels, such as *Fae–Fal*. Although we are used to seeing these at the top of the pages of dictionaries and telephone directories, we are more likely to estimate the place we are trying to find on the basis of bulk, rather than going strictly by the tabs. Moreover, if the interface presents a sequence of such decisions during the process of locating a single item (e.g., *F*, *Fa–Far*, *Fae–Fal*, . . . ,) it is a tedious way of narrowing down the search. It forces you to think about what you are doing in a rather unnatural way.

The final tab, *0–9*, indicates another snag with this scheme. There is no knowing what letters titles may start with!—they may even include punctuation characters or arithmetic operators. This is not a big problem in English because such documents rarely occur, and when they do they can be included in a single Miscellaneous tab at the end.

Ordering lists of words in Chinese

Some languages are not alphabetic. Chinese has no single universally used way of ordering text strings analogous to alphabetic ordering in European languages. Several different ordering schemes are used as the basis of printed dictionaries and telephone directories. For example, characters, or *ideographs*, can be ordered according to the number of strokes they contain. Or they can be ordered according to their *radical*, which is a core symbol on which they are built. Or they can be ordered according to a standard alphabetical representation called *Pinyin*, where each ideograph is given a one- to six-letter equivalent. Stroke ordering is probably the most natural way of ordering character strings for Chinese users, although many educated users prefer Pinyin (not all Chinese people know Pinyin). Browsers for these languages call for special design.

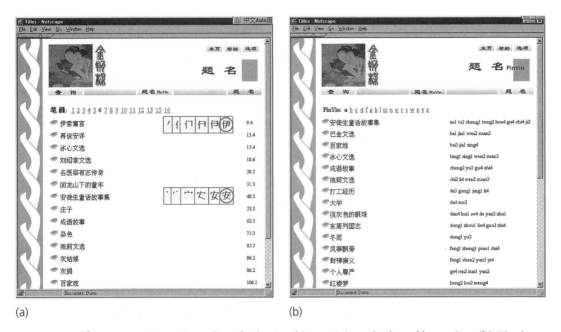

(a)   (b)

Figure 3.20 Browsing a list of titles in Chinese: (a) stroke-based browsing; (b) Pinyin browsing.

For an appreciation of the issues involved, see Figure 3.20, which shows a list for browsing titles in a large collection of Chinese books and articles. In Figure 3.20a, which is invoked by the rightmost of the three buttons on the access bar near the top, titles are ordered by the number of strokes contained in their first character when written. The number of strokes is given across the top: the user has selected six. The first character in all the book titles that follow has six strokes. If you don't know Chinese this will not be obvious from the display: you can only count the number of strokes in a character if you know how the character is written. To illustrate this, the initial characters for the first and seventh titles are singled out and their writing sequence is superimposed on the screen shot: the first stroke, the first two strokes, the first three strokes, and so on, ending with the complete character, which is circled. All people who read Chinese are easily able to work out the number of strokes required to write any particular character.

In most cases there are more than 200 characters corresponding to a given number of strokes, almost any of which could occur as the first character of a book title. Hence the titles in each group are displayed in a particular conventional order, again determined by their first character. This ordering is a little more complex. With each character is associated a radical, or basic structure that is contained in it. For example, in the first example singled out in Figure 3.20a (the first title), the radical is the pattern corresponding to its initial two strokes, which in this case form the left-hand part of the character. Radicals have a conventional ordering that is well known to educated Chinese; this particular one is number 9 in the Unicode sequence. Because this character requires four more strokes than its radical, it is designated by the two-part code 9.4. In the second example singled out in Figure 3.20a (the seventh title), the radical corresponds to the initial three strokes, which form the top part of the character, and is number 40; thus this character receives the designation 40.3. These codes are shown to the right of Figure 3.20a; they would not form part of the actual Web page display.

The codes form the key on which titles are sorted. Characters are grouped first by radical number, then by how many strokes are added to the radical to make the character. Ambiguity occasionally arises: the code 86.2, for example, appears twice. In these cases the tie is broken randomly.

The stroke-based ordering scheme is quite complex. In practice, Chinese readers have to work harder to identify an item in an ordered list than we do. It is easy to decide on the number of strokes. Once a page like Figure 3.20a is reached, however, people often simply scan it linearly. One strength of computer displays is that they can at least offer a choice of access methods.

The central button in the navigation bar near the top of Figure 3.20 invokes the Pinyin browser shown in Figure 3.20b. This orders characters alphabetically by their Pinyin equivalent. The Pinyin codes for the titles are shown to the right of the figure; they would not form part of the actual Web page display. Obviously this kind of display is much easier for Westerners to comprehend.

Browsing by date

Figure 3.21 shows newspapers being browsed by date. An automatically generated selector at the top gives a choice of years; within each range the newspapers are laid out by month. Just as Figure 3.19 was created automatically based on *Title* metadata, so Figure 3.21 was created automatically based on *Date* metadata. Again the year ranges are chosen by the computer to ensure that a reasonable number of items appear on each page.

Hierarchical classification structures

The browsers we have seen are essentially linear, and this restricts them to situations where the number of documents is not excessive. Hierarchical classification structures are standard tools in any area where significant numbers of objects are being considered. In the library world, the Library of Congress classification and the Dewey Decimal classification are used to arrange printed books in categories, the intention being to place volumes treating the same or

Figure 3.21 Browsing by date.

similar subjects next to each other on the library shelves. These schemes are hierarchical: the early parts of the code provide a rough categorization that is refined by the later characters.

Figure 3.22 shows a hierarchical display according to a particular classification scheme that was used for the Humanity Development Library. Nodes of the hierarchy are represented as bookshelves. Clicking one opens it up and displays all documents that occur at that level, as well as all nodes that lie underneath it. For example, node 2.00, shown in Figure 3.22b, contains one document and eight subsidiary nodes, of which one—node 2.06—is shown in Figure 3.22c. Just as bookshelf icons represent internal nodes of the hierarchy, so book icons represent documents, the leaves of the classification tree. One is visible in Figure 3.22b for the *Earth Summit Report*, which is the only document with classification 2.00.

This browsing structure was generated automatically from metadata associated with each document. Consider the information that must be given to the system to allow the hierarchical display to be built. Each document must have associated with it its position in the hierarchy. In fact, in this classification scheme an individual document may appear in different places, so there needs to be a way to specify classification information multiple times for a single document. In addition to the hierarchical information, names must be provided for the interior nodes—so that all the "bookshelf" nodes in Figure 3.22 can be labeled appropriately. This involves a separate file of information, distinct from the document collection itself.

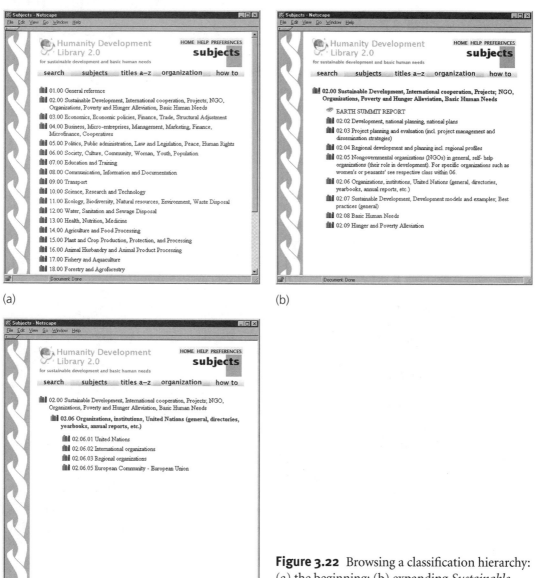

(a)

(b)

(c)

Figure 3.22 Browsing a classification hierarchy: (a) the beginning; (b) expanding *Sustainable development;* (c) expanding *Organizations, institutions.*

The classification scheme in Figure 3.22 is nonstandard. It was chosen by the collection editor as being the most appropriate for the collection's intended users. Implementers of digital library systems have to decide whether to try to impose uniformity on the people who build collections, or whether instead to provide flexibility for them to organize things in the way they see fit. Opting for the latter gives librarians freedom to exercise their professional judgment effectively.

3.5   Phrase browsing

Naturally people often want to browse information collections based on their subject matter. As we have seen, this kind of browsing is well supported by displays based on hierarchical classification metadata that is associated with each document. But manual classification is expensive and tedious for large document collections. What if this information is not available? To address this problem, one can build topical browsing interfaces based on phrase metadata, where the phrases have been extracted automatically from the full text of the documents themselves.

A phrase browsing interface

The browser illustrated in Figure 3.23 is an interactive interface to a phrase hierarchy that has been extracted automatically from the full text of a document collection. In this case the collection is simply a Web site: the site of the United Nations Food and Agriculture Organization (FAO). As we pointed out earlier, Web sites are not usually digital libraries. Even though they may be well organized, the organization is provided by a manual insertion of links, which conflicts with an essential feature of libraries: that new material can be added easily and virtually automatically, merely by supplying appropriate metadata. However, digital libraries can certainly be created from Web sites by adding automatically generated organization, and this collection is a good example. Figure 3.23c (and also Figure 3.24b) shows typical target documents. They are just Web pages, complete with all internal and external links, which are fully functional.

This interface is designed to resemble a paper-based subject index or thesaurus. In Figure 3.23a the user enters an initial word in the search box at the top—in this case the word *locust*. On pressing the Search button the upper of the two panels appears. This shows the phrases at the top level in the hierarchy that contain the search term. The list is sorted by phrase frequency; on the right is the number of times the phrase appears in the entire document collection, and beside that is the number of documents in which the phrase appears.

Only the first 10 phrases are shown, because it is impractical with a Web interface to download a large number of phrases, and many of these phrase lists are huge. At the end of the list is an item that reads *Get more phrases* (displayed in a distinctive color); clicking this will download another 10 phrases, and so on. The interface accumulates the phrases: a scroll bar appears to the right for use when more than 10 phrases are displayed. The number of phrases appears above the list: in this case there are 102 top-level phrases that contain the term *locust*.

So far we have only described the upper panel in Figure 3.23a. The lower one appears as soon as the user clicks one of the phrases in the upper list. In this case

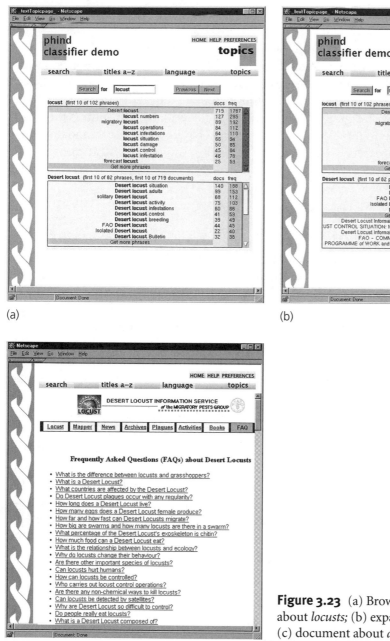

(a)

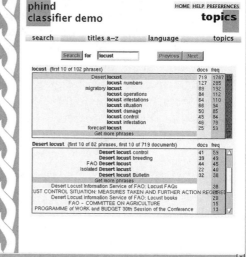

(b)

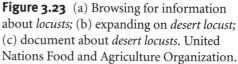

(c)

Figure 3.23 (a) Browsing for information about *locusts;* (b) expanding on *desert locust;* (c) document about *desert locusts.* United Nations Food and Agriculture Organization.

the user has clicked *Desert locust* (which is why the first line is highlighted in the upper panel), causing phrases containing the string *Desert locust* to be displayed in the lower panel.

If you continue to descend through the phrase hierarchy, eventually the leaves will be reached. In this system any sequence of words is a "phrase" if it appears more than once in the entire document collection. Thus a leaf corresponds to a phrase that occurs in a unique context somewhere in the collection (although the document that contains that contextually unique occurrence may include several other occurrences too). In this case the text above the lower panel shows that the phrase *Desert locust* appears in 82 longer phrases and also in 719 documents. These 719 documents each contain the phrase in some unique context. The first 10 documents are visible when the list is scrolled down, as is shown in Figure 3.23b.

In effect both panels show a phrase list followed by a document list. Either list may be empty: in fact the document list is empty in the upper panel because every context in which the word *locust* occurs appears more than once in the collection. The document list displays the titles of the documents.

In both panels of Figures 3.22a and b, you can click *Get more phrases* to increase the number of phrases that are shown in the list. In the lower panels you can also click *Get more documents* (again it is displayed at the end of the list in a distinctive color, but to see that entry you must scroll the panel down a little more) to increase the number of documents shown.

Clicking on a phrase expands that phrase. The page holds only two panels, and if a phrase in the lower one is clicked, the contents of that panel move up to the top to make space for the phrase's expansion. Alternatively clicking on a document opens that document in a new window. In fact the user in Figure 3.23b has clicked on *Desert Locust Information Service of FAO: Locust FAQs*, and this brings up the page shown in Figure 3.23c. As Figure 3.23b indicates, that document contains 38 occurrences of the phrase *Desert locust*.

Figure 3.24 shows another example of the interface in use. In this case a French user has entered the word *poisson*, exposing a weakness of the phrase extraction algorithm. The FAO Web site contains documents in French, but the phrase extraction system is tailored for English. The French phrases displayed are of much lower quality than the English ones shown earlier; of the ten phrases in the upper panel, only four are useful. Phrases like *du poisson* (meaning "of fish") are not useful and can obscure more interesting material. However, the system is still usable. Here the user has expanded *commercialisation du poisson* and, in the lower panel, has clicked on a document titled INFOPECHE which is shown in Figure 3.24b.

Utilizing phrases extracted automatically from the document text, as these example phrases are, has the great advantage that no manual processing is needed

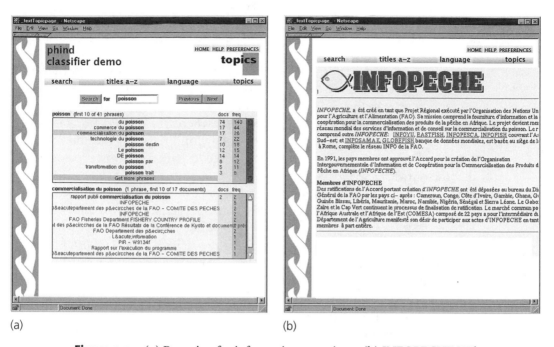

(a)   (b)

Figure 3.24 (a) Browsing for information on *poisson;* (b) INFOPECHE Web page.

to generate these indexes. However, the amount of computer processing required is substantial. This phrase interface has the advantage that it is readily comprehensible by users. The notion of browsing documents based on phrases that they contain has great intuitive appeal because you are in direct contact with the raw material of the documents themselves, without any intermediary operations that you may only dimly understand.

An important feature of this interface is that it scales up to large collections. Other browsing techniques, such as alphabetic lists of titles and authors, do not scale well: ranges of letters are uncomfortable to use for large collections. Hierarchical classification schemes scale well, but require manual classification of each document. This phrase interface is easy to browse even for colossal collections, and users are not overwhelmed with information, nor with difficult choices. It is unique in being both scalable and automatically generated. We return to the question of how to generate the phrase hierarchy at the end of Section 5.6.

Key phrases

The phrase browsing interface is based on a staggeringly large number of phrases—essentially all those that appear in the full text of the documents. Sometimes it helps to be more selective, choosing perhaps half a dozen representative phrases for each document. Such phrases are usually called *key phrases.*

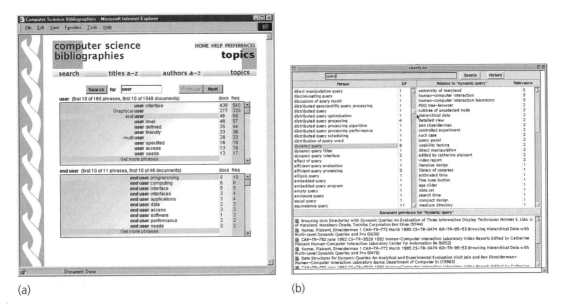

(a)   (b)

Figure 3.25 Browsing interfaces based on key phrases: (a) hierarchical browser; (b) document explorer.

Authors of scholarly or academic documents often provide accompanying key phrases, particularly in scientific and technological disciplines.

Figure 3.25a shows a hierarchical phrase browser just like that in Figures 3.23 and 3.24—except that in this case the phrases are author-assigned key phrases, rather than being taken automatically from the full text of the documents. Not surprisingly these key phrases are of much higher quality. In fact this example shows a collection of bibliographic entries in the computer science area: the full text is not available, just the bibliographic references and author-supplied key phrases.

The person using this interface has entered the term *user*, and the key phrases that contain this word are shown in the upper panel. There are 165 of them in total; only the 10 most frequent are shown. Of these, *end user* has been selected, and the phrases that appear below give a good synopsis of the way the term is used in the computer science literature. The key phrases are all high quality because they have been carefully chosen by the papers' authors, and the result is an excellent interactive taxonomy of terms and concepts in the field of computer science. Although the key-phrase metadata is supplied manually, the hierarchy is constructed automatically.

Figure 3.25b shows a different style of interface to a document collection, also based on key phrases. At the very top the user has typed the word *query*. Underneath are three large panels. The left-hand one displays all key phrases in the document collection that contain the word *query*. Unlike the earlier displays, this is not hierarchical—the number of key phrases is not so great that a hierarchy is necessary, although, as Figure 3.25a illustrates, it could be helpful. The user has selected one of these phrases, *dynamic query;* the number beside it indicates that it has been identified as a key phrase for eight documents. In the bottom panel appear the titles of these eight documents (only six are visible). Clicking on a document icon displays that document.

Whereas hierarchical phrase browsers allow users to focus on a particular area by selecting more and more specific terms from the choices that are offered, this interface provides a good way of broadening the concepts being considered. The panel at the right of Figure 3.25b gives the *other* key phrases that are associated with these eight documents. In a sense these key phrases "share a document" with the selected phrase *dynamic query.* The fact that *Library of Congress* appears in this list, for example, indicates that there is a document—namely, one of the eight displayed—that has both *dynamic query* and *Library of Congress* assigned to it as key phrases. Clicking on *Library of Congress* would transfer these words to the query box at the top of the screen, and then any key phrases containing them would be displayed in the panel on the left, with associated documents underneath.

The scheme in Figure 3.25b provides another convenient way to explore a document collection. Unlike the other interfaces in this chapter, it is not Web-based and does not operate in a Web browser. However, it could easily be reengineered to do so.

3.6 Browsing using extracted metadata

The browsing methods we have examined all rely on metadata that must be provided for all documents in the collection. With the exception of the phrase hierarchy metadata, which is extracted from the document text, metadata must be entered manually for each document. This is a tedious and time-consuming chore, which makes you wonder whether metadata can be automatically extracted from the documents' full text.

For example, titles may be identified by seeking capitalized text close to the beginning of documents—and if information about font size is available, it provides extra clues.

Names may be identified in the text of all documents by looking for the capitalization and punctuation patterns that characterize forms such as *Surname, Forename* and *Forename Initial. Surname.* Once this metadata is available, a browsing index could be provided that allows you to look through all people who are mentioned in the document collection and check references to them. Even if the method used to extract name metadata had some deficiencies, so that some names were omitted and some non-names included, the browsing facility could still be useful.

Dates that appear in documents could be identified. In historical collections it is useful to be able to restrict searches to documents that describe events within a certain time period—searching for information about *Trade Unions* in the 1930s, for example. Of course, dates of historical events must be distinguished from other dates—particularly ones that give the publication date of references. In many cases this distinction can be made automatically on the basis of punctuation, such as parentheses, that typically appears in references (e.g., dates are often included in brackets). Again, some errors in date identification are not necessarily disastrous.

Acronyms

We end our tour of browsing interfaces with two unusual examples based on metadata extraction. Figure 3.26a shows a list of acronyms in a document collection, along with their definitions. The tabs at the top allow you to select alphabetic ranges—although in this case there are only two. Where an acronym is defined in more than one document, a bookshelf is shown, with the number of documents in parentheses; clicking on the bookshelf will bring up the list of documents.

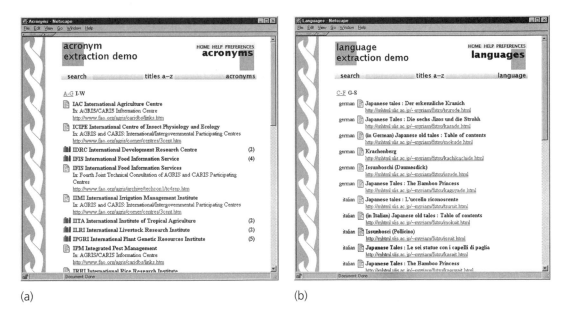

(a)   (b)

Figure 3.26 Browsing based on information mined from the document collection: (a) acronyms; (b) language identification.

These acronyms were extracted automatically from the full text of the document collection using a technique described in Chapter 5 (Section 5.6). Essentially the idea is to look for a word containing (mostly) uppercase letters—the acronym—preceded or followed by a sequence of words that begins with those letters, generally capitalized. Although the results are not perfect, the acronym browser is particularly useful for political and scientific documents. Because the information is mined automatically, no human effort at all goes into creating browsers for new collections.

Language identification

Figure 3.26b shows another example of metadata extraction in which documents are grouped by language, the language of each document having been identified automatically. This collection comprises a set of Japanese folktales that have been translated into a variety of languages. The same language metadata could be used to provide a separate subcollection for each language, in which the language could be selected when searching.

The language of each document was automatically identified by a system that looks at letter patterns, described in Section 5.6. For example, *yes* is characteristic of English, whereas *oui* is French and *ja* is German. However, instead of looking at complete words, the system looks at groups of up to five letters—because these are more general and sensitive indicators of language. Particular words may not occur in a given document (*yes* does not occur often in this book), yet it is hard to imagine any stretch of English writing that does not include the characters *the*. (Hard, but not impossible—surprising as it may seem, a complete book has been written that does not use the letter *e*!)

3.7   Notes and sources

"Begin at the beginning" is what the King of Hearts said to the White Rabbit in the trial scene in *Alice in Wonderland*. The screen shot in Figure 3.1, like most of the figures in this chapter, came from a collection in the New Zealand Digital Library Project, which is publicly accessible on the Web at *www.nzdl.org*. All these collections are created and served using the Greenstone Digital Library Software.

Collections

The Kids' Digital Library in Figure 3.2a is from a project at Middlesex University, London, that also uses Greenstone (*http://kidsdl.mdx.ac.uk/kidslibrary*). The Humanity Development Library in Figure 3.3 is mentioned in the "Notes and sources" of Chapter 1 (Section 1.6); it is available both on CD-ROM and at *www.nzdl.org.* More information about the Gutenberg Project from which Figure 3.1 comes can be found at *www.promo.net/pg.*

The *New Zealand School Journal* is produced by the Ministry of Education and published by Learning Media Ltd. in Wellington, New Zealand. Figures 3.2b and 3.5 are taken from a prototype collection containing a few sample journals across the entire range of years from 1907 to 1998; it was designed by Mankelow (1999). For copyright reasons, this collection is not publicly available. Note that Figure 3.5b is a fake: while we have worked on software to highlight words in images, this is not at present incorporated into the School Journal collection.

Information on the "Niupepa" (the Māori word for "newspapers") collection of historical New Zealand newspapers in Figure 3.6 is given in Chapter 2's "Notes and sources" (Section 2.5). The Oral History collection in Figure 3.7 was originally produced on audiotapes by Hamilton Public Library; Bainbridge and Cunningham (1998) describe its conversion into digital form. Work on music collections and music searching, some of which is illustrated in Figure 3.8, is described by McNab et al. (1996) and Bainbridge et al. (1999).

The Sahel Point Doc collection shown in Figure 3.9a is on a CD-ROM of the same name distributed by UNESCO; it also appears at *www.nzdl.org.* The collection of Tang Dynasty rubbings in Figure 3.10a was produced in conjunction with the Chinese Department of Peking University; it can be found on the Web at *http://162.105.138.23/tapian/tp.htm.* The collection of Chinese literature in Figure 3.10b, and the Arabic collection in Figure 3.11, are small demonstrations built out of material gathered from the Web.

Metadata

Figure 3.12 comes from a large collection of computer science bibliographies assembled and maintained by Alf-Christian Achilles at the University of Karlsruhe, Germany. The original source is at *http://liinwww.ira.uka.de/bibliography;* this material has been mirrored as a Greenstone collection. Figure 3.13a was obtained from the Library of Congress using the Z39.50 client that is embedded in the Greenstone software. This feature makes it possible to reach any Z39.50 server from a Greenstone installation. Figure 3.13b is from a large collection of the BBC radio and television archives with around one million entries. It was produced for the BBC in the form of a coordinated set of five CD-ROMs that can be loaded onto disk and searched either individually or together in a seamlessly coordinated fashion, making any laptop into a full catalog server.

Searching

Much of the material on searching is taken from the book *Managing Gigabytes* (Witten, Moffat, and Bell, 1999), which gives a comprehensive and detailed technical account of how to compress documents and indexes, yet make them rapidly accessible through full-text queries. There are many standard reference works covering the area of information retrieval; the best-known are Salton (1989), Salton and McGill (1983), van Rijsbergen (1979), Frakes and Baeza-Yates (1992), Korfhage (1997), and Baeza-Yates and Ribeiro-Neto (1999). Lovins (1968) and Porter (1980) are two of many authors who have produced particular algorithms for stemming. Frakes surveys this area in a chapter of a book that he coedited (Frakes, 1992); Lennon et al. (1981) have also examined the problem. We return to the topic of text searching, briefly, in Chapter 4 (Section 4.2).

Alan Kay, quoted near the beginning of Section 3.3, is a guru in the interactive computing world; an interesting article about him appeared in *New Scientist* (Davidson, 1993). George Santayana, who feared that those who ignored history would have to relive (not retype!) it, was a philosopher, poet, critic, and best-selling novelist (Santayana, 1932). Oscar Wilde, on the other hand, said that "the one duty we owe to history is to rewrite it." Perhaps it doesn't do to take these *bon mots* too seriously!

Browsing

Chang and Rice (1993) examine the activity of browsing from a broad interdisciplinary point of view. Hyman (1972) discusses how the notion of browsing in traditional libraries was linked to the rise of the open-stack organization; the quotation at the beginning of Section 3.4 about the "patron's random examination of library materials" is his. The brief characterization of browsing is from our favorite dictionary, the *Houghton Mifflin Canadian Dictionary of the English Language;* the longer one is from *Webster's Third New International Dictionary.*

The list of titles in Figure 3.19a shows the Demo collection, which is supplied with every Greenstone installation and contains a small subset of the Humanity Development Library; Figure 3.19b is from the full Humanity Development Library, as is Figure 3.22. The Chinese title browsers in Figure 3.20 are mock-ups and have not yet been implemented, although the Greenstone structure makes it easy to add new browsers like this by adding a new "classifier" module (see Sections 6.6 and 6.7 of Chapter 6). The date list in Figure 3.21 was generated within the Niupepa collection noted earlier.

Phrase browsing is a topic of lively current interest. The interface shown in Figures 3.23 and 3.24 has developed over several years; the current version is described in Paynter et al. (2000). Much work has gone into algorithms for extracting hierarchies of phrases from large document collections, and we return to this topic in Chapter 5 (Section 5.6). The collection is built from the FAO Web site at *www.fao.org*, which contains the documents shown.

Key-phrase browsing is another burning issue. The illustration in Figure 3.25a is from Alf-Christian Achilles' Computer Science Bibliography collection mentioned earlier. Figure 3.25b is taken from a collection of Computer Science Technical Reports that includes author-assigned key phrases. The interface is described by Gutwin et al. (1999); similar ones are described by Jones and Paynter (1999). Although these collections have manually assigned key-phrase metadata, key phrases can be extracted automatically from the full text of documents with a surprising degree of success, as we shall see in Section 5.6.

The acronym extraction software, and the interface shown in Figure 3.26a, is described by Yeates, Bainbridge, and Witten (1999); the collection used to illustrate it is a subset of the FAO Web site. The methods used to identify languages and extract acronyms are described further in Chapter 5 (Section 5.6).The illustration in Figure 3.26b is built from the material at *http://mhtml.ulis.ac.jp/ ~myriam/deuxgb.html*, a site that contains a charming collection of old Japanese folktales in different languages (Dartois et al., 1997). The book without any *e*'s is *Gadsby*, by E. V. Wright (1939).

4 Documents

The raw material

Documents are the digital library's building blocks. It is time to step down from our high-level discussion of digital libraries—what they are, how they are organized, and what they look like—to nitty-gritty details of how to represent the documents they contain. To do a thorough job we will have to descend even further and look at the representation of the characters that make up textual documents and the fonts in which those characters are portrayed. For audio, images, and video we examine the interplay among signal quantization, sampling rate, and internal redundancy that underlies multimedia representations.

A great practical problem we face when writing about how digital libraries work inside is the dizzying rate of change in the core technologies. Perhaps the most striking feature of the digital library field, at least from an academic point of view, is the inherent tension between two extremes: the very fast pace of technological change and the very long-term view that libraries must take. We must reconcile any aspirations to surf the leading edge of technology with the literally static ideal of archiving material "for ever and a day."

Document formats are where the rubber meets the road. Over the last decade a cornucopia of different representations have emerged. Some have become established as standards, either official or de facto, and it is on these that we focus. There are plenty of them: the nice thing about standards, they say, is that there are so many different ones to choose from!

Internationalization is an important component of the vision of digital libraries that motivates this book, and in the last chapter we saw examples of collections and interfaces in many different languages. It is all too easy from the native English speaker's perspective (which includes most of our readers and both this book's authors) to sweep under the carpet the many challenging problems of representing text in other languages. The standard ASCII code used on computers (the *A* stands for "American," of course) has been extended in dozens of different and often incompatible ways to deal with other character sets—including, for example, ISCII for Hindi and related languages, where the initial *I* stands for "Indian." To take a simple example, imagine searching for an accented word like *détente* in French text where the non-ASCII character *é* is sometimes represented as a single character in *extended ASCII*, sometimes in regular *7-bit ASCII* as *e* followed by a backspace followed by ´, and sometimes by the HTML incantation &*eacute*;. Or suppose the character set is specified explicitly: Web pages often do this. Internet Explorer recognizes over 100 different character sets, mostly extensions of ASCII and EBCDIC, some of which have half a dozen different names. Without a unified coding scheme, search programs must know about all of this to work correctly under every circumstance.

Fortunately there is an international standard called Unicode which aims to represent all the characters used in all the world's languages. Unicode emerged over the last 10 years and is beginning to be widely used. It is quite stable, although it is still being extended and developed to cover languages and character sets of scholarly interest. It allows the content of digital libraries, and their user interfaces, to be internationalized. Using it, text stored in digital libraries can be displayed and searched properly. We describe Unicode in the next section. Of course it only helps with character *representation*. Language translation and cross-language searching are thorny matters of computational linguistics that lie completely outside its scope (and outside this book's scope too).

Section 4.2 discusses the representation of documents in text form—plain text. Even ASCII presents ambiguities in interpretation (you might have wondered about the difference between the ASCII and binary modes in the FTP file transfer protocol, or encountered the junk characters ^*M* at the end of each line in a TELNET window). We also sketch how an index can be created for textual documents that contains for each word a list of documents it occurs in, and perhaps even the positions where it occurs, in order to facilitate rapid full-text searching. Before creating the index the input must be split into words. This involves a few mundane practical decisions—and introduces some deeper issues for some languages, such as Chinese and Japanese, that are not traditionally written with spaces between words.

Desktop publishing empowers ordinary people to create carefully designed and lavishly illustrated documents and publish them electronically, often dispensing with print altogether. In a short space of time we have become accustomed to reading publication-quality documents online. It is worth reflecting on the extraordinary sea change in our expectations of online document presentation since, say, 1990. This revolution has been fueled largely by Adobe's Post-Script language and its successor, PDF or Portable Document Format. These are both *page description* languages: they combine text and graphics by treating the glyphs that comprise text as little pictures in their own right and allowing them to be described, denoted, and placed on an electronic page alongside conventional illustrations.

Page description languages portray finished documents, ones that are not intended to be edited. In contrast, word processors represent documents in ways that are expressly designed to support interactive creation and editing. As society's notion of *document* has become more fluid—from painstakingly engraved Chinese steles, literally "carved in stone," to hand-copied medieval manuscripts; from the interminable revisions of loose-leaf computer manuals in the 1960s and 1970s to continually evolving Web sites whose pages are dynamically composed on demand from online databases—it seems inevitable that more and more documents will be handed around in word-processor formats.

As examples of word-processor documents we describe the ubiquitous Microsoft Word format and Rich Text Format (RTF). Word is intended to represent working documents inside a word processor. It is a proprietary format that depends strongly on the exact version of Microsoft Word that was used and is not always backward compatible. RTF is more portable, intended to transmit documents to other computers and other versions of the software. It is an open standard, defined by Microsoft, for exchanging word-processor documents between different applications. We also describe the format used by the LaTeX document processing system, which is widely used to represent documents in the scientific and mathematical community.

The final part of the chapter describes image, audio, and multimedia formats. There is less variation here in the basic representation of the data. But because of the raw, quasi-analog nature of these media, file size bloats quickly and so compression schemes are often built into the formats. However, as well as simply making files smaller, compression has side effects that need to be considered when designing digital libraries.

For image data we describe the GIF, PNG, and JPEG formats. The first two are suitable for representing artificially produced images such as text, computer-generated artwork, and logos. JPEG is designed for continuous-tone images such as photographic portraits and landscapes. Multimedia encompasses both video and audio formats: we focus principally on the open MPEG standard, which includes the MP3 scheme that is widely used for music representation. We also mention Apple's QuickTime and Microsoft's AVI formats for multimedia, and WAV, AIFF, and AU for audio.

We warned at the outset that this chapter gets down to details, the dirty details (where the devil is). You will probably find the level uncomfortably low. Why do you need to know all this? The answer is that when building digital libraries you will be presented with documents in many different formats, yet you will yearn for standardization. You have to understand how different formats work in order to appreciate their strengths and limitations. Examples? When converted from PDF to PostScript, documents lose interactive features such as hyperlinks. Converting images from GIF to JPEG often reduces file size but degrades picture quality irreversibly. Converting HTML to PostScript is easy (your browser does it every time you print a Web page), but converting an arbitrary PostScript file to HTML is next to impossible if you want a completely accurate visual replica.

Even if your project starts with paper documents, you still need to know about online document formats. The optical character recognition process may produce Microsoft Word documents, retaining much of the formatting in the original and leaving illustrations and pictures in situ. But how easy is it to extract the plain text for indexing purposes? To highlight search terms in the text? To display individual pages? Perhaps another format is preferable?

4.1 Representing characters

Way back in 1963, at the dawn of interactive computing, the American National Standards Institute (ANSI) began work on a character set that would standardize text representation across a range of computing equipment and printers. At the time, a variety of codes were in use by different computer manufacturers, such as an extension of a *binary-coded decimal* punched card code to deal with letters (EBCDIC, or Extended Binary Coded Decimal for Information Interchange), and the European Baudot code for teleprinters that accommodated mixed-case text by switching between upper- and lowercase modes. In 1968 ANSI finally ratified the result, called ASCII: American Standard Code for Information Interchange.

Until recently ASCII dominated text representation in computing. Table 4.1 shows the character set, with code values in decimal, octal, and hexadecimal. Codes 65–90 (decimal) represent the uppercase letters of the Roman alphabet, while codes 97–122 are lowercase letters. Codes 48–57 give the digits zero through nine. Codes 0–32 and 127 are *control characters* that have no printed form. Some of these govern physical aspects of the printer—for instance, BEL rings the bell (now downgraded to a rude electronic beep), BS backspaces the print head (now the cursor position). Others indicate parts of a communication protocol: SOH starts the header, STX starts the transmission. Interspersed between these blocks are sequences of punctuation and other nonletter symbols

Table 4.1 The ASCII character set.

Dec	Oct	Hex	Char	Dec	Oct	Hex	Char
0	000	00	NUL	35	043	23	#
1	001	01	SOH	36	044	24	$
2	002	02	STX	37	045	25	%
3	003	03	ETX	38	046	26	&
4	004	04	EOT	39	047	27	'
5	005	05	ENQ	40	050	28	(
6	006	06	ACK	41	051	29	)
7	007	07	BEL	42	052	2A	*
8	010	08	BS	43	053	2B	+
9	011	09	HT	44	054	2C	,
10	012	0A	LF	45	055	2D	-
11	013	0B	VT	46	056	2E	.
12	014	0C	FF	47	057	2F	/
13	015	0D	CR	48	060	30	0
14	016	0E	SO	49	061	31	1
15	017	0F	SI	50	062	32	2
16	020	10	DLE	51	063	33	3
17	021	11	DC1	52	064	34	4
18	022	12	DC2	53	065	35	5
19	023	13	DC3	54	066	36	6
20	024	14	DC4	55	067	37	7
21	025	15	NAK	56	070	38	8
22	026	16	SYN	57	071	39	9
23	027	17	ETB	58	072	3A	:
24	030	18	CAN	59	073	3B	;
25	031	19	EM	60	074	3C	<
26	032	1A	SUB	61	075	3D	=
27	033	1B	ESC	62	076	3E	>
28	034	1C	FS	63	077	3F	?
29	035	1D	GS]	64	100	40	@
30	036	1E	RS	65	101	41	A
31	037	1F	US	66	102	42	B
32	040	20	SPAC	67	103	43	C
33	041	21	!	68	104	44	D
34	042	22	"	69	105	45	E

(continued on the following page)

Table 4.1 The ASCII character set (continued).

Dec	Oct	Hex	Char	Dec	Oct	Hex	Char
70	106	46	F	99	143	63	c
71	107	47	G	100	144	64	d
72	110	48	H	101	145	65	e
73	111	49	I	102	146	66	f
74	112	4A	J	103	147	67	g
75	113	4B	K	104	150	68	h
76	114	4C	L	105	151	69	i
77	115	4D	M	106	152	6A	j
78	116	4E	N	107	153	6B	k
79	117	4F	O	108	154	6C	l
80	120	50	P	109	155	6D	m
81	121	51	Q	110	156	6E	n
82	122	52	R	111	157	6F	o
83	123	53	S	112	160	70	p
84	124	54	T	113	161	71	q
85	125	55	U	114	162	72	r
86	126	56	V	115	163	73	s
87	127	57	W	116	164	74	t
88	130	58	X	117	165	75	u
89	131	59	Y	118	166	76	v
90	132	5A	Z	119	167	77	w
91	133	5B	[	120	170	78	x
92	134	5C	\	121	171	79	y
93	135	5D	]	122	172	7A	z
94	136	5E	^	123	173	7B	{
95	137	5F	_	124	174	7C		
96	140	60	`	125	175	7D	}
97	141	61	a	126	176	7E	~
98	142	62	b	127	177	7F	DEL

(codes 33–47, 58–64, 91–96, 123–126). Each code is represented in seven bits, which fits into a computer byte with one bit (the top bit) free. In the original vision for ASCII, this was earmarked for a parity check.

ASCII was a great step forward. It helped computers evolve over the following decades from scientific number-crunchers and fixed-format card-image data processors to interactive information appliances that permeate all walks of life. However, it has proved a great source of frustration to speakers of other languages. Many different extensions have been made to the basic character set, using codes 128–255 to specify accented and non-Roman characters for particular languages. ISO 8859-1, from the International Standards Organization (the international counterpart of the American standards organization, ANSI), extends ASCII for Western European languages. For example, it represents *é* as the single decimal value 233 rather than the clumsy ASCII sequence "*e* followed by backspace followed by ´." The latter is alien to the French way of thinking, for *é* is really a single character, generated by a single keystroke on French keyboards. For non-European languages such as Hebrew and Chinese, ASCII is irrelevant. Here other schemes have arisen: for example, GB and Big-5 are competing standards for Chinese, the former used in the People's Republic of China and the latter in Taiwan and Hong Kong.

As the Internet exploded into the World Wide Web and burst into all countries and all corners of our lives, the situation became untenable. The world needed a new way of representing text.

Unicode

In 1988 Apple and Xerox began work on Unicode, a successor to ASCII that aimed to represent all the characters used in all the world's languages. As word spread, a consortium of international and multinational companies, government organizations, and other interested parties was formed in 1991. The result was a new standard, ISO-10646, ratified by the International Standards Organization in 1993. In fact the standard melded the Unicode Consortium's specification with ISO's own work in this area.

Unicode continues to evolve. The main goal of representing the scripts of languages in use around the world has been achieved. Current work is addressing historic languages such as Egyptian hieroglyphics and Indo-European languages, and notations such as music. There is a steady stream of additions, clarifications, and amendments which eventually lead to new published versions of the standard. Of course backwards compatibility with the existing standard is taken for granted.

A standard is sterile unless it is adopted by vendors and users. Recent programming languages—notably Java—have built-in Unicode support. Earlier ones—C, Perl, Python, to name a few—have standard Unicode libraries. All principal operating systems support Unicode, and application programs, including Web browsers, have passed on the benefits to the end user. Unicode is the default encoding for HTML and XML. People of the world, rejoice.

Unicode is universal: any document in an existing character set can be mapped into Unicode. But it also satisfies a stronger requirement: the resulting

Unicode file can be mapped back to the original character set without any loss of information. This requirement is called *round-trip compatibility* with existing coding schemes, and it is central to Unicode's design. If a letter with an accent is represented as a single character in some existing character set, then an equivalent must also be placed in the Unicode set, even though there might be another way to achieve the same visual effect. Because there is an existing character set that includes *é* as a single character, it must be represented as a single Unicode character—even if an identical glyph can be generated using a sequence along the lines of "*e* followed by backspace followed by ´." The idea of round-trip compatibility is an attractive way to facilitate integration with existing software and was most likely motivated by the pressing need for a nascent standard to gain wide acceptance. You can safely convert any document to Unicode, knowing that it can always be converted back again if necessary to work with legacy software. This is indeed a useful property. However, multiple representations for the same character can cause complications, as we shall see.

The Unicode character set

The Unicode standard is massive. It comes in two parts (ISO 10646-1 and ISO 10646-2), specifying a total of 94,000 characters. The first part focuses on commonly used living languages and is called (for reasons to be explained shortly) the *Basic Multilingual Plane*. It weighs in at 1,000 pages and contains 49,000 characters.

Table 4.2 breaks down the ISO 10646-1 code space into different scripts, showing how many codes are allocated to each (unassigned codes are shown in parentheses). Unicode's scope is impressive: it covers Western and Middle Eastern languages such as Latin, Greek, Cyrillic, Hebrew, and Arabic; the so-called CJK (Chinese-Japanese-Korean) ideographs comprising Chinese, Japanese, and the Korean Hangul characters; and other scripts such as (to name just a few) Bengali, Thai, and Ethiopic. Also included are Braille, mathematical symbols, and a host of other shapes.

Table 4.2 divides the Unicode code space into five zones: alphabetic scripts, ideographic scripts, other characters, surrogates, and reserved codes. Falling within the first zone are the broad areas of general scripts, symbols, and CJK phonetics and symbols. The reserved blocks are intended to help Unicode's designers respond to unforeseen circumstances.

Unicode distinguishes characters by script, and those pertaining to a distinct script are blocked together in contiguous numeric sequences: Greek, Cyrillic, Hebrew, and so on. However, characters are not distinguished by language. For example, the excerpt from the Unicode standard in Figure 4.1 shows the Basic Latin (or standard ASCII) and Latin-1 Supplement (an ASCII extension) char-

Table 4.2 Unicode Part 1: The basic multilingual plane.

Zone	Area	Code	Script	Number of codes
Alphabetic	General scripts	0000	Basic Latin (US-ASCII)	128
		0080	Latin-1 (ISO-8859-1)	128
		0100	Latin Extended	336
		0250	IPA Extensions	96
		02B0	Spacing Modifier Letters	80
		0300	Combining Diacritical Marks	112
		0370	Greek	144
		0400	Cyrillic	256
			–	(48)
		0530	Armenian	96
		0590	Hebrew	112
		0600	Arabic	256
		0700	Syriac	78
			–	(50)
		0780	Thaana	50
			–	(334)
		0900	ISCII Indic Scripts	
		0900	Devanagari	128
		0980	Bengali	128
		0A00	Gurmukhi	128
		0A80	Gujarati	128
		0B00	Oriya	128
		0B80	Tamil	128
		0C00	Telugu	128
		0C80	Kannada	128
		0D00	Malayalam	128
		0D80	Sinhalese	128
		0E00	Thai	128
		0E80	Lao	128
		0F00	Tibetan	192
			–	(64)
		1000	Mongolian	160
		10A0	Georgian	96
		1100	Hangul Jamo	256

(continued on the following page)

Table 4.2 Unicode Part 1: The basic multilingual plane (continued).

Zone	Area	Code	Script	Number of codes
Alphabetic	General scripts (continued)	1200	Ethiopic	384
			–	(32)
		13A0	Cherokee	96
		1400	Canadian Syllabics	640
		1680	Ogham	32
		16A0	Runic	96
		1700	Burmese	90
			–	(38)
		1780	Khmer	106
			–	(1558)
		1E00	Latin Extended Additional	256
		1F00	Greek Extended	256
	Symbols	2000	General Punctuation	112
		2070	Superscripts and Subscripts	48
		20A0	Currency Symbols	48
		20D0	Combining Marks for Symbols	48
		2100	Letterlike Symbols	80
		2150	Number Forms	64
		2190	Arrows	112
		2200	Mathematical Operators	256
		2300	Miscellaneous Technical	256
		2400	Control Pictures	64
		2440	Optical Character Recognition	32
		2460	Enclosed Alphanumerics	160
		2500	Box Drawing	128
		2580	Block Elements	32
		25A0	Geometric Shapes	96
		2600	Miscellaneous Symbols	256
		2700	Dingbats	192
			–	(64)
		2800	Braille Pattern Symbols	256
			–	(1536)

(continued on the following page)

Table 4.2 Unicode Part 1: The basic multilingual plane (continued).

Zone	Area	Code	Script	Number of codes
	CJK phonetics and symbols	2F00	KangXi radicals	214
			–	(42)
		3000	CJK Symbols and Punctuation	64
		3040	Hiragana	96
		30A0	Katakana	96
		3100	Bopomofo	48
		3130	Hangul Compatibility Jamo	96
		3190	Kanbun	16
			–	(96)
		3200	Enclosed CJK Letters and Months	256
		3300	CJK Compatibility	256
Ideographic		3400	CJK Unified Ideographs, Extension A	6656
		4E00	CJK Unified Ideographs	20902
			–	(90)
Other		A000	Yi	1225
			–	(1847)
		AC00	Hangul Symbols	11172
			–	(92)
Surrogates		D800	High Surrogates	1024
		DC00	Low Surrogates	1024
Reserved	Private use	E000		6400
	Compatibility and specials	F900	CJK Compatibility Ideographs	512
		FB00	Alphabetic Presentation Forms	80
		FB50	Arabic Presentation Forms-A	688
			–	(32)
		FE20	Combining Half Marks	16
		FE30	CJK Compatibility Forms	32
		FE50	Small Form Variants	32
		FE70	Arabic Presentation Forms-B	144
		FF00	Halfwidth and Fullwidth Forms	240
		FFF0	Specials	16

	0	1	2	3	4	5	6	7	8	9	a	b	c	d	e	f
000	NUL	SOH	STX	ETX	EOT	ENQ	ACK	BEL	BS	HT	LF	VT	FF	CR	SO	SI
010	DLE	DC1	DC2	DC3	DC4	NAK	SYN	ETB	CAN	EM	SUB	ESC	FS	GS	RS	US
020	SP	!	"	#	$	%	&	'	(	)	*	+	,	-	.	/
030	0	1	2	3	4	5	6	7	8	9	:	;	<	=	>	?
040	@	A	B	C	D	E	F	G	H	I	J	K	L	M	N	O
050	P	Q	R	S	T	U	V	W	X	Y	Z	[	\	]	^	_
060	`	A	b	c	d	e	f	g	h	i	j	k	l	m	n	o
070	p	Q	r	s	T	u	v	w	x	y	z	{	|	}	~	DEL
080	XXX	XXX	BPH	NBH	XXX	NEL	SSA	ESA	HTS	HTJ	VTS	PLD	PLU	RI	SS2	SS3
090	DCS	PU1	PU2	STS	CCH	MW	SPA	EPA	SOS	XXX	SCI	CSI	ST	OSC	PM	APC
0a0	NB/SP	¡	¢	£		¥	_	§	¨	©	a	«	¬	SHY	®	¯
0b0	°	±	_	_	´	µ	¶	·	¸	_	o	»	_	_	_	¿
0c0	À	Á	Â	Ã	Ä	Å	Æ	Ç	È	É	Ê	Ë	Ì	Í	Î	Ï
0d0	_	Ñ	Ò	Ó	Ô	Õ	Ö	_	Ø	Ù	Ú	Û	Ü	_	_	ß
0e0	à	Á	â	ã	ä	å	æ	ç	è	é	ê	ë	ì	í	î	ï
0f0	_	Ñ	ò	ó	ô	õ	ö	÷	ø	ù	ú	û	ü	_	_	ÿ

Figure 4.1 Unicode excerpt: Basic Latin and Latin-1 Supplement (U+0000–U+00FF).

acters, which are used for most European languages. The capital *A* in French is the same character as the one in English. Only the accented letters that are used in European languages are included in the Latin-1 Supplement; the basic character forms are not redefined.

Punctuation is also shared among different scripts. The ASCII period (i.e., full stop) in Figure 4.1 is used in Greek and Cyrillic text too. However, periods in languages such as Armenian, Arabic, Ethiopic, Chinese, and Korean are shaped differently and have their own Unicode representations. The multifunction ASCII hyphen is retained for the purpose of round-trip compatibility, but new codes are defined under "general punctuation" (codes 2000 and up in Table 4.2) to distinguish among the hyphen (-), en-dash (–), and em-dash (—). The minus sign, which is not usually distinguished typographically from the en-dash, has its own symbol as a "mathematical operator" (codes 2200 and up in Table 4.2).

Unicode does distinguish letters from different scripts even though they may look identical. For example, the Greek capital alpha looks just like the Roman capital *A*, but receives its own code in the Greek block (codes 0370 and up in Table 4.2). This allows you to downcase capital alpha to α, and capital *A* to *a*, without worrying about exceptions.

The characters at the core of Unicode are called the *universal character set*, and the standard is essentially a suite of lookup tables that specify which character is displayed for a given numeric code. What are all these characters, and what do they look like? Every one tells a story: its historical origin, how it changed

100	Ā	Ā	Ă	ă	Ą	ą	Ć	ć	Ĉ	ĉ	Ċ	ċ	Č	č	Ď	ď
110	Đ	Đ	Ē	ē	Ĕ	ĕ	Ė	ė	Ę	ę	Ě	ě	Ĝ	ĝ	Ğ	ğ
120	Ġ	Ġ	Ģ	ģ	Ĥ	ĥ	Ħ	ħ	Ĩ	ĩ	Ī	ī	Ĭ	ĭ	Į	į
130	İ	ı	Ĳ	ĳ	Ĵ	ĵ	Ķ	ķ	ĸ	Ĺ	ĺ	Ļ	ļ	Ľ	ľ	Ŀ
140	ŀ	Ł	ł	Ń	ń	Ņ	ņ	Ň	ň	ŉ	Ŋ	ŋ	Ō	ō	Ŏ	ŏ
150	Ő	ő	Œ	œ	Ŕ	ŕ	Ŗ	ŗ	Ř	ř	Ś	ś	Ŝ	ŝ	Ş	ş
160	Š	š	Ţ	ţ	Ť	ť	Ŧ	ŧ	Ũ	ũ	Ū	ū	Ŭ	ŭ	Ů	ů
170	Ű	ű	Ų	ų	Ŵ	ŵ	Ŷ	ŷ	Ÿ	Ź	ź	Ż	ż	Ž	ž	ſ

(a)

400		Ё	Ђ	Ѓ	Є	Ѕ	І	Ї	Ј	Љ	Њ	Ћ	Ќ		Ў	Џ
410	А	Б	В	Г	Д	Е	Ж	З	И	Й	К	Л	М	Н	О	П
420	Р	С	Т	У	Ф	Х	Ц	Ч	Ш	Щ	Ъ	Ы	Ь	Э	Ю	Я
430	а	б	в	г	д	е	ж	з	и	й	к	л	м	н	о	п
440	р	с	т	у	ф	х	ц	ч	ш	щ	ъ	ы	ь	э	ю	я
450		ё	ђ	ѓ	є	ѕ	і	ї	ј	љ	њ	ћ	ќ		ў	џ

(b)

Figure 4.2 Unicode excerpts: (a) Latin Extended A (U+0100–U+017F); (b) Cyrillic (U+0400–U+045F).

along the way, what languages it is used in, how it relates to other characters, how it can be transliterated or transcribed. We cannot tell these stories here: to hear them you will have to refer to other sources.

As an example of diversity, Figure 4.2a shows some of the Extended Latin characters, while Figure 4.2b shows part of the Cyrillic section. As you can see, some Cyrillic letters duplicate identical-looking Latin equivalents.

Composite and combining characters

In ordinary usage the word *character* refers to various things: a letter of an alphabet, a particular mark on a page, a symbol in a certain language, and so on. In Unicode the term refers to the abstract form of a letter, but still in a broad sense so that it can encompass the fabulous diversity of the world's writing systems. More precise terminology is employed to cover particular forms of use.

A *glyph* refers to a particular rendition of a character (or composite character) on a page or screen. Different fonts create different glyphs. For example, the character *a* in 12-point Helvetica is one glyph; in 12-point Times it is another. Unicode does not distinguish between different glyphs. It treats characters as abstract members of linguistic scripts, not as graphic entities.

A *code point* is a Unicode value, specified by prefixing *U+* to the numeric value given in hexadecimal. LATIN CAPITAL LETTER G (as the Unicode description goes) is U+0047. A *code range* gives a range of values: for example, the characters corresponding to ASCII are located at U+0000–U+007F and are called Basic Latin.

A code point does not necessarily represent an individual character. Some code points correspond to more than one character. For example, the code point U+FB01, which is called LATIN SMALL LIGATURE FI, represents the sequence *f* followed by *i*, which in most printing is joined together into a single symbol that is technically called a *ligature*, *fi*. Other code points specify part of a character. For example, U+0308 is called COMBINING DIAERESIS, and—at least in normal language—is always accompanied by another symbol to form a single unit such as *ü*, *ë*, or *ï*.

The COMBINING DIAERESIS is an example of what Unicode calls a *combining character*. To produce the single unit *ü*, the Latin small letter *u* (which is U+0075) is directly followed by the code for the combining diaeresis (which is U+0308) to form the sequence U+0075 U+0308. This is the handwriting sequence: first draw the base letter, then place the accent. Combining characters occupy no space of their own: they share the space of the character they combine with. They also may alter the base character's shape: when *i* is followed by the same combining diaeresis the result looks like *ï*—the original dot in the base letter is omitted. Drawing Unicode characters is not straightforward: it is necessary to be able to place accents over, under, and even through arbitrary characters—which may already be accented—and still produce acceptable spacing and appearance.

Because of the requirement to be round-trip compatible with existing character sets, Unicode also has single code points that correspond to precisely the same units as character combinations—in fact, they are part of the Latin-1 supplement shown in Figure 4.2a. This means that certain characters have more than one representation. For example, the middle letter of *naïve* could be represented using the combining character approach by U+0069 U+0308, or as a single, precomposed unit using the already prepared character U+00EF. Around 500 precomposed Latin letters in the Unicode standard are superfluous in that they can be represented using combining character sequences.

Combining characters allow many character shapes to be represented within a limited code range. They also help compensate for omissions: for example, the Guaraní Latin small *g* with tilde can be expressed without embarking upon a lengthy standardization process to add this previously overlooked character to Unicode. Combining characters are an important mechanism in intricate writing systems such as Hangul, the Korean syllabic script. In Unicode, Hangul is covered by 11,172 precomposed symbols (codes AC00 and up in Table 4.2), each of which represents a syllable. Syllables are made up of *Jamo*, which is the Korean name for a single element of the Hangul script. Each Unicode Hangul syllable has an alternative representation as a composition of Jamo, and these are also represented in Unicode (codes 1100 and up in Table 4.2). The rules for combining Jamo are complex, however—which is why the precomposed symbols are included. But to type medieval Hangul, even more combinations are needed, and these are not available in precomposed form.

The existence of composite and combining characters complicates the processing of Unicode text. When searching for a particular word, alternate forms must be considered. String comparison with regular expressions presents a knottier challenge. Even sorting text into lexicographic order becomes nontrivial. Algorithmically all these problems can be reduced to comparing two strings of text—which is far easier if the text is represented in some kind of normalized form.

Unicode defines four normalized forms using two orthogonal notions: *canonical* and *compatibility* equivalence. Canonical equivalence relates code points to sequences of code points that produce the same character—as in the case discussed earlier, where the combination U+0069 U+0308 and the single precomposed character U+00EF both represent *ï*. *Canonical composition* is the process of turning combining character sequences into their precomposed counterparts; *canonical decomposition* is the inverse.

Compatibility equivalence relates ligatures to their constituents, such as the ligature *fi* (U+FB01) and its components *f* (U+0066) and *i* (U+0069). Decomposing ligatures simplifies string comparison, but the new representation no longer maintains a one-to-one character-by-character mapping with the original encoding.

The four normalized forms defined by the Unicode standard are

- canonical decomposition
- canonical decomposition followed by canonical composition
- compatibility decomposition
- compatibility decomposition followed by canonical composition

Certain Unicode characters are officially *deprecated*, which means that although present in the standard they are not supposed to be used. This is how mistakes are dealt with. Once a character has been defined, it cannot be removed from the standard (for that would sacrifice backward compatibility); the solution is to deprecate it. For example, there are two different Unicode characters that generate the symbol Å, Latin capital letter A with ring above (U+00C5) and Angstrom sign (U+212B); the latter is officially deprecated. Deprecated characters are avoided in all normalized forms.

Further complications, which we only mention in passing, are caused by directionality of writing. Hebrew and Arabic are written right to left, but when numbers or foreign words appear they flow in the opposite direction; thus bidirectional processing may be required within each horizontal line. The Mongolian script can only be written in vertical rows. Another issue is the fact that complex scripts, such as Arabic and Indic scripts, include a plethora of ligatures, and contextual analysis is needed to select the correct glyph.

Because of the complexity of Unicode, particularly with regard to composite characters, three implementation levels are defined:

- Level 1 forms the base implementation, excluding combining characters and the Korean Hangul Jamo characters.
- Level 2 permits a fixed list of combining characters, adding, for example, the capability to express Hebrew, Arabic, Bengali, Tamil, Thai, and Lao.
- Level 3 is the full implementation.

Unicode character encodings

With future expansion in mind, the ISO standard formally specifies that Unicode characters are represented by 32 bits each. However, all characters so far envisaged fit into the first 21 bits. In fact the Unicode consortium differs from the ISO standard by limiting the range of values prescribed to the 21-bit range U+000000–10FFFF. The discrepancy is of minor importance; we follow the Unicode route.

So-called planes of 65,536 characters are defined; there are 32 of them in the 21-bit address space. All the examples discussed above lie in the Basic Multilingual Plane, which represents the range U+0000–U+FFFF and contains virtually all characters used in living languages. The Supplementary Multilingual Plane, which ranges from U+10000–U+1FFFF, contains historic scripts, special alphabets designed for use in mathematics, and musical symbols. Next comes the Supplementary Ideographic Plane (U+20000–U+2FFFF), which contains 40,000-odd additional Chinese ideographs that were used in ancient times but have fallen out of current use. The Supplementary Special-Purpose Plane (U+E0000–U+EFFFF), or Plane 14, contains a set of tag characters for language identification, to be used with special protocols.

Given the ISO 32-bit upper bound, the obvious encoding of Unicode uses 4-byte values for each character. This scheme is known as UTF-32, where UTF stands for "UCS Transformation Format" (a nested acronym: UCS is Unicode Character Set)—so called because Unicode characters are "transformed" into this encoding format. A complication arises from the different byte ordering that computers use to store integers: *big-endian* (where the 4 bytes in each word are ordered from most significant to least significant) versus *little-endian* (where they are stored in the reverse order), and the standard includes a mechanism to disambiguate the two.

The Basic Multilingual Plane is a 16-bit representation, so a restricted version of Unicode can use 2-byte characters. In fact a special escape mechanism called *surrogate characters* (explained below) is used to extend the basic 2-byte representation to accommodate the full 21 bits. This scheme is known as UTF-16. It also is complicated by the endian question, which is resolved in the same way. For almost all text the UTF-16 encoding requires half the space needed for UTF-32.

It is convenient to define a variant of Unicode that extends ASCII—which, as we have seen, is a 7-bit representation where each character occupies an individual byte—in a straightforward way. UTF-8 is a variable-length encoding scheme where the basic entity is a byte. ASCII characters are automatically 1-byte UTF-8 codes; existing ASCII files are valid UTF-8. Being byte-oriented, this scheme avoids the endian issue that complicates UTF-32 and UTF-16. We explain these more fully in the following sections.

UTF-32

In Figure 4.3 the word *Welcome* in five different languages has been converted to Unicode (Figure 4.3a) and encoded in the three different UTF methods (Figure 4.3b). UTF-32 maps the universal character set to 4-byte integers, and Unicode is turned into UTF-32 by dropping the *U+* prefix.

		Unicode
Welcome	(English)	U+0057 U+0065 U+006C U+0063 ...
Haere mai	(Māori)	U+0048 U+0061 U+0065 U+0072 ...
Wilkommen	(German)	U+0057 U+0069 U+006C U+006B ...
Bienvenue	(French)	U+0042 U+0069 U+0065 U+006E ...
Akwäba	(Fante from Ghana)	U+0041 U+006B U+0077 U+00E4 ...

(a)

	UTF-32	UTF-16	UTF-8
Welcome	00000057000000650000006C00000063 ...	00570065006C0063 ...	57656C63 ...
Haere mai	00000048000000610000006500000072 ...	0048006100650072 ...	48616572 ...
Wilkommen	00000057000000690000006C0000006B ...	00570069006C006B ...	57696C6B ...
Bienvenue	00000042000000690000006500000006E ...	004200690065006E ...	4269656E ...
Akwäba	000000410000006B0000007700000E4 ...	0041006B007700E4 ...	416B77C3A4...

(b)

Figure 4.3 Encoding *Welcome* in (a) Unicode; (b) UTF-32, UTF-16, and UTF-8.

Byte order is irrelevant when data is generated and handled internally in memory; it only becomes an issue when serializing information for transfer to a disk or transmission over a byte-oriented protocol. In the Unicode standard the big-endian format is preferred, bytes being ordered from most significant to least significant—just as they are when writing out the number in hexadecimal, left to right. This is what is shown in Figure 4.3b. However, two variants are defined: UTF-32BE and UTF-32LE for big-endian and little-endian, respectively.

A UTF-32 file can be either. Working within a single computer system, it does not matter which ordering is used—the system will be internally consistent. If necessary, however, UTF-32 encoding can include a *byte-order mark* to differentiate the two cases. This character, from the Reserved zone in Table 4.2, is defined as "zero-width no-break space." Its byte-for-byte transpose is carefully defined to be an invalid character. This means that software that does not expect a byte-order mark will be fail-safe, since a correctly matched endian system displays the byte-order mark as a zero-width space, and a mismatched one immediately detects an incompatibility through the presence of the invalid character.

In practice it is rare to encounter UTF-32 data because it makes inefficient use of storage. If text is constrained to the basic multilingual plane (and it usually is), the top two bytes of every character are zero.

UTF-16

In UTF-16 characters within the Basic Multilingual Plane are stored as 2-byte integers, as can easily be discerned in Figure 4.3b. The same byte-order mark as above is used to distinguish the UTF-16BE and UTF-16LE variants.

To represent code points outside the Basic Multilingual Plane, specially reserved values called *surrogate characters* are used. Two 16-bit values, both from the Surrogates zone in Table 4.2, are used to specify a 21-bit value in the range U+10000–U+10FFFF (a subset of the full 21-bit range, which goes up to 1FFFFF). Here are the details: the 21-bit number is divided into 11 and 10 bits, respectively, and to each is added a predetermined offset to make them fall into the appropriate region of the surrogate zone. This is a kind of "escape" mechanism, where a special code is used to signify that the following value should be treated differently. However, the surrogate approach is more robust than regular escaping: it allows recovery from errors in a corrupted file because it does not overload values from the nonescaped range, and thus the meaning cannot be confused even if the first surrogate character is corrupted. Inevitably robustness comes at a cost—fewer values can be encoded than with conventional escaping.

UTF-8

UTF-8 is a byte-based variable-length scheme that encodes the same 21-bit character range as UTF-16 and UTF-32. Code lengths vary from one byte for ASCII values through four bytes for values outside the Basic Multilingual Plane.

Table 4.3 Encoding the Unicode character set as UTF-8.

Unicode value	21-bit binary code	UTF-8 code			
U+00000000 – U+0000007F	00000000000000wwwwwww	0wwwwwww			
U+00000080 – U+000007FF	0000000000wwwwwxxxxxx	110wwwww	10xxxxxx		
U+00000800 – U+0000FFFF	00000wwwwxxxxxxyyyyyy	1110wwww	10xxxxxx	10yyyyyy	
U+00010000 – U+001FFFFF	wwwxxxxxxyyyyyyzzzzzz	11110www	10xxxxxx	10yyyyyy	10zzzzzz

If the top bit of a UTF-8 byte is 0, that byte stands alone as a Unicode character, making the encoding backward compatible with 7-bit ASCII. Otherwise, when the byte begins with a 1 bit, the leading 1 bits in it are counted, and their number signals the number of bytes in the code—11 for two bytes, 111 for three, and 1111 for four. The four possibilities are illustrated in Table 4.3. Subsequent bytes in that character's code set their two top bits to 10—so that they can be recognized as continuation bytes even out of context—and use the remaining six bits to encode the value.

Figure 4.3b shows the *Welcome* example in UTF-8. Of interest is the last line, which is one byte longer than the others. This is because the encoding for *ä* falls outside the ASCII range: Unicode U+00E4 is represented as the two bytes C3 A4, in accordance with the second entry of Table 4.3.

To eliminate ambiguity the Unicode standard states that UTF-8 must use the shortest possible encoding. For example, writing UTF-8 F0 80 80 C7 encodes U+0047 in a way that satisfies the rules, but it is invalid because 47 is a shorter representation.

Hindi and related scripts

Unicode is advertised as a uniform way of representing all the characters used in all the world's languages. Unicode fonts exist and are used by some commercial word processors and Web browsers. It is natural for people—particularly people from Western linguistic backgrounds—to assume that all problems associated with representing different languages on computers have been solved. Unfortunately today's Unicode-compliant applications fall far short of providing a satisfactory solution for languages with intricate scripts.

We use Hindi and related Indic scripts as an example. These languages raise subtle problems that are difficult for people of European background to appreciate, and we can only give a glimpse of the complexities involved. As Table 4.2 shows, the Unicode space from 0900 to 0DFF is reserved for ten Indic scripts. Although many hundreds of different languages are spoken in India, the principal officially recognized ones are Hindi, Marathi, Sanskrit, Punjabi, Bengali, Gujarati,

Devanagari	अ आ इ ई उ ऊ ऋ ऌ ऍ ऎ ए ऐ ऑ ऒ ओ औ क ख ग घ ङ च छ ज झ
Bengali	অ আ ই ঈ উ ঊ খা ৯ এ ঐ ও ঔ ক খ গ ঘ ঙ চ ছ জ ঝ ঞ ট ঠ ড
Gurmukhi	ਅ ਆ ਇ ਈ ਉ ਊ ਏ ਐ ਓ ਔ ਕ ਖ ਗ ਘ ਙ ਚ ਛ ਜ ਝ ਞ ਟ ਠ ਡ ਢ ਣ ਤ ਥ
Gujarati	અ આ ઇ ઈ ઉ ઊ ઋ ઍ એ ઐ ઑ ઓ ઔ ક ખ ગ ઘ ઙ ચ છ જ ઝ ઞ ટ ઠ
Oriya	ଅ ଆ ଇ ଈ ଉ ଊ ଋ ଌ ଏ ଐ ଓ ଔ କ ଖ ଗ ଘ ଙ ଚ ଛ ଜ ଝ ଞ ଟ ଠ ଡ ଢ ଣ
Tamil	அ ஆ இ ஃ உ ஊ எ ஏ ஐ ஒ ஓ ஔ க ங ச ஜ ஞ ட ண த ந
Telugu	అ ఆ ఇ ఈ ఉ ఊ ఋ ఌ ఎ ఏ ఐ ఒ ఓ ఔ క ఖ గ ఘ ఙ చ ఛ జ ఝ
Kannada	ಅ ಆ ಇ ಈ ಉ ಊ ಋ ಌ ಎ ಏ ಐ ಒ ಓ ಔ ಕ ಖ ಗ ಘ ಙ ಚ ಛ ಜ ಝ ಞ
Malayalam	അ ആ ഇ ഈ ഉ ഊ ഋ ഌ എ ഏ ഐ ഒ ഓ ഔ ക ഖ ഗ ഘ ങ

Figure 4.4 Examples of characters in Indic scripts.

Oriya, Assamese, Tamil, Telugu, Kannada, Malayalam, Urdu, Sindhi, and Kashmiri. The first twelve of these are written in one of nine writing systems that have evolved from the ancient Brahmi script. The remaining three, Urdu, Sindhi, and Kashmiri, are primarily written in Persian Arabic scripts, but can be written in Devanagari too (Sindhi is also written in the Gujarati script). The nine scripts are Devanagari, Bengali, Gujarati, Oriya and Gurmukhi (northern or *Aryan* scripts), and Tamil, Telugu, Kannada, Malayalam (southern or *Dravidian* ones). Figure 4.4 gives some characters in each of these. As you can see, the characters are rather beautiful—and the scripts are quite different from one another. Unicode also includes a script for Sinhalese, the official language of Sri Lanka.

Hindi, the official language of India, is written in Devanagari,[3] which is used for writing Marathi and Sanskrit too. (It is also the official script of Nepal.) The Punjabi language is written in Gurmukhi. Assamese is written in a script that is very similar to Bengali, but there is one additional glyph and another glyph is different. In Unicode the two scripts are merged, with distinctive code points for the two Assamese glyphs. Thus the Unicode scripts cover all 12 of the official Indian languages that are not written in Persian Arabic. All these scripts derive from Brahmi, and all are phonetically based. In fact the printing press did not reach the Indian subcontinent until missionaries arrived from Europe. The languages had a long time to evolve before they were fixed in print, which contributes to their diversity.

---

3. Pronounced *Dayv'nagri*, with the accent on the second *a*.

Since the 1970s various committees of the Indian Department of Official Languages and Department of Electronics have worked on devising codes and keyboards that cater to all official Indic scripts. A standard keyboard layout was developed that provides a uniform way of entering them all. A common code was defined so that any software that was developed could be used universally. This is possible because, despite the very different scripts, the alphabets are phonetic and have a common Brahmi root that was used for the ancient Sanskrit. The simultaneous availability of multiple Indic languages was intended to accelerate technological development and facilitate national integration in India.

The result was ISCII, the Indian Script Code for Information Interchange. Announced in 1983 (and revised in 1988), it is an extension of the ASCII code set that, like other extensions, places new characters in the upper region of the code space. The code table caters for all the characters required in the Brahmi-based Indic scripts. Figure 4.5a shows the ISCII code table for the Devanagari script; code tables for the other scripts in Figure 4.4 are similar but contain differently shaped characters (and some entries are missing because there is no equivalent character in that script). The code table contains 56 characters, 10 digits (in the last line of Figure 4.5a), and 18 accents and combining characters. There are also three special escape codes, but we will not go into their meaning here.

The Unicode developers adopted ISCII lock, stock, and barrel—they had to, because of their policy of round-trip compatibility with existing coding methods. They used different parts of the code space for the various scripts, which means that (in contrast to ISCII) documents containing multiple scripts can easily be represented. However, they also included some extra characters—about 10 of them—which in the original ISCII design were supposed to be formed from combinations of other keystrokes. Figure 4.5b shows the Unicode code table for the Devanagari script.

Most of the extra characters give a shorthand for frequently used characters, and they differ from one language to another. An example in Devanagari is the character Om, a Hindu religious symbol:

ॐ   (Unicode U+0950)

Although not part of the ISCII character set, this can be created from the keyboard by typing the sequence of characters

उ ॕ   (ISCII A8 A1 E9)

The third character (ISCII E9) is a special diacritic sign called the *Nukta* (which phonetically represents nasalization of the preceding vowel). ISCII defines Nukta as an operator used to derive some little-used Sanskrit characters that are not otherwise available from the keyboard, such as Om. However, Unicode includes these

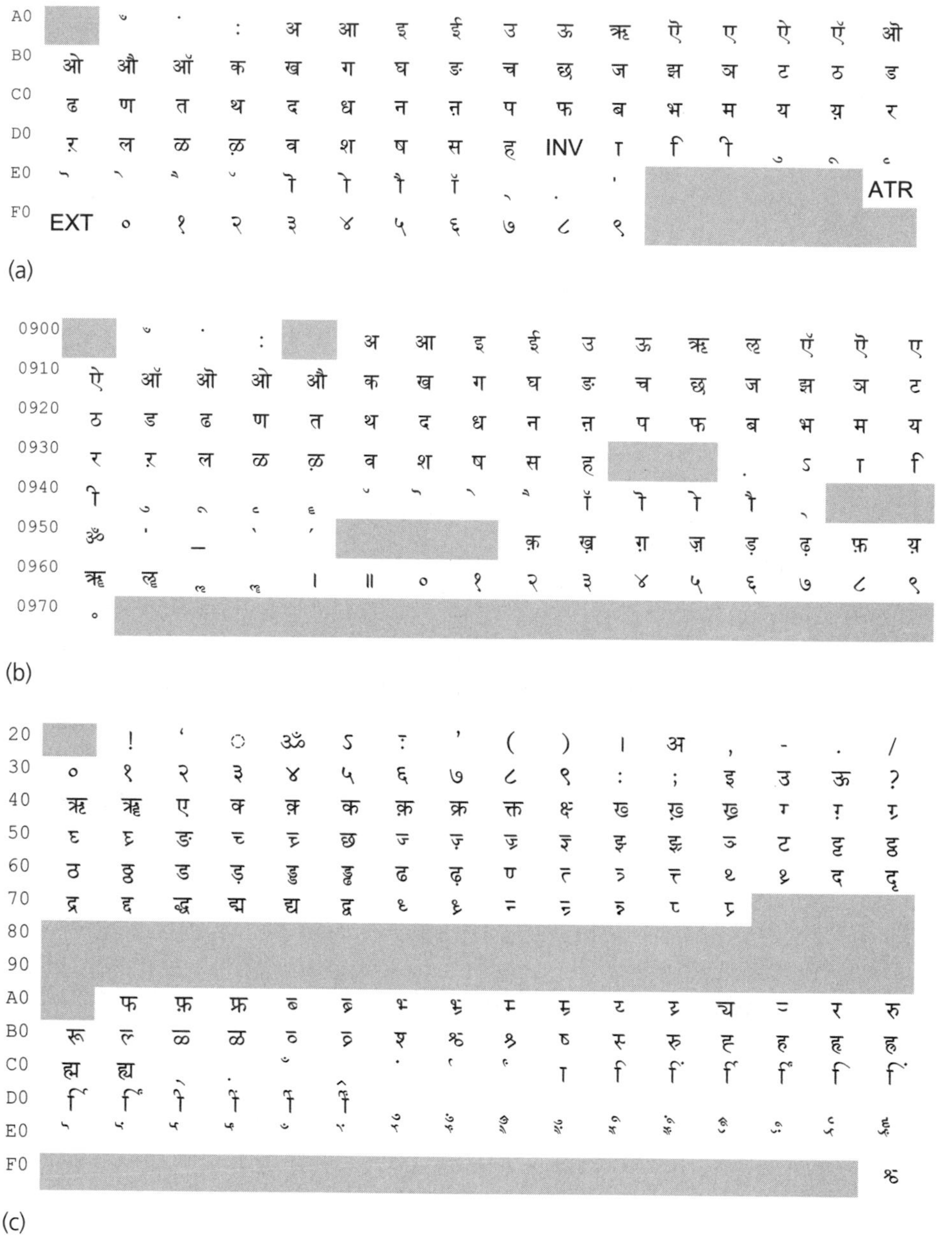

(a)

(b)

(c)

Figure 4.5 Devanagari script: (a) ISCII; (b) Unicode (U+0900–U+0970); (c) code table for the Surekh font.

lesser-used characters as part of the character set (U+0950 and U+0958 through U+095F).

Although the Unicode solution is designed to adequately represent all the Indic scripts, it has not yet found widespread acceptance. A practical problem is that the Indic scripts contain numerous conjuncts, which are clusters of two to four consonants without any intervening vowels. Conjuncts are the same idea as the ligatures discussed earlier, characters represented by a single glyph whose shape differs from the shapes of the constituent consonants—just as the sequence *f* followed by *i* is joined together into the single ligature *fi* in the font used for this book. Indic scripts contain far more of these, and there is a greater variation in shape. For example, the conjunct

ऌ

is equivalent to the two-character combination

ल ॢ . (Unicode U+0932 U+0943)

In this particular case, the conjunct happens to be defined as a separate code in Unicode (U+090C)—just as the ligature *fi* has its own code (U+FB01). The problem is that this is not always the case. In the ISCII design *all* conjuncts are formed by placing a special character between the constituent consonants, in accordance with the ISCII design goal of a uniform representation for input of all Indic languages on a single keyboard. In Unicode some conjuncts are given their own code—like the one above—but others are not.

Figure 4.5c shows the code table for a particular commercially available Devanagari font, Surekh (a member of the ISFOC family of fonts). Although there is much overlap, there is certainly not a one-to-one correspondence between the Unicode and Surekh characters, as can be seen in Figures 4.5b and c. Some conjuncts, represented by two to four Unicode codes, correspond to a single glyph that does not have a separate Unicode representation but does have a corresponding entry in the font. And in fact the converse is true: there are single glyphs in the Unicode table that are produced using the font by generating pairs of characters. For example, the Unicode symbol

ऒ (Unicode U+0912)

is drawn by specifying a sequence of three codes in the Surekh font.

We cannot give a more detailed explanation of why such choices have been made—this is a controversial subject, and a full discussion would require a book in itself. However, the fact is that the adoption of Unicode in India has been delayed because some people feel that it represents an uncomfortable compromise between the clear but spare design principles of ISCII and the practical requirements of actual fonts. They prefer to represent their texts in the original ISCII because they feel it is conceptually cleaner.

The problem is compounded by the fact that today's word processors and Web browsers take a simplistic view of fonts. In reality combination rules are required—and were foreseen by the designers of Unicode—that take a sequence of Unicode characters and produce the corresponding single glyph from Figure 4.5c. We will learn in Section 4.3 how such rules can be embodied in "composite fonts." But ligatures in English, such as *fi*, have their own Unicode entry, which makes things much easier. For example, the "insert-symbol" function of word processors implements a one-to-one correspondence between Unicode codes and the glyphs on the page.

The upshot is that languages such as Hindi are not properly supported by current Unicode-compliant applications. A table of glyphs, one for each Unicode value, is insufficient to depict text in Hindi script. To make matters worse, in practice some Hindi documents are represented using ISCII while others are represented using raw font codes like that of Figure 4.5c, which are specific to the particular font manufacturer. Different practices have grown up for different scripts. For example, the majority of documents in the Kannada language on the Web seem to be represented using ISCII codes, whereas for the Malayalam language diverse font-specific codes are used. To read a new Malayalam newspaper in your Web browser often involves downloading a new font!

To accommodate such documents in a digital library that represents documents internally in Unicode, it is necessary to implement several mappings:

1. from ISCII to Unicode, so that ISCII documents can be incorporated
2. from various different font representations (such as ISFOC, used for the Surekh font) to Unicode, so that documents in other formats can be accommodated
3. from Unicode to various different font representations (such as ISFOC), so that the documents can be displayed on computer systems with different fonts

The first is a simple transliteration because Unicode was designed for round-trip compatibility. However, both the other mappings involve translating sequences of codes in one space into corresponding sequences in the other space (although all sequences involved are very short). Figure 4.6 shows an example page produced by such a scheme.

Using Unicode in a digital library

Unicode encoding may seem complex, but it is straightforward to use in digital library software. Every string can be declared as an array of 16-bit integers and used to hold the UTF-16 encoding of the characters. In Java this is exactly what the built-in *String* type does. In C and C++ the data type *short* is a 16-bit integer, so UTF-16 can be supported by declaring all strings to be *unsigned short*. Read-

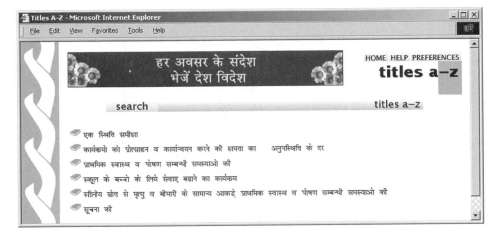

Figure 4.6 Page produced by a digital library in Devanagari script.

ability is improved by building a new type that encapsulates this. In C++ a new class can be built that provides appropriate functionality. Alternatively a support library, such as the type *wchar_t* defined in the ANSI/ISO standard to represent "wide" characters, can be used.

Further work is necessary to treat surrogate characters properly. But usually operation can safely be restricted to the Basic Multilingual Plane, which covers all living languages—more than enough for most applications. A further practical restriction is to avoid combining characters and work with Unicode level 1— which makes it far easier to implement string matching operations. For higher Unicode levels you should seek library support for normalization and matching.

When writing Unicode data structures to disk, it is easy to convert the 16-bit characters to UTF-8, reversing the process when reading. In most common situations this greatly reduces file size and also increases portability because the files do not depend on endianness.

Care is necessary to display and print Unicode characters properly. Most Unicode-enabled applications incorporate an arsenal of fonts and use a lookup table to map each Unicode character to a displayable character in a known font. Complications include composite Unicode characters and the direction in which the character sequence is displayed. By working through a modern Web browser, digital libraries can avoid having to deal with these issues explicitly.

4.2   Representing documents

Unicode provides an all-encompassing form for representing characters, including manipulation, searching, storage, and transmission. Now we turn our attention to document representation. The lowest common denominator for documents on computers has traditionally been plain, simple, raw ASCII text. Although there is no formal standard for this, certain conventions have grown up.

Plain text

A text document comprises a sequence of character values interpreted in ordinary reading order: left to right, top to bottom. There is no header to denote the character set used. While 7-bit ASCII is the baseline, the 8-bit ISO ASCII extensions are often used, particularly for non-English text. This works well when text is processed by just one application program on a single computer, but when transferring between different applications—perhaps through e-mail, news, http, or FTP—the various programs involved may make different assumptions. These alphabet mismatches often mean that character values in the range 128–255 are displayed incorrectly.

Formatting within such a document is rudimentary. Explicit line breaks are usually included. Paragraphs are separated by two consecutive line breaks, or the first line is indented. Tabs are frequently used for indentation and alignment. A fixed-width font is assumed; tab stops usually occur at every eighth character position. Common typing conventions are adopted to represent characters such as dashes (two hyphens in a row). Headings are underlined manually using rows of hyphens, or equal signs for double underlining. Emphasis is often indicated by surrounding text with a single underscore (_like this_), or by flanking words with asterisks (*like* *this*).

Different operating systems have adopted conflicting conventions for specifying line breaks. Historically teletypes were modeled after typewriters. The line-feed character (ASCII 10, *LF* in Table 4.1) moves the paper up one line but retains the position of the print head. The carriage-return character (ASCII 13, *CR* in Table 4.1) returns the print head to the left margin but does not move the paper. A new line is constructed by issuing *carriage return* followed by *line feed* (logically the reverse order could be used, but the *carriage return line feed* sequence is conventional, and universally relied upon). Microsoft DOS (and Windows) use this teletype-oriented interpretation. However, Unix and the Apple Macintosh adopt a different convention: the ASCII line-feed character moves to the next line *and* returns the print head to the left margin. This difference in interpretation can produce a strange-looking control character at the end of every line.[4] While the meaning of the message is not obscured, the effect is rather distracting.

---

4. ^*M* or "carriage return." Observe that *CR* and *M* are in the same row of Table 4.1. Control characters in the first column are often made visible by prefixing the corresponding character in the second column with ^.

People who use the standard Internet file transfer protocol (FTP) sometimes wonder why it has separate ASCII and binary modes. The difference is that in ASCII mode, new lines are correctly translated when copying files between different systems. It would be wrong to apply this transformation to binary files, however. Modern text-handling programs conceal the difference from users by automatically detecting which new-line convention is being used and behaving accordingly. Of course, this can lead to brittleness: if assumptions break down, all line breaks are messed up and users become mystified.

In a digital library, plain text is a simple, straightforward, but impoverished representation of documents. Metadata cannot be included explicitly (except, possibly, as part of the file name). However, automatic processing is sometimes used to extract title, author, date, and so on. Extraction methods rely on informal document structuring conventions. The more consistent the structure, the easier this becomes. Conversely the simpler the extraction technique, the more seriously things break down when formatting quirks are encountered. Unfortunately you cannot normally expect complete consistency and accuracy in large document collections.

Indexing

Rapid searching of the full text of large document collections for particular words, sets or words, or sequences of words is a core function of digital libraries that distinguishes them from physical libraries. The ability to search full text adds great value to documents used for study or reference, although it is rarely applicable to recreational reading, which normally takes place sequentially, in one pass.

Before computers, full-text searching was confined to highly valued—often sacred—works for which a concordance had already been prepared. For example, some 300,000 word appearances are indexed in Cruden's concordance of the Bible, printed on 774 pages. They are arranged alphabetically, from *Aaron* to *Zuzims*, and any particular word can be located quickly using a binary search. Each probe into the index halves the number of potential locations for the target, and the correct page for an entry can be located by looking at no more than 10 pages—fewer if the searcher interpolates the position of an entry from the position of its initial letter in the alphabet. A term can usually be located in a few seconds, which is not bad considering that only elementary manual technology is being employed. Once an entry has been located, it gives a list of references that the searcher can follow up. Figure 4.7 shows some of Cruden's concordance entries for the word *search*.

In digital libraries searching is done by a computer rather than a person, but essentially the same techniques are used. The difference is that things happen a

search
enquire and made *s.*   *Deut* 13:14
that *s.* may be made in.   *Ezra* 4:15
                                    5:17
s. hath been made, and it. 4:19; 6:1
prepare thyself to the *s.*   *Job* 8:8
hast thou walked in the *s.*?   38:16*
accomplish a diligent *s.*   *Ps* 64:6
my spirit made diligent *s.*   77:6
not found it by secret *s.*   *Jer* 2:34

search, *verb*
he shall not *s.* whether.   *Lev* 27:33
to *s.* out a resting place. *Num* 10:33
that they may *s.* the land.   13:2
which we have gone to *s.* it.   32
passed through to *s.* it, is.   14:7
of the men that went to *s.*   38
men, and they shall *s.*   *Deut* 1:22
before to *s.* you out a place.   33
men to *s.* the country.   *Josh* 2:2, 3
the Danites sent men to *s. Judg* 18:2
land, I will *s.* him out. *1 Sam* 23:23
servants unto thee to *s.* the city ?
              2 Sam 10:3; *1 Chr* 19:3
servants, and they shall *s. 1 Ki* 20:6
s. that none of the servants.
                         2 Ki 10:23
is it good that he should *s.*? *Job* 13:9
shall not God *s.* this out ? *Ps* 44:21

Figure 4.7 Entries for the word *search* in a
biblical concordance. *Cruden's Complete
Concordance to the Old and New Testaments* by
A. Cruden, C. J. Orwom, A. D. Adams, and S. A.
Waters. 1941, Lutterworth Press.

little faster. Usually it is possible to keep a list of terms in the computer's main
memory, and this can be searched in a matter of microseconds. The computer's
equivalent of the concordance entry may be too large to store in main memory,
in which case an access to secondary storage (usually disk) is required to obtain
the list of references. Then each of the references must be retrieved from the
disk, which typically takes a few milliseconds.

A full-text index to a document collection gives for each word in the collection the position of every occurrence of that word in the collection's text. A
moment's reflection shows that the size of the index is commensurate with the
size of the text, because an occurrence position is likely to occupy roughly the
same number of bytes as a word in the text. (Four-byte integers, which are convenient in practice, are able to specify word positions in a 4-billion-word corpus. Conversely an average English word has five or six characters and so also
occupies a few bytes, the exact number depending on how it is stored and

whether it is compressed.) We have implicitly assumed a word-level index, where occurrence positions give actual word locations in the collection. Space will be saved if locations are recorded to within a unit such as a paragraph, chapter, or document, yielding a coarser index—partly because pointers can be smaller, but chiefly because if a particular word occurs several times in the same unit, only one pointer is required for that unit.

A comprehensive index, capable of rapidly accessing all documents that satisfy a particular query, is a large data structure. Size, as well as being a drawback in its own right, also affects retrieval time, for the computer must read and interpret appropriate parts of the index to locate the desired information. Fortunately there are interesting data structures and algorithms that can be applied to solve these problems. They are beyond the scope of this book, but references can be found in the "Notes and sources" section at the end of the chapter (Section 4.7).

The basic function of a full-text index is to provide, given any particular query term, a list of all the units that contain it, along with (for reasons to be explained shortly) the number of times it occurs in each unit on the list. It's simplest to think of the "units" as being documents, although the granularity of the index may be paragraphs or chapters instead—or even individual words, in which case what is returned is a list of the word numbers corresponding to the query term. And it's simplest to think of the query term as a word, although if stemming or case-folding is in effect, the term may correspond to several different words. For example, with stemming the term *computer* may correspond to the words *computer, computers, computation, compute,* and so on; and with case-folding it may correspond to *computer, Computer, COMPUTER,* and even *CoMpUtEr* (an unusual enough word, but not completely unknown—for example, it appears in this book!).

When one indexes a large text, it rapidly becomes clear that just a few common words—such as *of, the,* and *and*—account for a large number of the entries in the index. People have argued that these words should be omitted, since they take up so much space and are not likely to be needed in queries, and for this reason they are often called *stop words*. However, some index compilers and users have observed that it is better to leave stop words in. Although a few dozen stop words may account for around 30 percent of the references that an index contains, it is possible to represent them in a way that consumes relatively little space.

A query to a full-text retrieval system usually contains several words. How they are interpreted depends on the type of query. Two common types, both explained in Chapter 3 (Section 3.3), are *Boolean queries* and *ranked queries*. In either case the process of responding to the query involves looking up, for each term, the list of documents it appears in, and performing logical operations on these lists. In the case of Boolean queries, the result is a list of documents that satisfies the query, and this list (or the first part of it) is displayed to the user.

In the case of ranked queries, the final list of documents must be sorted according to the ranking heuristic that is in place. As Section 3.3 explains, these heuristics gauge the similarity of each document to the set of terms that constitute the query. For each term they weigh the frequency with which it appears in the document being considered (the more it is mentioned, the greater the similarity) against its frequency in the document collection as a whole (common terms are less significant). This is why the index stores the number of times each word appears in each document. A great many documents—perhaps all documents in the collection—may satisfy a particular ranked query (if the query contains the word *the*, all English documents would probably qualify). Retrieval systems take great pains to work efficiently even on such queries; they use techniques that avoid the need to sort the list fully in order to find the top few elements.

In effect the indexing process treats each document (or whatever the unit of granularity is) as a "bag of words." What matters is the words that appear in the document and (for ranked queries) the frequency with which they appear. The query is also treated as a bag of words. This representation provides the foundation for full-text indexing. Whenever documents are presented in forms other than word-delineated plain text, they must be reduced to this form so that the corresponding bag of words can be determined.

Word segmentation

Before creating an index the text must first be divided into words. A word is a sequence of alphanumeric characters surrounded by white space or punctuation. Usually some large limit is placed on the length of words—perhaps 16 characters, or 256 characters. Another practical rule of thumb is to limit numbers to a far smaller size—perhaps four numeric characters, only indexing numbers less than 9,999. Without this restriction the size of the vocabulary might be artificially inflated—for example, a long document with numbered paragraphs could contain hundreds of thousands of different integers—which negatively impacts certain technical aspects of the indexing procedure. Years, however, at four digits, should be preserved as single words.

In some languages plain text presents special problems. Languages such as Chinese and Japanese are written without using any spaces or other word delimiters (except for punctuation marks)—indeed, the Western notion of a *word boundary* is literally alien. Nevertheless these languages do contain words. Most Chinese words comprise several characters: two, three, or four. Five-character words also exist, but they are rare. Many characters can stand alone as words in themselves, while on other occasions the same character is the first or second component of a two-character word, and on still others it participates as a component of a three- or four-character word.

This causes obvious problems in full-text indexing: to get a bag of words we have to identify the words first. One possibility is to treat each character as an individual word. However, this produces poor retrieval results. An extreme analogy is an English-language retrieval system that, instead of finding all documents containing the words *digital library*, found all documents containing the constituent letters *a b d g i l r t y*. Of course you receive all sought-after documents, but they are diluted with countless others. And ranking would be based on letter frequencies, not word frequencies. The situation in Chinese is not so bad, for individual characters are far more numerous, and more meaningful, than individual letters in English. But they are less meaningful than words.

Readers unfamiliar with Chinese can gain an appreciation of the problem of multiple interpretations from Figure 4.8a, which shows two alternative interpretations of the same character sequence. The text is a joke that relies on the ambiguity of phrasing. Once upon a time, the story goes, a man set out on a long journey. But before he could return home the rainy season began, and he had to take shelter at a friend's house. As the rains continued he overstayed his welcome, and his friend wrote him a note: the first line in Figure 4.8a. The intended interpretation is shown in the second line, which means "It is raining, the god would like the guest to stay. Although the god wants you to stay, I do not!" On seeing the note, the visitor added the punctuation shown in the third line, making three sentences whose meaning is totally different—"The rainy day, the staying day.

下雨天留客天留我不留	Unpunctuated Chinese sentence
下雨、天留客。天留、我不留！	*It is raining, the god would like the guest to stay. Although the god wants you to stay, I do not!*
下雨天、留客天。留我不？留！	*The rainy day, the staying day. Would you like me to stay? Sure!*

(a)

我喜欢新西兰花	Unsegmented Chinese sentence
我　喜欢　新西兰　花	*I like New Zealand flowers*
我　喜欢　新　西兰花	*I like fresh broccoli*

(b)

Figure 4.8 Alternative interpretations of two Chinese sentences: (a) ambiguity caused by phrasing; (b) ambiguity caused by word boundaries.

Would you like me to stay? Sure!" (Nevertheless, according to the story he did take the hint, leaving the amended note as a joke.)

This example relies on ambiguity of phrasing, but the same kind of problem can arise with word segmentation. Figure 4.8b shows a more prosaic example. For the ordinary sentence on the first line, there are two different interpretations, depending on the context: "I like New Zealand flowers" and "I like fresh broccoli."

Written Chinese documents are unsegmented, and Chinese readers are accustomed to inferring the corresponding sequence of words as they read. Accordingly machine-readable versions are invariably stored in unsegmented form. If they are to be incorporated into a digital library that offers full-text retrieval, a segmentation scheme should be used to insert word boundaries at appropriate positions when the text is indexed.

One way of segmenting text is to use a language dictionary. Boundaries are inserted to maximize the number of the words in the text that are also present in the dictionary. Of course there may be more than one valid segmentation, and heuristics must be sought to resolve ambiguities.

Another segmentation method is based on the insight that text divided into words is more compressible than text that lacks word boundaries. You can see this with a simple experiment. Take a text file, compress it with any standard compression utility (such as gzip), and measure the compression ratio. Then remove all the spaces from the file, making it considerably smaller (about 17% smaller, because in English approximately one letter in six is a space). When you compress this smaller file the compression ratio is noticeably worse than for the original file. Inserting word boundaries improves compressibility.

This fact can be used to divide text into words, based on a large corpus of training data that has been segmented by hand. Between every pair of characters lies a potential space. Segmentation can be achieved by training a text compression model on presegmented text and using a search algorithm to interpolate spaces in a way that maximizes the overall compression of the text. The "Notes and sources" section at the end of the chapter (Section 4.7) points to a fuller explanation of the technique.

For non-Chinese readers, the success of the space-insertion method can be illustrated by applying it to English text. Table 4.4 shows, at the top, some original text, with spaces in the proper places. Below is the input to the segmentation procedure. Underneath that is the output of a dictionary word-based segmentation scheme and of a character-based one that uses the compression method. The training text was a substantial sample of English, although far smaller than the corpus used to produce the dictionary for the word-based method.

Word-based segmentation fails badly when the words are not in the dictionary. In this case neither *crocidolite* nor *Micronite* were, and they are segmented incorrectly. In addition, *inits* is treated as a single word because it occurred that

Table 4.4 Segmenting words in English text.	
Original text	The unit of New York-based Loews Corp that makes Kent cigarettes stopped using crocidolite in its Micronite cigarette filters in 1956.
Without spaces	TheunitofNewYork-basedLoewsCorpthatmakesKentcig arettesstoppedusingcrocidoliteinitsMicronitecigarettef iltersin1956.
Word-based segmentation	The unit of New York-based Loews Corp that makes Kent cigarettes stopped using c roc id o lite inits Micron it e cigarette filters in 1956.
Character-based segmentation	The unit of New York-based LoewsCorp that makes Kent cigarettes stopped using croc idolite in its Micronite cigarette filters in 1956.

way in the text from which the dictionary was created, and in cases of ambiguity the algorithm prefers longer words. The strength of the compression-based method is that it performs well on unknown words. Although *Micronite* does not occur in the training corpus, it is correctly segmented. This method makes two errors, however. First, a space was not inserted into *LoewsCorp* because it happens to require fewer bits to encode than *Loews Corp*. Second, an extra space was added to *crocidolite* because that also reduced the number of bits required.

This brings to a close our discussion on plain text documents. We now move on to richer document representations that cater to combined text and graphics.

4.3 Page description languages: PostScript and PDF

Page description languages allow typeset pages to be expressed in a way that is independent of the particular output device being used. Early word-processing programs and drawing packages incorporated code for output to particular printers and could not be used with other devices. With the advent of page description languages, programs can generate graphical documents in a device-independent format which will print on any device equipped with a driver for that language.

Most of the time digital libraries can treat documents in these languages by processing them using standard "black boxes": generate this report in a particular language, display it here, transfer it there, and print. However, to build coherent collections out of the documents, you need internal knowledge of these formats to understand what can and cannot be accomplished: whether the text can be indexed, bookmarks inserted, images extracted, and so on. For this reason we now describe some page description languages in detail.

PostScript

PostScript, the first commercially developed page description language, was released in 1985, whereupon it was rapidly adopted by software companies and printer manufacturers as a platform-independent way of describing printed pages that could include both text and graphics. Soon it was being coupled with software applications (notably, in the early days, PageMaker on the Apple Macintosh) that ensure that "what you see" graphically on the computer's raster display is "what you get" on the printed page.

PostScript files comprise a sequence of graphical drawing instructions, including ones that draw particular letters from particular fonts. The instructions are like this: move to the point defined by these x and y coordinates and then draw a straight line to here; using the following x and y coordinates as control points, draw a smooth curve around them with such-and-such a thickness; display a character from this font at this position and in this point size; display the following image data, scaled and rotated by this amount. Instructions are included to specify such things as page size, clipping away all parts of a picture that lie outside a given region, and when to move to the next page.

But PostScript is more than just a file format. It is a high-level programming language that supports diverse data types and operations on them. Variables and predefined operators allow the usual kinds of data manipulation. New operations can be encapsulated as user-defined functions. Data can be stored in files and retrieved. A PostScript document is more accurately referred to as a PostScript *program*. It is printed or displayed by passing it to a PostScript interpreter, a full programming language interpreter.

Being a programming language, PostScript allows print-quality documents that compose text and graphical components to be expressed in an exceptionally versatile way. Ultimately, when interpreted, the abstract PostScript description is converted into a matrix of dots or *pixels* through a process known as *rasterization* or *rendering*. The dot structure is imperceptible to the eye—commonly available printers have a resolution of 300 to 600 dpi, and publishing houses use 1,200 dpi and above (see Table 2.4 in Chapter 2). This very book is an example of what can be described using the language.

Modern computers are sufficiently powerful that a PostScript description can be quickly rasterized and displayed on the screen. This adds an important dimension to online document management: computers without the original software used to compose a document can still display the finished product exactly how it was intended. Indeed, in the late 1980s one computer manufacturer took the idea to an extreme by developing an operating system (called NeXT) in which the display was controlled entirely from PostScript, and all applications generated their on-screen results in this form.

However, PostScript was not designed for screen displays. As we saw with ASCII, limitations often arise when a standard is put to use in situations for which it was not designed. Just as ASCII is being superseded by Unicode, a scheme called the Portable Document Format (PDF) has been devised as the successor to PostScript (see subsection "Portable Document Format: PDF") for online documents.

PostScript graphics

PostScript is page based. Graphical marks are drawn one by one until an operator called *showpage* is encountered, whereupon the page is presented. When one page is complete, the next is begun. Placement is like painting: if a new mark covers a previously painted area, it completely obliterates the old paint. Marks can be black and white, grayscale, or color. They are "clipped" to fit within a given area (not necessarily the page boundary) before being placed on the page. This process defines the *imaging model* used by PostScript.

Table 4.5 summarizes PostScript's main graphical components. Various geometric primitives are supplied. Circles and ellipses can be produced using the *arc* primitive; general curves are drawn using *splines*, a type of well-defined curved line whose shape is controlled precisely by a number of control points. A *path* is a sequence of graphical primitives interspersed with geometric operations and stylistic attributes. Once a path has been defined, it is necessary to specify how it is to be painted: for example, *stroke* for a line or *fill* for a solid shape. The *moveto* operator moves the pen without actually drawing, so that paths do not have to prescribe contiguous runs of paint. An operator called *closepath* forms a closed shape by generating a line from the latest point back to the last location moved to. The origin of coordinates is located at the bottom left-hand corner of a page, and the unit of distance is set to be one *printer's point*, a typographical measure whose size is 1/72 inch.

In PostScript, text characters are just another graphical primitive and can be rotated, translated, scaled, and colored just like any other object. However,

Table 4.5 Graphical components in PostScript.

Component	Description
Graphical primitives	Straight lines, arcs, general curves, sampled images, and text
Geometrical operations	Scale, translate, and rotate
Line attributes	Width, dashed, start and end caps, joining lines/corner mitre style
Font attributes	Font, typeface, size
Color	Color currently in use
Paths	Sequence of graphical primitives and attributes
Rendering	How to render paths: grayscale, color, or outline
Clipping	Restricts what is shown of the path

because of its importance, text comes in for some special treatment. The Post-Script interpreter stores information about the current font: font type, typeface, point size, and so on, and operators such as *findfont* and *scalefont* are provided to manipulate these components.

There is also a special operator called *image* for sampled images.

The PostScript language

Files containing PostScript programs are represented in 7-bit ASCII, but this does not restrict the fonts and characters that can be displayed on a page. A percentage symbol (%) indicates that the remainder of the line contains a comment; however, comments marked with a double percent (%%) extend the language by giving structured information that can be utilized by a PostScript interpreter.

Figure 4.9b shows a simple PostScript program that, when executed, produces the result in Figure 4.9a, which contains the greeting *Welcome* in the five languages we used earlier to illustrate Unicode. The first line, which is technically a comment but must be present in all PostScript programs, defines the file to be of type PostScript. The next two lines set the font to be 14-point Helvetica, and then the current path is moved to a position (10,10) points from the lower left-hand corner of the page.

The five *show* lines display the *Welcome* text (plus a space). PostScript, unlike many computer languages, uses a stack-based form of notation where commands *follow* their arguments. The *show* commands "show" the text that precedes them; parentheses are used to group characters together into text strings. In the fifth example, the text *Akw* is "shown" or painted on the page; then there is a relative move (*rmoveto*) of the current position forward two printer's points (the coordinate specification (2, 0)); then the character \310 is painted (octal 310, which is in fact an umlaut in the Latin-1 extension of ASCII); the current position is moved back six points; and the characters *aba* are "shown." The effect is to generate the composite character *ä* in the middle of the word. Finally the *showpage* operator is issued, causing the graphics that have been painted on the virtual page to be printed on a physical page.

The PostScript program in Figure 4.9b handles the composite character *ä* inelegantly. It depends on the spacing embodied in the particular font chosen—on the fact that moving forward two points, printing an umlaut, and moving back six points will position the forthcoming *a* directly underneath. There are better ways to accomplish this, using, for instance, ISOLatin1Encoding or composite fonts, but they require syntax beyond the scope of this simple example.

Levels of PostScript

Standards and formats evolve. There is a tension between stability, an important feature for any language, and currency, or the need to extend in response to the

Welcome Haere mai Wilkommen Bienvenue Akwäba

(a)

```
%!PS-Adobe-3.0
/Helvetica findfont
14 scalefont
setfont
10 10 moveto
(Welcome ) show
(Haere mai ) show
(Wilkommen ) show
(Bienvenue ) show
(Akw) show 2 0 rmoveto (\310) show -6 0 rmoveto (aba ) show
showpage
```

(b)

```
%!PS-Adobe-3.0 EPSF-3.0
%%Creator: Dr David Bainbridge
%%Title: Welcome example
%%BoundingBox: 0 0 350 35
%%DocumentFonts: Helvetica
%%EndComments
/Helvetica findfont
14 scalefont
setfont
10 10 moveto
(Welcome ) show
(Haere mai ) show
(Wilkommen ) show
(Bienvenue ) show
(Akw) show 2 0 rmoveto (\310) show -6 0 rmoveto (aba ) show
showpage
```

(c)

Figure 4.9 (a) Result of executing a PostScript program; (b) the PostScript program; (c) Encapsulated PostScript version; (d) PDF version; (e) network of objects in the PDF version; (f) RTF specification of the same document. (continued on the following pages)

ever-changing face of computing technology. To help resolve the tension, *levels* of PostScript are defined. The conformance level of a file is encoded in its first line, as can been seen in Figure 4.9b (*PS-Adobe-3.0* means Level 3 PostScript). Care is taken to ensure that levels are backward compatible.

What we have described so far is basic Level 1 PostScript. Level 2 includes

- improved virtual memory management
- device-independent color
- composite fonts
- filters

```
%PDF-1.3                              5 0 obj
1 0 obj                               [ /PDF /Text ]
<< /Type /Catalog                     endobj
   /Pages 2 0 R
>>                                    6 0 obj
endobj                                << /Type /Font
                                         /Subtype /Type1
2 0 obj                                  /Name /F1
<< /Type /Pages                          /BaseFont /Helvetica
   /Kids [3 0 R]                          /Encoding /WinAnsiEncoding
   /Count 1                           >>
>>                                    endobj
endobj
                                      xref
3 0 obj                               0 7
<< /Type /Page                        0000000000 65535 f
   /Parent 2 0 R                      0000000009 00000 n
   /MediaBox [0 0 612 792]            0000000062 00000 n
   /Contents 4 0 R                    0000000126 00000 n
   /Resources << /ProcSet 5 0 R       0000000311 00000 n
                 /Font << /F1 6 0 R >> 0000000480 00000 n
              >>                      0000000511 00000 n
>>
endobj                                trailer
                                      << /Size 7
4 0 obj                                  /Root 1 0 R
<< /Length 118 >>                     >>
stream                                startxref
BT                                    631
  /F1 14 Tf                           %%EOF
  10 10 Td
  (Welcome ) Tj
  (Haere mai ) Tj
  (Wilkommen ) Tj
  (Bienvenue ) Tj
  (Akw\344ba ) Tj
ET
endstream
endobj
```

(d)

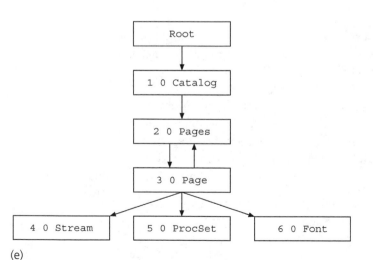

(e)

Figure 4.9 (continued)

```
{\rtf1\ansi\deff0{\fonttbl{\f0\froman Times;}{\f1\fswiss Helvetica;}}
{\info{\title Welcome example}{\creatim\yr2001\mo8\dy10}{\nofpages1}
}\pard\plain\f1\fs28\uc0
Welcome
 Haere mai
 Wilkommen
 Bienvenue
 Akw\u228ba
\par}
```

(f)

Figure 4.9 (continued)

The virtual memory enhancements use whatever memory space is available more efficiently, which is advantageous because PostScript printers sometimes run out of memory when processing certain documents. Composite fonts, which significantly help internationalization, are described below. Filters provide built-in support for compression, decompression, and other common ways of encoding information.

Level 2 was announced in 1991, six years after PostScript's original introduction. The additions were quite substantial, and it was a long time before it became widely adopted. Level 3 (sometimes called PostScript 3) was introduced in 1998. Its additions are minor by comparison, and include

- more fonts, and provision for describing them more concisely
- improved color control, and smoother shading
- advanced processing methods that accelerate rendering

Document structuring conventions

While PostScript per se does not enforce an overall structure to a document, applications can take advantage of a prescribed set of rules known as the *document structuring conventions* (DSC). These divide documents into three sections: a prologue, document pages, and a trailer. The divisions are expressed as PostScript "comments." For example, *%%BeginProlog* and *%%Trailer* define section boundaries. Other conventions are embedded in the document—such as *%%BoundingBox*, discussed below. There are around 40 document structuring commands in all.

Document structuring commands provide additional information about the document, but do not affect how it is rendered. Since the commands are couched as comments, applications that do not use the conventions are unaffected. However, other applications can take advantage of the information.

Applications such as word processors that generate PostScript commonly use the prologue to define procedures that are helpful in generating document pages, and use the trailer to tidy up any global operations associated with the document or to include information (such as a list of all fonts used) that is not known until the end of the file. This convention enables pages to be expressed more concisely and clearly.

Encapsulated PostScript

Encapsulated PostScript is a variant of PostScript designed for expressing documents of a single page or less. It is widely used to incorporate artwork created using one software application, such as a drawing package, into a larger document, such as a report being composed in a word processor. Encapsulated PostScript is built on top of the document structuring conventions.

Figure 4.9c shows the *Welcome* example expressed in Encapsulated PostScript. The first line is augmented to reflect this (the encapsulation convention has levels as well; this is EPSF-3.0). The *%%BoundingBox* command that specifies the drawing size is mandatory in Encapsulated PostScript. Calculated in points from the origin (bottom left-hand corner), it defines the smallest rectangle that entirely encloses the marks constituting the rendered picture. The rectangle is specified by four numbers: the first pair give the coordinates of the lower left corner, and the second pair define the upper right corner. Figure 4.9c also shows document structuring commands for the creator of the document (more commonly it gives the name and version number of the software application that generated the file), a suitable title for it, and a list of fonts used (in this case just Helvetica).

An Encapsulated PostScript file—which contains raw PostScript along with a few special comments—can be embedded verbatim, header and all, into a context that is also PostScript. For this to work properly, operators that affect the global state of the rendering process must be avoided. These restrictions are listed in the specification for Encapsulated PostScript, and in practice are not unduly limiting.

Fonts

PostScript supports two broad categories of fonts: base and composite fonts. Base fonts accommodate alphabets up to 256 characters. Composite fonts extend the character set beyond this point and also permit several glyphs to be combined into a single composite character—making them suitable for languages with large alphabets, such as Chinese, and with frequent character combinations, such as Korean.

In the *Welcome* example of Figure 4.9b, the *findfont* operator is used to set the font to Helvetica. This searches PostScript's font directory for the named font (*/Helvetica*), returning a *font dictionary* that contains all the information necessary to render characters in that font. Most PostScript products have a built-in font directory with descriptions of 13 standard fonts from the Times, Helvetica, Courier, and Symbol families. Helvetica is an example of a base font format.

The execution of a *show* command such as (*Welcome*) *show* takes place in two steps. For each character, its numeric value (0–255) is used to access an array known as the *encoding vector*. This provides a name such as /W (or, for nonalphabetic characters, a name such as /hyphen). This name is then used to look up a glyph description in a subsidiary dictionary. A *name* is one of the basic PostScript types: it is a label that binds itself to an object. The act of executing the glyph object renders the required mark. The font dictionary is a top-level object that binds these operations together.

In addition to the built-in font directory, PostScript lets you provide your own graphical descriptions for the glyphs, which are then embedded in the PostScript file. You can also change the encoding vector.

Base font formats

The original specification for PostScript included a means for defining typographical fonts. At the time there were no standard formats for describing character forms digitally. PostScript fonts, which were built into the LaserWriter printer in 1985 and subsequently adopted in virtually all typesetting devices, sparked a revolution in printing technology. However, to protect its investment the company that introduced PostScript, Adobe, kept the font specification secret. This spurred Apple to introduce a new font description format six years later, which was subsequently adopted by the Windows operating system. Adobe then published its format.

Level 3 PostScript incorporates both ways of defining fonts. The original method is called Type 1; the rival scheme is TrueType. For example, Times Roman, Helvetica, and Courier are Type 1 fonts, while Times New Roman, Arial, and Courier New are the TrueType equivalents.

Technically the two font description schemes have much in common. Both describe glyphs in terms of the straight lines and curves that make up the outline of the character. This means that standard geometric transformations—translation, scaling, rotation—can be applied to text as well as to graphic primitives. One difference between Type 1 and TrueType is the way in which curves are specified. Both use spline curves, but the former uses a kind of cubic spline called a *Bézier curve* whereas the latter uses a kind of quadratic spline called a *B-spline*. From a user perspective these differences are minimal—but they do create incompatibilities.

Both representations are resolution independent. Characters may be resized by scaling the outlines up or down—although a particular implementation may impose practical upper and lower limits. It is difficult to scale down to very small sizes. When a glyph comprises only a few dots, inconsistencies arise in certain letter features depending on where they are placed on the page, because even though the glyphs are the same size and shape, they sit differently on the pixel grid. For example, the width of letter stems may vary from one instance of a letter to another; worse still, when scaled down key features may disappear altogether.

Both Type 1 and TrueType deal with this problem by putting additional information called *hints* into fonts to make it possible to render small glyphs consistently. However, the way that hints are specified is different in each case. Type 1 fonts give hints for vertical and horizontal features, overshoots, snapping stems to the pixel grid, and so on, and in many cases there is a threshold pixel size at which they are activated. TrueType hints define flexible instructions that can do much more. They give the font producer fine control over what happens when characters are rendered under different conditions. But to use them to full advantage, individual glyphs must be manually coded. This is such a daunting undertaking that, in practice, many fonts omit this level of detail. Of course this does not usually affect printed text because even tiny fonts can be displayed accurately, without hinting, on a 600-dpi device. Hinting is more important for screen displays.

Composite fonts

The essence of composite fonts, which became standard in Level 3 PostScript, boils down to two key concepts. First, instead of mapping character values through a single dictionary as base fonts do, there is now a hierarchy of dictionaries. At its root a composite font dictionary directs character mappings to subsidiary dictionaries. These can either contain base fonts or further composite fonts (up to a depth limit of five).

Second, the *show* operator no longer decodes its argument one byte at a time. Instead a *font number* and *character selector* pair are used. The font number locates a font dictionary within the hierarchy, while the character selector uses the encoding vector stored with that dictionary to select a glyph description name to use when rendering the character. This latter step is analogous to the way base fonts are used.

The arguments of *show* can be decoded in several ways. Options include 16 bits per font number and character selector pair, separated into one byte each (note that this differs from a Unicode representation); or using an escape character to change the current font dictionary. The method used is determined by a value in the root dictionary.

Compatibility with Unicode

Character-identifier keyed, or *CID-keyed*, fonts provide a newer format designed for use with Unicode. They map multiple byte values to character codes in much the same way that the encoding vector works in base fonts—except that the mapping is not restricted to 256 entries. The CID-keyed font specification is independent of PostScript and can be used in other environments. The data is also external to the document file: font and encoding-vector resources are accessed by reading external files into dictionaries.

OpenType is a new font description that goes beyond the provisions of CID-keyed fonts. It encapsulates Type 1 and TrueType fonts into the same kind of wrapper, yielding a portable, scalable font platform that is backward compatible. The basic approach of CID-keyed fonts is used to map numeric identifiers to character codes. OpenType includes multilingual character sets with full Unicode support, and extended character sets which support small caps, ligatures, and fractions—all within the same font. It includes a way of automatically substituting a single glyph for a given sequence (e.g., the ligature *fi* can be substituted for the sequence *f* followed by *i*) and vice versa. Substitution can be context sensitive. For example, a *swash* letter, which is an ornamental letter—often a decorated italic capital—used to open paragraphs, can be introduced automatically at the beginning of words or lines.

Text extraction

It is useful to be able to extract plain text from PostScript files. To build a full-text index for a digital library, the raw text needs to be available. An approximation to the formatting information may be useful too—perhaps to display HTML versions of documents in a Web browser. For this, structural features such as paragraph boundaries and font characteristics must be identified from PostScript.

Although PostScript allows complete flexibility in how documents are described (for example, the characters do not even have to be in any particular order), actual PostScript documents tend to be more constrained. However, the text they contain is often fragmented and inextricably muddled up with other character strings that do not appear in the output. Figure 4.10 shows an example, along with the text extracted from it. Characters to be placed on the page appear in the PostScript file as parenthesized strings. But font names, file names, and other internal information are represented in the same way—examples can be seen in the first few lines of the figure. Also the division of text into words is not immediately apparent. Spaces are implied by the character positions rather than being present explicitly. Text is written out in fragments, and each parenthetical string sometimes represents only part of a word. Deciding which fragments to concatenate together is difficult. Although heuristics might be devised to cover common cases, they are unlikely to lead to a robust solution that can deal satisfactorily with the wide variety of files found in practice.

This is why text extraction based on scanning a PostScript document for strings of text meets with limited success. It also fails to extract any formatting information. Above all it does not address the fundamental issue that PostScript is a programming language whose output, in principle, cannot be determined merely by scanning the file—for example, in a PostScript document the raw text could be (and often is) compressed, to be decompressed by the interpreter every time the document is displayed. As it happens, this deep-rooted issue leads to a solution that is far more robust than scanning for text, can account for formatting information, and decodes any programmed information.

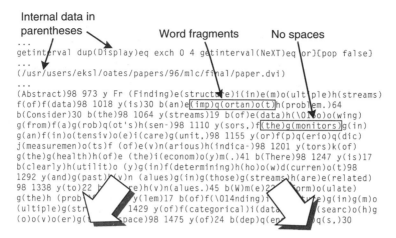

Figure 4.10 A PostScript document and the text extracted from it.

By prepending a PostScript code fragment to a document and then running it through a standard PostScript interpreter, the placement of text characters can be intercepted, producing text in a file rather than pixels on a page. The central trick is to redefine the PostScript *show* operator, which is responsible for placing text on the page. Regardless of how a program is constructed, all printed text passes through this operator (or a variant, as mentioned later). The new code fragment redefines it to write its argument, a text string, to a file instead of rendering it on the screen. Then when the document is executed, a text file is produced instead of the usual physical pages.

A simple text extraction program

The idea can be illustrated by a simple program. Prepending the incantation */show { print } def*, shown in Figure 4.11a, to the document of Figure 4.10 redefines the *show* operator. The effect is to define the name *show* to read *print* instead—and therefore print the characters to a file. The result appears at the right of Figure 4.11a. One problem has been solved: winnowing the text destined for a page from the remainder of the parenthesized text in the original file.

```
/show { print } def
```

Findingstructureinmultiplestreamsofdataisanimportant problem.Considerthestreamsofdataflowingfromarobot' ssensors,themonitorsinanintensivecareunit,orperiodic measurementsofvariousindicatorsofthehealthoftheeco nomy.Thereisclearlyutilityindetermininghowcurrentand pastvaluesinthosestreamsarerelatedtofuturevalues

(a)

```
/show { print ( ) print } def
```

Finding structure in m ultiple streams of data is an imp ortan t problem. Consider the streams of data flo wing from a rob ot's sensors, the monitors in an in tensiv e care unit, or p erio dic measuremen ts of v arious indicators of the health of the econom y . There is clearly utilit y in determining ho w curren t and past v alues in those streams are related to future v alues

(b)

```
/X 0 def

/show {
  currentpoint pop
  X sub 5 gt { ( )  print } if
  dup print
  systemdict /show get exec
  currentpoint pop /X exch def
} def
```

Finding structure in multiple streams of data is an important problem. Consider the streams of data flowing from a robot's sensors, the monitors in an intensive care unit, or periodic measurements of various indicators of the health of the economy. There is clearly utility in determining how current and past values in those streams are related to future values.

(c)

```
/X 0 def

/protoshow {
  currentpoint pop
  X sub 5 gt { ( )  print } if
  dup print
  systemdict exch get exec
  currentpoint pop /X exch def
} def
```

```
/show        { /show      protoshow } def
/kshow       { /kshow     protoshow } def
/widthshow   { /widthshow protoshow } def
/ashow       { /ashow     protoshow } def
/awidthshow  { /awidthshow protoshow } def
```

(d)

Figure 4.11 Extracting text from PostScript: (a) printing all fragments rendered by *show*; (b) putting spaces between every pair of fragments; (c) putting spaces between fragments with a separation of at least five points; (d) catering for variants of the *show* operator.

The problem of identifying whole words from fragments must still be addressed, for the text in Figure 4.11a contains no spaces. Printing a space between each fragment yields the text in Figure 4.11b. Spaces do appear between each word, but they also appear within words, such as *m ultiple* and *imp ortan t.*

To put spaces in their proper places, it is necessary to consider where fragments are placed on the page. Between adjacent characters, the print position moves only a short distance from one fragment to the next, whereas if a space intervenes the distance is larger. An appropriate threshold will depend on the type size and should be chosen accordingly; however, a fixed value will be used for illustration.

The program fragment in Figure 4.11c implements this modification. The symbol X records the horizontal coordinate of the right-hand side of the previous fragment. The new *show* procedure obtains the current x coordinate using the *currentpoint* operator (the *pop* discards the y coordinate) and subtracts the previous coordinate held in X. If the difference exceeds a preset threshold—in this case five points—a space is printed. Then the fragment itself is printed.

In order to record the new x coordinate, the fragment must actually be rendered. Unfortunately Figures 4.11a and b have suppressed rendering by redefining the *show* operator. The line *systemdict /show get exec* retrieves the original definition of *show* from the system dictionary and executes it with the original string as argument. This renders the text and updates the current point, which is recorded in X on the next line. Executing the original *show* operator provides a foolproof way of updating coordinates exactly as they are when the text is rendered. This new procedure produces the text at the right of Figure 4.11c, in which all words are segmented correctly. Line breaks are detected by analyzing vertical coordinates in the same way and comparing the difference with another fixed threshold.

PostScript (to be precise, Level 1 PostScript) has four variants of the *show* command—*ashow*, *widthshow*, *awidthshow*, and *kshow*—and they should all be treated similarly. In Figure 4.11d a procedure is defined to do the work. It is called with two arguments, the text string and the name of the appropriate *show* variant. Just before it returns, the code for the appropriate command is located in the system dictionary and executed.

Improving the output

Notwithstanding the use of fixed thresholds for word and line breaks, this scheme is quite effective at extracting text from many PostScript documents. However, several enhancements can be made to improve the quality of the output. First, fixed thresholds fail when the text is printed in an unusually large or small font. With large fonts, interfragment gaps are mistakenly identified as interword gaps, and words break up. With small ones, interword gaps are mistaken for interfragment gaps, and words run together.

To solve this problem the word-space threshold can be expressed as a fraction of the average character width. This is calculated for the fragments on each side of the break by dividing the rendered width of the fragment by the number of characters in it. As a rule of thumb, the interword threshold should be about 30 percent greater than the average character width.

Second, line breaks in PostScript documents are designed for typeset text with proportionally spaced fonts. The corresponding lines of plain text are rarely all of the same length. Moreover, the best line wrapping often depends on context—such as the width of the window that displays the text. Paragraph breaks, on the other hand, have significance in terms of document content and should be preserved.

Line and paragraph breaks can be distinguished in two ways. Usually paragraphs are separated by more vertical space than lines are. In this case any advance that exceeds the nominal line space can be treated as a paragraph break. The nominal spacing can be taken as the most common nontrivial change in y coordinate throughout the document.

Sometimes paragraphs are distinguished by horizontal indentation rather than by vertical spacing. Treating indented lines as paragraph breaks sometimes fails, however—for example, quotations and bulleted text are often indented too. Additional heuristics are needed to detect these cases. For example, an indented line may open a new paragraph if it starts with a capital letter; if its right margin and the right margin of the following line are at about the same place; and if the following line is not also indented. Although not infallible, these rules work reasonably well in practice.

Third, more complex processing is needed to deal properly with different fonts. For instance, ligatures, bullets, and printer's quotes (" ' ' " rather than ' ") are non-ASCII values that can be recognized and mapped appropriately. Mathematical formulas with complex sub-line spacing, Greek letters, and special mathematical symbols are difficult to deal with satisfactorily. A simple dodge is to flag unknown characters with a question mark because there is no truly satisfactory plain-text representation for mathematics.

Fourth, when documents are justified to a fixed right margin, words are often hyphenated. Output will be improved if this process is reversed. But simply deleting hyphens from the end of lines inadvertently removes hyphens from compound words that happen to straddle line breaks.

Finally, printed pages often appear in reverse order. This is for mechanical convenience: when pages are placed face up on the output tray, the first one produced should be the last page of the document. PostScript's document structuring conventions include a way of specifying page ordering, but it is often not followed in actual document files.

Of several possible heuristics for detecting page order, a robust one is to extract numbers from the text adjacent to page breaks. These are usually page numbers, and you can tell that a document is reversed because they decrease rather than increase. Even if some numbers in the text are erroneously identified as page numbers, the method is quite reliable if the final decision is based on the overall majority.

Using PostScript in a digital library

Digital libraries are often built from PostScript source documents. PostScript's ability to display print-quality documents using a variety of fonts and graphics on virtually any computer platform is a wonderful feature. Because the files are 7-bit ASCII, they can be distributed electronically using lowest-common-denominator e-mail protocols. And although PostScript predates Unicode, characters from different character sets can be freely mixed because documents can contain many different fonts. Embedding fonts in documents makes them faithfully reproducible even when sent to printers and computer systems that lack the necessary fonts.

The fact that PostScript is a programming language, however, introduces problems that are not normally associated with documents. A document is a program. And programs crash for a variety of obscure reasons, leaving the user with at best an incomplete document and no clear recovery options. Although PostScript is supposed to be portable, in practice people often experience difficulty with printing—particularly on different computer platforms. When a document crashes it does not necessarily mean that the file is corrupt. Just as subtle differences occur among compilers for high-level languages such as C++, the behavior of PostScript interpreters can differ in unpredictable ways. Life was simpler in the early days, when there was one level of Postscript and a small set of different interpreters. Now with a proliferation of PostScript support, any laxity in the code an application generates may not surface locally, but instead cause unpredictable problems at a different time on a computer far away.

Trouble often surfaces as a *stack overflow* or *stack underflow* error. Overflow means that the available memory has been exceeded on the particular machine that is executing the document. Underflow occurs when an insufficient number of elements are left on the stack to satisfy the operator currently being executed. For example, if the stack contains a single value when the *add* operator is issued, a stack underflow error occurs. Other complications can be triggered by conflicting definitions of what a "new-line" character means on a given operating system—something we have already encountered with plain text files. Even though PostScript classes both the carriage-return and line-feed characters (*CR* and *LF* in Table 4.1) as white space (along with "tab" and "space," *HT* and *SPAC*, respectively), not all interpreters honor this.

PostScript versions of word-processor files are invariably far larger than the native format, particularly when they include uncompressed sampled images.

Level 1 does not explicitly provide compressed data formats. However, PostScript is a programming language and so this ability can be programmed in. A document can incorporate compressed data so long as it also includes a decompression routine that is called whenever the compressed data is handled. This keeps image data compact, yet retains Level 1 compatibility. Drawbacks are that every document duplicates the decompression program, and decompression is slow because it is performed by an interpreted program rather than a precompiled one. These are not usually serious. When the document is displayed online, only the current page's images need be decompressed, and when it is printed, decompression is quick compared with the physical printing time. Note that digital library repositories commonly include legacy documents in Level 1 PostScript.

The ideas behind PostScript make it attractive for digital libraries. However, there are caveats. First, it was not designed for online display. Second, because documents are programs, they do not necessarily produce the same result when run on different interpreters. Third, if advantage is taken of additions and upgrades, such as those embodied in comments, encapsulated PostScript, and higher levels of PostScript, digital library users must upgrade their viewing software accordingly—or more likely some will encounter mysterious errors when viewing certain documents. Fourth, extracting text for indexing purposes is not trivial, and the problem is compounded by international character sets and creative typography.

Portable Document Format: PDF

PDF, for Portable Document Format, is a page description language that arose out of PostScript and addresses many of its shortcomings. It has precisely the same imaging model. Page-based, it paints sequences of graphical primitives, modified by transformations and clipping. It has the same graphical shapes—lines, curves, text, and sampled images. Again text and images receive special attention, as befits their leading role in documents. The concept of *current path*, stroked or filled, also recurs. PDF is device independent, and expressed in ASCII.

There are two major differences. First, PDF is not a full-scale programming language. In reality, as we have seen, this feature limits PostScript's portability. Gone are procedures, variables, and control structures. Features such as compression and encryption are built in—for there is no opportunity to program them. Second, PDF includes new features for interactive display. The overall file structure is imposed rather than being embodied in document structuring conventions as in PostScript. This provides random access to pages, hierarchically structured content, and navigation within a document. Also, hyperlinks are supported.

There are many less significant differences. Operators are still postfix—that is, they come after their arguments—but their names are shorter and more cryptic, often only one letter such as *S* for stroke and *f* for fill. To avoid confusion among the different conventions of different operating systems, the nature and use of white space is carefully specified. PDF files include byte offsets to other parts of the file and are always generated by software applications rather than being written by hand as small PostScript programs occasionally are.

Inside a PDF file

Figure 4.9d is a PDF file that produces an exact replica of Figure 4.9a. The first line encodes the type and version as a comment, in the same way that PostScript does. Five lines near the end of the first column specify the text *Welcome* in several languages. The glyph *ä* is generated as the character *\344* in the Windows extended 8-bit character set (selected by the line starting */Encoding* in the second column), and *Tj* is equivalent to PostScript's *show*. Beyond these similarities, the PDF syntax is far removed from its PostScript counterpart.

PDF files split into four sections: header, objects, cross-references, and trailer. The header is the first line of Figure 4.9d. The object section follows and accounts for most of the file. Here it comprises a sequence of six objects in the form *<num> <num> obj . . . endobj*; these define a graph structure (explained below). Then follows the cross-reference section, with numbers (eight lines of them) that give the position of each object in the file as a byte offset from the beginning. The first line says how many entries there are; subsequent ones provide the lookup information (we expand on this later). Finally comes the trailer, which specifies the root of the graph structure, followed by the byte offset of the beginning of the cross-reference section.

The object section in Figure 4.9d defines the graph structure in Figure 4.9e. The root points to a *Catalog* object (number 1), which in turn points to a *Pages* object, which points to (in this case) a single *Page* object. The *Page* object (number 3) contains a pointer back to its parent. Its definition in Figure 4.9d also includes pointers to *Contents*, which in this case is a *Stream* object that produces the actual text, and two *Resources*, one of which (*Font*, object 6) selects a particular font and size (14-point Helvetica), while the other (*ProcSet*, object 5) is an array called the *procedure set* array that is used when the document is printed.

A rendered document is the result of traversing this network of objects. Only one of the six objects in Figure 4.9d generates actual marks on the page (object 4, *stream*). Every object has a unique numeric identifier within the file (the first of the *<num>* fields). Statements such as *5 0 R* (occurring in object 3) define references to other objects—object 5 in this case. The 0 that follows each object number is its *generation number*. Applications that allow documents to be updated incrementally alter this number when defining new versions of objects.

Object networks are hierarchical graph structures that reflect the nature of documents. Of course they are generally far more complex than the simple example in Figure 4.9e. Most documents are composed of pages; many pages have a header, the main text, and a footer; documents often include nested sections. The physical page structure and the logical section structure usually represent parallel hierarchical structures, and the object network is specifically designed for describing such structures—indeed, any number of parallel structures can be built. These object networks are quite different from the linear interpretation sequence of PostScript programs. They save space by eliminating duplication (of headers and footers, for example). But most importantly they support the development of online reading aids that navigate around the structure and display appropriate parts of it, as described in the next subsection.

The network's root is specified in the trailer section. The cross-reference section provides random access to all objects. Objects are numbered from zero upward (some, such as object 0, may not be specified in the object section). The cross-reference section includes one line for each, giving the byte offset of its beginning, the generation number, and its status (*n* means it is in use, *f* means it is free). Object 0 is always free and has a generation number of 65,536. Each line in the cross-reference section is padded to exactly 20 bytes with leading zeros.

To render a PDF document you start at the very end. PDF files always end with *%%EOF*—otherwise they are malformed and an error is issued. The preceding *startxref* statement gives the byte offset of the cross-reference section, which shows where each object begins. The *trailer* statement specifies the root node.

The example in Figure 4.9d contains various data types: *number* (integer or real), *string* (array of unsigned 8-bit values), *name, array, dictionary,* and *stream.* All but the last have their origin in PostScript. A dictionary is delimited by double angle brackets, <<...>>—a notational convenience that was introduced in PostScript Level 2. The *stream* type specifies a "raw" data section delimited by *stream . . . endstream.* It includes a dictionary (delimited by angle brackets in object 4 of Figure 4.9d) that contains associated elements. The preceding */Length* gives the length of the raw data, 118 bytes. Optional elements that perform processing operations on the stream may also be included—*/Filter,* for example, specifies how to decode it.

PDF has types for *Boolean, date,* and specialized composite types such as *rectangle*—an array of four numbers. There is a *text* type that contains 16-bit unsigned values that can be used for UTF-16 text, although non-Unicode extensions are also supported.

Features of PDF

The PDF object network supports a variety of different browsing features. Figure 4.12 shows a document—which is in fact the language reference manual—displayed using the Acrobat PDF reader. The navigation panel on the left presents a hierarchical structure of section headings known as *bookmarks,* which

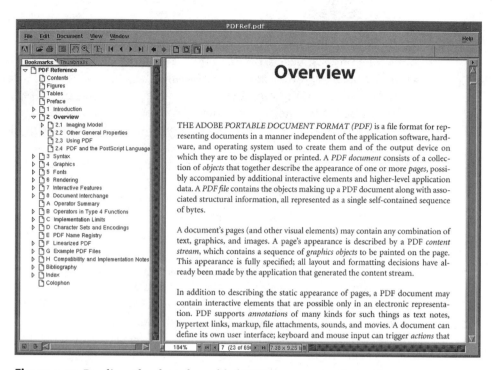

Figure 4.12 Reading a bookmark-enabled PDF document with Acrobat.

the user can expand and contract at will and use to bring up particular sections of the document in the main panel. This simply corresponds to displaying different parts of the object network tree illustrated in Figure 4.9e, at different levels of detail. Bookmarks are implemented using the PDF object type Outline.

Thumbnail pictures of each page can also be included in this panel. These images can be embedded in the PDF file at the time it is created, by creating new objects and linking them into the network appropriately. Some PDF readers are capable of generating thumbnail images on the fly even if they are not explicitly included in the PDF file. Hyperlinks can be placed in the main text so that you can jump from one document to another. For each navigational feature, corresponding objects must appear in the PDF network, such as the Outline objects mentioned earlier that represent bookmarks.

PDF has a *searchable image* option that is particularly relevant to collections derived from paper documents. Using it, invisible characters can be overlaid on top of an image. Highlighting and searching operations utilize the hidden information, but the visual appearance is that of the image. Using this option a PDF document can comprise the original scanned page, backed up by text generated by optical character recognition. Errors in the text do not mar the document's appearance at all. The overall result combines the accuracy of image display with the flexibility of textual operations such as searching and highlighting. In terms of implementation, PDF files containing searchable images are typically generated as an output option by OCR programs. They specify each entire page as a single image, linked into the object network in such a way that it is displayed as a background to the text of the page.

There are many other interactive features. PDF provides a means of annotation that includes video and audio as well as text. Actions can be specified that launch an application. Forms can be defined for gathering fielded information. PDF has moved a long way from its origins in document printing, and its interactive capabilities rival those of HTML.

Compression is an integral part of the language and is more convenient to use than the piecemeal development found in PostScript. It can be applied to individual stream components and helps reduce overall storage requirements and minimize download times—important factors for a digital library.

Linearized PDF

The regular PDF file structure makes it impossible to display the opening pages of documents until the complete file has been received. Even with compression, large documents can take a long time to arrive. *Linearization* is an extension that allows parts of the document to be shown before downloading finishes. Linearized PDF documents obey rules governing object order but include more than one cross-reference section.

The integrity of the PDF format is maintained: any PDF viewer can display linearized documents. However, applications can take advantage of the additional information to produce pages faster. The display order can be tailored to the document—the first pages displayed are not necessarily the document's opening pages, and images can be deferred to later.

PDF and PostScript

PDF is a sophisticated document description language that was developed by Adobe, the same company that developed PostScript, as a successor to it. PDF addresses various serious deficiencies that had arisen with PostScript, principally lack of portability. While PostScript is really a programming language, PDF is a format, and this bestows the advantage of increased robustness in rendering. Also, PostScript has a reputation for verbosity that PDF has avoided (PostScript now incorporates compression, but not all software uses it).

PDF incorporates additional features that support online display. Its design draws on expertise that ranges from traditional printing right through to hypertext and structured document display. PDF is a complex format that presents challenging programming problems. However, a wide selection of software tools is readily available.

There are utilities that convert between PostScript and PDF. Because they share the same imaging model, the documents' printed forms are equivalent. PDF is not a full programming language, however, so when converting Post-Script to it, loops and other constructs must be explicitly unwound. In PostScript, PDF's interactive features are lost.

Today PDF is the format of choice for presenting finished documents online. But PostScript is pervasive. Any application that can print a document can save it as a PostScript file, whereas standard desktop environments lack software to generate PDF. However, the world is changing: the Apple Macintosh computer now displays all online graphics as PDF. (Recall the parallel, mentioned earlier, of a 1980s operating system that controlled the display entirely from PostScript.)

From a digital library perspective, collections frequently contain a mixture of PostScript and PDF documents. The problems of extracting text for indexing purposes are similar and can be solved in the same way. Some software viewers can display both formats.

4.4 Word-processor documents

When word processors store documents, they store them in ways that are specifically designed to allow the documents to be edited. There are numerous different formats: we will take Microsoft Word—currently a leading product—as an illustrative example. This has two different styles of document format: Rich Text Format (RTF), a widely published specification dating from 1987, and a proprietary internal format that we call simply *native Word*. As an example of a completely different style of document description language, we end this section by describing LaTeX, which is widely used in the scientific and mathematical community. LaTeX is very flexible and is capable of producing documents of excellent quality; however, it has the reputation of being rather difficult to learn and is unsuitable for casual use.

RTF is designed to allow word-processor documents to be transferred between applications. Like PostScript and PDF, it uses ASCII text to describe page-based documents that contain a mixture of formatted text and graphics. Unlike them, it is specifically designed to support the editing features we have come to expect in word processors. For example, when Word reads an RTF document generated by WordPerfect or PowerPoint (or vice versa), the file must contain enough information to allow the program to edit the text, change the typesetting, and adjust the pictures and tables. This contrasts with PostScript, where the typography of the document might as well be engraved on one of those Chinese stone tablets. PDF, as we have seen, supports limited forms of editing—adding annotations or page numbers, for example—but is not designed to have anything like the flexibility of RTF.

Many online documents are in native Word format. Because it is a binary format, it is far more compact than RTF—which translates to faster download and display times. Native Word also supports a wider range of features and is tightly coupled with Internet Explorer, Microsoft's Web browser, so that a Web-based digital library using Word documents can present a seamless interface. But there are disadvantages. Non-Microsoft communities may be locked out of digital libraries unless other formats are offered. Although documents can be converted to forms such as HTML using scriptable utilities, Word's proprietary nature makes this a challenging task—and it is hard to keep up to date. Even Microsoft products sometimes can't read Word documents properly. Native Word is really a family of formats rather than a single one and has nasty legacy problems.

Rich Text Format

Figure 4.9f recasts the *Welcome* example in minimal RTF form. It renders the same text in the same font and size as the PostScript and PDF versions, although it relies on defaults for such things as page margins, line spacing, and foreground and background colors.

RTF uses the backslash (\) to denote the start of formatting commands. Commands contain letters only, so when a number (positive or negative) occurs, it is interpreted as a command parameter—thus \yr2001 invokes the \yr command with the value 2001. The command name can also be delimited by a single space, and any symbols that follow—even subsequent spaces—are part of the parameter. For example, {\title Welcome example} is a \title command with the parameter *Welcome example*.

Braces {...} group together logical units, which can themselves contain further groups. This allows hierarchical structure and permits the effects of formatting instructions to be lexically scoped. An inheritance mechanism is used. For example, if a formatting instruction is not explicitly specified at the current level of the hierarchy, a value that is specified at a higher level will be used instead.

Line 1 of Figure 4.9f gives an RTF header and specifies the character encoding (ANSI 7-bit ASCII), default font number (0), and a series of fonts that can be used in the document's body. The remaining lines represent the document's content, including some basic metadata. On line 3, in preparation for generating text, \pard sets the paragraph mode to its default, while \plain initializes the font character properties. Next, \f1 makes entry 1 in the font table—which was set to Helvetica in the header—the currently active font. This overrides the default, set up in our example to be font entry 0 (Times Roman). Following this, the command \fs28—whose units are measured in half points—sets the character size to 14 points.

Text that appears in the body of an RTF file but is not a command parameter is part of the document content and is rendered accordingly. Thus lines 4 through 8 produce the greeting in several languages. Characters outside the 7-bit ASCII range are accessed using backslash commands. Unicode is specified by \u: here we see it used to specify the decimal value 228, which is LATIN SMALL LETTER A WITH DIAERESIS, the fourth letter of *Akwäba*.

This is a small example. Real documents have headers with more controlling parameters, and the body is far larger. Even so, it is enough to illustrate that RTF, unlike PostScript, is not intended to be laid out visually. Rather it is designed to make it easy to write software tools that parse document files quickly and efficiently.

RTF has evolved through many revisions—over the years its specification has grown from 34 pages to over 240. Additions are backward compatible to avoid disturbing existing files. In Figure 4.9f's opening line, the numeric parameter of \rtf1 gives the version number, 1. The format has grown rapidly because, as well as keeping up with developments such as Unicode in the print world, it must support an ever-expanding set of word-processor features, a trend that continues.

Basic types

Now we flesh out some of the details. While RTF's basic syntax has not changed since its inception, the command repertoire continues to grow. There are five basic types of command: *flag*, *toggle*, *value*, *destination*, and *symbol*.

A *flag* command has no argument. (If present, arguments are ignored.) One example is \box, which generates a border around the current paragraph; another is \pard, which—as we have seen—sets the paragraph mode to its default. A *toggle* command has two states. No argument (or any nonzero value) turns it on; zero turns it off. For example, \b and \b0 switch boldface on and off, respectively. A *value* command sets a variable to the value of the argument. The \deff0 in Figure 4.9f is a value command that sets the default font to entry zero in the font table.

A *destination* command has a text parameter. That text may be used elsewhere, at a different destination (hence the command's name)—or not at all. For example, text given to the \footnote command appears at the bottom of the page; the argument supplied to \author defines metadata which does not actually appear in the document. Destination commands must be grouped in braces with their parameter—which might itself be a group. Both commands specified in {\info{\title Welcome example}} are destination commands.

A *symbol* command represents a single character. For instance, \bullet generates the bullet symbol (●), and \{ and \} produce braces, escaping their special grouping property in RTF.

Backward compatibility

An important symbol command that was built in from the beginning is *. Placed in front of any destination command, it signals that if the command is unrecognized it should be ignored. The aim is to maintain backward compatibility with old RTF applications.

For instance, there was no Unicode when RTF was born. An old application would choke on the *Welcome* example of Figure 4.9f because the \u command is a recent addition. In fact it would ignore it, producing *Akwba*—not a good approximation.

The * command provides a better solution. As well as \u, two further new commands are added for Unicode support. Rather than generating *Akwäba* by writing *Akw\u228ba*—which works correctly if Unicode support is present but produces *Akwba* otherwise—one instead writes

```
{\upr{Akwaba}{\*\ud{Akw\u228ba}}}
```

The actions performed by the two new commands \upr and \ud are very simple, but before revealing what they are, consider the effect of this command sequence on an older RTF reader that does not know about them. Unknown commands are ignored but their text arguments are printed, so when the reader works its way through the two destination commands, the first generates the text *Akwaba* while the second is ignored because it starts with *. This text is a far more satisfactory approximation than *Akwba*. Now consider the action of a current reader that knows how to process these directives. The first directive, \upr, ignores its first argument and processes the second one. The second directive, \ud, just outputs its argument—it is really a null operator and is only present to satisfy the constraint that * is followed by a destination command.

File structure

Figure 4.13 shows the structure of an RTF file. Braces enclose the entire description, which is divided into two parts: header followed by body. We have already encountered some header components; there are many others. A commonly used construct is *table*, which reserves space and initializes data—the font table, for example. The *table* command takes a sequence of items—each a group in its own right, or separated using a delimiter such as semicolon—and stores the information away so that other parts of the document can access it. A variety of techniques are deployed to retrieve the information. In a delimited list an increasing sequence of numeric values is implied for storage, while other tables permit each item to designate its numeric label, and still others support textual labels.

The first command in the header must be \rtf, which encodes the version number followed by the character set used in the file. The default is ASCII, but other encoding schemes can be used. Next, font data is initialized. There are two parts: the default font number (optional) and the font table (mandatory). Both appear in the *Welcome* example, although the font table has many more capabilities, including the ability to embed fonts.

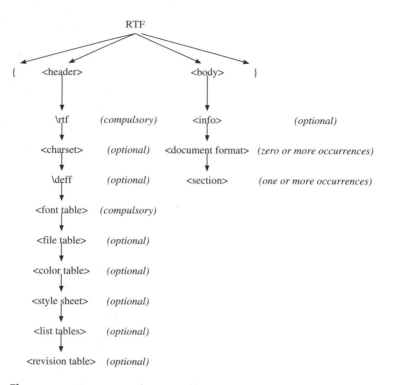

Figure 4.13 Structure of an RTF file.

The remaining tables are optional. The file table is a mechanism for naming related files and is only used when the document consists of subdocuments in separate files. The color table comprises *red*, *green*, and *blue* value commands, which can then be used to select foreground and background colors through commands such as \cf1 and \cb2, respectively. The style sheet is also a form of table. It corresponds to the notion of *styles* in word processing. Each item specifies a collection of character, paragraph, and section formatting. Items can be labeled; they may define a new style or augment an existing one. When specified in the document body, the appropriate formatting instructions are brought to the fore. List tables provide a mechanism for bulleted and enumerated lists (which can be hierarchically nested). Revision tables provide a way of tracking revisions of a document by multiple authors.

The document body contains three parts, shown in Figure 4.13: top-level information, document formatting, and a sequence of sections (there must be at least one). It begins with an optional information group that specifies document-level metadata—in our example this was used to specify the title. There are over 20 fields, among them author, organization, keywords, subject, version number, creation time, revision time, last time printed, number of pages, and word count.

Next comes a sequence of formatting commands (also optional). Again there are dozens of possible commands: they govern such things as the direction of the text, how words are hyphenated, whether backups are made automatically, and the default tab size (measured in *twips*, an interestingly named unit that corresponds to one-twentieth of a point).

Finally, in the last part of the body the document text is specified. Even here the actual text is surrounded by multiple layers of structure. First the document can be split into a series of sections, each of which consists of paragraphs (at least one). *Sections* here correspond to section breaks inserted by an author using, for instance, Microsoft Word. Sections and paragraphs can both begin with formatting instructions. For sections, these control such things as the number and size of columns on a page, page layout, page numbering, borders, and text flow and are followed by commands that specify headers and footers. For paragraphs, they include tab settings, revision marks, indenting, spacing, borders, shading, text wrapping, and so forth. Eventually you get down to the actual text. Further formatting instructions can be interspersed to change such things as the active font size.

Other features

So far we have described how RTF describes typographic text, based around the structure of sections and paragraphs. There are many other features. Different sampled image formats are supported, including open standards such as JPEG and PNG (described in Section 4.5) and proprietary formats such as Microsoft's Windows Metafile and Macintosh's PICT. The raw image data can be specified in hexadecimal using plain text (the default) or as raw binary. In the latter case care must be taken when transferring the file between operating systems (recall the discussion of FTP's new-line handling in Section 4.2).

Many word processors incorporate a built-in tool that draws lines, boxes, arcs, splines, filled-in shapes, text, and other vector graphic primitives. To support this RTF contains over 100 commands to draw, color, fill, group, and transform such shapes. These resemble the graphical shapes that can be described in PostScript and PDF—not surprisingly, considering that all artwork will ultimately be converted to one of these forms for printing or viewing.

Authors use annotations to add comments to a document. RTF can embed within a paragraph a destination command with two parts: a comment and an identifying label (typically used to name the person responsible for the annotation).

Field entities introduce dynamically calculated values, interactive features, and other objects requiring interpretation. They are used to embed the current date, current page, mathematical equations, and hyperlinks into a paragraph. They bind a field instruction command together with its most recently calculated value—which provides backup should an application fail to recognize the field. Accompanying parameters influence what information is displayed, and how. Using fields, metadata such as title and author can be associated with a document, and this information is stored in the RTF file in the form of an *\info* command. RTF also supports an index of entries and a table of contents, which are also implemented using the field mechanism.

In a word-processor document, bookmarks are a means of navigation. RTF includes *begin-* and *end-bookmark* commands that mark segments of the text along with text labels, accessible through the word-processing application.

Microsoft has a scheme called *object linking and embedding* (OLE) which places information created by one application within another. For example, an Excel document can be incorporated into a Word file and still function as a spreadsheet. RTF calls such entities *objects* and provides commands that wrap the data with basic information such as the object's width and height and whether it is linked or embedded.

Commands in the document format section control the overall formatting of footnotes (which in RTF terminology includes endnotes). The *\footnote* command is then used within paragraphs to provide a footnote mark and the accompanying text.

RTF tables are produced by commands that define cells, rows, and the table itself. Formatting commands control each component's dimensions and govern how text items are displayed—pad all cells by 20 twips, set this cell's width to 720 twips and center its text, and so on. However, there is a twist. While the other entities described earlier are embedded within a paragraph, an RTF table *is* a paragraph and cannot be embedded in one—this definition reflects the practice visible in Word, where inserting a table always introduces a new paragraph.

Use in digital libraries

When building a digital library collection from RTF documents, the format's editable nature is of minor importance. Digital libraries generally deal with completed documents—information that is ready to be shared with others. What matters is how to index the text and display the document.

To extract rudimentary text from an RTF file, simply ignore the backslash commands. The quality of the output improves if other factors, such as the character set, are taken into account. Ultimately full-text extraction involves parsing the file. RTF was designed to be easy to parse. Three golden rules are emphasized in the specification:

- Ignore control words that you don't understand.
- Always understand *.
- Remember that binary data can occur when skipping over information.

RTF files can usually be viewed on Macintosh and Windows computers. For other platforms or for speedier access, you might consider offering documents in a different format. For example, software is available to convert an RTF document to an approximate equivalent in HTML.

Native Word formats

The native Microsoft Word format is proprietary and its details are shrouded in mystery. Although Microsoft has published "as is" their internal technical manual for the Word 97 version, the format continues to evolve. Primarily a binary format, the abstract structures deployed reflect those of RTF. Documents include summary information, font information, style sheets, sections, paragraphs, headers, footers, bookmarks, annotations, footnotes, embedded pictures—the list goes on. The native Word representation provides more functionality than RTF and is therefore more intricate.

A serious complication is that documents can be written to disk in Fast Save mode, which no longer preserves the order of the text. Instead new edits are appended, and whatever program reads the file must reconstruct its current state. If this feature has been used, the header marks the file type as "complex."

Use in digital libraries

To extract text from Word documents for indexing, one solution is to first convert them to RTF, whose format is better described. The Save As option in Microsoft Word does this, and the process can be automated through scripting. (Visual Basic is well suited to this task.) It may be more expeditious to deliver native Word than RTF because it is more compact. However, non-Microsoft users will need a more widely supported option.

Word has a Save As HTML option. While the result displays well in Microsoft's Internet Explorer browser, it is generally less pleasing in other browsers (although it can be improved by performing certain postprocessing operations). Public domain conversion software cannot fully implement the Fast Save format because of lack of documentation and may generate all the text in the file rather than in the final version. The solution is simple: switch this option off and resave all documents (using scripting).

LaTeX format

LaTeX—pronounced *la-tech* or *lay-tech*—takes a different approach to document representation. Word processors present users with a "what you see is what you get" interface that is dedicated specifically to hiding the gory details of internal representation. In contrast, LaTeX documents are expressed in plain ASCII text and contain typed formatting commands: they explicitly and intentionally give the user direct access to all the details of internal representation. Any text editor on any platform can be used to compose a LaTeX document. To view the formatted document, or to generate hard copy, the LaTeX program converts it to a page description language—generally PostScript, but PDF and HTML are possible too.

LaTeX is versatile, flexible, and powerful and can generate documents of exceptionally high typographical quality. The downside, however, is an esoteric syntax that many people find unsettling and hard to learn. It is particularly good for mathematical typesetting and has been adopted enthusiastically by members of the academic scientific and technical community. It is a nonproprietary system, and excellent implementations are freely available.

Figure 4.14 shows a simple example that we use for illustration. Commands in the LaTeX source (Figure 4.14a) are prefixed by the backslash character, \. All LaTeX documents have the same overall structure. They open with *documentclass*, which specifies the document's principal characteristics—whether an article, report, book, and so forth—and gives options such as paper size, base font size, whether single-sided or back-to-back. Then follows a preamble which gives

```
\documentclass[a4paper,11pt]{article}
% This is a comment
\author{I. H. Witten and D. Bainbridge}
\title{Welcome example}
\date{10 August 2001}

\begin{document}

\maketitle
\section{Introduction}

% This is another comment.

Welcome, Haere mai, Wilkommen, Bienvenue, Akw\"aba

\section{Syntax}

LaTeX syntax is a little bit like RTF. It uses the $\backslash$
character for special formatting commands: what you
see as the end result is certainly \emph{not} what you type.  One
important difference from RTF is that it is designed to be generated
by people, not automatically generated by computer.  This means that
a written file can be more liberal with  its  use   of white    space
and this does not affect the overall prose.
If you really need extra spaces you need to do it \ \ like \ \ this.

Special symbols include: \{ \} \% \_ \# \&.
Speech marks are done ``like this''.

A blank line is used to separate paragraphs. It supports all the
usual document structures:
\begin{itemize}
\item bullet point list
\item enumerated list
\item tables and figures
\item drawn graphics
\item \ldots
\end{itemize}
In particular Latex has a powerful maths mode capable of expressing
complex equations. A rudimentary example is:
\begin{displaymath}
   x \geq \sum_{i=0}^{\infty}\frac{1}{i^2\pi}
\end{displaymath}

\end{document}
```

(a)

Welcome example

I. H. Witten and D. Bainbridge

10 August 2001

1 Introduction

Welcome, Haere mai, Wilkommen, Bienvenue, Akwäba

2 Syntax

Latex syntax is little bit like RTF. It uses the \ character for special formatting commands: what you see as the end result is certainly *not* what you type. One important difference from RTF is that it is designed to be generated by people, not automatically generated by computer. This means that a written file can be more liberal with its use of white space and this does not affect the overall prose. If you really need extra spaces you need to do it   like   this.

Special symbols include: { } % _ # &. Speech marks are done "like this".

A blank line is used to separate paragraphs. It supports all the usual document structures:

- bullet point list
- enumerated list
- tables and figures
- drawn graphics
- ...

In particular Latex has a powerful maths mode capable of expressing complex equations. A rudimentary example is:

$$x \geq \sum_{i=0}^{\infty} \frac{1}{i^2 \pi}$$

1

(b)

Figure 4.14 (a) LaTeX source document; (b) printed result.

an opportunity to set up global features before the document content begins. Here "packages" of code can be included. For example, *usepackage*{*epsfig*} allows Encapsulated PostScript files, generally containing artwork, to be included.

The document content lies between *begin*{*document*} and *end*{*document*} commands. This *begin* . . . *end* structure is used to encapsulate many structural items: tables, figures, lists, bibliography, abstract. The list is endless, because LaTeX allows users to define their own commands. Furthermore, you can wrap up useful features and publish them on standard Internet sites so that others can download them and access them through *usepackage*.

When writing a document most text is entered normally. Blank lines are used to separate paragraphs. A few characters carry special meaning and must therefore be "escaped" by a preceding backslash whenever they occur in the text; Figure 4.14 contains examples. Structural commands include *section*, which makes an automatically numbered section heading (*section** omits the numbering, and *subsection*, *subsubsection*, . . . are used for nested headings). Formatting commands include *emph*, which uses italics to emphasize text, and \\", which superimposes an umlaut on the character that follows. There are hundreds more.

The last part of Figure 4.14a specifies a mathematical expression. The *begin*{*displaymath*} and *end*{*displaymath*} commands switch to a mode that is tuned to represent formulas, which enables new commands suited to this purpose. LaTeX contains many shortcuts—for example, math mode can alternatively be entered by using dollar signs as delimiters.

LaTeX and digital libraries

LaTeX is a prime source format for collections of mathematical and scientific documents. Of course these documents can be converted to PostScript or PDF form and handled in this form instead—which allows them to be mixed with documents produced by other means. However, this lowest-common-denominator approach loses structural and metadata information. In the case of LaTeX, such information is signaled by commands for title, abstract, nested section headings, and so on.

If, on the other hand, the source documents are obtained in LaTeX form and parsed to extract such information, the digital library collection will be richer and provide its users with more support. It is easy to parse LaTeX to identify plain text, commands and their arguments, and the document's block structure.

However, there are two problems. The first is that documents no longer occupy a single file—they use external files such as the "packages" mentioned earlier—and even the document content can be split over several files if desired. In practice it can be surprisingly difficult to lay hands on the exact set of supporting files that were intended to be used with a particular document. Experience with writing LaTeX documents is necessary to understand what files need copying and, in the case of extra packages, where they might be installed.

The second problem is that LaTeX is highly customizable, and different authors adapt standard commands and invent new ones as they see fit. This makes it difficult to know in advance which commands to seek to extract standard metadata. However, new commands in LaTeX are composites of existing ones, and one solution is to expand all commands to use only built-in LaTeX features.

4.5 Representing images

An image displayed on the screen or printed to paper is formed by a regular matrix of tightly packed dots, black-and-white or colored, called picture elements or *pixels*. Picture quality is determined by the number of pixels per linear unit, usually expressed in dots per inch (dpi), and the number of bits used to represent each pixel's color—typically 1 bit per pixel for black-and-white, 8 bits for grayscale, and anywhere from 8 to 32 bits for full color. Table 2.4 in Chapter 2 shows the typical resolution of an assortment of devices.

Represented in a computer file in the obvious way, images can occupy an inordinate amount of space. When a standard $8\frac{1}{2} \times 11$ inch page is scanned with 1 bit per pixel at a resolution of 300 dpi, a file of just over 1 Mb is produced. Using 8-bit grayscale yields a 9-Mb file; a 24-bit full-color image occupies 28 Mb. Higher spatial resolution greatly amplifies the problem: a 600-dpi scanner will quadruple file size to over 100 Mb in the full-color case. Even a 100-Gb disk can only hold 1,000 such images.

Images are not normally stored this way on disk. Usually they are compressed, and an important component of an image file format is the particular compression method used. Compression does not necessarily imply degradation in image quality. There are two broad classes: *lossless* and *lossy*. Lossless compression ensures that the decompressed file is exactly the same—bit for bit—as the original. For text compression this technique is always used because even a minor change (such as adding a zero at the end of a sum of money) can have a marked effect on the meaning. Lossy compression does not guarantee that the decompressed file will be exactly the same as the original, but tries to ensure that any errors are hard to discern. Its use is confined to applications where small errors are permissible. Often they are completely imperceptible.

Both kinds of compression are used for images. Scanned images may contain *digitization noise*, artifacts caused by the process of digitization itself. If a compression scheme can eliminate these, it will achieve economy while simultaneously *increasing* image quality. Lossy techniques can be used to obtain remarkably compact representations, particularly for grayscale and photographic images. Depending on the image content, each pixel can sometimes be compressed from its original representation (one to four bytes) to well under a single bit, with a barely perceptible loss of quality. However, there are many situations in which exact representation is deemed essential, and lossless compression must be used. For example, some image data must be certified as an exact copy for medical or legal reasons. Archival storage of historical documents needs to be lossless because the requirements of future scholars cannot be anticipated.

A rudimentary approach to compressing images is to apply a standard utility designed for general-purpose compression of computer files. This treats the file as a one-dimensional sequence of bytes. Compression can be greatly improved by acknowledging the two-dimensional image structure and exploiting spatial characteristics of the data. For example, most images contain large areas whose color and texture is constant or slowly varying, interrupted by regions of abrupt change such as lines or edges. Sophisticated image compression algorithms identify these regions and exploit them for compression.

There are countless image-compression formats, so we restrict attention to a few that are in widespread use today in Web applications and digitization projects. We begin by describing the GIF and PNG formats for lossless images, and then proceed to review JPEG, a comprehensive international standard for high-performance lossy compression of photographic images. Next we discuss an important technique called *progressive refinement* which allows an image to be displayed rough-hewn before it has been received in full. GIF, PNG, and JPEG all have progressive refinement modes.

Lossless image compression: GIF and PNG

Two lossless image compression formats are in widespread use today: the pervasive (but proprietary) Graphics Interchange Format or GIF (usually pronounced *jiff*) and an open standard called Portable Network Graphics or PNG (pronounced *ping*).

GIF: Graphics Interchange Format

Originally specified in 1987, GIF was for many years the most widely used lossless image compression format. It was intended as an exchange medium for graphic images that could be displayed on a variety of graphics hardware platforms and was adopted by CompuServe in order to minimize the time required to download pictures over modem links.

GIF applies to images in which each pixel is represented by eight bits (or less). The code for a pixel can either be a grayscale value in its own right or an index into a table called a *color map* or *color lookup table* that represents a palette of colors for the image. The color map, which is stored with the image, comprises up to 256 different colors (corresponding to 8-bit pixel codes) and contains a full 24-bit color specification for each—eight bits for each of the three primary colors, red, green, and blue. Thus color images are represented in terms of a small palette whose values are chosen from the full range of possible colors. In a subsequent modification to the original GIF specification, one of the 256 colors is reserved as a "transparent" value which lets the background on which the image appears show through.

The GIF format allows the color map to be tailored specifically for each individual image and given along with it as a prefix to the image file. Alternatively a group of images can share the same color map, or the map can be omitted entirely. If present, the color map is uncompressed and occupies up to 768 bytes (3 bytes for each of 256 possible colors).

The sequence of 8-bit pixel values that represent the image content is compressed using a general-purpose scheme called LZW (for Lempel Ziv Welch, the names of its inventors). It was designed for text compression, not images, and exploits the fact that in text many short "phrases" (a few letters, or a few words, long) tend to repeat. However, it does not use a fixed dictionary of phrases like some compression methods. Instead it accumulates a list of phrases as they are encountered in the text file being processed. This strategy of adapting to the particular input file makes it language independent and also means that it can be sensibly applied to files other than text—images, for instance.

GIF files can contain either a single image or a sequence of images. A feature is included to make it easy to skip through the sequence without having to decompress each individual image.

In 1995 Unisys announced that royalties would be levied on programs implementing GIF because of a long-standing patent they held on the LZW compression scheme that lies at its core. This caused widespread dismay because GIF was at the time the primary means of storing images on the World Wide Web. Unisys has since refined its position. Now the vendor of any software product capable of generating GIF files must negotiate a license; users of the product are then free to create all the files they like. As a result of the uncertainty instilled by the original announcements, many developers remain wary of using GIF images. Furthermore, the same patent issue also applies to other formats that incorporate LZW compression, including TIFF, PDF, and PostScript (Level 2 and above).

PNG: Portable Network Graphics

Unisys's surprise announcement catalyzed the development of a new lossless image format, PNG, intended specifically for the public domain. At its core is a general-purpose compression scheme called *gzip*. This is a public-domain open-source compression utility, based on an earlier scheme called LZ77 (after the same Lempel and Ziv cited previously). Gzip performs better than LZW, and PNG usually achieves greater compression than GIF.

A more important factor in compression, however, is the fact that PNG works in a way that acknowledges the two-dimensional structure of the image, rather than treating it simply as a one-dimensional sequence of bytes. It defines a small number of "filters" that can be applied to the pixel values before compression. The *horizontal difference* filter subtracts the previous pixel value from the current one, so that pixel differences are encoded rather than pixel values.[5] The *vertical difference* filter subtracts the value of its neighbor in the row above. The *average difference* filter subtracts the average of the neighbors above and to the left. A further filter performs a slightly more complex operation involving a nonlinear function of the neighboring pixel values.

It is up to the encoder how it uses these filters—or indeed whether it uses them at all. The PNG standard recommends that encoders optimize the filter for each scan-line by trying all possibilities and using a heuristic criterion to select the best, possibly choosing a different filter for each scan-line. Combining this improvement with what is achieved by using gzip instead of LZW, PNG improves compression by around 10 to 30 percent over GIF, depending on the particular image being encoded.

PNG incorporates several other practical improvements. Pixels are not restricted to 8-bit values: they can be drawn from a 256-color palette, but they can alternatively include up to 16 bits of grayscale, or 48 bits of full-color information. There are 256 possible transparency values, so a picture can fade gradually into the background. There is a *gamma correction* feature that helps compensate for differences in how computer monitors interpret color values.

One restriction is that while GIF supports animated images, PNG does not—that is left to a different standard, Multiple-image Network Graphics or MNG (pronounced *ming*). Another caveat is that although all modern Web browsers can display PNG images, ancient ones cannot.

Lossy image compression: JPEG

JPEG, named after the Joint Photographic Experts Group that designed it, is a comprehensive standard intended for representing compressed continuous-tone images. It is general purpose and underlies a gamut of image communication services and image applications—desktop publishing, graphic arts, color facsimile, newspaper wirephoto transmission, and medical imaging—as well as hardware devices such as digital cameras. It is complex, and a great deal of care went into its specification. It has become the standard technique for compressing still images and is universally used for representing photographic images on the Web.

---

5. In fact, the difference operation is applied to individual bytes rather than to pixel values. Each pixel may be represented by more than one byte, in which case the difference is taken between corresponding bytes. All PNG filters operate byte-wise.

JPEG's compression algorithm works well enough to produce excellent image quality at around 1 bit per pixel—the same as an uncompressed bilevel image. This represents impressive compression: grayscale or color images are digitized at anything from 8 to 32 bits per pixel. No lossless image compression scheme could reduce continuous-tone pictures to anything like this level. At this rate some loss is inevitable—you have to accept approximate rather than exact reproduction. Consequently JPEG does not reconstruct the original image exactly (although the standard incorporates an alternative coding method, called JPEG-Lossless, that does). The compression method was selected from among many candidates, based on an assessment of subjective picture quality.

JPEG is divided into a baseline system that offers a limited set of capabilities, and a set of optional extended features. The baseline gives a plain, lossy, high-compression image coding and decoding capability.

The JPEG compression method

Baseline JPEG operates on images in which each pixel is represented by 8 bits. The algorithm encodes color image components independently and is suitable for use with commonly used color spaces such as red, green, and blue (RGB) and CMYK (cyan, magenta, yellow, and black). Higher-resolution options, with more bits per pixel, are among the extended system features.

Figure 4.15 depicts the encoding and decoding processes. Images are first divided into 8×8 pixel blocks. Each block is subjected to a signal-processing technique known as the *discrete cosine transform*, which maps the 64 pixel values into 64 numbers called *spatial frequency coefficients*. The transform is reversible: these 64 coefficients characterize the input block exactly and can be used to faithfully reproduce it. They represent image components at different spatial frequencies.

Transforming one set of 64 numbers into another set of 64 numbers does not seem to achieve much. However, the spatial frequency coefficients are far more suitable for lossy quantization than the pixel values themselves. There are blocks in which sample values vary slowly from point to point—indeed this is the case for most parts of nearly all images, particularly ones of natural objects—and in these the transformation concentrates most of the signal in the lower spatial frequencies. For a typical 8×8 sample block from a typical source image, many of the higher spatial frequencies have zero or negligible amplitude and need not be encoded at all. Some pictures do have significant higher spatial frequencies—for example, ones that contain regular patterns such as brick walls or tiled roofs—but these are the exception rather for the rule, particularly for natural images.

To show what the discrete cosine transform coefficients mean, Figure 4.16 presents an image after each successive coefficient has been calculated. The original 512×512 image has been divided into an 8×8 matrix of blocks, each block having 64×64 pixels. JPEG actually uses blocks of 8×8 pixels, but we use larger

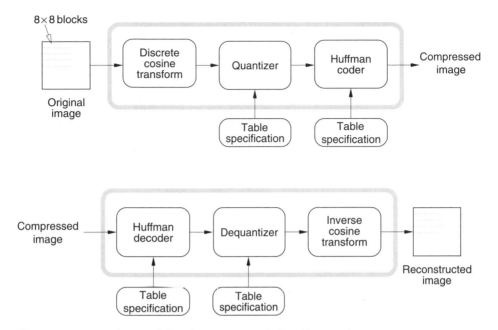

Figure 4.15 Encoding and decoding processes in baseline JPEG.

ones to demonstrate the effect. The first version of the image is made from each block's zero-frequency coefficient. This represents the overall grayness of the block, so at this stage each block is a uniform shade of gray. After inclusion of the second coefficient for each block, horizontal cross-sections through the blocks still have uniform shading, although vertical cross-sections do not. By the time the 32nd coefficient is combined, the image is starting to look much like the final version. However, it would require $64 \times 64 = 4,096$ coefficients per block for full, error-free reconstruction of our example picture. The corresponding figure for JPEG is $8 \times 8 = 64$ coefficients.

Following the discrete cosine transform, the nonzero coefficients are independently rounded to discrete values by a uniform quantizer—this is the lossy part. The quantizer step size—that is, the difference between successive levels—is different for each coefficient. The encoder may specify with each picture the quantization tables that are to be used for that picture—they could be derived for each picture independently and included with it. Alternatively it may specify that previously installed tables are to be used instead. The JPEG standard includes an example set of quantization tables that are particularly appropriate for natural scenery.

The zero-frequency coefficient is highly correlated from block to block because it is basically the average intensity over the block. Hence it is differentially encoded—in other words, it is represented by the difference between the

 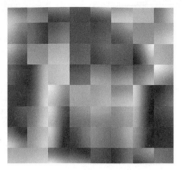

1 coefficient   2 coefficients   3 coefficients

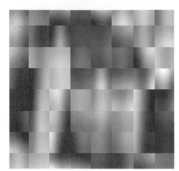 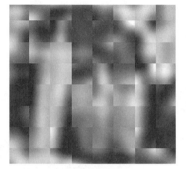 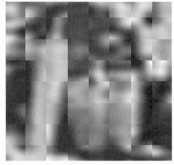

4 coefficients   6 coefficients   8 coefficients

10 coefficients   12 coefficients   16 coefficients

20 coefficients   32 coefficients   original (4,096 coefficients)

Figure 4.16 Transform-coded images reconstructed from a few coefficients. University of Southern California Image Processing Institute (USC-IPI) image database.

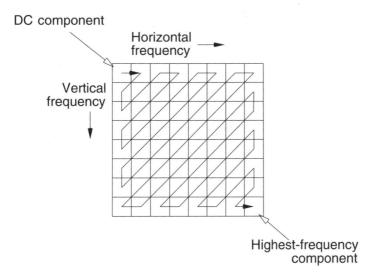

Figure 4.17 Zigzag encoding sequence.

zero-frequency value of this block and the previous one. The other 63 coefficients are not differentially encoded. They are sorted from low to high frequency using the zigzag sequence of Figure 4.17, in the order indicated by the arrowheads; then they are coded to reduce statistical redundancy.

The baseline system uses a standard scheme called *Huffman coding* to code the coefficients. First, since many of the coefficients are zero, the number of zero coefficients before the next nonzero one is specified—a kind of run-length encoding. Then the nonzero coefficients are Huffman coded. Huffman coding works by using a code table that gives each coefficient value a particular code. An example code table is provided in the JPEG specification, but the encoder can determine codes appropriate to the particular picture and embed them in the compressed data stream.

JPEG picture quality

A key feature of JPEG is its ability to control the number of bits per pixel used to represent an image. It accomplishes this by varying the amount of detail lost, which has a corresponding effect on the overall quality of the reconstructed image. Figure 4.18 shows three stages of lossy transmission from a JPEG-like encoding scheme, at 0.1, 0.2, and 1.0 bit/pixel, respectively. The differences in resolution are just discernible—despite the low-quality halftone reproduction—if you look closely, particularly around the straight edges in the pictures. The JPEG standard describes a postprocessing operation that can be used to suppress blocking artifacts and improve quality at low bit rates; it is not used in these examples.

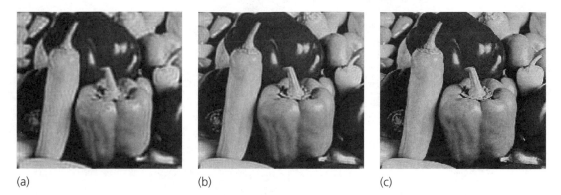

(a)   (b)   (c)

Figure 4.18 Images reconstructed from different numbers of bits: (a) 0.1 bit/pixel; (b) 0.2 bit/pixel; (c) 1.0 bit/pixel. USC-IPI image database.

Although JPEG is a complex format, well-engineered implementations can keep pace with 64 Kbit/second communication channels. This makes it suitable for interactive use. For example, compressed to 1 bit per pixel, a 720×576 pixel image takes 6.5 seconds to transmit over a 64-Kbit/second line, a tolerable delay for occasional image viewing.

As a general guide to the results attainable with a lossy compression method, for color images of moderately complex scenes, various levels of picture quality can be obtained at different compression factors:

- 0.25–0.5 bit/pixel: moderate to good quality, sufficient for some applications
- 0.5–0.75 bit/pixel: good to very good quality, sufficient for many applications
- 0.75–1.5 bit/pixel: excellent quality, sufficient for most applications
- 1.5–2 bits/pixel: usually indistinguishable from the original, sufficient for the most demanding applications

JPEG extensions and additions

The JPEG standard defines many extensions to baseline JPEG. Although the baseline system uses Huffman coding, the standard accommodates a different option called *arithmetic coding* which yields slightly greater compression at the expense of execution speed. The Huffman coding method is about twice as fast as arithmetic coding, but—at least in software implementations—throughput is dominated by other parts of the JPEG scheme, so the overall difference is not so great in practice. Arithmetic coding gives about a 10 percent compression advantage over Huffman coding for high-quality reconstructions of the relatively noisy test images used to develop JPEG. For lower bit rates and cleaner images, its benefit is even greater.

Although the baseline system is lossy, JPEG also defines a lossless variant. In the original JPEG definition, this was not a very effective compression scheme, and so a separate JPEG-Lossless standard was developed that provides an excellent but rather complex scheme for lossless compression of continuous-tone images.

There is a newer version of JPEG called JPEG-2000 whose main advance is to use an improved basis for compression, called *wavelets*, that avoids the tendency toward visible artifacts that can result from dividing an image into discrete blocks, as illustrated in Figure 4.16. This yields a 20 percent improvement in compression over the earlier scheme and also allows a smoother integration of lossless compression. JPEG-2000 incorporates other new features. The user can control how much resolution to download (so-called level of interest access), and there is increased flexibility in specifying color information.

Progressive refinement

Pictures on a conventional TV or printer are drawn in raster order—left to right, top to bottom, and across the screen or page. But when transmission is slow, there are advantages to creating the image in a different way. For example, 10 percent of the way through a raster transmission of an ordinary image format over the Web, only the top tenth of the picture can be seen, and this is not usually very informative. Users would generally prefer to see the whole picture at a tenth of the final resolution instead. This technique is called *progressive refinement*.

Figure 4.19 shows a picture that builds up gradually to the full resolution and contrasts it with ordinary raster transmission. The final picture is hardly distinguishable from the version created from only 10 percent of the information. Progressive refinement is also clearly advantageous in an interactive situation where one has an opportunity to stop transmission if the wrong picture appears, or when browsing casually through many pictures. Even with no such opportunity to cancel transmission, it is much less frustrating to see an initial image that is progressively refined than it is to have it revealed, slowly and tantalizingly, line by line.

A crude but effective form of progressive display called *interlacing* is used in television to reduce flicker by increasing the apparent rate at which successive images appear. The picture formed from the odd-numbered scan-lines is transmitted first, followed by the even-numbered scan-lines. An extension of this technique is used by both GIF and PNG to give a form of progressive display. When compressed, pictures can be stored in "interlaced order" instead of conventional order, so that when the file is read and transmitted over a network, an approximate version of the image is seen initially.

In GIF, data is interlaced by row and is stored in four "passes" over the image. Every eighth row is stored first, starting with row 0. Next comes every eighth row starting with row 4. Then every fourth row starting with row 2 is stored,

Progressive
transmission

After 1%

After 2%

After 5%

After 10%

After 100%

Raster
transmission

After 1%

After 2%

After 5%

After 10%

After 100%

Figure 4.19 Progressive versus raster transmission. USC-IPI image database.

1	6	4	6	2	6	4	6
7	7	7	7	7	7	7	7
5	6	5	6	5	6	5	6
7	7	7	7	7	7	7	7
3	6	4	6	3	6	4	6
7	7	7	7	7	7	7	7
5	6	5	6	5	6	5	6
7	7	7	7	7	7	7	7

Figure 4.20 8×8 tiled template used to generate a PNG interlaced file.

and finally every second row starting with row 1 fills in the missing lines. When the picture is read from this file, one-eighth of it is present by the end of the first pass, one-quarter by the end of the second, one-half by the end of the third, and the full image by the end of the fourth. When the picture is transmitted and displayed, corresponding amounts can be viewed—although just because an image is transmitted in an interlaced format does not mean the application at the receiving end must display it progressively.

PNG supports a two-dimensional interlacing scheme based around the 8×8 template shown in Figure 4.20 which provides a superior form of progressive display. The template is tiled over the whole image. The image is represented in seven pieces, and in each one the values of the correspondingly numbered pixels in Figure 4.20 are stored. The first piece, comprising pixels numbered 1 in the figure, stores $\frac{1}{64}$ of the information, the second (pixels numbered 2) $\frac{1}{32}$, and so on, until all information is complete by the end of the seventh piece (pixels numbered 7). When the picture is transmitted, a reasonable approximation can be drawn as soon as the first piece is received and improves with each new piece. Naturally this scheme impacts compression efficiency, and file size is slightly increased over the noninterlaced version.

One of the extended-feature options in the JPEG standard is a sophisticated form of progressive refinement. The image is approximated by low-frequency terms that are gradually refined to produce the final version. The process usually ends when the image is the same as would have been transmitted in the normal (lossy) case, but there is a further option of progressive *lossless coding*, which continues until the final picture is almost identical with the original—the only discrepancies being due to the finite-precision arithmetic employed in the encoder and decoder. This final stage involves sending a spatial correction signal that gives the difference between the final lossy image and the original one, pixel by pixel.

Recall that JPEG works by obtaining spatial frequency coefficients using the discrete cosine transform and quantizing them. With progressive refinement, instead of transmitting all coefficients for each block, in turn many passes are made through the picture, and successively higher bands of coefficients are transmitted at each pass. In early passes the low-frequency, or rough-detail, information is sent, leaving for later the high-frequency, fine-detail information. This is called the *spectral selection* method of progressive refinement. An alternative, called *successive approximation*, is also specified in which the coefficients are first sent with reduced precision. Successive approximation yields much better visual quality at low bit rates, but the number of progressive stages is limited. Spectral selection allows more progressive stages and, since it is a simple extension of the sequential mode, is easier to implement. Successive approximation—particularly, it turns out, the Huffman coding version—is more difficult to achieve.

4.6 Representing audio and video

Some digital library documents contain audio and video. These media consume even more space than images—by several orders of magnitude—because they represent the evolution of signals over time. Telephone-quality speech uses 8,000 8-bit samples per second, while CD-quality music needs 44,000 16-bit samples per second. Video requires at least 24 frames per second for the eye not to perceive flicker. Practical formats use compression to maximize the amount that can stream through a network of given bandwidth or be stored in given disk space.

Documents are coded for transmission (or storage) and decoded upon reception (or retrieval). The coder/decoder (equivalently, the compressor/decompressor) is generally called a *codec*. Codecs can be applied to audio or video information individually or packaged together to provide audiovisual delivery. Video coders achieve compression by exploiting spatial and temporal coherence; audio coders likewise exploit acoustic and temporal redundancy. The decoder reverses the compression process. High compression rates can be achieved, but the process is lossy. Lossless methods could be used, but their gain is slight in comparison.

Many codecs are asymmetric in that they take different times, or different resources, for encoding and decoding. Often it is worth expending more effort in coding if that achieves greater compression. For example, most video footage is generated once but viewed many times, or broadcast once and viewed simultaneously at many different locations. In both cases high compression brings great benefits. For online operation, encoding (and, less frequently, decoding) is often hardware assisted. Manufacturers produce a wide range of hardware options for desktop computers—right through to video editing studios.

Some multimedia architectures allow encoders to be upgraded to take advantage of new techniques, but remain backward compatible by ensuring that unmodified decoders can still decompress the data they generate. The upgraded system produces shorter files which can still be transported to other sites for playback by existing decoder software.

The dominant international standard for audiovisual material is MPEG, devised by the ISO Moving Picture Experts Group. We also discuss some popular proprietary formats: AVI, QuickTime, and RealSystem. The WAV, AIFF, and AU formats are widely used for information that is solely audio.

Multimedia compression: MPEG

The original aim of MPEG, formulated in 1988, was to develop an open digital format, comparable to the popular analog home video system VHS, that could be read from storage devices such as CD-ROM. A format was devised that enabled digital audio and video data to be combined with a target rate of 1.5 Mbit/second. The effort snowballed, attracting great interest from industry, and its goals expanded. There are now several formats that constitute the MPEG family. MPEG-1, MPEG-2, and MPEG-4 form the core; MPEG-3 has been abandoned; MPEG-7 incorporates metadata; and MPEG-21 supports the life cycle of multimedia information.

The original format, MPEG-1, was designed for color pictures with 352×240 pixel resolution shown at 30 frames a second, accompanied by audio of near CD quality. Not only did this come within the 1.5 Mbit/second target, but it could be decompressed in hardware with 512 Kbytes of memory (which corresponded to cost-effective VLSI design in the early 1990s). The frame rate, picture resolution, and audio sampling can be varied to give other bit rates, although these are less common. Data can be uni-media, comprising just sound or just pictures. Audio can be mono or stereo and has various options or "layers" designed for particular purposes (speech and music of different qualities). Of these, the third layer, more popularly called MP3, is widely used to represent digitized music on the Web.

MPEG-2 is designed for higher-quality video representation and forms the basis of DVD video. It can be transported over error-prone networks and supports interlaced images (making it suitable for broadcast TV) and multichannel audio. Decoders are backward compatible with MPEG-1 and can play back both formats. However, MPEG-2 has not superseded MPEG-1 because the earlier standard's performance is superior at lower bit rates. Users choose whichever version best suits their needs. The next standard, MPEG-3, was intended for high-definition television (HDTV), but it transpired that the MPEG-2 structure scaled well enough, and the new work was merged with the existing standard.

MPEG-4 is designed for low-bandwidth networks such as mobile communications and the World Wide Web. It is based on objects rather than signals and includes synthetic objects such as computer-generated text, graphics, and sound. It incorporates interactive capabilities, and the bit rate can be adjusted dynamically to suit the transportation medium.

The naming convention for succeeding MPEG standards is bizarre.[6] MPEG-7 allows the description of metadata for multimedia content that is conveyed by MPEG-1, 2, and 4; we explain it in Chapter 5 (Section 5.5). MPEG-21 is intended to provide a framework that integrates all elements of the multimedia life cycle, from content creation and production through distribution to end users with their specific needs. Its designers liaise with other standards bodies, drawing upon existing standards where they exist and defining complementary standards to bridge the gaps. In the context of digital libraries, MPEG-21 amounts to a form of interoperability for multimedia documents.

Inside MPEG

Before digging into the internal details of MPEG, we briefly review pertinent television standards for color, sample rate, and picture resolution. MPEG-1 was influenced by prior work on visual telephony, by the JPEG format for image data, and by various audio techniques. It in turn has influenced proprietary formats, and these commercial decisions have fed back into subsequent MPEG development. Note that there are two different formats for analog television in widespread use today: NTSC, originating in North America, and PAL, originating in Europe.

MPEG arose out of the same ISO working group as JPEG, but they quickly separated. Although an independent standard, it does reuse many concepts and idioms. Indeed there is a variant of JPEG called Motion JPEG or Moving JPEG, often used for video editing, which extends this standard to support videos by storing each frame in JPEG format—but this is quite different from MPEG.

Part of MPEG is based on a downsampled version of an international standard used in digital television and video equipment, CCIR 601, which is designed to be compatible with popular analog formats. Table 4.6 summarizes the principal analog television formats used around the world. In an NTSC environment, for example, CCIR 601 delivers a 720×486 picture that is interlaced, sending 720×243 half-frames 60 times per second. Because analog NTSC video reserves many lines for control information, CCIR 601's effective display area is the same even though it specifies fewer lines.

---

6. The reason for skipping the intervening numbers is that "cybersquatters" registered the corresponding domain names in anticipation of being able to sell them when new versions of the standard emerged.

Table 4.6 International television formats and their relationship with CCIR 601.

Format	Abbreviation	Transmission rate	Origin	CCIR 601 rate
National Television System Committee	NTSC	525 lines at 60 Hz (interlaced)	United States	720 × 486 (interlaced)
Phase Alternation Line	PAL	625 lines at 50 Hz (interlaced)	Europe	720 × 576 (interlaced)
Séquentiel Couleur Avec Mémoire (Sequential Color with Memory)	SECAM	625 lines at 50 Hz (interlaced)	Europe	720 × 576 (interlaced)

CCIR 601 represents color using the YUV model, rather than the RGB (red-green-blue) scheme commonly used by computers. This encodes brightness (luminance) in the Y parameter, and color difference (chrominance) in the two parameters U and V. It is preferred over RGB because the resolution for chromatic parameters can be reduced (and therefore expressed more compactly), with imperceptible loss of viewing quality.

There is a mathematical mapping that converts one color representation to the other. The three YUV components can be quantized into the same number of bits (e.g., 8 bits, or 10 bits for higher color resolution). Alternatively the U and V components can be downsampled—that is, transmitted every second, or every fourth, sample in the horizontal direction, or every second sample in both horizontal and vertical directions. To reconstruct the image, intermediate values are interpolated.

In MPEG terminology, a picture comparable to analog television is obtained by delivering, noninterlaced, a 352 × 240 pixel color image at 30 frames per second (NTSC flavor) or 352 × 288 pixels at 25 frames per second (PAL flavor). Taking into account rounding to the nearest multiple of 8 to simplify implementation (whether software or hardware), this configuration halves the resolution and sample rate of CCIR 601 and is known as the Standard Interchange Format (SIF). Both settings conveniently yield the same data rate in pixels/second (because 352 × 240 × 30 = 352 × 288 × 25 = 2,534,400).

Although PAL and NTSC videotapes are physically the same size, they require different equipment for playback (of course, dual players exist). For MPEG, the NTSC- and PAL-flavored SIF settings are purely for convenience—they do not pose a problem for playback because the differences can be overcome dynamically, in software. MPEG data that conforms to one of these variants most likely reflects the capture equipment used.

We begin by describing MPEG-1. The general ideas carry over to MPEG-2 and MPEG-4, and we summarize the differences later.

MPEG video

Video—a sequence of pictures—is represented in MPEG as a progression of graphical frames, processed into a bitstream. The frames may not be in the same order as the sequence of pictures in the original video, however. There are three types of frame.

An *intra frame* or *I-frame* provides a fixed point in the image sequence. It exploits spatial but not temporal coherence. In rough outline it follows JPEG: a discrete cosine transform is applied to 8×8 blocks, values are Huffman coded using fixed tables specially designed for two-dimensional data, and the zero-frequency coefficients are differentially encoded.

A *predicted frame* or *P-frame* is derived from the most recent I- or P-frame. It encodes differences between frames and therefore exploits temporal as well as spatial coherence. P-frames are compressed using motion predictors that work with 16×16 blocks in the luminance (Y) channel and can exploit similarity in data translated between one frame and the next.

A *bidirectional frame* or *B-frame* is based on a previous frame (most recent I or P), a future frame (next closest I or P), or the average of the two. The data is compressed along similar lines to the P-frame.

I-frames are an important feature of MPEG because they allow a form of random access playback. Because they contain all the information necessary to reconstruct that particular image, and subsequent frames (P or B) cannot reference a frame further back in time, a playback application can skip to an I-frame and start playing from that point.

Figure 4.21a shows a cyclic pattern of 12 I, P, and B-frames that works well in practice. The display can be restarted at the beginning of any cycle—every 0.4 second at a frame rate of 30 frames per second. However, for easy decompression, the frames are not encoded in numerical order. Frames 2 and 3, for instance, rely on frames 1 and 4; consequently they are reordered as shown in Figure 4.21b. Note that this makes the first I-frame cycle different from the next one. The first cycle starts with an I-frame followed by a P-frame, but the second one has two B-frames belonging to the previous cycle slotted between this I-P pair. This second pattern of frame numbers repeats until the final cycle. B-frames complicate life, but they also bring space savings and a degree of noise reduction. Implementers of MPEG encoders can choose not to use them, but compliant decoders must be able to handle them.

This last point illustrates a fundamental issue. While MPEG decoding is a well-defined deterministic process, there is great scope for variation in encoders—particularly with regard to motion prediction. Implementing a good encoder is a specialized skill that involves far more than the familiar speed verses compression tradeoff. Deficiencies in design yield poor-quality video playback that no decoder, however smart, can fix.

Frame number	1	2	3	4	5	6	7	8	9	10	11	12	13	14	15	16	17	18	...
Frame type	I	B	B	P	B	B	P	B	B	P	B	B	I	B	B	P	B	B	...

$\longleftarrow$ 12-unit cycle $\longrightarrow$$\longleftarrow$

(a)

Encoded frame order	1	4	2	3	7	5	6	10	8	9	13	11	12	16	...
Frame type	I	P	B	B	P	B	B	P	B	B	I	B	B	P	...

(b)

Figure 4.21 (a) Frame sequence for MPEG; (b) reordering for sequential transmission.

MPEG audio

MPEG compresses audio using a lossy technique that can achieve near-perfect CD-quality playback when reduced to $\frac{1}{12}$ of the original size. It exploits a phenomenon known as *acoustic masking:* the human auditory system cannot perceive low-amplitude frequency components that are dominated by nearby high-amplitude components. These masked frequencies can be dropped entirely or encoded using fewer bits than normal.

MPEG incorporates three different schemes—known as *layers*—for compression, all based on the acoustic masking principle. Higher layers are more complex and take more resources (time and memory) to encode and decode. Layer I is designed to be easy to implement and fast to process and has a target rate of 192 Kbit/second per channel. Layers II and III are 128 and 64 Kbit/second per channel, respectively.

All three layers support sample rates of 32 kHz, 44.1 kHz, and 48 kHz. The encoding process first performs a discrete cosine transform and then divides the frequency spectrum into 32 bands, which are analyzed to identify masked frequencies. Next the coefficients are quantized and encoded. The first two layers have equal frequency bands, while the third uses unequal ones. In addition, Layers II and III exploit temporal masking, and Layer III takes into account stereo redundancy. Layers are designed so that decoders are backward compatible: Layer II decoders can also handle Layer I data, and Layer III decoders handle all layers. Decoders are easier to write than encoders.

The audio quality of MPEG has been evaluated in extensive perceptual tests. Listeners are played three versions of several audio recordings: first the original, and then the MPEG encoding and the original randomly transposed. They are asked to score the second and third versions using a standard scale of impairment that ranges from "very annoying" to "perfect." At a rate of 128 Kbit/second per channel (6:1 compression), even experts cannot reliably distinguish MPEG from the original recording. At 64 Kbit/second per channel, Layer II was judged to lie between "annoying" and "slightly annoying." The same rate with Layer III scored significantly higher—"just noticeably different." This result has lead to the widely quoted claim that CD-quality audio encoded as MP3 (that is, MPEG Layer III audio) achieves minimal perceptible degradation with only 8 percent of the original file size.

As with video, the MPEG standard defines audio decoding fully, but leaves encoding open-ended. Future encoders may well improve on these quality ratings.

Mixing media

To combine video and audio bitstreams, each one is broken into packets that are multiplexed into a single stream. Packets are time-stamped to ensure correct synchronization.

MPEG-1 can cope with a range of audio sampling rates and a range of image frame sizes and rates. For instance, it is entirely possible to generate video with dimensions 4,096 × 4,096 delivered at 60 Hz. However, special significance is given to particular sets of parameter values that provide good tradeoffs between decoder computational complexity, buffer size, and memory bandwidth while still addressing a wide range of applications. One configuration is known as the *constrained parameter bitstream* (CPB). The upper limit of each parameter is shown in Table 4.7 (not all limits can be attained simultaneously). The maximum rate in pixels/second corresponds to the rate for the Standard Interchange Format (SIF) mentioned earlier. In a typical configuration, video uses around 1.2 Mbit/second, and audio uses around 0.3 Mbit/second.

MPEG-2

MPEG-2 incorporates several improvements. Images can be interlaced; audio can have multiple channels; data can be transported over an error-prone network; and delivery is scalable. Also included are low-level implementation enhancements that improve the overall compression factor (however, they restrict picture dimensions to multiples of 16).

Interlaced images make MPEG-2 suitable for broadcast television, but the extra complexity hinders compression. There are two audio extensions. One, which is backward compatible with MPEG-1, provides five main channels and a low-frequency enhancement channel; a typical application is surround sound. The other is a state-of-the-art technique called *advanced audio compression* that adds a raft of intricate encoding options but is not backward compatible.

MPEG-1 combines video and audio into a single bitstream. MPEG-2 refines the notion of stream to work in error-prone environments using fixed-size

Table 4.7 Upper limits for MPEG-1's constrained parameter bitstream.

Parameter	Limit
Pixels per line	704
Lines per frame	576
Pixels per frame	101,376
Frames per second	30
Pixels per second	2,534,400
Bit rate	1.86 Mbit/second
Buffer size	40 Kb

packets, as well as in error-free ones with arbitrary sized packets. Data can be prioritized by separating it into constituent bitstreams, which helps support heterogeneous environments. For example, a high-definition television (HDTV) signal can be decomposed into a 720 × 480 pixel baseline bitstream and a 1,440 × 960 pixel bitstream that encodes the differences between the two resolutions. This enables either a standard-resolution (CCIR 601) or a high-definition television to display a suitable picture.

MPEG-2 defines many implementation options, and encoders and decoders need not support all of them. Part of the standard specifies a real-time interface for video on demand, but particular implementations may not include it. In subsequent MPEG developments this piecewise trend evolved into a toolbox approach, where implementations are not expected to support all constituent parts.

MPEG-4

Whereas MPEG-2 is an extension of MPEG-1—for example, its decoder can handle MPEG-1 data—MPEG-4 represents a radical departure. It embodies a broader concept of multimedia document and is designed for use over the Web and low-bandwidth networks such as mobile communications. To video and audio it adds still images, synthetically generated graphics and sound, and text. These primitive data types can be composed hierarchically into objects. Objects supplant streams as the key structure, offering more expressive power than before. For example, footage can be created that composes live video (its background masked off to save space) with a two- or three-dimensional computer-generated backdrop and a synthesized music soundtrack.

MPEG-4 is a vast standard. It can deliver a quality of service that adapts to available network bandwidth. It allows users to interact with the composed scene. It also lets users implement strategies for identifying and managing intellectual property.

Other multimedia formats

Although it is an open standard, MPEG does embody some patented techniques (as indeed does JPEG). The International Standards Organization resolves the conflict by requiring all components used in its standards to be licensable on "fair and equal terms." The intention is to define standards that not only facilitate data interchange, but use techniques whose performance rivals state-of-the-art proprietary systems. A side benefit is that companies are more likely to support the standards.

There are some multimedia formats that are fully proprietary. In the age of universal access this seems to defy commercial sense because to play such material you must possess a particular program. However, a particular playback application for one proprietary format can incorporate modules to play rival formats too. To include such modules a licensing agreement is required—and the more popular the format, the more the company owning the technology can charge.

Video and audio

The Audio Video Interleave (AVI) format from Microsoft uses containers to represent data, which nicely matches this modular approach. The file header contains a code that determines which codec to use to process the data that follows. Codecs (there are over 20) range from a simple "device-independent bitmap" that represents frames using RGB color values and performs no compression whatsoever through to sophisticated approaches such as MPEG-4. A proprietary codec for a format derived from QuickTime, mentioned later in this subsection, is included—a popular choice in practice.

AVI files are device independent, and there are players for all major computer platforms. Because of the many different codecs, however, a particular installation often lacks the necessary module, prompting a diagnostic message. If the missing codec exists for that platform, installation is straightforward.

The long-established QuickTime format from Apple (also available for Windows) comes with a full programming environment. Independent software vendors can use this to parse multimedia files and develop graphical applications that access the media interactively. Because its programming environment extends well beyond basic audio and video manipulation, QuickTime is like an operating system in its own right, providing platform independence between Macintosh and Windows personal computers. A wide variety of codecs are supported. There is also a close relationship between MPEG-4 and QuickTime 5.

Application programs for multimedia were originally oriented for work on a single computer. However, there is a high and growing demand for making multimedia objects available over the Internet, where bandwidth is somewhat restricted and very unpredictable. Real-time delivery of multimedia over networks is called *streaming:* the information arrives in a continual stream rather than being received in its entirety before presentation begins. A format called RealSystems—also packaged individually as RealAudio and RealVideo—is specifically designed to stream multimedia over the Internet. Available on all major computers, it supports a wide variety of codecs, including MPEG, with an emphasis on real-time delivery over networks.

Audio only

There are several formats designed exclusively for audio—for example, WAV (Microsoft and IBM), AIFF (Apple), and AU (Sun Microsystems). These date back to the early desktop computers, and although each one originated on a particular computer, today they are platform independent. They use similar representations, with a header to encode sample rate and quantization details, followed by the data itself. The compression techniques are rudimentary—reflecting the need in the early days for computational algorithms that could handle the data at an appropriate rate—and their details are public knowledge. Many audio players can load and save files in these different formats.

Commonly used compression techniques are Huffman encoding, companding, adaptive differential pulse code modulation, and linear predictive coding. Huffman coding (mentioned in Section 4.5 with regard to JPEG) is lossless and therefore achieves limited compression on inherently noisy signals. *Companding* is a standard technique in telecommunications that uses logarithmic quantization—the μ-law in the U.S. and the A-law in Europe—to obtain better perceptual quality for a given bit rate. *Adaptive differential pulse code modulation* predicts the value of the signal based on preceding samples and encodes the difference using dynamically varying quantization steps. Speech data is unique because it is always produced by a particular system—the human vocal tract—that, while certainly not fixed, does not vary all that much from one individual to another. The technique of *linear predictive coding* takes advantage of this domain specificity to accomplish greater compression.

Using multimedia in a digital library

Audio, video, and multimedia digital libraries raise a wide range of interesting and challenging issues. Here are a few: How is the collection to be searched or browsed? How are users to access different parts of a document? What does it mean to provide a summary of an audio document, or a video document, or a multimedia document? Can summaries be produced accurately? How accurate does the digitization process need to be?

One approach is to build the indexing and browsing structures around textual metadata, and deliver multimedia material—once it has been located—through the Web browser. More ambitious is to combine signal processing algorithms (image, audio, or both) with graphical displays to provide a richer environment in which items can be located, played or displayed, and manipulated more directly. For truly flexible access, it should be possible to search and browse summaries of audio and video and to combine operations on different media. Developing usable tools for these more ambitious features remains a research problem. In the short term, practical digital library systems will likely take advantage of whatever direct access methods are available, including the use of textual metadata as an intermediary means of access, while in the longer term they will come to grips with the true multimedia nature of the material and also cater to the differing needs of individual users.

It is not easy to digitize physical signals, and considerable expertise and attention to detail is needed. Good results depend on suitable lighting conditions and audio recording levels. Technical parameters include linear resolution, color depth, frame rate, and audio sample rate. The output file format also affects how much detail is preserved. When designing a multimedia collection, a critical issue is whether lossy representations are acceptable. For some preservation purposes no loss can be tolerated, even though this greatly increases storage requirements.

Lossless representations make editing operations easier—and safer. Although there are tools that permit playback and editing of compressed formats, quality inevitably suffers if the process involves lossy decompression followed by lossy recompression. Repeated editing may even render the material unusable. Audio editors commonly use formats such as WAV, AIFF, and AU, whose rudimentary codecs suffer less from quality loss. Only when editing is complete is the data converted to a highly compressed format such as MP3.

Two other issues arise: How widespread is the software that can replay the material, and what are the bandwidth implications for delivery? Early multimedia applications involved individual computers with material stored locally on disk. However, today's users expect cross-platform support and network access. Rather than imposing a particular fixed solution, users can select a desired format and the digital library can convert the material on the server. This lets users access the material in the most convenient form, taking into account the bandwidth available for downloading.

4.7   Notes and sources

The ASCII code is central to many pieces of hardware and software, and the code table turns up everywhere in reference material, printed manuals and online help pages, Web sites, and even this book! At its inception, few could have predicted how widely it would spread. Of historical interest is the ANSI (American National Standards Institute, 1968) standard itself, a version of which was published (prior to final ratification) in *Communications of the ACM* (Gorn, Bemer, and Green, 1963).

The principal aim of ASCII was to unify the coding of numeric and textual information—the digits and the Roman alphabet—between different kinds of computer equipment. However, decisions over other symbols have had a subtle yet profound influence. Few keyboards in the 1960s possessed a backslash key, yet so ingrained is its use today to convey special meanings—such as a directory separator and to protect the meaning of certain characters in certain contexts—that computing would be almost inconceivable without it. It is here that the concept of *escaping* appeared for the first time.

The official title for Unicode is tongue-twisting and mind-boggling: The International Standard ISO/IEC 10646-1, Information Technology—Universal Multiple-Octet Coded Character Set (UCS)—Part 1: Architecture and Basic Multilingual Plane. Part 1 covers the values U+000000–U+10FFFF; further values are covered by Part 2. We mentioned that the ISO standard and the Unicode Consortium differ inconsequently over the size of the character space. Another difference is that Unicode augments its definition with functional descriptions to help programmers develop compatible software. For example, it defines an algorithm for displaying bidirectional text (Unicode Consortium, 2000). The consortium uses the Web site *www.unicode.org* to expedite the release of versions, revisions, and amendments to the standard, and information about Unicode version 3.0 through to version 3.2 is available there.

Technical details of searching and indexing are presented in *Managing Gigabytes* (Witten, Moffat, and Bell, 1999), which gives a comprehensive and detailed technical account of how to index documents and make them rapidly accessible through full-text queries. This and other relevant books on information retrieval are mentioned in the "Notes and sources" section of Chapter 3 (Section 3.7). The material on segmenting Chinese text is from Teahan et al. (2000), while Table 4.4, giving English segmentation results, is due to Teahan (1997).

Different scholars transcribe the Fante word for *welcome* in different ways. We have chosen the version with an umlaut above the second *a* to illustrate interesting text representation issues. Other common renderings are *akwāba* and *akwaaba*.

All file formats described in this chapter are well documented, except where commercial interests prevail. There is a rich vein of online resources, as you might expect from the area and the working habits of those in it, which are easy to find using Internet classification directories. On both Google and Yahoo, file formats are classed under *Computer*, then *Data formats*. Although slightly dated, Kientzle's (1995) *Internet File Formats* is an excellent compendium that brings together a wide sweep of formats in one place. Its covers the same major topics as this chapter, but in more detail, and describes other widely used formats not discussed here.

The definitive guides to PostScript and PDF are the reference manuals produced by Adobe (1999, 2000), the company responsible for these formats. They practice what they preach, putting their manuals online (in PDF format) on their Web site (*www.adobe.com*). A supplementary tutorial and cookbook (Adobe, 1985) gives worked examples in the PostScript language. Aladdin Enterprises' *ghostscript* is a software PostScript interpreter that provides a useful means of experimentation. Released under the GNU Public License, it is available for all popular platforms (*www.ghostscript.com*). Our description of PostScript and PDF mentions several graphics techniques, such as transformations, clipping, and spline curves, that are explained in standard textbooks on computer graphics (e.g., Foley et al., 1990). The technique for extracting plain text from PostScript files is described by Nevill-Manning, Reed, and Witten (1998).

An initial description of Microsoft's RTF format appears in *Microsoft Systems Journal* (Andrews, 1987), and its continued expansion is documented through the Microsoft Developers' Network. Subscribers receive updates on CD-ROM, while the same information is provided for general consumption at *http://msdn. microsoft.com*. At one stage an internal technical document describing the native Word format was published through this outlet, but that has since been discontinued. LaTeX, which is based on the TeX system invented by Knuth (1986), is described in many books, such as Lamport (1994). A useful online source is Tobias Oetiker's *Not so short introduction to LaTeX2e* at *http://people.ee.ethz. ch/~oetiker/lshort*. Bountiful collections of packages can be found on Internet sites such as the Comprehensive TeX Archive Network (*www.ctan.org/*).

For an introduction to the general area of multimedia systems (image, sound, and video), we recommend Chapman and Chapman's (2000) *Digital Multimedia*. This useful text also discusses HTML, XML, and cascading style sheets, topics that appear in the next chapter. More specific to images, Murray and van Ryper's (1996) *Encyclopedia of Graphics File Formats* covers an extensive range— not just the three representative formats described here. It also includes broad-brush descriptions of PostScript, RTF, MPEG, QuickTime, and AVI, for all of these qualify as graphics formats at some level. For a comprehensive explanation of the JPEG standard, see Pennebaker and Mitchell (1993). The LZW compression scheme used for the GIF image format is due to Welch (1984), while the earlier LZ77 that underlies gzip is the classic work of Ziv and Lempel (1977).

Video Demystified (Jack, 2001), written with an engineering bias, explains the labyrinth of video and TV standards, with separate chapters on MPEG-1 and MPEG-2. The International Telecommunication Union (ITU) is now responsible for both CCIR and CCITT standards, since these two bodies joined forces. The definitive references for MPEG are the standards themselves: MPEG-1 is ISO/IEC 11172; MPEG-2 is ISO/IEC 13818; and MPEG-4 is ISO/IEC 14496. Microsoft's Audio Video Interleave (AVI) format is subsumed by its fully fledged Advanced Streaming Format (ASF) for streaming audio and video over the

4.7 NOTES AND SOURCES **219**

Internet. This is an integral part of its "media technologies": a software development kit and applications that also run on the Apple Macintosh.

Pohlman's (2000) *Principles of Digital Audio* is a comprehensive resource for audio that moves from introductory material, through hardware and formats (including streaming), to signal processing techniques. For a text that is more focused on formats and practical programming, see Kientzle's (1997) *A Programmer's Guide to Sound*.

Carnegie Mellon's InforMedia digital video library project (*www.informedia. cs.cmu.edu*), a substantial project that has run for many years, is an excellent and mature example of a multimedia digital library.

5
Markup and metadata

Elements of organization

If documents are the digital library's basic building blocks, markup and metadata are its basic elements of organization. Markup is used to specify the structure of individual documents and control how they look when presented to the user. Metadata is used to expedite access to relevant parts of the collection through searching and browsing. Part of the job of markup is to identify metadata.

Markup controls two complementary aspects of an electronic document: structure and appearance. Structural markup makes certain aspects of the document structure explicit: typically section divisions, headings, subsection structure, enumerated and bulleted lists, emphasized and quoted text, footnotes, tabular material, and so on; these structural items can be considered metadata for the document. Appearance is controlled by *presentation* or *formatting* markup which dictates how the document appears typographically: page size, page headers and footers, fonts, line spacing, how section headers look, where figures appear, and so on. Structure and appearance are related by the design of the document, that is, a catalog—often called a *style sheet*—of how each structural item should be presented.

The traditional art of typography is nicely defined by Stanley Morison, the doyen of 20th-century British typographers, as

> the art of rightly disposing printed material in accordance with specific purpose; of so arranging the letters, distributing the space and controlling the type as to aid to the maximum the reader's comprehension of the text.

There is a strong link between structure and presentation: both are intended to aid the reader's comprehension "to the maximum." However, sometimes the author's requirements for certain elements of a document violate the usual distinction between form and content, or physical and logical structure. For example, eye-catching posters reflect the content in the structure to produce an attractive, evocative, and informative whole. Sometimes the medium is a goodly part of the message.

It can be difficult to divorce content from presentation—the message from the medium. Particularly in these days of electronic publishing, authors become fond of determining exactly how their work is presented on the page or screen. To them, editors and collection-builders seem inordinately obsessed with uniformity, seeking a Procrustean mold into which all documents must fit. We see the tension between the two points of view in this chapter in the development of HTML and the emergence of style sheets and XML.

The term *metadata* has already been used frequently throughout this book. It sounds impressive—we have heard it described, tongue firmly in cheek, as "cataloging for men." It was introduced in Chapter 1 using the catchphrase "data about data." This is glib but not very enlightening—in some sense, *all* data is about data. Where does data end and metadata begin?

The notion of metadata is not absolute but relative. It is only really meaningful in a context that makes clear what the data itself is. Metadata is generally taken to be structured information about a particular information resource. Information is "structured" if it can be meaningfully manipulated without understanding its content. For example, given a collection of source documents, bibliographic information about each document would be metadata for the collection—the structure is made plain, in terms of which pieces of text represent author names, which represent titles, and so on. But given a collection of bibliographic information, metadata might comprise some information about each bibliographic item, such as who compiled it and when.

Different kinds of metadata are designed for different purposes. Markup—particularly structural markup—is metadata that is intended to assist users in navigating around documents, as well as in comprehending the structure of the information they contain. Formatting markup, on the other hand, is more likely to be regarded as part of the document content than as metadata.

Another kind of metadata is information designed to assist in discovering relevant documents by searching and browsing around information collections.

Names of authors, titles, key phrases, and so on come into this category. Often called metadata for *resource discovery*, this is most important for our purposes, because the value of information in digital libraries depends on how easily it can be located. Another kind of metadata gives information about rights management and access control—policies that define rights, restrictions, and the rules that govern who can do what with digital resources. A final kind is metadata for administration and preservation: all the information that might be necessary to preserve the integrity and functionality of a digital resource over an extended period of time.

There is an important distinction between *explicit* and *extracted* metadata. Explicit metadata is determined by a person after careful examination and analysis of the document. Creating a traditional library catalog entry (a MARC record, which we discuss later in this section) is a job for a well-trained cataloger: it takes between one and two hours to generate a new entry. A large set of bibliographic records is thus a substantial investment. For example, in 1997 the Library of Congress cataloged nearly 300,000 bibliographic entries, at a total cost of around 25 million dollars. The Online Computer Library Center (OCLC), a central cataloging organization in the U.S., has about 34 million MARC records—representing an investment of some 30,000 years of human labor! It shares these records, so that member libraries can reuse the information when they acquire a new book that has been cataloged elsewhere.

Extracted metadata is obtained automatically from the document's contents. This is usually hard to do reliably, and although extracted metadata is cheap, it is often of questionable accuracy. *Text mining*, which may be defined as the process of analyzing text to extract information that is useful for particular purposes, is a hot research topic nowadays.

This chapter begins by looking at markup and then progresses to metadata. We first describe HTML, the Hypertext Markup Language, which was designed specifically to allow references, or *hyperlinks*, to other files—including picture files, giving a natural way to embed illustrations in the body of an otherwise textual document. It quickly became augmented (some would say "contaminated") with a host of other facilities, many of which provide formatting rather than structural markup.

Whatever its faults, HTML, being the foundation for the Web, is a phenomenally successful way of representing documents. It includes a basic facility for expressing associated metadata. However, when dealing with collections of documents, different ways of expressing formatting and metadata in HTML tend to generate inconsistencies—even though the documents may look the same. Although these inconsistencies matter little to human readers, they are a bane for automatic processing of document collections. The real advantage of structural markup is that it encourages document structure to be expressed the same way, and achieves consistency in appearance automatically, using machine-readable style sheets.

XML is an *extensible* markup language that allows you to declare what syntactic rules govern a particular group of files. More precisely, it is referred to as a *metalanguage*—a language used to define other languages. XML provides a flexible framework for describing document structure and metadata, making it ideally suited to digital libraries. It has achieved widespread use in a short period of time—reflecting a great demand for standard ways of incorporating metadata into documents—and underpins many other standards. Among these are ways of specifying style sheets that define how particular families of XML documents should appear on the screen or printed page.

There are several widely used standards for representing bibliographic metadata. The *machine-readable cataloging* (MARC) standard is a rich and complex format with hundreds of different fields and subfields. Developed by the library community, it has formed the basis of library catalogs since the 1970s. The Dublin Core is a more recent development, intended specifically for describing electronic documents and widely used in digital library projects. It adopts a minimalist approach, defining only 15 items for describing facets of documents. BibTeX and Refer are formats for bibliographic metadata which, although not designed by information science professionals, are widely used in technical fields, particularly mathematics, physics, and computer science. There are many large databases, and collections of databases, that include bibliographic information in these forms.

We also cover some metadata standards designed specifically for nontextual material. TIFF is a widely used file structure that accommodates numerous different formats for images, and it includes a descriptive metadata facility. MPEG-7 is an emerging standard for describing multimedia documents.

Finally we examine some techniques for extracting metadata from document text. These are advanced topics that do not necessarily impact the practical construction of digital libraries, and readers who are keen to get ahead and build their own digital libraries can safely skip them. However, this section describes the methods underlying some of the facilities in the Greenstone digital library software, which we will meet in the next chapter, and you should plan to return to it later if you become curious about how they work.

5.1 Hypertext markup language: HTML

HTML, or the Hypertext Markup Language, is the underlying document format of the World Wide Web, which makes it a baseline for interactive viewing. Like all major document formats, it has undergone growing pains, and its history reflects the anarchy that characterized the Web's evolution. Since the conception of HTML in 1989, its development has been driven by software vendors who compete for the Web browser market by inventing new features to make their product distinctive—the "browser wars."

Many new features play on people's desires to exert more control over how their documents appear. To take a simple example, who gets to control font attributes such as typeface and size—writer or reader? (If you think this is a rather trivial issue, imagine what it means for the visually disabled.) Allowing authors to dictate details of how their documents appear conflicts sharply with the original vision for HTML, which divorced document structure from presentation and left decisions about rendering documents to the browser itself. It makes the pages less predictable because viewing platforms may differ in the support they provide. For example, in HTML text can be marked up as "emphasized," and while it is common practice to render such items in italics, there is no requirement to follow this convention: boldface would convey the same intention.

Out of the maelstrom an HTML standard has emerged. Consolidated through successive versions, the situation continues to develop. In this section we describe the HTML language. The story is continued in the next section when we present the background to XML.

Basic HTML

Modern markup languages use words enclosed in angle brackets as tags to annotate text. For example, *<title>A really exciting story</title>* defines the title of an HTML document. In HTML, tag names are case insensitive. For each tag the language defines a "closing" version, which gives the tag name preceded by a slash character (/). However, closing tags in certain situations can be omitted—a practice that some decry as impure while others endorse as legitimate shorthand. For example, *<p>* is used to mark up paragraphs, and subsequent *<p>*s are assumed to automatically end the previous paragraph—no intervening *</p>* is necessary. The shortcut is only possible because nesting a paragraph within a paragraph—the only other plausible interpretation on encountering the second *<p>*—is invalid in HTML.

Opening tags can include a list of qualifiers known as *attributes*. These have the form *name="value"*. For example, *<img src="gsdl.gif" width="537" height="17">* specifies an image with a given source file name (*gsdl.gif*) and given dimensions (537 × 17 pixels).

Because the language uses characters such as <, >, and " as special markers, a way is needed to display these characters literally. In HTML these characters are represented as special forms called *entities* and given names like < for "less than" (<) and > for "greater than" (>). This convention makes ampersand (&) into a special character, which is displayed by & when it appears literally in documents. The semicolon needs no such treatment because its literal use and its use as a terminator are syntactically distinct. The same kind of special form is used for characters in extended fonts, such as è for è.

```html
<html>
<head>
  <title>Greenstone Digital Library Software</title>
  <meta name="Creator" content="The New Zealand Digital Library project">
  <meta http-equiv="Content-Type" content="text/html; charset=utf-8">
</head>

<!-- Set background to Maori motif -->
<body bgcolor="#ffffff" text="#000000" background="heke.gif">

  <center>
  <table width="537">
    <tr><td><center><img src="divb.gif" width=537 height=17></center>

    <table>
    <tr valign=top>
      <td><br>
          <h2>Kia papapounamu te moana</h2>
          <p> kia hora te marino,<br>
              kia tere te karohirohi,<br>
              kia papapounamu te moana

          <p> may peace and calmness surround you,<br>
              may you reside in the warmth of a summer's haze,<br>
              may the ocean of your travels be as smooth as the polished
                greenstone.
      </td>
      <td>
        <img src="gsdl.gif" width="140" height="77" border="0"
        alt="Greenstone Digital Library Software" hspace=0>
      </td>
    </tr>
    </table>

    <p> Greenstone is a semi-precious stone that (like this software)
    is sourced in New Zealand.  In traditional Maori society it was the
    most highly prized and sought after of all substances.  It can absorb
    and hold <i>wairua</i>, which is a spirit or life force ...

    <ul>
      <li>Some special symbols: &lt; &amp; &quot; &auml; &#257; ; #
    </ul>

    <p><center><img src="divb.gif" width=537 height=17></center>
    <p><a href="http://www.nzdl.org">New Zealand Digital Library Project</a>

  </table>
  </center>
</body>
<html>
```

(a)

Figure 5.1 (a) Sample HTML code involving graphics, text, and some special symbols; (b) snapshot rendered by a Web browser. (continued on following page)

Figure 5.1 shows a sample page that illustrates several parts of HTML, along with a snapshot of how it is rendered by a Web browser—it contains "typical" HTML code that you find on the Web, rather than exemplary HTML. Documents are divided into a header and a body. The header gives global information: the title of the document, the character encoding scheme, any metadata. The

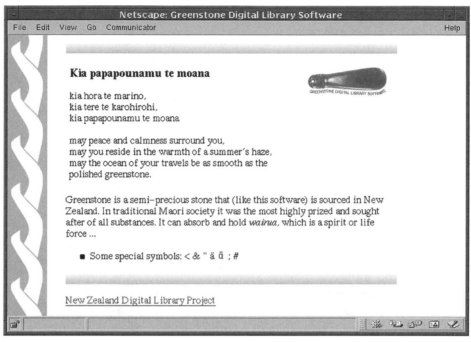

(b)

Figure 5.1 (continued)

<meta> tag is used in Figure 5.1a to acknowledge the New Zealand Digital Library Project as the document's creator. *Creator* imitates the Dublin Core element (see Section 5.4) that is used to represent the name of the entity responsible for generating a document, be it a person, organization, or software application; however, there is no requirement in HTML to conform to such standards. Following the header is a comment and a command that sets the background to a Polynesian motif.

This particular page is laid out as two tables. The first controls the main layout. The second, nested within it, lays out the poem and the image of a greenstone pendant. The tags *<tr>* and *<td>* are used to mark table rows and cells, respectively. The list item *<li>* near the end illustrates various special characters. Most take the &...; form, but the last two (; and #) do not need to be escaped because their normal meaning is syntactically unambiguous. To generate the letter *a* with a line above (called a *macron* and used in the Māori language), the appropriate Unicode UTF-8 value is given in decimal (#257), demonstrating one way of specifying non-ASCII characters. The example illustrates several other features, including images specified by the *<img>* tag, paragraphs beginning with *<p>*, italicized words given by *<i>*, and a bulleted list introduced by *<ul>* (for "unordered list"), along with a *<li>* tag for each list item (just one in this case).

Hyperlinks are an important feature of HTML. In the example the tag pair <*a*> . . . </*a*> near the end defines a link *anchor*. The document to link to—in this case, another page on the Web—is specified as an attribute. Hyperlinks can reference audio and video material and PDF documents—formats for these were covered in Chapter 4—as well as many others. For instance, the Virtual Reality Modeling Language, VRML, specifies a navigable virtual reality experience. Browsers display the anchor text—the text appearing between the start and end hyperlink tag—differently to emphasize the presence of a hyperlink. When clicked, the browser loads the new document.

HTML was originally encoded in ASCII for transmission over byte-oriented protocols. However, with the advent of Unicode the default has been changed to UTF-8, which, as we learned in Chapter 4 (Section 4.1), is backward compatible with ASCII. Other encoding schemes are supported by setting the *charset* attribute in a header element to the appropriate encoding name. In Figure 5.1a, line 5 sets it explicitly to UTF-8. Since it is the default, the behavior would be the same if the attribute were omitted.

HTML has many more features. For example, locally defined link anchors permit navigation within a single document. Fonts, colors, and page backgrounds can be specified explicitly. *Forms* can be created that collect data from the user—such as text data, fielded data, and selections from lists of items.

A mechanism called *frames* allows an HTML document to be tiled into smaller, independent segments, each an HTML page in its own right. A set of frames, called a *frameset*, can be displayed simultaneously. This is often used to add a navigation bar to every page of a Web site, along the top or down the side of the browser pane. When a link in the navigation bar is clicked, a new page is loaded into the main display frame, and the bar remains in place. Clicking on a link in the main display frame also loads the new page into the main frame.

Frames were introduced by one vendor during the "browser wars" and soon became supported by other browsers too. However, they have serious drawbacks. For instance, now that a browser can display more than one HTML document at a time, what happens when you create a bookmark? People often click around a site to reach an interesting document, then bookmark it in the usual way—only to find that the bookmark returns not to the intended page but to the point where the site split into frames instead. This can be very frustrating.

Many of the effects for which frames are currently used—such as persistent navigation bars—can also be accomplished by the newer and more principled mechanism of style sheets, avoiding the problems of frames. We describe style sheets in Section 5.3.

Using HTML in a digital library

As the lingua franca for the Web, HTML underpins virtually all digital library interfaces. Moreover, digital library source documents are often presented in

HTML form. This eliminates most of the difficulties with the plain text representation introduced in Chapter 4 (Section 4.2)—for example, the HTML header disambiguates the character set, while the <br> and <p> tags disambiguate line and paragraph breaks.

To extract text from HTML documents for indexing purposes, the obvious strategy of parsing them according to a well-defined grammar quickly runs into difficulty. The permissive nature of Web browsers encourages authors to depart from the defined standard. A better way to identify and remove tags is to write them in the form of "regular expressions" (a scheme described in the next section), and this generally achieves greater success for less effort. An alternative is to use the very kind of application that caused the complication in the first place: Web browsers. The plain text browser *lynx* provides a fast and reliable method of extracting text from HTML documents—you give it a command-line argument (*dump*) and a URL, and it dumps out the contents of that URL in the form of plain text.

As the example in Figure 5.1 illustrates, HTML allows metadata to be specified explicitly using <meta> tags. However, the mechanism it provides is rather limited. For one thing, you might hesitate before tampering with source documents by inserting new metadata (perhaps determined separately, perhaps mined from the document content) in this way. When developing a digital library you need to consider whether it is wise to add new information that cannot be disentangled from that present in the source document, or whether it is acceptable to serve up an altered version in place of the original.

5.2   Extensible markup language: XML

During the 1970s and 1980s a generalized system for structural markup was developed called the Standard Generalized Markup Language or SGML; it was ratified as an ISO international standard in 1986. SGML is not a markup language but a metalanguage for describing markup formats. It is popular among large organizations such as government offices and the military. However, it is rather intricate, and it has proven difficult to develop flexible software tools for the fully blown standard. This fact was the catalyst for the "extensible markup language," XML.

XML is a simplified version of SGML designed specifically for interoperability over the Web. Informally speaking it is a dialect of SGML, whereas HTML is an example of a markup language that SGML can describe. It provides a flexible way of characterizing document structure and metadata, making it well suited to digital libraries. It has achieved widespread use in an astonishingly short stretch of time.

XML has strict syntactic conventions that make it impossible for it to describe ancient forms of HTML exactly. The differences expose parts of the early specifications that were loosely formed—ones that cause difficulty when parsing and processing documents. However, with a little trickery—for example, judicious placement of white space—it is possible to generate an XML specification of an extremely close approximation to HTML. Put another way, you can take advantage of HTML's sloppy specification to produce files that are valid XML. Such files have twin virtues: they can be viewed in any Web browser, and they can be parsed and processed by XML tools.

Development of markup and stylesheet languages

Web culture has advanced at an extraordinary pace, creating a melee of incremental—and at times conflicting—additions and revisions to HTML, XML, and related standards. Figure 5.2 summarizes the main developments by year.

Although it has been retrospectively fitted with XML descriptions, HTML was created before XML was conceived and drew on the more general expressive capabilities of SGML. It was also forged in the heat of the browser wars, in which Web browsers sprouted a proliferation of innovative nonstandard features that vendors thought would make their products more appealing. As a result browsers became forgiving: they process files that flagrantly violate SGML syntax. One example is tag scope overlap—writing *<i>one two </i>three * to produce *one* ***two*** **three**—despite SGML's requirement that tags be strictly nested. During subsequent attempts at standardization, more tags were added that control typeface and layout, features deliberately excluded from HTML's original design.

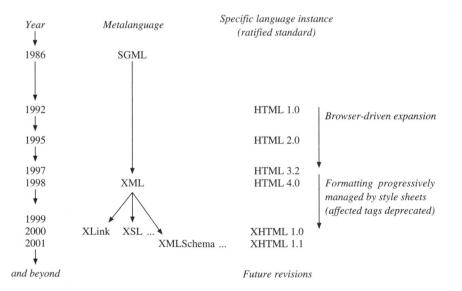

Figure 5.2 The relationship between XML, SGML, and HTML.

The notion of *style sheets* was introduced to resolve the conflict between presentation and structure by moving formatting and layout specifications to a separate file. They purify the HTML markup to reflect, once again, nothing but document structure. Different documents can share a uniform appearance by adopting the same style sheet. Equally, different style sheets can be associated with the same document. Style sheets specify a sequence—a *cascade*—of inherited stylistic properties and are dubbed *cascading style sheets*.

Cascading style sheets were first specified in 1996, quickly followed by an expanded backward-compatible version two years later. Style sheets can be adapted to different media by including formatting commands that are grouped together and associated with a given medium—screen, print, projector, handheld device, and so on. Guided by the user (or otherwise), applications that process the document use the relevant set of style commands. A Web browser might choose *screen* for online display but switch to *print* when rendering the document in PostScript.

HTML version 4 promotes the use of style sheets. Moreover, it encourages them by officially deprecating formatting tags and other elements that affect presentation rather than structure. This is accomplished through three subcategories to the standard. *Strict* HTML excludes all frameset commands and all deprecated tags and elements listed in the standard. Layout is expressed only through style sheets. *Transitional* HTML shuns framesets but allows deprecated commands. Style sheets are the principal way of specifying layout, but deprecated commands may also be included to provide compatibility with older browsers. *Frameset* HTML permits both frameset commands and deprecated tags and elements. HTML 4 files declare their subcategory at the start of the document. The format also adds improved support for multidirectional text (not just left to right) and enhancements for improved access by people with disabilities.

With the emergence of XML, an HTML subset called XHTML has been defined that obeys the stricter syntactic rules imposed by the XML metalanguage. For instance, tags in XML are case sensitive, so XHTML tags and attributes are defined to be lowercase. Attributes within a tag must be enclosed in quotes. Each opening tag must be balanced by a corresponding closing tag (or be a single tag that combines opening and closing, with its own special syntax).

The power and flexibility of XML is further increased by related standards. Three are given in Figure 5.2 (there are others). The "extensible stylesheet language" XSL represents a more sophisticated approach than cascading style sheets: it can also transform data. The "XML linking language" XLink provides a more powerful method for connecting resources than HTML hyperlinks: it has bidirectional links, can link more than two entities, and associates metadata with links. Finally, XML Schema provides a rich mechanism for combining components and controlling the overall structure, attributes, and data types used in a document. In this chapter we concentrate on the XML extensions that yield presentation capabilities comparable to HTML. In Chapter 8 we discuss advanced features of this family that take documents well beyond the boundaries of HTML.

From a technical standpoint it is easier to work with XHTML and its siblings than HTML because they conform more strictly to a defined syntax and are therefore easier to parse. In reality, however, digital libraries have to handle legacy material gracefully. Today's browsers do in fact cope remarkably well with the wide range of HTML files: they take backward compatibility to impressive levels. To help promote standardization a software utility called HTML Tidy converts older formats. The process is largely automatic, but human intervention may be required if files deviate radically from recognized norms.

The XML metalanguage

Figure 5.3 shows an example that encodes a formatted list of information about United Nations agencies in XML. For each agency the file records its full name, an optional abbreviation, and the URL of a photograph of its headquarters. Included with the name is the address of the headquarters, stored as an attribute.

The file contains three broad sections, separated by comments in the form <!-- . . . -->. Line 1 is a header: it uses the special notation <? . . . ?> to denote an application-processing instruction. This syntax originates in SGML, which uses it to embed information for specific application programs that process the document. Here it is used to declare the version of XML, the character encoding (UTF-8), and whether or not external files are used. Lines 5 to 19 dictate the syntactic structure in which the remainder of the file is expressed, in the form of a Document Type Definition (DTD). Lines 21 to 44 provide the content of the document.

The style of the content section is reminiscent of HTML. The tag specifications have the same syntactic conventions, and many tags are identical—examples are *<Head>*, *<Title>*, and *<Body>*. However, in lines 27 to 40 the markup forms structures that HTML cannot represent.

Being a metalanguage, XML gives document designers a great deal of freedom. Here the designer has chosen to make the main document structure resemble HTML, but there is no requirement to do so. Not only could one choose different tag names, but different ways could be used to express the information. For example, Figure 5.3 gives the headquarters address as the *hq* attribute of the *<Name>* tag. Instead a new tag pair could have been defined to contain this information. It could be forced to appear immediately following the *<Name>* element, or left optional, or sited anywhere within the *<Agency>* element.

```
1   <?xml version="1.0" encoding="UTF-8" standalone="yes"?>
2   <!--
3     Document Type Definition (DTD) for Non-Government Organizations (NGOs)
4     -->
5   <!DOCTYPE NGODoc [
6   <!ELEMENT NGODoc (Head,Body)>
7   <!ELEMENT Head    (Title)>
8   <!ELEMENT Body    (#PCDATA|Agency)*>
9   <!ELEMENT Agency (Name,(Abbrev?|Photo*)+)>
10  <!ELEMENT Title   (#PCDATA)>
11  <!ELEMENT Name    (#PCDATA)>
12  <!ATTLIST Name
13           hq CDATA #IMPLIED>
14  <!ELEMENT Abbrev (#PCDATA)>
15  <!ELEMENT Photo  EMPTY>
16  <!ATTLIST Photo
17           src  CDATA #REQUIRED
18           desc CDATA "A photo">
19  ]>
20  <!-- Sample content conforming to DTD -->
21  <NGODoc>
22  <Head>
23    <Title>Agencies of the United Nations</Title>
24  </Head>
25  <Body>
26    <Agency>
27      <Name hq="Paris, France">United Nations Educational, Scientific
28          and Cultural Organization</Name>
29      <Abbrev>UNESCO</Abbrev>
30      <Photo src="photos/unesco_hq.jpg"
31          desc="Aerial photo of main UNESCO building"/>
32    </Agency>
33    <Agency>
34      <Name hq="Rome, Italy">Food and Agricultural Organization</Name>
35      <Abbrev>FAO</Abbrev>
36      <Photo src="photos/fao_hq.jpg"/>
37    </Agency>
38    <Agency>
39      <Name hq="Washington, USA">World Bank</Name>
40      <Photo src="photos/worldbank_hq.jpg"/>
41    </Agency>
42    <!-- and so on ... -->
43  </Body>
44  </NGODoc>
```

Figure 5.3 Sample XML document.

Such structural decisions are recorded in the DTD (lines 5–19). DTD tags use the special syntax <! . . . > and express keywords in block capitals. For example, *ELEMENT* and *ATTLIST* are used to define tags and tag attributes. Our document designer decided to capitalize the initial letter of all document tags and leave attributes in lowercase. This improves the legibility of Figure 5.3 considerably.

Line 5 starts the DTD, and the square bracket syntax [. . .] indicates that the DTD will appear in-line. (It must, for line 1 declared that the file stands alone.) Alternatively the DTD can be placed in an external file, referred to by a URL— and this is normally desirable in practice.

New elements are introduced in lines 6 to 11 by the keyword *ELEMENT*, followed by the new tag name and a description of what the element may contain. A *leaf* is an element that comprises plain text, with no markup. This is accomplished through *parsed character data* and declared as *#PCDATA*. Despite its primitive nature, special characters may be included. For example, when the *<Title>* tag defined on line 10 is used, any of the special markup characters may appear in the title's text. These are encoded in the familiar HTML way—<; &; and so on. (This convention originated in SGML.)

Lines 6 to 9 describe nonleaf structures. These are defined in a form known as a *regular expression*. Here a comma signifies an ordered sequence: line 6 declares that the top-level element *<NGODoc>* contains a *<Head>* element followed by a *<Body>* element. A vertical bar (|) represents a choice of one element from a sequence of named elements, and an asterisk (*) indicates zero or more occurrences. Thus *<Body>* (line 8) is a mixture of parsed character data and *<Agency>* elements where it is permissible for nothing at all to appear. A plus (+) means one or more occurrences, and a question mark (?) signifies either nothing or just one occurrence. Line 9 includes all four symbols, |, *, +, and ?: it declares that *<Agency>* must include a name element, but that *<Abbrev>* is optional and there can be zero or more occurrences of *<Photo>* (the example is contrived: there are more concise ways of expressing the same thing). The inner pair of brackets to the expression bind these last two tags together, adding the extra stipulation that there must be one or more occurrences of these *<Abbrev>* and *<Photo>* options.

Attributes also give a set of possible values, but here there is no nesting. Lines 12 and 13 show an example. The attribute is signaled by the keyword *ATTLIST*, followed by the element to which it applies (*Name*), the attribute's name (*hq*), its type (*character* data), and any appearance restrictions (this one is optional). Lines 16 to 18 show another example, which introduces two attributes of the element *Photo*. Line 17 states that the *src* attribute is required, while line 18 provides a default value (namely "*A photo*") for the *desc* attribute.

In addition to <; and &; XML incorporates definitions for >; '; and ";. These are called *entities*, and new ones can be added in the DTD using the syntax *ENTITY name "value"*. For instance, although XML does not have a definition for *à* as HTML does, one can be defined by <!*ENTITY agrave "à">*, which relies on the Unicode standard for the numeric value. Entities are not restricted to single characters, but can be used for any excerpt of text (even if it is marked up). For example, <!*ENTITY howto "How to Build a Digital Library">* is a shorthand way of encoding the title of this book.

If several elements were to share exactly the same attributes, it would be tedious (and error-prone) to repeat the attribute definitions in each element. In XML this can be handled using a special type of entity known as a *parameter entity*. To illustrate it, Figure 5.4 shows a modified and slightly restructured version of the DTD in Figure 5.3 that defines two attributes *ident* and *style* under

```
1    <?xml version="1.0" encoding="UTF-8" standalone="yes"?>
2    <!DOCTYPE NGODoc [
3    <!ENTITY % sharedattrib
4      " style NMTOKEN #IMPLIED
5        ident ID #IMPLIED ">
6    <!ELEMENT NGODoc (Title,Body)>
7    <!ELEMENT Body    (Name|Abbrev)+>
8    <!ELEMENT Title   (#PCDATA)>
9    <!ELEMENT Name    (#PCDATA)>
10   <!ELEMENT Abbrev  (#PCDATA)>
11   <!ATTLIST Title   %sharedattrib;>
12   <!ATTLIST Abbrev  %sharedattrib;>
13   <!ATTLIST Name    %sharedattrib;
14             HQ CDATA #IMPLIED>
15   ]>
```

Figure 5.4 Sample DTD using a parameterized entity.

the name *sharedattrib* (lines 3–5), which is then used to bestow these attributes on the <*Title*>, <*Abbrev*>, and <*Name*> elements (lines 11–14). Parameter entities are signaled using the percent symbol (%) and provide a form of shorthand for use within a DTD.

Declaring the shared attribute *style* as *NMTOKEN* (line 4) restricts this attribute's characters to alphanumeric characters plus period (.), colon (:), hyphen (-), and underscore (_), where the first character must be a letter. Its twin *ident* is defined as *ID* (line 5), which is the same as *NMTOKEN* with the additional constraint that no two such attributes in the document can have the same value. *ID* therefore provides a mechanism for uniquely identifying its elements. The concept is already present in HTML for any attribute with the particular name *id*. In XML uniqueness can be bestowed on any attribute, whatever its name—such as *ident*.

DTD syntax also supports enumerated types, although none are present in the example. It is also permissible to have lists of tokens separated by white space (*NMTOKENS*) and attributes that are references to *ID* attributes (*IDREF*).

Parsing XML

A document that conforms to XML syntax but does not supply a DTD is said to be *well formed*. One that conforms to XML syntax and does supply a DTD is said to be *valid*—providing the content does indeed abide by the syntactic constraints defined in the DTD. It is also possible to store a DTD externally, replacing the bracketed section in lines 5 to 19 of Figure 5.3 by a URL. This allows documents of the same structure to be shared within an organization or, if the DTD is publicly available, between organizations.

XML allows you to define new languages. It is easy to develop parsers for them. Moreover, because of the syntactic constraints imposed by XML, generic parsers are available that are capable of parsing *any* XML file. If a DTD is present, such parsers can also check that the file is valid. However, merely parsing a document—even with respect to a DTD—is of limited utility. The result of a parser is just a yes/no indication of whether the document conforms to the general rules of XML or not (or the more specific DTD or not).

Far more useful would be a way of specifying what the generic parser should do with the data it is processing. This is arranged by having the generic tool build a parse tree and providing a programming interface—commonly called an API or "application program interface"—that lets the user traverse the tree and retrieve the data it contains.

The result of parsing any XML file is a root node whose descendants reflect both text content and nested tags. At each tag's node are stored the values of the tag's attributes. There is a cross-platform and cross-language API called the *document object model* (DOM) which allows you to write programs that access and modify the document's content, structure, and style.

The XML language includes defaults, so that if a particular value is missing, the standard describes what value it should take. For example, if no encoding is mentioned in the XML header declaration line, UTF-8 is assumed.

Using XML in a digital library

XML is a powerful tool. It allows file formats within an organization, such as a digital library, to be rationalized and shared. Alongside any material they publish, organizations can provide an explanation of the structures used in the form of a DTD. Different organizations can develop comprehensive formats for sharing information by formulating appropriate DTDs.

A notable example is the Text Encoding Initiative (TEI), founded in 1987, which developed a set of DTDs for representing scholarly texts in the humanities and social sciences. SGML was the implementation backbone, but the work has since been reconciled with XML. These DTDs are widely used by universities, museums, and commercial organizations to represent museum and archival information, classical and medieval works, dictionaries and lexicographies, religious tracts, legal documents, and many other forms of writing.

Examples are legion. The Oxford Text Archive is a nonprofit group that has provided long-term storage and maintenance of electronic texts for scholars over the last quarter-century. Perseus is a pioneering digital library project, dating from 1985, that focuses upon the ancient Greek world. Der Junge Goethe in Seiner Zeit is a collection of early works—poems, essays, legal writings, and letters—by the great German writer Johann von Goethe (1749–1832). The Japanese Text Initiative is a collaborative project that makes available a steadily increasing set of Japanese literature, accompanied by English, French, and German translations.

Various related standards increase XML's power and expand its applicability. Used on its own, XML provides a syntax for expressing structural information, or metadata. But recall that whether information is metadata or not is really a matter of perspective. Combined with additional standards, XML goes much further: it supports document restructuring, querying, information extraction, and formatting. The next section expands on the formatting standards, which equip XML with display capabilities comparable with HTML. In Chapter 8 we return to XML and complete our discussion of its relatives.

5.3 Presenting marked-up documents

There are two kinds of style sheet that can be used to control the presentation of marked-up documents. *Cascading style sheets* produce presentable documents with minimal effort and work with both HTML and XML. The *extensible stylesheet language* adds further power by allowing the document structure to be altered dynamically—for example, a particular element type can be constrained to appear at the top of the page, regardless of where it is actually defined—but only works with XML (and versions of HTML that are XML compliant).

Cascading style sheets: CSS

Figure 5.5 shows what the document of Figure 5.3 looks like when displayed using Mozilla, an XML-capable Web browser. The display is rudimentary. All the text that appears between tag names is run together in one paragraph, in a default font. Information stored as attributes does not appear anywhere.

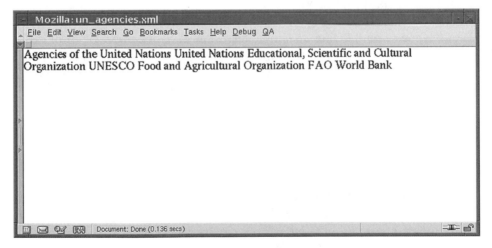

Figure 5.5 Sample XML document, viewed in a Web browser.

Basic CSS

Figure 5.6a gives a basic style sheet for the same example. It is included by adding the line

```
<?xml-stylesheet href="un_basic.css" type="text/css"?>
```

just after the XML header declaration in Figure 5.3 (the text of Figure 5.6a resides in a file called *un_basic.css*). Figure 5.6b shows the result. The document's background is now explicitly set to white; a different font and type size are used to distinguish its title; and improved line formatting makes the individual records easier to read.

Style sheets specify a series of rules using *selector-declaration* pairs. Here is an example:

```
NGODoc { background: white }
```

The selector, here *NGODoc,* relates the style to the document being viewed by naming one or more tags. There can be several rules for a given tag name—Figure 5.6a includes two for *NGODoc.* The declaration that follows, enclosed in braces, gives formatting commands that apply to the named tag or tags—in this case setting the document background to white. Declarations consist of one or more *property-value* pairs separated by semicolons, each with a colon to distinguish the property from the value.

Cascading style sheets provide an inheritance mechanism based upon the hierarchical document model that underpins XML. If formatting for a tag is specified in the style sheet, nested tags—tags that come beneath it in the document tree—inherit that specification. This makes style sheets concise and perspicuous. It is easy to override inherited behavior: just supply further rules at the appropriate level.

Although inheritance is the norm, some properties are explicitly defined to be noninheriting. In simple terms, what happens can be informally characterized as "intuitive inheritance" because exceptions to the rule make things behave more naturally. For example, if a background image is specified, it is tiled over the entire page. However, if nested tags inherited the background, they would break up the pattern by restarting the image at every hierarchical block and subblock. Thus the *background-image* property is not inherited. For completeness you can override the default inheritance behavior by explicitly specifying certain properties to be inheritable (and vice versa).

Returning to the example style sheet in Figure 5.6a, the first rule causes the entire document to be formatted in a block. The same selector name is used for the second rule—part of which has already been discussed. This rule augments this tag's formatting to include a white background and sets the block's width to 7.5 inches. The third rule declares the *Title* font to be Times, 25 point, boldface. The declarations in the fourth rule place the *Agency* record in a paragraph block with

```
/* Cascading Style Sheet for UN Example */

NGODoc          { display: block }

NGODoc          { background: white; width: 7.5in }

Title           { font-family: times; /* Set font type to Times */
                  font-size: 25pt;     /* Set font size to 25 point */
                  font-style: bold }   /* and so on ... */

Agency          { display: block;
                  margin-top: 8pt; margin-bottom: 3pt;
                  font-size: 16pt;
                  font-family: helvetica }

Head, Body      { display: block;
                  margin-top: 6pt;
                  margin-left: 0.2in;
                  margin-right: 5mm }

Abbrev          { display: inline; font-style: italic }

Abbrev:before { content: "(" }
Abbrev:after  { content: ")" }
```

(a)

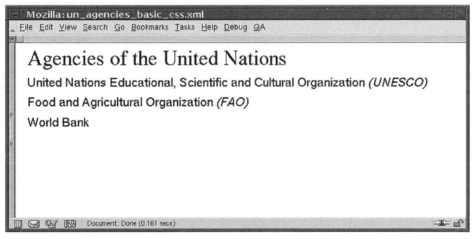

(b)

Figure 5.6 (a) Basic CSS style sheet for the United Nations Agencies example;
(b) viewing the result in an XML-enabled Web browser.

8-point spacing above and 3-point spacing below, typeset as 16-point Helvetica. The inheritance mechanism ensures that nested tags also share this typeface.

In rule five, two tag names are specified as the selector, *Head* and *Body*, and both are assigned top, left, and right margins of 6 points, 0.2 inch, and 5 mm, respectively. Referring to the DTD that begins Figure 5.3, the *Head* specification applies to the document's *Title*, and the *Body* applies to the *Agency* node. Since the two specifications are the same, this effect could have been achieved more concisely by setting these properties in the *NGODoc* node, but this would not have illustrated the comma selector syntax. Rule six adds italics to *Abbrev*, which already inherits a 16-point Helvetica typeface from *Agency*.

The last two rules use a construct known as *pseudo-elements*. The tag name is qualified by :*before* and :*after*, which cause stylistic operations to be performed before and after the *Abbrev* tag is processed. In this case the effect is to place parentheses around the abbreviation. Other pseudo-elements give access to the first character and first line of a block. Pseudo-classes, a related construct, can distinguish between links that have been visited and ones that have not, and support interactive response to events such as the cursor hovering over a location.

In general the ordering of rules in a style sheet is immaterial because every rule that matches any selector is applied. However, it is possible for rules to be contradictory—for example, the background color may be set to both red and blue. The CSS specification includes an algorithm that resolves ambiguity based upon ordering and precedence values.

The same separation of structural markup and formatting instructions in HTML is achieved using a *<link>* tag in the document's *<head>*, like this:

```
<link ref="stylesheet" type="text/css" href="example_style.css">
```

This is just like the processing-application instruction used to augment the XML example with a style sheet. Also cascading style sheet instructions can be embedded in an HTML document by enclosing them within *<style type="text/css">* . . . *</style>* tags.

Tables and lists

Style sheets are *cascaded* when several are applied to the same document. Figure 5.7a shows how the records in the United Nations Agencies example can be embedded in a table and the document title formatted with a bullet point. The result, viewed in a Web browser, appears in Figure 5.7b. Following the opening comment, the special command *@import* directs the application processing the style sheet to use the earlier style file (Figure 5.6a) to provide a base layer of formatting rules. These are augmented by the rules that follow the *@import* command. New properties take precedence: if they conflict with existing ones, the existing ones are overridden. The style sheet in Figure 5.7a also demonstrates some of the table and list features of CSS.

The first rule augments the formatting of the *Title* tag—Times font, 25 point, boldface, as defined in Figure 5.6a—with new rules: the display type is set to *list item*, a bullet point (*disk*) is chosen as the list item to display, and a left-hand margin of 0.2 inch is used to indent the bullet slightly. These new rules create no conflict.

```
/* Table and List item Cascading Style Sheet for UN Example */

@import url("un_basic.css");

Title    { display: list-item;
           list-item: disk;
           margin-left: 0.2in; }

Body     { display: table;
           table-layout: auto;
           background: silver;
           border: outset 5pt;
           border-collapse: separate;
           border-spacing: 10pt }

Agency   { display: table-row; }

Name     { display: table-cell;
           padding: 4pt;
           background: white;
           border: inset 2pt;}

Abbrev   { display: table-cell;
           padding: 4pt;
           background: white;
           border: dotted black;
           text-align: center;
           vertical-align: middle; }

Photo    { display: table-cell;
           width: 60pt;
           background: white;
           vertical-align: middle }

Photo:before { content: "photo available"; }
```

(a)

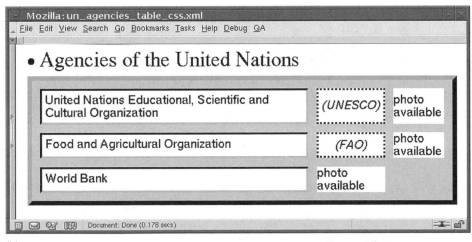

(b)

Figure 5.7 (a) CSS style sheet illustrating tables and lists; (b) viewing the result in an XML-enabled Web browser.

CSS allows you to choose the symbol used for bullet points, use enumeration rather than bullets, and alter the style of enumeration (alphabetic, roman, etc.). A counter mechanism allows such things as nested section numbering.

The other rules in Figure 5.7a present the document's information in tabular form. To do this the style file must map tag names to the display settings *table*, *table-row*, and *table-cell* and supply appropriate stylistic parameters for each. First the *Body* element is mapped to *table*, along with values for background color and border style and size. The table layout mode is set to *auto*, which causes the cell dimensions to be calculated automatically to make best use of available space. (The alternative is to specify the layout to be *fixed* and give cell width and height explicitly.) The value *separate* for *border-collapse* separates the borders of the individual cells.

The next rule maps the *Agency* node to *table-row*, so that each agency's information is displayed in its own row. The following three rules define *Name*, *Abbrev*, and *Photo* to be table cells and specify some properties intended to give a pleasing result: the background is *white*, the border styles are *inset*, *dotted*, and (by omission) *plain*, the *Name* and *Abbrev* cells are padded to leave space inside the border, and the text in *Abbrev* is horizontally and vertically centered using *text-align: center* and *vertical-align: middle*, respectively.

Although the *Photo* elements in the XML document do not explicitly provide text information between tag pairs, they are defined as type *table-cell*, and so the table will include empty cells of width 60 points. This has been done to illustrate a further point: the pseudo-element *before* fills the empty cell with the text *photo available*.

The end result in Figure 5.7b exhibits a small glitch: the *photo available* message on the last line appears in the second column, not the third. This reflects the structure of the XML document in Figure 5.3, which lacks an abbreviation for the World Bank. This serves to remind us that CSS does not provide a general mechanism for altering document structure, although some manipulation is possible using pseudo-elements. In contrast, XSL is a more expressive language that is explicitly designed to allow the document structure to be altered.

Figure 5.7a gives a mere taste of CSS's table model. Tables can have headers, footers, captions, or sections grouped by row or column, and they can all be structured hierarchically into the final table. CSS, HTML, and XSL share the same model for table formatting, and concepts map naturally between the three representations. This general trend underlies the design of CSS and XSL; we return to this point later when we move on to XSL.

Context-sensitive formatting

So far we have seen some of what cascading style sheets can do. But there's more—context-sensitive formatting. Using compound selectors, rules can detect when descendant or sibling tags match a particular pattern and produce different effects. Rules can also trigger when attributes match particular patterns, and this facility can be combined with compound selectors.

Figure 5.8a introduces some contrived formatting instructions into the running example to illustrate some of these points. Figure 5.8b shows the result. Again through the *@import* command, the new style incorporates the formatting instructions of Figure 5.6a.

Using the pseudo-element *before*, the first rule tailors the content of a *Photo* according to the value of the *desc* attribute—but only when the *Photo* is a child of *Agency*. Omitting the > symbol would change the meaning to "descendant"

```
/* Contextual Cascading Style Sheet instructions for UN Example */

@import url("un_basic.css");

Agency > Photo[desc]:before   { content: "Available: " attr(desc) }

Body Photo[desc="A photo"]    { display: none }

Agency + Agency               { color: red;
                                background: #ffa080 }

Name[hq="Rome, Italy"]        { background: rgb(%0,%50,%0);
                                color: rgb(255,160,80) }

Agency                        { font-size: 20pt; }
```

(a)

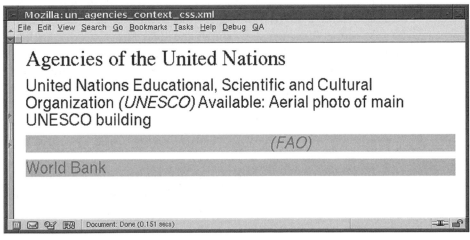

(b)

Figure 5.8 (a) CSS style sheet illustrating context-sensitive formatting; (b) viewing the result in an XML-enabled Web browser.

rather than "child" and would trigger if the *Photo* node appeared anywhere beneath an *Agency* node.

The second rule suppresses the *Photo* text if its *desc* attribute matches the string *A photo*. If the first rule appeared without the second, the result would show the text *A photo* for both the FAO and the World Bank records because the document's DTD supplies this text as the default value for *desc*.

The third rule demonstrates the + syntax that is used to specify sibling context. When one *Agency* node follows another at the same level in the document tree, this rule alters its background and foreground colors. In the XML document of Figure 5.3, only the first *Agency* record in the document retains its default coloring. The rule also illustrates two different ways of specifying color: by name (*red*) and by specifying red, green, and blue components in hexadecimal.

The next rule prints the full name of the FAO in the same color as the background,[7] because its *hq* attribute in the *Name* tag matches *Rome, Italy*. It uses a third form of color specification: the *rgb*() function, which gives color components in decimal—and these in fact specify the same color as in the previous hexadecimal assignment. This rule makes no sense in practice, but it explains why *(FAO)* is placed far to the right in Figure 5.8b, because it is preceded by the now-invisible name.

The last rule further illustrates inheritance by setting the font size for *Agency* text to 20 points. This overrides the 16-point value set in the initial style sheet and is inherited by descendant nodes.

Media-dependent formatting

A key feature of cascading style sheets is the ability to handle different media such as screen, print, handheld devices, computer projectors, text-only display, Braille, and audio. Figure 5.9 shows the idea. The *@media* command names the media type or types and gives rules, scoped to that media, within braces. The example first sets the *Agency* node globally to be a block with specified margins. Then for screen and projection media, the font is set to 16-point Helvetica, while for print it is 12-point Times.

An *@import* command can be augmented to restrict the media type it applies to, for example:

```
@import url("un_audio.css") aural;
```

CSS continues to be developed. Like XHTML, the trend is to modularize the specification so it is easier for a software implementer to clarify what support is given.

---

7. The example would be more realistic if different colors were used here, but in this book we are restricted to black and white.

```
/* Different styles for different media */

Agency          { display: block;
                  margin-top: 8pt;
                  margin-bottom: 3pt }

@media screen, projection
{
  Agency        { font-size: 16pt;
                  font-family: helvetica }
}

@media print
{
  Agency        { font-size: 12pt;
                  font-family: times }

}
```

Figure 5.9   Using CSS to specify different formatting styles for different media.

Extensible stylesheet language: XSL

Cascading style sheets were developed principally in support of HTML. A parallel development is XSL, the extensible stylesheet language for XML. It performs the same kind of services as CSS but expresses the style sheet in XML form. To illustrate the similarities and differences, we work through XSL versions of the above three examples—Figures 5.6, 5.7, and 5.8.

XSL transcends the functionality of CSS. It allows the style sheet designer to transform documents quite radically. Parts can be duplicated, tables of contents can be created automatically, lists can be sorted. A price is paid for this expressive power—complexity.

CSS and XSL share a common heritage and are based on the same formatting model. We have already mentioned that they embody the same framework for tables (also in this case shared with HTML 4.0). Another commonality is the notion of a rectangular block of content, padded all around by specified amounts of white space and encased within four borders, which are themselves enclosed by margins. In CSS this is called a *box*, in XSL an *area*.

The XSL specification is divided into three parts: formatting objects (FO), XSL transformations (XSLT), and XPath (a way of selecting parts of a document). Derived from the same model as CSS, formatting objects map closely to the instructions we have already seen and use the same property names wherever possible. XSL transformations manipulate the document tree, while XPath selects parts to transform. We expand on these later in this section.

It is a potentially confusing fact that CSS can be combined with facilities such as Web-page scripting and the document object model mentioned in Section 5.2 (under "Parsing XML") to provide comparable functionality to XSL—this combination is sometimes dubbed *dynamic HTML*. Experts fiercely debate which is the better approach! We think you should know about both, for the wider context in which you work often dictates the path you must tread. There is one key difference between the two approaches. Because XSL is designed to work with XML, it cannot be used with all forms of HTML—because not all forms are XML compliant. CSS, in comparison, operates in either setting: HTML, for which it was designed, and XML, because there is no restriction in the tag names that CSS can provide rules for.

We introduce the XSL formatting capabilities by working through the examples used to illustrate CSS. However, Formatting Objects transcend CSS's functionality in several ways by extending the suite of formatting objects and formatting properties. For example, they include a model for pagination and layout that extends the simple page-by-page structure of paper documents to provide an equivalent to the "frames" that are used in Web pages. They also adopt a more internationally oriented naming convention: *padding-left* becomes *padding-start* so the term makes more sense when dealing with languages such as Arabic that are written right to left. Similarly named attributes exist to control the space above, below, and at the end of text, although XSL also includes the old names for backward compatibility.

Basic XSL

Figure 5.10 shows an XSL file for the initial version of the United Nations example in Figure 5.6b. It is much longer that its CSS counterpart (Figure 5.6a) and uses XML syntax. Take some comfort from the fact that, beyond the initial *NGODoc* declaration, it includes many of the keywords we have seen in the earlier version. For example, the *font-size: 25pt* specification that appeared in CSS's rule for the *Title* node now comes between nested tags whose inner and outer elements include the attributes *font-size="25pt"* and *match="Title"*, respectively. The CSS style sheet in Figure 5.6a (called *un_basic.css*) was included by adding the line

```
<?xml-stylesheet href="un_basic.css" type="text/css"?>
```

just after the XML header declaration in Figure 5.3, and the XSL style sheet (*un_basic.xsl*) is added with essentially the same line:

```
<?xml-stylesheet href="un_basic.xsl" type="text/xsl"?>
```

The result is a replica of Figure 5.6b, although both standards are complex and it is not uncommon to encounter small discrepancies.

Figure 5.10 begins with the obligatory XML processing application statement, followed by an *<xsl:stylesheet>* tag. As usual this is a top-level root element that encloses all the other tags. Its attributes declare two namespaces: one for XSL itself; the other for Formatting Objects (FO). Namespaces are an XML extension that keep sets of tags designed for particular purposes separate—otherwise confusion would occur if both XSL and FO happened to include a tag with the same

```
<?xml version="1.0" encoding="utf-8"?>
<xsl:stylesheet
xmlns:xsl="http://www.w3.org/1999/XSL/Transform"
xmlns:fo="http://www.w3.org/1999/XSL/Format"
version="1.0">

<xsl:output method="xml"/>

<xsl:template match="NGODoc">
  <fo:root xmlns:fo="http://www.w3.org/1999/XSL/Format">
    <fo:layout-master-set>
      <fo:simple-page-master master-name="UN-page" page-width="7.5in">
        <fo:region-body/>
      </fo:simple-page-master>
    </fo:layout-master-set>
    <fo:page-sequence master-name="UN-page">
      <fo:flow flow-name="xsl-region-body" background-color="white">
  <xsl:apply-templates/>
      </fo:flow>
    </fo:page-sequence>
  </fo:root>
</xsl:template>

<xsl:template match="Title">
  <fo:block font-family="Times" font-size="25pt"
            margin-left="0.2in" margin-right="5mm">
    <xsl:apply-templates/>
  </fo:block>
</xsl:template>

<xsl:template match="Agency">
  <fo:block space-before="8pt" space-after="3pt" font-size="16pt"
            font-family="Helvetica"
            margin-left="0.2in" margin-right="5mm">
    <xsl:apply-templates/>
  </fo:block>
</xsl:template>

<xsl:template match="Head|Body">
  <fo:block margin-left="0.2in" margin-right="5mm" space-before="6pt">
    <xsl:apply-templates/>
  </fo:block>
</xsl:template>

<xsl:template match="Abbrev">
  <fo:inline font-style="italic">
    (<xsl:value-of select="."/>)
  </fo:inline>
</xsl:template>

</xsl:stylesheet>
```

Figure 5.10 XSL style sheet for the basic United Nations Agencies example.

name (such as *block*). The ambiguity is resolved by assigning special meaning to any attribute qualified by *xmlns*. Thus Figure 5.10 sets up two namespaces called *xsl* and *fo*, and thereafter *<xsl:block>* specifies the XSL *block* tag while *<fo:block>* specifies the Formatting Objects tag.

Namespaces also bring semantic information into play. If an FO-aware application encounters a namespace declaration whose value is *http://www.w3c.org/*

1999/XSL/Format, it interprets subsequent tag names according to a published specification. In the following discussion we focus on a subset of Formatting Object tags typically used in document-related XML style sheets. The full specification is more comprehensive.

Returning to the example, the next tag sets the document's output type. The XSL style sheet is used to transform the XML source into another document. Because our style sheet is designed to format the document using Formatting Object tags, the output is set to *xml*. Other choices are *html*, in which case all the *fo:* scoped tags in the XSL file would need to be replaced with HTML tags, and *text*.

Transformation involves matching the input document against the style sheet and building a new document tree based on the result. First the document's root node is compared with the XSL file's *<xsl:template>* nodes until one is found whose *match* attribute corresponds to the node's name. Then the body of the XSL *template* tag is used to construct the tags in the output tree. If *apply-templates* is encountered, matching continues recursively on that document node's children (or as we shall see later, on some other selected part of the document), and further child nodes in the output tree are built as a result.

In the example the document's root node matches *<xsl:template match="NGODoc">*. This adds several *fo* tags to the output tree—tags that initialize the page layout of the final document. Eventually *<xsl:apply-templates>* is encountered, which causes the document's children *<Head>* and *<Body>* to be processed by the XSL file. When the matching operation has run its course, the document tree that it generates is rendered for viewing.

The fourth template rule specifies its *match* attribute as *Head|Body* to catch *Head* or *Body* nodes. This specification achieves the same effect as the comma syntax in CSS. However, as we shall see shortly, this new syntax is part of a more powerful and general standard called XPath. The last template rule also introduces brackets around the abbreviation. The

```
<xsl:value-of select="."/>
```

is again XPath syntax. The "." is a way of selecting the current position, or "here"—in this context it selects the text of the current node (*Abbrev*). This usage is adapted from the use of a period (.) in a file name to specify the current directory.

Tables and lists

Formatting Objects provide similar capabilities to those expressible in CSS: margins, borders, padding, foreground and background color, blocks, in-line text, tables with rows and cells, and so on. Many CSS declarations are simply mapped into *fo* tag names and attributes with the same name.

Figure 5.11 shows an XSL style sheet for the version of the United Nations Agencies example illustrated in Figure 5.7b, with records embedded in a table

```xml
<?xml version="1.0" encoding="utf-8"?>
<xsl:stylesheet
        xmlns:xsl="http://www.w3.org/1999/XSL/Transform"
        xmlns:fo="http://www.w3.org/1999/XSL/Format"
        version="1.0">

<xsl:import href="un_basic.xsl"/>

<xsl:template match="Title">
  <fo:list-block>
    <fo:list-item>
      <fo:list-item-label end-indent="label-end()">
        <fo:block font-family="ZapfDingbats" font-size="9pt">
        &#9679;
        </fo:block>
      </fo:list-item-label>

      <fo:list-item-body start-indent="body-start()">
        <fo:block>
          <xsl:apply-imports/>
        </fo:block>
      </fo:list-item-body>
    </fo:list-item>
  </fo:list-block>
</xsl:template>

<xsl:template match="Body">
  <fo:table table-layout="auto" background-color="silver"
    border-style="outset 5pt" border-collapse="separate"
            Border-spacing="10pt">
    <fo:table-body>
      <xsl:apply-templates/>
    </fo:table-body>
  </fo:table>
</xsl:template>

<xsl:template match="Agency">
  <fo:table-row space-before="8pt" space-after="3pt"
      font-size="16pt" font-family="Helvetica"
      margin-left="0.2in" margin-right="5mm">
    <xsl:apply-templates/>
  </fo:table-row>
</xsl:template>

<xsl:template match="Name">
  <fo:table-cell padding="4pt" background-color="white"
      border-style="inset 2pt" display-align="center">
    <fo:block>
      <xsl:apply-imports/>
    </fo:block>
  </fo:table-cell>
</xsl:template>

<xsl:template match="Abbrev">
  <fo:table-cell padding="4pt" background-color="white"
      border-style="dotted black" text-align="center"
      display-align="center">
    <fo:block>
      <xsl:apply-imports/>
    </fo:block>
  </fo:table-cell>
</xsl:template>
```

Figure 5.11 XSL style sheet illustrating tables and lists. (continued on the following page)

```
<xsl:template match="Photo">
  <fo:table-cell width="60pt" background-color="white"
        display-align="center">
    <fo:block>
        Photo available <xsl:apply-imports/>
    </fo:block>
  </fo:table-cell>
</xsl:template>

</xsl:stylesheet>
```

Figure 5.11 (continued)

and the title formatted with a bullet point. Like the CSS version, the file inherits from the basic XSL style sheet. This is done using the *<xsl:import>* tag, whose *href* attribute supplies the appropriate URL.

The first template rule processes the *<Title>* node, which starts by wrapping a *list-block* and *list-item* around the core information. Using a Unicode character that lies beyond the normal ASCII range, it then inserts a *list-item-label* whose content is a bullet point, before setting up the *list-item-body* with the content of the *Title* tag.

Next, instead of using *<apply-templates>* to recursively process any nested tags as was done in the first XSL example, this rule specifies *<apply-imports>*. This looks in prior imported files (in the order that they were imported) for a rule that also matches the current tag (*Title*) and applies that rule as well. The result is to nest settings given in the *Title* rule of *un_basic.xsl* inside the current formatting, and then fire the *<apply-templates>* statement that that rule specifies. The overall effect provides an inheritance facility similar to that of CSS.

The remaining template rules have *fo:* tags for table, table row, and table cell that correspond to the same entities in CSS and are "bound" to the same tag names in the source document. Attributes within these tags provide similar table formatting: an overall silver-colored table with white cells using a mixture of border styles and padding.

Some complications in the example stem from the stricter requirements of the Formatting Objects specification. First, tables must include a table body, whereas the equivalent structure in CSS is optional. In the example the table body element appears in the rule for *Body*, so this rule encodes both *table* and *table-body* elements. This is not possible in the CSS example because these two table structures are set by the *display* property, and this would therefore conflict in the file. To avoid the conflict the source document would need two tag names: one mapping to *table* and the other to *table-body*.

A second complication is that *fo:blocks* cannot be placed immediately within *fo:table-body* and *fo:table-row* tags. This is why the two rules containing these elements must resort to *<xsl:apply-templates>* in their recursive processing of the document instead of *<apply-imports>* and duplicate the formatting attributes already present in the imported file.

Contextual matching

Figure 5.12 reworks as an XSL file the Figure 5.8 version of the United Nations example, which illustrates context-based matching using contrived formatting instructions.

The key to context-based matching in XSL is the XPath mechanism. In many operating system interfaces, multiple files can be selected using wild card characters—for example, *project/*/file.html* selects all files of this name within any subdirectory of *project*. XPath generalizes this to select individual sections of a document. This is done by mapping nodes in the document tree into a string that defines their position in the hierarchy. These strings are expressed just as file names are in a directory hierarchy, with node names separated by slashes. For example, in our document *NGODoc/Body/** returns all the *Agency* nodes.

```
<?xml version="1.0" encoding="utf-8"?>
<xsl:stylesheet
        xmlns:xsl="http://www.w3.org/1999/XSL/Transform"
        xmlns:fo="http://www.w3.org/1999/XSL/Format"
        version="1.0">

<xsl:import href="un_basic.xsl"/>

<xsl:template match="Agency/Photo[@desc]">
    Available: <xsl:value-of select="@desc"/>
</xsl:template>

<xsl:template match="Agency/Photo[@desc='A photo']">
</xsl:template>

<xsl:template match="Agency">
  <fo:block space-before="8pt" space-after="3pt" font-size="20pt"
            font-family="Helvetica"
            margin-left="0.2in" margin-right="5mm">
      <xsl:apply-templates select="." mode="Extra Color"/>
  </fo:block>
</xsl:template>

<xsl:template match="Agency[position()>1]" mode="Extra Color">
   <xsl:attribute name="background-color">#ffa080</xsl:attribute>
   <xsl:attribute name="color">red</xsl:attribute>
   <xsl:apply-templates/>
</xsl:template>

<xsl:template match="Name[@hq='Rome, Italy']">
  <fo:inline color="rgb(255,160,80)">
     <xsl:apply-templates/>
  </fo:inline>
</xsl:template>

</xsl:stylesheet>
```

Figure 5.12 XSL style sheet illustrating context-sensitive formatting.

This idea is augmented to condition access on attributes stored at nodes. For example, *Name[@desc]* matches a *Name* node only if it has a *desc* attribute defined. Built-in predicates are supplied to check the position of a node in the tree—for example, whether it is the first or last in a chain of siblings.

The first template rule in Figure 5.12 inserts into the document the text that is stored as a *Photo* node's *desc* attribute, prefixed by *Available:*. The second is more selective and only matches if the *Photo* node's *desc* attribute contains the text *A photo*—which happens to coincide with its default given in the DTD. If it does match, no text is displayed, and recursive template matching down that part of the tree is abandoned.

The third rule, which works in conjunction with the fourth, demonstrates XSL modes. When an *Agency* node is first encountered, rule 3 fires and sets up the basic formatting for the block. When it comes to recursively applying the template match, it selects itself with *select=".",* switches the mode to *Extra Color*, and then rematches on *Agency*. This time only rule 4 can match (because of the mode), which enforces the additional requirement that *Agency* must be at least the second node in the file. If so, the rule uses *<xsl:attribute>* tags to augment the closest enclosing tag (the main *block* for *Agency*) with attributes for foreground and background colors.

Finally, the remaining rule sets the foreground color the same as the background color for any *Name* node whose *hq* attribute matches *Rome, Italy*.

Media-dependent formatting

XSL supports different output media—screen, printer, and so on—using the *media* attribute of *<xsl:output>*, which we have already seen used to set the output type to XML. For example, to restrict a style sheet setting to printers, add

```
<xsl:output output="xml" media="printer">.
```

Sorting

Our examples so far have shown XSL's ability to transform the source document, but the changes have been slight (such as putting brackets around the content of an *Abbrev* tag) and could all have been achieved using CSS. Figure 5.13 shows an XSL style sheet that sorts the UN agencies alphabetically for display, something that CSS can't do. It follows a similar pattern to the last two examples, importing *un_basic.xsl* to provide some general formatting. It then defines a rule for *Body* that performs the sorting, overriding the match that would have occurred against *Head|Body* in the imported file.

First a block is created that maintains the same margins and spacing provided by the basic style file. Then a recursive match is initiated on all *Agency* nodes that are descendants of the *Body* node. In earlier examples matching has been expressed by combining the opening and closing tags, as in *<xsl:apply-templates/>*. This shorthand notation is convenient for straightforward matches.

```
<?xml version="1.0" encoding="utf-8"?>
<xsl:stylesheet
        xmlns:xsl="http://www.w3.org/1999/XSL/Transform"
        xmlns:fo="http://www.w3.org/1999/XSL/Format"
        version="1.0">

<xsl:import href="un_basic.xsl"/>

<xsl:template match="Body">
  <fo:block margin-left="0.2in" margin-right="5mm" space-before="6pt">
    <xsl:apply-templates select="Agency">
      <xsl:sort data-type="string" select="./Name"/>
    </xsl:apply-templates>
  </fo:block>
</xsl:template>

</xsl:stylesheet>
```

Figure 5.13 XSL style sheet that sorts UN agencies alphabetically.

Here we split this element into its opening and closing parts and supply the criteria for sorting through the tag *xsl:sort*, nested inside. To accomplish the desired result, the example sets the data type to *string* and specifies a sort on child nodes of *Agency* called *Name*.

This example really only scratches the surface of what you can do with XSL. It can encode a vast array of transformations. Even within sorting there are many more attributes that can control the ordering. There are many other language constructs: variables, *if* statements, and *for* statements are just three. XSL contains many elements of programming languages, making it impressively versatile. It is finding use in places that even the designers did not envisage.

5.4   Bibliographic metadata

Anyone working with digital libraries needs to know about two different standard methods for representing document metadata: the machine-readable cataloging (MARC) format and the Dublin Core. They represent opposite ends of the complexity spectrum. MARC is a comprehensive, well-developed, carefully controlled scheme intended to be generated by professional catalogers for use in libraries. Dublin Core is an intentionally minimalist standard intended to be applied to a wide range of digital library materials by people who are not trained in library cataloging. These two schemes are of interest not only for their practical value, but also to highlight diametrically opposed underlying philosophies. The discussion in the next subsection follows on from Section 2.2 of Chapter 2, and you might want to review that section before continuing. We also include descriptions of two bibliographic metadata formats that are in common use among document authors in scientific and technical fields, BibTeX and Refer.

MARC

The MARC standard was developed in the late 1960s at the Library of Congress to promote the sharing of catalog entries among libraries. It is a comprehensive and detailed standard whose use is carefully controlled and transmitted to budding librarians in library science courses. Most of us are well accustomed to seeing MARC records when consulting online catalogs in academic libraries.

Table 5.1 shows an entry that was obtained from the Library of Congress online catalog. It gives the complete bibliographic record for the book *The Development of the English Traction Engine*. The information includes the author, type of material, information about the physical book itself, publisher, some notes, and various identification numbers. We discussed these bibliographic entities in Chapter 2 (Section 2.2). We also discussed the Library of Congress Subject Headings. *The Development of the English Traction Engine* falls under the subject heading *Agricultural Machinery* listed in Table 2.3, as well as under the heading *Traction-engines*. Incidentally, bibliographic records such as this provide an additional linking mechanism between different subject headings: the fact that these two headings both describe a particular book creates a bond between them that is not reflected in the *Library of Congress Subject Headings* "red books" mentioned in Section 2.2. The record in Table 5.1 also includes the subject classification according to the Dewey Decimal System.

Producing a MARC record for a particular publication is an onerous undertaking that is governed by a detailed set of rules and guidelines called the *Anglo-American Cataloging Rules*, familiarly referred to by librarians as *AACR2R* (the *2* stands for second edition, the final *R* for revised). These rules, inscribed in a formidable handbook, are divided into two parts: Part 1 applies mostly to the description of documents; Part 2 to the description of works. Part 2, for example,

Table 5.1 Library catalog record.

Type of Material	Book (Print, Microform, Electronic, etc.)
Personal Name	Clark, Ronald H. (Ronald Harry), 1903-
Main Title	The development of the English traction engine.
Published/Created	Norwich [Eng.] Goose [1960]
Description	xxv, 390 p. illus., facsims. 29 cm.
Notes	Errata slip inserted. Bibliography: p. 346-347.
Subjects	Traction-engines. Agricultural machinery.
LC Classification	TJ700 .C52
Dewey Class No.	621.14
National Bib. No.	GB60-15328
Other System No.	(OCoLC)3942065

treats *Headings*, *Uniform titles*, and *References* (i.e., entries starting with "See …" that capture relationships between works). Under *Headings* there are sections on how to write people's names, geographic names, and corporate bodies. Appendices describe rules for capitalization, abbreviations, and numerals.

The rules in *AACR2R* are highly detailed, almost persnickety. It is hard to convey their flavor in a few words. Here is one example: how should you name a local church? Rules under *corporate bodies* give the answer. The first choice of name is that "of the person(s), object(s), place(s), or event(s) to which the local church … is dedicated or after which it is named." The second is "a name beginning with a word or phrase descriptive of a type of local church." The third is "a name beginning with the name of the place in which the local church … is situated." Now you know. If rules like this interest you, there are thousands more in *AACR2R*.

Internally MARC records are stored as a collection of tagged fields in a fairly complex format. Table 5.2 gives something close to the internal representation of the catalog record presented earlier, while Table 5.3 lists some of the field codes

---

Table 5.2 MARC fields in the record of Table 5.1.

001	8901720
005	19980421194037.0
008	780531s1960 enkah b 000 0 eng
035	(DLC) 61026816
906	**la** 7 **lb** cbc **lc** oclcrpl **ld** u **le** ncip **lf** 19 **lg** y-gencatlg
010	**la** 61026816
015	**la** GB60-15328
035	**la** (OCoLC)3942065
040	**la** DLC **lc** NcRS **ld** NcRS **ld** Uk **ld** DLC
050	**la** TJ700 **lb** .C52
082	**la** 621.14
100	**la** Clark, Ronald H. **lq** (Ronald Harry), **ld** 1903-
245	**la** The development of the English traction engine.
260	**la** Norwich [Eng.] **lb** Goose **lc** [1960]
300	**la** xxv, 390 p. **lb** illus., facsims. **lc** 29 cm.
500	**la** Errata slip inserted.
504	**la** Bibliography: p. 346-347.
650	**la** Traction-engines.
650	**la** Agricultural machinery.
985	**le** OCLC REPLACEMENT
991	**lb** c-GenColl **lh** TJ700 **li** .C52 **lt** Copy 1 **lw** OCLCREP

Table 5.3 Meaning of some MARC fields.	
001	Control number uniquely identifying the record
005	Date and time that the record was last modified
008	Fixed fields
010	Library of Congress control number
015	National Bibliographic number
035	System control number
040	Cataloging source
050	Library of Congress classification
082	Dewey classification
100	Main entry—personal name
245	Title
260	Imprint: place of publication, publisher, date
300	Physical description
500	General note
504	Bibliography note
650	Subject entry
906	Tags in the 900 range are reserved for local use and are
985	used by vendors, systems, or individual libraries to
991	exchange additional data

and their meaning. Many of the fields contain various identification codes. For example, field 008 contains fixed-length data elements such as the source of the cataloging for the item and the language in which the book is written. Many of the variable-length fields contain subfields, which are labeled *a*, *b*, *c*, and so on, each with their own distinct meaning (in the computer file they are separated by a special subfield delimiter character). For example, field 100 is the personal name of the author, with subfields indicating the standard form of the name, full forenames, and dates. Field 260 gives the imprint, with subfields indicating the place of publication, publisher, and date. The information in the more legible representation of Table 5.1 is evident in the coded form of Table 5.2. Note that some fields can occur more than once, such as the subject headings stored in field 650.

The MARC format covers more than just bibliographic records. It is also used to represent authority records—that is, standardized forms that are part of the librarian's controlled vocabulary. One authority file is for personal names and maps all versions of a person's name (like those for *Muammar Qaddafi* in Table 2.1 of Chapter 2) into one standardized form. Another is for the Library of Congress Subject Headings illustrated in Table 2.3.

Dublin Core

The Dublin Core is a set of metadata elements that are designed specifically for nonspecialist use. It is intended for use when people describe electronic materials, such as those they have created—which, being electronic materials, will almost certainly not receive a full MARC catalog entry. The result of a collaborative effort by a large group of people, it is named not for the capital of Ireland but after Dublin, Ohio, where the first meeting was held in 1995. It received the approval of ANSI, the American National Standards Organization, in 2001.

Compared with the MARC format, Dublin Core has a refreshing simplicity. Table 5.4 summarizes the metadata elements it contains: just fifteen rather than the several hundred used by MARC. As the name implies, these are intended to form a "core" element set that may be augmented by additional elements for local purposes. In addition, the existing elements can be refined through the use of qualifiers. All elements can be repeated where this is appropriate.

Chapter 2 described how librarians struggled over the document versus work distinction and then ended up adopting the term *entity* when defining the objectives of bibliographic systems. The Dublin Core uses the general term *resource*—

Table 5.4 Dublin Core metadata standard.

Metadata	Definition
Title	The name given to the resource by the creator or publisher
Creator	The person or organization primarily responsible for the intellectual content of the resource
Subject	The topic of the resource
Description	A textual description of the content of the resource
Publisher	The entity responsible for making the resource available
Contributor	A person or organization (other than the Creator) who is responsible for making significant contributions to the intellectual content of the resource
Date	A date associated with the creation or availability of the resource
Type	The nature or genre of the content of the resource
Format	The physical or digital manifestation of the resource
Identifier	An unambiguous reference that uniquely identifies the resource within a given context
Source	A reference to a second resource from which the present resource is derived
Language	The language of the intellectual content of the resource
Relation	A reference to a related resource, and the nature of its relationship
Coverage	Spatial locations and temporal durations characteristic of the content of the resource
Rights	Link to a copyright notice or rights management statement

which subsumes pictures, illustrations, movies, animations, simulations, even virtual reality artifacts, as well as textual documents. Indeed, a resource has been defined in Dublin Core documents as "anything that has identity."

The *Creator* might be a photographer, an illustrator, or an author. The *Subject* is typically expressed as a keyword or phrase that describes the topic or the content of the resource. The *Description* might be an abstract of a textual document, or a textual account of a nontextual resource such as a picture or animation. The *Publisher* is generally a publishing house, a university department, or a corporation. A *Contributor* could be an editor, a translator, or an illustrator. The *Date* is the date of resource creation, not the date or dates covered by its contents. For example, a history book will have an associated *Coverage* date range that defines the historical time period it covers, as well as a publication *Date*. Alternatively (or in addition), *Coverage* might be defined in terms of geographical locations that pertain to the content of the resource. The *Type* might indicate a home page, research report, working paper, poem, or any of the media types listed above. The *Format* is used to identify software systems needed to run the resource.

The Dublin Core does not impose any kind of vocabulary control or authority files: two different people might easily generate quite different descriptions of the same resource. However, it is an evolving standard, and current work is aimed at specifying recommended sets of values for certain elements, as a way of encouraging uniformity. For example, the Library of Congress Subject Headings are encouraged as one way of specifying the *Subject*, along with some other classification standards such as the Library of Congress classification system (which, as the "Subject classifications" subsection of Section 2.2 explained, differs from the Library of Congress Subject Headings) and the Dewey Decimal classification. There are standard ways of encoding dates whose use is encouraged and ways of encoding languages too.

Also, certain Dublin Core fields can be refined, and efforts are underway to standardize this. For example, the *Date* can be qualified as *date created*, *date valid*, *date available*, *date issued*, or *date modified*; multiple specifications are possible. The *Description* element can be couched as an *abstract* or a *table of contents*. Standard refinements of the *Relation* field include *is version of*, *is part of*, *replaces*, *requires*, *references*—along with the inverse relations.

BibTeX

Scientific and technical authors, particularly those using mathematical notation, often favor a widely used generalized document-processing system called TeX (pronounced *tech*), or a customized version called LaTeX (*la-tech*), which was described in Section 4.4. This freely available package contains a subsystem called BibTeX (*bib-tech*) that manages bibliographic data and references within documents.

```
@article{Gettys90,
    author = {Jim Gettys and Phil Karlton and McGregor, Scott},
    title = {The {X} Window System, Version 11},
    journal = "Software Practice and Experience",
    volume = 20,
    number = {S2},
    month = nov,
    year = 1990,
    abstract = {A technical overview of the X11 functionality.  This is an update
                of the X10 TOG paper by Scheifler and Gettys.}
```

Figure 5.14 Bibliography item in BibTeX format.

Figure 5.14 shows a record in BibTeX format. Records are grouped into files, and files can be brought together to form a database. Each field can flow freely over line boundaries—extra white space is ignored. Records begin with the @ symbol followed by a keyword naming the record type: article, book, and so forth. The content follows in braces and starts with an alphanumeric string that acts as a key for the record. Keys in a BibTeX database must be unique. Within a record, individual fields take the form *name=value,* with a comma separating entries. Names specify bibliographic entities such as author, publisher, address, and year of publication. Each item type can be included only once, and values are typically enclosed in double quotation marks or braces to protect spaces. Certain standard abbreviations such as month names can be used, and users can define their own abbreviations.

Two items in Figure 5.14 deserve explanation. First, the *author* field is used for multiple authors, and names are separated by the word *and* rather than by commas with a final *and* as in ordinary English prose. This is because the tools that process BibTeX files incorporate bibliographic standards for presenting names. The fact that McGregor's name in the example uses a different convention is of no consequence: like the other names it will be presented correctly in whatever style has been chosen for the document. Second, the *title* field contains an extra pair of braces around the *X*. This is because titles are also presented in whatever style has been chosen for the document—for example, only the first word may be capitalized, or all content words may be capitalized—regardless of how they appear in the bibliography file. Braces override this and preserve the original capitalization, so that the proper noun *X* appears correctly capitalized in the document.

Unlike other bibliographic standards, the set of attribute names is determined by a style file named in the source document and used to formulate citations in the text and format the references as footnotes or in a list of references. The style file is couched in a full programming language and can support any vocabulary. However, there is general consensus in the TeX community over what keywords to use. Advantage can be taken of TeX's programmability to generate XML syntax instead; alternatively there are many stand-alone applications that simply parse BibTeX source files.

Academic authors often create BibTeX bibliographic collections for publications in their area of expertise, accumulating references over the years into large and authoritative repositories of metadata. Aided by software heuristics to identify duplicate entries, these constitute a useful resource for digital libraries in scientific and technical areas.

Refer

The Refer format has many similarities to BibTeX. Originally designed by computer scientists for use by mainly scientific and technical researchers, it was built to complement a Unix document-formatting tool called Troff that is now nearly obsolete. However, it has gained a new lease on life as the basis of the popular bibliographic tool EndNote, which augments Microsoft Word with an interactive tool for compiling and maintaining bibliographic databases and can export databases in the Refer format.

Figure 5.15 shows the same bibliographic record as Figure 5.14, but couched in Refer rather than BibTeX. It is formatted line by line, and records are separated with a blank line. Each line starts with a key character, introduced by a percent symbol, that signals the kind of information the line contains. The rest of the line gives the data itself.

Refer has the fixed set of keywords listed in Table 5.5. Unlike BibTeX the author field (%A) is repeated for multiple authors; the ordering reflects the document's authorship. Only one organizational author (%Q) may appear; versions of Refer vary in whether they permit multiple editors (%E). Dates (%D) specify the year in full, but months can be abbreviated.

In BibTeX, the type of bibliographic record (an article, in our example) is given at the beginning (@article). There is no provision for this in the original Refer format—programs must infer how to format a reference from the fields it contains. However, the EndNote version includes a new keyword (%0, or percent zero) which appears as the first line of a record to make the type explicit—*%0 Journal Article* in our example. In the original Refer, names are not

```
%A Jim Gettys
%A Phil Karlton
%A Scott McGregor
%T The X Window System, Version 11
%J Software Practice and Experience
%V 20
%N S2
%D 1990
%X A technical overview of the X11 functionality.  This is an update ...
```

Figure 5.15 Bibliography item in Refer format.

Table 5.5 The basic keywords used by the Refer bibliographic format.

Tag	Description
%A	Author
%B	Book title (for an article that is part of a book)
%C	Place (city) of publication
%D	Date of publication
%E	Editor (for an article that is part of a book)
%G	Government ordering number (United States)
%I	Publisher (issuer)
%J	Journal name (for an article in a journal)
%K	Keywords
%L	Label
%N	Number of journal issue
%O	Other information (usually printed at the end of the reference)
%P	Page number; a range of pages can be specified as m-n
%Q	The name of the author, if the author is not a person
%R	Technical report number
%S	Series name
%T	Title
%V	Volume number of the journal or book
%X	Annotation

processed but are printed in exactly the form in which they are given, whereas the EndNote version specifies that names should be written as *surname, comma, first names.* It also includes new keywords for captions (*%F*), URL (*%U*), price (*%$*), and copyright information (*%**).

5.5 Metadata for images and multimedia

The idea of metadata is by no means confined to textual documents. In fact, because it is much harder to search the content of image, audio, or multimedia data than to search full text, flexible ways of specifying metadata become even more important for locating these resources.

The image file formats described in Chapter 4 (Section 4.5) incorporate some rather limited ways of specifying image-related metadata. For example, GIF and PNG files include the height and width of the image (in pixels), and the *bit depth* or number of bits per pixel (up to 8 for GIF, 48 for PNG). PNG specifies the color representation (palletized, grayscale, or true color) and includes the ability to store text strings representing metadata. JPEG also specifies the horizontal and vertical resolution. But these formats do not include provision for other kinds of structured metadata, and when they are used in a digital library, image metadata is usually put elsewhere.

We describe two widely differing metadata formats for images and multimedia. The Tagged Image File Format, or TIFF, is a practical scheme for associating metadata with image files that has been in widespread use for well over a decade. This is how images—including document images—are stored in today's digital libraries. MPEG-7 is a far more sophisticated and ambitious scheme for defining and storing metadata associated with any multimedia information. It is still in the process of being standardized and is highly general and extensible. We describe TIFF in specific detail and then go on to outline the facilities that MPEG-7 provides.

Image metadata: TIFF

The Tagged Image File Format or TIFF is a public-domain file format for raster images that incorporates extensive facilities for descriptive metadata. It is used to describe image data that typically comes from scanners, frame-grabbers, paint programs, and photo-retouching programs. It is a rich format that can take advantage of the varying image requirements but is not tied to particular input or output devices. It provides numerous options—for example, several different compression schemes, and comprehensive information for color calibration. It is designed so that private and special-purpose information can be included.

TIFF was originally specified in 1986 by Aldus (now owned by Adobe Systems) and Microsoft, and several revisions have appeared since then. TIFF is under continual development, and backward compatibility is, of course, a high priority. The large number of options and the fluidity of the standard does create problems with TIFF readers that cannot process all options. While it is easy to write a TIFF writer, it is difficult to write a fully compliant TIFF reader.

TIFF is a byte-oriented format, which (like Unicode) is designed for compatibility between big-endian and little-endian computers (although some implementations do not accommodate both). The first two bytes of a TIFF file determine endianness. A single TIFF file can include several images. Images are characterized by sets of *tags* whose values define particular properties of the image. Most tags contain integers, but some contain ASCII text—and provision is made for tags containing floating-point and rational numbers.

Baseline TIFF caters to four different image types: bilevel, grayscale, palette-color, and full-color images. There are a dozen or so mandatory tags that give physical characteristics and features of images: their dimensions, compression, various metrics associated with the color specification, and information about where they are stored in the file.

Table 5.6 shows some TIFF tags, of which all but the last group are mandatory. The first tags specify the dimensions of the image in pixels, along with enough information to allow them to be converted to physical units where possible. All images are rectangular. The second group of tags gives color information. For bilevel images, this is just whether they are standard black-on-white or reversed; for grayscale it is the number of bits per pixel; for palette images, it is where the color palette is specified. The third group specifies the compression method—only extremely simple schemes are allowed in baseline TIFF. Finally, TIFF allows an image to be broken into separate strips for efficient input/output buffering, and the last group of mandatory tags specifies the location and size of each strip.

Additional features go far beyond the baseline illustrated by Table 5.6. Different color spaces are supported. Compression types include the LZW scheme, used in GIF,[8] and JPEG. Users can define new TIFF tags and compression types and can register their definitions so that others can share them. You can also register private tag data centrally, thereby reserving new tag codes for private use. More radical extensions of TIFF include GeoTIFF, which permits the addition of geographic information associated with cartographic raster data and remote sensing applications, such as projections and datum reference points. Many digital cameras produce TIFF files, and Kodak has a PhotoCD file format (called *pcd*) based on TIFF with proprietary color space and compression methods.

Most digital library projects that work with images use the TIFF format to store and archive the original captured images, even though they may convert them to other formats for display. At the bottom of Table 5.6 are some optional fields that are widely used in digital library work. The first two, the name of the program that generated the image and the date and time when it was generated, are usually filled in automatically by scanner programs and other image creation software. Digital library projects often establish conventions for the use of the other fields; for example, in a digitization project the *Document name* field might contain the catalog ID of the original document. These fields are coded in ASCII, but there is no reason why they should not contain data that is further structured. For example, the *Image description* field might contain an XML specification that itself includes several subfields.

Multimedia metadata: MPEG-7

We learned about the MPEG family of standards in Chapter 4 (Section 4.6). MPEG-7, which is formally called the *multimedia content description interface*, is intended to provide a set of tools to describe multimedia content. The idea is that

---

8. The inclusion of LZW means that TIFF raises the same licensing issues as were discussed for GIF in Chapter 4 (Section 4.5).

Table 5.6 TIFF tags.

Dimensions

Image width	in pixels
Image length	(as above)
Resolution unit	none, inch, cm
X resolution	pixels per resolution unit
Y resolution	(as above)

Color

Photometric interpretation	(black-on-white or white-on-black)
Bits per sample	(1 for bilevel, 4 or 8 for grayscale)
Samples per pixel (RGB only)	normally 3 for RGB images
Color map (palette-color only)	specifies a color table for the image

Compression

Bilevel	▪ uncompressed
	▪ packed into bytes as tightly as possible
	▪ CCITT compression (as used in fax machines)
	▪ byte-oriented run-length coding
Others	▪ uncompressed
	▪ byte-oriented run-length coding

Location of the data

Rows per strip
Strip offsets
Strip byte counts

Optional fields

Software	program that generated the image
Date and time	when it was generated
Document name	name of the document
Page name	typically used for the page number
Artist	creator
Image description	free-form textual description

you can search for audiovisual material that has associated MPEG-7 metadata. The material can include still pictures, graphics, 3D models, audio, speech, video, and any combination of these elements in a multimedia presentation. It can be information that is stored, or streamed from an online real-time source. The standard is being put together by broadcasters, electronics manufacturers, content creators and managers, publishers, and telecommunication service providers under the aegis of the International Standards Organization.

MPEG-7 has exceptionally wide scope. For example, it is envisaged that metadata may be used to answer queries such as these:

- Play a few notes on a keyboard and retrieve musical pieces with similar melodies, rhythms, or emotions.
- Draw a few lines on a screen and retrieve images containing similar graphics, logos, or ideograms.
- Define objects, including color or texture patches, and retrieve similar examples.
- Describe movements and relations between a set of given multimedia objects and retrieve animations that exhibit them.
- Describe actions and retrieve scenarios containing them.
- Using an excerpt of Pavarotti's voice, obtain a list of his records and video clips and photographic material portraying him.

However, the way in which MPEG-7 metadata will be used to answer such queries is beyond the scope of the standard.

MPEG-7 is a complex and extensible standard that is still under development, and we can only sketch its structure here. At its core is an extensible description language called DDL ("description definition language"), which allows users to create their own metadata format. DDL uses XML syntax and is a form of XML Schema, which we describe in Chapter 8. XML Schema alone is not flexible enough to handle low-level audiovisual forms, so DDL was formulated to address these needs.

The DDL links together *descriptors*, which bind a feature to a set of values, and *description schemas*, which specify the types of descriptors that can be used and the relationships between them or between other description schemas. Descriptors represent low-level features, the fundamental qualities of audiovisual content. They range from statistical models of signal amplitude to the fundamental frequency of a signal, from emotional content to parameters of an explicit sound-effect model.

DDLs are able to express spatial, temporal, structural, cardinality, and data type relationships between descriptors and description schemas. For example, structural constraints specify the rules that a valid description should obey: what children elements must be present for each node, or what attributes must be associated with elements. Cardinality constraints specify the number of times an element may occur. Data type constraints specify the type and the possible values for data or descriptors within the description.

There are different descriptors for audio, visual, and multimedia data. The audio description framework operates both in the temporal and spectral dimensions, the former for sequences of sounds or sound samples and the latter for frequency spectra that comprise different components. At the lowest level you can represent such things as instantaneous waveform and power values, various features of frequency spectra, fundamental frequency of quasi-periodic signals, a measure of spectral flatness, and so on. There is a way of constructing a temporal *series* of values from a set of individual samples, and a spectral *vector* of values such as a sampled frequency spectrum. At a higher level, description tools are envisaged for sound effects, instrumental timbre, spoken content, and melodic descriptors to facilitate query-by-humming.

In the visual domain, basic features include color, texture, region-based and contour-based shapes, and camera and object motion. Another basic feature is a notion of *localization* in both time and space, and these dimensions can be combined together into the form of a space-time trajectory. These basic features can be built into structures such as a grid of pixels or a time series of video frames.

Multimedia features include low-level audiovisual attributes such as color, texture, motion, and audio energy; high-level features of objects, events, and abstract concepts; and information about compression and storage media. Browsing and retrieval of audiovisual content can be facilitated by defining summaries, partitions, and decompositions. Summaries, for example, allow an audiovisual object to be navigated in either a hierarchical or a sequential fashion. For hierarchical navigation, material is organized into successive levels that describe it at different levels of detail, from coarse to fine. For sequential navigation, sequences can be created of images or video frames, possibly synchronized with audio and text that compose a slide show or audiovisual synopsis.

MPEG-7 descriptions can be entered by hand or extracted automatically from the signal. Some features (color, texture) can best be extracted automatically, while for others ("this scene contains three shoes," "that music was recorded in 1995") this is effectively impossible.

The application areas envisaged for MPEG-7 are many and varied and stretch well beyond the ambit of what most people mean by digital libraries. They will include education, journalism, tourist information, cultural services, entertainment, geographical information systems, remote sensing, surveillance, biomedical applications, shopping, architecture, real estate, interior design, film, video and radio archives, and even dating services.

5.6 Extracting metadata

We now turn to the business of extracting metadata automatically from a document's contents. Automatic extraction of information from text—*text mining*, as it is often called—is a hot research topic. The ready availability of huge amounts of textual information on the Web has placed a high premium on automatic extraction techniques. In this area there is hardly any underlying theory, and existing methods use heuristics that are complex, detailed, and difficult to replicate and evaluate.

Plain text documents are designed for people. Readers extract information by *understanding* their content. Indeed text comprehension skills—reading documents and then being able to answer questions about them—have always been a central component of grade-school education. Over the past several decades, computer techniques for text analysis have been developed that can achieve impressive results in constrained domains. Nevertheless fully automatic comprehension of arbitrary documents is well beyond their reach and will likely remain so for the foreseeable future.

Structured markup languages such as XML help make key aspects of documents accessible to computers and people alike. They encode certain kinds of information explicitly in such a way that it can be extracted easily by parsing the document structure. Of course, except for the simplest of documents, this information falls far short of that conveyed by a complete and comprehensive understanding of the text.

Relatively few documents today contain explicitly encoded metadata. The balance will shift as authors recognize the added value of metadata, standards for its encoding become widespread, and improved interfaces reduce the mechanical effort required to supply it. However, although their role may diminish, schemes for extracting metadata from raw text will never be completely replaced by explicit provision of metadata.

Fortunately it is often unnecessary to understand a document in order to extract useful metadata from it. In the following discussion we give several examples that indicate the breadth of what can be done, although we do not describe the techniques in full detail because they usually require considerable tuning to the problem at hand. The first three sections, extracting document metadata, generic entities, and bibliography entries, describe useful general techniques. The last four sections, language identification, extracting acronyms and key phrases, and generating phrase hierarchies, are facilities that are included in the Greenstone software described in subsequent chapters. This material pushes beyond the boundaries of what is conventionally meant by "metadata"—our focus is on extracting information that is generally of use in digital libraries rather than on any narrow interpretation of the term.

Extracting document metadata

Basic metadata about a document—its title, author, publisher, date of publication, keywords, and abstract—is often present on the first page for all to see. Moreover, it is frequently presented in a fairly uniform way: the title first, centered, followed by some white space and then the authors' names and affiliations, also centered, followed by the publication date, keywords preceded by the word *Keywords*, and abstract preceded by the word *Abstract* or *Summary*. Document families bear family resemblances. Different type sizes or typefaces may be used for different elements of the title page.

Such structure is easy to spot for a well-defined and tightly controlled family of documents. However, doing it in a general way is not so easy, and the appropriate heuristics depend very much on the situation. Practical document collections often contain exceptions that go unnoticed by human readers but confound extraction heuristics. For example, HTML provides a *title* tag that allows authors to identify the title of their document explicitly for use by the browser, but even this explicit mechanism is frequently ignored, misused, or abused in actual Web documents.

There is little to be said in general about extracting document metadata automatically because it depends too much on the format of the documents and the uniformity of the collection. Some of the techniques used for generic entity extraction, described in the next subsection, may be applicable in particular situations.

Generic entity extraction

Some information is easy to extract from plain text documents because it is expressed in a fixed syntax that is easy to recognize automatically. E-mail addresses and Web URLs are good examples. Of course these are both products of the Internet era in which computers commonly handle free text: they are explicitly designed for automatic recognition and processing.

Other artificial entities are also readily recognized, although slightly less reliably. Sums of money, times of day, and dates are good examples. There are well-known variants—dates can be expressed in several different ways. These sometimes cause ambiguity—as with date formats such as 9/9/99, and time specifications using the 12- versus 24-hour clock. Some differences are cultural—for example, when sums of money are specified in decimal currency, the English-speaking world reverses the common European usage of comma and period.

Names of people, places, and companies are an important kind of semistructured data, and it is often useful to identify them as metadata. Names can be recognized partly by intrinsic and partly by extrinsic properties. They almost always begin with capital letters. (But not quite always, as the class of archaic English surnames such as ffoulkes, the avant-garde poet e e cummings, and the contemporary singer k d lang all testify. Also, this fact loses much of its practical value in languages such as German that capitalize all nouns.) Indeed the statistical patterns in which letters appear differ between names and ordinary language, a trend that is accentuated by globalization, with the increasing incidence of foreign names in

Western documents. People's names are commonly preceded by forenames and may contain initials. There are numerous honorific prefixes such as Mr., Ms., Dr., and Prof. Names may also include baronial prefixes such as *von*, *van*, or *de*, and other miscellaneous qualifiers such as *Jr.* or *Sr.*

Extrinsic properties constrain the contexts in which names occur in text. People's names are often recognizable because they are introduced by phrases such as "according to . . . " or " . . . said." Similar stock phrases characterize company names and place names. Indeed sometimes entity names can be distinguished from people's names only by the surrounding words. When a string such as *Norman* occurs, context provides the only clue as to whether it is the place Norman, Oklahoma, a person such as Don Norman, or the race of Normans. (Notice that this last sentence itself uses context to make the referents clear.)

Subsequent references to an already mentioned entity provide a further dimension of richness. Once a document has mentioned a person, place, or company, subsequent references may be abbreviated. Here, for example, it should be clear who cummings or lang is.

The task of identifying entities such as times, dates, sums of money, and different kinds of names in running text is called *generic entity extraction*. There are many systems that use heuristics to detect these entities; some pointers are given in "Notes and sources" (Section 5.7). One important distinction is between methods that use preprogrammed heuristics, those that can accommodate different textual conventions using manually tagged training data, and ones that can self-adapt using untagged data.

When heuristics are preprogrammed, human intelligence is used to refine the extraction scheme manually to take account of the vagaries of natural language usage. On the other hand, heuristic entity extraction systems are never finished, and modifying such systems manually to take account of newly discovered problems can be daunting—they quickly become practically unmanageable.

Some adaptive systems use training data in which the entities in question have been tagged manually. These systems embody a predefined generic structure that can adapt to the kinds of textual patterns that are actually encountered. Adaptation consists of adjusting parameters in accordance with pretagged training documents. This gives an easy way of catering to newly discovered variants: add some appropriate examples, manually tagged, to the training data.

Tagging training data is a boring, laborious, and error-prone task—particularly since large amounts are often needed for adequate training. Some current research focuses on *self-adaptive* techniques. These are ones that, once primed, can work autonomously through large volumes of untagged documents to improve their performance. This approach promises good performance with a minimum of manual effort. However, its inherent limitations are not yet known.

Bibliographic references

Most academic documents contain bibliographic references, and these constitute an important kind of metadata—though now we are beginning to push the conventional meaning of the term—that is extremely useful both for characterizing the topic of the article and for linking it to related articles. Traditional citation indexes identify the citations that a document makes and link them with the cited works. A key advantage is navigation forward in time, through listing articles that cite the current one, as well as backward through the list of cited articles. Scholars find citation indexes useful for many purposes, including locating related literature, placing given articles in context, evaluating their scientific influence, and analyzing general research trends to identify emerging areas.

It is not hard to automatically determine where the list of references occurs in the plain text of a document with a reasonable degree of accuracy. Then each reference is parsed individually to extract its title, author, year of publication, page numbers, and so on, and the tag that is used to cite it in the body of the document (e.g., [1]). The special structure of references makes this easier than the general problem of generic entity extraction. When parsing a reference, fields that have relatively little variation in syntax and position, given the result of previous parsing, should be identified next. For example, the citation tag always comes first, and its format is the same for all references. Once the more regular features of a reference have been identified, the usual relative position of not-yet-identified fields can be exploited to predict where desired fields occur (if they are present at all). For example, author information almost always precedes titles, and publisher almost always comes after. Databases of author's names, journal names, and so on can be used to help identify the fields of the reference.

The power of a citation index depends on the ability to identify the article that is being referenced and recognize different references to the same article. To do this references must be normalized and heuristics used to identify when they refer to the same article.

Language identification

Two important pieces of metadata that can be readily and reliably derived from a document's content are the language in which it is written and the encoding scheme used. This is a problem of text categorization, in which an incoming document is assigned to some preexisting category. Because category boundaries are almost never clear-cut, it is necessary to be able to recognize when a given document does not match any category, or when it falls between two categories. Also, to be useful it must be robust to spelling and grammatical errors in text, and to character recognition errors in OCR'd documents.

A standard technique for text categorization is to characterize each document by a profile that consists of the "*n*-grams," or sequences of *n* consecutive letters, that appear in it. A training set containing several documents in each possible category is assembled, where the category values are known for each training document. A profile is obtained for each category by including the *n*-grams that appear in all documents in that category. Then, given an unknown document, the system calculates a distance measure between that document's profile and each of the category profiles and selects the category whose profile is closest—or no category if none is sufficiently close.

It is sufficient for successful language identification to consider just the individual words that make up the documents—the effects of word sequences can be neglected. Documents are preprocessed by splitting the text into separate word tokens consisting only of letters and apostrophes (the usage of digits and punctuation is not especially language-dependent). The tokens are padded with a sufficient number of spaces, and then all possible *n*-grams of length 1 to 5 are generated for each word in the document. These *n*-grams are counted and sorted into frequency order to yield the document profile.

In document profiles the most frequent 300 or so *n*-grams are highly correlated with the language. The highest ranking ones are mostly unigrams consisting of one character only, and simply reflect the distribution of the letters of the alphabet in the document's language. Starting around rank 300 or so, the frequency profile begins to be more specific to the topic of the document.

A simple metric for comparing a document profile to a category profile is to calculate, for each document *n*-gram, the difference between its positions in the two profiles—how far "out of place" it is. Document *n*-grams that do not appear in the category profile are given some maximum value. The total of these "out of place" figures gives a measure of the overall difference. An unknown document is assigned to the category to which its profile is closest.

A small experiment gives an indication of the accuracy of this method. About 3,500 articles in Internet newsgroups were obtained, written in eight different languages—Dutch, English, French, German, Italian, Polish, Portuguese, and Spanish. An independent training set contained a modest sample of each category, ranging from 20K to 120K bytes in length. Only the most frequent 400 *n*-grams in each category profile were used. The system misclassified only seven articles, yielding an overall classification accuracy of 99.8 percent. This provides an accurate way of assigning language metadata to documents.

Acronym extraction

Technical, commercial, and political documents make extensive use of acronyms. A list of acronyms and their definitions can assist document presentation by allowing users to click on an acronym to see its expansion and help check whether acronyms are being used consistently in a document collection. Identifying acronyms, and their definitions, in documents is a good example of a metadata extraction problem that can be tackled using heuristics.

The dictionary definition of *acronym* is

> a word formed from the first (or first few) letters of a series of words, as *radar*, from radio detecting and ranging.

Acronyms are often defined by preceding or following their first use with a textual explanation, as in this example. Finding all acronyms, along with their definitions, in a particular technical document is a problem that can be tackled using heuristics. The information desired—acronyms and their definitions—is relational, which distinguishes it from many other information extraction problems.

One heuristic way of identifying acronyms is to encode potential acronyms with respect to the initial letters of neighboring words. With a well-chosen coding scheme, this should achieve a more efficient representation that can be detected by measuring the compression achieved. The criterion is whether a candidate acronym could be coded more efficiently using a special model than it is using a regular text compression scheme. A phrase is declared to be an acronym definition if the discrepancy between the number of bits required to code it using a general-purpose compressor and code it using the acronym model exceeds a certain threshold.

The first step is to identify candidates for acronyms—for example, by taking all words that are expressed in uppercase only. The acronym definition may precede or follow the acronym itself and invariably occurs within a window of a fixed number of preceding or following words—say 16 words.

Candidate acronyms are expressed in terms of the leading letters of the words on either side. The technical details of the coding are not particularly interesting and are omitted here. After compressing the acronym candidates with respect to their context, all legal encodings for each acronym are compared and the one that compresses best is selected. For comparison, the acronym is compressed using a generic text model, taking the preceding context into account. The candidate is declared to be an acronym if the ratio between the two compression figures exceeds some predetermined threshold. Incidentally it is a curious fact that, using a standard text model, longer acronyms tend to compress into fewer bits than do shorter ones. The reason is connected to the fact that whereas short acronyms are often spelled out, long ones tend to be pronounced as words. This affects the choice of letters: longer acronyms more closely resemble "natural" words.

Needless to say acronym extraction is not entirely perfect. Figure 3.26a (Chapter 3) showed an example of a browser based on it, and here *IFIS* for *International Food Information Service* and *International Food Information Services* should have been treated as a single acronym—not because the acronym is the same, for there are many acronyms that have several different interpretations, but because the definitions are so similar. However, experiments on a sizable sample of technical reports show that this kind of scheme performs well and provides a viable basis for extracting acronyms and their definitions from plain text.

Key-phrase extraction

In the scientific and technical literature, keywords and key phrases are often attached to documents to provide a brief synopsis of what they are about. (Henceforth we use the term *key phrase* to subsume keywords, that is, one-word key phrases.) Key phrases are a useful form of metadata because they condense documents into a few pithy phrases that can be interpreted individually and independently of one another. Their brevity and precision make them useful in a variety of information-retrieval tasks: to describe the documents returned by a query, as the basis for search indexes, as a means of browsing an information collection, and as a document clustering technique. Key phrases can be used to help users get a feel for the content of an information collection; provide sensible entry points into it; show ways in which queries can sensibly be extended; support novel browsing techniques with appropriate linkage structures; facilitate document skimming by emphasizing important phrases visually. They also provide a way of measuring similarity among documents.

The key phrases that accompany articles are chosen manually. In academia authors assign key phrases to documents they have written. Professional indexers often choose phrases from a "controlled vocabulary" that is predefined for the domain at hand—one example is the Library of Congress Subject Headings introduced in Chapter 2 (Section 2.2). However, the great majority of documents come without key phrases, and assigning them manually is a laborious process that requires careful study of the document and a thorough knowledge of the subject matter.

Surprisingly, perhaps, key-phrase metadata can be obtained automatically from documents with a considerable degree of success. There are two fundamentally different approaches: key-phrase *assignment* and key-phrase *extraction*. Both require for training purposes a set of documents to which key phrases have already been attached manually. The training set needs to be far more extensive and pertinent in the case of key-phrase assignment than it does for extraction.

In key-phrase assignment the training documents provide a predefined set of key phrases from which all key phrases for new documents are chosen—a controlled vocabulary. For each key phrase the training data defines a set of documents that are associated with it. For each key phrase standard machine-learning techniques are used to create a "classifier" from all training documents, using the ones associated with it as positive examples and the remainder as negative examples. Given a new document, it is processed by each key phrase's classifier.

Some classify it positively—in other words, it belongs to the set of documents associated with that key phrase—while others classify it negatively—it does not. Key phrases are assigned to the new document accordingly.

In the other kind of technique, key-phrase extraction, all the phrases that occur in the document are listed, and information retrieval heuristics are used to select those that seem to characterize it best. Most key phrases are noun phrases, and syntactic techniques may be used to identify these and ensure that the set of candidates contains only noun phrases. The heuristics used for selection range from simple ones, such as the position of the phrase's first occurrence in the document, to more complex ones, such as the occurrence frequency of the phrase in the document versus its occurrence frequency in a corpus of other documents in the subject area. The training set is used to tune the parameters that balance these different factors.

With key-phrase assignment, the only key phrases that can be assigned are ones that have already been used for training documents. This has the advantage that all key phrases are well formed, but the disadvantage that novel topics cannot be accommodated. The training set of documents must therefore be large and comprehensive. In contrast, key-phrase extraction is open-ended: it selects phrases from the document text itself. There is no particular problem with novel topics, but malformed key phrases may be assigned. The training set does not need to be large and comprehensive because it is only used to set parameters for the algorithm.

Key-phrase assignment employs methods of machine learning, and it would take us too far off track to describe them here. Its success depends critically on the coverage of the training corpus and its appropriateness for the documents under consideration. Given the right conditions, key-phrase assignment can be quite accurate—considerably more so than key-phrase extraction. But it is harder to do in a general way.

We will explain key-phrase extraction in a little more detail. Suppose a well-tuned extraction algorithm is used to select half a dozen key phrases for a particular document, and these are compared with phrases selected manually by the document's author. Generally speaking one might expect one or two of the key phrases to match exactly or almost exactly, one or two others to be plausible phrases that the document author happened not to choose, and the remaining two or three to be less satisfactory key phrases.

As an example, Table 5.7 shows the output of a particular extraction algorithm for three research papers in computer science. For each paper the title is shown, along with two sets of key phrases. One set gives the key phrases assigned by its author, and the other gives key phrases assigned by an automatic procedure. Phrases in common between the two sets are italicized. It is not hard to guess that the key phrases on the left are the author's, while those on the right are assigned automatically. Although many of the automatically extracted key phrases are

Table 5.7   Titles and key phrases—author- and machine-assigned—for three papers.

Protocols for secure, atomic transaction execution in electronic commerce

Author-assigned	Machine-assigned
anonymity	*atomicity*
atomicity	*auction*
auction	customer
electronic commerce	*electronic commerce*
privacy	intruder
real-time	merchant
security	protocol
transaction	*security*
	third party
	transaction

Neural multigrid for gauge theories and other disordered systems

Author-assigned	Machine-assigned
disordered systems	disordered
gauge fields	gauge
multigrid	*gauge fields*
neural multigrid	interpolation kernels
neural networks	length scale
	multigrid
	smooth

Proof nets, garbage, and computations

Author-assigned	Machine-assigned
cut-elimination	cut
linear logic	*cut elimination*
proof nets	garbage
sharing graphs	proof net
typed lambda-calculus	weakening

plausible, some are rather strange. Examples are *gauge* and *smooth* for the second paper. Smooth is not even a noun phrase—clearly this particular extraction algorithm did not use syntactic analysis to identify the candidate key phrases. The key phrase *garbage* for the third paper is a complete giveaway—while that word may be used repeatedly in a computer science paper, and even displayed prominently in the title, no author is likely to choose it as a keyword for their paper! Although automatically extracted key-phrase metadata may not reflect exactly what the author might have chosen, it is useful for many purposes.

There are three stages in the overall process used for key-phrase extraction.

- Use a corpus of text to produce a set of frequencies with which candidate phrases are likely to occur in documents.
- Use training data—that is, a set of documents with key phrases already assigned—to create a "model" for key-phrase identification.
- Process an individual document to identify key phrases in it, using the results of the previous two stages.

All three stages begin by choosing a set of phrases from each document that are potential key phrases. The second and third stages then generate features for each candidate phrase. Note that subphrases of candidate phrases are often candidates themselves. Thus the input is not "segmented" into key phrases: as candidate phrases are generated, all subphrases are tested to see if they also should join the list of candidates.

The extraction process hinges on the features that are used to characterize phrases and select key phrases from all the candidate phrases in the document. Three features are particularly useful. The first is the position of the phrase's first occurrence in the document. Phrases that occur early on are more likely to be key phrases—particularly if they occur in the title or abstract, or early in the introduction. If these sections are identified in the document structure, they could be weighted accordingly; otherwise a simple measure of distance from the start of the document (as a proportion of document length) will do.

The second feature weighs two factors against each other: first, phrases used frequently throughout a document are more likely to be key phrases; and second, phrases that are common in a corpus of similar documents are less likely to be key phrases for any particular document. The situation is similar to the ranked queries discussed in Chapter 3 (Section 3.3). There we noted that ranking techniques assign a numeric weight to each query term based on its frequency in the document collection—common terms receive low weight—and also compensate for the length of the document so that long ones are not automatically favored. Exactly the same kind of metric can be used to assess key phrases. In order to calculate this feature, a large corpus of cognate text must be available—but note that it does not have to consist of documents with key phrases already assigned. For example, if key phrases are being assigned to documents in a digital library collection, then the raw text in that collection will suffice.

A third feature is helpful in situations where there is a large training set of documents with manually assigned key phrases. It records for each candidate phrase the number of documents in the training set for which it is already a key phrase. Using this feature makes the assignment process somewhat conservative: phrases that have been used before as key phrases are automatically more likely to be used again. Tests have shown that while the first two features alone give good performance (the examples in Table 5.7 were based on just two features), using the third improves performance if a large and relevant training set happens to be available.

In order to weigh these three features, a machine-learning technique is used to create a model for key-phrase identification based on the training data. The model is a simple statistical one that weighs the features described above in a way that gives good performance on the training documents. It is a simple matter to apply the model to the candidate key phrases identified in a new document to produce a measure of "keyphrase-ness" for each one, and choose the most likely few as key phrases for the document.

Phrase hierarchies

Key phrases consist of a few well-chosen words that characterize the document under consideration. It is also useful to extract a structure that contains *all* phrases in the documents. In Chapter 3 (Section 3.5), we saw how a hierarchical structure of phrases can support a useful style of browsing around a digital library collection. As an example, Figure 3.23 shows an interactive interface to a phrase hierarchy that has been extracted automatically from the full text of a document collection. Although describing such a phrase hierarchy as "metadata" is stretching the term beyond its conventional usage, we will nevertheless take this opportunity to say something about how such a structure can be obtained from the full text of a document collection—a nontrivial task, particularly for large collections.

Identifying phrases

Underlying the user interface is a hierarchy of phrases that appear in the document collection. For present purposes a *phrase* is a sequence of words that occurs more than once in the text—that is, we are talking about any phrases that repeat. Thus all the phrases visible in Figures 3.23a and b—*Desert locust, Desert locust situation, Desert locust adults*, and so on—occur more than once in the document collection.

However, to include *every* such phrase would clutter the interface with trivial phrases, so three further conditions are added. Phrases must begin and end with a *content word*, must not contain *phrase delimiters*, and must be *maximal length*.

Many trivial phrases can be suppressed by imposing the condition that phrases must begin and end with "content words." Function words such as *the*, *of*, and *and* occur frequently (in English) but have no intrinsic semantic value. Without special treatment, the phrases that are extracted would include a myriad of trivial expansions such as *the locust* and *of locusts*—which would displace more useful terms by taking up space in the phrase list. For each language we further expand phrases whose first or last word appears in a predefined list of stop words. Figure 3.24a shows the consequences of not giving stop words special treatment. The stop-word list should contain *du, le, de*, and *par*, and the phrases *du poisson, Le poisson, DE poisson*, and *poisson par* would not appear in the upper panel—they would be further expanded into longer phrases such as *commercialization de poisson*.

If the text were treated as an undifferentiated stream of words, many of the phrases extracted from it would cross syntactic boundaries. For example, the last word of one sentence and the first word of the next are unlikely to form a meaningful two-word phrase. For this reason phrases may not include delimiters. Delimiters are defined, broadly speaking, as any punctuation characters, but the rule is tuned to account for common (and language-dependent) usage. In English, for example, neither the apostrophe in *don't* nor the hyphen in *language-dependent* count as phrase boundaries.

Phrases are *maximal-length* sequences if they occur in more than one context, where by *context* we mean the words that flank the phrase where it appears in the text. Phrases that are not maximal length—ones that occur in a single unique context, that is, ones that are flanked by the same two words wherever they appear—are expanded to encompass that context.

The phrase extraction process

At the core of the phrase extraction process is a program that extracts the phrase hierarchy from a sequence of input symbols. It must identify the set of phrases that occur more than once, are maximal length, do not contain delimiters, and begin and end with content words. This is a lengthy process and is performed as part of the collection-building procedure.

The result is a data structure that supports the runtime browsing interface. In addition to the text of the phrases, the interface needs to know the structure defined by the subphrase relation and what documents each phrase occurs in. For each word and phrase there is a list of phrases in which that word or phrase occurs, and with each word or phrase is stored a list of the documents in which it occurs.

The output of the phrase extraction process has an entry for every phrase that has been identified. Each entry contains a unique phrase identifier, the sequence of words that comprise the phrase, and the number of times it occurs in the entire collection. It also includes the number of expansions of the phrase, a list containing the identifier of each expansion, the number of documents in which the phrase occurs, and a list of document numbers in which it appears.

Building a phrase hierarchy

Although it sounds easy to identify repeated phrases and structure them into a phrase hierarchy, it is surprisingly difficult to do so efficiently on large text collections. There are several different possible techniques, but each is fairly complex.

One widely used basis for text compression is to build a dictionary of phrases that occur in the input and replace all phrases by references to dictionary entries, forming each new phrase by adding a single terminal symbol to an existing dictionary entry. This generates a hierarchical dictionary: each entry (except for the first few) points to another entry that is one character shorter. The hierarchy of repetitions is a simple one—embedding can only occur on the left—but unfortunately this is not a useful structure for phrase browsing.

Another idea is to form a rule for the most frequently occurring pair of words or *digram*, substituting a new symbol for that digram in the input string, and continue until no digram appears more than once. This algorithm is inefficient because it makes multiple passes over the string, recalculating digram frequencies from scratch every time a new rule is created. However, there is an efficient algorithm that creates the same structure of rules in a time that increases in proportion to the length of the input string. We will not describe this algorithm; it is quite complex.

Another algorithm creates a hierarchical dictionary for a given string in a greedy left-to-right fashion. It builds the hierarchy of phrases by forming a new rule out of existing pairs of symbols, including nonterminal symbols. Rules that become nonproductive—in that they do not yield a net space saving—are deleted, and where they occur they are replaced by the symbols that comprise the right-hand side of the deleted rules. This is how rules involving more than two symbols are formed. This method also operates in time proportional to the length of the input string.

The methods described above segment the input string into a nonoverlapping sequence of constituent phrases, each of which may itself be divided into a nonoverlapping sequence of subphrases. The emphasis on segmentation arises out of the fact that they were devised in the context of text compression, where an economical representation of the original string is the ultimate goal. In such a context it is appropriate to restrict consideration to nonoverlapping phrases. However, the restriction is unnecessary if the aim is to infer a useful phrase structure.

The solution is to consider all potential phrases—including ones that overlap—rather than segmenting the input into phrases. Although it seems simple, overlapping phrase extraction is computationally far harder than segmented phrase extraction. A document collection containing several gigabytes of text may have a vocabulary of several hundred thousand words, and exponentially more phrases. Over an N-word vocabulary there are potentially N^2 two-word phrases, N^3 three-word phrases, and so on. In practice the growth is less extreme—otherwise there would be no repeated phrases to browse! The algorithms mentioned above achieve linear complexity by removing many potential phrases from consideration.

Advanced algorithms for overlapping phrases use a data structure called a *suffix tree* to address the complexity issue. Suffix trees can be built in time proportional to the length of the input; however, they take a great deal of space. More economical in space—but rather slower—is a different structure, roughly equivalent in functionality, called a *suffix array*. Even here memory requirements constrain the size of document collections that can be processed because the entire input must be stored along with the suffix and prefix arrays—which are themselves large.

5.7   Notes and sources

Stanley Morison's definition is from *First Principles of Typography* (Morison, 1954). It was Marshall McLuhan (1964) who coined the phrase "the medium is the message" in his book *Understanding Media*: "In a culture like ours, long accustomed to splitting and dividing all things as a means of control, it is sometimes a bit of a shock to be reminded that, in operational and practical fact, the medium is the message."

Lagoze and Payette (2000) give an interesting and enlightening discussion of metadata. They point out that the term is meaningful only in a context that makes clear what the data itself is, and they discuss the different kinds of metadata identified at the start of this chapter.

You will find in your local bookstore many books that teach how to use the HTML markup language. The definitive reference source on the Web for HTML matters is the World Wide Web Consortium (W3C) at *www.w3c.org*. You can find the lynx text browser, which is a fast and reliable method of extracting text from HTML documents, at *http://lynx.browser.org*. The most comprehensive reference source for SGML is Goldfarb (1990), while Bryan (1988) gives a gentler introduction. The Text Encoding Initiative is described by Sperberg-McQueen and Burnard (1999).

There are many excellent accounts of XML and related standards. A comprehensive one is Harold's (2001) *The XML Bible*, which uses many worked examples to convey the points and has strong coverage of XSL. The World Wide Web Consortium is responsible not only for the development of HTML, but also for other standards such as XML, CSS, XSL, the document object model DOM, and formatting objects FO. They publish specifications for all these standards on their Web site, cited above.

The Oxford Text Archive at *http://ota.ahds.ac.uk* is a nonprofit group that has provided long-term storage and maintenance of electronic texts for scholars since 1976. Perseus at *www.perseus.tufts.edu* is a pioneering digital library project, dating from 1985, that originally focused upon the ancient Greek world but now has wider coverage (Crane, 1998). Der Junge Goethe in Seiner Zeit at *www.jgoethe.uni-muenchen.de* is a collection of early works (poems, essays, legal writings and letters) by the great German writer Johann von Goethe (1749–1832), best known internationally for his poem *Faust*, which inspired Gounod's opera of the same name. The Japanese Text Initiative at *http://etext.lib.virginia.edu/japanese* is a collaborative project that makes available a steadily increasing set of Japanese literature, accompanied by English, French, and German translations.

Turning to bibliographic metadata, details of the MARC record structure are presented in books on library automation—for example, Cooper (1996). The *AACR2R* cataloging rules are published by the American Library Association (Gorman and Winkler, 1988). Svenonius (2000) gives a readable account of them, and she quoted the extract about naming a local church. The Dublin Core metadata initiative is described by Weibel (1999), and the standard is available at *www.niso.org*. Thiele (1998) gives a review of related topics, while current developments are documented on the official Dublin Core Web site *http://purl.org/dc* run by the Online Computer Library Center (OCLC).

BibTeX, part of the TeX system invented by Knuth (1986), is covered by Lamport (1994). A description of Refer is included in the Unix manual pages. The EndNote bibliographic system, a commercial reference database and bibliographic software program, can be obtained from ISI ResearchSoft at *www.isiresearchsoft.com*.

The TIFF specification is provided online by Adobe and can be found at *http://partners.adobe.com/asn/developer/technotes/prepress.html*. A readable early account of the MPEG-7 metadata standard for multimedia is given by Nack and Lindsay (1999a, 1999b).

A series of Message Understanding Conferences (MUC) has been held at irregular intervals: the last was MUC-7 in 1998. They provide an ongoing forum for assessing the state of the art and practice in text analysis technology and include formulations and extensive studies of the generic entity extraction task. Many extraction systems are described in the conference proceedings. An account of an excellent and widely used automatic citation indexing system which embodies the techniques mentioned for extracting bibliographic references is given by Giles, Bollacker, and Lawrence (1998).

The method described for language identification was developed and investigated by Cavnar and Trenkle (1994) and implemented in a system called TextCat. The acronym extraction algorithm was developed and evaluated by Stuart Yeates (Yeates, Bainbridge, and Witten, 2000). Different systems for browsing using key phrases are described by Gutwin et al. (1999) and Jones and Paynter (1999).

Dumais et al. (1998) describe state-of-the-art text classification techniques for key-phrase assignment, while Frank et al. (1999) and Turney (2000) describe key-phrase extraction. The standard text-compression technique that builds a dictionary of phrases is due to Ziv and Lempel (1978). The earliest known description of the repeated-digram-substitution algorithm—which has been reinvented many times—is Wolff's (1975), while the more complex implementation that operates in linear time is due to Larsson and Moffat (1999). Finally, the greedy algorithm that creates a hierarchical dictionary is described by Nevill-Manning and Witten (1997). Nevill-Manning and Witten (2000) summarize various computationally efficient techniques for inferring phrase hierarchies from large amounts of text.

6 Construction

Building collections with Greenstone

We briefly met the Greenstone software in Chapter 1, and Section 1.4 reviewed its features to help convey the breadth of requirements for digital library software. Chapter 3 introduced different user interfaces, virtually all of which showed actual Greenstone collections. In Chapter 4 we met different document formats, all of which the software supports. Although all these things are supported by Greenstone, up to this point we have tried to be quite general: with few exceptions our account of digital libraries has not been tied to any particular system.

Now, in this chapter and the next, we focus specifically on Greenstone: how to use it and how it operates. We assume that you have installed it on your computer, be it Windows or Unix; the procedure is introduced in the Appendix. This is a very simple operation—particularly if you accept the standard default configuration—and takes only a few minutes. The starting page of your Greenstone installation, which we call the Greenstone home page, gives access to a small demonstration collection that we call the Demo collection: it is a small subset of the Humanity Development Library with which the book opened.

In any digital library there is an important distinction between the processes involved in *building* collections and those involved in *delivering* the information they contain to users. Computer scientists will recognize this as the classic compile-time versus runtime distinction in conventional computer programming. To serve users effectively, information structures usually have to be prepared in advance. Whereas faster computers may alter the tradeoff by allowing more latitude to postpone operations until runtime, the sheer size of digital library collections makes it unrealistic ever to envisage a fully interpreted service, one without any advance preparation at all. The most we can expect is a kind of incremental operation wherein collections can be augmented without a full recompilation or rebuilding.

We begin by describing Greenstone's facilities and how it helps you organize information and briefly review how to access the information in the Demo collection. Then this chapter focuses on the building aspect: what is involved in creating a collection. Chapter 7 describes what happens at runtime.

It's easy to build simple collections with Greenstone. A subsystem called the Collector leads you step by step through the necessary operations. No programming is required, and it takes just a few minutes to build a plain but utilitarian collection containing your own material. Section 6.2 leads you through the process. We assume that you already have identified some information on your computer (or on the Web) from which you will build your first collection—in formats such as plain text, HTML, Microsoft Word, PDF, or standard e-mail files.

The Collector interface is specifically designed to conceal details of what happens behind the scenes. For more advanced work it is necessary to understand just what building digital library collections entails, and in Section 6.3 we walk through the operations involved in building a collection manually, rather than automatically. Every real-life digital library project presents unique requirements and problems. Expect the unexpected: exceptions are routine—or, to quote a succinctly ominous warning posted at a Tasmanian blowhole, "freak waves are common" (see Figure 6.1). To crest freak waves in a digital library without being overwhelmed, you need to understand the system and how it works.

Figure 6.1 Sign at a Tasmanian blowhole.

Section 6.4 describes the building process in more detail. Before beginning we learn about the directory structure in which digital library collections and the Greenstone software are both stored. Documents are identified throughout the system by object identifiers or OIDs, and we examine how these are assigned and maintained. In order to promote extensibility, the work of format conversion and metadata extraction is handled by software modules called *plug-ins*. Finally we focus on the two key subprocesses of building: importing documents into the system and constructing searching and browsing indexes.

Documents and metadata are stored internally in an XML-based file format called the Greenstone Archive Format, described in Section 6.5. Each collection's structure is defined by a file called the *collection configuration file* that governs how the collection is built and how it appears to users. Sections 6.6 and 6.7 tell you more about how to deal with the novel problems—the freak waves—that most digital library applications pose. The chief mechanisms used to extend the capabilities of Greenstone are the just-mentioned plug-ins, which handle document and metadata formats; classifiers, which handle different kinds of browsing structures; and format statements, which govern the content and appearance of the Web pages that comprise the user interface. Finally Section 6.8 introduces a more advanced graphical user interface that assists in building collections—a possible successor to the Collector.

6.1   Why Greenstone?

Greenstone is a comprehensive system for constructing and presenting collections of thousands or millions of documents, including text, images, audio, and video. A typical digital library contains many collections, individually organized—although they bear a strong family resemblance. Easily maintained, collections can be augmented and rebuilt automatically.

Collections are designed to be easy to use. Web-based and CD-ROM versions have interfaces that are identical. Greenstone can be installed on any Windows or Linux computer; a standard installation program is used which includes precompiled binaries. Collections can be used locally on the computer where the software is installed; also, if this computer is connected to a network, remote users can access them using an ordinary Web browser.

What it does

One of Greenstone's noteworthy design features is that each collection can be organized differently. Requirements vary from collection to collection in several ways. One is the format (or formats) in which the source documents are supplied—whether plain text, HTML, PostScript, PDF, Word, e-mail, or some other file type. Images may be associated with documents—for example, page images of OCR'd documents or cover images of books. Video or audio versions may be supplied too. A second dimension of variation is what metadata is available and how it is supplied—whether embedded in the document itself, perhaps using metadata expressed as "fields" in Microsoft Word or <*meta*> tags in HTML, or information coded into the file name and its enclosing directories, or available separately as a spreadsheet or other data file, or in an explicitly designed metadata format such as MARC. A third kind of variation is the directory structure in which the information is provided. A fourth is the structure of the documents themselves: are they flat, divided sequentially into pages, or organized hierarchically, with metadata (such as title) available at each level? Further dimensions concern the services that are offered by the digital library: searching (what indexes?—what hierarchical levels?—what metadata?), browsing (what metadata?—what kind of browser?), and so on. Still others concern presentation: what formats are target documents shown in?—the search results page?—the various metadata browsers?—what is the default interface language? Auxiliary services might also be required (such as user logging).

Many digital library systems take a Procrustean view: documents must be supplied in such-and-such a format (or converted before entering the system), certain metadata must be available (e.g., Dublin Core) and supplied in a standard way, and so on. In contrast, in Greenstone the structure of a collection is defined by a *collection configuration file*. Creating a collection involves *design* as well as gathering together the raw material, and the result of the design process resides in this file.

On the front page of each collection is a statement of its purpose and coverage (as recommended in Section 2.1) and an explanation of how it is organized. Most collections can be accessed by both *searching* and *browsing:* we encountered many examples in Chapter 3.

When searching, users can choose between indexes built from different parts of the documents. Some collections have an index of entire documents, an index of paragraphs, and an index of titles, each of which can be searched for particular words or phrases. Using these you can find all documents that contain a particular set of words (they might be scattered far and wide throughout the document), or all paragraphs that contain the words (which must all appear in the same paragraph), or all documents whose titles contain the words (which must all appear in the document's title). There may be other indexes, perhaps an index of sections, or an index of section headings, or an index of figure captions.

Browsing involves lists that the user can examine: lists of authors, lists of titles, lists of dates, hierarchical classification structures, and so on. Different collections incorporate different browsing facilities (such as those in Section 3.4).

Organization

As Chapter 3 illustrates there are several ways to find information in Greenstone collections. You can search for particular words that appear in the document text and can often restrict the search to a particular section. You can generally browse documents by title: click on the book icon to read the book. You can sometimes browse documents by subject. Subjects are represented by book-shelves: click on one to look at the books. Where appropriate, documents come complete with a table of contents: you can click on a chapter or subsection to open it, expand the full table of contents, or expand the entire document into your browser window (useful for printing).

All index structures are created automatically from the documents and supporting files: nothing is done manually. If new documents in the same format become available, they can be merged into the collection automatically. Indeed, for many collections this is done by processes that awake regularly, scout for new material, and rebuild the indexes—all without manual intervention.

Document formats

Source documents come in a variety of formats and are converted into a standard XML form for indexing using *plug-ins*. Standard plug-ins process plain text, HTML, Word and PDF documents, and Usenet and e-mail messages—and new ones can be written for different document types. To build browsing structures from metadata, modules called *classifiers* are used to create browsers of various kinds: scrollable lists, alphabetic selectors, dates, and arbitrary hierarchies. Programmers can write new classifiers that create novel browsing structures.

Multimedia and multilingual documents

Collections can contain text, pictures, audio, and video. Nontextual material is either linked into the textual documents or accompanied by textual descriptions (such as figure captions) to allow full-text searching and browsing.

Unicode is used throughout to represent document text and metadata. This allows any language to be processed and displayed in a consistent manner. Collections have been built containing Arabic, Chinese, English, French, Māori, Russian, and Spanish. Multilingual collections embody automatic language recognition, and the interface is available in all these languages (and more).

Distributing collections

Collections can be accessed over the Internet or published, in precisely the same form, on a self-installing Windows CD-ROM. Compression is used to compact the text and indexes. Collections can be distributed among several different computers on a network (such as the Internet) using a CORBA-based protocol, which also supports the construction of graphical query interfaces.

The New Zealand Digital Library (*www.nzdl.org*) provides many examples, including collections of historical documents, humanitarian and development information, technical reports and bibliographies, literary works, and magazines.

Being open source, the software is readily extensible and benefits from the inclusion of GNU-licensed modules for full-text retrieval, database management, and text extraction from proprietary document formats.

How to use it

The searching and browsing facilities that are provided have already been described in Chapter 3. We briefly review them here, focusing on the Demo collection, a small subset of the Humanity Development Library supplied with the Greenstone system. Other collections offer similar facilities; if you can use one, you can use them all.

Exploring the interface

The easiest way to learn how to use the interface is to try it out. Click liberally: all images that appear on the screen are clickable. If you hold the mouse stationary over an image, most browsers will soon pop up a "mouse-over" message that tells you what will happen if you click. Experiment! Choose common words such as *the* and *and* to search for—that should evoke some response, and nothing will break. (Note: Greenstone indexes all words; there are no stop words.)

Each digital library system usually contains several separate collections—for example, computer science technical reports, literary works, Internet FAQs, and magazines. A home page for the digital library system allows you to consult any publicly accessible collection; in addition each collection has its own About page that gives information about it. To return to this page at any time, click on the collection icon that appears at the top left of all searching and browsing pages.

Figure 6.2 shows a screen shot of the Demo collection. All icons are clickable. Several appear at the top of almost every page; Table 6.1 defines what they mean. The *search . . . subjects . . . titles a-z . . . organization . . . how to* navigation bar at the top of the figure gives access to the searching and browsing facilities. The leftmost button is for searching, and the others—four, in this collection—evoke different browsing facilities. These differ from one collection to another.

Table 6.2 summarizes the different ways to find information in the Demo collection, most of which have already been encountered in Chapter 3. You can search for particular words that appear in the text from the Search page. (This is just like the About page shown in Figure 6.2, except that it doesn't show the *about this collection* text.) The Search page can be reached from other pages by pressing the Search button. You can access publications by subject by pressing the Subjects button. This brings up a list of subjects, represented by bookshelves

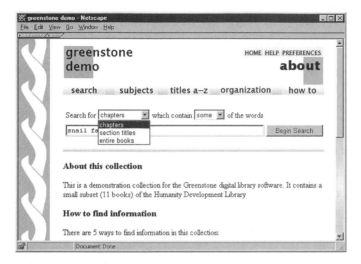

Figure 6.2 Using the Demo collection.

Table 6.1 What the icons at the top of each page mean.

greenstone demo	Takes you to the About page
HOME	Takes you to the Digital Library's home page
HELP	Provides help text
PREFERENCES	Allows you to set user interface and searching options

Table 6.2 What the icons on the search/browse bar mean.

search	Search for particular words
subjects	Access publications by subject
titles a–z	Access publications by title
organization	Access publications by organization
how to	Access publications by "how to" listing

that can be further expanded by clicking on them. You can access publications by title by pressing the Titles A-Z button. This brings up a list of books in alphabetic order. You can access publications by organization by pressing the Organization button, which brings up a list of organizations. You can access publications by "how to" listing by pressing the How To button, which brings up a list of "how to" hints. All these buttons are visible in Figure 6.2.

Table 6.3 Icons that you will encounter when browsing.	
	Click on a book icon to read the corresponding book
	Click on a bookshelf icon to look at books on that subject
	View this document
	Open this folder and view contents
	Click on this icon to close the book
	Click on this icon to close the folder
	Click on the arrow to go on to the next section ...
	... or back to the previous section
DETACH	Open this page in a new window
EXPAND CONTENTS	Expand the table of contents
EXPAND TEXT	Display all text
HIGH- LIGHTING	Highlight search terms

You can tell when you have arrived at an individual book because there is a photograph of its front cover. Figure 3.3 showed a particular book and explained how you can click around the table of contents and read the various sections. At the end of each section are arrows that take you on to the next one or back to the previous one. In some collections the documents do not have a hierarchical chapter/section structure; in these cases no table of contents is displayed when you get to an individual document—just the document text. In other cases the document is split into pages, and you can read sequentially or jump around from one page to another.

While browsing through the collection, you will encounter the icons shown in Table 6.3.

Searching

Small details were omitted from the discussion of searching in Section 3.3. Search terms in Greenstone contain only alphabetic characters and digits and are separated by white space. If other characters such as punctuation appear, they serve to separate terms just as though they were spaces—and then they are ignored. You can't search for words that include punctuation (unless you couch them as a phrase search). For example, the query

```
Agro-forestry in the Pacific Islands: Systems for
Sustainability (1993)
```

is treated the same as

```
Agro forestry in the Pacific Islands Systems for Sustainability
1993
```

Section 3.3 explained two different types of query, ranked and Boolean. The Greenstone interface gives a simplified set of choices:

- queries for all the words
- queries for some of the words

The first is interpreted as a Boolean AND query, the second as a ranked one. Users are encouraged to employ as many search terms as they like—a whole sentence, even a whole paragraph. Phrase searching is included and is implemented by a postretrieval scan as described in Section 3.3.

In most collections you can choose different indexes to search. For example, there might be author and title indexes. Or there might be chapter and paragraph indexes. In most collections the full matching document is returned regardless of which index you search, although this need not be the case.

Preferences

More advanced control over the search operation can be obtained using the Preferences page, shown in Figure 3.15. These facilities were discussed in Section 3.3 and include control over case-folding and stemming, an advanced query mode that allows users to specify Boolean operators, a large-query interface, and a mode that displays search history.

The Preferences page also allows you to change other features of the interface to suit your own requirements. Some collections comprise several subcollections that can be searched independently or together as one unit. If so, you can select from the Preferences page which subcollections to include in your searches.

Each collection has a default presentation language, but you can choose a different one if you like. You can also alter the encoding scheme used by Greenstone for communicating with the browser—the software chooses sensible defaults, but with some browsers better visual results are obtained by switching to a different encoding scheme. All collections allow you to choose a textual interface format rather than the standard one, which is useful for visually impaired users who use large screen fonts or speech synthesizers.

Depending on the collection, there may be other options that control the presentation. In some collections of Web pages, you can suppress the navigation bar at the top of each document page, so that clicking on a search result lands you at the Web page that matches, without any Greenstone header. Then to do another search you would have to use the browser's Back button. In these collections you can also suppress the system's alert message that appears when you click a link that leads out of the digital library collection and on to the Web itself. In some Web collections you can control whether the links on the Search Results page take you straight to the actual URL in question, rather than to the digital library's own copy of the page.

6.2 Using the Collector

Greenstone's Collector subsystem is a facility that helps you create new collections, modify or add to existing ones, and delete collections. Like the rest of Greenstone, it operates through a Web interface, whether you are working locally on your own computer or remotely on someone else's. The Collector helps by guiding you through a sequence of pages that request the information needed for your collection. The sequence is almost self-explanatory: this section runs through it in detail. You can create collections on any computer that is running Greenstone, whether it is your own laptop or workstation or a remote machine that you are interacting with over the Internet—provided you are an authorized user, of course. In either case the entire interaction takes place using a standard Web browser.

Having installed Greenstone on your computer using the procedure introduced in the Appendix, you will be presented with the default Greenstone home page. Access the Collector by clicking the appropriate link on this page.

In Greenstone the structure of each digital library collection is determined at the time the collection is set up. Included in this structure are such things as the format of the source documents, how they are to be displayed on the screen, the source of metadata, what browsing facilities are provided, what search indexes are available, and how the search results and target documents are displayed. Once the collection has been constructed, it is easy to add new documents to it—so long as they are in the same format as the existing ones and the same metadata is provided in exactly the same way. Whenever you add new documents, you need to initiate a "rebuilding" process to recreate the searching and browsing indexes.

The Collector's main purpose is to enable you to build a new collection. It also allows you to modify an existing one: you can add new material to it, alter its structure, delete it, or write it onto a self-contained, self-installing CD-ROM. Even when creating a brand-new collection, the simplest way to proceed is to copy the structure of an existing collection and replace its contents with new material. Later you might want to adapt its structure as well. This is *copy and edit*, a paradigm that underlies most practical computer work: you start with what already exists and rework it into something new. We describe in this section how to do the "copy" part, which is very easy indeed. The rest of the book elaborates on the "edit" part, which is where you tailor the information collection to particular requirements, determined partly by its content and partly by the way you want it to appear to the digital library's user.

Whenever you use the Collector, you need to log in before proceeding. This may seem superfluous when working on your own computer. However, the Collector, like the rest of the Greenstone interface, operates through a Web browser. Web browsers do not provide authentication—the browser does not know that it is *you*, the computer's local user, that is accessing the browser and not someone else at another site, and programs that the browser invokes cannot know this either. People often use Greenstone's collection-building facility to build new collections on a remote computer; the fact that you can do so is a major strength of the design.

Of course it is inappropriate to let arbitrary Internet users build collections on your computer—for reasons of propriety if nothing else. For this reason Greenstone embodies a security system that forces people who want to build collections to log in first. In this way a central system can offer a service to authorized users wishing to build information collections and make them available to others via that central server. For example, you can let your friends log on to your Greenstone system and build their own collections on your computer. You yourself will probably be building collections locally, but you still have to log in because other people using Greenstone on your computer should not be allowed to build collections indiscriminately.

You can create accounts for other people on your Greenstone system. When the software is installed, an initial account is set up for a user called *admin*, whose password is set during the installation procedure.

Creating a new collection

We will describe how to use the Collector to create a new information collection, your own personal digital library. In our example the collection builder will create a collection from some files that are stored on the disk locally, plus other files on a remote Web site. In our example the raw material is HTML, although it is just as easy to accommodate other file types too. We suppose that when remote files are served up by the digital library system, the collection builder wants them to be fetched from the remote site where the original resides, rather than showing a locally cached copy. This will help to make it clear to end users that these files belong elsewhere and are merely *indexed* by the digital library. It also leaves full control of the information with the original site, where files can be edited or deleted at any time. However, the remote files will have to be downloaded for indexing purposes.

Figure 6.3a shows how the interaction starts. You first decide whether to build a new collection or work with an existing one; in our case the user opts to create a new collection. Then the user name is entered (the *admin* user is shown in Figure 6.3a), along with the corresponding password.

Dialog structure

After logging in, the page in Figure 6.3b appears. This shows the sequence of steps that are involved in collection building. They are

1. supplying collection information
2. specifying source data
3. configuring the collection
4. building the collection
5. viewing the collection

The first step is to give the collection's name and associated information. The second is to specify where the source data is to come from. The third is to adjust the configuration options, a step that becomes more useful as you gain experience with Greenstone. The fourth step is where all the (computer's) work is done. During this building process the system makes all the indexes and gathers together any other information that is required to make the collection operate. The fifth step is to check out the collection that has been created.

These five steps are displayed as a sequence of gray buttons at the bottom of the screen in Figure 6.3b and at the bottom of all other pages generated by the Collector. This display helps you keep track of where you are in the process. The button that should be clicked to continue the sequence is shown in green (Collection Information in Figure 6.3b). The gray buttons (all the others, in Figure 6.3b) are inactive. The buttons change to yellow as you proceed through the sequence, and you can return to an earlier step by clicking the corresponding yellow button in the diagram. This display is modeled after the "wizards" that are widely used in commercial software to guide end users through the steps involved in installing new software.

Supplying the collection information

The next step in the sequence, supplying the collection information, is shown in Figure 6.3c. When creating a new collection, you need to enter some information about it:

- title
- contact e-mail address
- brief description

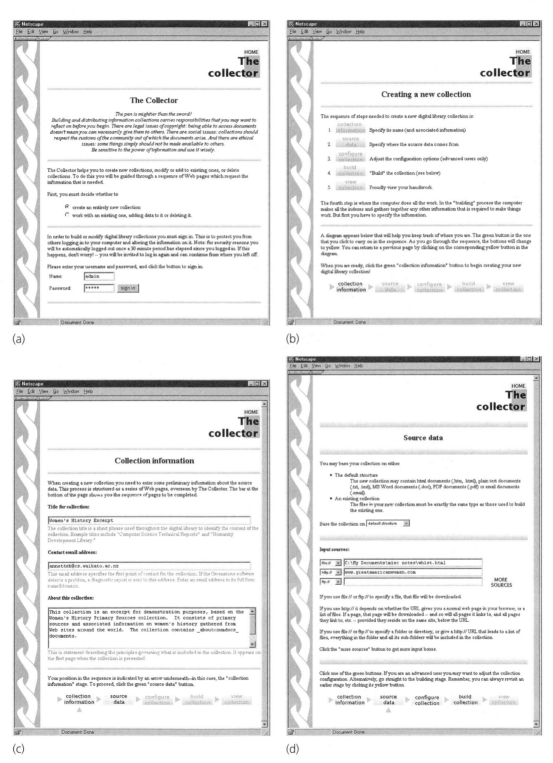

Figure 6.3 Using the Collector to build a new collection. (continued on following page)

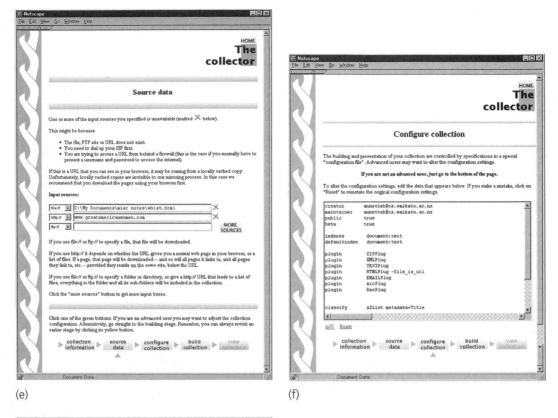

(e)

(f)

(g)

Figure 6.3 (continued)

The collection title is a short phrase used throughout the digital library to iden-tify the collection. Examples include the *Food and Nutrition Library*, *World Environmental Library*, *Humanity Development Library*, and so on. The e-mail address gives the first point of contact for any problems encountered with the collection. If the Greenstone software detects a problem, a diagnostic report may be sent to this address. Finally, the brief description sets out the principles that govern what is included in the collection. It appears under the heading *About this collection* on the first page when the collection is presented. Section 2.1 of Chapter 2, under "Ideology," explained the importance of including this kind of information with every digital library collection.

The user's current position in the collection-building sequence is indicated by an arrow that appears in the display at the bottom of each screen—in this case, as Figure 6.3c shows, the collection information stage. The user proceeds to the stage shown in Figure 6.3d by clicking the green Source Data button.

Specifying the source data

Figure 6.3d shows the point at which the user specifies the source text for the collection. You can either create a completely new collection or "clone" an exist-ing one—that is, base the structure of your new collection on one that exists already.

If you clone a collection, you need to specify (on a pull-down menu) which one you want to clone. Note that some collections use nonstandard input file formats, while others use metadata specified in auxiliary files. If your new input lacks this information, some browsing facilities may not work properly. For example, if you clone the Demo collection (one of the collections provided in the Greenstone distribution) you may find that the Subjects, Organization, and How To buttons don't work.

The alternative to cloning an existing collection is to create a completely new one. A bland collection configuration file is provided that accepts a wide range of different document types and generates a searchable index of the full text and an alphabetic title browser. More information about the different document for-mats that can be accommodated is given in the subsection "Document Formats."

Boxes are provided to indicate where the source documents are located: up to three separate input sources can be specified in Figure 6.3d. If you need more, just click the More Sources button.

There are three kinds of specification:

- a directory name on the Greenstone server system (beginning with *file://*)
- an address beginning with *http://* for files to be downloaded from the Web
- an address beginning with *ftp://* for files to be downloaded using FTP

You can specify sources of more than one type. If you use *file://* or *ftp://* to spec-ify a file, that file will be downloaded. If you use *http://* it depends on whether the URL gives you a normal Web page in your browser or a list of files. If a page, that page will be downloaded—and so will all pages it links to, and all pages they link to, and so on—provided they reside on the same site, below the URL. If you use *file://* or *ftp://* to specify a folder or directory, or give an *http://* URL that leads to a list of files, everything in the folder and all its subfolders will be included in the collection.

In this case (Figure 6.3d) the new collection comprises documents taken from a local file system as well as a remote Web site. The documents on the remote site will be copied, or *mirrored*, to the local site during the building process.

When you click the Configure Collection button to proceed to the next stage of building, the Collector checks that all the sources of input you specified can be reached. This might take a few seconds, or even a few minutes if you have specified several sources. If one or more of the input sources you specified is unavailable, you will be presented with a page like that in Figure 6.3e, where the unavailable sources are marked (both of them in this case).

Sources might be unavailable because

- the file, FTP site, or URL does not exist (or the name has been entered incorrectly)
- you need to dial up your Internet Service Provider (ISP) first
- you are trying to access a URL from behind a firewall on your own computer
- the URL you are trying to access is behind a firewall on the remote computer

The last case is potentially the most mysterious. It occurs if you normally have to present a username and password to access the Internet. Sometimes it happens that you can see the page from your Web browser if you enter the URL, but the Collector claims that it is unavailable. The explanation is that the page in your browser may be coming from a locally cached copy. Unfortunately, locally cached copies are invisible to the Collector. In this case we recommend that you first download the pages individually using your browser and save them locally.

Configuring the collection

Figure 6.3f shows the next stage. The construction and presentation of all collections are controlled by specifications in a special collection configuration file (discussed later). Advanced users may use this page to alter the configuration settings. Most, however, will proceed directly to the final stage. Indeed, in Figure 6.3d both the Configure Collection and Build Collection buttons are displayed in green, signifying that step 3 can be bypassed completely.

In this case the user has made a small modification to the default configuration file by including a *file_is_url* switch with the HTML plug-in. This flag causes URL metadata to be inserted into each document, based on the file-name convention that is adopted by the mirroring package. The collection uses this metadata to allow readers to refer to the original source material rather than a local copy.

Building the collection

Figure 6.3g shows the building stage. Until now the responses to the dialog have merely been recorded in a temporary file. The building stage is where the action takes place.

During building, indexes for both browsing and searching are constructed according to instructions in the collection configuration file. The building process takes some time: minutes to hours, depending on the size of the collection and the speed of your computer. Some large collections take a day or more to build.

When you reach this stage in the interaction, a status line at the bottom of the Web page gives feedback on how the operation is progressing, updated every five seconds. The message visible in Figure 6.3g indicates that when the snapshot was taken, *Title* metadata was being extracted from an input file.

Warnings are written if input files or URLs are requested that do not exist, or exist but there is no plug-in that can process them, or the plug-in cannot find an associated file—such as an image file embedded in an HTML document. The intention is that you will monitor progress by keeping this window open in your browser. If any errors cause the process to terminate, they are recorded in this status area.

You can cancel the building process at any time by clicking on the Stop Building button in Figure 6.3g. If you leave the Web page (and have not canceled the building process), the building operation will continue, and the new collection will be installed when the operation completes.

If you do experience problems with the Collector, or if you are working with large collections or more advanced projects, you can build collections from the command line. Section 6.3 gives a detailed walkthrough of how this is done.

Viewing the collection

When the collection is built and installed, the sequence of buttons visible at the bottom of Figures 6.3b–f appears again at the bottom of Figure 6.3g, with the View Collection button active. This takes you directly to the newly built collection.

To help monitor the creation of new collections, e-mail can be sent to the collection's contact address, and to the system administrator, whenever a collection is created (or modified). This allows those responsible to check when changes occur and to monitor what is happening on the system. The facility is disabled by default but can be enabled by editing the *main.cfg* configuration file (see Section 7.4).

Working with existing collections

When you enter the Collector, you have to specify whether you want to create an entirely new collection or work with an existing one, adding data to it or deleting it. Updating an existing collection with new material is an automatic process rather than the tedious manual procedure that is usually involved when updating a richly linked Web site. Greenstone creates all searching and browsing structures automatically from the documents themselves. Because no links are inserted by hand, when new documents in the same format become available they can be merged into the collection automatically.

Although our purpose in this section is to create a brand-new collection, we take this opportunity to explain briefly what can be done with existing collections. First you select the collection from a list that is provided. Some collections are "write protected" and cannot be altered: these don't appear in the selection list. With the selected collection, you can

- add more material and rebuild the collection
- edit the configuration file to modify the collection's structure
- delete the collection entirely
- export the collection to a self-contained, self-installing CD-ROM

When adding new material, you are taken straight to the stage of the dialog depicted in Figure 6.3d, where you can specify new files that will be added to the collection. Make sure that you do not respecify files that are already present—otherwise the collection will include duplicate copies. You specify directories and files just as you do when building a new collection: files are identified by their full path name, Web pages by their absolute Web address. If you add data to a collection and for some reason the building process fails, the old version of the collection remains unchanged.

The structure of a collection can be modified by editing its configuration file. This option takes you straight to the stage of the dialog depicted in Figure 6.3f. Simple changes can be made at this stage, such as adding new plug-ins (such as the PDF and Word plug-ins mentioned in the next subsection) or adding an option to a plug-in (earlier we added *file_is_url* to the HTML plug-in). More radical alterations to the configuration file are best undertaken outside the Collector interface, as described in Section 6.3.

If you specify that you want to delete a collection, you will be asked to confirm whether you really want to do so. Once deleted, Greenstone cannot bring collections back!

Finally you can export the collection in a form that allows it to be written to a self-contained, self-installing Greenstone CD-ROM for Windows. When you export the collection, the dialog informs you of the directory name in which the result has been placed. The entire contents of the directory are then written to CD-ROM using a standard CD-writing utility.

Document formats

When building collections Greenstone processes each source document by seeking a plug-in that can deal with that particular format. Plug-ins are specified in the collection configuration file. Greenstone generally uses the file name to determine document format—for example, *foo.txt* is processed as a text file, *foo.html* as HTML, and *foo.doc* as a Word file—because the plug-ins are written to seek these particular file name patterns.

Here is a summary of the plug-ins that are available for widely used document formats, including the file names that each one processes. Most plug-ins allow you to specify various options. More detail about plug-ins and their options, and further plug-ins for less commonly used formats, can be found in Section 6.7.

TEXTPlug (*.txt, *.text)
TEXTPlug interprets a plain text file as a simple document. It adds *Title* metadata based on the first line of the file.

HTMLPlug (*.htm, *.html; also .shtml, .shm, .asp, .php, .cgi)
HTMLPlug processes HTML files. It extracts *Title* metadata based on the HTML <*title*> tag; other metadata expressed using HTML's metatag syntax can be extracted too. It also parses and processes any links that the file contains. Links to other files in the collection are trapped and replaced by references to the corresponding documents within the digital library. Several options are available with this plug-in, including the *file_is_url* switch mentioned earlier.

WORDPlug (*.doc)
WORDPlug imports Microsoft Word documents. There are many different variants on the Word format—even Microsoft programs sometimes have conversion problems. Greenstone uses independent programs to convert Word files to HTML. For some older Word formats, the system resorts to a simple extraction algorithm that finds all text strings in the input file.

PDFPlug (*.pdf)
PDFPlug imports documents stored as PDF files, Adobe's Portable Document Format. Like WORDPlug, it uses an independent program to convert files to HTML.

PSPlug (*.*ps*)

PSPlug imports documents stored as PostScript files. It works best if a standard conversion program is already installed on your computer. These are available on most Linux installations, but not on Windows. If no conversion program is present, the system resorts to a simple text extraction algorithm.

EMAILPlug (*.*email*)

EMAILPlug imports files containing e-mail and deals with common formats such as are used by the Netscape, Eudora, and Unix mail readers. Each source document is examined to see if it contains an e-mail, or several e-mails joined together in one file, and if so the contents are processed. The plug-in extracts *Subject*, *To*, *From*, and *Date* metadata.

ZIPPlug (*.gz, .z, .tgz, .taz, .bz, .zip, .tar*)

ZIPPlug handles several compressed and/or archived input formats. It relies on standard utility programs being present.

6.3 Building collections manually: A walkthrough

Now it is time to walk through the operations involved in building a Greenstone collection from the command line, to help understand the process better. The collection used as an example contains the Web home pages of people who have worked on the New Zealand Digital Library project. As we go we will take the opportunity to explain some general features and design principles, as well as the specific steps involved in building a collection.

We have talked loosely about "building" a collection as the process of taking a set of documents and metadata information and creating all the indexes and data structures that support the searching, browsing, and viewing operations that the collection offers. This process is broken down into four phases. First we make a skeleton framework structure that will contain the collection. Then we import the documents and metadata specifications from the form in which they are provided to a Greenstone standard form. Next we build the required indexes and data structures. Finally we install the collection so that it becomes operational. We refer to these operations as *make*, *import*, *build*, and *install*, respectively. The terminology is potentially confusing: we use *make* because the English language does not have a specific verb for creating a skeleton or framework, and—worse still—*build* is used in two different senses, one that encompasses the whole process and another that refers to a particular subprocess. Provided the distinction is kept in mind, it should be clear from the context whether *build* refers to the general process of building-in-the-large or the specific one of building-in-the-small.

Table 6.4 The collection-building process.

Step	Function
1. `cd "C:\Program Files\gsdl"`	Assumes that Greenstone is installed in the default location.
2. `setup.bat`	This makes Greenstone programs available. On Unix, use *source setup.bash* or *source setup.csh* instead, depending on the shell you are using.
3. `perl -S mkcol.pl` `-creator me@cs.waikato.ac.nz dlpeople`	Create a skeleton framework of initial files and directories. We called our collection dlpeople.

4. Copy source files into
    `C:\Program Files\gsdl\`
        `collect\dlpeople\import`
	Populate the collection with sample documents. On Windows, select the files and drag them. On Unix, use the *cp* command.

5. Edit the file
    `C:\Program Files\gsdl\`
        `collect\dlpeople\etc\collect.cfg`
	Customize the collection by editing the collection-level metadata in the configuration file. Alter *collectionname*, *collectionextra*, and *collectionicon*.

6. `perl -S import.pl dlpeople`	Convert the source documents and metadata specifications to the Greenstone standard form.
7. `perl -S buildcol.pl dlpeople`	Build the indexes and data structures that make the collection work.
8. Replace the contents of the collection's index directory with that of the building directory	On Windows, select the files and drag them. On Unix, use the *mv* command.

If you can, follow along on your own computer. We use Windows terminology. The process for Unix is virtually identical; the differences are mentioned in Table 6.4. You may think that some operations are unnecessary, but their role becomes clear later. Remember that our purpose is not to provide a streamlined way of building collections—for that, use the Collector instead—but to explain the collection-building procedure, a powerful and flexible process that provides a basis for building all sorts of different collections with radically different structures. Table 6.4 summarizes the procedure, for reference.

Getting started

The first challenge when working from the command line under Windows is to locate the *command prompt*, the place where you type commands. Look in the

Start menu, or under the Programs submenu, for an entry such as MS-DOS Prompt, DOS Prompt, or Command Prompt. If you can't find one, invoke the Run entry and type *cmd* (or, on Windows 95/98 systems, *command*) in the dialog box. If all else fails, seek help from one who knows—perhaps your system administrator.

Change into the directory in which Greenstone has been installed. Assuming it was placed in its default location, you can move there by typing

```
cd "C:\Program Files\gsdl"
```

(We show the quotation marks because in some circumstances you need them to protect the space in *Program Files*.) Next, at the prompt type

```
setup.bat
```

This batch file (which you can read if you like) tells the system where to look for Greenstone programs and other parts of the digital library file structure by setting the variable *GSDLHOME* to the Greenstone home directory.[9] If later on you want to return to this place, type

```
cd "%GSDLHOME%"
```

(again, the quotation marks are there to protect spaces in the file name). If you close the DOS window and open another one, you must invoke *setup.bat* again.

Making a framework for the collection

Now you are in a position to make, import, build and install collections. The first operation creates an empty framework structure for a collection and is accomplished by the Perl program *mkcol.pl*—the name stands for "make a collection." Cryptic abbreviations are used because Greenstone runs on systems right down to Windows 3.1, which imposes an eight-character limit on all file and directory names.

First run the program by typing *perl –S mkcol.pl.* (If your environment is set up to associate the Perl application with files ending in *.pl*, you can drop the *perl* preamble and simply type *mkcol.pl.*) All Greenstone programs take at least one argument—the name of the collection being operated on. Running them without arguments causes a description of usage and a list of arguments to appear on the screen.

---

9. On Windows 95/98 systems running *setup.bat* may fail with an "Out of environment space" error. If this happens, you should edit your system's *config.sys* file (normally found at *C:\config.sys*) and add the line *shell=C:\command.com /e:4096 /p* (where *C:* is your system drive letter) to expand the size of the environment table. You'll need to reboot for this change to take effect, and then repeat the steps above for Greenstone.

The usage statement explains that *mkcol* requires just one argument, the collection name. It also shows an extensive list of options, which are arguments that are preceded by a minus sign (−). One of these options, *creator*, must be present—it is used to specify who built the collection. (The notion of a "required option" may be a contradiction in terms but we use it all the same.) This illustrates a general principle: sensible defaults are provided wherever possible, so that only a minimum of information needs to be specified explicitly—in accordance with the maxim "Simple things should be simple; complex things should be possible." Every Perl program in Greenstone has many options, of which virtually all have default values. The fact that you can always obtain a usage summary by invoking the program without arguments provides up-to-date documentation for an evolving system.

We now use *mkcol.pl* to create a framework of initial files and subdirectories for our new collection. To assign the collection the name *dlpeople*, type

```
perl -S mkcol.pl -creator me@cs.waikato.ac.nz dlpeople
```

(If Perl is associated with the *.pl* file extension, use the corresponding short form *mkcol.pl −creator me@cs.waikato.ac.nz dlpeople*). The creator's e-mail address is needed because any problems that arise with the collection are automatically notified (although this facility is switched off by default). Please substitute your address for the one shown.

To examine the new file structure, move to the newly created collection directory by typing

```
cd "%GSDLHOME%\collect\dlpeople"
```

(Again the quotation marks protect spaces in *GSDLHOME*.) List the contents of this directory by typing *dir*. The *mkcol.pl* program has created seven subdirectories: *archives, building, etc, images, import, index* and *perllib*. We learn about their roles shortly.

In the new collection's *etc* directory, *mkcol* has placed a collection configuration file called *collect.cfg*. Figure 6.4 shows the one created by the above *mkcol* command. The e-mail address that was specified has been placed in the *creator* and *maintainer* lines, and the collection name appears in one of the *collection-meta* lines, which give metadata concerning the collection as a whole. The configuration file includes a liberal selection of plug-ins.

Importing the documents

The next step is to populate the collection with documents. In our case, source material for the new collection resides in a series of directories, one for each of the people concerned. These directories contain a mixture of HTML files and associated GIF or JPEG image files, along with the occasional PDF file. They also

```
creator         me@cs.waikato.ac.nz
maintainer      me@cs.waikato.ac.nz
public          true

indexes         document:text
collectionmeta .document:text      "documents"
defaultindex    document:text

plugin          ZIPPlug
plugin          GAPlug
plugin          TEXTPlug
plugin          HTMLPlug
plugin          EMAILPlug
plugin          PDFPlug
plugin          RTFPlug
plugin          WORDPlug
plugin          ArcPlug
plugin          RecPlug

classify        AZList -metadata "Title"

collectionmeta collectionname     "dlpeople"
collectionmeta iconcollection     ""
collectionmeta collectionextra    ""
```

Figure 6.4 Collection configuration file created by *mkcol.pl*.

contain subdirectories, each containing the same kind of mixture, and possibly further subdirectories as well. The whole structure is messy and disorganized, which is typical of the file structures that people present you with when building digital libraries.

The file structure containing the source material should be placed in the new collection's *import* directory. Just drag the directory containing the source material into the *dlpeople* collection's *import* directory. It doesn't matter if the directory represents a whole hierarchy, or if you put more than one source directory into the *import* directory.

Because *mkcol* has included a wide selection of plug-ins in the configuration file in Figure 6.4, the file structure you place in *import* can include many file types: PDF documents (with extension *.pdf*), RTF documents (*.rtf*), Word documents (*.doc*), e-mail documents (*.email*) from Netscape, Eudora, or Unix e-mail files, as well as plain text documents (*.txt* or *.text*) and HTML (*.htm* or *.html*) files (along with associated images). They will all be included in the collection.

Now you are ready to perform the import process. This brings the documents into the Greenstone system, standardizing their format, the way that metadata is specified, and the file structure that contains the documents. In different collections source metadata is provided in different ways. Most plug-ins extract whatever metadata they can from the document files—for example, the HTML plug-in extracts *Title* metadata and any metadata specified with HTML's *<meta>* syntax. The best way to learn about what the other plug-ins do is to try them and see! It is also possible to provide metadata explicitly (see Section 6.7).

Type *perl –S import.pl* at the prompt to get a list of options for the import program. Then issue the basic command

```
perl -S import.pl dlpeople
```

Text scrolls past, reporting the progress of the import operation. Some warnings may appear—for example, when there are files that no plug-in can process. You can ignore warnings—in this case these files will simply be ignored. The *dlpeople* file structure contains about 300 files in about 40 folders, occupying a total of about 6 Mb. Importing it on an ordinary laptop takes a minute or two—correspondingly longer on slower machines. You do not have to be in any particular directory when the *import* command is issued because the software works out where everything is from the Greenstone home directory and the collection's name.

Building the indexes

The next step is to build the indexes and data structures that make the collection work. This is building-in-the-small (as opposed to building-in-the-large, which refers to the whole process of making, importing, building, and installing). With a small nod toward the ambiguity of the term *build*, the relevant program is called *buildcol.pl*.

But first let's customize the new collection's appearance by altering the collection-level metadata shown at the end of the configuration file in Figure 6.4. (You can omit this step if you like.) Give the collection a less cryptic name by editing the *collectionname* line to *collectionmeta collectionname "The People of the NZDL project"*. Web browsers receive this name as the title of the collection's front page. Add a description between the quotes of the *collectionextra* line—for example, "This collection is made up of the home pages of some of the people who have worked on the NZDL project." (For real collections you should use a more informative description.) This text appears under *About this collection* on the collection's home page. It should be entered as a single line in the editor,

Figure 6.5 Collection icon.

without pressing the Enter key, because each line of the configuration file is treated as a new command.

Give the collection an icon. (In its absence, the collection's name is used instead.) Any picture viewable in a Web browser is suitable—Figure 6.5 shows ours. Put the image's location between the quotes in the *iconcollection* line. We named the image *icon.gif* and placed it in the collection's *images* directory, that is, *collect\dlpeople\images*. For the icon to be correctly located through a Web browser, we use the string *_httpprefix_/collect/dlpeople/images/icon.gif* as the value of *iconcollection*. The word *_httpprefix_* is a shorthand way of beginning any URL that points within the Greenstone file area. Notice that forward slashes are used for URLs, not the familiar Windows backslashes; this is standard in Web-serving software.

Having edited the collection configuration file, save and close it.

Now "build" the collection. First type *perl –S buildcol.pl* at the command prompt for a list of collection-building options (these options are explained more fully in Section 6.4). Then, sticking to the defaults, type

```
perl -S buildcol.pl dlpeople
```

Again "progress report" text scrolls past, which under normal conditions can be ignored. (Any serious problem will cause the program to be terminated immediately with an error message.) The building process takes about a minute.

Installing the collection

Although it has been built, the collection is not yet "live"—users of your Greenstone system cannot see it. Building takes place in a special area, and the result must be moved to the proper place before the collection can be used. This is because some collections take hours—or days—to build, and during that period an existing version of the collection may continue to serve users. Building is done in the *building* directory, whereas collections are served from their *index* directory.

To make the collection operational, select the contents of the *dlpeople* collection's *building* directory, and drag them into the *index* directory. If *index* already contains some files, remove them first.

The newly built collection can now be invoked from the digital library home page. If you are using the Local Library version of Greenstone (this is explained in the installation instructions), you will have to restart the library program. Otherwise you need only reload the home page (although caching may conceal the change, in which case you should close the browser and restart it). To view the new collection, click on its icon. The result is shown in Figure 6.6. If the collection doesn't appear on the Greenstone home page, the most common cause is omitting to move the contents of the *building* directory into *index*.

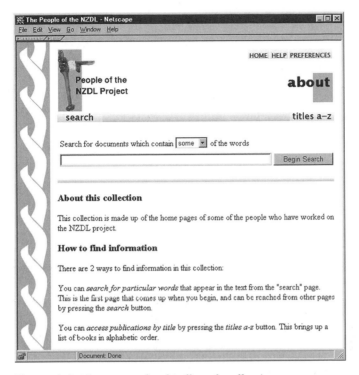

Figure 6.6   About page for the *dlpeople* collection.

6.4   Importing and building

There are two main parts to the collection-building process that we walked through earlier: importing (*import.pl*) and building in the narrow sense (*build-col.pl*). The import process brings documents and metadata into the system in a standardized XML form that is used internally, the Greenstone Archive Format. Afterward the original material can safely be deleted because the collection can be rebuilt from the archive files. The original material is placed in the collection's *import* directory, and the import process transforms it to files in the *archives* directory. To add new material to the collection, put it into *import* and reexecute the import process. The new material will find its way into *archives*, along with any files that are already there. To keep a collection in "source" form so that it can be augmented and rebuilt later, do not delete the *archives*.

The build process (*buildcol.pl*) creates the indexes and data structures needed to make the collection operational. The building process does not work incrementally (although the import process does): indexes for the whole collection are built all at once. If you add new material to *archives* as described earlier, you then have to rebuild the collection from scratch by reissuing *buildcol.pl*. This

Table 6.5 Options for the import and build processes.

Option	Argument	Function
−verbosity	Number 0–3	Control how much information about the process is printed to standard error; 0 gives a little, 3 gives lots.
−archivedir	Directory name	Specify the location of the archives—where *import.pl* puts them and where *buildcol.pl* finds them (default *archives*).
−maxdocs	Number	Specify the maximum number of documents to be processed.
−collectdir	Directory name	Specify the collection's location (default *collect*).
−out	Filename	Specify a file to which all output messages are written (defaults to standard error—the screen).
−keepold	–	Do not remove the result of the previous import (*archives* directory) or build (*building* directory).
−debug	–	Print plug-in output to standard output.

nonincremental operation is a less serious limitation than might appear at first sight. Most collections can be rebuilt overnight—this suffices for collections with up to a gigabyte or so of text (depending on the number of indexes). If necessary, a two-part collection with a main and an auxiliary part can be used, with new material added to the latter. Greenstone can be set up to search multiple collections and present them as though they were a single collection.

The import and build processes have many similarities and take many of the same options, described in Table 6.5. Remember that to see the options for any Greenstone script, type its name at the command prompt.

Many of the options in Table 6.5 assist with debugging. *Verbosity* determines how much information, if any, is produced during the process. The *maxdocs* parameter selects just the first few documents for importing or building. This is useful when debugging new collections and new plug-ins. The *out* specification allows debugging information to be written to a file for later analysis. The *debug* option allows you to see the output of each plug-in rather than having it written to a file.

Files and directories

Before going any further you need to learn how to find your way around the software. Figure 6.7 shows the structure of the Greenstone home directory, including one collection—the newly built *dlpeople*.

We begin with the *collect* directory, which, as we have seen, contains the digital library collections in this Greenstone installation. Each collection has the same structure: just one, *dlpeople*, is shown here. The *dlpeople* directory com-

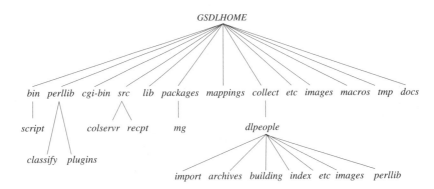

Figure 6.7 Structure of the Greenstone home directory.

prises an *import* directory where the original source material is placed and an *archives* directory where the import process's result goes. The *building* directory is used temporarily during building, whereupon its contents are moved manually into *index*. It is *index* that contains the bulk of the information that is served to users—the *import*, *archives*, and *building* directories can be deleted after the build is complete. The *etc* directory contains the collection's configuration file and, if necessary, other miscellaneous information associated with it. Finally *images* holds specific images that are used in the collection—such as the collection icon in Figure 6.5—while *perllib* contains any Perl programs that are specific to the collection.

Having covered the *collect* directory, we turn to the remainder of Figure 6.7. To the left of *collect* is the Greenstone program code. *Bin* contains the programs that are used in the building process (broadly defined). There are subdirectories for Windows and Unix (not shown), and a *script* subdirectory that holds the Perl programs used for creating and building collections—for example, *mkcol.pl*, *import.pl*, and *buildcol.pl*. For an account of how to use any Perl program, type its name at the command prompt.

The *perllib* directory contains Perl modules that are used when building. Plug-ins and classifiers are placed in the corresponding subdirectory. They are discussed further in Section 6.7.

The *cgi-bin* directory contains the software that implements the Greenstone runtime system, which is the subject of Chapter 7 (except that in the Local Library version of Greenstone mentioned earlier, *cgi-bin* is absent, and the software is placed in the top-level Greenstone directory instead). This software is written in the C++ language. *Src* contains the source code. The main part comprises the "collection server" and the "receptionist"—these are explained in Chapter 7—but there are also several auxiliary programs. Common software that is used by both components is placed in *lib*.

Packages holds the source code for various external software packages, all distributed under the GNU Public License, that Greenstone uses. Their functions vary widely, from MG, an indexing and compression program, to GDBM, a standard database manager program; from Web mirroring programs to ones that support standard library protocols; from encryption modules for password protection to utilities that convert PDF and Microsoft Word documents to HTML. Each package is stored in a directory of its own, with a *readme* file that gives more information about it. The corresponding executable programs are placed in the *bin* directory when Greenstone is compiled and installed. The *mappings* directory holds Unicode translation tables.

Just as the *etc* subdirectories of *collect* holds the collection configuration files, so the main Greenstone *etc* directory holds configuration files for the entire system. It also includes initialization and error logs and the user authorization database. The main *images* directory stores images used in the user interface, among them the icons shown in Tables 6.1–6.3. The user interface is driven by small code fragments called *macros*, and these are placed in the *macros* directory. *Tmp* is used for storing temporary files. Also, some programs make *tmp* subdirectories of individual collection directories for temporary files. Finally, *docs* contains the documentation for the system.

Object identifiers

Every document has an associated object identifier or OID that is used to identify it within the system. This identifier is *persistent:* that is, it is intended as a permanent name for the document. For example, suppose a user is reviewing a list of search results and at precisely that time, unbeknownst to him or her, a new version of the same collection is installed. When the user clicks one of the documents, the correct document will still be displayed, despite the fact that all the underlying data structures have changed, because it is identified internally by its OID—and object identifiers remain the same when collections are rebuilt.

Assigning object identifiers to documents is one of the import process's major functions. The OID is assigned and stored as an attribute in the document's archive file. If the import process is reexecuted, documents receive the same OID. To ensure this, OIDs are obtained by calculating a random number based on the content of the document—called *hashing*. If the content changes, the OID changes. If it does not, the OID remains the same. Identical copies of a document will be assigned the same OID and will thereafter be treated by the system as one. The same document can appear in two different collections: if it does, searching both collections will return just one copy of the document.

OIDs are character strings starting with the letters *HASH*: for example, *HASH0109d3850a6de4440c4d1ca2*. They are long enough that the chance of two documents receiving the same OID is vanishingly small, and this possibility is ignored in the system.

By default the hashing method is used to assign OIDs. When a document is imported, its OID is stored in the archive file that represents the document. But the OID could be overridden by altering it in the file—perhaps to take advantage of an existing identifier. Documents are not usually reimported when adding new material to a collection, so if their OIDs have been overridden in the archive file, they will stay that way.

Hashing the contents of documents is slow and can easily dominate the import process. A simpler alternative is provided which instead numbers the documents sequentially in the order in which they are imported (specified by the *OIDtype* argument in Table 6.6 below). This makes importing faster, but the hashing method should be used if you intend to add documents to the collection later. If you were to use sequential numbering and add documents without reimporting, OID conflicts would arise; if you did reimport the existing documents, their OIDs would change.

Each document's archive file occupies its own directory in the archives structure, along with any files associated with the document—such as image files included in it. OIDs are used to name this directory. File-system limitations may be encountered when storing large collections on primitive computers: the length of file names may be limited; the number of files in a directory may be limited; there may be a restriction on the maximum nesting depth of directories. (Early Windows systems impose an eight-character limit on file names and cannot read CD-ROMs that have more than eight nested directories.)

For all these reasons OIDs are not used as file names directly. Instead they serve to define an efficient directory hierarchy that respects these limitations. The details are mundane. Briefly, the OID's first eight characters are used as the document's directory: thus the above document would be stored in directory *HASH0109*. If a second document's OID begins with the same eight characters— say *HASH010942bbf9c1376e9489c29c*—it is stored in a subdirectory named by the next eight characters, in this case *HASH0109/42bbf9c1*. If the following eight characters clash with a third document's OID, the policy continues. This produces a maximum of four nested directories—e.g., *HASH0109/42bbf9c1/376e9489/c29c*, if the directory names end up being spelled out in full. Combined with the standard prefix *GSDLHOME/collect/collection-name/archives*, this comes just inside an eight-level maximum nesting depth.

Plug-ins

Most of the import process's work is accomplished by plug-ins. These operate in the order in which they occur in the collection's configuration file. An input file is passed to each plug-in in turn until one is found that can process it—thus earlier plug-ins take priority over later ones. A document's file name is generally used to determine its format—for example, *foo.txt* is processed as a text file, *foo.html* as HTML, and *foo.doc* as a Word file—because the plug-ins are written to detect these particular file name patterns. However, it is possible to write plug-ins that examine a document's content before deciding whether to process it. If there is no plug-in that can process the file, a warning is printed and attention passes to the next file.

One plug-in can inherit the functionality of another. For example, WORD-Plug inherits from HTMLPlug the ability to process HTML files and works by converting Word documents to an intermediate HTML form.

The traversal of the subdirectory structure in the *import* directory is also determined by plug-ins. We have explained that you begin by placing the whole file structure containing the source material into *import*. A special plug-in called RecPlug is provided that recurses through directory structures. This plug-in only processes directories. It operates by creating a list of all the files they contain (including subdirectories) and passing the name of each back through the plug-in list. The effect is to expand all directories in the hierarchy. RecPlug is normally included in all collection configuration files as the last member of the plug-in list. The fact that subdirectories are traversed by a plug-in opens up the possibility of having different schemes for working through the files. It also means that metadata could be assigned to documents based on where they occur in the *import* directory hierarchy.

Two other special plug-ins are included in every collection configuration file: GAPlug and ArcPlug. GAPlug processes Greenstone Archive Format documents. These do not occur in the *import* files, but they certainly do occur in the *archives* directory structure. The import and build phases use the same plug-in list, so GAPlug must be included for use when building. ArcPlug is also used during building only: it processes the list of document OIDs that were produced during importing (the list is stored in the *archives.inf* file mentioned in the next subsection).

The import process

The import process converts documents from their native format to the Greenstone Archive Format. This format also includes all metadata that pertains to the document. Reading any metadata files that are supplied with the collection, decoding their format, and inserting the information into the appropriate archive files are all part of the import process.

Figure 6.8 depicts the import process. Each oval represents a specific module that resides in the *perllib* directory. There are many options: Table 6.5 shows

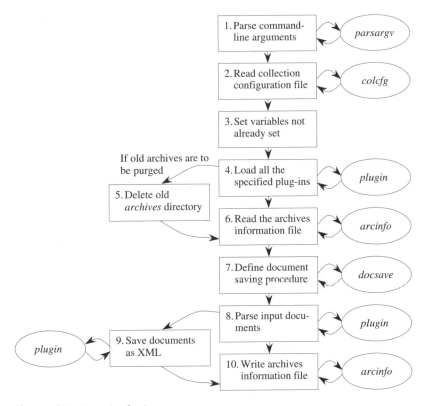

Figure 6.8 Steps in the import process.

those that are common to both import and build; Table 6.6 lists import-specific ones.

The first step in Figure 6.8 is to parse the command line arguments to identify which options are in effect. Next the collection configuration file is read. Some parameters of the import process can be set either in the collection configuration file or in the command line. Command-line settings are useful for debugging purposes and take precedence in case of conflict. For example, the names of the *import* and *archives* directories can be overridden using the *importdir* and *archivedir* variables—either in the collection configuration file or on the command line.

Plug-ins are loaded in step 4. They can either be general ones or collection-specific versions. Any general plug-in—say HTMLPlug—can be overridden by a particular collection with nonstandard needs—like a private convention for specifying metadata in an HTML file. General plug-ins are found in a standard place in the top-level Greenstone directory: *perllib/plugins*. However, if there is a directory called *perllib/plugins* in the collection's own space—for example,

Table 6.6 Additional options for the import process.

Option	Argument	Function
–importdir	Directory name	Specify the location of material to be imported (default *import*).
–removeold	None	Remove the contents of the *archives* directory before importing.
–gzip	None	Zip up the archive documents produced by *import*.
–groupsize	Number > 0	Specify the number of documents put into each archive file (default 1).
–sortmeta	Metadata tag name	Sort the documents alphabetically by the named metadata tag.
–OIDtype	*hash* or *incremental*	Specify the method of creating OIDs for documents.

dlpeople/perllib/plugins for the *dlpeople* collection—step 4 also checks there for collection-specific plug-ins, which override general ones of the same name.

In step 5, the *removeold* option (Table 6.6) determines whether the result of importing is added to or replaces any existing material in the archive. Step 6 reads the archives information file (*archives.inf*), which lists any documents that are already present in the *archives* directory, in order to speed up subsequent processing; steps 8 and 10 append new files to this list. Each document is stored in the archives as the file *doc.xml* in a directory (or a series of nested directories) that is calculated from its OID as explained earlier. The *archives.inf* file contains one line for each document, giving its OID and the directory in which it is stored. In the previous example, it would include the lines

```
HASH0109d3850a6de4440c4d1ca2   HASH0109
HASH010942bbf9c1376e9489c29c   HASH0109/42bbf9c1
```

Step 7 creates an object that determines where and how documents are to be saved. Their location is given by the variable *archivedir* (Table 6.5). The *sortmeta* switch (Table 6.6) sorts documents according to a specified metadata tag, and this determines the order in which they are presented as the result of a Boolean search. It operates by sorting the contents of *archives.inf*.

The actual work is done in step 8. The plug-ins operate on each document and generate corresponding archive files, along with any associated files (such as images). Some plug-ins assign metadata to documents rather than processing the document text itself; their effect is to include that information in the archive file. At the end of the import process, each document appears in its own directory as an archive file that includes all the metadata that pertains to it. All files associated with the document are included in the directory too.

Step 9 writes the archive documents using the object created in step 7. The final step is to write the *archives.inf* file that lists the documents for use during the build process.

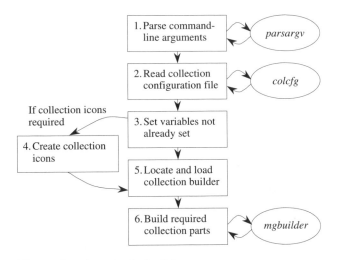

Figure 6.9 Steps in the build process.

Two further functions in Table 6.6 deserve mention. The *gzip* option compresses the archive documents using gzip (which must be installed on your machine). To ensure that compressed documents can be uncompressed at build time, ZIPPlug should be included in the plug-in list. The *groupsize* option groups several documents together into each archive file. Normally there is one file for each document. In collections with many very small documents, processing time can be dominated by file operations, and it is advantageous to group documents together. The Greenstone Archive plug-in automatically recognizes grouped files and processes them correctly.

The build process

The build process (*buildcol.pl*) builds all the indexes and data structures needed to make the collection work. It also compresses the text of the documents. The full-text indexes that are required are specified by a line in the collection configuration file (see Section 6.6); most collections have multiple indexes. In addition to full-text indexes, other information about how the collection is to appear on the Web is precalculated and incorporated into the collection—for example, information about icons and titles and information produced by classifiers.

The process operates in several passes. Two passes are required to compress the text, two for each index included in the collection, and a final pass to produce the collection information database. Every document is read and processed during each pass. This is the main reason for separating the import and build processes: it means that the work of converting the text from its original encoding into UTF-8, and calculating the OID, and processing the metadata, is only done once.

Table 6.7 Additional options for the build process.

Option	Argument	Function
–builddir	Directory name	Where the result of building is stored (default *building*)
–index	Index name	Which indexes to build (default: all indexes in the collection configuration file)
–allclassifications	None	Include all classifications, even empty ones
–create_images	None	Create collection icons automatically
–mode	*all, compress_text, infodb,* or *build_index*	Determine what components are built (default *all*)
–no_text	None	Don't store compressed text

The diagram in Figure 6.9 represents the execution of *buildcol.pl,* while Table 6.7 shows the options unique to building. Options shared by the import process have already been discussed.

Step 4 (to the left) is the first one in Figure 6.9 that is not common to the import process, and it is performed only if the *create_images* option has been set. It invokes a function that creates an icon for the collection and registers it in the configuration file (which must have write permission set). The image is created by GIMP, the GNU Image Manipulation Program that runs on Linux, and the GIMP Perl module must be installed and properly configured.[10] The image created looks like the greenstone demo icon at the top left of the screen in Figure 6.2, but with text appropriate for the new collection.

Step 5 checks for a collection-specific build procedure. Some collections are built by a special nonstandard program, which is placed in the collection's *perllib* directory and named by the collection name with *builder* suffixed. The basic build procedure is called *mgbuilder,* and collection-specific builders are derived from it. In step 5 the builder, whether the general version or a collection-specific one, is initialized with relevant parameters: how many documents are to be included, whether or not the old version of the collection is to be retained, and where the *building* and *archive* directories are located.

In step 6, the building step, the document text is compressed and indexed, collection titles and icons are stored in a collection information database, and data structures are constructed to support the classifiers that are specified in the collection's configuration file. All these operations are handled by the builder program. The default one, *mgbuilder,* uses the Managing Gigabytes software (mentioned in the "Notes and sources" sections of Chapters 3 and 4) for com-

---

10. This external paint package also runs under Windows, so in principle it is possible to augment the Windows version of Greenstone with this service too.

pressing and indexing. The collection information database (described in more detail in Section 7.2) stores all information pertaining to the collection—its name, icons, document OIDs, associated files, and structures that define the classifiers.

Generally all components of the collection are built together—compressed text, indexes, and collection information database. However, for debugging purposes the operation can be restricted to certain components using the *mode* switch: the document text only (*compress_text*), the collection information database (*infodb*), or the indexes specified in the collection configuration file (*build_index*). Just one index can be built by specifying it on the command line. For example, *–index section:Title* will build just an index of section titles. The syntax for specifying indexes will be discussed in Section 6.6.

The building process normally suppresses classifiers that include no documents—for example, if no titles begin with the letter *X*, the *X* tab under the Titles A-Z button will be suppressed. The *allclassifications* switch overrides this behavior and does not suppress empty classifiers. Sometimes the user is shown the original documents rather than the digital library's local version—collections can be set up this way by including a specification in the configuration file. Then there is no point in storing the compressed text, and the *no_text* option can be used to suppress it, reducing the size of the built collection.

Once it has been built, to make a collection available over the Web you must move the contents of the *building* directory into the *index* directory. As explained earlier, collections are not built directly into *index* to ensure that any existing version remains accessible during the building process.

6.5   Greenstone archive documents

Source documents are brought into the Greenstone system by converting them to a format known as the Greenstone Archive Format. This divides documents into sections and stores metadata at the document or section level. One design requirement is to be able to represent any previously marked-up document that uses HTML tags, even if the markup is sloppy. Another is that archive documents can be parsed very rapidly. The archive is an XML-compliant syntax that contains explicit top-level markup for sectioning and metadata and can also embed HTML-style markup that is not interpreted at the top level.

In XML, tags are enclosed in angle brackets for markup, just like HTML tags. The archive format encodes documents that are already in HTML by escaping any embedded left or right angle bracket (<, >), or quote (") characters within the original text using the standard codes <, > and ".

A *<Section>* tag signals the start of each document section, and the corresponding closing tag marks the end of that section. Each section begins with a metadata block that defines metadata pertinent to that section. There can be any number of metadata specifications, each of which gives the metadata name and its value. In addition to regular metadata, the file that contains the original document can be specified as *gsdlsourcefilename*, and files that are associated with the document, such as image files, can be specified as *gsdlassocfile*.

Figure 6.10a gives the XML Document Type Definition (DTD) for the Greenstone Archive Format. Basically a document is split up into *Sections*, which can be nested. Each *Section* has a *Description* that comprises zero or more *Metadata* items, and a *Content* part (which may be null)—this is where the actual document's contents go. A name attribute and some textual data are associated with each *Metadata* element (the name can be anything). In XML, *PCDATA* stands for "parsed character data": basically Unicode text in this case.

Figure 6.10b shows a simple document in this format, comprising a short book with two associated images. The book has two sections called *Preface* and *First and only chapter*, respectively; the latter has two subsections. Note that a chapter is represented simply as a top-level section.

Document metadata

Metadata is descriptive information about author, title, date, keywords, and so on, associated with a document. As Figure 6.10 shows, it is stored at the beginning of the section along with the metadata name. One example is the line *<Metadata name="Title">Freshwater Resources in Arid Lands</Metadata>* in Figure 6.10b.

The Dublin Core standard described in Chapter 5 (Section 5.4) is used for defining metadata types. However, in keeping with Greenstone's permissive philosophy, the metadata types are not restricted to those in Table 5.4. If there is no type that aptly describes a particular kind of metadata, a new one can be freely invented and used. For example, the Demo collection contains *Magazine* and *how to* metadata.[11] Magazines form a subclass of the alphabetic title browser, and *how to* metadata has its own browsing tag in the access bar at the top of Figure 6.2 (we return to these in Section 6.7). Any subtags that appear in an archive file other than *gsdlsourcefilename* or *gsdlassocfile* are treated as metadata. Allowing metadata types to be freely invented has the downside that typographical errors in attribute names are treated as novel metadata types. However, in Greenstone metadata is normally assigned by some automatic process rather than being entered manually, which reduces the chance of misspelling.

---

11. Internally, *how to* metadata is called *Howto*—metadata types must not contain spaces.

```
<!DOCTYPE GreenstoneArchive [
  <!ELEMENT Section (Description,Content,Section*)>
  <!ELEMENT Description (Metadata*)>
  <!ELEMENT Content (#PCDATA)>
  <!ELEMENT Metadata (#PCDATA)>
  <ATTLIST Metadata name CDATA #REQUIRED>
]>
```

(a)

```
<?xml version="1.0" ?>
<!DOCTYPE GreenstoneArchive SYSTEM
"http://greenstone.org/dtd/GreenstoneArchive/1.0/GreenstoneArchive.dtd">
<Section>
  <Description>
    <Metadata name="gsdlsourcefilename">ec158e.txt</Metadata>
    <Metadata name="Title">Freshwater Resources in Arid Lands</Metadata>
    <Metadata name="Identifier">HASH0158f56086efffe592636058</Metadata>
    <Metadata name="gsdlassocfile">cover.jpg:image/jpeg:</Metadata>
    <Metadata name="gsdlassocfile">p07a.png:image/png:</Metadata>
  </Description>
  <Section>
    <Description>
      <Metadata name="Title">Preface</Metadata>
    </Description>
    <Content>
          This is the text of the preface
    </Content>
  </Section>
  <Section>
    <Description>
      <Metadata name="Title">First and only chapter</Metadata>
    </Description>
    <Section>
      <Description>
        <Metadata name="Title">Part 1</Metadata>
      </Description>
      <Content>
          This is the first part of the first and only chapter
      </Content>
    </Section>
    <Section>
     <Description>
       <Metadata name="Title">Part 2</Metadata>
     </Description>
     <Content>
          This is the second part of the first and only chapter
     </Content>
    </Section>
  </Section>
</Section>
```

(b)

Figure 6.10 Greenstone Archive Format: (a) Document Type Definition (DTD); (b) example document.

Inside the documents

The Greenstone Archive Format imposes a limited amount of structure within each document. Documents can be split hierarchically into sections and subsections, and these may be nested to any depth.

In some collections documents are split into pages. These are simply treated as sections. For example, a book might have first-level sections that correspond to chapters, within each of which are defined a number of "sections" that actually denote individual pages of the chapter. Just as chapter-level sections normally have *Title* metadata, in page-level ones the *Title* is set to the page number. There is no provision for defining parallel structures, such as a logical chapter/section/subsection hierarchy that coexists with a division into physical pages.

The document structure serves two purposes. First, it allows readers to browse around inside documents once they have been found. When you open a book, the table of contents shows the section hierarchy. Figure 3.3 (Chapter 3) illustrates browsing within a book that has a hierarchical table of contents showing chapters, sections, and subsections. In some collections documents are split into pages instead. Figure 3.1 shows (at the top right) a page selector for such a document. Chapters, sections, subsections, and pages are all "sections."

The second use of document structure is for searchable indexes. There are three levels of index: *document*, *section*, and *paragraph*, and most collections use more than one. A *document* index relates to complete documents—you use it to find all documents that contain a particular set of words. When a *section* index is created, each portion of text that is indexed stretches from one *Section* tag to the next—thus a chapter that immediately begins with a new section will produce an empty document in the index (that document will never be visible to the user). Sections and subsections are treated alike: the hierarchical document structure is flattened for the purposes of creating searchable indexes. Paragraph-level indexes treat each paragraph as a separate document and are used for more focused searches.

The pull-down menu in Figure 6.2 shows the searchable indexes in the Demo collection. *Chapters* and *section titles* are section-level indexes, while *entire books* is a document-level one. *Section titles* is an index of document metadata rather than document content. In fact indexes of any kind of metadata can be created—the mechanism for doing this is described in the next section.

As explained earlier, each document has an object identifier or OID. Identifiers are extended to individual sections of a document using integers separated by periods. For example, if the OID of the document in Figure 6.9b were *HASHa723e7e164df07c833bfc4*, the OID of the first of the two subsections of the *First and only chapter* would be *HASHa723e7e164df07c833bfc4.2.1*—because that chapter is the second in its enclosing *Section*, and the relevant subsection is the first in *its* enclosing *Section*. Section-level OIDs are not stored explicitly, but are used internally within the system to represent individual document sections that are returned as the result of a search. They do not necessarily coincide with the logical numbering of chapters and sections—documents often include unnumbered chapters, such as a preface—but are only for internal use.

6.6 Collection configuration file

The configuration file governs the structure of a collection. It allows you to customize the look and feel of the collection and the way in which its documents are processed and presented. When you run *mkcol* to make an initial skeleton structure for a new collection, one of the things it does is create a default collection configuration file. The configuration file is called *collect.cfg* and resides in the collection's *etc* directory.

Each line of a collection configuration file specifies an *attribute, value* pair. Attributes give pieces of information that affect how documents are processed and how the collection will look. Table 6.8 shows the items that can be included in a configuration file and what each is used for. In addition, all the command-line options for importing and building (Tables 6.5, 6.6, and 6.7) may be specified in the configuration file—for example, a line reading *no_text true* will set the *no_text* building option (Table 6.7).

Table 6.8   Items in the collection configuration file.

Item	Function
creator	E-mail address of the collection's creator
maintainer	E-mail address of the collection's maintainer
public	Whether collection is to be made public or not
indexes	List of indexes to build
defaultindex	The default index
subcollection	Define a subcollection based on metadata
indexsubcollections	Specify which subcollections to index
defaultsubcollection	The default *indexsubcollection*
languages	List of languages to build indexes in
defaultlanguage	Default index language
collectionmeta	Defines collection-level metadata
plugin	Specify a plug-in to use at build time
format	A format string
classify	Specify a classifier to use at build time

Default configuration file

The configuration file created by *mkcol* is shown in Figure 6.4. It is a simple one that includes a bare minimum of information. The first two lines both reflect the *creator* value supplied to the *mkcol.pl* program; however, the person responsible for maintaining the collection need not necessarily be its creator. The next line indicates whether the collection, when built, will be available to the public—that is, placed on the home page of your Greenstone installation. This is useful when building test collections or collections for personal use.

The *indexes* line determines what full-text indexes are created at build time. In Figure 6.4 there is just one: the document text, but most collections contain more than one index. For example, the line

```
indexes   section:text section:Title document:text
```

specifies the three indexes shown in the pull-down menu in Figure 6.2. In each specification the part before the colon is the "level" of the index: it must be one of *paragraph*, *section*, or *document*. The part after the colon gives the material to be included in the index: either the word *text* or the name of a kind of metadata that occurs in the collection. Thus *section:text* defines a section-level index comprising full text—given a query, the search engine seeks document sections that match it. More than one type of data can be included in the same index by separating the data types with commas. For example, to create a section-level index of text plus *Title* and *Date* metadata, specify *section:text,Title,Date*.

The first and last items in the specification just cited both index the document's text. The difference is that the first seeks matching *sections* whereas the last seeks matching *documents*. The search process returns the OID of the matching unit, be it section or document; Greenstone normally presents the whole document that contains the match (or makes it easy to get to the whole document). The index *section:Title* contains metadata comprising all section titles. The order of the three indexes in the specification under discussion determines the order in which they appear on the menu in Figure 6.2.

Returning to the configuration file in Figure 6.4, the "collection-level metadata" in the next line gives the name of that index as it appears in the search menu. There should be one such line for each index: Figure 6.4 specifies just one index. However, there are three indexes in Figure 6.2, and this is where the words *chapters*, *section titles*, and *entire books* arise in the pull-down menu of Figure 6.2. The following line specifies the default index. In Figure 6.2 it was specified as *section:text*, which is named *chapters*.

The next group of lines specify which plug-ins to use when converting documents and metadata to the archive format and when building collections from archive files.

The *classify* line creates an alphabetic list of titles for browsing. Browsing structures are constructed by modules called *classifiers;* Section 6.7 explains how they work.

The last three lines give collection-level metadata. The *collectionname* is the long form of the collection's name, which is used as its "title" for the Web browser—although in the simple configuration file in Figure 6.4 the short name is used instead. The *collectionicon* gives the URL of the collection's icon. The *collectionextra* metadata gives the *About this collection* text.

Whenever text that goes on Web pages produced by Greenstone is specified in the collection configuration file, it is couched in a particular language. To make a collection appear correct in several different languages, you need to be able to put in different versions of such things as *collectionextra* for different interface languages. This is done by adding a language specification in square brackets— for example,

```
collectionmeta collectionextra "collection description"
collectionmeta collectionextra [l=fr] "description in French"
collectionmeta collectionextra [l=mi] "description in Maori"
```

If the interface language is set to *fr* or *mi*, the appropriate version of the description will be displayed. For other languages the default version will appear.

Subcollections and supercollections

There are other features of collection configuration files that do not appear in Figure 6.4. One is that you can define subcollections and build separate indexes for each subcollection. For example, one collection contains a large subset of documents called Food and Nutrition Bulletin. This collection has three indexcs, all at the section level: one for the whole collection, one for the Food and Nutrition Bulletin subcollection, and the third for the remaining documents. Here are the relevant lines from the configuration file:

```
indexes              section:text
subcollection        fn "Title/^Food and Nutrition Bulletin/i"
subcollection        other "!Title/^Food and Nutrition Bulletin/i"
indexsubcollections  fn other fn,other
```

The second and third lines define subcollections called *fn*, which contains the Food and Nutrition Bulletin, and *other*, which contains the remaining documents. The quoted text in these definitions identifies the subsets using *Title* metadata: we seek titles that begin with *Food and Nutrition Bulletin* in the first case and ones that do not in the second. To do this, a "regular expression" in the

Perl language is used. The caret (^) specifies that the *Title* must start with the characters shown, the terminating *i* makes the comparison case insensitive, and the exclamation point (!) that begins the second string represents negation. The metadata name, in this case *Title*, can be any metadata type, or *Filename*, which matches against the document's original file name.

The fourth line, *indexsubcollections*, specifies three indexes: one for the *fn* subcollection, one for the *other* subcollection, and the third for both subcollections (i.e., all the documents). Note that if two entries had been given on the *indexes* line, the total number of indexes generated would have been six rather than three because a version of each index is created for every subcollection.

If collections contain documents in different languages, separate indexes can be built for each language. *Language* is a metadata item that Greenstone derives automatically for each document using a built-in language identification module (although you can override it by explicitly specifying this metadata). Its values are specified using two-letter codes—for example, *en* is English, *zh* is Chinese, and *mi* is Māori. In fact these codes follow the international standard ISO 639. Since metadata values can be specified at the section level, parts of a document can be in different languages.

Suppose the configuration file contained

```
indexes section:text section:Title document:text paragraph:text
languages en zh mi
```

Section text, section title, document text, and paragraph text indexes would be created for English, Chinese, and Māori—12 indexes altogether. Adding a couple of subcollections multiplies the number of indexes again. Take care to guard against index bloat!

Alternatively this index specification could be defined using the *subcollection* facility rather than the *languages* facility. However, you cannot create subcollections of subcollections, so it would then be impossible to index each language in the subcollections separately.

Cross-collection searching is a way of forming supercollections by searching several collections at once. Search results are combined behind the scenes as though you were searching a single unified collection. If a supercollection is defined from a set of collections, any combination of the original collections can also be searched—the Preferences page allows you to choose which ones are included.

Cross-collection searching is enabled by this line in the collection configuration file:

```
supercollection col_1 col_2 …
```

The collections involved are called *col_1*, *col_2*, and so on. The same line should appear in the configuration file of every collection that is involved.

6.7 Getting the most out of your documents

Collections can be tailored to make the information they contain accessible in different ways. Greenstone incorporates three mechanisms for doing this. *Plug-ins* extract information from source documents and metadata specifications and regularize the input in the form of archive files. *Classifiers* create browsing structures from metadata and place them in the collection information database so that they can be used at runtime. And *format statements* dictate what information will appear on the user's screen and how it appears. This section describes these mechanisms in turn.

Plug-ins

Plug-ins translate the source documents into a common form and extract metadata from them. For example, the HTML plug-in converts Web pages to the archive format and extracts metadata that is explicit in the original document—such as titles, signaled by the *<title>* tag. Plug-ins all derive from a basic plug-in called BasPlug, which performs universally required operations such as creating a new archive document to work with, assigning an object identifier (OID), and handling the sections in a document. Plug-ins are written in the Perl language and are stored in the *perllib/plugins* directory.

A utility program called pluginfo gives information about individual plug-ins. To learn about the HTML plug-in, type *pluginfo.pl HTMLPlug* at the command prompt. (You need to invoke the *setup* script first, if you haven't already, and on Windows you need to type *perl –S pluginfo.pl HTMLPlug* if your environment is not set up to process files ending in *.pl* appropriately.) Pluginfo displays information about the plug-in's options on the screen.

With a working knowledge of the Perl language, you can write new plug-ins that process document formats not handled by existing ones, format documents in some special way, assign metadata specified in new formats, or even extract new kinds of metadata from the document text. The best way to write a new plug-in is to find an existing one that does something similar and modify it—the "copy and edit" paradigm that underlies much of practical computer science.

Basic plug-in options

Several features are common to all plug-ins. All of them can handle different character encodings for the source documents, such as ASCII, and different variants of Unicode. They can all accept and reject files with different file name patterns, such as names ending with *.html* for HTMLPlug. Finally there are several extraction algorithms that derive metadata from the text of any document

Table 6.9 Options applicable to all plug-ins.

Option	Function
input_encoding	Character encoding of the source documents.
default_encoding	Used if *input_encoding* is *auto* and automatic encoding detection fails.
process_exp	A Perl regular expression to match against file names.
block_exp	Specify file names that are to be blocked from further processing.
first	Extract the initial text as *First* metadata.
cover_image	Associate a *.jpg* cover image with each document.
extract_language	Identify each document's language.
default_language	This value is used if automatic language extraction fails.
extract_email	Extract e-mail addresses.
extract_acronyms	Extract acronym definitions.
markup_acronyms	Add acronym information into document text.
extract_date	Extract dates relating to the content of historical documents.

and are implemented as plug-in options. All these features are implemented in BasPlug, and all derived plug-ins inherit them.

Table 6.9 shows the basic options. The *input_encoding* option specifies the kind of character encoding used for source documents. As well as ASCII and Unicode, there are some 30 other possible values—use *pluginfo.pl BasPlug* for a full list—including about 15 for particular languages such as Chinese, Cyrillic, Greek, Hebrew; five ISO standards; and 10 different Windows standards. The default value, *auto*, automatically determines the character encoding for each document individually. This rarely fails, but if it does, the value of *default_encoding* is used. *Input_encoding* defaults to *auto*, but it is sometimes useful to set it explicitly. For example, if you know that all your documents are plain ASCII, choosing *ascii* greatly increases the speed at which documents are imported and built.

The value of *process_exp* dictates which files a plug-in processes and is used to specify a certain file extension. Each plug-in has a default value. HTMLPlug's default is an expression that includes any file names with the extension *.htm* or *.html*—use *pluginfo* to learn how it is expressed as a "regular expression." In a similar way *block_exp* specifies files that are not to be passed further down the list of plug-ins. If a file reaches the end of the list without having been processed by any plug-in, a warning message is generated. *Block_exp* is used to prevent annoying error messages about files that might be present but don't need processing. HTMLPlug blocks files with such extensions as *.gif*, *.png*, and *.jpg* because they do not contain any text or metadata but are embedded in documents when they are viewed.

The remaining options to BasPlug identify certain features that occur within documents and add them to the documents as metadata. A document's opening words are often used as a title substitute if *Title* metadata is unavailable, so the *First* option extracts the first stretch of text and adds it as metadata. For example, *–first 50* adds to each document metadata called *First50*, which contains the document's opening 50 characters. A heuristic language-extraction program can be used to identify the language in which each document is written: the *extract_language* option invokes this and puts the result into the documents as metadata. (If *input_encoding* is *auto*, this is done automatically as part of the encoding detection.) E-mail addresses can be extracted automatically and added to the document as *emailAddress* metadata. Similarly acronyms and their definitions can be extracted and added as *Acronym* metadata. It is sometimes useful to annotate all occurrences of acronyms with their definitions.[12] A final option is to extract dates (in years) relating to the content of historical documents and add them as *Coverage* metadata.

Document processing plug-ins

The plug-ins are listed in Table 6.10 for reference: we have already encountered many of them. The first three were mentioned earlier (Section 6.4, under "Plug-ins"). RecPlug recurses through a directory structure. If the *use_metadata_files* option is set and metadata files are present, RecPlug also reads XML metadata files and assigns metadata to each document (described in the subsection "Assigning metadata from a file"). ArcPlug processes files named in *archives.inf*, which is used to communicate between the import and build processes. GAPlug processes archive files generated by the import process. These three plug-ins are normally included in every collection.

Many individual plug-ins were introduced at the end of Section 6.2. The plug-ins BibTexPlug and ReferPlug for processing bibliography files were not mentioned there. Neither was SplitPlug, which provides a general facility for dividing input files into stretches that represent individual documents—for example, it is used to split files containing many e-mails into individual messages. It should not be called directly, but may be inherited by plug-ins that need to process files containing multiple documents.

Some plug-ins use external programs that parse specific proprietary formats—for example, Word or PDF—into either plain text or HTML. A general plug-in called ConvertToPlug invokes one or more conversion programs and passes the result to either TEXTPlug or HTMLPlug. We describe this in more detail shortly. Conversion under all circumstances is a difficult job, and in some

---

12. They are marked up in such a way that the definition appears as "mouse-over" text at each occurrence of the acronym.

Table 6.10 Standard plug-ins.

	Plug-in	Purpose	File types	Ignores files
General	RecPlug	Recurses through a directory structure	—	—
	ArcPlug	Processes files named in *archives.inf*	—	—
	GAPlug	Processes Greenstone archive files	*.xml*	—
	TEXTPlug	Plain text	*.txt, .text*	—
	HTMLPlug	HTML, replacing hyperlinks appropriately	*.htm, .html, .cgi, .php, .asp, .shm, .shtml*	*gif, .jpeg, .jpg, .png, .css, .rtf*
	WordPlug	Microsoft Word documents, extracting author and title	*.doc*	*.gif, .jpeg, .jpg, .png, .css, .rtf*
	PDFPlug	PDF documents, extracting the first line of text as a title	*.pdf*	*.gif, .jpeg, .jpg, .png, .css, .rtf*
	PSPlug	PostScript documents	*.ps*	*.eps*
	EMAILPlug	E-mail messages, recognizing author, subject, date, etc.	Must end in digits or digits followed by .Email	—
	BibTexPlug	Bibliography files in BibTeX format	*.bib*	—
	ReferPlug	Bibliography files in refer format	*.bib*	—
	SRCPlug	Source code files	*Makefile, Readme, .c, .cc, .cpp, .h, .hpp, .pl, .pm, .sh*	*.o, .obj, .a, .so, .dll*
	ImagePlug	Image files for creating a library of images (restricted to Unix)	*.jpeg, .jpg, .gif, .png, .bmp, .xbm, .tif, .tiff*	—
	SplitPlug	Splits a document file into parts.	—	—
	ZIPPlug	Uncompresses files (requires the appropriate GNU tool to be available)	*.gzip, .bzip, .zip, .tar, .gz, .bz, .tgz, .taz*	—
Collection Specific	GBPlug	Project Gutenberg e-text	*.txt.gz, .html, .htm*	—
	TCCPlug	E-mail documents from *Computists' Weekly*	Must begin with *tcc* or *cw*	—
	PrePlug	HTML output from the PRESCRIPT program.	*.html, .html.gz*	—

cases these external programs fail—in which case ConvertToPlug automatically reverts to a simpler method.

Some plug-ins are written for specific collections that have an idiosyncratic document format not found elsewhere. Examples include the e-text used in the

Gutenberg collection, which includes manually entered title information, and the e-mailed issues of the *Computists' Weekly* electronic publication. Others perform special functions, such as splitting documents into pages for the Computer Science Technical Reports collection (PrePlug). Collection-specific plug-ins can be placed in the collection's *perllib/plugins* directory and override general plug-ins with the same name.

Many plug-ins have their own specific options that control what they do. Use *pluginfo* to find out about these.

As an example, HTMLPlug has a plethora of options, listed in Table 6.11. These illustrate details (the dirty details!) buried deep within the digital library system. Some are provided to accelerate processing of very large document collections. What should be done with HTML hyperlinks to other documents in the collection—including internal links within a document? It seems appropriate to trap them and replace them with a link to the same document within the digital library—and this is what HTMLPlug does. However, the *nolinks* option suppresses this. It speeds up importing, but any internal links will be broken. The *no_metadata* option is also provided to speed up importing.

Other options concern metadata. In Chapter 5, we met HTML's *<meta>* syntax for defining metadata; such metadata can be extracted using the *metadata_fields* option. To rename it in the archive file (perhaps to use Dublin Core names instead of ad hoc ones in the HTML), use *tag<newname>* where *tag* is the HTML tag and *newname* its new name. *Hunt_creator_metadata* finds as much metadata as possible about authorship and inserts it as *Creator* metadata in the archive file. For this to work, *Creator* should be included using the *metadata_fields* option. The *description_tags* option is described in the subsection "Tagging document files."

Table 6.11 Plug-in–specific options for HTMLPlug.

Option	Function
nolinks	Do not trap links within the collection.
keep_head	Do not strip out HTML headers.
no_metadata	Do not seek any metadata.
metadata_fields	Take a comma-separated list of metadata types to extract (default *Title*).
hunt_creator_metadata	Extract *creator* metadata.
description_tags	Interpret tagged document files.
file_is_url	Treat file names in *import* as though they were URLs.
assoc_files	Redefine the list of associated files (default *.jpg, .jpeg, .gif, .png, .css*).
rename_assoc_files	Rename files associated with documents.
title_sub	Perl substitution expression to modify titles.

Further options determine how files are handled. Source documents for HTMLPlug are often brought in by a Web mirroring program which uses a special URL-based scheme for file names, and the *file_is_url* option treats these file names appropriately. Certain file types in an HTML collection are treated as associated files, including *.gif*, *.png*, and *.jpg* files; *assoc_files* allows this default list to be overridden. When discussing the OID scheme in Section 6.4, we observed that some systems place restrictions on the maximum depth of directory hierarchies. Unfortunately an HTML collection may utilize its own nested directory structure for images and other associated files, which can break the limit. *Rename_assoc_files* renames associated files to make a suitably shallow directory hierarchy.

Finally, there is an option that allows you to modify all titles according to a specified regular expression. This is useful if many of the titles in your collection include an extraneous character string. We mentioned in Section 6.6 a collection that contained many documents in the *Food and Nutrition Bulletin* whose titles all began with that string. If left unmodified, these would all appear under the letter *F* in an alphabetic title browser.

Plug-ins for proprietary formats

Proprietary formats pose a challenge to any digital library system. Even when documentation about how they work is available, they may change without notice and it is hard to keep abreast of changes. In Greenstone, open-source GPL (Gnu Public License) conversion utilities are used that have been written by people committed to the task.

Utilities to process Word and PDF formats are included in the *packages* directory. These convert documents to either HTML or text form. Then HTMLPlug or TEXTPlug is used to further transform them to the archive format. Sometimes there is more than one converter for what is ostensibly the same format, and they are tried successively on each document. For example, the preferred Word converter wvWare does not cope with documents prior to Word 6, and a different program, which just extracts whatever text strings it can, is used to process the Word 5 format.

The conversion utilities are invoked by a general plug-in called ConvertToPlug. Like BasPlug it is never called directly but forms a basis for other plug-ins.

Greenstone users may occasionally have to add new plug-ins that use external converters to process a particular format. The process of extending ConvertToPlug is as follows:

1. Put the new conversion utility in the *packages* directory and install it.
2. Alter the program *gsConvert.pl* (in *bin/script*) to use the new utility.
3. Write a plug-in that inherits from ConvertToPlug to catch the format and pass it on.

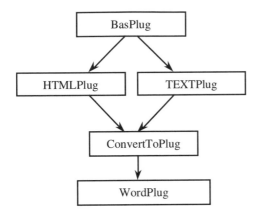

Figure 6.11 Plug-in inheritance hierarchy.

To see how this works, you need to understand how ConvertToPlug is structured. The process is rather intricate, and many readers may wish to skip the remainder of this subsection. The "dynamic inheritance" facility in the Perl language is used to inherit from either TEXTPlug or HTMLPlug, depending on the format to which source documents are converted. Figure 6.11 shows the inheritance path.

When it receives a document, ConvertToPlug calls *gsConvert.pl* to invoke the appropriate conversion utility. Step 2 of the process involves adding a new clause calling the utility to the *if* statement in the main function. Documents, when converted, are returned to ConvertToPlug, which invokes the HTML or text plug-in as appropriate. Any plug-in derived from ConvertToPlug has a *convert_to* option that specifies which intermediate format is preferred, either *text* or *html*. Text may be faster, but HTML usually looks better—and includes pictures.

Assigning metadata from a file

It is often necessary to assign metadata to documents from a manually created file. For example, information pertaining to a document collection might be available in a standard form such as MARC records. In order to use it you have to somehow get the metadata into each individual document's archive file during the import process. Once there, it can be freely used to define searchable indexes and browsing structures.

The standard plug-in RecPlug also incorporates a way of assigning metadata to documents from manually (or automatically) created XML files. We describe this in some detail, so that you can create metadata files in the appropriate format. If the *use_metadata_files* option is specified, RecPlug uses an auxiliary metadata file called *metadata.xml*. Figure 6.12a shows the XML Document Type

```
<!DOCTYPE DirectoryMetadata [
  <!ELEMENT DirectoryMetadata (FileSet*)>
  <!ELEMENT FileSet (FileName+,Description)>
  <!ELEMENT FileName (#PCDATA)>
  <!ELEMENT Description (Metadata*)>
  <!ELEMENT Metadata (#PCDATA)>
  <ATTLIST Metadata name CDATA #REQUIRED>
  <ATTLIST Metadata mode (accumulate|override) "override">
]>
```

(a)

```
<?xml version="1.0" ?>
<!DOCTYPE DirectoryMetadata SYSTEM
"http://greenstone.org/dtd/DirectoryMetadata/1.0/DirectoryMetadata.dtd">
<DirectoryMetadata>
  <FileSet>
    <FileName>nugget.*</FileName>
    <Description>
      <Metadata name="Title">Nugget Point, The Catlins</Metadata>
      <Metadata name="Place" mode="accumulate">Nugget Point</Metadata>
    </Description>
  </FileSet>
  <FileSet>
    <FileName>nugget-point-1.jpg</FileName>
    <Description>
      <Metadata name="Title">Nugget Point Lighthouse</Metadata>
      <Metadata name="Subject">Lighthouse</Metadata>
    </Description>
  </FileSet>
</DirectoryMetadata>
```

(b)

Figure 6.12 XML format: (a) Document Type Definition (DTD); (b) example metadata file.

Definition (DTD) for the metadata file format, while Figure 6.12b shows an example *metadata.xml* file.

The example file contains two metadata structures. In each one the *filename* element describes files to which the metadata applies, in the form of a regular expression. Thus *<FileName>nugget.*</FileName>* indicates that the first metadata record applies to every file whose name starts with *nugget*.[13] For these files *Title* metadata is set to "Nugget Point, The Catlins."

Metadata elements are processed in the order in which they appear. The second structure sets *Title* metadata for the file named *nugget-point-1.jpg* to "Nugget Point Lighthouse," overriding the previous specification. It also adds a *Subject* metadata field.

13. Note that in Greenstone regular expressions are interpreted in the Perl language, which is subtly different from some other conventions. For example, an asterisk (*) matches zero or more occurrences of the previous character, while a period (.) matches any character—so *nugget.** matches any string with prefix *nugget*, whether or not it contains a period after the prefix. To insist on a period you would need to escape it, and write *nugget\..** instead.

Sometimes metadata is multivalued, and new values should accumulate rather than overriding previous ones. The *mode=accumulate* attribute does this. It is applied to *Place* metadata in Figure 6.12b, which will therefore be multivalued. To revert to a single metadata element, write *<Metadata name="Place" mode="override">New Zealand</Metadata>*. In fact you could omit this mode specification because every element overrides unless otherwise specified. To accumulate metadata for some field, *mode=accumulate* must be specified in every occurrence.

When its *use_metadata_files* option is set, RecPlug checks each input directory for an XML file called *metadata.xml* and applies its contents to all the directory's files and subdirectories.

The *metadata.xml* mechanism embodied in RecPlug is just one way of specifying metadata for documents. It is easy to write different plug-ins that accept metadata specifications in completely different formats.

Tagging document files

Source documents often need to be structured into sections and subsections, and this information needs to be communicated to Greenstone so that it can preserve the hierarchical structure. Also, metadata—typically the title—might be associated with each section and subsection.

The simplest way of doing this is often just to edit the source files manually. The HTML plug-in has a *description_tags* option that processes tags in the text like this:

```
<!--
<Section>
  <Description>
    <Metadata name="Title"> Realizing human rights for
         poor people: Strategies for achieving the
         international development targets </Metadata>
  </Description>
-->

    (text of section goes here)

<!--
</Section>
-->
```

The <!-- ... --> markers are used because they indicate comments in HTML; thus these section tags will not affect document formatting. In the *Description* part other kinds of metadata can be specified, but this is not done for the style of collection we are describing here. Also, the tags can be nested, so the line marked *text of section goes here* in the code just cited can itself include further subsections, such as

(text of first part of section goes here)

```
<!--
<Section>
  <Description>
    <Metadata name="Title"> The international
         development targets </Metadata>
  </Description>
-->
```

(text of subsection goes here)

```
<!--
</Section>
-->
```

(text of last part of section goes here)

This functionality is inherited by any plug-ins that use HTMLPlug. In particular, the Word plug-in converts its input to HTML form, and so exactly the same way of specifying metadata can be used in Word (and RTF) files. (In order to make this operate properly, Greenstone has to do some work behind the scenes. When Word documents are converted to HTML, care is normally taken to neutralize HTML's special interpretation of stray angle brackets, < and >. But Greenstone overrides this in the case of the previous specifications.) Note that exactly the same format as shown here is used, even in Word files, including the surrounding symbols <!-- and -->. Font and spacing is ignored.

Classifiers

Classifiers are programs that build a collection's browsing indexes. We have seen many examples in Chapter 3. The navigation bar near the top of the screen shots shown in Chapter 3 always includes a Search button, and this is followed by buttons for any classifiers that have been defined. For example, Figure 3.1 shows the *titles A-Z* and *authors A-Z* indexes in the Project Gutenberg collection; Figure 3.3 shows *subjects*, *titles A-Z*, *organization*, and *how to* indexes in the Humanity Development Library; Figure 3.5 shows *title*, *journal*, and *year* indexes in the School Journal collection; and Figure 3.6 shows *series* and *dates* indexes in the Historic Māori Newspaper collection. All these browsing functions are called *classifiers*.

Like plug-ins, classifiers are specified by lines in the collection configuration file. Each line starts with the keyword *classify*, followed by the name of the classifier and any relevant options. The basic configuration file (Figure 6.4) discussed in

Section 6.3 includes the line *classify AZList –metadata "Title"*, which makes an alphabetic list of titles by taking all those with a *Title* metadata field, sorting them, and splitting them into alphabetic ranges. An example is shown in Figure 6.13a.

Unlike plug-ins, which are used in the import phase of the collection-building process, classifiers are called in the building phase. They are invoked by *buildcol.pl* to produce the information necessary to support browsing and store it in the collection information database.

Examples of classifiers

A basic *List* classifier is illustrated in Figure 6.13b. It displays a sorted list of a given metadata element without any alphabetic tabs. The example shows the Demo collection's *how to* metadata, which is produced by the line *classify List –metadata Howto* in the configuration file.

The *AZList* in Figure 6.13a is a variant of *List*. The alphabetic ranges (five in this case) are generated automatically by the classifier, and the number of alphabetic buckets is designed to place a sensible number of documents in each. Figure 3.19b (Chapter 3) was generated by the same *AZList* specification but has

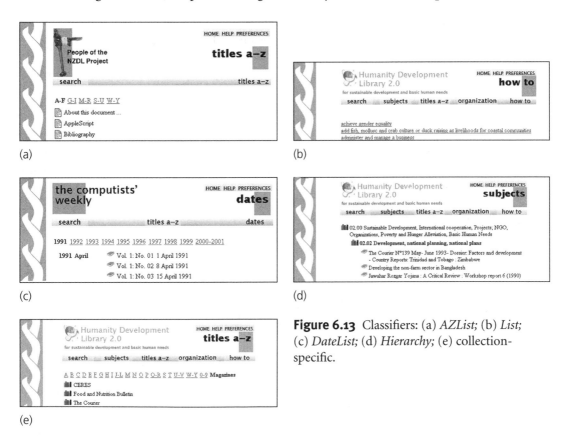

(a)

(b)

(c)

(d)

(e)

Figure 6.13 Classifiers: (a) *AZList*; (b) *List*; (c) *DateList*; (d) *Hierarchy*; (e) collection-specific.

20 buckets. Figure 3.19a shows a degenerate case that was generated by the same specification but has so few documents that no alphabetic divisions are created at all.

Another variant of *List* is *DateList*, illustrated in Figure 6.13c, which generates a selection list of date ranges. Figure 3.21 (Chapter 3) shows another example. Again the ranges (of years in this case) are generated automatically to place a sensible number of items in each.

Other classifiers generate browsing structures that are hierarchical. These are used for subject classifications and organizational hierarchies. Figure 6.13d shows a snapshot of the *subjects* browser for the Demo collection. The bookshelf with a bold title is the one currently being perused; above it you can see the subject classification to which it belongs. A more extensive example of the same hierarchy appears in Figure 3.22 (Chapter 3).

These examples of hierarchical classifiers are based on *Subject* metadata. The collection configuration file in this case contains the line *classify Hierarchy –hfile sub.txt –metadata Subject –sort Title*, and the role of the *hfile* argument is to specify a file in which the hierarchy is stored (in this case *sub.txt*, stored in the collection's *etc* directory). We describe the file format later.

Figure 6.13e shows a classifier that is very similar to *AZList* but contains an additional tab for *Magazines* to the right of the alphabetic list which has been clicked to reveal a bookshelf for each magazine. This is an example of an ad hoc collection-specific classifier that is a variant of a standard one; we discuss it further in the following subsection.

The structure of classifiers

The standard classifiers are listed in Table 6.12a. There are several types of list, and a single *Hierarchy* classifier. All of them—including list classifiers, which are not overtly hierarchical—generate a hierarchical structure that is used for browsing. The hierarchy's lowest levels (i.e., leaves) are usually documents, but in some cases they are individual sections. They are represented internally as OIDs.

There are three possible types for the internal nodes of the hierarchy: *Vlist*, *Hlist*, and *Datelist*. A *Vlist* is a list of items displayed vertically down the page, such as the *how to* index in the Demo collection (Figure 6.13b). An *Hlist* is displayed horizontally. For example, the *AZList* display in Figure 6.13a is a two-level hierarchy of internal nodes consisting of an *Hlist* (the A–Z selector) whose children are *Vlists*—and their children, in turn, are documents. A *Datelist* (Figure 6.13c) is a special kind of *Vlist* that allows selection by year and month.

Table 6.12b shows the options that classifiers support. Just as you can use the *pluginfo.pl* program to find out about any plug-in, a *classinfo.pl* program gives information about the options provided by classifiers.

Table 6.12 (a) Greenstone classifiers; (b) their options.

Classifier	Function		
(a) *List*	Alphabetic list of documents		
SectionList	List of sections in documents		
AZList	List of documents split into alphabetical ranges		
AZSectionList	Like *AZList* but includes every section of the document		
DateList	Similar to *AZList* but sorted by date		
Hierarchy	Hierarchical classification		
(b) *All classifiers*	*metadata*	Include documents containing this metadata element	
	buttonname	Name of button used to access this classifier (defaults to value of metadata argument)	
Hierarchy classifiers	*hfile*	Classification file	
	sort	Metadata element used to sort documents within leaves (default *Title*)	

The line used to specify classifiers in collection configuration files normally contains a *metadata* argument that determines what metadata governs the classification. Any document for which this metadata is undefined will be silently omitted from the classifier. (The document remains in the collection—it is still indexed and can be found in a full-text search—but is invisible under that classifier.)

In the case of the list classifiers, documents are sorted by the *metadata* argument. If none is specified, all documents are included in the classifier, in the order in which are encountered during the building process. This provides a list of all documents in the collection, with none omitted. The *Hierarchy* classifier has a separate *sort* parameter that defines the order in which documents at the leaves are presented. If omitted, this defaults to the *Title* metadata value.

The navigation button that invokes a classifier is labeled by the classifier's metadata argument. Buttons are provided for each Dublin Core type and for some other types of metadata. You can redefine the label for individual classifiers using the *buttonname* argument.

Collection-specific classifiers are stored in the collection's *perllib/classify* directory. For example, the Humanity Development Library has a classifier called *HDLList*, which is a minor variant of *AZList*. Shown in Figure 6.13e, it includes an additional nonalphabetic classification for *Magazines*. This was produced by making a small change (two lines of Perl) to the code for the basic *AZList*. The modification uses *Magazine* metadata (which says whether a document is a magazine or not) to determine whether to place the document in its alphabetic position or include it under the *Magazines* tab instead. This illustrates how to cope with the kind of minor ad hoc variant of a basic structure that pervades practical digital library applications. Freak waves are common.

List classifiers

Table 6.12a shows several variants of the basic list classifier. Some collections, such as newsletters, need a browsing list of sections because these represent independent articles on different topics. A *SectionList* is a *List* whose leaves are sections rather than documents: all document sections are included except the top level. An *AZList*, as we have seen, generates a two-level hierarchy comprising an *HList* whose children are *VLists*, whose children are documents. The *HList* is an A–Z selector that sorts the documents and divides them into alphabetic ranges. An *AZSectionList* is an *AZList* whose leaves are sections rather than documents. Finally, *DateList* is like *AZList* except that the top-level *HList* allows selection by year and its children are *DateLists* rather than *VLists*. The metadata argument defaults to *Date*.

The *hierarchy* classifier

All classifiers are hierarchical. However, list classifiers have a fixed number of levels, whereas the *hierarchy* classifiers described in this section have an arbitrary number and are consequently more complex to specify.

The hierarchy is based on a particular kind of metadata—*Subject*, in the case of Figure 6.13d. The metadata values could be anything, and further information is required to translate each particular value into an appropriate position in the hierarchy. This is accomplished by a file that defines the metadata hierarchy, whose name is given by the *hfile* argument.

Each line of the metadata hierarchy file describes one classification and has three parts:

- Identifier, which matches the value of the metadata to the classification
- Position-in-hierarchy marker in multi-part numeric form (e.g., 2, 2.12, 2.12.6)
- Name of the classification (if this contains spaces, it should be quoted)

Figure 6.14 shows part of the *sub.txt* file used to create the subject hierarchy in Figure 6.13d. This example is slightly confusing because documents in this collection specify the metadata type *Hierarchy* not as a text string, but as a value that is already in hierarchical numeric form. The number representing the hierarchy appears twice on each line of Figure 6.14. The first occurrence is the value of the *Hierarchy* metadata type (which can be any text string); the second is the structured identifier used to determine the hierarchical position of that metadata value. For example, in a collection of television items, the *Hierarchy* metadata values

```
1        1        "General reference"
1.2      1.2      "Dictionaries, glossaries, language courses, terminology (all languages)"
2        2        "Sustainable Development, International cooperation, Projects; NGO, Organizations, Povert
2.1      2.1      "Development policy and theory, international cooperation, national planning, national pl
2.2      2.2      "Development, national planning, national plans"
2.3      2.3      "Project planning and evaluation (incl. project management and dissemination strategies)"
2.4      2.4      "Regional development and planning incl. regional profiles"
2.5      2.5      "Nongovernmental organizations (NGOs) in general, self- help organizations (their role in
2.6      2.6      "Organizations, institutions, United Nations (general, directories, yearbooks, annual rep
2.6.1    2.6.1    "United Nations"
2.6.2    2.6.2    "International organizations"
2.6.3    2.6.3    "Regional organizations"
2.6.5    2.6.5    "European Community - European Union"
2.7      2.7      "Sustainable Development, Development models and examples; Best practices (general)"
2.8      2.8      "Basic Human Needs"
2.9      2.9      "Hunger and Poverty Alleviation"
```

Figure 6.14 Part of the file *sub.txt.*

might be such things as *tv*, *tv.news*, *tv.news.political*, and *tv.drama*, while the corresponding position identifiers would be such things as 1, 1.1, 1.1.1, and 1.2.

Ordering at internal nodes of the hierarchy is determined by the order in which items are specified in the hierarchy file. The classifier's *sort* option determines how documents at the leaves are ordered.

How classifiers work

Classifiers are Perl objects derived from a basic classifier called *BasClas.pm*. When they are executed, the following steps occur.

1. The *new* method creates a classifier object.
2. The *init* method initializes the object with parameters such as metadata type, button name, and sort criterion.
3. The *classify* method is invoked once for each document and stores information about the document's classification.
4. The *get_classify_info* method returns the locally stored classification information, which the build process then writes to the collection information database.

The *classify* method retrieves each document's OID, the metadata value on which the document is to be classified, and, where necessary, the metadata value on which the documents are to be sorted. The *get_classify_info* method performs all sorting and other classifier-specific manipulation. In the case of *AZList*, for example, it splits the list into ranges.

The building process reads whatever classifiers are needed from the collection configuration file and initializes each one. Classifications are created by a building module called *classify.pm*.

Format statements

The Web pages you see when you use Greenstone are not prestored but are generated on the fly as they are needed. Their content and appearance are controlled using *format statements*. These belong in the collection configuration file and are introduced by the keyword *format*, followed by the name of the element to which the format applies. Format statements are interpreted at the time that pages are displayed, and changes take effect as soon as the collection configuration file is saved. For the Local Library version of Greenstone, this means that you can see the changes when you restart Greenstone; for other versions they appear immediately, without restarting. This makes experimenting with format statements quick and easy.

Two different kinds of element are controlled by format statements. The first are the items on the page that show documents or parts of documents; the second are the lists produced by classifiers and searches. We deal with them in turn. The details of format statements are messy: you should consider skipping this section unless you have specific display requirements in a particular collection you are working on.

Formatting documents

To review the effect of the first kind of format specifier, look again at the figures in Chapter 3 that show the beginning of documents—for example, Figures 3.1, 3.3a, and 3.3b. Format statements control whether the title (Figure 3.1) or a cover image (Figure 3.3) is displayed, and in the former case it can be different metadata, formatted differently (such as Figure 3.6). The document in Figure 3.1 is page-structured, whereas the one in Figure 3.3 is hierarchical: format statements determine whether the page selector or table of contents structure appears or not. Beneath the title (Figure 3.1) or cover image (Figure 3.3) are some buttons (Expand Text, Expand Contents, Detach, No Highlighting): which ones appear is determined by a format statement. How the entire text of the document is formatted is also controllable, as is the presence of little arrows that appear at the end of the text to take you on to the next page or back to the previous one.

Table 6.13 shows how these things are controlled. The first four items affect the heading, before the text of the document starts. The *DocumentImages* statement either displays a cover image at the top left (Figures 3.3a and b) or it does not, in which case some text is displayed instead (Figure 3.1, where the text is *Alice's Adventures in Wonderland*, and Figure 3.6, where it is *Vol. 1 No. 1 21 August 1978*). The metadata chosen for display, along with its formatting, is determined by the *DocumentHeading* statement. By default the table of contents is shown for hierarchical documents (Figures 3.3a and b); otherwise the display is paginated and includes a page selector (Figure 3.1). *DocumentContents*

Table 6.13 The format options.	

Option	Function
format DocumentImages true/false	Display cover image at the top left of the document page (default *false*).
format DocumentHeading formatstring	Defines the document header shown at the top left of the document page (default *[Title]*).
format DocumentContents true/false	Display table of contents (hierarchical documents) or page selector (nonhierarchical ones), or not.
format DocumentButtons string	Determines which buttons are displayed on a document page (default *Detach/Highlight*).
format DocumentText formatstring	Format of the document text: default
	* <table width=537>*
	<tr><td>[Text]</td></tr>
	*</table> *
format DocumentArrowsBottom true/false	Display next/previous section arrows at bottom of document page (default *true*).
format DocumentUseHTML true/false	If *true*, each document is displayed inside a separate frame (default *false*).

switches these off. The *DocumentButtons* option controls which buttons appear on a document page. Here *string* is a list of button names (separated by |), and possible values are *Detach*, *Highlight*, *Expand Text*, and *Expand Contents*. The entire list must be quoted. Reordering the list reorders the buttons.

The remaining three items affect the body of the document, below the header. *DocumentText* determines how (or whether!) the text is displayed. This is done by defining a *format string* that is basically a fragment of HTML. The default is to display the document's text in a fixed-width single-column table, but this can be changed. Indeed it is not necessarily the document text that is shown: any metadata—or any combination of text and metadata—can appear instead. In Figure 3.13b the header comprises just the first line, *Newsnight New Zealand Anti-nuclear Policy*, and the remaining text is all determined by the *DocumentText* format string. The next subsections describe how to express these specifications, but for a simple display the document's text is generated by the specifier *[Text]*. *DocumentArrowsBottom* determines whether next- and previous-section arrows appear at the bottom of the document page.

By default Greenstone does not use frames. However, if *DocumentUseHTML* is set, each document is displayed within a separate frame. This also causes a slight change to the Preferences page, adding options that apply specifically to collections of HTML documents. For example, one option is to go directly to the original source document (anywhere on the Web) rather than to the digital library's copy. This gives the interface a search-engine style—an index to a collection of documents on the Web rather than private copies in a stand-alone digital library.

Formatting lists

The second kind of format statement defines strings that determine the appearance of lists produced by searches and classifiers. Format strings can apply at different levels of the display structure. They can alter all lists of a certain type—for example, all of the elements in the *DateList* generated by a date classifier. Or they can alter all parts of a list—for example, all the entries in the list of search results. Or they can alter specific parts of a certain list—for example, the horizontal part of an *AZList* title classifier that shows the alphabetic selector, or the vertical part that shows the titles themselves.

These format statements need to specify the list to which the format applies. The list generated by a search is called *Search*. Classifiers are numbered by their position in the collection configuration file—for example, the third classifier specified in *collect.cfg* is called *CL3*. Thus the list of names is *Search*, *CL1*, *CL2*, *CL3*, ... These names can be qualified by the part of the list to which the formatting is to apply—*HList* for horizontal list, like the A–Z selector in an *AZList*; *VList* for vertical list, like the list of titles under an *AZList*; or *DateList*. For example:

format CL4VList ...	applies to all *VLists* in classifier 4
format CL2HList ...	applies to all *HLists* in classifier 2
format CL1DateList ...	applies to all *DateLists* in classifier 1
format SearchVList ...	applies to the search results list
format CL3 ...	applies to all nodes in classifier 3
format VList ...	applies to all *VLists* in all classifiers

General statements are overridden by more specific ones. If the first and last of the above statements were both included, the first would override for classifier 4 the more general *Vlist* specification given by the last.

The final part of a format statement—which is omitted from the previous examples and shown merely as an ellipsis (...)—is a string that controls the information displayed and its layout. It comprises plain text and HTML tags. Also, the value of any metadata item can be interpolated by putting the metadata name within square brackets. Some other items may appear in format strings: the document text itself, an HTML link to the document, the internal document number (useful for debugging), or an icon appropriate to the document (for example, the little text icon in a *Search results* string). These items are

Table 6.14 Items appearing in format strings.	
Item	Function
[Text]	The document's text
[link] ... [/link]	HTML link to the document
[num]	Internal document number
[icon]	An icon
[metadata-name]	The value of this metadata element for the document, e.g., *[Title]*

```
classify  Hierarchy      -hfile sub.txt -metadata Subject -sort Title
classify  AZList         -metadata Title
classify  Hierarchy      -hfile org.txt -metadata Organisation -sort Title
classify  List           -metadata Howto

format  SearchVList     "<td valign=top [link] [icon] [/link]</td><td>{If}
                        {[parent(All':'):Title],[parent(All':'):Title]:}
                        [link][Title][/link]</td>"
format  CL4Vlist        "<br>[link] [Howto] [/link]"
format  DocumentImages  true
format  DocumentText    "<h3>[Title]</h3>\\n\\n<p>[Text]"
format  DocumentButtons "Expand Text|Expand contents|Detach|Highlight"
```

Figure 6.15 Excerpt from the Demo collection's *collect.cfg*.

summarized in Table 6.14. The syntax for format strings also includes a conditional statement, which is illustrated later in this subsection.

Recall that all classifiers produce hierarchies. Each level of the hierarchy is displayed in one of four ways. We have already encountered *HList*, *VList*, and *DateList*. The final possibility is *Invisible*, which is how the very top levels are displayed—because the name of the classifier is already shown separately on the Greenstone navigation bar.

Examples of format strings

Figure 6.15 shows part of the configuration file for the Demo collection. This is a good example because it has several classifiers that are richly formatted. Note that statements in collection configuration files must not contain new-line characters—in the figure, longer lines are broken up for readability.

Line 4 defines the Demo collection's *how to* classifier. This is the fourth one in the configuration file and is referred to as *CL4*. The corresponding format statement is line 6 of Figure 6.15. The *how to* browser is generated by the *List* classifier, and its structure is the plain list of titles in Figure 6.13b. The titles are linked to the documents themselves: clicking a title brings up the relevant document. The children of the hierarchy's top level are displayed as a *VList* that lists the sections vertically. As dictated by the format statement in line 6, each element of the list appears on a new line ("*
*") and contains the *Howto* text, hyperlinked to the document itself.

The first line defines the Demo collection's *Subject* classification, referred to as *CL1* (the first in the configuration file), and the third the *Organization* classification, *CL3*. Both are generated by the *Hierarchy* classifier and therefore comprise a hierarchical structure of *VLists*.

The second line defines the remaining classification for the Demo collection, *Titles A–Z* (*CL2*). Note that there are no format strings for *CL1*, *CL2*, or *CL3*. There are built-in defaults for each classifier type. You need not define a format string unless you want to override the default.

This accounts for the four *classify* lines in Figure 6.15. There are five format statements. We have already discussed one, for *CL4Vlist*. The last three are format statements of the first type, documented in Table 6.13. Line 7 places the cover image at the top left of each document page. Line 8 formats the actual document text, preceded by the title of the relevant chapter or section. The effect of these is illustrated in Figure 6.16a.

Line 5 of Figure 6.15 is a formidable specification that governs the query result list returned by a search. Its parts are illustrated in Figure 6.16b. A simplified version of this format string is

```
<td valign=top>[link][icon][/link]</td>
<td>[link][Title][/link]</td>
```

Items on the query results list are designed to appear as a table row. This specification gives a small icon followed by the value of the *Title* metadata. Both are hyperlinked to the document itself.

In this collection documents are hierarchical: they contain sections, subsections, and so on. In fact, the second hyperlink anchor above evaluates to the title of the section returned by the query. It would be better to augment it with the title of the enclosing section, the enclosing chapter, and the book in which it occurs. For this purpose there is a special pseudo-metadata item, *parent*, which is not stored in documents but is implicit in any hierarchical document. It returns either the parent document or, if used with the qualifier *All*, the list of hierarchically enclosing parents, separated by a character string that can appear after the *All* qualifier. Thus

```
<td valign=top>[link][icon][/link]</td>
<td>[parent(All': '):Title]: [link][Title][/link]</td>
```

has the effect of generating a list containing the book title, chapter title, and so on that enclose the target section, separated by colons, with a further colon followed by a hyperlink to the target section's title.

Unfortunately, if the target is itself a book, there is no parent and so an empty string will appear, followed by a colon. To circumvent this the conditional *if* and *or … else* statements can be used in a format string:

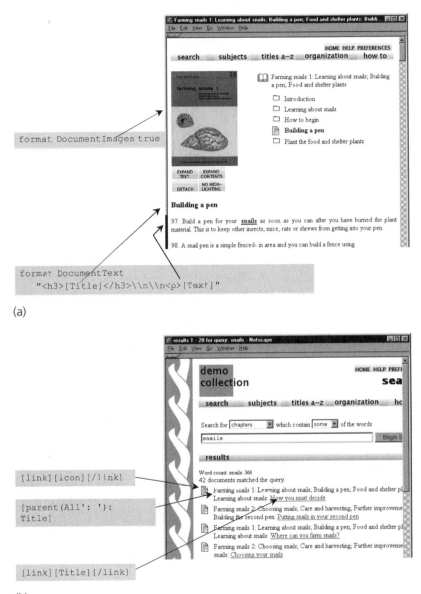

Figure 6.16 The effect of format statements on (a) the document itself; (b) the search results.

```
{If}{[metadata], action-if-non-null, action-if-null}
{Or}{action, else another-action, else another-action, etc}
```

Braces are used to signal that the statements should be interpreted and not printed out as text. *If* tests whether the metadata is non-null. If so it takes the first clause; otherwise the second (if it exists). Any metadata item can be used, including the pseudo-metadata *parent*. *Or* evaluates each action in turn until one is found that is non-null. It sends that to the output and skips the remaining actions.

Returning to line 5 of Figure 6.15, the full, unexpurgated, format string is

```
<td valign=top>[link][icon][/link]</td>
<td>{If}{[parent(All': '):Title],
        [parent(All': '):Title]:}
    [link][Title][/link]</td>
```

The *parent* specification is preceded by a conditional that checks whether the result is empty and only generates the parent string when it is present. Incidentally, *parent* can be qualified by *Top* instead of *All*, which gives the top-level document name that encloses a section—in this case the book name. No separating string is necessary with *Top*.

As a final example, Figure 6.13c shows the *Dates* classification of the Computists' Weekly collection. The classifier and format specifications are given below (it happens to be the second classifier, *CL2*). The *DateList* classifier differs from *AZList* in that, by default, it sorts by *Date* metadata, and the browsing hierarchy's leaves use *DateList* instead of *Vlist*—which causes the year and month to be added to the left of the document.

```
classify DateList
format CL2DateList "<td>[link][icon][/link]</td>
                    <td>[Title]</td>
                    <td>[Date]</td>"
```

In this case the *Title* metadata for an issue gives its volume and number, while *Date* gives its date. The result can be seen in Figure 6.13c.

The format-string mechanism is flexible, but rather tricky. The best way to learn it is by experimenting and studying existing collection configuration files.

Linking to different document versions

Greenstone pages often include hyperlinks to the document text, so that when the link is clicked, the HTML version of the document is displayed. This is accomplished by the *[link] . . . [/link]* notation in format strings, as described earlier. However, in some collections it is useful to be able to display other versions of the document. For example, in a collection of Microsoft Word files, the Word version of documents could be displayed rather than (or as well as) the HTML version derived from them.

The key to gaining access to different versions of a document is to embed information about where they reside into the Greenstone Archive Format. This information is represented as metadata. Recall that putting

```
[link][Title][/link]
```

into a format string creates a link to the HTML version of the document, whose anchor text is the document's title. The Word and PDF plug-ins both generate *srclink* metadata. If you put

```
[srclink] [Title] [/srclink]
```

into a format string, it makes a link to the original Word or PDF version of the document. Again the anchor here is the document's title—but it need not be. These plug-ins also generate *srcicon* metadata, which displays the appropriate icon for Word and PDF documents. Thus

```
[srclink] [srcicon] [/srclink]
```

creates a link labeled by the standard Word or PDF icon (whichever is appropriate), rather than the document's title.

6.8   Building collections graphically

We have now seen most of the major facilities of Greenstone for building and customizing collections. Executing command-line scripts and editing configuration files gives close control over the structure and appearance of collections. It is always possible to customize further by digging into the program code itself and modifying it to add new facilities—this is how it evolves to meet new requirements. However, most users will not want to do this, nor should they need to. Many will be satisfied with the Collector's visual interface, which is easier to use for simple building tasks but only really lets you copy the structure of existing collections.

It is instructive to learn about the internal operation of the system and how to invoke and customize the various operations using command-line scripts and configuration files. However, powerful systems do not have to be complex to use, and more comprehensive capabilities could certainly be incorporated within an easily accessible end-user interface. Figures 6.17 through 6.19 show an interaction with a prototype successor to the Collector in which a user collates pages from various Web sites, augments them with metadata, and then builds a collection. Like the original Collector, it runs on the system that hosts Greenstone. However, it is implemented in Java, which provides greater control over user interaction than the HTML forms used so far.

In Figure 6.17 the user has started to develop a new collection using the File menu (top left). A box has popped up requesting the collection's title, the creator's e-mail address, and a brief description of what it includes—exactly the information that the Collector solicits when it starts (Figure 6.3c). As in Section 6.2, the collection being built is about women in history, based on primary source documents.

Figure 6.17 Starting to build a collection.

Notice the Browse, Mirror, MetaEdit, and Options tabs under the address box in the main window. These open up a user-interface panel for the corresponding task. The initial task is Browse: from here you can browse around the Web. Enter a URL in the address box and that page appears in the Browse panel. For example, you may bring up a search engine and use it to hunt for relevant documents and sites.

The Mirror facility is used to copy an interesting document, or Web site, to the local computer for inclusion in the collection. In Figure 6.18 this tab has been selected for the home page of the Great American Women project. A Download button appears to the right of the address box, and the user has clicked it. The Options panel (not shown) allows control over such things as the mirroring depth. In our example the user has chosen to download the home page and pages one link away that lie within the same Internet domain.

Figure 6.18 Mirroring a site.

It may be that not every page copied should be included in the digital library collection. First, mirrored files are copied into an area labeled *Private Workspace* (lower panel on the left). There documents or folders can be selected in an interactive tree display and brought into the collection area (upper panel on the left) using the Collect button beneath the tree display area. A Remove button below the collection area reverses the process. In Figure 6.18 this step has already been performed, and all downloaded documents have been transferred to the collection area. The last line of the message area at the bottom of the screen reports that 42 files have been moved into the collection.

The next step is to enrich the files by entering metadata, a process that the original Collector does not allow. The MetaEdit panel is used for this. Figure 6.19 shows the screen partway through the process. The user has selected the file *anthony.htm* from the collection area (upper left); chosen the *Creator* metadata type from a pull-down menu of Dublin Core categories (lower right); and

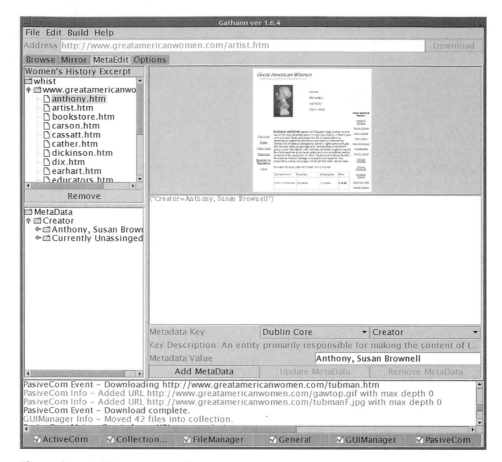

Figure 6.19 Adding new metadata.

entered "Anthony, Susan Brownell" as its value. Several documents can be selected at once and metadata assigned to them all in one step. Thumbnails of the selected documents, and their metadata so far, are displayed in the top and bottom halves of the horizontally split main panel.

When you are satisfied with the metadata, you can build the collection using options listed in the Build menu. This offers facilities similar to those of the Collector. When the process is complete, the About this Collection page appears in the Browse panel. You can save your work at any stage using the File menu. You can also continue browsing and adding metadata while documents are being mirrored or the collection is being built.

Future versions of this tool will allow interactive control over the elements in the collection configuration file itself—what indexes are to be included, what plug-ins may be required, what classifiers to include and the metadata values that they should work on, what collection-level metadata is needed (such as icons for the collection and the default interface language). You will even be able to control the format of the collection's pages using a special-purpose interactive page editor.

Why should building a digital library be difficult?

6.9   Notes and sources

The Greenstone Collector subsystem that gives ordinary people the power to build high-quality digital library collections is described in a paper called "Power to the people" by Witten, Bainbridge, and Boddie (2001).

7 Delivery

How Greenstone works

We explained in Chapter 6 the distinction between *building* digital library collections and *delivering* to users the information they contain. Building prepares information structures in advance that expedite searching and browsing the information collection. Delivering interacts with digital library users on the one hand, and on the other it utilizes the information structures to find out the information the users need. Building is a compile-time process; delivery is a runtime one—it's what users see when they use the digital library.

You need to understand the building process if you want to be able to create new digital library collections. That is why we delved into it in such great and laborious detail in the last chapter. Understanding how building works empowers you to create effective collections very quickly.

The same is not true for the delivery process—you need not understand Greenstone's runtime system in order to build or use collections. However, because the software is "open source"—that is, it is available to you in source code form—you can augment and extend its capabilities, tailoring them to new situations and new requirements. To do this you will have to learn about the runtime system. If you're not interested in technical details of how digital library systems work—and, you may ask, why should you be?—skip this chapter.

Here we explain how the runtime system operates in sufficient detail that you can begin to work with it yourself. We start by outlining its overall structure.

Then we study two major components that are needed to understand its operation: the macro language, which is how all Web pages are expressed internally, and the collection information database, which records information produced during the building operation for use at runtime. Next we examine what is involved when the system responds to user requests. Following that we describe operational aspects of the digital library system—in particular, how it can be configured for different situations.

7.1 Processes and protocols

Figure 7.1 shows three users, represented by computer terminals at the top of the diagram, accessing three different collections at the bottom. Before going online, these collections have undergone the processes described in Chapter 6. This is depicted at the bottom. Source documents are imported into the Greenstone archive language, then from these files are built various searchable indexes

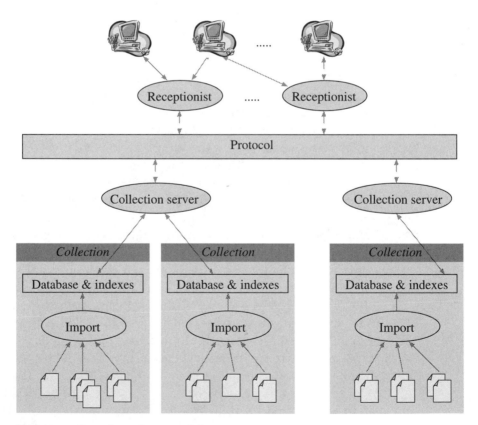

Figure 7.1 Overview of a general Greenstone system.

and a collection information database that includes structures to support browsing. Then the collection is ready to go online and respond to requests from users for information.

Processes

Two software processes are central to the design of the runtime system: *receptionists* and *collection servers*. From a user's point of view, a receptionist is the point of contact with the digital library—although users need know nothing about the software architecture in order to use the system. The receptionist accepts user input, typically in the form of keyboard entry and mouse clicks communicated via a Web browser, analyzes it, and dispatches a request to the appropriate collection server (or servers). Collection servers interact with the data structures that have been produced by the building process. They locate the requested piece of information and return it to the receptionist for transmission to the user's Web browser and presentation to the user. Collection servers provide an abstract mechanism to handle the content of the collection, while receptionists are responsible for the user interface.

Different users can share a receptionist—and if you access a Greenstone digital library Web site, you are likely sharing the receptionist with many other users. Also, different collections can share a collection server—for example, most Greenstone sites have only one server that handles all the collections they offer. But each receptionist has the potential to communicate with several different collection servers, and each server can serve several different receptionists. The architecture is flexible.

The null protocol implementation

As Figure 7.1 illustrates, receptionists communicate with collection servers through a defined protocol. The implementation of the protocol depends on whether the digital library system is run on a distributed system with several networked processors. The most common case, and the simplest, is when there is one receptionist and one collection server and both run on the same computer. This is what you get when you install Greenstone. In this case the two processes are combined to form a single executable program. This reduces the protocol to a simple matter of making function calls—although all communication between the two modules goes through this protocol interface. We call this implementation the *null protocol*, and it forms the basis for the standard out-of-the-box Greenstone system. Figure 7.2 illustrates how the receptionist, protocol, and collection server are bound together as one entity, which is called the *library* program. The aim of this chapter is to show how it works.

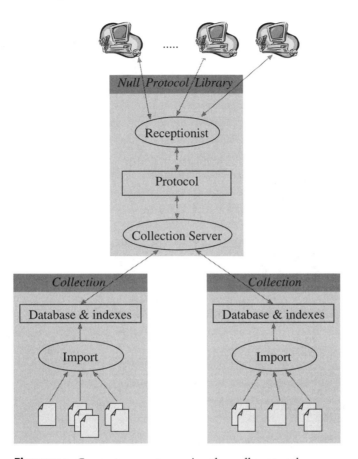

Figure 7.2 Greenstone system using the null protocol.

Usually a *server* is a persistent process that, once started, runs indefinitely, responding to any requests that arise. Despite its name, however, the collection server in the null protocol configuration is not a server in this sense. In fact, every time any Web page is requested, the *library* program is started up, responds to the request, and then exits. This is accomplished by the CGI mechanism that is widely used by Web servers to communicate with application programs. We call the collection server a *server* because it is also designed to work in the more general configuration of Figure 7.1.

This start-up, process, and exit cycle is not as slow as one might expect and results in a perfectly usable service. However, it is clearly inefficient. There is a scheme called Fast-CGI that provides a middle ground. Using it, the *library* program, once executed, remains in memory and subsequent sets of arguments are fed to it, thereby avoiding repeated initialization overheads. This provides essentially the same behavior as a server. Using Fast-CGI is an option that you can enable when compiling (or recompiling) the source code.

The CORBA protocol implementation

Exactly the same protocol is also implemented using the CORBA scheme. CORBA uses a unified object-oriented paradigm to enable different processes, running on different computer platforms and implemented in different programming languages, to access the same set of distributed objects over the Internet (or any other network). With it, scenarios like the one in Figure 7.1 can be fully realized, with receptionists and collection servers running on different computers.

Using the CORBA implementation of the Greenstone protocol, far more sophisticated interfaces can be connected to exactly the same digital library collections. As an example, Figure 7.3 shows an experimental graphical query interface, based on Venn diagrams, which lets users manipulate Boolean queries directly. Users type query terms, whereupon the system places them in the workspace in the form of a circle, annotated by the number of matching documents. Users can move them around interactively and form logical combina-

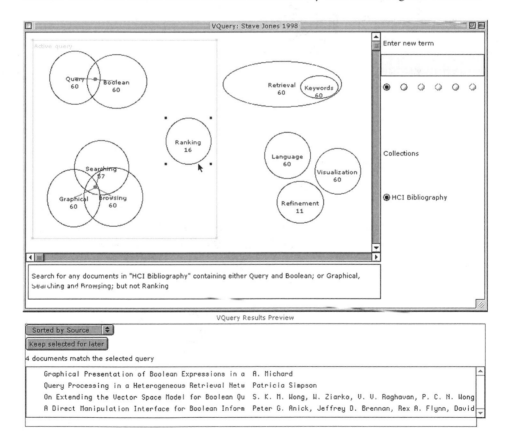

Figure 7.3 Graphical query interface to a Greenstone collection.

tions—for example, in Figure 7.3 the user has constructed the query (*Query* OR *Boolean*) AND (*Graphical* OR *Searching* OR *Browsing*) AND (NOT *Ranking*).

More interesting than the interface itself—at least from our present perspective—is how the software works behind the scenes. Written in Java, the interface runs locally on the user's own computer. Using the CORBA protocol, it accesses a remote collection server, written in C++. It presents a radically different interface—far beyond what is possible with the format statement mechanism in Chapter 6—that harnesses the power of the digital library "back end" and the documents it contains.

In most of this chapter we assume the null protocol. However, in Section 7.3, after peeling back one layer of Greenstone by showing how user requests, represented as arguments, drive the standard receptionist, we describe two CORBA-based examples and explain how the distributed version of the protocol is used to support them.

7.2 Preliminaries

Before getting underway we describe two software components that are central to the runtime system: the macro language, which creates all pages in the user interface, and the collection information database, which communicates information about collections—including the structure of classifiers—between the building and delivery phases.

The macro language

All Web pages in the user interface are created on the fly: none are stored in advance. They are generated using *macros* written in a simple language specially designed for the job. The purpose is to make things easy (although admittedly it makes it harder at first to understand what is going on). Macros are inline scripts that perform textual replacement—one piece of text, the macro name, is replaced by another, its content.

One reason macros are used is that the interface comes in many different languages. All the text fragments are couched as macro definitions. To add a new language, you need only translate these macros—you don't have to rework all the Web pages. Every page displayed by the system is passed through a *macro interpreter* that expands all the macros on the page. The interpreter checks a language variable and uses the macro definitions pertaining to it. This loads the page in the appropriate language.

Macros can have parameters. In this case the parameter is the language variable: this causes the appropriate text fragment to be used for the macro's expansion. If there is no Arabic version for a particular macro, the macro interpreter will automatically substitute the default version (English). This lets system developers experiment with the interface without having to worry about translating every little bit of new text immediately. Defaulting to English is not ideal—it reflects an Anglo-centric mind-set—but it seems better than displaying nothing. However, if "nothing" were preferred, it would be a simple matter to alter the software to default to the empty language!

Macros are also used to deal with display variables. Whenever a Web page contains information that is not known in advance—such as the number of documents returned by a search, or the value of a particular metadata item, or the content of a document page—a macro name is used in the page description. Unlike language macros, these macros are *dynamic:* their content is not stored in advance but is generated by the system in accordance with the value of the variable in question.

Introducing macros

Macros contain the pieces of text and data used on the Web pages. For example, Figure 7.4a shows the About This Collection page of a particular collection (the Project Gutenberg collection). The layout of this page is encoded in the file *about.dm* given in Figure 7.4b. (The suffix *.dm* indicates a macro file.) Macros come in *packages*, each containing a series of macros used for a single purpose; what Figure 7.4b shows is the *about* package. Headers, footers, and the background image are not mentioned in *about.dm* because they are located in the *Global* macro package.

Macro names begin and end with an underscore, and their content is defined using curly braces. The content can be plain text, HTML (including links to Java applets and JavaScript), macro names, or any combination of these. Lines beginning with the hash symbol (#) are comments.

Three macros are defined in Figure 7.4b: _pagetitle_, _content_, and _textabout_. The *pagetitle* macro (we leave off the underscores) defines the title of the page in the Web browser—how the page is identified in the browser's history list, for example. Note that the *about* package is not specific to any particular collection, yet the collection's name must appear as this page's title. The About page is unusual in this regard. Other page titles do not depend on the collection—the Search page, for example, is always called "Search page." To accomplish this, *pagetitle* is defined for the About page as a dynamic macro, *collectionname*, whose content is generated by the system—it gives the name of the collection from the collection configuration file.

The *content* macro is used for the page body. It is defined mostly in terms of other macros, but some HTML appears—*<center>*, *<p>*, *<h3>*. First comes the navigation bar—dynamically defined, because the browsing buttons depend on what classifiers are present in the collection. The incantation *query:queryform*

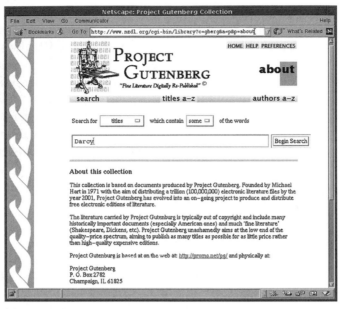

(a)

```
package about

########################################
# "about page" content
########################################

_pagetitle_ {_collectionname_}

_content_ {
<center>
_navigationbar_
</center>
_query:queryform_
<p>_iconblankbar_
<p>_textabout_
_textsubcollections_
<h3>_help:textsimplehelpheading_</h3>
_help:simplehelp_
}

_textabout_ {
<h3>_textabcol_</h3>
_Global:collectionextra_
}
```

(b)

Figure 7.4 (a) About This Collection page; (b) part of the macro file that generates it.

generates the query structure near the top of Figure 7.4a. Here *queryform* is the macro name; the preceding word indicates that it comes from a macro package defined elsewhere called *query*. There are several forms that queries can take (described in Chapter 3): it depends on whether the user has specified in his or her Preferences a large query box (Figure 3.16), a query with history (Figure 3.17), or a form query (Figure 3.18). The *query* macro package sorts these out.

Returning to Figure 7.4, *iconblankbar* is the thin line that follows the query box in Figure 7.4a. Then comes *textabout*, which is defined at the bottom of Figure 7.4b as an HTML heading (*<h3>*) followed by the *collectionextra* text from the *Global* macro package. Next comes text about subcollections (there are none in the Gutenberg collection). Help text follows (not visible in Figure 7.4a).

The About text for a particular collection is not known in advance, but is placed at runtime in a special dynamic macro named *collectionextra* in the *Global* macro package. (Incidentally this same name was used to express the About text when customizing the collection's appearance in the walkthrough of Chapter 6, Section 6.3.)

Language macros

There is no actual text in the macro file of Figure 7.4b—even the heading *About this collection*, which is visible in Figure 7.4a, is encapsulated in another macro *textabcol* mentioned near the bottom. The reason is that the text depends on the interface language, which is determined by the user's Preferences. A macro file called *english.dm* contains this line,

```
_textabcol_ {About this collection}
```

which defines the macro in question. However, for the Dutch language there is another file, *dutch.dm*, with the line

```
_textabcol_ [l=nl] {informatie over deze collectie}
```

The specification *l=nl* is a parameter in the macro language; parameters always appear in square brackets. This macro definition is to be used when the language variable (*l*) is Dutch (*nl*). An appropriately parameterized version of the *textabcol* macro appears in every language file. Examples are

spanish.dm	(*l=es*)	Acerca de esta colección
russian.dm	(*l=ru*)	Немного о коллекции
arabic.dm	(*l=ar*)	حول هذه المجموعة

When a macro is to be expanded and no suitably parameterized version exists, the default is to omit that parameter. For example, suppose *chinese.dm* lacked the appropriate specification for *textabcol* with the *l=zh* parameter value. Then the parameterless version, which expands to the English text cited earlier, would automatically be substituted.

Examples of macros

Like classifiers and plug-ins, all macros are constructed from a predefined basis, in this case the file *base.dm*. This file is read before any other macro file. When macros are redefined, later definitions supersede earlier ones—and many of the definitions in *base.dm* are designed to be overridden. For example, to define the content of a page in the absence of any overriding macro, *base.dm* contains

```
_content_ {<p><h2>Oops</h2>_textdefaultcontent_}
```

The page, which is never supposed to be seen, shows the heading "Oops" followed by *textdefaultcontent*, which is defined, in English, to be "The requested page could not be found. Please use your browser's 'back' button or the home button to return to the Greenstone Digital Library." Just as *about.dm* in Figure 7.4b overrides this macro for the About page, so all other pages' macro packages override it—or are supposed to. If they do not, you will see the above *Oops* message.

The macros *textdefaultcontent* and *content* are both defined in the *Global* package because they are required by all parts of the user interface. All the language macros are in this package too. Package definitions may span more than one file.

When macros from packages other than the one being defined are used, their names must be prefixed by the package name. For example, this definition of *collectionextra* occurs in *english.dm*:

```
_collectionextra_ {This collection contains
_about:numdocs_ documents. It was last built
_about:builddate_ days ago.)
```

It is used as the default description of a collection in case nothing is specified in the configuration file and is part of the *Global* package. However, because *numdocs* and *builddate* are both in the *about* package, their names are preceded by *about*.

Macros often contain conditionals. The basic form is *_If_(x,y,z)*, where *x* is a condition and *y* and *z* contain the text to use if it is true and false, respectively. The condition can use standard comparison operators *less than*, *greater than*, *equals*, and *not equals*.

For example, at the top left of each page is a collection icon—like the picture of the little printing press and the text "Project Gutenberg" in Figure 7.4a—which normally links to the collection's About page. This macro from *base.dm* is used to display the image:

```
_imagecollection_ {
    _If_ ("_iconcollection_" ne "",
        <a href = "_httppageabout_">
            <img src = "_iconcollection_" border = 0>
            </a>,
        _imagecollectionv_)
}
```

Here *iconcollection* resolves to the name of the file containing the collection icon if one has been defined, and the empty string if not. The code can be paraphrased like this:

> If there is a collection image, display it with a link to the About This Collection page (referred to by *httppageabout*); otherwise use the alternative *macro imagecollectionv*.

The fallback substitutes the collection name in text form for the image.

As it happens, the collection icon in Figure 7.4a does *not* link to the About This Collection page, because this *is* the About This Collection page. So the *imagecollection* macro is overridden by a definition in *about.dm*. We have to confess that Figure 7.4b does not tell the whole truth: header items have been omitted for simplicity.

Page parameters

As we saw when we met language macros, macros can take a language parameter *l*, specified in square brackets. We call this a *page parameter* because it affects how every page in the interface is generated. There are two other page parameters. One contains the name of the current collection (*c*). The second determines whether the macro will be expanded in graphical or text-only mode (*v*). The interface has a switch (set on the Preferences page) that provides a text-only version intended for visually impaired people who use large-font displays or speech synthesizers for output. In this mode all images are suppressed from the interface.

Immediately following the above *imagecollection* macro is a text-only version:

```
_imagecollection_[v=1]{_imagecollectionv_}
```

The argument *v*=1 ensures that this more specialized definition, which is the same as the previous one but suppresses the collection image, is used when the system is running in text-only mode. If it is unspecified, or if it is given the value *v*=0 (which amounts to the same thing), the macro will be expanded in regular, graphical mode.

If a parameter is missing from a macro when it is called, the parameter-free version of the macro is used instead (if one exists). The question arises, what precedence is given to the parameters when there is more than one? Figure 7.5 shows a series of macro definitions that use all three page parameters. For

```
package query
_header_  []                        {_querytitle_}
_header_  [l=en]                     {Search page}
_header_  [v=1]                      {_textquery_}
_header_  [c=demo]                   {<table bgcolor=green>
                                         <tr><td>_querytitle_</td></tr>
                                     </table>}

_header_  [l=fr,v=1,c=hdl] {HDL Page de recherche}
```

Figure 7.5 Illustration of macro precedence.

example, the last line of Figure 7.5 will be used if all three values are specified. But if only two are, say *l=en* and *c=demo*, which version should be used for expansion—the second, which specifies *l=en*, or the fourth, which specifies *c=demo*?

In fact this situation rarely arises. Figure 7.5 purports to be a fragment from the *query* package that defines a *header* macro. It shows a specific exception for the HDL collection which, if generated in French text-only mode, will be headed *HDL Page de recherche*. Another special case is made for the Demo collection. Otherwise the fragment is unremarkable. The text-only mode is special-cased, and a specification for the page title is given in the English language—presumably the macro files for other languages will contain corresponding definitions. In fact, however, this is a made-up example: collection-specific processing is avoided in generic macro packages, and language-specific text is confined to the language macro files.

When conflicts do arise, macro precedence is defined as follows: the *c* (collection) parameter takes precedence over the *v* (graphical vs. text-only interface) one, which takes precedence over the *l* (language) parameter. The definitions in Figure 7.5 happen to fall in reverse preference order. The last is used if it is applicable, otherwise the second last, otherwise the third last, and so on. (However, ordering is *not* used to govern precedence because different parts of a package may be in different macro files.) For example, if the parameter values were *c=hdl*, *v=1*, and *l=en*, the *v=1* version of the *header* macro would be used. It is preferred over the *l=en* version because *v* has a higher precedence than *l*. The specific version with all three arguments set would not be selected because the parameter value for *l* is different.

Like many aspects of Greenstone, the order of macro precedence is not fixed but can be changed. Every site has a configuration file called *main.cfg*, which is discussed in Section 7.4. Macro precedence is governed by a statement in this file that gives the preference order among the three parameters.

Personalizing using macros
Macros are powerful but seem mysterious at first. With a working knowledge of HTML and some practice, they are a quick and easy way to customize your site.

Macros are stored in the top-level *macros* directory. To change the overall look and feel, you can edit the *base* and *style* packages. To change the query page, edit *query.dm*.

Suppose you wanted to personalize the Greenstone home page. Figure 7.6 shows how it looks when you install the software; altering it is one of the first things you will want to do. The relevant macro file is *home.dm*. Instead of editing that, we recommend creating a new file, say *yourhome.dm*, which defines the *home* package in a different way.

Figure 7.7 shows a new home page along with the corresponding *yourhome.dm* file. You can use it as a template for creating your own home page. Each of the *Click here* links takes you to the appropriate page. Figure 7.7b defines a macro called *content*. You can change the text inside the braces to make the page look however you wish. You can include hyperlinks and use all the other facilities that HTML provides. Note that the special characters {, }, \, and _ must be escaped with a backslash to prevent them from being processed by the macro language interpreter.

To make your new home page link in with other digital library pages, you need to use appropriate macros. These appear in Figure 7.7b: *httppagehome*

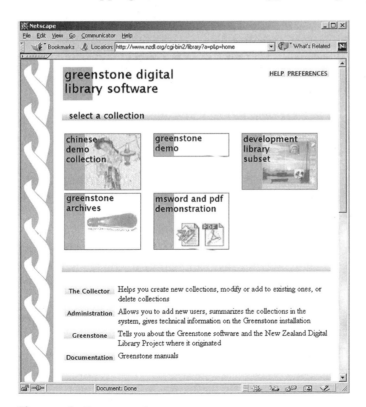

Figure 7.6 Greenstone home page.

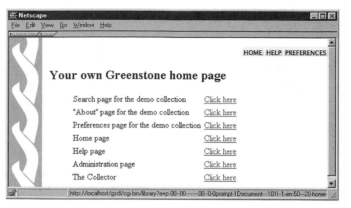

(a)

```
package home
_content_ {

<h2>Your own Greenstone home page</h2>

<ul>
<table>
<tr valign=top><td>Search page for the demo collection<br></td>
    <td><a href="_httpquery_&c=demo">Click here</a></td></tr>

<tr><td>"About" page for the demo collection</td>
    <td><a href="_httppageabout_&c=demo">Click here</a></td></tr>

<tr><td>Preferences page for the demo collection</td>
    <td><a href="_httppagepref_&c=demo">Click here</a></td></tr>

<tr><td>Home page</td>
    <td><a href="_httppagehome_">Click here</a></td></tr>

<tr><td>Help page</td>
    <td><a href="_httppagehelp_">Click here</a></td></tr>

<tr><td>Administration page</td>
    <td><a href="_httppagestatus_">Click here</a></td></tr>

<tr><td>The Collector</td>
    <td><a href="_httppagecollector_">Click here</a></td></tr>

</table>
</ul>

}

# if you dislike the squirly green bar down the left-hand side of the
# page, uncomment these lines:

# _header_ {
#          }
```

(b)

Figure 7.7 Personalizing the home page: (a) new version; (b) *yourhome.dm* file used to create it.

takes you to the home page, *httppagehelp* to the help page, and so on. For some macros you must include a collection name. For example, *_httpquery_&c=demo* specifies the Search page for the Demo collection; for other collections, replace *demo* by the collection name.

The *content* macro does not define any HTML header or footer. To change these on the home page, you must define *header* and *footer* macros in *yourhome.dm*. For example, the squirly green bar down the left-hand side of Greenstone pages is defined in the *header* macro. Making this macro null will remove it, as indicated at the end of Figure 7.7b.

Making macros work

The system reads in the macro files specified in the main configuration file *main.cfg* (see Section 7.4). Name clashes are handled sensibly: the most recent definition takes precedence. To make the system replace the normal home page by that in Figure 7.7, first put *yourhome.dm* into the *macros* directory. Then edit the *main.cfg* configuration file to replace *home.dm* with *yourhome.dm* in the list of macro files that are loaded at start-up.

Macros, like format statements, are interpreted when pages are displayed, so when you alter them the change appears instantly. For the Local Library version you need to restart the system; with other versions changes appear as soon as you reload the page. This makes it easy to experiment with macro definitions.

The collection information database

For each collection there is a database that holds information needed when serving the collection to users. Passing mention was made of this several times in Chapter 6. When describing the building process (Section 6.3), we learned that this database stores all information pertaining to the collection—its name, icons, document OIDs, associated files, and structures that define the classifiers it contains. Now is the time to look at the details of how things are stored.

The collection information database is stored using GDBM, the GNU database manager program (*www.gnu.org*). GDBM implements a flat record structure of key/data pairs, with operations that include storage, retrieval and deletion of records by key, and an unordered traversal of all keys.

Figure 7.8 shows an excerpt from the collection information database that is created when building the Gutenberg collection. (It resides in the collection's *index/text* directory under the collection name with extension *.ldb* or *.bdb*, depending on whether the computer's native format is little-endian or big-endian.) The excerpt was produced using the Greenstone utility program db2txt, which converts the binary database format into the textual form shown. Figure 7.8 contains three records, separated by horizontal rules. The first is a

```
<doctype>doc
<hastxt>1
<Title>The Golf Course Mystery
<Creator>Steele
<archivedir>HASH51e5/98821ed6.dir
<thistype>Paged
<childtype>Paged
<contains>".1;".2;".3;".4;".5;".6;".7;".8;".9;".10;".11;".12;          \
        ".13;".14;".15;".16;".17;".18;".19;".20;".21;".22;            \
        ".23;".24;".25;".26;".27;".28;".29;".30;".31;".32;            \
        ".33;".34;".35;".36;".37;".38;".39;".40;".41;".42;            \
        ".43;".44;".45;".46;".47;".48;".49;".50;".51;".52;            \
        ".53;".54;".55;".56;".57;".58;".59;".60;".61;".62;            \
        ".63;".64;".65;".66;".67;".68;".69;".70;".71;".72;            \
        ".73;".74;".75;".76;".77;".78;".79;".80;".81;".82;            \
        ".83;".84;".85;".86;".87;".88;".89;".90;".91;".92;            \
        ".93;".94;".95;".96;".97;".98;".99;".100;".101;               \
        ".102;".103;".104
<docnum>162283
-----------------------------------------------------------------------
[CL1]
<doctype>classify
<hastxt>0
<childtype>HList
<Title>Title
<numleafdocs>1818
<thistype>Invisible
<contains>".1;".2;".3;".4;".5;".6;".7;".8;".9;".10;".11;".12;          \
        ".13;".14;".15;".16;".17;".18;".19;".20;".21;".22;            \
        ".23;".24
-----------------------------------------------------------------------
[CL1.11]
<doctype>classify
<hastxt>0
<childtype>VList
<Title>K
<numleafdocs>22
<contains>HASH78255bb10d6d5bf3947084;HASH5a36c85ebfb4d7e1056120;        \
        HASHcb6f357d99ff1df380aeb8;HASHfa3f78c1f57b35a354a908;         \
        HASH357fc236dd8d818ba6af1b;HASH0175e5199e2070e0a2e21670;       \
        HASHee1ecd06e6207a5533c3ab;HASH01a8447e42650115258f38ab;       \
        HASH014a624729d626537a24e403;HASH01f2d49d40e3bb7ea4196c08;    \
        HASHbaff553d55b7158b9cbfd4;HASHc6291d49cfadf0cc0257c6;         \
        HASHeb1f590550508a8d8fb3a9;HASHd231b27a93712882a4d3e4;         \
        HASH01b7b0bbe4329d32541cabf5;HASH012d721262a55518dbcab629;    \
        HASH0bb624976dd0effcf94d0c;HASH011ca220779aeaeb17e1ec9a;       \
        HASH017d084491f8d22a791e795d;HASH94166c1a8389842e0ef140;       \
        HASH01eb4615549775aee8e62494;HASH019b46470c94f68a5aa5edc5
```

Figure 7.8 GDBM database for the Gutenberg collection (excerpt).

document entry; the other two are part of the hierarchy created by the *AZList* classifier for titles in the collection. The first line of each record is its key.

The document record relates to the document shown in Figure 7.9 (*The Golf Course Mystery*). It stores the book's title, author, and any other metadata provided (or extracted) when the collection was built. It also records values for internal use: where files associated with this document reside (*archivedir*) and (at the end of the record) the document number used internally by the MG system that is used for full-text retrieval (*docnum*). Note that this is different from

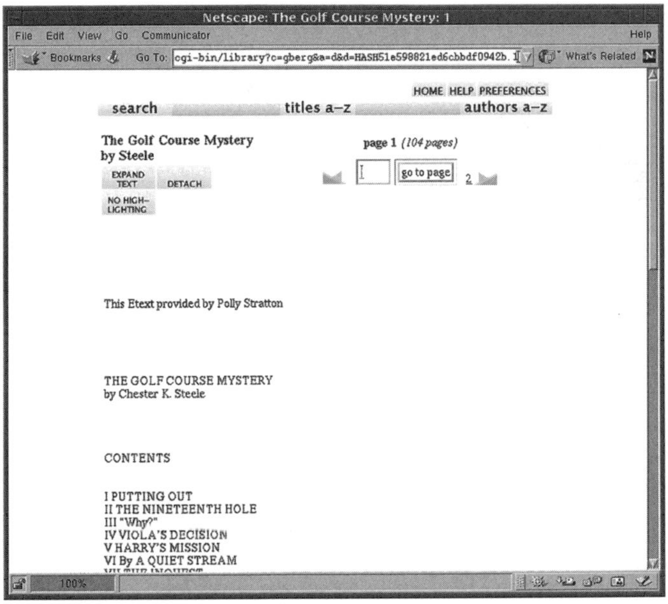

Figure 7.9 *The Golf Course Mystery.*

the OID for the document because MG reallocates document numbers when collections are rebuilt and hence these identifiers are not persistent. Also recorded is the fact that the document contains some text (*hastxt*). The reason for this is that some document sections begin at once with a subsection header. These contain no text themselves—although they do contain subsections—and for them the *hastxt* flag will be 0.

The *contains* field stores a list of elements, separated by semicolons, that point to related records in the database. There is a document record for each individual section and subsection of each document. In the document record the *contains* field is used to point to the nested sections. Subsequent record keys are formed by concatenating the current key with one of the child elements (separated by a period) because this is how OIDs are formed for nested documents. These keys begin with a quotation mark (") because they are expressed relative to the current key. Other database records use absolute keys.

The second record in Figure 7.8 is the top node for the classification hierarchy of *titles A–Z*. In fact, it corresponds to the alphabetic selector list near the top of Figure 7.10. Its children, accessed through the *<contains>* field, include *CL1.1*, *CL1.2*, *CL1.3*, and so on, and correspond to the individual pages for the letters *A*, *B*, *C*, and so on. There are only 24 children rather than the 26 letters of the alphabet: the *AZList* classifier merged the *Q–R* and *Y–Z* entries because they covered only a few titles. There is no text corresponding to this node (*hastxt*=0), and it is a horizontal list (*Hlist*), which is why the alphabetic list appears hori-

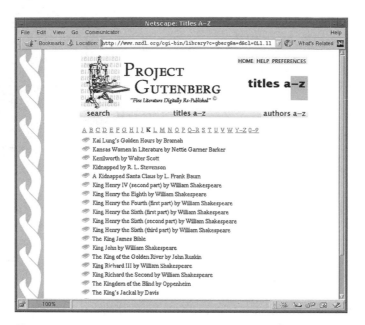

Figure 7.10 Browsing titles in the Gutenberg collection.

zontally. A total of 1,818 documents (*numleafdocs*) are covered by this node. Its type is set to *Invisible*. The reason for this is slightly obscure: in fact it is because the heading for this node is not displayed—it corresponds to the Titles A–Z button in Figure 7.10.

The third record is part of the same classification hierarchy. It describes the 11th child, or node *CL1.11*, of the classifier described in the previous paragraph. This corresponds to the letter *K* in the *AZList* classifier, which is shown as the vertical list (*Vlist*) of titles in Figure 7.10. The children in its *contains* field are the documents themselves: there are 22 of them (although only 18 are visible in Figure 7.10).

More complicated structures are possible. The *contains* field can include a mixture of documents and further *CL* nodes. An example of this can be seen in Figure 3.22b in Chapter 3: this shows a vertical list containing a single document (*Earth Summit Report*) along with eight further *CL* nodes. Arbitrary structures of horizontal and vertical lists (*Hlists* and *Vlists*) are supported by the runtime system, although existing classifiers only put horizontal lists at the uppermost level.

7.3 Responding to user requests

We now describe how the runtime system responds to user requests, using the About page in Figure 7.4a as an example. Unlike other screen shots in this book, this one shows the URL at the top. As the URL indicates, the page is generated as a result of running the CGI script *library*. This is the program mentioned in Section 7.1 that comprises a receptionist and collection server connected by the null protocol.

The arguments to *library* can also be seen in the URL. They are *c=gberg*, *a=p*, and *p=about* and can be interpreted as follows:

> For the Project Gutenberg collection (collection *c=gberg*), the action is to generate a page (action *a=p*), and the page to generate is called "about" (page *p=about*).

Collection, *action*, and *page* are standard arguments used in URLs to communicate with the *library* program. Incidentally we have already encountered the *c* argument in the discussion in Section 7.2 of the macro language. The other two values used as macro parameters, *l* for the language specification and *v* for text-only mode, may also appear in URLs (although they need not because they have standard defaults). There are many other possible arguments to the *library* program that can be supplied using the CGI mechanism by embedding them within a URL.

Figure 7.11 illustrates the main components of the runtime system. Both receptionist and collection server comprise a number of separate modules that

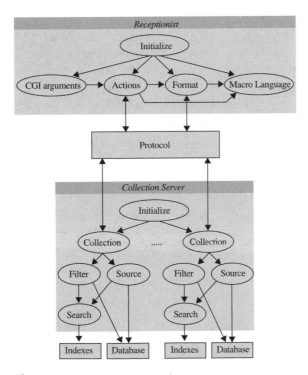

Figure 7.11 Greenstone runtime system.

we call *objects*. At the top, the receptionist first initializes its objects, then parses the CGI arguments to decide which action to call. The *action* argument determines what the program is supposed to do and affects how the other arguments are processed. In performing the action, the receptionist uses the protocol to communicate with the collection server, which is responsible for accessing the content of the collection. The result, aided by the format and macro language components, is used to generate a Web page in response to the original request.

The macro language is used to ensure that the Web pages have a consistent style. Interacting with the library generates the bare bones of Web pages; the macros wrap them in flesh. During initialization, the Macro Language object in Figure 7.11 reads the macro files, parses them, and stores the result in memory. Any action can use the Macro Language object to expand a macro. It can even create new macro definitions and override existing ones, adding a dynamic dimension to macro use. Special *dynamic macros* are how the receptionist gets results onto Web pages.

When the receptionist generates the page in Figure 7.4a, it uses the protocol to retrieve the "About this collection" text from the collection server and stores it as the special dynamic macro *collectionextra*. The content of the About page is created by expanding the *content* macro in Figure 7.4b. This in turn expands *textabout*, which itself accesses *collectionextra*, which had just been dynamically defined by the receptionist. Voilà.

The receptionist's remaining component is the Format object in Figure 7.11. Chapter 6 described how format statements in the collection configuration file affect the presentation of particular pieces of information. The Format object's main task is to parse and evaluate these statements. As we learned in Section 6.6, these can include references to metadata in square brackets (e.g., *[Title]*), which need to be retrieved from the collection server. The Format object and the Macro Language object interact with each other, because format statements can include macros that, when expanded, include metadata, which when expanded include macros, and so on.

The collection server is shown in the lower part of Figure 7.11. It too undergoes an initialization process, setting up Filter and Source objects to respond to incoming protocol requests, and a Search object to assist in this task. Ultimately these access the indexes and the collection information database, both formed during collection building.

To encourage extensibility and flexibility, inheritance is used widely—particularly within Action, Filter, Source, and Search objects. For a simple digital library dedicated to text-based collections, this means that you need to learn slightly more to program the system. However, it also means that the MG and GDBM subsystems could easily be replaced should the need arise. Furthermore, the software architecture is rich enough to support full multimedia capabilities, such as controlling the interface through speech input or submitting queries as graphically drawn pictures.

Next we work through examples of a user interacting with the system and describe what goes on behind the scenes. We assume that all objects are correctly initialized; initialization is a rather intricate procedure.

Performing a search

When a user submits a query by pressing Begin Search on the Search page, a new action is invoked that ends up by generating a new Web page using the macro language. Figure 7.12 shows the result of searching the Project Gutenberg collection for the name *Darcy*. Buried deep within the HTML of the original Search page is the statement $a=q$. When the Search button is pressed, this statement is activated and sets the new action to be a query action. Executing this sets up a call through the protocol to the designated collection's Filter object ($c=gberg$).

Filters are a central function of collection servers. Designed to fulfill the requirements of both searching and browsing activities, they provide a way of selecting a subset of information from a collection. There are two types of filter: *query* filters and *browse* filters. Query filters are implemented using the MG full-text search system, and browse filters are implemented using the GDBM database scheme to access the collection information database—but the software

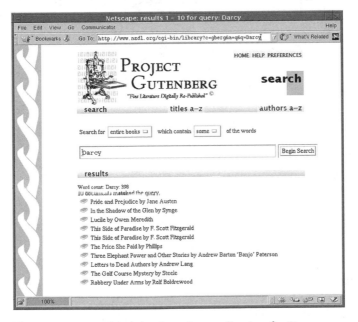

Figure 7.12 Searching the Gutenberg collection for *Darcy*.

uses the mechanism of virtual inheritance to ensure that other schemes can equally well be used.

In this case the query action sets up a filter request by

- setting the filter request to have the type *Query Filter*
- storing the user's search preferences—case-folding, stemming, and so on—in the filter request
- calling the *filter*() function using the null protocol

Calls to the protocol are synchronous. The receptionist is blocked until the filter request has been processed by the collection server and any data generated has been returned.

When a protocol call of type *QueryFilter* is made, the Filter object (in Figure 7.11) decodes the options and makes a call to the Search object, which uses MG to do the actual search. The role of the Search object is to provide an abstract program interface that supports searching, regardless of the underlying search tool being used. The format used to return results also enforces abstraction, requiring the Search object to translate the data generated by the search tool into a standard form.

Once the search results have been returned to the receptionist, the action proceeds by formatting the results for display, using the Format object and the Macro Language. As Figure 7.12 shows, this involves generating the standard header, footer, navigation bar, and background; repeating the main part of the query page just beneath the navigation bar; and displaying a book icon, title, and author for each matching entry. The format of this last part is governed by the *format SearchVList* statement in the collection configuration file. Before *Title* and *Author* metadata can be displayed, they must be retrieved from the collection server. This requires further calls to the protocol, this time using *Browse-Filter*.

Retrieving a document

Following the previous query for *Darcy*, consider what happens when a document is displayed. Figure 7.9 shows the result of clicking on the icon beside *The Golf Course Mystery* in Figure 7.12.

The source text for the Gutenberg collection comprises one long file per book. At build time these files are split into separate pages every 200 lines or so, and relevant information for each page is stored in the indexes and collection information database. The top of Figure 7.9 shows that this book contains 104 computer-generated pages, and below it is the beginning of page one: who entered it, the title, the author, and the beginnings of a table of contents (this table forms part of the Gutenberg source text and was not generated by Greenstone). At the top left are buttons that control the document's appearance. At the top right is a navigation aid for reaching other pages in the book.

The action for retrieving documents is specified by setting $a=d$ and takes several additional arguments. Most important is the document to retrieve: this document is specified through the d variable. In Figure 7.9 it is set to $d=HASH51e598821ed6cbbdf0942b.1$ to retrieve the first page of the document with the identifier $HASH51e598821ed6cbbdf0942b$, known in more friendly terms as *The Golf Course Mystery*. There are further variables: whether query term highlighting is on or off (hl) and which page within a book is displayed (gt). These variables are used to support the activities offered by the buttons in Figure 7.9; defaults are used if any variables are omitted.

The action follows a similar procedure to the query action: appraise the CGI arguments, access the collection server using the protocol, and use the result to generate a Web page. Options relating to the document are decoded from the arguments and stored for further work. To retrieve the document from the collection server, only the document identifier is needed to set up the protocol call to *get_document*(). Once the text is returned, it is formatted. To achieve this the code for the document action accesses the stored arguments and makes use of the Format object and the Macro Language.

Browsing a hierarchical classifier

Figure 7.10 shows an example of browsing, where the user has chosen *Titles A-Z* and accessed the hyperlink for the letter *K*. The action that supports this is also the document action, given by the argument $a=d$ as before. However, whereas before a *d* variable was included, this time there is none. Instead the relevant node of the classification hierarchy is specified by the variable *cl*. In our case this represents titles grouped under the letter *K*. This list was formed at build time and stored in the collection information database. The numbering scheme for classifiers was described in Chapter 6 (Section 6.7, under "Formatting Lists"). The top-level classifier node for titles in our example is *CL1*, and the page sought is generated by setting $cl=CL1.11$, the bucket for *K* being the 11th in the alphabetic list. This can be seen in the URL at the top of Figure 7.10.

To process a *cl* document request, the Filter object is used to retrieve the node over the protocol. Depending on the data returned, further protocol calls are made to obtain document metadata. In this case the titles of the books are retrieved. However, if the node were an interior one whose children are themselves nodes, the titles of the child nodes would be retrieved. From a coding point of view, this amounts to the same thing and is handled by the same mechanism.

Finally all the retrieved information is bound together using the macro language to produce the Web page shown in Figure 7.10.

Generating the home page

As a final example, we look at generating the Greenstone home page. Figure 7.6 shows the home page of the default installation after some test collections have been installed. Its URL, visible at the top of the screen, includes the arguments $a=p$ and $p=home$. Like the About This Collection page, this is generated by a page action ($a=p$), but this time the page to produce is *home* ($p=home$). The macro language therefore accesses the content of *home.dm*. There is no need to use the c variable to specify a collection.

The purpose of the home page is to show what collections are available. Clicking on each icon takes the user to the About This Collection page for that collection. The menu of collections is dynamically generated every time the page is loaded, based on those that are in the file system at that time. When a new collection comes online, it automatically appears on the home page when that page is reloaded (provided the collection is stipulated to be "public").

To do this the receptionist again uses the protocol. As part of appraising the arguments, the page action code is programmed to detect the special case when $p=home$. Then the action uses the protocol call *get_collection_list*() to establish the current set of online collections. For each of these it calls *get_collectinfo*() to obtain information about it. This information includes whether the collection is publicly available, when it was last built, how many documents it contains, the URL for the collection's icon (if any), and the collection's full name. This information is used to generate an appropriate entry for the collection on the home page.

Using the protocol

Having now had a glimpse of how the interaction between receptionist and collection server works, we can complete our description of the protocol. Table 7.1 lists the function calls to the protocol, with a summary for each entry.

Some of these have already been mentioned. Given an OID, *get_document*() retrieves the corresponding document or document section from the collection server. As we have just seen, *get_collection_list*() returns a list of collections, while *get_collectinfo*() gives information about an individual collection.

Filter(), also mentioned earlier, supports searching and browsing. Given a Filter type and option settings, it accesses the content of the named collections to produce a result set that is filtered in accordance with the options. The options also determine what data is returned: examples include query term frequency and document metadata—we expand upon this later. Two protocol calls are provided to allow a receptionist to interrogate a collection server to find out what filters and options are supported and so dynamically configure itself to take full advantage of the services offered by a particular server: *get_filterinfo*()

Table 7.1 List of protocol calls.

Protocol call	Function
get_protocol_name()	Returns the name of this protocol.
get_collection_list()	Returns the list of collections that this protocol knows about.
get_collectinfo()	Obtains general information about the named collection.
has_collection()	Returns *true* if the protocol can communicate with the named collection.
ping()	Returns *true* if a successful connection was made to the named collection.
filter()	Supports searching and browsing by filtering the result set as specified.
get_filterinfo()	Gets a list of all filters for the named collection.
get_filteroptions()	Gets all options for a particular filter within the named collection.
get_document()	Gets a document or section of a document.

and *get_filteroptions*(). The former returns a list of all Filters for the named collection; the latter returns a list of options for a particular Filter.

Of the protocol calls in Table 7.1 that have not already been mentioned, *has_collection*() and *ping*() provide yes/no answers to questions about individual collections: "Does the collection exist on this server?" and "Is it running?" respectively.

The purpose of *get_protocol_name*() is to support multiple protocols. Two protocols were mentioned in Section 7.1: the null protocol and the CORBA scheme that allows a set of collections to be distributed over a network. A third is Z39.50, a standard communications protocol used by library systems internationally to give users and other libraries remote access to catalog records (see Section 8.5). *Get_protocol_name*() returns a value that identifies which protocol is being used and is called by protocol-sensitive parts of the runtime system to decide which piece of code to execute.

Figure 7.13 shows the software interface to the filter mechanism. For example, by setting the filter name to *QueryFilter*, specifying the collection name to be *oralhist*, and storing the query string *VE day* in *filterOptions*, the Oral History collection is searched for those words. (In fact, Figure 3.7 in Chapter 3 showed one of the results for that query.) Defaults are used throughout to supply any unspecified options. In this case stemming defaults to *on* and case-matching to *off*.

Information returned by *filter*() is stored in two variables: *response* and *error*. The code fragment in Figure 7.13 would be followed by a check to determine whether an error had occurred, and if not, the document identifiers returned in *response* would be accessed. Depending on the desired output, further calls to *filter*() might be made to retrieve additional document details and metadata. Alternatively the document retrieval part of the protocol could be used to access

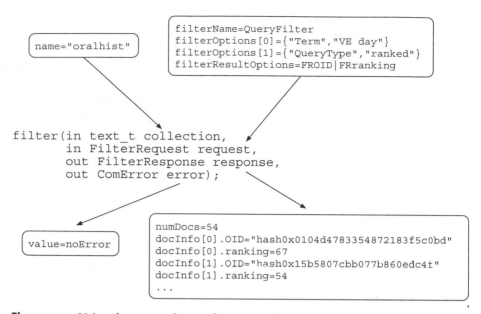

Figure 7.13 Using the protocol to perform a search.

the contents of individual documents. Control is provided over the document type, format, and sections returned.

The protocol is stateless, or—to be more accurate—designed for a stateless server. This simplifies the server code but complicates life for receptionists because they must store the state of play if a continuous interactive session is to be supported.

The following subsections present two examples that demonstrate use of the Greenstone protocol. The first is a C++ receptionist similar to the null protocol receptionist, augmented to access remote collections as well as local ones. The second is an interactive client application written in Java for accessing bibliographic records. Both use CORBA to communicate with remote Greenstone collection servers.

Remote access through a C++ receptionist

Figure 7.14 shows a personal page of the Kids' Digital Library (the home page was depicted in Figure 3.2 of Chapter 3). It has a C++ receptionist that integrates local and remote collections. The local collections are small and personalized; the remote ones are larger and more bountiful.

The home page has been stylized by modifying the macro files. The set of links in the center show the collections available to the pupil. On the left are support services: a workspace for creative writing, a submission process for completed stories and poems, a bulletin board where selected works are dis-

Figure 7.14 Kids' Digital Library. Middlesex University,
London, England.

cussed and annotated, and training packages to help users learn about the working environment. The receptionist asks the user—Jamie, in this case—to log in
first. The class teacher has a special account from which collections can be
updated with new stories, usernames can be created for new pupils, and so
forth.

From this page a pupil can view the collections or access the support services
just mentioned. Poems and Short Stories are collections of finished works by the
pupils, vetted by the teacher. They can be searched by full text, author, and title,
or browsed by author and title. Pictures & Images, Audio Sounds, and Ideas are
collections pulled together from various sources to provide resources and ideas
for students; they too are searchable and browsable. Finally, the Personal Bookmarks collection, which is specific to each particular user, is formed by downloading every page mentioned in the user's bookmark files. The collection is
fully indexed and browsable by title and subject folder.

The idea behind the Bookmarks collection is that pupils browse the Web
using a variety of strategies for finding information pertinent to their work,
bookmarking relevant pages. Upon activating "rebuild this collection" through
a hyperlink on the collection's page, new Web pages are downloaded, any existing ones that have changed are updated, and the collection is rebuilt.

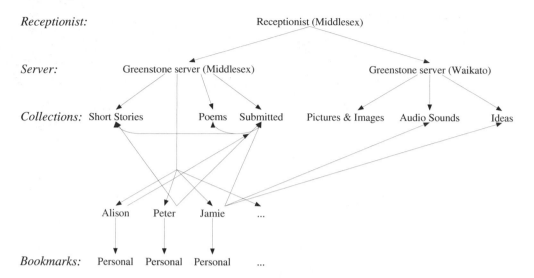

Receptionist:

Server:

Collections:

Bookmarks:

Figure 7.15 Implementing the Kids' Digital Library using the protocol.

Figure 7.15 shows the structures underlying the Kids' Digital Library environment. Behind the scenes, collections are accessed from two servers: one local, the other remote. Small collections that are rebuilt frequently, such as personal bookmarks, short stories, and the bulletin board, are served locally (in London, as it happens). The larger collections—intended as a source of inspiration—do not change so rapidly and are served remotely by a computer (in New Zealand) that is dedicated to supporting digital library collections. In Figure 7.15 Jamie is accessing the remote Sounds and Ideas collections as a basis for creative writing, and submitting his composition for the teacher's perusal.

This integrated environment was easily constructed. Support for multiple protocols is already built into Greenstone. Instead of creating a single object of type Null Protocol, as C++ receptionists usually do, the Kids' Digital Library receptionist creates both a Null Protocol object for local collections and a CORBA Protocol object connected to the New Zealand Digital Library server. Both are stored in the protocol list, which is available to the rest of the receptionist code.

By default, receptionists iterate through the list of protocols, seeking the right object to respond to the CGI arguments that have been supplied, or (if appropriate) making calls to every protocol object in the list. In the standard C++ receptionist this list contains just one item, but in the Kids' Digital Library receptionist, it has two. To generate the home page in Figure 7.14, for example, the receptionist first calls *get_collection_list*() for the null protocol, returning the collections that are available locally, and then calls *get_collection_list*() for the CORBA-based protocol, returning the publicly available collections on the New

Zealand Digital Library server. The information that is returned is then combined into a suitable HTML page.

In Greenstone, client-side authentication is built into the receptionist's actions, while server-side authentication is supported using external mechanisms. In Chapter 8 we encounter systems that take a different approach, embedding authentication in the protocol itself.

Remote access through a Java receptionist

Figure 7.16 illustrates a Greenstone receptionist written in Java that implements a client-side bibliographic search tool. The protocol is used to access a collection server that contains citations on human-computer interaction; the receptionist displays the search results graphically, based on year of publication and the matching relevance score. The display is enhanced by color: each query term is colored differently, and citations that include it are displayed in that color. For documents that contain more than one query term, the box is divided into colored strips (like the two boxes at the top right). The scroll bars let you zoom and pan around the search set; clicking on a document box pops up a new window that includes its full citation.

The implementation works like this. When the receptionist is started, it establishes contact with the remote site named in its configuration file through

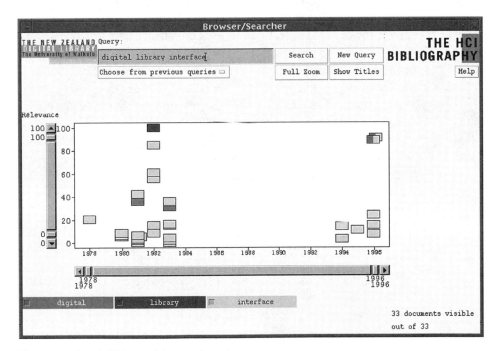

Figure 7.16 A bibliographic search tool.

CORBA-specific initialization code, whereupon a search window appears. (If the remote server is not running or cannot be contacted, an error message is produced and the application terminates.) When a user enters a query and presses the Search button, a Filter object of type *QueryFilter* is created (like that shown in Figure 7.13) and initialized to request a case-insensitive ranked query with no stemming. This is dispatched through CORBA as a *filter*() call.

The response—which is synchronous, meaning that the client application is blocked until the reply is received—returns either an error condition or the information requested. Assuming no errors, the receptionist stores the information in its own data structures. Given this data, it can assign colors to the search terms, produce the graphical display of results, and respond to further user interaction. When the user zooms or pans, the graph is redrawn from the stored information. When one of the document boxes is clicked, a further protocol request is made, this time using *get_document*() to obtain the full citation. The data returned is displayed in a popup window.

Actions

Everything the null protocol receptionist does begins as a specification of an "action" as one of the arguments of a Greenstone URL. We have already met three: page actions, document actions, and query actions. Page actions generate HTML Web pages in conjunction with the Macro object. Document actions retrieve documents or document sections. They also retrieve other information provided by the collection server, such as parts of the classification hierarchy, or formatting information. Query actions perform a search. Table 7.2 lists the actions that are implemented.

All actions derive from a single base action using a programming mechanism called *virtual inheritance* to aid extensibility.

Other actions are concerned with authentication. The *authen* action prompts the user for a user name and password and checks whether they are valid. Subsequent *authen* actions in the same dialog will succeed automatically, except that authentication expires and the user has to log in again if sufficient time elapses. The *users* action supports the addition of new users and removal of existing ones; it also allows a user's permissions to be altered. The first step in executing a *users* action is to issue an *authen* action to check that the current user has permission to make the change.

The Collector subsystem is implemented using a *collector* action. Here also the first step is to issue an *authen* action to check that the user has permission to build collections.

The remaining actions perform miscellaneous tasks. Greenstone has an administrator facility (mentioned in the next section) that gives information about the

Table 7.2 Action.

Actions	Function
action	Base class for virtual inheritance.
page	Generate a Web page.
document	Retrieve items from a collection server.
query	Perform a search.
authen	Authenticate the user.
users	Add and delete users and their access permissions.
collector	Generate the pages for the Collector.
status	Generate the administration pages.
extlink	Take a user to an external URL.
ping	Check to see whether a collection is online.
tip	Bring up a random tip for the user.

system; this is handled by the *status* action. Sometimes collections take a user directly to a URL that is external to a collection, and this may, depending on a setting on the Preferences page, generate an alert page first: this is handled by the *extlink* action. Finally, *ping* checks to see whether a particular collection is online.

7.4 Operational aspects

Many aspects of a digital library site need to be set up individually for each installation. Some, like the name of the directory where the software is kept and the HTTP address of the system, define the whereabouts of the system—what logical space it occupies. Others concern people and how they are treated: the e-mail address of the system maintainer, whether logs of user activity are kept, and whether Internet "cookies" are used to identify users. Still others control what users can do with the system—such as whether the Collector subsystem is enabled, which lets authorized users create new collections and modify existing ones as described in Chapter 6 (Section 6.2).

Just as the structure of each individual collection is governed by a collection configuration file, these global aspects of system operation are also determined by configuration files. There are two. One, the *site configuration file* (*gsdlsite.cfg*, found in the Greenstone *cgi-bin* directory), defines parameters that are particular to a given site, thereby tailoring the software to work at that site. The other, the *main configuration file* (*main.cfg*, found in the top-level *etc* directory), sets parameters for the receptionist and contains information common to the interface of all collections served by the site. With it you can control such things as the languages that the interface can use and what logs of user activity are kept.

Greenstone also has an administrator facility that gives information about the entire system, including all collections it offers. It displays the installation's configuration files and allows them to be modified. It allows you to examine the user logs that record usage and the error logs that record internal errors. It enables you to authorize others to build collections and add new material to existing ones—in other words, it is used to set up the Collector's login accounts that we met at the beginning of Section 6.2. All these facilities are accessed interactively from the menu items. Of course they can only be accessed by a person who has been authorized to act as system administrator: just as access to the Collector is restricted to authorized users, so is access to the administrator facility.

This section describes the structure and content of the configuration files, since they affect the operation of the system at delivery time.

Configuring the receptionist

Table 7.3 shows the items that can occur in the main configuration file. They concern site maintenance and logging, language support, and default values for page parameters and CGI arguments. In addition, another one—the first in Table 7.3—determines which macros are loaded; this was mentioned at the end of the description of the macro language in Section 7.2.

The best way to learn about the various configuration options possible is to experiment with the *main.cfg* file itself. Note that if you are using the "local library" version, you need to restart the server before any configuration changes take effect.

Site maintenance

Each digital library installation has a person who is responsible for maintaining it. The maintainer checks the log file, which records internal errors—such as when a collection is inaccessible or a user sees the "Oops" text in the *content* macro shown earlier. This person also receives mail relating to the operation of the system—for example, when the Collector is used to build new collections or delete old ones. The maintainer's e-mail address is specified in the configuration file (if it is null, mail events are disabled). The mail server can also be specified. If it is null, the domain of the *maintainer* is used (e.g., if the maintainer is *me@example.com*, the default is *mail.example.com*). If this does not resolve to a valid mail server, automatic e-mail notification will not work.

Just as automatic e-mail notifications help a system maintainer to keep an installation in good working order, the Collector subsystem automatically sends notification of certain events to those in charge of particular collections, such as someone adding information to the collection, or rebuilding it. These events are

Table 7.3 Configuration options for site maintenance and logging.

Option	Value	Purpose
macrofiles	list of macro file names	Specify macros loaded by the receptionist
maintainer	e-mail address	Specify e-mail address of the site maintainer to be used for notification purposes
MailServer	mail server name	Specify outgoing mail server for this site
EmailUserEvents	*enabled* or *disabled*	Notify a collection's maintainer of changes to that collection
EmailEvents	*enabled* or *disabled*	Mail the system maintainer every time an event occurs for any collection
collector	*enabled* or *disabled*	Specify whether to make the Collector available
status	*enabled* or *disabled*	Specify whether to make the Administrator pages available
LogEvents	*AllEvents, CollectorEvents,* or *disabled*	Specify whether to log certain events
logcgiargs	*true* or *false*	Specify whether to log usage in *usage.txt*
usecookies	*true* or *false*	Specify whether to log information about users (using cookies)
LogDateFormat	*LocalTime, UTCTime,* or *Absolute*	Specify format for logging time stamps
Encoding	*shortname, longname, map,* and *multibyte*	Specify a possible character encoding for the interface
Language	*shortname, longname,* and *default_encoding*	Specify a possible language for the interface
pageparam	*l, c,* or *v*	Specify a default for a page parameter
macroprecedence	list of *l, c,* and *v*	Specify parameter precedence when expanding macros
cgiarg	*shortname, longname, multiplechar, argdefault, defaultstatus,* and *savedarginfo*	Define defaults for a CGI argument

recorded in a log file (see next subsection); in addition, an automatic e-mail notification can be sent whenever an item is logged. Because this can become a burden for active experimental systems, particularly during the debugging and commissioning stages, it can be controlled by switches in the configuration file that enable or disable automatic notification of events related to a particular collection to its maintainer (*EmailUserEvents*). These are events that the maintainer of a multiuser digital library might want to monitor, and events for all collections can be sent to the system maintainer (*EmailEvents*).

Various other components of the digital library system can be enabled or disabled. Sites that aim to offer a comprehensive, polished service to others will probably prefer not to enable the Collector subsystem because under no circumstances would end users be permitted to build collections on such sites. Similarly, the administrative facility described earlier can be turned off.

Logging

Three kinds of log are maintained: an error log, an events log, and a usage log (recorded in the files *errors.txt*, *events.txt*, and *usage.txt* in the *etc* subdirectory of the file structure). The error log, which is permanently enabled, contains messages relating to initialization and operational errors: it is only really of interest to people maintaining the software.

We have mentioned events: they are generated by the Collector when people build, delete, or modify collections. They can be logged with messages such as "sjboddie just successfully built a collection" in the events log file (controlled by the *LogEvents* switch). The collection maintainer or system maintainer can be automatically notified of logged events as described previously.

All user activity—every page that each user visits—can be recorded by the Greenstone software, although no personal names are included in the logs. Each user action is effectively defined by the set of CGI arguments that characterizes that action, and these are what is logged. Disabled by default, logging is enabled using the switches *logcgiargs* and *usecookies* in the main configuration file. Both options are false by default: no logging is done unless they are set. It is the first option that actually turns logging on and off. If the second is activated as well, a unique identification code is assigned to each user, which enables individual users' interactions to be traced through the log file.

Each line in the user log records a page visited. Each entry contains a time stamp, the address of the user's computer, the name of the user's Web browser, the name of the library program being run, and the arguments transmitted to that program by the CGI mechanism. The format used for the time stamp can be altered with *LogDateFormat*—the local time in the format "Thu Dec 07 12:34 NZDT 2000," the UTC time which is the same format but expressed as Greenwich Mean Time, or as an integer representing the number of seconds since 00:00:00 01/01/1970 GMT.

Figure 7.17 shows an example log entry, split up into these components. This entry, which occurred on 7 Dec 2000 from a site at *massey.ac.nz*, is displaying a page (action *a=p*) which is the home page (page *p=home*) of the Māori newspaper collection (collection *c=niupepa*). Many of the other arguments have default values—for example, the language is English (*l=en*) and the display is not text-only (*v=0*). The user's browser is Netscape (internally, Netscape is called "Mozilla"). The last CGI argument, *z*, is an identification code or *cookie* gener-

```
/fast-cgi-bin/niupepalibrary                                    Library program
its-www1.massey.ac.nz                                           User's computer


[Thu Dec 07 23:47:00 NZDT 2000]                                 Time stamp
(a=p, b=0, bcp=, beu=, c=niupepa, cc=, ccp=0, ccs=0, cl=, cm=, cq2=, d=, e=,     Arguments
er=, f=0, fc=1, gc=0, gg=text, gt=0, h=, h2=, hl=1, hp=, il=1, j=, j2=, k=1,
ky=, l=en, m=50, n=, n2=, o=20, p=home, pw=, q=, q2=, r=1, s=0, sp=frameset,
t=1, ua=, uan=, ug=, uma=listusers, umc=, umnpw1=, umnpw2=, umpw=, umug=,
umun=, umus=, un=, us=invalid, v=0, w=w, x=0, z=130.123.128.4-950647871)
"Mozilla/4.08 [en] (Win95; I ;Nav)"                             User's browser
```

Figure 7.17 Entry in the usage log.

ated by the user's browser: it comprises the computer's IP number followed by the time stamp when the user first accessed the digital library.

When logging is enabled, every action by every user is logged—even the pages generated to inspect the log files!

Language support

Two entries in the main configuration file control the way that languages are handled by determining which encodings and languages can be chosen on the Preferences page.

Encoding statements specify the different types of character encoding that can be selected. The UTF-8 version of Unicode, which has standard ASCII as a subset, is handled internally and should always be enabled. But there are many other possible encodings. For example, the Big-5 encoding scheme is frequently used for traditional Chinese text. The standard file *main.cfg* specifies many encodings, most of which are commented out. To enable an encoding, remove the comment character (#).

Each encoding statement in the main configuration file relates to a particular coding method and defines four attributes. First comes the standard short label for the encoding. This must always be specified. For the Big-5 encoding, for example, it is *big5*. Second comes the "long" name of the encoding, the name that will be displayed in the menu on the Preferences page. If it is absent, the standard label is used instead. For the Big-5 encoding, the long name is given as *Chinese Traditional (Big5)*. Third is the name of a mapping file that converts the encoding to and from Unicode; these are kept in the top-level *mappings* directory. This value is mandatory for everything except UTF-8. Fourth is a flag that indicates that the character set requires more than one byte per character—which, for example, Big-5 does.

The second kind of language-related configuration file entry specifies what user interface languages can be selected. Language macros must be specified for each named language. Again many examples appear in the standard main configuration file.

Each language statement relates to a particular language and specifies three attributes. The first is a standard label for the language—in this case the ISO 639 two-letter language symbol—and must be specified, while the second is the name used for the language in the Preferences menu, and defaults to the short name if absent. Finally comes the preferred encoding for this language.

Page parameters

Page parameters are the three parameters in the macro files that affect the display of each page produced in the interface, introduced in Section 7.2. One (l) determines the interface language, another (c) the current collection, and the third (v) whether the interface is graphical or text-only.

It is sometimes useful to be able to change the default values for page parameters. For example, to change the default interface language to French, which would be appropriate for an installation in France, the language parameter should default to French rather than the built-in default, which is English. This can be accomplished by a statement in the main configuration file:

```
pageparam l fr
```

This mechanism avoids the need to change the default settings given in the source code and recompile it.

We already mentioned when discussing macros (Section 7.2) that the order of macro precedence is not fixed but can be changed by a *macroprecedence* statement in the main configuration file. The line

```
macroprecedence c,v,l
```

defines the ordering normally used, c (the collection) taking precedence over v (graphical vs. text-only interface) taking precedence over l (the language).

CGI arguments

The receptionist program takes parameter values supplied in the form of CGI arguments—page parameters are a special case. There are many different parameters—as the log entry in Figure 7.17 shows—and the software defines default values for all of them. But sometimes it is useful to change the defaults. For example, if the URL of the *library* program is given without any arguments, which page should be displayed? To ensure that the default is to display the home page, the *action* argument should default to generating a page (action $a=p$), and the page to generate should default to the home page (page $p=home$). This is accomplished by these two statements in the main configuration file:

```
cgiarg shortname=a argdefault=p
cgiarg shortname=p argdefault=home
```

The *cgiarg* configuration option takes up to six different values, of which *short-name* and *argdefault* are two. These values correspond to different properties of the CGI argument. The other four include a more meaningful description of the action, in the form of its long name; whether it represents a single or multiple character value; what happens when more than one default value is supplied (since defaults can also be set in collection configuration files); and whether or not the value is preserved at the end of this action.

Configuring the site

The site configuration file sets variables that are used by the library software and Web server at runtime, and it resides in the same directory as the *library* program. The install procedure creates a generic site configuration file based on your installation choices. Table 7.4 describes the lines in this file. In addition, for the system to work properly, access permissions for certain files must be set up appropriately.

The first line in Table 7.4 simply points to the directory in which the software is installed (on the default Windows installation, this is *C:\Program Files\gsdl*). The second line gives the Web address of this directory: this ensures that Greenstone URLs are directed to the correct place. You do not need this if the document root on your Web server is set to the Greenstone home directory. The third gives the Web address of the directory containing the images for the user interface (*C:\Program Files\gsdl\images* in the default installation). In the standard installation this is *httpprefix/images*. The fourth gives the Web address of the Greenstone CGI program, called *library*. This is not required by most Web servers (including Apache).

The final entry in Table 7.4 is only used by versions that are compiled with the Fast-CGI option enabled. The standard binary distribution does not include this option because not all Web servers are configured to support it; in this case the *maxrequests* statement should be ignored. If available, Fast-CGI speeds up the execution of CGI programs by keeping them in memory between invoca-

Table 7.4 Lines in *gsdlsite.cfg*.

Line	Function
gsdlhome	A path to the Greenstone home directory
httpprefix	The Web address of the Greenstone home directory
httpimage	The Web address of the directory containing the images for the user interface
gwcgi	The Web address of the *library* CGI script
maxrequests	The number of requests Fast-CGI should process before it exits

tions rather than loading them from disk every time a Web page is requested. However, the amount of memory used grows steadily while the program remains in memory. Once a certain number of pages (*maxrequests*) have been generated, the program quits, freeing all space, and on the next request for a Web page it is reinitialized. If you use Fast-CGI, set this parameter to a large value, such as 10,000 (unless you are debugging modifications to the *library* program).

7.5   Notes and sources

The Greenstone software is written in C++ and makes extensive use of virtual inheritance. To understand the details you will need at least a superficial knowledge of this language and of the C++ Standard Template Library, which provides a foundation for the runtime system. To learn more about this language, Deitel and Deitel (2001) provide a comprehensive tutorial, while Stroustrup (2001) is the definitive reference. The Standard Template Library (STL) C++ library is from Silicon Graphics (*www.sgi.com*). For a full description you should consult the official STL reference manual, available online at *www.sgi.com*, or one of the many STL textbooks—for example, Josuttis (1999).

The Venn diagram interface for graphical Boolean queries is called Vquery and is described by Jones, McInnes, and Staveley (1999). The Fast-CGI scheme for running CGI scripts without them having to reinitialize each time is described at *www.fastcgi.com*. Slama, Garbis, and Russell (1999) give a thorough account of the CORBA protocol and its use.

Bainbridge et al. (2001) give more information about the Greenstone protocol. The Managing Gigabytes compression and indexing software is thoroughly described by Witten, Moffat, and Bell (1999).

8 Interoperability

Standards and protocols

We complained at the beginning of Chapter 4 that it is difficult to write a book about how to build digital libraries because the field is in flux and the ground shifts under your feet as you work. It is even more difficult to provide a comprehensive software system to illustrate the ideas in the book and form a basis for the reader's own library because reliable software takes time to build and is inevitably based on a design that was made some time ago. We have done our best to show you how to build a digital library and provide a state-of-the-art software system to use as a foundation for your own work. Now, however, it is time to look around and see what news is breaking and what people will be doing next.

We learned in Chapter 5 about the extensible markup language, XML, and the family of open standards that have built up around it. XML is a flexible framework for describing document structure and metadata. In fact, there are other developments centered upon XML, which will probably also have far-reaching effects on digital libraries of the future. We describe some of them in this chapter. One concerns naming: how are we to name documents in this brave new Web world, where so much changes so quickly? Another concerns linking. The "hyperlink" has served us well as a central feature of the Web, but plain hyperlinks are rather rudimentary—far more can be done. Historically hypertext predates the Web, and researchers were busily pursuing the idea when the Web burst onto the scene in 1993. It was like a supernova exploding in the sky nearby: the effect was so dramatic that other work in the area was outshone, virtually obliterated. We were blinded! But the Web as we know it uses hyperlinks in a primitive way, and by now our eyes have accommodated to the point where we can see what to do next. A final issue is data types. In essence the document type description (DTD) describes a data type that represents a document, but more general data needs richer facilities. Also, DTDs, although they resemble it closely, are not written in proper XML, an inelegance that a later development has rectified.

A digital library is a collection of "resources." So are a database, a shopping catalog, an atlas, an FTP site, and a list of e-mail addresses. There are countless collections of resources, and people often need to describe them in terms of what information they contain. A standard way of doing this has been devised called the *resource description framework*, and it is being used to describe digital library collections. Again it is based on the XML family.

Digital libraries contain electronic books. Although we have not yet mentioned them, schemes—and standards—for electronic books are emerging. Some are proprietary, but there is an open standard, Open eBook, that is based on the XML family. We meet it in this chapter. Open eBooks contain not just the text, and pictures, and title page, and table of contents, and index, and colophon, but also the reading order, and they can even include different "tours" through the book.

The query is another important part of a digital library. Why should we have to learn different ways of querying when we move from one digital library, or Web search engine, to another? There are standard ways of expressing queries, and we describe two of them. One, the common command language (CCL), arose out of the library world, and variants have been in use for library catalog searching for years. The other, XQuery, is part of the brave new world of XML and provides an exceptionally powerful framework for issuing queries and having the results composed into lists and even documents—documents that are generated dynamically on demand by accessing the contents of a digital library or any other information collection.

Interoperability is the name of the game for libraries. An important part of traditional library culture is the ability to locate copies of information in other libraries and receive them on loan—interlibrary loan. Libraries work together to provide a truly universal international information service. The degree of cooperation is enormous, and laudable. What other large organizations cooperate in this way?

For digital libraries to communicate with one another, standards are needed for representing *documents*, *metadata*, and *queries*. We studied documents and metadata in Chapters 4 and 5, and queries are what we have just been talking about! The components are in place. What we need are *protocols* that put them all together to achieve effective and widespread communication.

Different protocols have sprung from the two different cultures upon which digital libraries are founded. We describe two principal ones: the Z39.50 protocol, developed by the library community and maintained by the Library of Congress, and the Open Archives Initiative (OAI) protocol, developed by members of various communities concerned with electronic documents. OAI draws upon the experience learned in a research project at Cornell University called Dienst, which we also summarize, along with Stanford University's protocol SDLIP.

8.1   More markup

Chapter 5 introduced XML and discussed some extensions that allow XML documents to be presented in ways comparable to HTML: the stylesheet languages CSS and XSL. However, as we intimated there, there are other extensions to XML that provide more advanced data representation and manipulation facilities. Because of XML's importance for future digital libraries, we expand on these developments here. But first we need to say something about naming resources on the Internet and namespaces in XML.

Names

Most people are acquainted with URLs—indeed it is hard to talk to friends about the Internet without mentioning them. The acronym stands for "uniform resource locator," where a "resource" is a piece of information, typically a Web page. However, a URL is useless if the resource it identifies is unavailable—and we know from bitter experience that this happens all the time. The problem is that a "locator" is a kind of address, and things often move around on the Web when sites are reorganized or information changes hands. People lose touch when they change addresses frequently, and the same is true of information.

What is needed is a way of naming resources so that, wherever they are, they can be found. Since the early 1990s people have debated how to identify resources on the Internet in a way that is both independent of location and persistent over time. But naming is a difficult business, and although technical people prefer technical solutions, making a name "persistent" is really an institutional matter rather than a technical one. For example, a "persistent URL" or PURL is one that is backed up by an institutional commitment to availability over an extended period of time.[14]

---

14. For example, the Online Computer Library Center (OCLC) that runs the official Dublin Core Web site is committed to persistent URLs registered through them.

The upshot of this debate has been a way of naming resources called a "universal resource name" or URN. Each URN includes within it a "naming authority" that is able to resolve the URN and provide the named information (or the address where it is currently stored).

Together URLs and URNs are types of URI, or "uniform resource identifier," and the term *URL* is now officially deprecated. In summary, there are three ways of naming resources.

- *URI (uniform resource identifier)*: the generic set of all names or addresses that are short strings referring to resources
- *URL (uniform resource locator)*: an informal term, no longer used in technical specifications, that is associated with popular URI schemes such as *http*, *ftp*, and *mailto*
- *URN (uniform resource name)*: either a URL that has an institutional commitment to persistence and availability (the PURL mentioned earlier), or a particular scheme intended to serve as a persistent, location-independent resource identifier

While *URL* is still widely used in practice, official standards increasingly use the term *URI* to specify such entities. As we said earlier, naming is a difficult business.

Namespaces

Namespaces help you to avoid mixing up XML tags that are designed for different purposes. We already encountered them in Chapter 5 (under "Basic XSL" in Section 5.3). For example, the style sheets in Figures 5.10 through 5.13 began with the lines

```
xmlns:xsl="http://www.w3.org/1999/XSL/Transform"
xmlns:fo="http://www.w3.org/1999/XSL/Format"
```

The *xmlns* qualifier sets up a namespace, so this example creates two namespaces called *xsl* and *fo* (for XML stylesheet language and Formatting Object, respectively). The same tag can occur in each namespace and yet retain distinct meanings. For example, *<xsl:block>* specifies an XSL tag called *block*, while *<fo:block>* specifies a Formatting Object tag of the same name. Namespaces can be used in XML documents and DTDs, as well as in XSL style sheets.

Namespaces have further features, which are used in examples in this chapter. First, namespace declarations (such as the previous two lines) can be embedded in any node of the tree that represents the document, not just the root node as they were in Figures 5.10 through 5.15. The fact that tags are nested ensures that each namespace's scope is well defined. Thus different blocks can make use of different namespaces.

You can also define a *global* namespace by simply omitting the label that follows the colon, as in

```
xmlns="http://www.openarchives.org/"
```

Tags from this namespace do not need to be qualified with a prefix—in fact there is no prefix name to use! The global namespace can be redefined at different points in the document: unqualified tags use the current global namespace. This encourages brevity.

Namespace prefixes are used to qualify tags. They can also be used to qualify attributes. Within a single tag, different attributes may even use different namespaces: they can be freely mixed. For example,

```
<MyTag a:att="XXX" b:att="YYY">Some text</MyTag>
```

has one attribute from the *a* namespace and a second from the *b* namespace.

Links

XML files can define connections between resources using two supporting standards, XLink and XPointer. These provide a linking scheme that is far more powerful than the unidirectional hyperlinks of HTML. Of course power does not necessarily guarantee success. The Text Encoding Initiative mentioned at the end of Section 5.2 (Chapter 5) incorporates a very rich linking ability—in fact XLink is based on it—yet because of its complexity, it is not used as much as it might be.

We met the XPath mechanism in Chapter 5. It is a way of selecting parts of documents, and we used it in conjunction with transformations in the XML stylesheet language to manipulate parts of the document tree. XPointer is a development of XPath that provides a finer degree of contol over the part or parts of the document being selected. XLink is a general way of connecting selected resources. Together XPointer and XLink provide a foundation for bidirectional links, multiway links, and annotated links. For example, they might be used to specify an algorithm for picking out a destination such as "the third section heading in the Appendix."

In this chapter we will continue to use the UN example that was introduced in Chapter 5 to illustrate XML and style sheets (see Figures 5.3–5.13). Figure 8.1 augments it to demonstrate XLink usage. A new *<Intro>* element has been added to include introductory text, which will require corresponding updates to the DTD and any style sheets used to display the example. However, we do not elaborate on these because they are not the focus of the example.

Within the introductory text is an *<HrefLink>* element that provides a link to the United Nations Web site rather like the HTML anchor hyperlink *<a href=…>*. The tag name *HrefLink* is of no consequence; it is intended merely to

```
<NGODoc>
<Head>
  <Title>Agencies of the United Nations</Title>
</Head>
<Body>
  <Intro>
    The <HrefLink xmlns:xlink="http://www.w3.org/1999/xlink"
     xlink:type="simple"
     xlink:href="http://www.un.org/"
     xlink:actuate="onRequest"
     xlink:show="replace">United Nations</HrefLink>
    consists of several agencies.
    Their basic details are as follows:
  </Intro>

  <Agency>
    <Name hq="Paris, France">United Nations Educational, Scientific
          and Cultural Organization</Name>
    <!-- ... -->
  </Agency>

  <!-- and so on -->

</NGODoc>
```

Figure 8.1 Adding an XLink to the UN example.

convey the intention to anyone reading the source file (you!). What is important is the declaration of the XLink namespace within the tag, and the attributes and values that follow.

In Xlink every link has a *type*. In Figure 8.1 it has the value *simple*, which indicates an ordinary link. There are five other possibilities: *extended*, which is another main form of link, and *arc*, *locator*, *resource*, and *title*, which play supporting roles. *Extended* links allow labeled directed graphs to be described, in which nodes represent resources and directional links hold annotations. *Simple* links provide a shorthand for the HTML link tags such as *<a>* and *<img>* (or any HTML tags that use *href* and *src*). You will appreciate the value of the shorthand when we move on to the example in Figure 8.2.

The *href* attribute of the *<HrefLink>* tag in Figure 8.1 indicates the resource that the link addresses—the destination of the link. Here it is the home page of the UN, but the destination can combine a URI with an XPointer specification to select a subset of a document. The *actuate* attribute determines when the destination resource is accessed. Here it is set to *onRequest*, which means that access occurs whenever the link is clicked. Another commonly used value is *onLoad*, which means that the linked resource is accessed when the document containing the link is loaded. The *show* attribute determines where the destination resource will be displayed. Here it is set to *replace*, which means that the window used to display the UN agencies will be updated to show the UN's home page when the link is clicked. Alternatively you can set *show* to open the destination resource in a *new* window, or to *embed* it in the current page, at the current position.

If a document includes several links, the XLink namespace could be specified higher up the hierarchy—for example, at the root node. In many cases only the *href* attribute differs from one link to another, and values for the other attributes could be provided in a DTD. This would reduce the tag to

```
<HrefLink xlink:href="http://www.un.org/">
```

—just like HTML.

Figure 8.1 shows four XLink attributes. There are ten possibilities altogether. They are listed in the leftmost column of Table 8.1, which also indicates (with ✓) those that can be used for various settings of the *type* attribute.

To illustrate the attributes and types, we extend the example to include a multiway link connecting the text *several agencies* to a list of Web sites, one for each agency. Here is what it will do. When the user clicks on the words *several agencies*, a popup window will appear that displays an informative list of agency names. When one of these is clicked, a new window displaying the appropriate home page will be opened. This behavior can be achieved using extended links. If only simple links were available, each agency's link would have to be embedded in the document, needlessly consuming screen space.

Figure 8.2 shows what must be done. Not surprisingly it is far more complex than the previous example. Figure 8.2 also includes an internal link that uses an XPointer to make an extra entry in the multiway link that takes the user to the start of the agency information in the current document.

The link is created by the tag named *<MultiwayLink>*—the actual name is immaterial and is chosen purely for readability. The link's type is *extended*, and its scope ends with the tag *</MultiwayLink>* near the end of the example. Contained within it are elements of type *resource*, *locator*, and *arc*. There is only one

Table 8.1 XLink attributes.

		_ simple	extended	_ locator	arc	resource	title
				Type of link			
	href	✓		✓			
	role	✓	✓	✓		✓	
	arcrole	✓			✓		
Attribute	*title*	✓	✓	✓	✓	✓	
	show	✓			✓		
	actuate	✓			✓		
	label			✓		✓	
	from				✓		
	to				✓		

```
<NGODoc>
<Head>
  <Title>Agencies of the United Nations</Title>
</Head>
<Body>

  <Intro>
    The United Nations consists of
    <MultiwayLink xmlns:xlink="http://www.w3.org/1999/xlink"
                  xlink:type="extended" xlink:title="Un Agencies">
      <SingleSource xlink:type="resource" xlink:label="source">
        several agencies</SingleSource>
      <Destination xlink:type="locator"
                 xlink:title="UNESCO Home Page"
                 xlink:label="unesco"
                 xlink:href="http://www.unesco.org/"/>
      <Destination xlink:type="locator"
                 xlink:title= "FAO Home Page"
                 xlink:label="fao"
                 xlink:href="http://www.fao.org/"/>
      <!-- ... -->
      <Internal xlink:type="locator"
                 xlink:title= "Start of records"
                 xlink:label="details"
                 xlink:href="#xpointer(/NGODoc/Agency[position()==1])"/>

      <ExternalConnection xlink:type="arc" xlink:from="source"
                 xlink:to="unesco"     xlink:show="new"
                 xlink:title = "Educational, Scientific and Cultural"
                 xlink:actuate="onRequest"/>
      <ExternalConnection xlink:type="arc" xlink:from="source"
                 xlink:to="fao"      xlink:show="new"
                 xlink:title = "Food and Agriculture"
                 xlink:actuate="onRequest"/>
      <!-- World Bank ... -->
      <InternalConnection xlink:type="arc" xlink:from="source"
                 xlink:to="details"     xlink:show="replace"
                 xlink:title = "Agency details"
                 xlink:actuate="onRequest"/>
    </MultiwayLink>
    Their basic details are as follows:
  </Intro>

  <Agency>
    <Name hq="Paris, France">United Nations Educational, Scientific
        and Cultural Organization</Name>
    <!-- ... -->
  </Agency>

  <!-- and so on -->
</Body>
</NGODoc>
```

Figure 8.2 Adding extended XLinks to the UN example.

resource here, *<SingleSource>*, and it represents the starting point of the multi-way link. The content of this tag, "several agencies," is the anchor text for the link—what you click on in the document. The *<SingleSource>* element sets its *xlink:label* to *source;* we explain this shortly.

The *<SingleSource>* element is followed by a series of *locator* elements called *<Destination>*, one for each of the UN agencies (plus a further one that demonstrates the use of an XPointer). These are used to specify external resources—in our case the targets of the link—and they too make use of the *xlink:label* attribute. Following them is a series of *arc* elements called *<ExternalConnection>*, each of which have *from* and *to* attributes that reference the labels given in the resource and locator elements.

The structure defined by this multiway link is represented by the directed graph shown in Figure 8.3. Nodes represent the one *resource* element *<SingleSource>* and all the *locator* elements, of which several are called *<Destination>* and one is called *<Internal>*. These nodes correspond to a document or part of a document. The graph's edges are formed by matching the *from* and *to* attributes of *arc* elements with the *label* attributes used in the node definitions, and are annotated with the *title* attributes of the *arc* definitions. The title information that the *locator* elements provide is associated with the destination documents. Being attributes, these titles cannot contain markup. However, there is a second form of title (not shown in the example) that is specified using an element of type *title*, and this construct can include markup. It can accompany elements of type *arc*, *locator*, and *extended* and can be repeated several times within one element.

Within the *locator* and *arc* segments of the extended link are two tags that have not yet been discussed: *<Internal>* and *<InternalConnection>*. Again the names are immaterial, but are there to aid comprehension. These constructs demonstrate the use of XPointers. The first has an *href* attribute whose value is

```
#xpointer(/NGODoc/Agency[position()==1])
```

Unlike the *href*s that we have encountered so far, this is not a simple URI. It is an XPointer that specifies a hierarchical position within the document called *NGODoc:* namely, the first *Agency* node. XPointers are a superset of the XPaths that we met in Chapter 5 and contain extra features such as the ability to specify ranges that cross node boundaries.

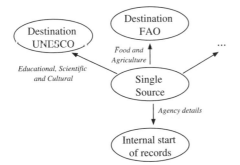

Figure 8.3 Directed graph for the XLink of Figure 8.2.

This particular XPointer is used to select an internal portion of the document. However, it can also be paired up with a URI to link to part of an external resource, as in

```
www.un.org/index.html#xpointer(html/body/table)
```

Recall that in HTML a hyperlink can be directed at a particular position in a document by embedding an anchor name such as *<a name="here">* in the destination document and using *<a href="...#here">* in the source document to link to that point. The same effect can be achieved in XML by combining a URI with an XPointer that names an *ID* attribute in the destination document. However, an XPointer can be more expressive than this: it can indicate a particular internal position by specifying a location in the hierarchical structure that represents the target document. This allows a position to be specified in the destination document without actually having to edit explicit anchors into the destination document.

The *role* and *arcrole* attributes are not used in this example. Like *title*, they are semantic attributes that help communicate the meaning of the link. *Title* gives the description directly, but *role* and *arcrole* specify URIs that point to resources containing the description.

This example gives a flavor of what is possible. Far more complex graphs than that of Figure 8.3 can be built. The graph description can even be included in an external file—a type of database describing, for example, the linking structure for a network of pages.

Types

Document type definitions were originally introduced for use with the standard generalized markup language SGML. XML has been applied to a wider set of problems, and this has exposed limitations in the expressiveness of DTDs. For instance, they can include only limited information about data types, and certain structures are convoluted and do not scale well. XML Schema was designed to address these deficiencies.

In addition to describing what structure is allowed in an XML file, XML Schema provides a rich array of basic types, including year, date, and URI, as well as textual patterns and ways of subtyping and defining new types. Types can be applied to the data that appears between tag pairs, or to the fields of attributes. Everything is expressed using the basic XML syntax. Note that DTDs do not themselves adhere to XML syntax, but are expressed using an add-on notation. Strictly speaking they do not contain properly formed tags.

We introduced DTDs in Section 5.2 (Chapter 5) using the United Nations example (Figures 5.3 and 5.4). Figure 8.4 reworks the example of Figure 5.3 to give the same result using XML Schema. Like other members of the XML brotherhood, XML Schema is defined using namespaces to prevent any clash of tags with other elements of a document.

The file in Figure 8.4 has the same structure as other standards built on the basic XML foundation. The root node specifies the XML Schema namespace, enabling applications to interpret subsequent nodes appropriately. Its children use *annotation*, *element*, and *complexType* elements. The first is a mechanism for embedding comments in the file in a more structured way than <!-- ... -->. The second defines an XML element: it performs the same function as <!*ELEMENT* ...> in a DTD. Structural information can be embedded inside the tag, as in the first occurrence of the *element* tag. Alternatively the definition can be deferred using the *type* attribute and the combined open/close tag syntax <.../> for empty elements, as in the second occurrence of the *element* tag. In the latter case the *complexType* element that provides the deferred definition need not follow the *element* node directly, although it does in our example.

The definition of the *NGODoc* element sets up a *sequence* comprising *Head* followed by *Body*. This construct forces elements to appear in the stated order. The attributes *minOccurs* and *maxOccurs* restrict the number of times each element may occur. In the *Head* element, both are set to 1. However, this is the default value and may be dropped—as it is in the definition of *Body*. Other numerical values can be used. For example, if *minOccurs* is 0 and *maxOccurs* is *unbounded*, any number of occurrences are allowed.

Within the scope of the *sequence* tag, two complementary tags may appear: *choice* and *all*. The last nesting group in Figure 8.4, which defines the *Agency* element, contains an example. In the lower half of the definition, *choice* is used to select an element from a list of potential candidates—in this case *Abbrev* and *Photo*. In the *choice* tag, *maxOccurs* is set to *unbounded*. This means that not only can *Abbrev* and *Photo* appear in any order, but any number of these element types can occur in any order. The *all* tag (not illustrated) means that all of the child elements must occur, but their order is immaterial. Constructs like these are difficult to define using DTDs.

To allow a mixture of parsed character data and tags within the *Body* element as the original DTD example did (Figure 5.4), *Body*'s definition sets the *mixed* attribute to *true*.

An element's attributes are defined using the *xsd:attribute* tag (equivalent to <!*ATTRIBUTE* ...> in a DTD). There are three examples in Figure 8.4. Defining attributes in XML Schema is decidedly self-referential because the construct uses attributes itself to define the name and type of the attribute being defined. However, it is fairly straightforward to deduce the meaning. For example, including

```
<xsd:attribute name="hq" type="xsd:string"/>
```

```xml
<?xml version="1.0"?>
<xsd:schema xmlns:xsd="http://www.w3.org/2001/XMLSchema">

  <xsd:annotation>
    <xsd:documentation xml:lang="en">
      XML Schema example for United Nations record example
    </xsd:documentation>
  </xsd:annotation>

  <xsd:element name="NGODoc">
    <xsd:complexType>
      <xsd:sequence>
        <xsd:element name="Head" type="HeadType" minOccurs="1" maxOccurs="1"/>
        <!-- minOccurs & maxOccurs default to 1 so same effect if omitted -->
        <xsd:element name="Body" type="BodyType"/>
      </xsd:sequence>
    </xsd:complexType>
  </xsd:element>

  <xsd:element name="Head" type="HeadType"/>
  <xsd:complexType name="HeadType">
    <xsd:sequence>
      <xsd:element name="Title"  type="xsd:string"/>
    </xsd:sequence>
  </xsd:complexType>

  <xsd:element name="Body" type="BodyType"/>
  <xsd:complexType name="BodyType" mixed="true">
    <xsd:sequence maxOccurs="unbounded">
      <xsd:element name="Agency" type="AgencyType" minOccurs="1"
          maxOccurs="unbounded"/>
    </xsd:sequence>
  </xsd:complexType>

  <xsd:element name="Agency" type="AgencyType"/>
  <xsd:complexType name="AgencyType">
    <xsd:sequence>
      <xsd:element name="Name">
        <xsd:complexType>
          <xsd:simpleContent>
            <xsd:extension base="xsd:string">
              <xsd:attribute name="hq" type="xsd:string"/>
            </xsd:extension>
          </xsd:simpleContent>
        </xsd:complexType>
      </xsd:element>

      <xsd:choice maxOccurs="unbounded">
        <xsd:element name="Abbrev" type="xsd:string" minOccurs="0"/>

        <xsd:element name="Photo"  minOccurs="0"     maxOccurs="unbounded">
          <xsd:complexType>
            <xsd:attribute name="src" type="xsd:string"  use="required"/>
            <xsd:attribute name="desc" type="xsd:string" use="optional"
                  default="A photo"/>
          </xsd:complexType>
        </xsd:element>

      </xsd:choice>
    </xsd:sequence>
  </xsd:complexType>
</xsd:schema>
```

Figure 8.4 XML Schema for the UN Agency example.

inside an *element* definition defines an attribute *hq* for that element. Here for the first time we encounter XML Schema's ability to specify type information. However, since this example matches an existing DTD, types are used in a simplistic way: they are all defined to be *string* to maintain compatibility with the character data (CDATA) used in the original DTD.

Attributes can be *optional* or *required*, and a *default* value can be supplied. These are handled within the construct using attributes of the same name.

A complication occurs when an element, defined to be a particular type, also has attributes. This occurs in the upper half of the *Agency* element definition (the last major nested group), when the *Name* element is defined. Its basic type is *string*, but it includes an *hq* attribute which is also defined to be *string*. The syntax necessary to achieve this is convoluted and uses the new tag types *simpleContent* and *extension*; nevertheless it is not hard to follow. *Extension* permits the type of the element to be specified through the *base* attribute; then within the scope of the *extension* tag the attribute is defined as before. Finally, because XML Schema does not permit *extension* to be embedded directly in *complexType* tags, it is necessary to wrap *extension* up in a *simpleContent* tag.

The XML Schema specification in Figure 8.4 is far longer than the DTD equivalent in Figure 5.4. Of course the example is tutorial and could be abbreviated somewhat using such things as default values—but it would still be longer. The benefit of XML Schema is that it provides greater control over the structures and values that constitute a valid document. And documents like the specification in Figure 8.4 are clearly intended to be created and displayed with a structured editor rather than in raw text form. This transfers the emphasis from readability to "parseability": from ease of reading by a person to ease of manipulation by a computer. There are generic tools that allow all members of the XML family to be read, parsed, and edited.

XML Schema has extensive facilities for data typing. We have already encountered the type *string*, which was used in the first example to provide a counterpart to CDATA. This is a built-in type. There are over 40 others, reflecting the wide range of information handled by XML. The main categories are *Boolean*, *numeric*, *time*, *string*, and *binary*. *Binary* data is encoded into printable plain text to meet the XML character-set requirement. The *numeric* category includes signed and unsigned numbers, integer and floating point numbers, finite and infinite precision. Within the *time* category, dates, months, and years can all be represented individually. There is also a built-in type for URIs (subsuming URLs and URNs), and for XML notation such as entities (e.g., ") and tokens. New types can be constructed that expand or restrict the set of permissible values.

To demonstrate the data-typing abilities, we extend the XML Schema example to include the year in which each UN agency was founded, and we constrain

```
<?xml version="1.0"?>
<xsd:schema xmlns:xsd="http://www.w3.org/2001/XMLSchema">

  <!--- annotation, and definition for NGODoc, Head, Body and Title omitted -->

  <xsd:element name="Agency" type="AgencyType"/>
  <xsd:complexType name="AgencyType">
    <xsd:sequence>
      <xsd:element name="Name">
        <xsd:complexType>
          <xsd:simpleContent>
            <xsd:extension base="xsd:string">
              <xsd:attribute name="hqcity"    type="CityType"/>
              <xsd:attribute name="hqcountry" type="UNCountryType"/>
            </xsd:extension>
          </xsd:simpleContent>
        </xsd:complexType>
      </xsd:element>

      <xsd:choice maxOccurs="unbounded">
        <xsd:element name="Abbrev" type="xsd:string" minOccurs="0"/>
        <xsd:element name="Founded" type="UNYear" minOccurs="0"/>

        <xsd:element name="Photo"  minOccurs="0"       maxOccurs="unbounded">
          <xsd:complexType>
            <xsd:attribute name="src" type="xsd:anyURI"  use="required"/>
            <xsd:attribute name="desc" type="xsd:string" use="optional"
                 default="A photo"/>
          </xsd:complexType>
        </xsd:element>

      </xsd:choice>
    </xsd:sequence>

  </xsd:complexType>

  <xsd:simpleType name="UNYear">
    <xsd:restriction base="xsd:gYear">
      <xsd:minInclusive value="1850"/>
    </xsd:restriction>
  </xsd:simpleType>

  <xsd:simpleType name="CityType">
    <xsd:restriction base="xsd:string">
      <xsd:minLength value="2"/>
      <xsd:pattern value="\p{Lu}\p{L}*"/>
    </xsd:restriction>
  </xsd:simpleType>

  <xsd:simpleType name="UNCountryType">
    <xsd:restriction base="xsd:string">
      <xsd:enumeration value="Afghanistan"/>
      <xsd:enumeration value="Albania"/>
      <xsd:enumeration value="Algeria"/>
      <!-- and so on ... -->
      <xsd:enumeration value="France"/>
      <!-- and so on ... -->
      <xsd:enumeration value="Italy"/>
      <!-- and so on ... -->
      <xsd:enumeration value="USA"/>
    </xsd:restriction>
  </xsd:simpleType>


</xsd:schema>
```

Figure 8.5 XML Schema that demonstrates data typing.

more tightly the value types that attributes can assume. The result is shown in Figure 8.5. The *simpleType* construct is used to define new types. The first example is *UNYear*, in the lower half of Figure 8.5. It is based on the built-in time structure *gYear* and is restricted to values greater than the year 1850. (The United Nations was founded in 1945, but some of the specialized agencies it contains—such as the Universal Postal Union and the International Labor Organization—predate it by a considerable margin.)

The second *simpleType* in Figure 8.5 is *CityType*, which is used as the type for the *hqcity* attribute of the *Agency* element (near the top of the figure). This illustrates the use of patterns, which are couched in the form of regular expressions. The type definition restricts the basic *string* type to contain an uppercase letter (\p{Lu}) followed by a sequence of any letters (\p{L}*). Regular expressions follow standard practice, with the usual special characters: ? (meaning an optional character), + (meaning a sequence of one or more characters), * (a sequence of zero or more characters), . (any character), [A-Z] (the uppercase letters), and so on. The \p{...} in the example is an extension of the notation that expresses sets of Unicode symbols: letters, numbers, punctuation, currency symbols, and so on. We could have specified a capital letter as [A-Z], but \p{Lu} is more general. The *minLength* tag in the type definition illustrates one way to specify bounds on string length. This could equally have been accomplished within the regular expression itself.

The last *simpleType* definition, *UNCountryType*, is an enumerated type. After specifying the base type to be *string*, a series of *enumeration* tags are used to restrict the permissible countries to a given set.

Another main form of type declaration is *complexType*, which is used to define compound types that include other elements. We have already encountered this construct in the previous XML Schema example, although we did not discuss it explicitly. It was used in Figure 8.4 to make *NGODoc* contain a *Head* followed by a *Body*, to make *Head* contain a *Title*, to make *Body* contain an unbounded sequence of *Agencies*, and to make each *Agency* a *Name* followed by any number of *Abbrevs* and *Photos*.

Putting all this type information together, we see that Figure 8.5 adds these restrictions to the UN schema:

- The *hq* attribute has been replaced with *hqcity* and *hqcountry*. The former must (unrealistically) contain just one word, starting with a capital letter and having at least one other letter. The latter must be one of a list of designated countries.
- There is now a *<Founded>* element, used to express years after 1850.
- The *src* attribute for *Photo* must now be a legal URI.

8.2 Resource description

The Resource Description Framework (RDF) is designed to facilitate the interoperability of metadata, particularly in the realm of the World Wide Web. Because metadata covers too great a variety of information to specify exhaustively and categorically, RDF follows the lead of XML: rather than providing a set of possibilities, it supplies a means for describing a valid system. It is expected that communities of users will assemble to establish RDF systems suited to their collective needs. They will have to agree on a vocabulary, its meaning, and the structures that can be formed from it. This is done by specifying an *RDF Schema*, just as DTDs and XML Schemas are used to control XML vocabulary and structure.

The Resource Description Framework is a way of modeling as a *resource* anything that can be represented as a URI—a Web page, part of a document, a set of pages, an FTP site, an e-mail address, and so on. These resources are *described* in a machine-readable fashion through a *framework* for specifying metadata. The framework is compositional: new resources can be built from existing ones.

Figure 8.6 uses RDF to give a graphical description of the very book you are holding in your hands. The book is represented by its ISBN (International Standard Book Number) in URI syntax—yes, even ISBNs are a form of URI. The top-level description comprises a title, two authors, and a publisher. The authors in turn are characterized by a name and an e-mail address.

As the figure illustrates, an RDF can be represented as a directed graph. Previously we saw how this ubiquitous structure can be used to describe a powerful form of hyperlinking. Here the aim is different and imposes different require-

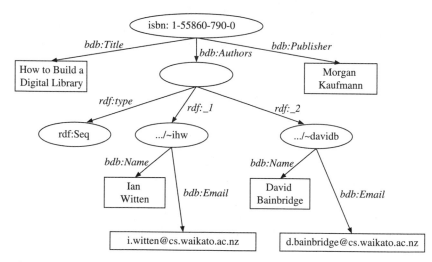

Figure 8.6 Modeling this book graphically using RDF.

ments on the syntactic structures used to express RDF—although, as we will shortly see, there is some similarity.

Mapping a picture into a character stream is a process of serialization, and for RDF the language of choice is (again) XML. Figure 8.7 shows the description of the example graph. This representation obscures some of the abstract aspects of RDF and makes it seem like just another example of an XML language—particularly as we have recently seen so many of them! When considering RDF, you should keep in mind that it is a sister format to XML, not a subsidiary. However, this medium bestows practical benefits: software support for parsing and editing, transparent handling of international characters, and so on.

The basic construction in RDF, as indeed in English, is to connect a subject to an object using a predicate. This is known as a *statement*. Subjects and objects are nodes in the graph. The directed arc that joins them shows the connection; a label on the arc identifies the predicate used. To take one example from Figure 8.6, *How to Build a Digital Library* (object) is the *Title* (predicate) of the resource *ISBN: 1-55860-790-0* (subject). The subject is a resource, represented in the diagram as an oval node. An object may be either a resource or a string literal. In our case it is a string, represented as a rectangular node.

We now match this up with the serialized form in Figure 8.7. It begins with the by now familiar processing instruction, and a root node that declares some namespaces. In this case there are two: one for RDF and another for "Book

```
<?xml version="1.0"?>
<rdf:RDF xmlns:rdf="http://www.w3.org/1999/02/22-rdf-syntax-ns#"
         xmlns:bdb="http://bookdatabase.org/schema/publications">

  <rdf:Description about="urn:isbn:1-55860-790-0">
    <bdb:Title>How to Build a Digital Library</bdb:Title>
    <bdb:Authors>
      <rdf:Seq>
        <rdf:li>
          <rdf:Description about="http://www.cs.waikato.ac.nz/~ihw">
            <bdb:Name>Ian Witten</bdb:Name>
            <bdb:Email>i.witten@cs.waikato.ac.nz</bdb:Email>
          </rdf:Description>
        </rdf:li>
        <rdf:li rdf:resource="http://www.cs.waikato.ac.nz/~davidb"/>
      </rdf:Seq>
    </bdb:Authors>
    <bdb:Publisher>Morgan Kaufmann</bdb:Publisher>
  </rdf:Description>

  <rdf:Description about="http://www.cs.waikato.ac.nz/~davidb">
    <bdb:Name>David Bainbridge</bdb:Name>
    <bdb:Email>d.bainbridge@cs.waikato.ac.nz</bdb:Email>
  </rdf:Description>

</rdf:RDF>
```

Figure 8.7 XML serialization of the example RDF model.

Database," denoted by the prefix *bdb*. This represents a hypothetical organization that has developed an XML schema for representing metadata about books in terms of titles, authors, names, e-mail addresses, and publishers.

The first child of the root node is an *rdf:Description* element that includes an *about* attribute to specify the resource as a URI that gives the ISBN. The *bdb:Title* tag that follows sets the predicate, and its content represents the string literal object which forms the title itself. Two other predicates connected to the ISBN resource are *Authors* and *Publisher*. The latter, like *Title*, declares a string literal object (the string "Morgan Kaufmann"); the former, however, is more complex. Thus we see how the top level of the tree in Figure 8.6 is constructed.

Not only is *bdb:Authors* the first object encountered in our explanation that is itself a resource, it is also an example of an *anonymous resource*—an intermediary node that has no specific resource name but is itself the subject of further qualifying statements. The counterpart in the graphical version of the model in Figure 8.6 is the node at the end of the *Authors* predicate, which is nameless.

The anonymous resource also demonstrates a new structure called a *container*, used to group resources together. RDF has three types of container: *bag*, *sequence*, and *alternative*. A *bag* is an unordered list of resources or string literals; a *sequence* is an ordered list; and an *alternative* represents the selection of just one item from the list. Each item in a *container* is denoted by an *rdf:li* tag. The example uses *rdf:Seq* to represent a sequence of authors because the order is significant. The container type is represented by the *rdf:type* predicate, and its contents are numbered *rdf:_1*, *rdf:_2*. These are implicitly inferred from the XML description (Figure 8.7) but shown explicitly in the pictorial version (Figure 8.6).

There are two list items in the example, one for each author, and both happen to be compound resources. They are introduced by the RDF list item tag *rdf:li*, and for illustrative purposes they are specified in different ways. The first is embedded in-line by starting a new *rdf:Description* tag. The second receives a more compact *rdf:li* tag that defers the resource's definition through the *rdf:resource* attribute. The missing detail is filled in when a resource description is encountered whose *rdf:about* attribute matches the named list item. This occurs in the lower third of the example.

RDF is a rich framework whose design draws upon structured documents, entity relationships, object orientation, and knowledge representation. We cannot illustrate all aspects here: the example is only intended to give an impression of what is possible.

Collection-level metadata

Just as document-level metadata is structured information about an individual document, so collection-level metadata is structured information about the entire content of a collection, treated as a single entity. This might include its coverage, the number of documents contained, access conditions, and so on. Collection-level metadata is an important category of resource in any digital library system. For example, it allows users to start their information gathering process one step earlier by interrogating a set of collections to determine which ones best suit their needs. For this to work across different digital library systems, standard terms and meaning are required. This is exactly what RDF is for.

One example of collection-level metadata is provided by the Research Support Libraries Programme (RSLP) Collection Description project. This uses a model that represents *Collections*, *Locations*, and *Agents* as RDF resources. There are three types of agent—*Collector*, *Owner*, and *Administrator*—reflecting the roles that people or organizations play in providing and maintaining a collection. The bulk of the detail is contained in the collection resource, which may in turn reference further resources, such as a location and a collector.

Figure 8.8 shows an abridged version of a description for the Morrison Collection of Chinese Books housed at the School of Oriental and African Studies Library in London, England. Four existing namespaces provide relevant elements and attributes: RDF (naturally), unqualified Dublin Core, qualified Dublin Core, and vCard, which is a namespace devised by the Internet Mail Consortium to represent fax numbers, phone numbers, and so on for electronic business cards. A further namespace for RSLP covers attributes and elements not defined elsewhere (prefix *cld:*).

The example contains four top-level resource descriptions: *Collection*, *Collector*, *Owner*, and *Location* (marked with XML comments). There is no administrator resource in this example. Most of the information supplied in the collection resource description is through Dublin Core. In particular the *<dc:subject>* element shown uses the *anonymous resource* mechanism mentioned earlier to embed another resource, which is a Library of Congress Subject Heading (LCSH), expressed using qualified Dublin Core.

About halfway down the collection resource description, the Dublin Core *<dc:type>* element is used to give the collection's type. The RSLP collection description defines an enumerated list of possible types, starting with broad classifications such as *Catalog* and *Index*, which become more specific with items such as *Library*, *Museum*, and *Archive*, and even more specific with items such as *Text*, *Image*, and *Sound*. A collection can be given more than one of these types by separating the terms by a period (.), as can be seen in the figure.

Elements *<dcq:hasPart>*, *<dcq:isPartOf>*, and *<cld:hasDescription>* are examples of external relationships. These identify or name other resources that have a bearing on the collection being described. There are seven external relationships in all. The ones appearing here are used to name subcollections (*hasPart*), the larger library this collection fits into (*isPartOf*), and where a description of the collection appears (*hasDescription*).

```
<?xml version="1.0"?>
<rdf:RDF
        xmlns:rdf   ="http://www.w3.org/1999/02/22-rdf-syntax-ns#"
        xmlns:dc    ="http://purl.org/dc/elements/1.1/"
        xmlns:dcq   ="http://purl.org/dc/qualifiers/1.0/"
        xmlns:vcard="http://www.imc.org/vcard/3.0/"
        xmlns:cld   ="http://www.ukoln.ac.uk/metadata/rslp/1.0/">

  <!-- Collection resource -->
  <rdf:Description about="urn:x-rslpcd:967715792-47835">
    <dc:title>Morrison Collection of Chinese Books</dc:title>
    <dc:description>
      This collection comprises the Chinese books accumulated by Dr.
          Robert Morrison (1782 - 1834), the first Protestant missionary to
          China, during his sixteen years residence in Guangzhou and Macao
          between 1807 and 1823. Ten thousand Chinese-style thread-bound
          volumes cover a broad spectrum of subjects from early and mid-Qing
          China.
    </dc:description>

    <dc:subject>
      <rdf:Description>
        <dcq:scheme>LCSH</dcq:scheme>
        <rdf:value>Missionaries -- China</rdf:value>
      </rdf:Description>
    </dc:subject>
    <!-- additional subject entries for "Rare Books - China - Bibliography --
          Catalogs" and "Chinese Imprints -- Catalogs" -->

    <cld:agentName>Morrison, Robert, 1782-1834.</cld:agentName>
    <!-- additional entries for cld:agent, dcq:place, dcq:time, cld:strength,
          dc:language, and dc:format -->

    <dc:type>Collection.Library.Special</dc:type>
    <cld:accumulationDateRange>1807-1823</cld:accumulationDateRange>
    <cld:contentsDateRange>1650-1825</cld:contentsDateRange>

    <dcq:hasPart>
      Literature collection within Morrison Collection of Chinese Books
    </dcq:hasPart>
    <!-- additional entries for dcq:hasPart, dcq:isPartOf, cld:hasDescription,
          cld:accrualStatus, cld:accessControl, cld:note -->

    <dc:creator resource="urn:x-rslpcd:967715792-32366"/>
    <cld:owner resource="urn:x-rslpcd:967715792-62789"/>
    <cld:hasLocation resource="urn:x-rslpcd:967715792-16277"/>
  </rdf:Description>

  <!-- Collector resource -->
  <rdf:Description about="urn:x-rslpcd:967715792-32366">
    <vcard:fn>Morrison, Robert, 1782-1834.</vcard:fn>
  </rdf:Description>

  <!-- Owner resource -->
  <rdf:Description about="urn:x-rslpcd:967715792-62789">
    <vcard:org>School of Oriental and African Studies Library</vcard:org>
    <vcard:voice>+44 207 898 4163</vcard:voice>
    <vcard:fax>+44 207 898 4159</vcard:fax>
    <vcard:email>libenquiry@soas.ac.uk</vcard:email>
  </rdf:Description>

  <!-- Location resource -->
  <rdf:Description about="urn:x-rslpcd:967715792-16277">
    <dc:title>School of Oriental and African Studies Library</dc:title>
    <!-- additional entries for cld:address, cld:postcode, cld:country,
          cld:accessConditions, cld:seeAlso -->
    <cld:isLocationOf resource="urn:x-rslpcd:967715792-47835"/>
  </rdf:Description>
</rdf:RDF>
```

Figure 8.8 RSLP description of the Morrison collection of Chinese books.

The lower part of the collection resource description contains references to the collector, owner, and location resources through *dc:creator*, *cld:owner*, and *cld:hasLocation*, respectively. The first two are examples of agents and make use of *vcard:* elements to supply the necessary information. A location can be electronic or physical, and most of its elements are defined by RSLP namespace elements.

8.3   Document exchange

The computer and publishing industries have come up with the concept of *electronic books* (eBooks) as an analog of paper books. Electronic books can be bought and sold, lent and read. Here we concentrate on the reading part, and let others worry about the publishers' business model.

Electronic books combine a rich mixture of text and graphics with hyperlinked navigation structures and a page-turning metaphor. Figure 8.9 shows one of the many eBook software applications—known simply as *readers*—being

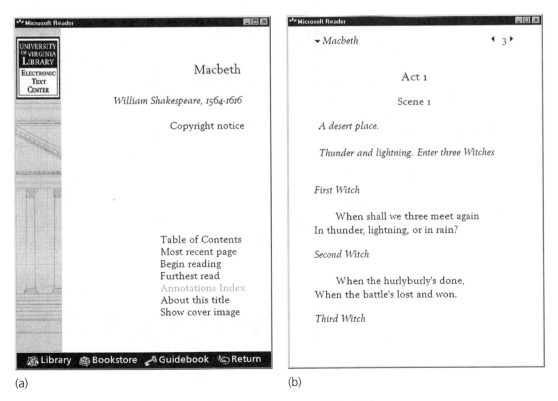

(a)   (b)

Figure 8.9 Reading an eBook of Shakespeare's *Macbeth*.

used to peruse a version of Shakespeare's play *Macbeth*. Some readers run on desktop PCs and run within their own window (which can be expanded to the full screen if desired). Others run on special electronic book hardware, or on handheld computers, and take over the whole screen.

The figure shows two snapshots. The first is the eBook's title page, which provides access to the table of contents and links to the start, end, and most recently read page (useful since electronic pages are not so easily dog-eared as paper ones). In many cases the title page also points to global resources such as the user's personal library, help documentation for the software application (expressed as an eBook, of course), and electronic bookstores. The second snapshot shows the start of Act I, Scene I, where the witches begin "When shall we three meet again. . . . " This particular reader displays one page at a time, but some readers show a two-page spread that reflects more strongly the book metaphor.[15]

Like HTML and PDF, eBook pages can contain text, graphics, and hyperlinks. It is also common to find facilities for active reading: annotation, highlighting, and bookmarking. The interaction adopts minimalist principles: self-explanatory keys move from one page to another (page-up/page-down or arrow keys). Clicking on a word typically brings up its dictionary entry. In the figure, you can click the little triangular shapes at the top of each page to transport yourself to bookmarked spots or to close the book and return to the reader's home page.

It would be nice to be able to share eBooks. Unfortunately commercial applications adopt proprietary formats, limiting portability. A standard called Open eBook is intended to become more catholic. It demonstrates how XML and its brethren can facilitate the exchange of information—one basic requirement of interoperability.

Open eBook

The Open eBook Forum is an association of hardware and software companies, publishers, authors, users, and related organizations whose goal is to establish common specifications for electronic book systems that will benefit content creators, manufacturers of readers, and—most importantly—consumers. The forum intends to catalyze the adoption of electronic books and increase awareness and acceptance of the emerging electronic publishing industry. The Open eBook standard is expressed in XML and makes use of namespaces, document type definitions, cascading style sheets, a subset of HTML 4.0/XHTML 1.0, the

---

15. In the Māori language of indigenous New Zealanders, the word for book is *pukapuka*. The *puka* is a plant whose large leaf is pale underneath, and the word represents two leaves side by side—an open book.

Dublin Core, Unicode, and a set of core MIME types that all compliant readers must support.

Each publication takes the form of a *package* file, normally given the file name extension *.opf*. It is expressed in XML and has six distinct parts:

- a *unique identity* for the publication
- *metadata* about it
- a *manifest* that lists all supporting files that comprise its content
- a *spine* that determines a linear reading order for the supporting files
- *tours* that permit different traversal patterns through the material
- a *guide* of structural components, such as the title page and table of contents

An Open eBook package must be expressed in either UTF-8 or UTF-16 and conform to the standard's document type definition. Figure 8.10 shows a hypothetical package that describes an eBook version of the book you are reading. We have deliberately set the encoding to UTF-8 (even though this is XML's default value) to emphasize the stricter encoding requirements of the Open eBook standard. The second line specifies the external DTD for the standard.

The six structural components are apparent in the XML file. The first is an attribute of the *package* tag, while the remainder are child elements of *package* whose names reflect their role. *Tours* and *guide* are optional; the rest are mandatory.

The *metadata* element must include a Dublin Core subelement, declared with the appropriate namespace. The standard also insists that the namespace *oebpackage* is included, for future compatibility. Within the Dublin Core element, *Title* and at least one *Identifier* are mandatory, the latter being used to connect the content of its element to the *unique-identifier* attribute in *<package>* using the same identifier—in this case *nzdl.org:howto_edition1*.

A selection of other Dublin Core elements are used to describe the book. Open eBook augments the *Creator* tags with optional attributes, *role* and *file-as*. The first attribute (which also applies to the *Contributor* metadata type) is used to provide more detail about the element by specifying a MARC "relator" code. There are more than 180 of these, including annotator (*ann*), editor (*edt*), illustrator (*ill*), musician (*mus*), translator (*trl*), and wood-engraver (*wde*). The second attribute is used to specify names in a normative form suitable for machine processing. Additional metadata that does not fit the Dublin Core model can be provided using *x-metadata*, which adopts the HTML convention of specifying metadata using *<meta>*. The example defines *Software* metadata whose value is a URL that points to the digital library software system used in this book.

The *manifest* element is used to list all the files that make up the book's content. In our example there is one HTML file per chapter. These files embed images for the various figures, and these must also be listed in the manifest.

```xml
<?xml version="1.0" encoding="utf-8" ?>
<!DOCTYPE package PUBLIC "+//ISBN 0-9673008-1-9//DTD OEB 1.0.1 Package//EN"
          "http://openebook.org/dtds/oeb-1.0.1/oebpkg1.dtd">
<package unique-identifier="nzdl.org:howto_edition1">
  <!-- Open eBook version of this text book -->
  <metadata>
    <dc-metadata xmlns:dc="http://purl.org/dc/elements/1.0/"
                 xmlns:oebpackage="http://openebook.org/namespaces/oeb-package/1.0/">
      <dc:Identifier id="nzdl.org:howto_edition1" scheme="ISBN">
        1-55860-790-0
      </dc:Identifier>
      <dc:Title>How to build a digital library</dc:Title>
      <dc:Creator role="aut" file-as="Witten, Ian H.">Ian H. Witten</dc:Creator>
      <dc:Creator role="aut" file-as="Bainbridge, David">David Bainbridge</dc:Creator>
      <dc:Rights>Copyright &copy; 2002 Morgan Kaufmann Publishers, Inc ...</dc:Rights>
      <!-- ... -->
      <dc:Language>en</dc:Language>
    </dc-metadata>
    <x-metadata>
      <!-- Additional, non-Dublin Core metadata -->
      <meta name="Software" content="www.greenstone.org" />
      <!-- ... -->
    </x-metadata>
  </metadata>

  <manifest>
    <!-- Chapters -->
    <item id="frontpage"   href="cover.html"        media-type="text/x-oeb1-document" />
    <item id="foreword"    href="frontmatter.html" media-type="text/x-oeb1-document" />
    <item id="orientation" href="chapter1.html"     media-type="text/x-oeb1-document" />
    <!-- and so through the chapters ... -->
    <!-- Figures -->
    <item id="f1_1_png" href="figs/1_1.png" media-type="image/png" />
    <item id="f1_1"     href="figs/1_1.svg" media-type="image/svg+xml"
          fallback="f1_1_png" />
    <!-- and so on through all the supporting figures in all the chapters ... -->

    <item id="toki"     href="toki.jpg"  media-type="image/jpeg" />
    <item id="toc"      href="toc.html"  media-type="text/x-oeb1-document" />
    <item id="glossary" href="glos.html" media-type="text/x-oeb1-document" />
    <!-- ... bibliography, index etc. -->
  </manifest>

  <spine>
    <itemref idref="frontpage" />
    <itemref idref="foreword" />
    <itemref idref="orientation" />
    <!-- ... -->
  </spine>

  <tours>
    <tour id="softwaretour" title="Using Greenstone">
      <site title="Introduction"          href="chapter1.html#greenstone" />
      <site title="Building collections" href="chapter6.html" />
      <site title="Serving collections"  href="chapter7.html" />
    </tour>
    <tour> <!-- Selected sections relating to the role of metadata ... --> </tour>
  </tours>

  <guide>
    <reference type="preface"  title="Preface"           href="frontmatter.html" />
    <reference type="toc"      title="Table of Contents" href="toc.html" />
    <reference type="glossary" title="Glossary"          href="glos.html" />
    <!-- ... bibliography, title-page, index etc. -->
  </guide>

</package>
```

Figure 8.10 Sample Open eBook package.

There are files for the title page, the table of contents, and so on. The idea is to declare an *item* for each file whose attributes define an identification label, a file name, and a MIME type.

The core MIME types in Open eBook are HTML 4.0, CSS, JPEG, and PNG. All have been introduced in previous chapters. HTML allows book content to be marked up, CSS takes care of formatting requirements, JPEG covers natural images, and PNG covers synthetic images. There is a caveat, however: the HTML and CSS specifications that are allowed in Open eBook publications are subsets of these standards and are represented with their own MIME types (*text/x-oeb1-document* and *text/x-oeb1-css*—the names are prefixed with *x* because they are as yet unregistered types). EBooks do not have the full generality of Web pages: the restrictions simplify rendering and encourage wider access. For each HTML tag the standard sets out conditions of use and restrictions. For example, the *http-equiv* attribute is omitted from *<meta>* because it serves no purpose, and *alt* attributes are compulsory in graphical elements such as *<img>*.

The *manifest* section of Figure 8.10 has examples of all core MIME types. Publications can draw on other types provided there is a fallback. In other words, any non-core material must be backed up with a *fallback* attribute giving the label of another *item* that can be used in its place should the reader fail to process it. Chains of fallbacks are allowed, but they must end in one of the core types.

For example, scalable vector graphics (SVG) is an XML-based language for describing two-dimensional graphics, comparable in many ways to PostScript. It allows high-quality artwork to be included in Web pages without resorting to raster images such as PNG. However, not all Web browsers support it. In Figure 8.10 the artwork for the first figure in the first chapter (*<item id=f1_1 ... />*) is given in this format. If the reader cannot display this, the *fallback* attribute directs it to the PNG version.

Following the manifest comes the *spine* element. This defines the logical order of the book using *itemref* tags whose *idref* attribute identifies items from the manifest. These items must be HTML—that is, their MIME type must be *text/x-oeb1-document*.

Figure 8.11 shows the file named by the third *itemref*—namely, *orientation*. Its header resembles the package header but names the external DTD for the modified version of HTML. Embedded in the document's *head* is a *style* element that encloses raw cascading stylesheet commands to format chapter headings, section headings, and the main text, as well as to set up margins and spacing between blocks. In the document's *body* appear *div* elements whose *class* attributes ensure that the appropriate formatting is applied.

Empty elements are one of the few real differences between XML and HTML. For example, *
* in HTML is written *
* in XML. This sometimes causes

```
<?xml version="1.0" encoding="utf-8" ?>
<!DOCTYPE html PUBLIC "+//ISBN 0-9673008-1-9//DTD OEB 1.0.1 Document//EN"
   "http://openebook.org/dtds/oeb-1.0.1/oebdoc1.dtd">
<html>
<head>
<title>How To Build a Digital Library: Orientation</title>
<style>
<!--
  body     { margin: 0.7in }
  div      { display: block; margin-bottom: 4pt }
  p        { text-align: justify; }
  .chapter { font-family: helvetica; font-size: 17pt; font-weight: bold   }
  .section { font-family: helvetica; font-size: 10pt; font-style:  italic }
  .para    { font-family: times;     font-size: 10pt; margin-left: 1.75in }
-->
</style>
</head>
<body>
<div class="chapter">Orientation: The world of digital libraries</div>

<div class="section">Example One: Supporting human development</div>

<div class="para">
<p> Kataayi is a grassroots cooperative organization based in the village
    of Kakunyu in rural Uganda. In recent years its enterprising members
    have built ferro-cement rainwater catchment tanks, utilized renewable
    energy technologies such as solar, wind, and biogas, and established a
    local industry making clay roofing tiles </p>
    ...
</div>

<!-- and so on ... -->

</body>
</html>
```

Figure 8.11 Inside an Open eBook.

problems when XML documents are processed by HTML applications. An informal convention has arisen to place a white space before the trailing slash, as in *
*, which usually allows applications from either world to parse the file correctly according to their interpretation of the rules. The Open eBook standard enforces the convention, and Figures 8.10 and 8.11 conform to this.

The *tours* element, if present, provides one or more alternative paths through the eBook. Each *tour* subelement defines one such route, including its *title* as an attribute and an embedded sequence of *site* elements as the route. Each *site* element specifies a resource using the *href* attribute. The first tour in Figure 8.10 is called *Using Greenstone* and comprises the introductory description of Greenstone in Chapter 1, followed by Chapters 6 and 7.

In the time-honored tradition of URLs, *href* attributes can target specific parts of a file by appending a hash character followed by an identifier. The Greenstone tour uses this to take the reader directly to *chapter1.html#greenstone*, which assumes that an identifier of the same name has been embedded at the beginning of the relevant section. Open eBook (versions 1.0 and 1.0.1) does not use XLink and Xpointer because they were insufficiently developed at the time of formulation.

The *guide* element, if present, identifies structural components commonly found in books: table of contents, list of illustrations, list of tables, copyright page, colophon, and so forth. The standard defines 17 types of component, each identified by a particular word or mnemonic. Components are defined by *reference* elements that name their type and provide a title and an *href* to the resource. Three examples appear in Figure 8.10.

8.4   Query languages

So far this chapter has described document structure and data control. The final element needed for interoperability in a distributed environment is an agreed way of specifying queries. As anyone who works with library computer systems or different Web portals knows, there are many different query languages in use today. We have discussed some examples in Chapter 3 (Section 3.3) and recapitulated the query syntax used in Greenstone in Chapter 6 (Section 6.1). As in many practical systems, this particular query mechanism owes much to the underlying information retrieval software used—in this case the MG search engine. To free users from having to learn different languages, and to promote interoperability, standards for querying are needed. We look at two: the common command language (CCL) and XML Query.

Common command language

The Common Command Language for Online Interactive Information Retrieval is an ANSI standard (labeled Z39.58) that defines an information retrieval cycle independent of the software used, although it inevitably makes some assumptions about what functionality is supported. A member of the Z39 family of library standards, it adopts an underlying state-based model. We will only describe the process of issuing a particular query, although the Z39.58 standard contains much more.

The Common Command Language contains commands that cover *starting* an interactive query session; *choosing* databases to query; *finding* documents using searches that can include field names, Boolean operators, word proximity, and wild character matching; *displaying* the result of a query by moving *forward* and *backward* through the items found and *sorting* or *printing* them; *reviewing* the queries entered so far; and when all is done, *stopping* the session. Each query issued is named, and combinations of them can be *saved* under a new name. Session parameters can be *seen* and *set* to different values; aliases to composite commands can be *defined*; and resources can be *deleted*. Finally, there is a *help*

Table 8.2 Common Command Language keywords, with abbreviations.

Keyword	Abbreviation	Keyword	Abbreviation	Keyword	Abbreviation
BACK	BAK	FIND	FIN	SAVE	SAV
CHOOSE	CHO	FORWARD	FOR	SCAN	SCA
DEFINE	DEF	HELP	HEL	SEE	SEE
DELETE	DEL	PRINT	PRI	SET	SET
DISPLAY	DIS	RELATE	REL	SORT	SOR
EXPLAIN	EXP	REVIEW	REV	START	STA
				STOP	STO

facility; an *explanation* of the services and databases available; and an ordered *scan* of terms in an index and how they *relate* to other terms.

The 19 italicized words above are CCL's fundamental commands. Table 8.2 lists the exact keywords along with their official three-letter abbreviations. Commands can be further abbreviated so long as they are unambiguous: FORWARD can be reduced to FORW or FO, but not to F since that could equally well represent FIND. Most keywords take additional arguments, although defaults are widely used.

Figure 8.12 shows a sample retrieval session. Before it begins the user must connect to a server that supports appropriate databases—we use the National Library of New Zealand's publicly available Z39.50 server (modified slightly for illustrative purposes). The CCL prompts have been added, and the results reformatted slightly for legibility. Keywords and operators are shown in block capitals, although the language is in fact case insensitive. User-specified arguments such as query terms are shown in mixed case, and system-specific parameters, such as representations for author and title fields, are shown in italics.

The first two commands (START and CHOOSE) pave the way for queries on databases named *newspapers* and *journals*, and evoke some feedback informing the user that default values are being used. The first query searches for documents by the author Sam Hunt (a contemporary New Zealand poet) and finds one match. The next command displays a brief summary of the record.[16] Both *AU* and *SHORT* are system-specific parameters and may not be supported by different CCL implementations—although there is wide agreement in practice on the terms used.

The second query reuses the first (which is represented by *S1*), adding a Boolean condition. Its result set comprises documents authored by Sam Hunt, or whose abstract contains the phrase "Sam Hunt." It returns six documents,

---

16. The format used in this example to display documents is the Simple Unstructured Text Record Syntax (SUTRS).

```
CCL 1> START
          Session parameters at default settings.
CCL 2> CHOOSE newspapers journals
CCL 3> FIND AU Sam Hunt
          Sent searchRequest.
          Received SearchResponse.
          Search was a success.
          Number of hits: 1, setno S1
CCL 4> DISPLAY SHORT
          Source-type: J - Journal.
          author: Hunt, Sam.
          title: Poetry: Some of the Plateau Songs (for Tom turning eleven).
          publicationDate: Apr 1988.
          Descriptor: POETRY.
          abstract:
CCL 5> FIND AB Sam Hunt OR S1
          Sent searchRequest.
          Received SearchResponse.
          Search was a success.
          Number of hits: 6, setno S2
CCL 6> SORT S2 TI
CCL 7> DISPLAY SHORT 1-2
          Source-type: J - Journal.
          author: Yuzwalk, Donna.
          title: Home movies.
          publicationDate: Aug 1988.
          Descriptor: TELEVISION REVIEWS.
          abstract: Reviews 'Catching the tide: Sam Hunt's Cook Strait'.
          ----
          Source-type: N - Newspaper.
          title: Minstrel makes trip alone.
          publicationDate: 21 Dec 1988.
          Descriptor: OBITUARIES; ANIMALS; POETRY.
          abstract: A notice on the dog belonging to poet Sam Hunt.
CCL 8> STOP
```

Figure 8.12 Using the Common Command Language.

which are sorted by title. The first two are viewed using a DISPLAY command with a numeric range. The SORT command need not have named the result set *S2* because it is the default at this point.

We will see in Section 8.5 that the same notion of a query session and the same types of services also underpin the Z39.50 standard for interoperability of online information repositories.

Full implementations of the complete CCL language are rare. However, the query part—the commands that begin with FIND—is more widespread. Online catalog systems often support such queries through an advanced query mode. The initial keyword is often omitted because it is redundant.

Figure 8.13 continues the CCL example, broadening the scope to classical poets. You might think that Query 1 searches the collection for documents by Keats or Wordsworth, but this requires parentheses as shown in Query 2. Query 1 in fact locates documents written by Keats, or documents whose entry in the default index contains *Wordsworth*. The default index need not be *AU*. Query 3 makes use of *?* to represent a variable number of characters—for instance *farm?* matches *farm*, *farmers*, and *farming*. The user is trying to locate documents by

```
CCL 1> FIND AU Keats OR Wordsworth
CCL 2> FIND AU (Keats OR Wordsworth)
CCL 3> FIND DE sonnet? AND AU shakespeare NOT compare thee
CCL 4> FIN  PD (GE 1600 AND LT 1606) AND AU shakespeare AND DE tragedy
CCL 5> FI   AU rob### burns AND TI rose N2 red
CCL 6> FI   AU rob### burns AND TI rose W2 red
CCL 7> FIND AU "W" W Shakespeare
CCL 8> FIND AU, AB Sam N Hunt AND PD 1946- AND TI ?2ternal
```

Figure 8.13 Various FIND commands.

Shakespeare that are described (*DE*) as a *sonnet* or *sonnets* and do not mention the phrase *compare thee* in the default field. Because CCL is case insensitive, proper names need not be entered with an initial capital letter.

Query 4 applies numeric constraints to locate Shakespearian tragedies published (*PD*) between 1600 and 1605 inclusive ("GE" means ≥, while "LT" means <). Queries 5 and 6 use single-character matching (the # character) to match both *Robert* and the more colloquial *Robbie* when seeking the Scottish poet Robert Burns. The last three queries demonstrate word proximity calculations using the *W* and *N* operators. With *W*, word order is important, and the term to the left must occur immediately before the one on the right. If a number is provided, as with *W2*, this limits how many words can intervene. *N* is similar except that word order is immaterial. Consequently Query 5 matches *My luve is like a red red rose*, while Query 6 does not.

Characters (or words) that have special meaning in CCL need to be enclosed in quotation marks if they are used in queries. Query 7 demonstrates this by locating documents whose author field matches *W* in immediate proximity to *Shakespeare*. Finally, ?, like *W*, can take a numeric value: this provides an upper bound to the number of matching characters. The last example seeks documents whose author (*AU*) or abstract (*AB*) field matches the words *Sam* and *Hunt* in either order, and whose title contains words such as *external*, *internal*, and *eternal*.

As these examples demonstrate, querying is a complex business and uses features that not all information retrieval software supports. Systems that conform to the official CCL standard must respond meaningfully to any valid command, but the reply might say "feature not supported." There is no minimal set of required features, and implementors are free to add extra commands as they see fit.

XML Query

XML Query (abbreviated to XQuery) is also designed for information retrieval without being tied to any specific implementation, but it takes a strikingly different approach, founded upon the extensible markup perspective. With the rider that all documents must be in XML, queries can be used to construct new documents, and no distinction is made between retrieval of documents and parts of documents.

XQuery is considerably more complex than CCL, involving its own functional programming language, and builds on XPath and XML Schema. The underlying data model (also shared by XPath) represents arbitrary sequences of documents, or parts of documents, as forests—lists of tree structures. The language consists of

- path expressions
- element constructors
- For-Let-Where-Return expressions
- quantified expressions
- operators and functions
- conditional expressions
- data types

The first two items are particular to XML; the third borrows heavily from the database query language SQL; and the last four are standard components of functional languages.

We demonstrate these parts through a series of examples based upon the resource outlined in Figure 8.14. Figure 8.14a represents the overall structure. The root node is *<Library>*, and its children represent publication categories (akin to the database names used in the CCL example). Within each category are the publications themselves, expressed as an XInclude statement that uses the *href* attribute to provide a URL for a particular publication. XInclude is a supplementary XML standard that acts just like the *include* statements of programming languages. It is self-explanatory. Triggered by the inclusion of its namespace, an XInclude-aware processing application interprets the *include* tags as textual substitution of the named resources.

Figure 8.14a embeds individual publications in an overall document type hierarchy. Figure 8.14b shows the first document, which reuses the Book Database schema from Section 8.2; the remaining publications follow the same pattern. In the example, a publication starts with a *Document* node, which includes *Metadata* and *Text* sections. Metadata includes *Title*, *Author*, and *Description* items, and the text is further marked up with *Poem*, *Chapter*, and other suitable elements. We could equally well have used the Open eBook standard, but this would unnecessarily complicate the XQuery illustrations.

Figure 8.15 shows XQuery statements that perform the same search as do the two examples of Figure 8.12: find documents with author Sam Hunt, and find documents authored by Sam Hunt, or whose abstract contains the phrase "Sam Hunt." The language's functional nature is very much in evidence, with keywords appearing in block capitals. It also has a scripting feel, variables being

```
<Library xmlns:xi="http://www.w3.org/1999/XML/xinclude">
  <Books>
    <xi:include href="bottle_creek.xml"/>
    <xi:include href="running_scared.xml"/>
    <!-- and so on ... -->
  </Books>

  <Journals>
    <!-- ... -->
  </Journals>
  <Newspapers>
    <!-- ... -->
  </Newspapers>

  <!-- ... -->
</Library>
```

(a)

```
<Document xmlns="http://bookdatabase.org/schema/publications">
  <Metadata>
    <Title>Bottle Creek</Title>
    <Author>Sam Hunt</Author>
    <Description>Poetry Collection</Description>
    <!-- ... -->
  </Metadata>
  <Text>
    <Poem Title="...">
      <!-- Stanzas for first poem ... -->
    </Poem>
    <Poem Title="...">
      <!-- Stanzas for second poem ... -->
    </Poem>
    <!-- and so on ... -->
  </Text>
</Document>
```

(b)

Figure 8.14 XML library of publications: (a) main XML file (*library.xml*);
(b) supporting file (*bottle_creek.xml*).

prefixed with $ and comments beginning with #. Both queries have the same
structure: FOR . . . WHERE . . . RETURN, a subset of the For-Let-Where-Return
or FLWR ("flower") expression. The first query uses three XPath expressions to
select subtrees in the XML library structure. They are easily recognizable
because they include slashes (/): the first is in the FOR line, the next in WHERE,
and the last in RETURN. The result of executing the query is this: for every *Document* node in the *Library* (represented by *library.xml*), locate every grandchild
Author (descending through *Metadata*) and check whether it contains the
phrase "Sam Hunt"; if so, return its *Title* element.

SOME . . . IN . . . SATISFIES . . . is an example of a qualified expression;
another form of qualified expression starts with EVERY. Our query finishes by
calling the built-in function *contains*(). The language also allows new functions

```
#--
# Comparable with FIND AU Sam Hunt
#--
FOR $d IN document("library.xml")/Library/*/Document
WHERE SOME $a IN $d/Metadata/Author SATISFIES
  contains($a,"Sam Hunt")
RETURN $d/Metadata/Title

#--
# Comparable with FIND AU Sam Hunt AND AB Sam Hunt
#--
FOR $d IN document("library.xml")/Library/*/Document
WHERE SOME $a IN $d/Metadata/(Author|Abstract) SATISFIES
  contains($a,"Sam Hunt")
RETURN $d/Metadata/Title
```

Figure 8.15 XQuery commands.

to be defined. Types are the same as the ones that XML Schema uses, augmented with operations for type casting (although none are present in the example).

Figure 8.16 shows two XQuery statements that show how elements can be constructed. The first example builds an XML document with the root *Library-Summary* that contains a *DocumentSummary* element which summarizes each document by recording its title and the number of authors. To do this, programming constructs are embedded into XML tags using braces {...}. These in turn can specify XML tags, and so on. A LET statement is used on the second line to gather all the *Author* nodes, which is later passed as an argument to the built-in function *count()*. This returns the number of items (authors) represented by the variable.

The second example builds an XML document that contains the poems that Sam Hunt published between 1980 and 1985. It uses a full FLWR statement, retrieving all documents *$d* with publication date *$p* that match the conditions expressed in the WHERE clause. The information that is extracted is packaged in *Document*, *Metadata*, and *Text* tags. Note the alternative method used to select the author. Instead of the protracted qualified clause *WHERE SOME . . . contains(...)* used in the Figure 8.15 example, the same effect is accomplished by the more concise XPath expression *$d/Metadata/[Author="Sam Hunt"]*. This is because we seek an exact match with the content of *Author*, not a substring match. FLWR expressions can be nested inside other expressions, including other FLWR expressions, although none of our examples requires this.

XQuery commands are considerably more lengthy than their CCL counterparts and require a more detailed knowledge of programming. A specialized environment might be set up for a particular community, so that members can achieve the results they need using simplified function calls defined in XQuery itself. For this to work, the various XML databases involved need to agree on the structures they use. That, of course, is what RDF, XML Schema, and DTDs are for.

```
#--
# Produce summary of all <Document> containing the <Title>
# and number of authors
#--
<LibrarySummary>
{
  FOR $d IN document("library.xml")/Library/*/Document
  LET $a := $d/Metadata/Author
  RETURN
     <DocumentSummary>
       { $d/Metadata/Title }
       <AuthorCount> { count($a) }
       </AuthorCount>
     </DocumentSummary>
}
</LibrarySummary>

#--
# Produce a new <Document> whose content represents poems
# by Sam Hunt published between 1980 and 1985
#--
<Document>
  <Metadata>
    <Title>Poems: 1980-1985</Title>
    <Author>Sam Hunt</Author>
    <!-- ... -->
  </Metadata>
{
  FOR $d IN document("library.xml")/Library/*/Document
  LET $p := $d/Metadata/Published
  WHERE $d/Metadata/[Author="Sam Hunt"]
    AND ($p >= 1980) AND ($p<=1985)
  RETURN
  <Text>
  {
     $d/Text/Poem
  }
  </Text>
  SORTBY(Poem/Title)
}
</Document>
```

Figure 8.16 XQuery commands that demonstrate element construction.

8.5 Protocols

As digital libraries pervade the workplace, the collective needs of users mushroom. The standard modus operandi of Web usage is to reach a new document by clicking on a button or hyperlink—and this is the classical form for a digital library too. How can we step outside this model in a flexible way that does not involve a heavy commitment to a particular alternative? The answer is to provide fine-grained interaction with the content of a digital library through a defined protocol that others can use. The interaction can be implemented using various different transport layers: sockets, which are typically supported by low-level Internet operations; HTTP, a more structured Web-based approach;

CORBA, a high-level architecture that supports a distributed object-oriented paradigm; and SOAP, which is based on XML.

Two prominent protocols used in digital libraries are the Z39.50 protocol and the Open Archives Initiative (OAI) protocol. These are separated historically by a decade and a half, culturally by the communities in which they arose, and ideologically by the approach taken. We also describe two other protocols developed by well-established digital library research groups—Cornell's Dienst project and Stanford's InfoBus project. Together these schemes represent a diverse range of philosophies and embody important ideas for future digital library protocols.

Z39.50 has been developed by standards committees whose members come from widely disparate backgrounds and have very different agendas. It supports a rich set of commands but is large and complex to implement. The other protocols, by comparison, are simpler and more focused on particular requirements. However, they all share the same aim of communicating with digital document repositories, and common elements and themes recur.

Z39.50

The Z39.50 standard defines a wide-ranging protocol for information retrieval between a client and a database server. Its origins stretch back to 1984, and progressive versions of the specification were ratified by standards committees in 1988, 1992, and 1995—a fourth (initiated in 2001) is nearing completion. It is administered by the Library of Congress.

Z39.50 is an example of an application layer of the Open System Interconnection (OSI) Reference Model, a comprehensive standard for networked computer environments. Message formats are specified using Abstract Syntax Notation One (ASN.1) and serialized for transmission over the OSI transport layer using Basic Encoding Rules (BER). The Transmission Control Protocol (TCP) is typically used for the actual information communication.

Accessing and retrieving heterogeneous data through a protocol in a way that promotes interoperability is a challenging problem. To address the broad spectrum of different domains where it might be used—such as bibliographic data, museum collection information, and geospatial metadata—Z39.50 includes a set of classes, called *registries*, that provide each domain with an agreed-upon structure and attributes. Registries cover query syntax, attribute fields, content retrieval formats, and diagnostic messages. For example, content retrieval formats include Simple Unstructured Text Record Syntax (SUTRS) and the various MARC formats.

The Z39.50 protocol is divided into 11 logical sections (called *facilities*) that each provide a broad set of services. We cannot do justice to the myriad details

Table 8.3 Facilities provided by Z39.50.

Z39.50 Facility	Client-side description
Initialization	Establish connection with server and set/request resource limits.
Search	Initiate search using a registered query syntax, generating a result set server-side.
Retrieval	Retrieve a set of records from a specified result set: a large record may be segmented and transmitted piecemeal.
Result-set-delete	Request deletion of server-side result set or sets.
Access Control	Server initiated authentication check.
Accounting & Resource Control	Request status reports of committed server resources and dictate if server is allowed to contact client when agreed limits are reached.
Sort	Specify how a result set should be sorted.
Browse	Access ordered lists such as title and subject metadata.
Explain	Interrogate server to discover supported services, registries, and so on.
Extended Services	Access services that continue beyond the life of this client-server exchange, such as persistent queries and database update.
Termination	Abruptly end client-server session: initiated by either client or server.

here, but instead convey some idea of the functionality supported. Table 8.3 gives a high-level summary of each category.

The protocol is predominantly client-driven; that is to say, a client initiates a request and the server responds. Only in a few places does the server demand information from the client—for example, the Access Control Facility might require the client to authenticate itself before a particular operation can be performed. Any server that implements the protocol must retain information about the client's state and apportion resources so it can respond sensibly to clients using the Initialization Facility, which sets resource limits. Mandatory search capabilities include fielded Boolean queries, which yield result sets that can be further processed by the Sort and Browse Facilities or canceled by the Result-set-delete Facility. Results themselves are returned through the Retrieval Facility. At any stage the response to a request might be an error diagnostic. This style of interaction is reflected in the common command language (CCL) query session shown in Figure 8.12.

Establishing which of the many Z39.50 options, registries, and domain-specific attributes are supported by a particular server is accomplished through the Explain Facility. The Extended Services Facility is a mechanism to access server functionality that persists beyond the duration of a given client-server session— for example, periodic search schedules and updating the database. The client-server session can be canceled immediately by either side through the Termination Facility.

A particular Z39.50 system need not implement all parts of the protocol. Indeed the protocol is so complex that full implementation is a daunting undertaking and may in any case be inappropriate for a particular digital library site. For this reason the standard specifies a minimal implementation, which comprises the Initialize Facility, the Search Facility, the Present Service (part of the Retrieval Facility), and Type 1 Queries (part of the registry).

Using this baseline implementation, a typical client-server exchange works as follows. First the client uses the Initialization Facility to establish contact with the server and negotiate values for certain resource limits. This puts the client in a position to transmit a Type 1 query using the Search Facility. The number of matching documents is returned, and the client then interacts with the Present Service to access the contents of desired documents.

Supporting the Z39.50 protocol

Support for Z39.50 in Greenstone is provided through YAZ, an open-source software library that can be used by both Z39.50 clients and servers. Using Greenstone's model of receptionists communicating with collection servers, a Z39.50 client is formed by inheriting a new receptionist from its base class and using YAZ as a back end to communicate with an existing Z39.50 server at the other end. Similarly Z39.50 serving capabilities are added to Greenstone by developing a new server that uses YAZ as a front end to accept requests from Z39.50 clients and translate them into requests that use the Greenstone protocol. The Greenstone response is then converted, through YAZ, into Z39.50 terms and returned to the client.

Figure 8.17 shows a snapshot of the Z39.50 client in use. It displays the result of searching the Library of Congress's publicly available catalog of bibliographic records for titles that include the word *Waikato* (a geographical region of New Zealand). The search is performed by the Library of Congress's computer, not the Greenstone site. The interaction style follows the standard Greenstone interface. After selecting the field to search—from the choices *any fields*, *title*, and *author*—and whether *some* or *all* of the words must be included, a search is initiated by pressing the Begin Search button. This loads a new page (shown) that repeats the query settings at the top and includes matching entries below. Clicking on the book icon beside a matching entry produces a new page giving the full catalog entry.

As with all Greenstone collections, further search options are available on the Preferences page, accessed by clicking on the Preferences button located in the top right-hand corner. Here the user can specify, among other things, whether matching is to be case sensitive or not, and whether Boolean operations are allowed.

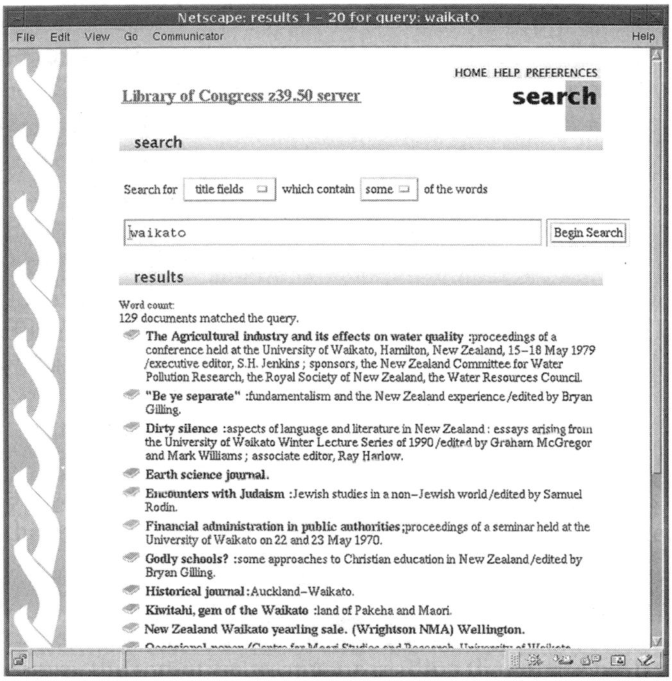

Figure 8.17 Interface to the Library of Congress using Z39.50.

Due to the complexity of the Z39.50 bibliography registry, *Title* metadata covers various different fields. However, for brevity, this system shows only one of these fields for each matching entry. Thus the display may not include the words in the query. For example, the second entry in Figure 8.17, *Be ye separate*, does not specifically mention *Waikato*. However, the term does appear in the full citation, as will be revealed by clicking on the book icon.

The Open Archives Initiative

The Open Archives Initiative (OAI) was motivated by the electronic print community, which has a strong desire to increase the availability of scholarly repositories and enhance access to them. Part of the initiative has been to devise a protocol for the efficient dissemination of content. It is intentionally broad and independent of content, making it useful to a wide range of areas, not just scholarly information.

The protocol supports interaction between a *data provider* and a *service provider*—a renaming of the client-server model which emphasizes that interaction is driven by the client and that the client alone has the onus of deciding what services are offered to users. Data providers, in contrast, are in the business of managing repositories. They do not have to perform text searching based on supplied query terms; they must merely export on demand data records in a standardized form, unencumbered by any consideration of how the information will be used. If text searching is to be supported, it must be performed by the service provider, not the data provider. Of course a site may choose to be both a service provider and a data provider. It may also manage more than one repository.

The OAI protocol is "open" in the sense that its definition is freely available and its use encouraged. The term *archive* should not be taken to imply only the compilation of digital material for historical purposes—although this is certainly one use.

A key technical goal of the protocol is to make it easy to implement using readily available software tools and support. The protocol provides a framework, borne over HTTP, in which requests are encoded in URLs and executed using CGI scripts in the normal way. Results are returned as XML records. Figure 8.18 shows the basic form of interaction using an example that requests a record pertaining to a particular document identifier and expressed using Dublin Core metadata. First the arguments are encoded into a URL (characters such as : and / must be specially coded) and dispatched over HTTP. The response is an XML document, which draws heavily on XML namespaces and schemas.

Recall from our earlier discussions that namespaces are a way of ensuring that markup tags intended for a particular purpose do not conflict with other tag sets, and XML Schema is a way of extending the idea of predefined tag sets and document structure with typed content. For example, *responseDate* in OAI is defined to be the complete date, including hours, minutes, and seconds, using the schema type *xsd:timeInstant*.

The top-level element in the example record is *GetRecord*. Through its attributes this sets up a suitable namespace using a URL in the Open Archives Web site and specifies the defining XML Schema stored at the same site. Nested deeper in the *GetRecord* structure is a *metadata* element. This uses the Dublin Core namespace and a schema specifically for this metadata standard that is defined at the Open Archives site.

Within the *metadata* element is the main content—expressed, as requested, using Dublin Core metadata—for the digital item that matches document identifier *oai:nzdl:hdl/018cf2f4256b4c8827e747b8*. The book is titled *Farming Snails* and was written for the Food and Agriculture Organization of the United Nations. Further information supplies a brief description of its content, gives the year of publication, declares that it is principally text, and states its format as HTML. This record is rich in metadata, but the protocol does not insist on this.

The protocol supports six services through the *verb* argument, and Table 8.4 summarizes them. *Identify* and *ListSets* are services that are typically called early on in a client's interchange with a server to establish a broad picture of the repository. *ListIdentifiers* is a way of receiving all the document identifiers or a

```
Request Arguments:
      verb=GetRecord
      identifier=oai:nzdl:hdl/018cf2f4256b4c8827e747b8
      metadataPrefix=oai_dc

Encoded URL:
http://www.nzdl.org/cgi-bin/oai/request?verb=GetRecord
          &identifier=oai%3Anzdl%3Ahdl%2F018cf2f4256b4c8827e747b8
          &metadataPrefix=oai_dc

Response :
<?xml version="1.0" encoding="UTF-8"?>
 <GetRecord
    xmlns="http://www.openarchives.org/OAI/1.0/OAI_GetRecord"
    xmlns:xsi="http://www.w3.org/2000/10/XMLSchema-instance"
    xsi:schemaLocation="http://www.openarchives.org/OAI/1.0/OAI_GetRecord
                http://www.openarchives.org/OAI/1.0/OAI_GetRecord.xsd">
  <responseDate>2001-06-16T13:15:42+00:00</responseDate>
  <requestURL>http://www.nzdl.org/cgi-bin/oai/request?verb=GetRecord
          &amp;identifier=oai%3Anzdl%3Ahdl%2F018cf2f4256b4c8827e747b8
          &amp;metadataPrefix=oai_dc</requestURL>
  <record>
   <header>
    <identifier>oai:nzdl:hdl/018cf2f4256b4c8827e747b8</identifier>
    <datestamp>1986-01-01</datestamp>
   </header>
   <metadata>
   <dc xmlns="http://purl.org/dc/elements/1.1/"
       xmlns:xsi="http://www.w3.org/2000/10/XMLSchema-instance"
       xsi:schemaLocation="http://purl.org/dc/elements/1.1/
                      http://www.openarchives.org/OAI/dc.xsd">
    <title>Farming Snails</title>
    <description>Learning about snails; Building a pen; Food
          and shelter plants</description>
    <creator>Food and Agriculture Organization of the United Nations</creator>
    <type>Text</type>
    <format>text/html</format>
    <date>1986-01-01</date>
    <identifier>
    http://www.nzdl.org/cgi-bin/library?&a=d&cl=search&d=HASH018cf2f4256b4c8827e747b8
    </identifier>

   </dc>
   </metadata>
  </record>
</GetRecord>
```

Figure 8.18 OAI *GetRecord* request and XML response.

group that matches a stipulated set name. *ListMetadataFormats* can be applied to the repository as a whole or to a particular document within it to establish which metadata formats are supported. Dublin Core is mandatory, but other formats such as MARC, which has the capacity to export a greater volume of metadata per record, may also be supported. We have already seen *GetRecord* in action in the example just given—*ListRecords* is similar except that more than one record can be returned, and group selection is possible with the same set-naming technique used by *ListIdentifiers*.

These are the general facilities supported by the protocol. Greater flexibility can be achieved using the input arguments and the set and resumption mecha-

Table 8.4 Open Archive Initiative protocol requests.

OAI protocol request	Description
Identify	Returns both fixed-format and domain-specific descriptions
ListSets	Returns the repository's classification hierarchy
ListIdentifiers	Returns a list of document identifiers
ListMetadataFormats	Returns the metadata formats supported by the repository in general or for a specific document
GetRecord	Returns the repository item specified by the document identifier in the requested format
ListRecords	Returns a list of repository items in the requested format

nisms. First, repository items can be categorized into sets—multiple hierarchies, where an item can be in more than one hierarchy or in none at all. Each node in the hierarchy has a set name, such as *beekeeping,* and a descriptive name, such as *Beekeeping and honey extraction.* Its hierarchical position is specified by concatenating set names separated by colons—like *husbandry:beekeeping. ListSets* returns this information for the complete repository, marked up as XML.

Now instead of retrieving all the document identifiers, a service provider can restrict the information returned by *ListIdentifiers* to a particular set. (The same applies to *ListRecords.*) Because records in the repository are date-stamped, the information returned can be restricted to a particular range of dates using *from* and *until* arguments. Even so, the list of data returned may still be excessively long. If so, a data provider might transmit part of the data and include a *resumption token* in the record. This mechanism enables the service provider to contact the data provider again and request the next installment (which might include another resumption token).

The OAI protocol makes use of the HTTP status code mechanism to indicate the success or failure of a request. Status code 400, in this context, indicates a syntactic error in the request, such as an invalid input argument. Other forms of failure, such as a repository item being unavailable in the requested metadata format, produce null data in the XML record that is returned.

Supporting the OAI protocol

For a given digital library site to become an OAI data provider, software needs to be written that can respond to CGI requests and access the database system that stores the documents. Many programming languages have library support for implementing CGI scripts—Perl, Python, Java, and C++, among others—although the database itself will probably dictate the most suitable choice. None of this should present much difficulty to an experienced programmer, who can quickly make the metadata in the digital library available to others using OAI.

Becoming a service provider is more challenging, although much depends on how much value is added to the data that is handled. Minimum requirements are safely encoding URLs, parsing the returned XML, and detecting error conditions. None of this is difficult. The challenges begin when services are extended beyond those provided by the basic OAI protocol—for instance, text searching. Of course managing such services is akin to building your own digital library using a suitable software tool—say Greenstone! Some format conversion may be required for both metadata and documents—this is precisely the role of plug-ins in Greenstone.

As an example we now describe the construction of a Greenstone digital library collection based on OAI exported data. There are two steps: obtaining the raw material from a data provider, and configuring a suitable collection. The first step is accomplished using the Greenstone script *getoai.pl*, which takes as arguments a base URL for an OAI site and a local collection name. The result is to place the exported data in the collection's *import* directory. OAI record identifiers encode hierarchical structure, and *getoai.pl* maps these into subdirectories of *import*. The script uses a Web mirroring package to handle access to the OAI site. If the Dublin Core section of an OAI record includes an *identifier* element whose content is a URL, and *getoai.pl* has the *retrieve document* option switched on, a follow-up call is made to the mirroring package to download that object too.

The second step is accomplished by augmenting the collection configuration file with the line

```
plugin OAIPlugin
```

which incorporates a plug-in designed to process files like that shown in Figure 8.18. Written in Perl like any plug-in, it uses a regular expression to locate the *metadata* element and turn each element into a metadata item in Greenstone. If a file named *identifier* can be located in the *import* area, this relationship is represented in Greenstone as an associated document.

With the issuing of the appropriate *import.pl* and *buildcol.pl* commands, the end result of these two stages is a searchable, browsable Greenstone collection based on the exported content. Further configuration of indexes and classifiers is possible depending on the metadata available.

8.6   Research protocols

We now introduce two long-standing digital library protocols from the research community that are designed to promote interoperability. The trouble with interoperability, though, is that the purpose is defeated if several groups pro-

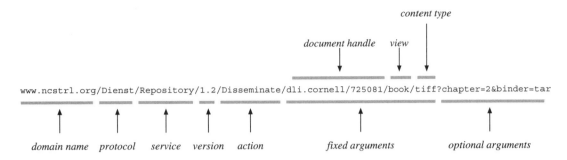

Figure 8.19 Using the Dienst protocol.

mote different interoperability schemes. We well remember a digital library conference in which so many people wanted to talk about interoperability that parallel sessions were set up in separate rooms. The irony seemed to be lost on most participants.

Dienst

Dienst, at Cornell University in the U.S., is one of the longest-running digital library projects in the research community: its origins stretch back to 1992. It has three facets: a conceptual architecture for distributed digital libraries, an open protocol for service communication, and a software system that implements the protocol.

The protocol supports search and retrieval of documents, browsing documents, adding new documents, and registering users. Each of these is an independent service, borne over HTTP. A digital library collection involves a combination of these services. There are six categories of service: *repository services* store digital documents and associated metadata; *index services* accept queries and return lists of document identifiers; *query mediator services* dispatch queries to the relevant index servers; *info services* return information about the state of a server; *collection services* provide information on how a set of services interact; and *registry services* store user information.

The repository service, a bidirectional link to a collection's content (or part of it), lies at the heart of the system. Figure 8.19 shows this service being used to export a set of images in TIFF format taken from the second chapter of the book identified by the handle *dli.cornell/725081*,[17] bound into one file using the *tar* format. Within the service area (*Repository* in our example), a particular action is specified using the argument *verb*. Here *Disseminate* is specified, because we wish to retrieve some document content. Earlier, in the description of the OAI protocol, we encountered

---

17. A *handle* is a form of URN.

a similar use of a CGI argument named *verb* (at the top of Figure 8.18). In fact the OAI designers drew on lessons learned from this protocol.

In Figure 8.19 the desired book's handle contains two parts separated by a slash character: a naming authority and an identifying string. The naming authority is used whenever the content of a repository is updated—whenever books are added or deleted. The details of the authentication mechanism are left to the service: for example, a simple policy would be to restrict access to a fixed set of the identifiers—called *IP numbers*—that are used on the Internet to identify individual computers.

HTTP messages are used to respond to service requests: they can take a variety of forms. In the example the returned message has MIME type *application/tar*. However, requests for information, such as lists of verbs and other options, are today more often encoded as XML.

Given that Dienst was a source of inspiration for the OAI protocol, it is not surprising to learn that several Dienst-based digital library sites are also OAI data providers and are switching to the new protocol.

Simple digital library interoperability protocol

Interoperation among distributed objects has been a central plank of Stanford University's digital library project, the Infobus. Many Infobus objects are in fact proxies to established information sources and services. The original CORBA-based Digital Library Interoperation Protocol (DLIOP) has since been superseded by the Simple Digital Library Interoperability Protocol (SDLIP), designed in collaboration with other U.S. research projects.

SDLIP places emphasis on a design that is scalable, permitting the development of digital library applications that run on handheld devices such as Palm Pilots, as well as workstation- and mainframe-based systems. There are two transport options, one based on CORBA, the other on HTTP, and applications can mix them freely.

The protocol supports both state-keeping and stateless exchanges on the server side, and both synchronous and asynchronous interactions between client and server. However, servers need not implement all these options. It is up to a client to establish, using the protocol, what functionality is supported.

There are four parts (called *interfaces*) to the protocol: *searching, accessing results, metadata,* and *delivery*. The *search* interface initiates a search. In a synchronous, stateless exchange, the client waits until all results are returned, but in a synchronous, state-keeping exchange, only some of the results need be returned as part of the search—the rest can be accessed through the *result access* interface. A server that supports asynchronous searches must by nature also be state-keeping. When the results of an asynchronous query become available, the server uses the *delivery* interface to notify the client. Finally the *source metadata*

Interface

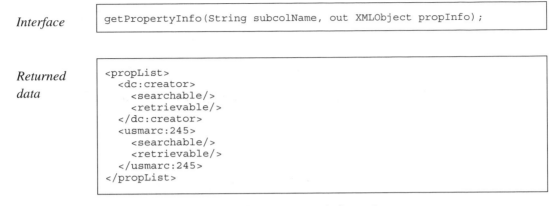

```
getPropertyInfo(String subcolName, out XMLObject propInfo);
```

Returned data

```
<propList>
  <dc:creator>
    <searchable/>
    <retrievable/>
  </dc:creator>
  <usmarc:245>
    <searchable/>
    <retrievable/>
  </usmarc:245>
</propList>
```

Figure 8.20 Using SDLIP to obtain property information.

interface provides a mechanism for clients to discover the functional capabilities of a server (including its version number), the collections stored there, and the metadata fields present in a particular collection.

Figure 8.20 shows the interface description language for *getPropertyInfo*(), part of the source metadata interface, along with some sample returned data. If *subcolName* is empty, property information about the default subcollection is returned, encoded as XML in the output variable *propInfo*. Otherwise a prior call to *getSubcollectionInfo*() must be made to establish the subcollection names. The property information returned in this example states that Dublin Core metadata for Creator is available, as is the author field in the Library of Congress's MARC attribute model (called USMARC). Both can be searched and retrieved.

Translating between protocols

The Stanford research group provides a Java-based software development kit to support SDLIP. To demonstrate the ease of protocol conversion, this was used to develop a translator that maps the SDLIP protocol calls pertaining to stateless synchronous interaction to Greenstone protocol calls. The translator runs as a server in its own right. As Figure 8.21 shows, it acts as an intermediary, accepting SDLIP requests transmitted either through CORBA or HTTP and passing them on to Greenstone's CORBA-based protocol. The translator server implements the intersection of the Greenstone protocol and SDLIP's *search* and *source metadata* interfaces.

The *search* interface maps to Greenstone's Filter and Document operations, while *source metadata* maps to various Greenstone calls (grouped as *general* in the figure). The remaining interfaces and services, such as the *result access* interface and *delivery* interface, are set up for trivial default behavior because they have no counterpart in a direct mapping to a synchronous stateless service.

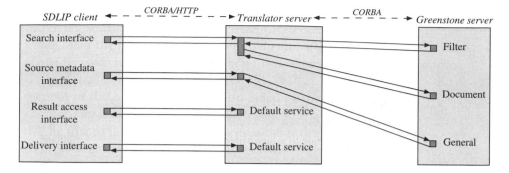

Figure 8.21 Mapping SDLIP calls to the Greenstone protocol.

Figure 8.22 shows the result of running a command-line SDLIP client provided by the Stanford research group. At the top we see diagnostic output from the SDLIP client; at the bottom is the diagnostic output from the SDLIP-to-Greenstone translator. We assume the existence of a Greenstone server (output not shown) whose location is specified when the translator server is started.

When the client program is run, it first connects to the SDLIP server specified on the command line (the translator in our case) and then calls the *search* interface with the remaining command-line arguments stored as the query. The translator server accepts these arguments and sets up a Filter call to emulate the call to SDLIP search. If the property list supplied by the SDLIP call specifies document text, a second call to Greenstone is made, this time using the Document part of the protocol, to access the necessary information. The data obtained from these calls is then collated and returned encoded as XML.

The translator example is intended for demonstration purposes only. A more sophisticated—and ultimately more desirable—approach is to enhance the translator with state-keeping capabilities. Just because the Greenstone server does not keep state does not mean that state-based SDLIP interactions cannot be supported. For instance, when query results are returned from the CORBA call to Greenstone, the translator server can store the result locally and assign it a result set identifier. It can use this to support subsequent calls to the *result access* interface—including query refinement. Other details that would need attention to make the demonstration practically useful include mapping more carefully the SDLIP-supported query syntax, which makes use of various standards, to the Greenstone query syntax.

Discussion

We have summarized the main features of four digital library protocols: Z39.50, Open Archives Initiative (OAI), Dienst, and SDLIP, along with the Greenstone protocol described in Chapter 7. All support browsing and document retrieval,

Client:

```
weka% java SimpleClient http://kiwi.cs.waikato.ac.nz:8282 "music style"
DOCUMENT: 1
        http://purl.org/metadata/dublin_core#Title
          = "Computer Graphic Aided Music Composition"
DOCUMENT: 2
        http://purl.org/metadata/dublin_core#Title
          = "Schenker s Theory of Tonal Music -- Its Explication ..."
DOCUMENT: 3
        http://purl.org/metadata/dublin_core#Title
          = "Andre Tchaikovsky Meets the Computer: A Concert ..."
```

Server:

```
kiwi% java SdlipToGsdl http://www.nzdl.org hcibib 8282
GreenstoneCorba Init on www.nzdl.org OK
hcibib OK
hcibib is public? ... yes
Starting DASL/HTTP server transport on port: 8282

[SDLIP/DASL Server Transport] request from: weka.cs.waikato.ac.nz
Query is:
<a:basicsearch xmlns:a="DAV:">
        <a:select>
                <a:allprop/>
        </a:select>
        <a:where>
                <a:contains>music style</a:contains>
        </a:where>
        <a:limit>
                <a:nresults>10</a:nresults>
        </a:limit>
</a:basicsearch>

Query string = music style
Title: Computer Graphic Aided Music Composition
Title: Schenker s Theory of Tonal Music -- Its Explication ...
Title: Andre Tchaikovsky Meets the Computer: A Concert ...
```

Figure 8.22 Using the SDLIP-to-Greenstone translator.

and all but OAI support searching. Text searching is relatively well under-
stood—all support ranked and Boolean queries, with a rich array of options:
fielded search, stemming, case matching, and so forth. The main divergence is
in the query syntax used. Z39.50 and SDLIP are notable in their use of existing
standards.

The role of browsing in a digital library is less clear-cut, and support varies.
Browsing is usually closely associated with metadata. OAI, with its focus on
metadata, and Greenstone appear to be more general than the others, both providing hierarchical browsing and exporting.

Document retrieval is well supported throughout. Different protocols assume
different models of document structure and different ways of enumerating docu-

ment formats and types. Dienst, with its ability to export logical structure in a variety of MIME types, seems to provide the richest functionality.

While not a core requirement, all protocols provide a way of determining which options the server supports and (with the exception of OAI) what services it offers. This enables clients to be written that configure themselves dynamically in response to different situations.

Other important elements are version control and authentication, and here the protocols differ. Version control is handled externally in Z39.50 by ratified standards. SDLIP, Dienst, and OAI build it into the protocol—a more ambitious aim, and one that places the onus on clients to resolve version conflicts. The Greenstone protocol provides no explicit version control. Because it is closely associated with the software architecture, this is not as limiting as it might at first seem. The application program interface gives latitude for backward-compatible extensions, and the filtering mechanism—the main part of the protocol that is likely to change—has been designed to be extensible. This is backed up by the Greenstone's Filter mechanism, which includes calls to list the filter types supported and the options they take.

Although a framework for authentication is part of Dienst, it is left up to the service provider to implement. In Z39.50, authentication is rigorously defined by an Access Control Facility, in stark contrast to SDLIP, Greenstone, and OAI, which have none. Of course these protocols do not rule out authentication—a security check can always be imposed using the transport layer when a client connects to a server.

8.7 Notes and sources

The World Wide Web Consortium's Web site (*www.w3.org*) is the definitive source for explanations of XML and its supporting specifications. The formulation of XML Schema started in the XML Developers' e-mail list, and preliminary forms were called XSchema and the Document Definition Markup Language (DDML) before being cast in the form described here.

RDF is also managed by the World Wide Web Consortium, and an even more ambitous project, called the Semantic Web, builds on its ideas to increase the opportunities for machine comprehension of Web documents. There is an introduction to RDF in *D-Lib Magazine* (Miller, 1998), and an article in *Scientific American* introduces the Semantic Web (Berners-Lee, Hendler, and Lassila, 2001).

The RSLP Collection Description project at the Research Support Libraries Programme based at the University of Bath, U.K., was motivated by a need to consistently describe all projects funded through their research program. However, what resulted is of far wider application. A detailed description of the project, along with an unabridged version of the Morrison Collection RDF example, appears in *D-Lib Magazine* (Miller, 2000). This is a special issue on collection-level metadata and contains other relevant papers. For additional information about RSLP projects, consult the Web site *www.rslp.ac.uk.*

Open eBook Forum publishes its work at *www.openebook.org.* They strongly advocate the idea of making online publications available to people with print disabilites. Version 2.0 of the standard is under development.

XML Query is required to be both human-readable and machine-readable. The examples given in this chapter are shown in the human-readable form. By *machine-readable* the specification means that the language should be valid XML, and clearly the programming language used in the examples is not valid XML. XQueryX is an equivalent version of the language that uses pure XML syntax, thus fulfilling the machine-readable requirement. However, it is verbose to write by hand and more convoluted to read—hence the XQuery form.

The home page for Z39.50 is located at the Library of Congress Web site at *www.loc.gov/z3950/agency.* There is an active group of online developers and implementers known as ZIG (for Z39.50 Implementers' Group). They maintain a ListServ for e-mail discussion and hold regular meetings.

Further information on the Open Archives Initiative can be found in an article by Lagoze and Van de Sompel (2001), and on the Web site *www.openarchives.org.* For the Dienst protocol see Lagoze and Fielding (1998); for SDLIP see Paepcke et al. (1999).

9 Visions

Future, past, and present

Whither digital libraries? Where are we headed, where have we come from, and what should we be doing now? This chapter looks at the past, present, and future—but not in that order.

We began this book with a whirlwind tour of the history of 25 centuries of physical libraries. A whirlwind tour of prognostications for the first 25 centuries of digital libraries, starting today, would be an excellent way to end. But technology predictions are futile. We cannot even foresee the next 25 years: in fact, given the rate of change in the field, 25 months seems sufficiently ambitious! Nevertheless we will present some visions of the digital library—images of today as well as visions of tomorrow. Digital libraries have certain obvious practical advantages over physical ones and seem to offer the promise of far greater universality. While all this is true, we believe that their real power lies elsewhere. In our own vision the digital library is like an all-encompassing information medium that will envelop us as we work—like air. Just as oxygen unobtrusively powers our body and brain, so digital libraries will unobtrusively empower our mind.

Having glimpsed the vision, we turn to a troubling but vital issue that threatens to jeopardize the whole enterprise: preserving the past. This is something that we have not mentioned so far. The mission of a library is twofold: to collect, organize, and provide access to information, and to pass it down to succeeding generations as a record of culture. In short, the librarian's twin duties are access and preservation: providing access to the world's literature for today's readers and preserving it for future generations. Libraries are containers for putting things in and getting them out again—at different points in the space-time continuum.

This book has talked a lot about access, but not at all about the problem of preservation. In truth there is not a lot we can say—except to recognize the problem, acknowledge its devastatingly serious nature, and point out that although it is caused by technology, it will not be solved by technology. Preservation is a social issue, not a technical one. In the history of libraries, a great deal has been destroyed forever. But some has been preserved. It is sobering to realize that if the ancients had possessed our technology, we would probably have even less record of the past.

What are the challenges for digital libraries? We focus on one: generalized documents. Today's collections are mostly text. They include pictures, of course, even audio and video—but these objects are subservient to text, in particular textual metadata. Of course some research projects do focus on, say, video libraries, but they neglect text and documents in other media. The real challenge is to create collections of digital documents in diverse media types, where each type is treated as a first-class citizen. One example we can point to is digital libraries of music, which allow you to search melodies directly, by humming or singing, and combine this with textual queries on lyrics or metadata. But designing searching and browsing strategies specifically for different media, and integrating them into a unified concept of "generalized documents," are key problems for current research.

Generalized documents raise some intriguing questions and possibilities. What is "literature" if documents are generalized? Can information collections be language-independent? Can digital libraries be used by people from oral cultures? Why not! Does this have implications for developing countries? You bet! And what about our own society, where text and sustained, coherent argument are increasingly being hijacked by imagery and sound bites?

Library traditions have long been influenced by the belief that libraries should serve democracy. As part of their mission to serve as resource centers for citizens, public libraries maintain collections of records, policy statements, government documents, and so on. The U.S. Library of Congress is the oldest cultural institution in the nation's capital and serves as a symbol of American democracy and faith in the power of learning. Indeed the library gained support during World War II by publicly defending American culture against the threat of totalitarianism in Europe.

We believe that future digital libraries will find a new role to play in helping to reduce the social inequity that haunts today's world, both within our own countries and between nations.

9.1   Libraries of the future

Digital libraries have the potential to be far more flexible than conventional ones. Of course they are portable: they will be with you whenever you want them to be: in the home, in the plane, at the beach, in a Ugandan village, on the street when you want to play your friends that new song. They will be large, giving access to your personal book collection, your town's public library, your university library. Not only this, but they will ultimately be seamlessly integrated with national and international sources of information—interlibrary loan at your fingertips. Like H. G. Wells's vision of a permanent world encyclopedia mentioned in Chapter 1, they will give access to the world's recorded knowledge. But they will certainly not be static. In 1931, shortly before Wells penned his vision, Ranganathan, an influential librarian and educator who is considered the father of library science in India, wrote as one of his "five laws of library science" that a library is a growing organism. The ultimate digital library will continually be revised and extended by original thinkers around the world.

But wait, there's more. Flexibility will extend well beyond matters of physical convenience. Future digital libraries will surround you with information in ways that we can yet only dimly perceive. When Karl Marx wrote *Das Kapital*, he worked in the reading room of the British Museum library. Not only will future revolutionaries use their laptop instead of Marx's pen and paper, they will work "inside" their digital libraries in a stronger and more visceral sense.

Today's visions

Figure 9.1 shows the reading room of the New York Public Library, which itself is depicted in Figure 1.3 (Chapter 1). This is a magnificent place: spacious and airy with bright yet soft lighting, comfortable furniture, warm tones of wood, leather, and books; the hushed sounds of people thinking and working. You can become absorbed in what you are reading, living in your own world shared between your head and the book you are holding, or your gaze can wander around the immense spaces above you, the massive windows, the huge chandeliers, the painted ceiling. But the space is impersonal, as any large physical library has to be. One size fits all. No matter how divergent your intellectual pursuits, you work in the same place as your neighbor. The most you might expect by way of personalization is an assigned carrel where you can leave your books and materials undisturbed until tomorrow. Is this the vision we seek for digital libraries?

Figure 9.2 shows an example digital library, one that forms part of the British National Library. It is just as impersonal as Figure 9.1, if not more so. You stand

Figure 9.1 New York Public Library reading room.

at the threshold and are confronted with row upon row of identical workstations. This space lacks the architectural beauty of the reading room in Figure 9.1—it looks utilitarian rather than spacious. We all know from bitter experience that the technology it contains, no matter how spiffy today, will appear old and jaded in just a few months. But perhaps the most striking thing about the vision is the staged nature of this publicity photograph: one man in an empty room, clearly posed as though at work. Every other workstation in the room shows the same screen—not only that, but beside each one, on a typing stand, is the same piece of paper. This Orwellian setting does not seem like a nice place to work. Is it the vision we seek?

A more engaging picture of a present-day digital library is Figure 9.3, which shows the computer room at the Kataayi cooperative in Uganda with which this book opened. From a Western perspective the image is decidedly low-tech. The computers are ancient, the furniture is shabby, the walls are bare, the setting is plain and utilitarian. But it looks as though it works. Here we see real people interacting with information in a real environment, rather than a publicity machine's conception of some kind of spine-chilling ideal. This picture serves as

Figure 9.2 Digital library in the British National Library. "The Virtue of Virtual Libraries" by Matt Jones. *The Independent*, 16 July 2001. London, England.

Figure 9.3 A peek inside the digital library at the Kataayi cooperative in Uganda.

a salutary reminder that libraries are about connecting people with the information they need. Kataayi's library may not be flashy, but it works.

Tomorrow's visions

So much for the present: what about the future? By way of—literally!—comic relief, Figure 9.4 shows a sci-fi artist's image of a digital library taken from a Marvel comic, the living computers of Xandar (dated 1979). On this planet they have stored the still-functioning brains of the population for more than 10,000 millennia, giving—as our guide explains—a complete record of all their history, all their science, all their *knowledge*. Is this the long-term prognosis that we

Figure 9.4 Xandar's digital library. Vol. 1, #25, 1979.
FANTASTIC FOUR™ © 2002 Marvel Characters, Inc.
Used with permission.

sought at the outset? (Note that our 25 centuries of libraries represent a mere eye-blink in Xandarian history.)

Here is a vision that emphasizes preservation over access. Xandarians can put the brains in, but can they get the knowledge out? It certainly appears from the illustration that their computer scientists have some work to do on the user interface. But the problem runs deeper. In storing living brains, what is lacking (or may be lacking—it's hard to tell from the picture!) is *librarianship*—the selection, organization, and maintenance in the definition of digital libraries in Chapter 1, the wisdom that librarians put into the library by making value judgments about what information is to be included and how it should be organized. Figure 9.4 is reminiscent of a historical archive of the Web. There is no organization, no quality control: a mere repository. This is not a library.

Our own vision of the digital library of the future is that it will be a personalized, comfortable space to work in. Think of it as more like a kitchen than a library—a kitchen for knowledge preparation. If you like cooking, you will have arranged your kitchen to suit what you do: utensils ready to hand, pots by the stove, spices for the kind of dishes you like to cook, and placed just where you need them. Left-handed?—change your kitchen around. Short?—adjust the work surfaces. Like wine?—keep a glass handy. Stir-frys?—here's the wok.

Figure 9.5 shows another workspace that illustrates the vision we are trying to convey. This carpenter's workshop, although perhaps a little stiff and idealized, is all set out as a comfortable, productive workplace. Hand tools are arranged in convenient clusters, bench tools such as vise and drill press are conveniently located, nails and screws are boxed and labeled, a well-positioned lamp illuminates the current job. This man knows where everything is, and the physical arrangement almost exudes productivity. Imagine how much better you could work here than in the messy corner, littered with assorted junk and half-finished projects, that most of us have in our garage. Imagine how this carpenter would feel if he had to carry all his tools into the New York Public Library reading room in Figure 9.1; unpack them, sort them, and arrange them before he began work; and pack them up again before lunch to leave the space clear for someone else.

Just so with the digital library. Inside the computer it will be *your* library, arranged the way you like it, personalized for the kind of things you do. Externally it may look like Figure 9.1 (just bring your laptop and plug it in), Figure 9.2 (hopefully a little more welcoming and ergonomic, with concealed computers, flat-panel screens, and wrist rests), or even Figure 9.3 (though with more powerful equipment). Inside it will not only give access to the world's recorded knowledge as Wells's vision did, but it will feel like Figure 9.5, arranged just for you and the kind of things you do.

You will need to invest in this personalization, just as our carpenter invested time and money establishing his workplace. And there are pitfalls aplenty, for

Figure 9.5 Carpenter's workshop. *Working in Wood* by
E. Scott. Putnam, 1980.

with the potential for flexibility comes the potential for confusion. A physical
environment makes the possibilities that it opens up for interaction—its "affor-
dances"—openly manifest. There is no user manual for Figure 9.5: you can step
into this environment and see immediately how it works. It will be harder to
make the intellectual environment your digital library provides so accessible
and transparent.

But we're dreaming of the future: these problems will be solved. The computers, so prominent in Figure 9.2, will disappear. There will still be an interface—
perhaps a screen, though it may disappear into the wall or into your spectacles;
perhaps a keyboard, though it may disappear into finger sensors or a microphone; perhaps a mouse, though it may be a wand or a wave of the hand. But
you will conceptualize this interface as a *library* rather than a *computer:* the
computer will become invisible just as the countless electric motors in your

house have become invisible, disappearing into hair dryers, fans, electric razors, kitchen appliances, CD players, and VCRs. Tomorrow's digital library will feel less like a computer, more like a kitchen or workshop.

As well as being personalized, your digital library will be dynamic. And not only in the sense that the information it contains will be bang up to date. The library will work alongside you, tracking your activity, unobtrusively rearranging itself to put what you might need in the context of what you are doing just there where you can see and read it. When you leave off for the day, it will continue to work for you, locating pertinent information, classifying and categorizing it, working through the implications, researching on your behalf, so that tomorrow when you recommence you will start well ahead of where you left off today.

Working inside the digital library

We said in Chapter 1 that digital libraries are libraries without walls, although they do need boundaries; we argued that the very notion of a collection implies a boundary. Paradoxically, perhaps, in the future we will work *inside* the digital library in a new sense of "in"-ness that we can barely glimpse today. The library will be an environment that surrounds you in an intellectual, not a physical, sense. But virtual reality means that intellectual experiences can easily be translated into physical ones. More or less immersive (you can choose), the library will be an environment that reacts and responds to what you are doing, making the right kind of information available to you as and when you need it, and in an appropriate form. It will surround your head.

Lest you feel you are being carried away by empty rhetoric, a system called Phrasier, conceived and constructed by Steve Jones of the University of Waikato, gives a glimpse of what we mean. Phrasier is an environment for reading and writing within a digital library. Figure 9.6 shows us at work writing this chapter. We are working in a digital library, and associated with every document in it are a handful of key phrases, perhaps assigned manually, perhaps extracted automatically from the text as described in Section 5.6 (Chapter 5). It is these that are used to connect the chapter being written with the documents in the library.

As Figure 9.6 shows, certain parts of the chapter's text are highlighted in boldface. These are phrases that appear as key phrases of other documents in the library. If a subject-matter thesaurus were available, phrases in it would be highlighted too, wherever they appeared in the chapter. The user can control the amount of highlighting and the tone of the non-highlighted text using the slider at the top of the page. Studies are underway to determine whether people can skim text faster, yet still gain some comprehension of it, if the text fades away into the background and only the key phrases are clearly visible.

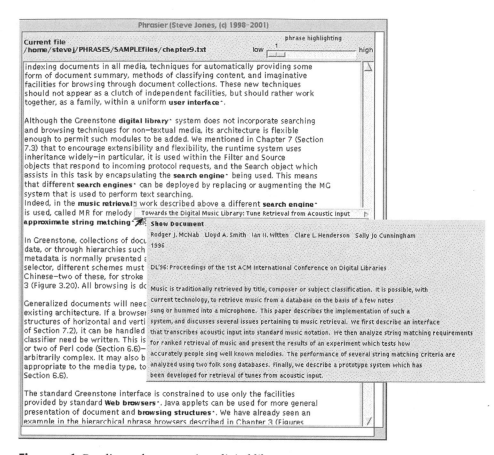

Figure 9.6 Reading a document in a digital library.

Mouse buttons can be used to focus on a phrase of interest that appears in the chapter and to examine the documents in the library for which it is a key phrase. A popup window contains titles of documents for which this is a key phrase. In this case the key phrase is *music retrieval*, and the list contains just one item. That document has been selected and is shown just beneath the item, in a second popup window.

In Figure 9.7 we have brought up another window (in the background) in which to examine related literature. We have focused on a particular area of the chapter—the three paragraphs in the middle—by highlighting it with the mouse (the highlighting is only faintly visible in the picture). In the background window there appears, on the left, a list of the key phrases that appear in that region (there are three), along with their frequency and the number of documents for which they are a key phrase. The system has used this set of key phrases as a query into the digital library and has retrieved a list of documents

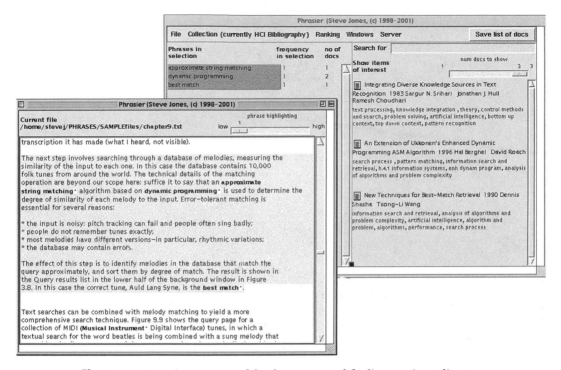

Figure 9.7 Focusing on part of the document and finding pertinent literature.

that relate to all of them, sorted into relevance order using the same kind of ranking heuristic that is used during full-text search. If the selected part of the chapter is the focus of interest, this list shows the relevant literature in the library. It appears in the right-hand panel; clicking on a document brings it up in a separate window.

As authors we often want to focus on a conceptual subtopic of the chapter's subject matter rather than on a spatial region like a particular paragraph or section. In Figure 9.8 the phrases in the background window's list are key phrases in the digital library that are mentioned anywhere in the chapter's text, not just in a particular subarea as before. Some are highlighted because we have selected them manually by clicking on them. This selection effectively defines a subtopic, or group of subtopics, that has been chosen as being of special interest. As before, a list of related documents appears in the right-hand window; but now it is the manually chosen key phrases that are used to select and rank them. This provides a reading list, ranked by relevance, for the conceptual subtopic that has been defined. Again, of course, the full text of each document is just a click away.

We have chosen to illustrate the Phrasier interface by describing how we might have written this chapter. As we type new material into the document window in Figures 9.6, 9.7, and 9.8, everything we have just described happens

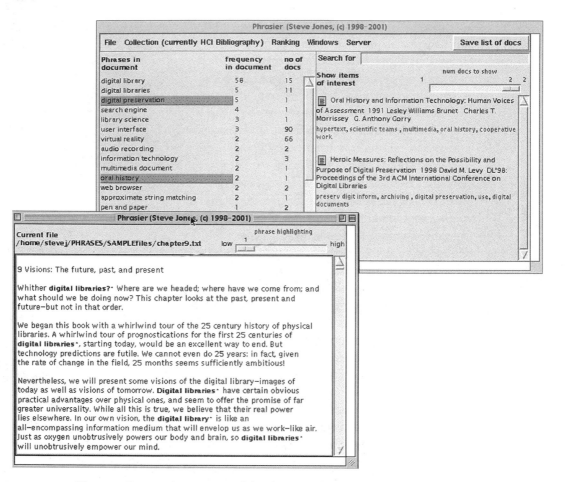

Figure 9.8 Focusing on part of the document's subject matter.

interactively. The new chapter is not only born digital, it is born in a library, fully contextualized and linked to the existing literature at birth.

Exactly the same system supports reading. You can load an article into the document window and read it "in" the library. The article could be taken from the library or downloaded from elsewhere. The entire contents of the library are available with no effort, in context, at your fingertips, on the fly, as you read and write. This is a library that works along with you.

9.2 Preserving the past

Libraries link the past and the future, and preservation has always been a key function. Whatever form the cultural record is in, libraries ensure that it is preserved and made available for later use. We learned in Chapter 1 of the tragic loss of the historic Alexandrian Library, willfully laid to waste during the decline of the Roman Empire. Acts of God—fires, floods, earthquakes—and acts of man—wars, revolutions—have damaged the holdings of many libraries, destroying forever much of the recorded history of human civilization. We gaze in awe at the stone steles of Xi'an (Figure 1.4) and the *Book of Kells* (Figure 1.8) not just because of their intrinsic beauty, but also because they have survived one or two millennia and have witnessed unimaginable strife and conflict.

The problem of preservation

The trouble with technological progress is that it seems to come at the expense of preservation. In Wolfenbüttel, Germany, Duke August's collection of 31,000 volumes of medieval literature with pale parchment bindings is still there for any visitor to see—in fact you can see them yourself in Figure 9.9—and, barring catastrophe, our descendants in years to come will be able to share this experience too. Xi'an's stone steles, older technology, have lasted longer. It is a tragic fact that your grandchildren and ours, while they can still visit Wolfenbüttel and

Figure 9.9 Medieval literature in the library at Wolfenbüttel. Herzog August Bibliothek Wolfenbüttel: Globenkabinett.

Xi'an, will not be able to see our own parents' and grandparents' literature—despite the fact that it is far more recent.

Why? The reason is paper technology. Until the middle of the 19th century, nearly all paper used for written or printed material was made from cotton or linen rags. This paper lasts for several hundred years without decomposing. Since then, however, ordinary paper has been made from wood pulp treated with acidic chemicals. The residual acid slowly decomposes the paper, causing it to become brittle and crumbly. The rate of decomposition depends on paper's original quality and the conditions under which it has been stored. Light, heat, and humidity all accelerate decomposition. After a period of only a few decades, books made with acid-based paper decompose to the point where they can crumble into pieces, even when handled carefully. If this technological "advance" had been made in medieval times, the Duke's collection would have disintegrated centuries ago.

The problem continues. Library organizations advise publishers to use acid-free paper when printing new books that are likely to have enduring value. However, fewer than 20 percent of hardcover books—and even fewer paperbacks—are printed on acid-free paper. Deacidification processes have been developed that help prolong the life of books printed on acid paper, but they are expensive and time-consuming.

Nor is paper the only—or even the principal—problem. Other parts of our heritage have been irretrievably lost. Until 1951 the only type of film that was available for movie production contained nitrate, which caused it to decay quickly, even in controlled environments. Today half of the 21,000 feature-length films made in the U.S. before 1951 no longer exist. Those that have not been lost or destroyed have decomposed beyond repair. Similarly, analog audio recordings on wax cylinders or magnetic tapes need to be preserved by transferring them onto digital formats such as CD-ROM. While CD-ROMs are not necessarily long-lasting—certainly not compared with the acid-free paper used in the old days—at least a process of regular copying can be established to preserve digital material without loss.

A tale of preservation in the digital era

Despite its very short history, computer technology has an unbelievably bad record when it comes to preservation. There are many examples. A 1990 U.S. government report cited several cases of significant digital records that had already been lost or were in serious danger of being lost. For example, the 1960 U.S. census narrowly escaped oblivion, for it was originally stored on tape that became obsolete faster than expected. We will describe in more detail a different case of near-loss, notable for its irony.

The year 1986 was the 900th anniversary of the Domesday Book, a document commissioned by William the Conqueror to provide a record of the land he had conquered 20 years before in 1066. The original book, handwritten on parchment by (probably) a single monk, still exists and is kept at the U.K.'s Public Record Office in Kew, near London. The book sets out a record of all the lands in the kingdom, and who held them. Of course, few subjects saw the results of this labor—most couldn't read.

The Domesday Project was a national information-gathering exercise conceived and coordinated by the BBC in London to commemorate the event. Schools around the U.K. were asked to survey their areas to produce a database of text and pictures that recorded how Britain looked to the British in 1986. This was combined with central statistical, written, and visual information. The idea was to capitalize on the wide base of microcomputers in British schools to capture and present this information in a uniform way.

This was a major project: over a million people took part in one way or another. The information was recorded on two interactive videodisks that were issued in 1986, and controlling software was produced for the BBC microcomputer in the BCPL language, an ancestor of C. The videodisk player was connected on a SCSI bus (very new at the time) and was made to look to the controlling computer like a very large read-only disk. A special version of the BBC microdisk filing system was used to organize the data.

Most of the people who contributed to the database never saw the result of their labors—even though they could read. The system was obsolete virtually from the moment it was released. Apparently it would take over seven years to look at everything on the disks—but you would have had to work fast, for long before that time had elapsed the system had vanished, almost without trace. The only place you might see it now is in a museum. The Science Museum in London has one, and there is rumored to be another at the Ontario Science Center in Toronto (although it was never intended as a permanent display).

In 1996, on the project's tenth anniversary, a plea went out for information on any installations that were still available for public or research access. It would be easier to go and see the original Domesday Book, then 910 years old.[18]

The digital dark ages

"Let us be absolutely clear from the outset," warns an article entitled "A Digital Dark Ages?," "no one understands how to archive digital documents." In stark, uncompromising language, it develops several points.

---

18. Although few scholars are allowed to see the original, a handsome facsimile is on display in the lobby of the Public Record Office.

First, with regard to preservation technology:

- Enormous amounts of digital information are already lost forever.
- Information technologies become obsolete very quickly.
- Document and media formats continue to proliferate.
- Technology standards will not solve fundamental issues in the preservation of digital information.

Second, with regard to the availability of material:

- Libraries will shortly see a demographic bulge of electronic material as the baby boom generation of authors and academics contribute material gathered during their careers.
- Much material will never make it into library collections for preservation because of increasingly restrictive intellectual property and licensing regimes.
- Archiving and preservation functions in a digital environment will increasingly become privatized as information continues to be commodified.

Third, with regard to the traditional library functions of archiving and preservation:

- Financial resources available to libraries and archives continue to decrease.
- Libraries and archives will be required to continue their existing archival and preservation practices as the current paper publishing boom continues.

This paints a gloomy picture. And it is not just one person's view. In 1996 the U.S. Commission on Preservation and Access issued the final report of a Task Force on the Archiving of Digital Information. An impressive group of 21 experts had spent a year studying the problem. The conclusion was alarming—there is, at present, no way to guarantee the preservation of digital information. The first line of defense against loss of valuable digital information rests with the creators, providers, and owners of that information. It's every man for himself.

This conclusion is borne out by today's best practice. From the U.K., a recent (2001) report by the British National Library records that

> At present, our preferred preservation medium is high-quality microform. Although we are researching and developing digital preservation strategies with other institutions it is difficult to predict when the preservation community will have sufficient confidence in digital preservation techniques for us to acquire the "born digital" as the preferred medium for preservation.

One of the practical problems with preservation is that issues arise at different time scales. Many organizations are faced with crisis: an urgent short-term need to save documents that are in imminent danger of becoming lost, documents that are already difficult to access. Fortunately the vast bulk of information is not usually in immediate danger, but for the medium term something must be done now to prevent them from being vulnerable to imminent loss in the near future. In the long term, strategies must be developed that do not require continual emergency operations to be mounted on an ad hoc basis—strategies that are robust to unexpected technical and, particularly, social changes. For once lost, material is gone forever.

Preservation strategies

Digital documents are vulnerable to loss because the media on which they are stored decays and becomes obsolete. They become inaccessible when the software needed to interpret them, or the hardware on which the software runs, becomes obsolete and is lost. A luminary in the field declared ironically that "digital information lasts forever—or five years, whichever comes first."

The situation is paradoxical. Digital formats have many advantages over analog ones, advantages that seem to *promote* preservation. They include

- ease of creation and copying
- independence of physical media
- constant improvement in hardware and software

The problem is that these apparent advantages actually make digital preservation even harder, as a little thought shows. Ease of creation causes information glut. Ease of copying means that it is not clear which is the original—so every "copy" seems dispensable. Independence of media means that it seems hardly worth expending effort on saving the physical artifact, even if that were possible. Constant improvement in hardware and software promotes obsolescence—cynics say this is what drives the computer industry.

"May all your problems be technical ones" is a blessing that nerds, among others, bestow upon one another. Computer people recognize that the technical stuff is the easy bit. It's the human part that causes problems. The human interface is by far the largest and most complex part of virtually all of today's software systems. Administrative problems consume time and beget frustration. Political processes such as standardization require negotiation, compromise, bargaining. It is the technical problems that have solutions which yield to honest intellectual work.

But preservation is not a technical problem, unfortunately. There are four basically different preservation strategies:

1. paper
2. museums
3. emulation
4. migration

The first two involve printing the material out on paper (or microfilm), and preserving the technology in museums, respectively. These are not usually taken seriously as long-term preservation strategies, although we have already encountered both. Printing is what the British National Library actually does today, while visiting a museum of technology is what you have to do if you want to see the Domesday Project.

The remaining methods highlight the distinction between preserving the physical stream of bits that constitutes each document, and preserving the logical means by which these bits are interpreted as a document. These two mechanisms are independent. Although retaining the integrity of the physical bitstream is what initially springs to mind when thinking about preservation, the second problem is the more taxing.

Emulation involves keeping the documents in exactly the same form as they are and emulating the functionality of the original, obsolete system on future, unknown systems, so that a digital document's original software can be run in the future despite being obsolete. To preserve the physical bitstream will involve regular copying to new media, the application of error detection to determine whether degradation is occurring, and error-correcting codes to ensure that new generations are faithful copies of the original. To preserve the logical interpretation requires emulating old interpreters on new hardware—either by incorporating backward compatibility into software, or compiling special "historic" versions of the software that emulate its functions. For example, current incarnations of Microsoft Word can read (most) old Word documents, even though the formats are quite different: this is backward compatibility. Although neither Microsoft nor Word may be around in fifty years, it should be possible to emulate the crucial parts of Word's functionality on then-current hardware and so read and display old documents.

This example highlights one of the problems. As we learned in Chapter 4, the Word format is proprietary. Without inside knowledge you cannot write software even today that reliably reads every Word file. An important feature of any format used for preserving documents is that it is *open:* the details are made publicly available. And as well as being open in principle, it must be open in practice: documented well enough for others to understand and build their own interpreters. PostScript and PDF are good examples.

Migration involves translating the document from the old format, designed for now-near-obsolete software, to one that is accepted by new software. This involves not just copying the physical bitstream to new media, but translating it at the same time into a new logical format. The difficulty of this operation depends on the details of the software upgrade, but it will normally be very easy. For example, you might go through all your old Microsoft Word files, reading them into Word and writing them out in the latest version of the format. Word provides this functionality of course—no one would upgrade to new versions if they were unable to read at least the last generation file format—and, for the same reason, virtually all serious software will always provide this facility.

Emulation or migration? There are arguments on both sides. Migration may be cheaper, for no special emulation software needs to be written. Conversion software is almost always available if it is invoked in a timely manner. But proponents of emulation point to the fact that conversion is a kind of translation, and translation often loses features of the data. If each translator in the chain were reversible, the original document could be reconstituted. But this is not necessarily the case—at best subtleties such as format, font, footnotes, cross-references, citations, headings, and color might be sacrificed; at worst entire segments such as graphics or sound might be omitted, or the whole document could be meaningless garbage. Would a modern version of the tale of *Beowulf* have the same literary impact if it had been translated through a series of intermediate languages rather than from the earliest surviving text in ancient Anglo-Saxon?

These copying operations are actually inexpensive, particularly for a digital library. It is not as though the documents have to be copied by hand, as the Alexandrian scribes did with the Athenian manuscripts, or individually deacidified, as conservationists are doing with yesterday's books. Once the procedure has been established, you can start a batch job that runs through all the documents and converts them. For a large collection the expense, amortized on a per-document basis, will be negligible. There will be ancillary costs of course. Newly converted documents must be sampled and checked manually against the originals to ensure that the procedure is operating properly. Safeguards must be put in place against unexpected problems. You will need to satisfy yourself that the new collection is complete and correct before finally destroying the old versions. You may need to change the digital library system to use the new format. But, again measured per document, the cost is minimal.

The danger is that you might miss a generation. When you come across that Word file from long ago, current versions may fail to read it. When you encounter that dusty old magnetic tape, the drive might be unable to read it for physical reasons, or you might not be able to find a suitable drive. All it takes is one broken link to lose the documents forever. Through fire and flood, pestilence and famine, war and revolution, the procedure must go on forever. Forever is a long time. The problem is administrative, institutional, and political, not technical.

And it is all very well to say that copying is inexpensive per document, but it is not so overall, and it is a continual operational expense rather than a capital cost. When it comes to copying from one media to another, and converting from one format to another, who will pay?

Today we are witnessing a great upsurge in nationally funded digital library projects, industriously putting content on the Web. Libraries, museums, and archives proudly declare that they are creating a national identity and putting it out on the Web for people to experience: a showcase of cultural memory. And cultural memory is indeed an integral and vital part of healthy modern societies which benefits people by contributing to their enjoyment and inspiration, promoting their sense of identity through shared values, and enriching their life-long learning potential. But what about sustainability? Underlying most of these projects is the tacit assumption, at least by the administrators and politicians who promote them, that once material is "on the Web" it will be there forever. Nothing could be further from the truth.

9.3   Generalized documents: A challenge for the present

The digital library technologies covered in this book are largely concerned with text documents. It is true that Chapter 3 described collections containing audio recordings, photographic material, videos, and music, and in Chapter 4 we learned how video and audio documents are represented. It is also true that the Greenstone software described in Chapters 6 and 7 can deal with multimedia collections. Nevertheless text remains the principal means of searching and browsing collections, even when they contain documents in other media. Multimedia documents can be present in the collection and displayed in the digital library user interface, but they are linked to textual documents—even if these contain just captions—and it is the textual material that is browsed and searched. If content is king, text is prince—and documents in other media are serfs.

For example, in Chapter 3 we saw a collection of page images of Māori newspapers (Figure 3.6). Although the target documents are images, they are accessed by searching text obtained from the images using OCR, and browsed using textual metadata such as newspaper title and date. We saw a collection of rubbings of Tang poetry (Figure 3.10); again it is not the images themselves that are searched, but text extracted from them, typed into the computer—although in this case this text stays in the background and is unseen by the library user. We saw a collection of oral history, including audiotapes and old photographs (Figure 3.7), but it is textual summaries that are searched, not the audio and photographic material itself.

Digital libraries of music

This book has mentioned just one case in which information in a nontextual medium is searched directly: the music collection in Chapter 3 (Figure 3.8).

Although this was not described in full, in Figure 3.8 the user is searching for a tune by humming, whistling, or singing a snatch of it (although without words), or entering it on a music or computer keyboard. The system is capable of interpreting audio input as a sequence of musical notes and searching for that sequence in a database of melodies.

The first stage in the process is to transcribe the acoustic query into symbolic musical notes. The background window in Figure 3.8 shows, on the left, the query in symbolic form. This has been produced by the computer from audio input captured by a special Web browser plug-in when the user sang into a microphone. The frequency profile of the input is analyzed by standard pitch tracking software, and the notes are segmented based on the amplitude profile to generate the musical representation shown. In fact the notes are a perfect transcription of the opening bars of *Auld Lang Syne*, rendered in a nice tenor voice. Buttons underneath allow the user to replay his vocal input (*What you sang*, visible in Figure 3.8) and play a computer synthesis of the transcription it has made (*What I heard*, not visible).

The next step involves searching through a database of melodies, measuring the similarity of the input to each one. In this case the database contains 10,000 folk tunes from around the world. The technical details of the matching operation are beyond our scope here: suffice it to say that an approximate string-matching algorithm based on dynamic programming is used to determine the degree of similarity of each melody to the input. Error-tolerant matching is essential for several reasons:

- The input is noisy: pitch tracking can fail and people often sing badly; people do not remember tunes exactly.
- Most melodies have different versions—in particular, rhythmic variations.
- The database may contain errors.

The effect of this step is to identify melodies in the database that match the query approximately, and sort them by degree of match. The result is shown in the *Query results* list in the lower half of the background window in Figure 3.8. In this case the correct tune, *Auld Lang Syne*, is the best match.

Text searches can be combined with melody matching to yield a more comprehensive search technique. Figure 9.10 shows the query page for a collection of MIDI (Musical Instrument Digital Interface) tunes, in which a textual search for the word *beatles* is being combined with a sung melody that resembles the first few notes of the tune *Yesterday*. The music displayed in the figure is the computer's rendition of the user's singing—note incidentally that the rhythm of the notes is disturbed because the output module, which resynthesizes the music-editor notation into an image for display, has assumed, incorrectly in this case, that the tune starts at the beginning of a bar. This misinterpretation does not affect the result of melody matching.

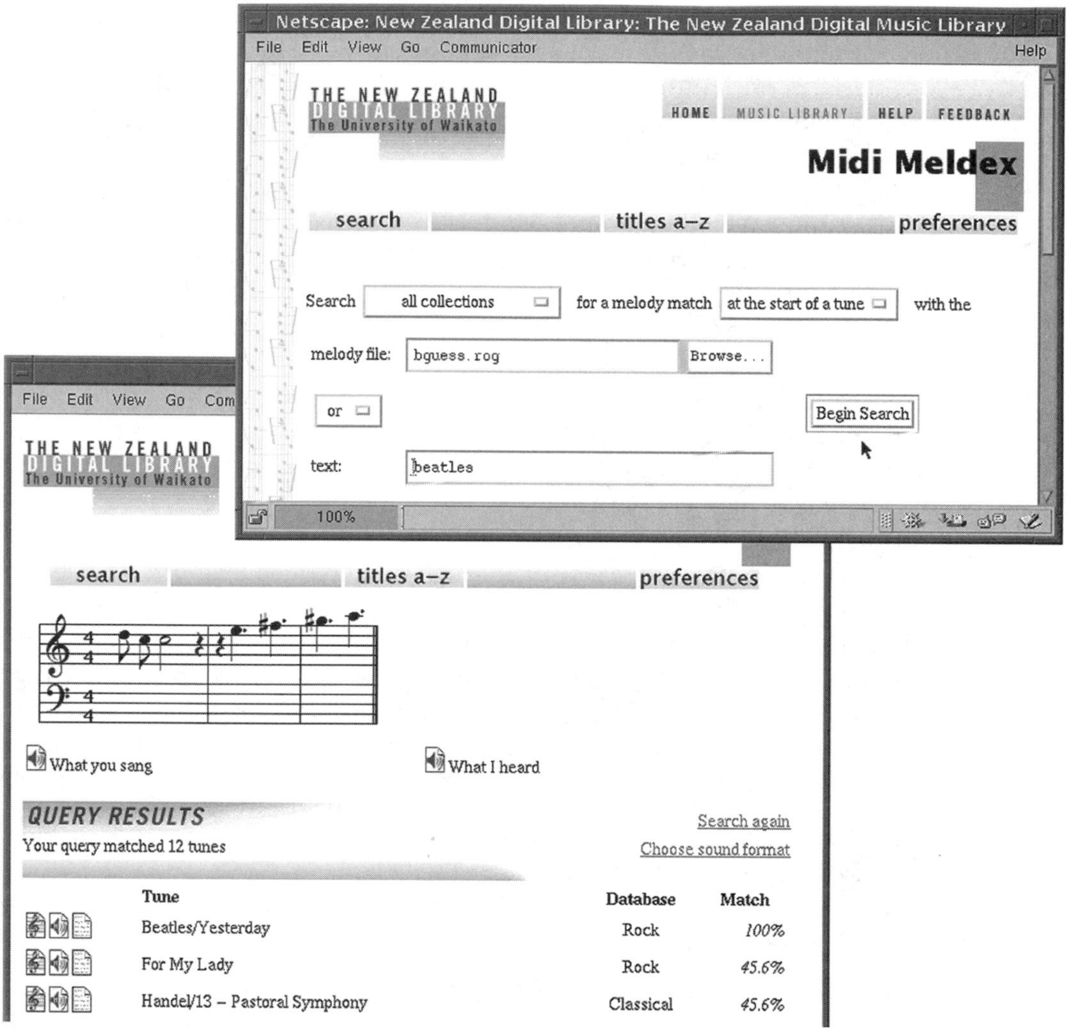

Figure 9.10 Combined music and text search.

Text matching is governed by options specified on the Preferences page—in this case matching is case insensitive with stemming disabled. Likewise music matching is also governed by options. In this case it is restricted to the start of each tune (ignoring leading rests), takes account of the interval between notes (rather than using simply the up-down-same "contour," which is more appropriate for poor singers), and ignores note duration. From the Query Results page, part of which is shown in Figure 9.10, items in the collection can be viewed in various forms, symbolized using icons to the left: the MIDI file reconstructed in the form of sheet music, audio playback of the MIDI file, and an HTML page showing the text that accompanies the song.

Music information retrieval is a fascinating area which involves many novel techniques. For example, it is useful to extract musical motifs—short sequences of notes that are repeated throughout a given tune. Motifs in music are analogous to key phrases in text, and the same techniques mentioned in Chapter 5 (Section 5.6) can be used to identify candidates. Coming up with an algorithm to identify just those motifs that are musically interesting is a challenging research problem. However, extracted motifs are useful even if they are diluted by many uninteresting ones. For example, searching can be accelerated by producing an index of motifs in advance, like the full-text indexes used for text. Motifs could form the basis of a musical browser, serve as brief surrogates for tunes, and even underpin musicological studies. Other fascinating problems are presented by polyphonic matching—most music comes in parallel streams of information played by different instruments but strongly coordinated in time— and rhythmic matching—as any dancer will confirm, music is characterized by different rhythmic patterns.

Another interesting area is the acquisition of music for digital libraries. We mentioned in Chapter 3 that copious quantities of files in MIDI notation can be found on the Web. We had no trouble in locating and downloading several hundred thousand of these to provide a basis for research on theme extraction. From these we selected 100,000 different files. Of course this collection still contains many duplicates. For example, there were 25 different arrangements of J. S. Bach's *Jesu, Joy of Man's Desiring*, and 27 versions of the Beatles' *Yesterday*. There is a tremendous variation in quality, ranging from puerile to excellent. One of the advantages of audio information is that it is very easy to scan, given a suitable interface. You can click quickly down the list of search results in Figures 3.8 and 9.10, listening to the beginning of each song, perhaps for half a second or less. Because the information on the screen stays the same, the visual context remains undisturbed—whereas when scanning text results it changes constantly, causing a far higher level of perceptual stress.

We also made passing mention of acquiring music using optical music recognition or OMR, the musical analog of OCR. Figure 9.11 shows an OMR system being applied to an excerpt of printed music to generate a symbolic form from which the score has been constructed for display. Although the notes are the same, they can now be manipulated in musical terms because the music is now represented in the computer symbolically rather than pictorially. Reconstruct-

Figure 9.11 Application of an optical music recognition system.

ing the image is just one example. The tune can also be played back, have its key altered, be searched for musical motifs, and so on.

Other media

To promote nontextual documents into first-class citizens, searching and browsing strategies must be devised specifically for different media. The music-searching capabilities described in the last section are just one example.

Images

Visual material can be rapidly browsed using *thumbnails*—miniature pictures, typically presented in a gallery on the screen. With a suitable interface users can page or scroll through these very quickly, looking for something in particular.

The simple device of cycling automatically through representative images is a powerful way of capturing the reader's attention and conveying a feeling for what an information collection contains. For example, Figure 9.12 shows the home page of the Humanity Development Library mentioned in Chapter 1. Just

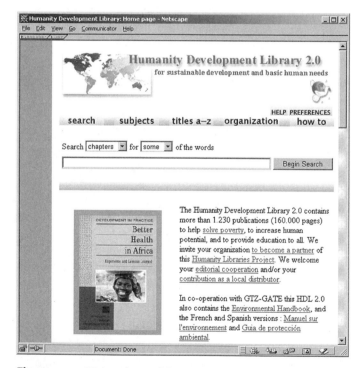

Figure 9.12 Home page of the Humanity Development Library.

as libraries display new acquisitions or special collections in the foyer to pique the reader's interest, this page highlights a particular book that changes every few seconds. The book can be opened by clicking on the image. This simple display is extraordinarily compelling. And just as libraries may display a special book in a glass case, open at a different page each day, a "gallery" screen could show an ever-changing mosaic of images from pages of the books, informative images that, when clicked, open the book to that page.

When it comes to automatically *searching* images rather than manually browsing through them, things become more difficult. Ideally one would like to be able to say, "Find me all images that show elephants," or "flashy cars," or "lovers on a tropical island." These simple questions require sophisticated image understanding that is not possible in the present state of the art. However, it is possible to answer questions such as "images that contain a large gray area," or "images with mostly sky at the top."

For example, there are many systems that can show images similar to a given example. Simple techniques such as matching the histogram of colors of an image's pixels against the histograms for other images often work surprisingly well, considering that the color histogram discards all shape and proximity information. Textures (a tiled roof or a field of corn) can be matched by computing what is known as the *optical flow* of an image. Shapes can be extracted and matched—simple ones such as lines and circles, or complex ones such as frogs and horses. Research on image retrieval has produced a host of techniques that are useful for digital libraries.

Videos

A video is just a sequence of pictures, and the same techniques apply. One of the key problems in video processing is *cut detection*—locating techniques where the shot, or scene, changes. There are several types of cut. *Sharp* cuts are easily detected because virtually all pixels change abruptly and at the same time. *Dissolves* change from one scene to another over a period of a second or so. *Wipes* reveal the new picture from the top down, or the bottom up, or diagonally, or from the center out—there are many possibilities. Sometimes it is hard to distinguish cuts from camera or object motion, or pinpoint individual cuts in a rapidly changing sequence. Yet automatic methods for cut detection are well developed and work well.

Cuts determine the different scenes in a movie. Movies can be browsed and manipulated using a succession of thumbnails representing the initial image in each scene—or perhaps a "typical" image extracted from each scene. And the techniques mentioned here for picture retrieval can be applied to these representative images.

Objects

Many libraries contain *realia*, or real artifacts. School libraries may include various kinds of rock for the study of geology; cultural libraries may possess objects such as the *toki* shown in Figure 1.10. Museums are institutions that house nothing but realia—objects of artistic, historic, or scientific interest, typically conserved and displayed for the edification and enjoyment of the public. While museums and libraries are ordinarily considered to be rather different kinds of institution, we can expect a convergence between them in the digital world.

Computer graphics techniques allow three-dimensional objects to be captured in the form of a data set that can be viewed under various lighting conditions and rotated or otherwise transformed interactively. Technology has been developed over the years to allow extremely realistic images to be rendered, including light and shade, surface characteristics, translucence, and specular and diffuse reflection. Realistic representations can be made even of objects that artists find challenging, such as liquids, glass, fire, plants, hair, clothing, and skin tones. As the movie industry has demonstrated, these objects can be animated realistically too.

In libraries and museums, artifacts are indexed and located on the basis of metadata rather than intrinsic characteristics such as shape and color. However, there are applications that need objects to be retrieved on the basis of physical similarity, whether three-dimensional size or shape or surface characteristics. Electronic commerce will probably spur rapid progress in this area because shoppers like to see what they are buying and need to be able to browse through similar items.

Books are a special case of artifacts that can be modeled as physical objects—a case that is of particular interest to libraries! Figure 9.13 shows an image from a system in which the book's pages can be turned by touching their edges and sliding your finger across the display screen—the page comes with you, revealing as it goes the page underneath, and as it passes the halfway point, the flip side of the page being turned comes into view. This provides a very effective feeling of working with a physical book.

Other document types

Many other useful document types can be distinguished. Here are some examples, each of which could form the basis of significant digital library collections.

Teaching material often involves multimedia elements: textbooks, diagrams and pictures, slide presentations, online presentations, educational videos, realia such as the rocks mentioned earlier, and audiovisual recordings of lectures.

Generations of scientists have recorded the results of their work in *laboratory notebooks*. These have proved invaluable for resolving patent issues, because a properly maintained inventor's laboratory notebook is often the first evidence

Figure 9.13 Modeling a book as a physical object. By Permission of the British Library.

of the conception of an idea. They have also been central in investigations of fraud. For example, in a long, bitter, and extremely complex investigation of scientific misconduct during the 1980s and 1990s that came to be known as the "Baltimore affair," the U.S. Secret Service analyzed laboratory notebooks to try to determine whether pages had been falsely backdated and new ones inserted to cover up weaknesses in the data.

Scientific and engineering data form another category of information that must be archived, searched, and browsed. This includes the results of scientific experiments, engineering design data such as the results of simulations, and social science data in the form of survey results and analysis. The information is heterogeneous and expressed in many different forms: spreadsheets, databases, engineering drawings, files from computer-assisted design and manufacturing systems, and so on.

Generalized documents in Greenstone

We defined a digital library in Chapter 1 as a "focused collection of digital objects, including text, video, and audio." A key challenge is to integrate objects of all kinds of media into digital libraries in such a way that each becomes a first-class citizen. In this book textual documents have been paramount; other media types are included in a secondary way as associated files. To meet the new challenge, we need to devise ways of searching and indexing documents in all media, techniques for automatically providing some form of document summary, methods of classifying content, and imaginative ways of browsing through document collections. These new techniques should not appear as a clutch of independent facilities, but should rather work together, as a family, within a uniform user interface.

Although the Greenstone digital library system does not incorporate searching and browsing techniques for nontextual media, its architecture is flexible enough to permit such modules to be added. We mentioned in Chapter 7 (Section 7.3) that to encourage extensibility and flexibility, the runtime system uses inheritance widely—in particular, it is used within the Filter and Source objects that respond to incoming protocol requests, and the Search object which assists in this task by encapsulating the search engine being used. This means that different search engines can be deployed by replacing or augmenting the MG system that is used to perform text searching. Indeed, in the music retrieval work described earlier, a different search engine is used, called MR for "melody retrieval," which implements an approximate string-matching algorithm for music.

In Greenstone, collections of documents are browsed by textual metadata, or by date, or through hierarchies such as subject classifications. Although textual metadata is normally presented alphabetically, often with an alphabetic *A–Z* selector, different schemes must be incorporated for ideographic languages such as Chinese—two of these, for stroke ordering and Pinyin, were described in Chapter 3 (Figure 3.20). All browsing is done through classifier modules.

Generalized documents will need different browsers, but these fit within the existing architecture. If a browser can be presented in terms of arbitrary structures of horizontal and vertical lists (mentioned in Chapter 7, at the end of Section 7.2), it can be handled by existing mechanisms, and only a new classifier need be written. This is normally a lightweight job involving a page or two of Perl code (Section 6.7)—plus the media-dependent part, which could be arbitrarily complex. It may also be necessary to add new facilities, appropriate to the media type, to the format mechanism (also described in Section 6.7).

The standard Greenstone interface is constrained to use only the facilities provided by standard Web browsers. Java applets can be used for more general presentation of document and browsing structures. We have already seen an example in the hierarchical phrase browsers described in Chapter 3 (Figures 3.23–3.25), which use an applet to present scrolling lists of phrases. For even more general interfaces (an example is shown in Figure 7.3), the CORBA implementation of the Greenstone protocol can be used. This allows any system to access a remote collection server and present a radically different interface—far beyond what is possible with the format statement mechanism—that harnesses the power of the digital library "back end" and the documents it contains.

A final task—or rather, the initial one—is to import multimedia documents into the collection. All documents are brought into Greenstone using plug-ins, and new plug-ins will be needed for different media types.

Ultimately, generalized documents may challenge the very notion of the *document* as the basic unit within a digital library. Why does everything have to hinge on discrete documents? Greenstone, along with other digital library systems, views its input as a collection of documents, documents that have their own internal structure in terms of sections and subsections. This view may be artificial and culture-dependent, stemming from traditional limitations involved in handling physical information objects.

If the input really is a long stream of text, perhaps it should be treated that way. Search engines could find those stretches that are most relevant to queries, without any regard for artificial document and section boundaries. Extending this vision to generalized documents may provide a uniform way of looking at digital collections that transcends current thinking.

Digital libraries for oral cultures

Libraries are about literature. Our dictionary defines *literature* as "the writings of a society, in prose or verse," and goes on to add, "Broadly speaking, literature includes all types of fiction and nonfiction writing intended for publication." This seems to be firmly dependent upon writing. But the earliest cultural tradition in New Zealand, for example, is that of the Māori, whose literature consisted of history, tales, poems, and myths handed down by oral tradition. It was only when missionaries arrived from Europe that these were written down and became "literature" by the dictionary definition. We have much to learn from early cultures. One trend in modern writing, for example—particularly Australian and North American—is to draw on the oral storytelling traditions of aboriginal cultures.

The ultimate aim of generalized documents is to give nontextual material first-class status in a digital library—if you like, first-class status in "the literature." This has important cultural ramifications. It should be possible to create digital library collections intended for use by people in oral cultures, who may be illiterate or semi-literate, or by people who, though they can read and write their own language, cannot speak or read the language of the digital library.

Imagine having access to collections that spring out of the rich cultures of China or Arabia, created by people who grew up in these cultures, without having to learn a new language. More practically—since you, dear reader, are culturally privileged and can probably access this kind of information in translation—imagine giving someone in the highlands of Peru, fluent and literate in her native language of Quechua, first-hand access to the information in humanitarian collections such as the Humanity Development Library (currently available only in English and French) or the Biblioteca Virtual de Desastres (a collection of information dealing with disasters and emergencies, currently mainly in Spanish).

If you find it difficult to imagine how serious practical information could possibly be conveyed in purely iconic form, look at Figure 9.14, which shows how to splint a broken forearm. It is taken from a 120-page manual on first aid that contains not a single written word. Literate as you undoubtedly are, in an emergency you might even prefer these pictures—which in the book are vividly colored, adding further clarity—to a textual account of how to deal with a medial radius fracture. Another striking example is the "user manual" for Mexico City's underground transport system: a brilliant iconic design, with no words whatever, that gives clear instructions for how to use the metro. A third example, and a historical precedent, are the so-called Beggar's Bibles (*Biblia pauperum*) which were designed in the Middle Ages for the religious instruction of illiterate believers. They used numerous illustrations to explain passages from

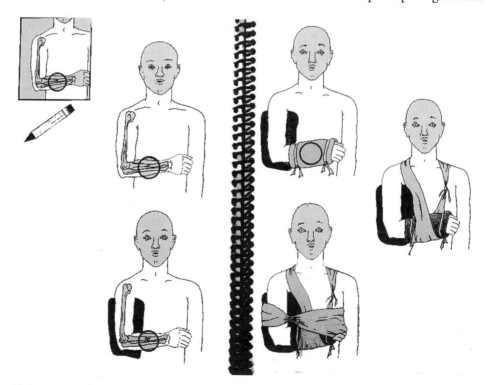

Figure 9.14 First aid in pictures: how to splint a broken arm. *First Aid in Pictures* by M. B. DeLong, J. G. Brady, L. D. Bourgeois, and L. J. Niemiec. Barbara A. Bear, Illustrator. Edward L. Meador, Editor. Vade Mecum Press, 1988.

the Bible and have been called prototypes of our present-day comics. Produced before Gutenberg, each printed page was carved in a woodblock. You can see them today at Wolfenbüttel.

These three examples are static images. Imagine what you could do with motion, sound, video, interaction, 3D objects, simulations, and virtual reality.

The apparently paradoxical notion of libraries for the illiterate has its resolution in the notion of generalized documents. The challenge is to design digital libraries in a way that they are usable by people from oral cultures—not so different from designing searching and browsing mechanisms for nontextual material. In fact it is even possible to imagine such people creating their own digital library collections. The LINCOS project, for example, equips villages in developing countries in Central and South America with information technology, housed in ordinary transportation containers. These units form a kind of "school," typically attended by children and elderly people—the economically active segment of the population does not enjoy the luxury of leisure time for continuing education. In them, people—including the semi-literate—enjoy learning to use computers for creative and artistic activities: drawing, capturing photographs, making movies. Suitably equipped, the modern microcomputer transcends text.

With the advent of low-cost consumer technology for image and movie capture, a quiet revolution is taking place in our homes. Now anyone can keep a photograph album on a home computer, or shoot video and use sophisticated editing techniques to produce a professional-quality movie, or make a CD-ROM of one's own music (or that of others). Ever since the advent of broadcast television, our text-dominated society has gradually become attuned to the more visceral medium of moving images. We book lovers may deplore the decline of the printed word, laud the sustained argument carefully built up over pages, and praise the power of the written word to conjure up far more imaginative and vivid imagery than any TV can. We may lament the decrease in attention span, the reduction of arguments to sound bites. We may wish that our children spent more time reading books, less time playing video games. But we must live in the world too, and the world is changing.

Perhaps digital libraries for people from oral cultures will find a place in our own society too and help reduce the various "digital divides" that cleave our world—the "social divide" between the information-rich and the information-poor in our own nations, the "democratic divide" between those who do and do not use the panoply of digital resources to engage, mobilize, and participate in public life, as well as the "global divide" that reflects the huge disparity in access to information between people in industrialized and developing societies.

Is this too much to hope?

9.4 Notes and sources

S. R. Ranganathan, the father of library science in India, began his classic book *The Five Laws of Library Science* (1931) with this quotation from Manu, an ancient Hindu philosopher and lawmaker: "To carry knowledge to the doors of those that lack it . . . even to give away the whole earth cannot equal that form of service." What an inspirational sentiment for budding digital librarians with a social conscience!

We have quoted one of Ranganathan's laws of library science. You might be interested in the others too:

1. Books are for use.
2. Every reader his book.
3. Every book his reader.
4. Save the reader's time.
5. The library is a growing organism.

We have to thank Rob Akscyn for the vision of digital libraries as kitchens for knowledge preparation; it has greatly influenced our thinking. And we are grateful to Steve Jones (Jones, 1999; Jones and Paynter, 1999; Jones and Staveley, 1999) for the Phrasier system depicted in Figures 9.6 to 9.8: it was he who had the original vision to which we so enthusiastically subscribe (and he who actually made the figures).

The changing world of preservation is a matter of serious concern for democratic societies. As George Orwell said in *Nineteen Eighty-Four* (published in 1949), "Who controls the past controls the future. Who controls the present controls the past." It was Jeff Rothenberg (1997) who quipped that "digital information lasts forever—or five years, whichever comes first." He has published an interesting *Scientific American* article about preservation called "Ensuring the longevity of digital documents" (Rothenberg, 1995) which promotes emulation as the only workable solution, and a more extended report that develops the same theme (Rothenberg, 1999).

The poem *Beowulf* survives in the British Museum manuscript Cotton Vitellius A.xv, probably written about 1000 A.D.; most scholars accept that it took its present form somewhere between 680 and 800 A.D. It opens with these words:

> Hwæt wē Gār-Dena in geārdagum,
> þēodcyninga þrym gefrūnon,
> hū ðā æþelingas ellen fremedon.

An eloquent translation by Crossley-Holland (1968) begins:

> Listen! The fame of Danish kings
> in days gone by, the daring feats
> worked by those heroes are well known to us.

Just thirty years later Seamus Heaney (1999) gave a fresh rendering:

> So. The Spear-Danes in days gone by
> and the kings who ruled them had courage and greatness.
> We have heard of those princes' heroic campaigns.

It is hard to imagine that such stirring words would ever have resulted from a sequence of paraphrasings of earlier interpretations.

The government report that cited cases of digital records that had been, or were about to be, lost—including the 1960 census results—was published by the U.S. Congress (1990). More studies of preservation and access can be found at the Web site of the U.S. Council on Library and Information Resources, *www.clir.org*. A report on the Domesday project appears at *www.atsf.co.uk/dottext/domesday.html*, written in 1996 by Andy Finney. The British National Library's report that documents their microfilm-based preservation strategy is entitled "New strategic directions" (British National Library, 2001). The ominous article on the digital dark ages is by Kuny (1998). Lynch (1999) has published an interesting analysis of the issues that arise when managing digital objects over time, in particular the need to track authenticity as part of an object's provenance, maintain its integrity and ensure the integrity of links to that object from other objects (or from metadata), and reformat the object without impacting its integrity.

The Baltimore affair is described by Kevles (1998) in a book entitled *The Baltimore Case: A Trial of Politics, Science, and Character*.

We gratefully acknowledge Dieter Fellner for sharing his visions for generalized documents, in particular ones that transcend the notion of *document* as a basic unit, and Maria Trujillo for helping us focus on digital libraries for oral cultures. Some search systems already treat text as a semi-infinite string (Salminen and Tompa, 1994; Clarke, Cormack, and Burkowski, 1995), and methods of finding arbitrary stretches of text that most closely match queries, independent of document boundaries, have been developed by de Kretser and Moffat (1999).

The image in Figure 9.13 comes from a British National Library project called Turning the Pages (*www.bl.uk/collections/treasures/digitisation.html*). This particular book is an extract from the Lindisfarne Gospels. The system is a two-dimensional rather than a three-dimensional simulation, created using Macromedia Director. Several intermediate images have been taken for each page turn—so the image in Figure 9.13, for example, is a stored image, not computed from a physical model of the book. This involves a lot of images—indeed the system consumes 304 Mb for only 20 pages (it includes zoomed-in versions of each page and accompanying audio). And it has some shortcomings—for example, the top of the page being turned is missing in the figure. But it gives an interesting preview of how books might be simulated as physical objects in the future.

The wonderful book from which Figure 9.14 is reproduced is *First Aid in Pictures* (DeLong et al., 1987). The mission of LINCOS, which stands for "little intelligent communities," is to help disadvantaged communities from developing countries to use a series of services and applications—telemedicine, the Internet, electronic communication, videoconferencing, electronic trade, and educational applications. You can find out more about this project at *www.lincos.net*. Finally digital divides and their ramifications are thoroughly discussed in a thought-provoking book by Norris (2001).

APPENDIX

Installing and operating Greenstone

Greenstone is a suite of software for building and distributing digital library collections. It provides a new way of organizing information and publishing it on the Internet or on CD-ROM. Greenstone is produced by the New Zealand Digital Library Project at the University of Waikato. It is free, open-source software, issued under the terms of the GNU General Public License. You can download it, along with documentation, from *www.greenstone.org*. Although this URL is hosted in New Zealand, your download may be automatically redirected elsewhere—normally to *http://sourceforge.net* in the U.S.—to expedite network access. We want to ensure that the software works well for you: please report any problems on the feedback form at *www.greenstone.org* or by e-mailing to *greenstone@cs. waikato.ac.nz*.

In cooperation with UNESCO and the Humanity Libraries Project, Greenstone is issued on a CD-ROM that includes documentation in English, French, and Spanish. If you do not have Internet access, you can obtain a copy of the CD-ROM, for a nominal charge that covers the cost of shipping and handling, by writing to Greenstone, Department of Computer Science, University of Waikato, Hamilton, New Zealand. However, you are encouraged to download the software if you possibly can rather than purchasing the CD-ROM; this puts you in touch with current developments and gives you the latest version of the software. *Everything on the CD-ROM is freely available on the Internet from* www.greenstone.org.

Greenstone runs on different platforms and in different configurations, as summarized in Figure A.1. There are many issues that affect (or might affect) the installation procedure. Before beginning the installation procedure, you should consider these questions:

- Are you using Windows or Unix?
- If Windows, are you using 3.1/3.11 or a more recent version? Although you can view collections under 3.1/3.11 and serve other computers on the network, you cannot build new collections. The full Greenstone software runs on Windows 95/98/Me and NT/2000/XP.
- If Unix, are you using Linux or another version of Unix? For Linux a binary version of the complete system is provided that is easy to install. For other types of Unix, you will have to install the source code and compile it.
- If Windows NT/2000 or Unix, can you log in as the system "administrator" or "root"? This may be required to configure a Web server.
- Do you want the source code? If you are using Windows or Linux, you can just install binaries. But you may want the source code as well—it's all in the Greenstone distribution.
- Do you want to build new digital library collections? If so, you need Perl, which is freely available for both Windows and Unix.

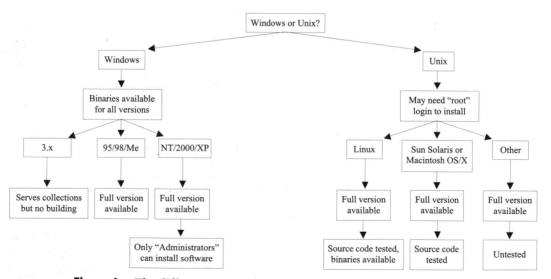

Figure A.1 The different options for Windows and Unix versions of Greenstone.

- Is your computer already running a Web server? The Windows version of Greenstone comes with a built-in Web server. However, if you are already running a Web server, you may want to stay with it. For Unix, you have to run a separate Web server.
- Do you know how to reconfigure your Web server? If you don't use the Greenstone Web server, you will have to reconfigure your existing one slightly to recognize the Greenstone software.

Versions of Greenstone are available for both Windows and Unix, as binaries and in source code form. The user interface uses a Web browser: Netscape Navigator and Internet Explorer (version 4.0 or greater in both cases) are both suitable. In case you're not connected to the Internet and don't already have a Web browser, a Windows version of Netscape is provided on the Greenstone CD-ROM.

To download Greenstone go to *www.greenstone.org,* where you will find full installation instructions and comprehensive documentation, as well as all versions of the code.

Glossary

AACR2R	*Anglo-American Cataloging Rules* (second edition, revised), published by the American Library Association
ASCII	American Standard Code for Information Exchange, a 1968 standard 7-bit code for representing the Roman alphabet plus numerals and special symbols
BibTeX	Scheme for managing bibliographic data and references within documents in the TeX format
Boolean query	Query to an information retrieval system that may contain AND, OR, NOT
Browsing	Accessing a collection by scanning an organized list of metadata values associated with the documents (such as author, title, date, and keywords)
buildcol.pl	Greenstone program used to build collections
Building	Process of creating the indexing and browsing structures that are used to access a collection
C++	Programming language in which the majority of the Greenstone software is written
Case-folding	Making uppercase and lowercase words look the same, for searching purposes
CCL	Common Command Language, a format used for expressing bibliographic queries

CD-ROM	Compact disk read-only memory, a 650 Mb disk that uses the same technology as audio CDs
CGI	Common Gateway Interface, a scheme that allows users to activate programs on the host computer by clicking on Web pages
cgi-bin	Directory in which CGI scripts are stored
CGI script	Code associated with a button, menu, or link on a Web page that specifies what the host computer is to do when clicked
Classifier	Greenstone code module that examines document metadata to form an index for browsing
Collection	Set of documents that are brought together under a uniform searching and browsing interface
Collection configuration file	File that specifies how a collection is to be imported and built, what indexes and language interfaces are to be provided, and so on
Collection information database	GDBM database that holds information needed when serving the collection to users
Collection server	Program responsible for providing access to a collection when it is being used
Collector	Greenstone subsystem that leads you interactively through the operations necessary to create a digital library collection
Configuration file	*See* Collection configuration file, Main configuration file, Site configuration file
CORBA	Common Object Request Broker Architecture, a protocol used to communicate between processes on different computers over the Internet
CSS	Cascading Style Sheets, a way of controlling the presentation of HTML and XML documents
db2txt	Greenstone tool for viewing a GDBM database as plain text
DDL	Description Definition Language, a form of XSchema used in MPEG-7 to allow users to create their own metadata format
DDML	Document Definition Markup Language, a preliminary form of XML Schema
Demo collection	A subset of the Humanities Development Library, distributed with the Greenstone software and used for illustration in this book

Dienst	Digital library protocol developed in a long-running research project at Cornell University
Digital library	Collection of digital objects (text, audio, video), along with methods for access and retrieval, and for selection, organization, and maintenance
Document	Basic unit from which digital library collections are constructed, which may include text, graphics, sound, and video
DTD	Document Type Definition, a specification used in XML (and also SGML) to express the structure of a particular set of documents
Dublin Core	An intentionally minimalist standard for describing metadata, designed to be applied to resources on the Web
DVD	Digital versatile disk, a disk format that can hold from 5 to 20 Gb of data
Dynamic HTML	Combination of HTML with CSS, Web-page scripting, and the document object model that provides functionality comparable to XSL
EBCDIC	Extended Binary Coded Decimal for Information Interchange, an alternative code to ASCII
Encapsulated PostScript	Variant of PostScript designed for expressing graphics of a single page or less that are to be included in other documents
FAO	United Nations Food and Agricultural Organization
Fast-CGI	Facility that allows CGI scripts to remain continuously active so that they do not have to be restarted from scratch every time they are invoked
Filter program	That part of a Greenstone collection server that implements querying and browsing operations
FO	Formatting Objects, the component of the XML specification that deals with the actual formatting
Format string	A string that specifies how documents and other listings are to be displayed in Greenstone
FTP	File transfer protocol
GB-encoding	Standard way of encoding the Chinese language
GDBM	GNU DataBase Manager, a program used within the Greenstone software to store metadata for each document
GIF	Graphics Image Format, a widely used compression scheme for lossless images

GIMP GNU Image-Manipulation Program, used (on Unix) to create icons in Greenstone

GNU Public License Software license that permits users to copy and distribute computer programs freely, and to modify them so long as all modifications are made publicly available

Greenstone The name of the digital library software used as an example in the book (*www.greenstone.org*)

GSDL Abbreviation for Greenstone Digital Library

%GSDLHOME% Operating system variable that represents the top-level directory in which all Greenstone programs and collections are stored (*$GSDLHOME* on Unix systems)

hashfile Greenstone program used at import or build time to generate the OID of each document

HDL Humanity Development Library, a collection of humanitarian information for developing countries

HTML HyperText Markup Language, the language in which Web documents are written

HTML Tidy Software utility that converts older HTML formats to XHTML

HTTP Hypertext transfer protocol

Hyperlink Link to another document or to another place in this document

Importing Process of bringing collections of documents into the Greenstone system

import.pl Greenstone program used to import documents

Index Information structure that is used for searching or browsing a collection

InstallShield Windows program, used by Greenstone CD-ROMs, that allows a system to be installed from a CD-ROM

ISBN International Standard Book Number

ISCII Indian Script Code for Information Interchange, an ASCII extension that incorporates Brahmi-based Indic scripts

JPEG Standard for (mainly) lossy image compression, named after the Joint Photographic Experts Group

JPEG-2000 Later version of the JPEG image compression standard

LCSH	Library of Congress Subject Headings, a controlled vocabulary for assigning subject descriptors
LZW	Lempel-Ziv-Welch compression scheme, patented by Unisys, used in GIF, TIFF, PDF, and PostScript Level 2 and above
Macro language	Language that allows the specification of textual replacements, used to generate all pages in the Greenstone user interface
Main configuration file	File that contains specifications common to all collections served by this site
MARC	Machine-readable cataloging format, a metadata scheme designed in the late 1960s for use by professional library catalogers
Metadata	Structured information, such as author, title, date, keywords, and so on, that is associated with a document (or document collection)
MG	Managing Gigabytes, a program used by the Greenstone system for full-text indexing, that incorporates compression techniques (Witten, Moffat, and Bell, 1999)
mgbuild	MG program for building a compressed full-text index
mgquery	MG program for querying a compressed full-text index
MIDI	Musical Instrument Digital Interface, a representation of music used by music synthesizers
MIME	Multipurpose Internet Mail Extensions, a standard for including different types of file—text, images, audio, video, or application-specific data—in e-mail messages
Mirror	The process of copying a Web site, or part of a Web site, to another location and making it available there
mkcol.pl	Greenstone program that creates and initializes the directory structure for a new collection
MPEG	Standard for representing multimedia material, named after the Motion Picture Experts Group
New Zealand Digital Library Project	Research project in the Computer Science Department at the University of Waikato, New Zealand, that created the Greenstone software (*www.nzdl.org*)
OAI	Open Archives Initiative, the name of a protocol designed for the efficient dissemination of digital library content

OCR   Optical Character Recognition, the process of producing a digital representation of the textual content of a document image

OID   Object Identifier, a unique identification code associated with a document or other digital object

OMR   Optical Music Recognition, the musical analog of OCR

Open eBook   An open standard for electronic books

PDF   Portable Document Format, a page description language designed for interactive use as a successor to PostScript

Perl   Programming language used for many of the text-processing operations that occur during the Greenstone building process

Phrasier   An environment for reading and writing within a digital library

Ping   Message sent to a system to determine whether it is running or not

Plug-in   Code module for handling documents of different formats, used during the importing and building processes

PNG   Portable Network Graphics, an open standard for lossless images

PostScript   The first page description language

Protocol   Set of conventions according to which two systems communicate (for example, a Greenstone receptionist and collection server)

PURL   Persistent URL, a particular style of URN

Ranked query   Natural-language query to an information retrieval system, for which the documents that match the query are sorted in order of relevance

RDF   Resource Description Framework, a scheme designed to facilitate the interoperability of metadata

Receptionist   Program that organizes the Greenstone user interface

Refer   Scheme for managing bibliographic data and references within documents

RLSP collection description   A particular application of RDF by the Research Support Libraries Program based at the University of Bath, U.K.

RTF   Rich Text Format, a standard format for interchange of text documents

SDLIP   Simple Digital Library Interoperability Protocol, developed by Stanford University

Searching	Accessing a collection through a full-text search of its contents (or parts of contents, such as section titles)
Server	*See* Collection server and Web server
setup.bat, setup.sh, setup.csh	Script used to set up your environment to recognize the Greenstone software
SGML	Standard Generalized Markup Language, a metalanguage for describing markup formats that was standardized in 1986 and forms a precursor to XML
Site configuration file	File that contains specifications used to configure the Greenstone software for the site on which it is installed
SQL	Structured Query Language, an industry-standard database-query language
Stemming	Stripping endings off a term to make it more general
STL	Standard Template Library, a widely available library of C++ code developed by Silicon Graphics
SVG	XML-based language for describing two-dimensional graphics
TEI	Text Encoding Initiative, a project founded in 1987 that developed SGML DTDs for representing scholarly texts in the humanities and social sciences
TIFF	Tagged Image File Format, a public-domain file format for raster images that incorporates facilities for descriptive metadata
txt2db	Greenstone program used at build time to create the GDBM database
UCS	Unicode Character Set, the set of characters supported by Unicode
UNESCO	United Nations Educational, Scientific and Cultural Organization
Unicode	Standard scheme for representing the character sets used in the world's languages
UNU	United Nations University; also used to refer to a Greenstone collection created for that organization
URI	Universal Resource Identifier, a generic name for URLs and URNs
URL	Universal Resource Locator, a standard way of addressing objects on the Web (but this term is supposed to be superseded by URI)
URN	Universal Resource Name, a way of naming resources instead of specifying their locations

UTF	UCS Transformation Format, a scheme for representing Unicode characters with three variants: UTF-32, UTF-16, and UTF-8
VRML	Virtual Reality Modeling Language, used for presenting virtual reality experiences on the Web
Web server	Standard program that computers use to make information accessible over the World Wide Web
Word	Microsoft Word, a widely used word processing program
XHTML	Modern version of HTML that incorporates the stricter syntactic rules of XML
XLink	XML linking language that provides a more powerful method for connecting resources than HTML hyperlinks
XML	Extensible Markup Language, a metalanguage for describing markup formats for structured documents and data on the Web
XML Schema	Way of specifying the structure of a particular set of documents that provides more expressive facilities for structures and data types than DTDs
XPath	Component of the XML specification that allows the selection of parts of a document
XPointer	Development of XPath that provides a finer degree of control over the parts of the document being selected
XQuery	Format used for expressing queries in the style of XML
XQueryX	Version of the XQuery language that is expressed in valid XML and is intended to be read by machines rather than by people
XSchema	Preliminary form of XML Schema
XSL	Extensible Stylesheet Language, a way of controlling the presentation of XML documents (and XML-compliant HTML ones) that is more expressive than CSS
XSLT	XSL Transformations, a component of the XML specification that allows you to manipulate parts of the document tree
YAZ	Open-source software library that implements the Z39.50 protocol
Z39.50	International standard communications protocol developed for use by library catalog systems

References

ABBYY Software (2000) *FineReader User's Guide*. ABBYY Software, 123015 Moscow, P.O. 72, Russia.

Adobe Systems Incorporated (1985) *PostScript Language Tutorial and Cookbook*. Addison Wesley, Boston, MA.

Adobe Systems Incorporated (1999) *PostScript Language Reference*, third edition. Addison Wesley, Boston, MA.

Adobe Systems Incorporated (2000) *PDF Reference*, second edition (version 1.3). Addison Wesley, Boston, MA.

Akscyn, R. M., and Witten, I. H. (1998) "Report on First Summit on International Cooperation on Digital Libraries." *http://ks.com/idla-wp-oct98*.

American National Standards Institute (1968) *American Standard Code for Information Interchange (ASCII)*, Standard No. X3.4–1968; updated as X3.4–1986.

Andrews, N. (1987) "Rich text format standard makes transferring text easier." *Microsoft Systems Journal*, Vol. 2, No. 1, pp. 63–67; March.

Apperley, M., Cunningham, S. J., Keegan, T., and Witten I. H. (2001) "Niupepa: A historical newspaper collection." *Communications of the ACM*, Vol. 44, No. 5, pp. 86–87; May.

Apperley, M., Keegan, T., Cunningham, S. J., and Witten, I. H. (in press) "Delivering the Maori language newspapers on the Internet." In *Maori Language Newspapers*, edited by J. McRae. Auckland University Press, New Zealand.

Arms, W. Y. (2000) *Digital Libraries*. MIT Press, Cambridge, MA.

Arunachalam, S. (1998) "How the Internet is failing the developing world." Presented at *Science Communication in the Next Millennium*, Egypt; June. Available at *www.abc.net.au/science/slab/infopoverty/story.htm.*

Atkinson, R. (1986) "Selection for preservation: A materialistic approach." *Library Resources and Technical Services* 30, pp. 344–348; October/December.

Baeza-Yates, R., and Ribeiro-Neto, B. (1999) *Modern Information Retrieval.* ACM Press, New York.

Bainbridge, D. (2000) "The role of music information retrieval in the New Zealand Digital Library project." *Proc International Symposium on Music Information Retrieval*; Plymouth, UK (3 pages).

Bainbridge, D., Buchanan, G., McPherson, J., Jones, S., Mahoui, A., and Witten, I. H. (2001) "Greenstone: A platform for distributed digital library applications." *Proc European Conference on Digital Libraries*, Darmstadt, Germany, pp. 137–148; September.

Bainbridge, D., and Cunningham, S. J. (1998) "Making oral history accessible over the World Wide Web." *History and Computing*, Vol. 10, No. 1/3, pp. 73–81.

Bainbridge, D., Nevill-Manning, C., Witten, I. H., Smith, L. A. and McNab, R. J. (1999) "Towards a digital library of popular music." *Proc ACM Digital Libraries*, Berkeley, CA, pp. 161–169.

Berners-Lee, T., Hendler, J., and Lassila, O. (2001) "The Semantic Web." *Scientific American*, Vol. 284, No. 5, pp. 34–43; May.

Borgman, C. L. (2000) *From Gutenberg to the Global Information Infrastructure: Access to Information in the Networked World.* MIT Press, Cambridge, MA.

Bowker, R. R. (1883) "The work of the nineteenth-century librarian for the librarian of the twentieth." *Library Journal*, Vol. 8, pp. 247–250; September–October.

Brassil, J. T., Low, S., Maxemchuk, N. F., and O'Gorman, L. (1994) "Electronic marking and identification techniques to discourage document copying." *Proc Infocom*, Toronto, Canada, pp. 1278–1287; June.

British National Library (2001) *New Strategic Directions.* British National Library, London.

Bryan, M. (1988) *SGML: An Author's Guide to the Standard Generalized Markup Language.* Addison Wesley, Boston, MA.

Bush, V. (1947) "As we may think." *The Atlantic Monthly*, Vol. 176, No. 1, pp. 101–108.

Cavnar, W. B., and Trenkle, J. M. (1994) "N-Gram-based text categorization." *Proc Symposium on Document Analysis and Information Retrieval*, Las Vegas, NV, pp. 161–175; April.

Chang, S. J., and Rice, R. E. (1993) "Browsing: A multidimensional framework." *Annual Review of Information Science and Technology*, Vol. 28, pp. 231–276.

Chapman, N., and Chapman, J. (2000) *Digital Multimedia.* Wiley, New York.

Chen, S. S. (1998) *Digital Libraries: The Life Cycle of Information.* BE (Better Earth) Publisher, Columbia, MO.

Clarke, C. L. A., Cormack, G.V., and Burkowski, F. J. (1995) "An algebra for structured text search and a framework for its implementation." *Computer Journal*, Vol. 38, No. 1, pp. 43–56.

Clinton, W., and Gore, A., Jr. (1993) *Technology for America's Economic Growth: A New Direction to Build Economic Strength*. Executive Office of the President, Washington, DC; February.

Committee on Intellectual Property Rights, Computer Science and Telecommunications Board (2000) *The Digital Dilemma: Intellectual Property in the Information Age*. National Academy Press, Washington, DC.

Cooper, M. D. (1996) *Design of Library Automation Systems*. Wiley, New York.

Cox, I., Miller, M., and Bloom, J. (2001) *Digital Watermarking*. Morgan Kaufmann, San Francisco.

Crane, G. (1998) "The Perseus project and beyond: How building a digital library challenges the humanities and technology." *D-Lib Magazine*, Vol. 4, No. 1; January.

Crawford, W., and Gorman, M. (1995) *Future Libraries: Dreams, Madness, and Reality*. American Library Association, Chicago.

Crossley-Holland, K. (Trans.) (1968) *Beowulf*. Folio Society, London.

Cutter, C. A. (1876) *Rules for a Printed Dictionary Catalog*. U.S. Bureau of Education special report on public libraries, Part II, U.S. Government Printing Office, Washington, DC.

Dartois, M., Maeda, A., Sakaguchi, T., Fujita, T., Sugimoto, S., and Tabata, K. (1997) "A multilingual electronic text collection of folk tales for casual users using off-the-shelf browsers." *D-Lib Magazine*, Vol. 3, No. 10; October.

Davidson, C. (1993) "The man who made computers personal." *New Scientist*, No. 1978, pp. 32–35; June.

de Kretser, O., and Moffat, A. (1999) "Effective document presentation with a locality-based similarity heuristic," *Proc ACM SIGIR Conference on Research and Development in Information Retrieval*, pp. 113–120. ACM Press, New York; August.

de Stefano, P. (2000) "Selection for digital conversion." In *Moving Theory into Practice: Digital Imaging for Libraries and Archives*, edited by A. R. Kenney and O. Y. Rieger. pp. 11–23. Research Libraries Group, Mountain View, CA.

Deitel, H. M., and Deitel, P. J. (2001) *C++ How to program*. Prentice Hall, Upper Saddle River, NJ.

DeLong, M. B., Brady, J. G., Bourgeois, L. D., and Niemiec, L. J. (1987) *First Aid in Pictures*. Vade Mecum Press, Sterling, VA.

Dumais, S. T., Platt, J., Heckerman, D., and Sahami, M. (1998) "Inductive learning algorithms and representations for text categorization." *Proc ACM Conf on Information and Knowledge Management*, pp. 148–155.

Duncker, E. (2000) "Cross-cultural use of colours and metaphors in information systems." *Proc Workshop on Cultural Issues in HCI*, University of Luton, UK; December.

Foley, J. D., van Dam, A., Feiner, S. K., and Hughes, J. F. (1990) *Computer Graphics: Principles and Practice in C.* Addison Wesley, Boston, MA.

Frakes, W. B. (1992) "Stemming algorithms." In Frakes and Baeza-Yates (1992), Chapter 8, pp. 131–160.

Frakes, W. B., and Baeza-Yates, R. (Eds.) (1992) *Information Retrieval: Data Structures and Algorithms.* Prentice Hall, Englewood Cliffs, NJ.

Frank, E., Paynter, G. W., Witten, I. H., Gutwin, C., and Nevill-Manning, C. (1999) "Domain-specific keyphrase extraction." *Proc International Joint Conference on Artificial Intelligence*, Stockholm, Sweden, pp. 668–673. Morgan Kaufmann, San Francisco, CA; July/August.

Gaines, B. R. (1993) "An agenda for digital journals: The socio-technical infrastructure of knowledge dissemination." *Journal of Organizational Computing*, Vol. 3, No. 2, pp. 135–193.

Gapen, D. K. (1993) "The virtual library: Knowledge, society, and the librarian." In *The Virtual Library: Visions and Realities*, edited by L. M. Saunders, pp. 1–14. Information Today, Medford, NJ.

Giles, C. L., Bollacker, K. D., and Lawrence, S. (1998) "CiteSeer: An automatic citation indexing system." *Proc ACM Digital Libraries*, Pittsburgh, PA, pp. 89–98; June.

Ginsparg, P. (1996) "Winners and losers in the global research village." Presented at UNESCO Conference on Electronic Publishing in Science, Paris; February. Available at *http://xxx.lanl.gov/blurb/pg96unesco.html*.

Goldfarb, C. F. (1990) *The SGML Handbook.* Oxford University Press, New York.

Goodman, H. J. A. (1987) "The 'world brain/world encyclopaedia' concept: Its historical roots and the contributions of H. J. A. Goodman to the ongoing evolution and implementation of the concept." In *Proc 50th Annual Meeting of the American Society for Information Science*, pages 91–98, Medford, NJ.

Gore, D. (Ed.) (1976a) *Farewell to Alexandria: Solutions to Space, Growth, and Performance Problems of Libraries.* Greenwood Press, Westport, CT.

Gore, D. (1976b) *Farewell to Alexandria: The Theory of the No-growth, High-performance Library.* Greenwood Press, Westport, CT, pages 164–180.

Gorman, M., and Winkler, P. W. (Eds.) (1988) *Anglo-American Cataloguing Rules*, second edition. American Library Association, Chicago.

Gorn, S., Bemer, R. W., and Green, J. (1963) "American standard code for information interchange." *Communications of the ACM*, Vol. 6, No. 8, pp. 422–426; August.

Gutwin, C., Paynter, G. W., Witten, I. H., Nevill-Manning, C., and Frank, E. (1999) "Improving browsing in digital libraries with keyphrase indexes." *Decision Support Systems*, Vol. 27, No. 1/2, pp. 81–104; November.

Harold, E. R. (2001) *XML Bible*, Gold edition. IDG Books, Boston, MA.

Heaney, S. (Trans.) (1999) *Beowulf.* Faber and Faber, London.

Hyman, R. J. (1972) *Access to Library Collections: An Inquiry into the Validity of the Direct Shelf Approach, with Special Reference to Browsing.* Scarecrow Press, Metuchen, NJ.

International Telecommunication Union (1998) *Universal Access to Basic Communication and Information Services.* World telecommunication development report, International Telecommunication Union, Geneva, Switzerland.

International Telecommunication Union (1999) *Mobile Cellular.* World telecommunication development report, International Telecommunication Union, Geneva, Switzerland.

Jack, K. (2001) *Video Demystified*, third edition. LLH Technology, Eagle Rock, VA.

Jones, S. (1999) "Phrasier: An interactive system for linking and browsing within document collections using keyphrases." *Proc IFIP Conference on Human-Computer Interaction*, Edinburgh, Scotland, pp. 483–490; August/September.

Jones, S., McInnes, S., and Staveley, M. S. (1999) "A graphical user interface for Boolean query specification." *International J Digital Libraries*, Vol. 2, No. 2/3, pp. 207–223.

Jones, S.. and Paynter, G. (1999) "Topic-based browsing within a digital library using keyphrases." *Proc ACM Digital Libraries*, Berkeley, CA, pp. 114–121; August.

Jones, S.. and Staveley, M. (1999) "Phrasier: A system for interactive document retrieval using keyphrases." *Proc ACM SIGIR Conference on Research and Development in Information Retrieval*, Berkeley, California, pp. 160–167; August.

Josuttis, N. M. (1999) *The C++ Standard Library: A Tutorial and Handbook.* Addison-Wesley, Reading, MA.

Kahle, B. (1997) "Preserving the Internet." *Scientific American*, Vol. 276, No. 3, pp. 82–83; March.

Katzenbeisser, S., and Petitcolas, F. A. P. (Eds.) (1999) *Information Hiding Techniques for Steganography and Digital Watermarking.* Artech House Books, Boston, MA.

Keegan, T., Apperley, M., Cunningham, S. J., and Witten, I. H. (2001) "The Niupepa collection: Opening the blinds on a window to the past." *Proc ICHIM Conference*, Milan, Italy, pp. 347–356; September.

Kevles, D. J. (1998) *The Baltimore Case: A Trial of Politics, Science, and Character.* Norton, New York.

Kientzle, T. (1995) *Internet File Formats: Your Complete Resource for Sending, Receiving, and Using Internet Files.* Coriolis Group, Scottsdale, AZ.

Kientzle, T. (1997) *A Programmer's Guide to Sound.* Addison Wesley, Boston, MA.

Knuth, D. E. (1986) *The TeXbook.* Addison Wesley, Boston, MA.

Korfhage, R. R. (1997) *Information Storage and Retrieval.* Wiley, New York.

Kruse, R. (1994) "Human skin book." Web posting to *Rare Books and Special Collections Forum*, 14 February 1994.

Kuny, T. (1998) "A digital dark ages? Challenges in the preservation of electronic information." *International Preservation News*, No. 17; May.

Lagoze, C., and Fielding, D. (1998) "Defining collections in distributed digital libraries." *D-Lib Magazine*, Vol. 4, No. 11; November.

Lagoze, C., and Payette, S. (2000) "Metadata: Principles, practices and challenges." In *Moving Theory into Practice: Digital Imaging for Libraries and Archives*, edited by A. R. Kenney and O. Y. Rieger, pp. 84–100. Research Libraries Group, Mountain View, CA.

Lagoze, C., and Van de Sompel, H. (2001) "The Open Archives Initiative: Building a low-barrier interoperability framework." *Proc Joint Conference on Digital Libraries*, Roanoke, VA, pp. 54–62; June.

Lamport, L. (1994) *LaTeX: A Document Preparation System User's Guide and Reference Manual*. Addison Wesley, Boston, MA.

Larsson, N. J., and Moffat, A. (1999) "Offline dictionary-based compression." *Proc Data Compression Conference*, pp. 296–305. IEEE Press, Los Alamitos, CA; March.

Lennon, M. D., Pierce, D., Tarry, B., and Willett, P. (1981) "An evaluation of some conflation algorithms for information retrieval." *Journal of Information Science*, Vol. 3, pp. 177–183.

Lesk, M. (1997) *Practical Digital Libraries: Books, Bytes, and Bucks*. Morgan Kaufmann, San Francisco.

Library of Congress (1998) *Library of Congress Subject Headings*, 21st edition. Library of Congress Cataloging Policy and Support Office, Washington, DC.

Licklider, J. C. R. (1960) "Man-computer symbiosis." *IRE Trans Human Factors in Electronics*, Vol. HFE-1, pp. 4–11.

Lovins, J. B. (1968) "Development of a stemming algorithm." *Mechanical Translation and Computation*, Vol. 11, No. 1–2, pp. 22–31.

Lynch, C. (1999) "Canonicalization: A fundamental tool to facilitate preservation and management of digital information." *D-Lib Magazine*, Vol. 5, No. 9; September.

Mankelow, T. (1999) "The New Zealand School Journal: A digital library for teachers and students." Department of Computer Science, University of Waikato; October.

Mann, T. (1993) *Library Research Models*. Oxford University Press, New York.

Mason, J., Mitchell, S., Mooney, M., Reasoner, L., and Rodriguez, C. (2000) "INFOMINE: Promising directions in virtual library development." *First Monday*, Vol. 5, No. 6; June.

McCallum, A. K., Nigam, K., Rennie, J., and Seymore, K. (2000) "Automating the construction of Internet portals with machine learning." *Information Retrieval*, Vol. 3, No. 2, pp. 127–163; July.

McLuhan, M. (1964) *Understanding Media: The Extensions of Man*. McGraw-Hill, New York; reprinted in 1994 by MIT Press, Cambridge, MA.

McNab, R. J., Smith, L. A., Witten, I. H., Henderson, C. L., and Cunningham, S. J. (1996) "Towards the digital music library: Tune retrieval from acoustic input." *Proc ACM Digital Libraries*, Bethesda, MD, pp. 11–18; March.

Miller, E. (1998) "An introduction to the resource description framework." *D-Lib Magazine*, Vol. 4, No. 5; May.

· Miller, P. (Ed.) (2000) *D-Lib Magazine Special Issue on Collection-Level Description*, Vol. 6, No. 9; September.

Morison, S. (1954) *First Principles of Typography*. Cambridge University Press, Cambridge, England.

Murray, J. D., and van Ryper, W. (1996) *Encyclopedia of Graphics File Formats*, second edition. O'Reilly and Associates, Sebastopol, CA.

Nack, F., and Lindsay, A. (1999a) "Everything you wanted to know about MPEG-7: Part I." *IEEE Multimedia*, Vol. 6, No. 3, pp. 65–77; July–September.

Nack, F., and Lindsay, A. (1999b) "Everything you wanted to know about MPEG-7: Part II." *IEEE Multimedia*, Vol. 6, No. 4, pp. 64–73; October–December.

Nevill-Manning, C. G., Reed, T., and Witten, I. H. (1998) "Extracting text from Post-Script." *Software—Practice and Experience*, Vol. 28, No. 5, pp. 481–491; April.

Nevill-Manning, C. G., and Witten, I. H. (1997) "Identifying hierarchical structure in sequences: A linear-time algorithm." *J. Artificial Intelligence Research*, Vol. 7, pp. 67–82.

Nevill-Manning, C. G., and Witten, I. H. (2000) "Online and offline heuristics for inferring hierarchies of repetitions in sequences." *Proceedings of the IEEE*, Vol. 88, No. 11, pp. 1745–1755; November.

Norris, P. (2001) *Digital Divide? Civic Engagement, Information Poverty and the Internet Worldwide*. Cambridge University Press, New York.

Orwell, G. (1949) *1984*. Martin Secker and Warburg, London.

Paepcke, A., Baldonado, M., Chang, C.-C. K., Cousins, S., and Garcia-Molina, H. (1999) "Using distributed objects to build the Stanford Digital Library Infobus." *IEEE Computer*, Vol. 32, No. 2, pp. 80–87; February.

Paynter, G. W., Witten, I. H., Cunningham, S. J., and Buchanan, G. (2000) "Scalable browsing for large collections: A case study." *Proc ACM Digital Libraries*, San Antonio, TX, pp. 215–223; June.

Pennebaker, W. B., and Mitchell, J. L. (1993) *JPEG: Still Image Data Compression Standard*. Van Nostrand Reinhold, New York.

Pohlmann, K. C. (2000) *Principles of Digital Audio*, fourth edition. McGraw Hill, New York.

Porter, M. F. (1980) "An algorithm for suffix stripping." *Program*, Vol. 13, No. 3, pp. 130–137; July.

Price-Wilkin, J. (2000) "Access to digital image collections: System building and image processing." In *Moving Theory into Practice: Digital Imaging for Libraries and Archives*, edited by A. R. Kenney and O. Y. Rieger, pp. 101–118. Research Libraries Group, Mountain View, CA.

Ranganathan, S. R. (1931) *The Five Laws of Library Science.* Madras Library Association, Madras.

Rothenberg, J. (1995) "Ensuring the longevity of digital documents." *Scientific American*, Vol. 272, No. 1, pp. 42–47; January.

Rothenberg, J. (1997) "Digital information lasts forever—or five years, whichever comes first." Rand Corporation Video V-079.

Rothenberg, J. (1999) "Avoiding technological quicksand: Finding a viable technical foundation for digital preservation." Technical Report Pub 77, Council on Library and Information Resources, Washington, DC; January.

Salminen, A., and Tompa, F. W. (1994) "PAT Expressions: An algebra for text search." *Acta Linguistica Hungarica*, Vol. 41, No. 1-4, pp. 277–306.

Salton, G. (1989) *Automatic Text Processing: The Transformation, Analysis, and Retrieval of Information by Computer.* Prentice Hall, Englewood Cliffs, NJ.

Salton, G., and McGill, M. J. (1983) *Introduction to Modern Information Retrieval.* McGraw-Hill, New York.

Samuelson, P. (1998) "Encoding the law into digital libraries." *Communications of the ACM*, Vol. 41, No. 4, pp. 13–18; April.

Samuelson, P., and Davis, R. (2000) "The digital dilemma: A perspective on intellectual property in the information age." Presented at the Telecommunications Policy Research Conference, Alexandria, VA; September.

Sanders, L. M. (Ed.) (1999) *The Evolving Virtual Library II: Practical and Philosophical Perspectives.* Information Today, Medford, NJ.

Santayana, G. (1932) *The Life of Reason in the Phases of Human Progress.* Scribner's, New York.

Slama, D., Garbis, J., and Russell, P. (1999) *Enterprise CORBA.* Prentice Hall, Upper Saddle River, NJ.

Sperberg-McQueen, C. M., and Burnard, L. (Editors) (1999) *Guidelines for Electronic Text Encoding and Interchange.* Text Encoding Initiative, Chicago and Oxford.

Stroustrup, B. (2001) *The C++ Programming* Language. Addison-Wesley, Reading, MA.

Sun Microsystems (2000) *The Digital Library Toolkit.* Sun Microsystems, Palo Alto, CA. Available at *www.sun.com/edu.*

Svenonius, E. (2000) *The Intellectual Foundation of Information Organization.* MIT Press, Cambridge, MA.

Teahan, W. J. (1997) "Modelling English text." Ph.D. thesis, Department of Computer Science, University of Waikato, New Zealand.

Teahan, W. J., Wen, Y. Y., McNab, R., and Witten, I. H. (2000) "A compression-based algorithm for Chinese word segmentation." *Computational Linguistics*, Vol. 26, No. 3, pp. 375–393; September.

Thiele, H. (1998) "The Dublin Core and Warwick Framework: A review of the literature, March 1995–September 1997." *D-Lib Magazine*, Vol. 4, No. 1; January.

Thompson, J. (1997) *A History of the Principles of Librarianship*. Clive Bingley, London.

Turney, P. D. (2000) "Learning algorithms for keyphrase extraction." *Information Retrieval*, Vol. 2, No. 4, pp. 303–336.

Unicode Consortium (2000) *The Unicode Standard, Version 3.0*. Addison Wesley, Reading, MA.

United Nations (1997) *Universal Access to Basic Communication and Information Services*. UN Administrative Committee on Coordination, New York.

United Nations (1999) *Human Development Report*. UN Development Programme, New York.

U.S. Congress (1990) *Taking a Byte Out of History: The Archival Preservation of Federal Computer Records*. House Committee on Government Operations Report 101-987, Washington, DC.

van Rijsbergen, C. J. (1979) *Information Retrieval*, second edition. Butterworths, London.

Weibel, S. (1999) "The state of the Dublin Core metadata initiative." *D-Lib Magazine*, Vol. 5, No. 4; April.

Welch, T. A. (1984) "A technique for high-performance data compression." *IEEE Computer*, Vol. 17, No. 6, pp. 8–20; June.

Wells, H. G. (1938) *World Brain*. Doubleday, New York.

White, J. (Ed.) (1999) *Intellectual Property in the Age of Universal Access*. ACM Press, New York.

Witten, I. H., Bainbridge, D., and Boddie, S. (2001) "Power to the people: end-user building of digital library collections." *Proc Joint Conference on Digital Libraries*, Roanoke, VA, pp. 94–103; June.

Witten, I. H., Loots, M., Trujillo, M. F., and Bainbridge, D. (2001) "The promise of digital libraries in developing countries." *Communications of the ACM*, Vol. 55, No. 5, pp. 82–85; May.

Witten, I. H., McNab, R. J., Boddie, S. J., and Bainbridge, D. (2000) "Greenstone: A comprehensive open-source digital library software system." *Proc ACM Digital Libraries*, San Antonio, TX, pp. 113–121; June.

Witten, I. H., McNab, R., Jones, S., Cunningham, S. J., Bainbridge, D., and Apperley, M. (1999) "Managing complexity in a distributed digital library." *IEEE Computer*, Vol. 32, No. 2, pp. 74–79; February.

Witten, I. H., Moffat, A., and Bell, T. C. (1999) *Managing Gigabytes: Compressing and Indexing Documents and Images*, second edition. Morgan Kaufmann, San Francisco, CA.

Wolff, J. G. (1975) "An algorithm for the segmentation of an artificial language ana-logue." *British J Psychology*, Vol. 66, pp. 79–90.

World Bank (1998/99) *World Development Report: Knowledge for Development.* World Bank, Washington, DC.

World Bank (2000) *World Development Indicators 2000.* World Bank, Washington, DC.

Wright, E. V. (1939) *Gadsby.* Wetzel, Los Angeles; reprinted by Kassel Books, Los Angeles.

Wu, J. (Ed.) (1999) *New Library Buildings of the World.* Shanghai Public Library, Shang-hai, China.

Yeates, S., Bainbridge, D., and Witten, I. H. (2000) "Using compression to identify acronyms in text." *Proc Data Compression Conference*, p. 582. IEEE Press, Los Alamitos, CA.

Ziv, J., and Lempel, A. (1977) "A universal algorithm for sequential data compression." *IEEE Trans Information Theory*, Vol. IT-23, No. 3, pp. 337–343; May.

Ziv, J., and Lempel, A. (1978) "Compression of individual sequences via variable-rate cod-ing." *IEEE Trans Information Theory*, Vol. IT-24, No. 5, pp. 530–536; September.

Index

About the authors

Ian H. Witten
www.cs.waikato.ac.nz/~ihw

Ian H. Witten is a professor of computer science at the University of Waikato in New Zealand. He directs the New Zealand Digital Library Project. His research interests include information retrieval, machine learning, text compression, and programming by demonstration. He received an M.A. in mathematics from Cambridge University, England; an M.Sc. in computer science from the University of Calgary, Canada; and a Ph.D. in electrical engineering from Essex University, England. He is a fellow of the ACM and of the Royal Society of New Zealand. He has published widely on digital libraries, machine learning, text compression, hypertext, speech synthesis and signal processing, and computer typography. He has written several books, the latest being *Managing Gigabytes* (1999) and *Data Mining* (2000), both from Morgan Kaufmann.

David Bainbridge
www.cs.waikato.ac.nz/~davidb

David Bainbridge is a senior lecturer in computer science at the University of Waikato, New Zealand. He holds a Ph.D. in computer science from the University of Canterbury, New Zealand, where he studied the problem of optical music recognition as a Commonwealth Scholar. Since moving to Waikato in 1996, he has continued to broaden his interest in digital media, while retaining a particular emphasis on music. An active member of the New Zealand Digital Library Project, he manages the group's digital music library project and has collaborated with several United Nations agencies, the BBC, and various public libraries. He has published in the areas of image processing, music information retrieval, digital libraries, data compression, and text mining. David has also worked as a research engineer for Thorn EMI in the area of photorealistic imaging and graduated from the University of Edinburgh in 1991 as the class medalist in computer science.